TALKING TEXTS

HOW SPEECH AND WRITING INTERACT
IN SCHOOL LEARNING

TALKING TEXTS

HOW SPEECH AND WRITING INTERACT
IN SCHOOL LEARNING

Edited by

Rosalind Horowitz
The University of Texas–San Antonio

LAWRENCE ERLBAUM ASSOCIATES, PUBLISHERS

2007   Mahwah, New Jersey   London

Cover design by Rosalind Horowitz and Tomai Maridou.

Lawrence Erlbaum Associates
Taylor & Francis Group
270 Madison Avenue
New York, NY 10016

Lawrence Erlbaum Associates
Taylor & Francis Group
2 Park Square
Milton Park, Abingdon
Oxon OX14 4RN

Printed in the United States of America on acid-free paper
10 9 8 7 6 5 4 3 2 1

International Standard Book Number-13: 978-0-8058-5305-6 (Softcover)

Library of Congress Cataloging-in-Publication Data

Talking texts : how speech and writing interact in school learning / edited by Rosalind Horowitz.
    p. cm.
   Includes bibliographical references and index.
   ISBN 978-0-8058-5304-9 -- 0-8058-5304-9 (cloth)
   ISBN 978-0-8058-5305-7 -- 0-8058-5305-6 (pbk.)
   1. Oral communication--Study and teaching. 2. Discourse analysis--Study and teaching. 3. Written communication--Study and teaching. 4. Rhetoric--Study and teaching. 5. Learning. I. Horowitz, Rosalind.

P95.3.T35 2007
371.102'2--dc22

                                         2006602121

Visit the Taylor & Francis Web site at
http://www.taylorandfrancis.com

This book is dedicated in blessed memory of my beloved brother

Searle Seymour Horowitz

(1947–1987)

Who treasured the language of music and song

לעד בכ' אישׁ הלדי פ

ל"בע שוליא' ממק קפ ישולד

So now, write this song for yourselves, and teach it to the
Children of Israel, place it in their mouth, so that this song shall
be for Me a witness on behalf of the Children of Israel.
Deuteronomy, Chapter 31, Verse 19

וְעַתָּה כִּתְבוּ לָכֶם֙ אֶת־
הַשִּׁירָה הַזֹּאת וְלַמְּדָהּ אֶת־בְּנֵי־יִשְׂרָאֵל שִׂימָהּ בְּפִיהֶם
לְמַ֫עַן תִּהְיֶה־לִּי הַשִּׁירָה הַזֹּאת לְעֵד בִּבְנֵי יִשְׂרָאֵל:

Scherman, N. (Ed.). (1993). *The Chumash. The Stone Edition*
(Art Scroll Series, pp. 1096–1097). Brooklyn, NY: Mesorah.

Contents

Preface

In the twentieth century, we witnessed a revolution in text studies. I was at the University of Minnesota in the 1970s to the early 1980s and vividly recall the exhilaration we felt about the range of possibilities in front of us, as we avidly pursued research on texts and comprehension. Attention to texts in the United States was influenced by the new theoretical work of European scholars. Teun A. van Dijk and Walter Kintsch had just produced *Strategies of Discourse Comprehension*—incidentally, a book that I nominated for the American Education Research Association's Outstanding Book Award and which, without hesitation by our Committee, won. Their volume added to James L. Kinneavy's seminal *A Theory of Discourse: The Aims of Discourse*, a model for cognitive and linguistic studies of text processing and examples of far-reaching scientific merit. It advocated for interdisciplinary studies in ways that stretched discourse and text scholarship internationally. Thus, in the 1980s and 1990s researchers attended to structural analysis of texts and the mental representations of propositions in written texts in ways that were unprecedented. It, however, became apparent that texts could not be studied in isolation from the social situation and cultural contexts in which they were produced or resided. Further, what was missing was, simply stated, the human element of text processing, the real time, evolutionary aspects of discourse processing that motivate today's learners and their development as they perform school tasks. By the close of the twentieth century, the conversational conventions among learners and teachers had gained heightened attention and a new research rigor.

We are now fascinated with oral discourse for its potential, in not only scaffolding understanding of texts, but also transforming the self—and mind.

Talking Texts presents oral discourse as central to the creation of knowledge. Throughout the volume are examples of natural, spontaneous student oral discourse guided by teacher-designed discourse that contribute to learning and knowledge building. More specifically, this volume examines how oral texts can be successfully interconnected to written texts that are used on a daily basis in schools. This book adds a semblance of balance and order to the past century's conflicting theories about oral and written language by presenting research that illuminates how they function in unison in multidimensional ways in school learning.

Rather than argue for the prominence of one over the other, as has been the case among linguists for many years, I hope the reader will come away from this book with a richer understanding of how inter-related and essential the oral *and* written are and how they might work together to create a new discourse (and mind) that ultimately creates new knowledge. In this book, authors present oral discourse, produced by teachers and students, as text types in relation to written-literate text types, advancing our definitions of the intertextuality of learning. Through talk (as text) that precedes, co-occurs, and comments upon written texts, students and teachers become co-constructors of meaning in domains of knowledge taught in schools. Today, written text is conceived of as more than what Aristotle and later Leonard Bloomfield characterized as "speech writ' down." Student written language is significantly influenced in content and style by words spoken or overheard (by adults or peers) that enter writing but take on a style of their own. Written language may be a result of a repetition or translation of spoken language, but now functioning in a new context for different purposes than the original oral source. Expressions spoken as part of a series of classroom events may be parroted with limited understanding by young children, but also quoted, paraphrased, and later more curiously interpreted or analyzed in writing or reading. We have yet to fully understand how a developing *writer* incorporates select features of the spoken language (e.g., vocabulary and voice) and cognitive processes associated with speaking (and listening). Similarly, developing *speakers* incorporate in oral texts features of writing (e.g., punctuation and paragraphing) and cognitive processes associated with writing (and reading). With time, students develop a sense of agency and academic identity as they discover how the above features of the oral and written work and intersect in specialized fields—whether presented on the printed page or computer screen.

But why should this matter? Why should how the oral and written evolve and interact be a question for study in a full-length volume of papers? While reading the chapters in this book, it should become apparent that how school communication develops (in the learner and teacher)—how the oral and the written interface (in talk or text)—will contribute to how children think and learn and approach the world. This book can be used as a tool for choosing and scaffolding classroom dialogue styles, whether by the teacher, tutor, or coach. These choices are not minor issues. Attention to how oral and written forms and styles of discourse overlap removes some of the folklore associated with a frozen, "correct" speech and "correct" written language of instruction. The book offers rich ways of thinking about children's incomplete thoughts or expressions. Applying what we know about oral-written interactions offers new possibilities for educating those children who find learning through reading and writing difficult.

In designing this volume, researchers and teachers were invited to present seminal lines of research that illustrate the way oral discourse evolves in dialogic communication. These researchers have not been assembled previously in one source. This volume, thus, allows the reader to compare and/or contrast how instructional speech styles mediate, through time, children's learning from textual sources.

Until children enter school, most of their language is oral. It is adapted to family members, peers, and other adults encountered, but limited in topic and content. In school, there are new subjects with advanced linguistic and cognitive requirements. As illustrated in this volume, children make linguistic adjustments to these new subjects based on classroom tasks. Theorists of child development from Jean Piaget to John Flavell have examined children's role taking, rhetorical stances, social perceptions, and awareness of self and audience—and, more recently, children's theories of mind. These approaches to speech and cognition are now being considered within the contexts of teacher-student talk. This book conveys that teacher speech, whether in the form of directions or assessments, will need to be fine-tuned to a child's everyday and school language to ensure the effectiveness of instruction.

Finally, this volume shows how oral discourse patterns can be used to support the teaching of domains of knowledge in academic contexts. Through talk and text, students are led from novice to expert thinking and doing. The chapters show how oral language is not only the foundation of literacy, but essential for thinking, reasoning, and acting in a range of scientific and humanities fields.

The first chapter of the book examines how talk, text, and meaning *evolve* in learning through a review of the chapters. The Postscript addresses the *interaction* of speech and writing in classroom discourse through a re-examination of the chapters.

The volume is divided into four sections. Part I introduces the book with the creating of discourse and mind. It presents historical background for the study of talk and text by reviewing a half-century of distinguished theory and research. It shows how talk, text, and meaning evolve beyond the constraints of recitation in the context of school learning. Discourse of the classroom is viewed as a unique and "peculiar" kind of discourse study developed through oral and written intertextuality and crediting of sources.

Part II presents examples of children's and adolescent's natural conversations as analyzed by linguists. Preschool children are studied as they use language persuasively to win a position in peer interactions, while teenage talk is analyzed as it evolves from an informal chat to a more controlled small-group discussion. Parent-child interactions at the dinner table and parental language choices are studied to show their influence on cultural membership and children's schooling within distinct communities.

Part III includes exemplars of forms of talk and their evolution inside school contexts. More specifically, this section adds to studies of school discourse by considering communication that is, at the same time, conversational *and* instructional, a style of talk that has been scientifically shown to draw students into content knowledge learning. A number of chapters concentrate on fourth-grade populations where a "slump" in reading and knowledge acquisition has been identified but not fully explained. This drop in school performance, with the potential of influencing the remainder of a child's education, has been linked to the transition children must make from narrative to descriptive writing styles, but is also influenced by logical and social reasoning abilities along with the reader-writer's ability to follow the flow of arguments.

Part IV addresses talk as it co-occurs and interfaces with domains of knowledge taught in schools. Covering a range of subject areas, from technicalities of engineering to the techniques of music instruction, these chapters show how talk is related to and may be influenced by the structure, language, and activities of a specific school discipline. Talk in these fields provides a means for the individual's objective and analytical inquiry but, as the chapters demonstrate, is also subject to the group assigned textbooks and the reading and writing mandated by the institution of schooling. A number of chapters illustrate how the teacher's questions and gradual withdrawal of direct control are critical in influencing how students interact with the text and what they take away from a text domain.

Finally, the study of learners immersed in talk and texts has been subject to some of the same challenges in the twenty-first century as other studies of human psychological and social behavior faced by researchers, educational policy leaders, and federal government officials. To what extent shall we use quantitative measures? And when shall we apply more humanistic, qualitative measures? And, most recently, when shall we apply multiple-method designs? Alexander Romanovich Luria (1902–1977) faced a similar dilemma. With a 60-year career influenced by Lev Vygotsky, Luria valued an experimental method but *also* pursued a humanistic approach to thought and behavior (Cole, 1976). There was a need to reconcile art and science, the quantitative and the qualitative-the affective, the descriptive, and the explanatory. Luria argued that to fully understand the mind, we needed to account for "the knowledge people have about the world and the motives that energize them as they put that knowledge to use" (p. 6). This is an approach not so far from Jerome Bruner's (1990) call for the cognitive *and* the cultural in his treatise on "The Proper Study of Man."

Speech, with its range of styles and cognitive outcomes, remains one of the most neglected and underfunded subjects in American educational research.

Yet the Russian psychologists, coupled with the work of North American scholars in argumentation and rhetoric, have taught us how vital oral discourse can be in the development of the human mind and of a culture and civilization.

In keeping with the theme of "talking texts," the cover design of this volume consists of five icons that are associated with different domains of knowledge and text types addressed in this book. At the top left is a line drawing of the Bactrian camel, one noted for its endurance of extreme temperatures-from the heat of Iran to the cold of Tibet. To the right of the camel is a technical illustration depicting an aberration in an optical system. This is a condition whereby a lens or mirror fails to bring parallel rays of light into focus, causing a blurring of an image. In the center figure are stereographic and orthographic map projections of the earth on a flat sheet of paper. On the bottom left is a lister, a plow used for agricultural purposes such as preparing shallow beds and planting seeds. The bottom right hand corner contains handwritten contrapuntal music, similar to the eighteenth-century classical music of Bach and Beethoven, composed by my grandfather Sam Horowitz over 70 years ago for the choir he conducted.

The dedication page makes reference to what was regarded in ancient times as the highest form of *"talking text"*—Song. According to Deuteronomy (*Devarim*), and related commentaries, a song signifies harmony as produced by all of the notes in the score of a complex musical piece—all the instruments of an orchestra, all of the voices in a choir coming together in harmonious cooperation, a goal to be sought and achieved in school-guided cognition and creativity.

ACKNOWLEDGMENTS

Talking Texts is based on what has been a life-long fascination with oral and written communication and learning. By the time I had finished writing and editing the chapters in *Comprehending Oral and Written Language* (1987), it became apparent that one could no longer study talk and written texts as separate entities. *Studies in Orality and Literacy: Critical Issues for the Practice of Schooling*, produced as a special issue of *Text* (1991), became a precursor to *Classroom Talk about Text: What Teenagers and Teachers Come to Know About the World Through Talk About Text* (1994). Upon completion of the latter project, Janet Binkley of the International Reading Association urged me to expand this work on classroom discourse by designing a book-length manuscript.

The Institute of Child Development at the University of Minnesota impressed upon me during graduate school how important it was to incorporate child and adolescent developmental perspectives in the studies of human learning. The present project is also the result of years of education and training with Gene L. Piché, Professor Emeritus, of the University of Minnesota, who enriched my vision of speech-communication and rhetoric and the study of composing processes. Loren Ekroth, my freshman-year speech-communications professor at the University of Minnesota, and later the Director of the Center for Teaching Excellence at the University of Hawaii-Manoa, continues to be a source of knowledge through his work and website on how everyday conversation matters. Finally, teacher and long-term collaborator, S. Jay Samuels, at the University of Minnesota, gave me the tools of the trade for analyzing reading research and discourse processes. His workbench was where I tackled real-world problems of the beginning reading acts that, with time, form a literate mind.

Over the past few years, I have met with colleagues and students who have contributed to my thinking about theoretical approaches to speech and written language as I gave lectures at Waseda University in Tokyo, Japan; Lviv Polytechnic National University in the Ukraine; the University of Utrecht in The Netherlands; the University of Amsterdam; and the University of Tel Aviv, Bar Ilan University, and Ben Gurion University, all in Israel. Travels to Russia and the Ukraine provided an opportunity to meet with linguists and teachers interested in language, speech, and identity formation including Andrej Kibrik, Moscow State University; Valentyna Pavlenko, University of Kharakov; and Lydia Velychko, an English as a second language teacher in Kiev, Ukraine.

Above all, this book was inspired by dialogues with David R. Olson at the Ontario Institute of Studies in Education (OISE) of the University of Toronto. Chapter 2 came about because of the gracious hospitality I received at OISE and by way of participation in doctoral seminars, discussions with Janet Astington and Nancy Torrance, and data collection in Toronto. Art Graesser's leadership of the Society for Text and Discourse helped establish discourse processes as a field of global study and continues to be influential. A National Academy of Education Spencer Fellowship provided funds that inaugurated this research trajectory, and yearly meetings provided opportunities to explore the insights reported in this book.

Contributors to this volume are international scholars who were invited to be part of the project because they have developed solid lines of research that will influence discourse studies for years to come. This book should be useful to researchers, teachers on the frontlines, graduate students beginning their education and careers, and advanced undergraduates. The scholars included herein were patient as we edited the chapters and added to fill in gaps in what became a seven-year project, sans Sabbatical or leave. I appreciate their contributions and am honored that they are part of this book.

I am grateful to my teacher and friend, Louise Androff Hopson, of blessed memory, who followed my scholarly interests for most of my life and epitomized the highest ideals of what a teacher should and could be.

I am grateful to those who faithfully supported me, to my friend Gus Shalchi— for constant caring and trusting in my dreams. I thank my students at The University of Texas–San Antonio who worked with dedication on various phases of this book. Cynthia Kennedy performed yeoman tasks. Bernice Cole, Elizabeth Seat, Ruby Kainth, Anna Brown, Adriana Campos, Anna Hernandez, and Nicole McLeod were loyal graduate students. Gayla Schill, Terry Jones and Tanya Figueroa were assistants who served as in-house editors, seeing to it that the book was complete and ready for the publishers. I thank Naomi Silverman, my editor, for unyielding faith and support, and Lawrence Erlbaum for wisdom that moved the publishing industry from the ordinary to the exceptional.

Above all, the memories of my beloved parents, Cantor Louis Horowitz and Fannie Hartman Horowitz, and brother, Searle Seymour Horowitz, to whom this book is dedicated, were a constant blessing and inspiration. It is their love of learning and education and their respect for human development that sustained me throughout this project.

—*Rosalind Horowitz*

REFERENCES

Bruner, J. S. (1990). The proper study of man. In *Acts of meaning* (pp. 1–32). Cambridge, MA: Harvard University Press.

Horowitz, R. (Ed.). (1994). Classroom talk about text: What teenagers and teachers come to know about the world through talk about texts [Special issue]. *Journal of Adolescent and Adult Literacy, 37*(7), 532–539.

Horowitz, R. (Ed.). (1991). Studies in orality and literacy: Critical issues for the practice of schooling [Special issue]. *Text, 11*(1), 1–166.

Horowitz, R., & Samuels, S. J. (Eds.). (1987). *Comprehending oral and written language.* San Diego, CA: Academic Press.

Kinneavy, J. L. (1980). *A theory of discourse: The aims of discourse.* New York: W. W. Norton.

Luria, A. R., Cole, M. (Ed.), & Cole, S. (Ed.). (1979). *The making of mind: A personal account of Soviet psychology.* Cambridge, MA: Harvard University Press.

van Dijk, T. A., & Kintsch, W. (1983). *Strategies of discourse comprehension.* New York: Academic Press.

I

Creating Discourse
and Mind

CHAPTER 1

Creating Discourse and Mind: How Talk, Text, and Meaning Evolve

Rosalind Horowitz

In 1992 I was commissioned by the president of my university to attend a six-week program at Bryn Mawr College on the outskirts of Philadelphia. This program was designed to address the workings of higher education for those who would serve in leadership roles. While there, I found a provocative poster advertising Bryn Mawr to prospective college students. It offered a guidepost for a college education: *Create a mind that you can live inside of for the rest of your life.* I asked myself, What would be the attributes of such a mind? How might faculty foster and students create such a mind? How might discourse best serve as a precursor to and instrument in the development of mind?

Speech and writing that occur in classrooms are the penultimate means by which students learn and form a persona for learning in academic fields. These are also the means by which students develop cognitively and linguistically. Just how talk and text are created and evolve to influence the development of meaning and mind in schools is a concern of this book.[1] This introductory chapter provides background for the present volume. It examines oral discourse styles, particularly those associated with domains of knowledge, and explores their relationships to academic uses of written texts. It also places the chapters that follow in the context of current scholarship on classroom discourse and learning in schools.

As was the case in *Comprehending Oral and Written Language* (1987), I use the terms *oral* and *written language, speech* and *writing*, and *spoken* and *written* language to refer to different systems of communication and, as M. A. K. Halliday calls them, "modes of meaning." The terms *oral* and *written language* have traditionally been used by scholars in the language arts and in English education and by many in English departments to refer to conversation, as opposed to written language, and to interpersonal communication, as opposed to text communication. *Speech* and *writing* and *spoken* and *written language* have traditionally been used by linguists or scholars with a linguistic bent, including speech-communication researchers, who are particularly concerned with the actual sound and rhythm of speech and with the relationships between patterns of sound and meaning. Often, all of the above phrases have been used to refer to the formal dimensions of language and language as an object as opposed to a process.

Talk and Text: Background and Basic Premises for School Learning

First, there can be no doubt that talk and text work in unison. Talk and texts contribute to what we know about disciplines in the sciences and arts and to the formation of original ideas across these fields. Through conversations about academic writings, students acquire new speech genres, what Richard Bauman (2004) defines as speech styles that are conventionalized and formalized. These speech genres are associated with scientific languages, historical discourses, musical and poetic patterns of expression, and, concomitantly, new forms of thinking. They develop through an education that encourages *argumentation, imagination,* and *inspiration* through oral and written-visual or technological sources (all treated in this book). Discussions in academic settings have the potential to stimulate students to learn expert-like ways of text processing and communicating. Discussions also teach students how to create and manipulate tools and symbols in order to solve complex problems. Dialogue, effectively orchestrated through pedagogical instruction, teaches students how to investigate controversies across spoken and written sources. This communication nurtures self-reflection, often among peers, whereby interlocutors decide what they believe and value. Through discipline-based critical discourse, albeit speech or writing-reading, students learn to determine the merits of scientific theory or applications and the logic and reasons for their beliefs.

Though often unrecognized, oral and written expression are also the most direct instrument of the human mind and spirit. While teaching, I have witnessed student conversations originate in serendipitous ways, yet unexpectedly, with time to yield clear thinking, build empathic understanding, and create affective intelligence. Through oral expression—albeit drama, poetry, or song, all of which are addressed in this volume—a range of emotions becomes visible. It is this intellectual *and* emotional knowledge, acquired through controlled use of talk and written text that guides interlocutors in how to resolve the most difficult questions, such as those encountered in the medical or legal professions or, for our purposes, the teaching profession.

Second, talk is a living, fleeting, dynamic form of expression that changes in style and content momentarily and is subject to the fluidity of context. This is evident in the dialogue of experts performing a series of professional tasks in real time. Imagine the talk of architects designing, newspaper reporters writing, engineers problem-solving, chefs cooking, or lawyers persuading judges in courtrooms. Everyday talk is a drama, continuously evolving, with one utterance leading to another in "varying temporalities"—with the speaker and listener *remembering, attending, anticipating* (Perinbanayagam, 1991, pp. 167–168). Talk also changes in content and form, at the blink of an eye, when relationships evolve and are transformed among interlocutors—e.g., friends become lovers or lovers, friends. In this regard, the creation of discourse in everyday life events is a dynamic process with moment-to-moment possibilities that alter life situations. But we must recognize that this fluidity of talk occurs in contexts that are also fluid and have their own motion and potential for creative expressions.

Further, different physical arrangements and stances may influence communication patterns and our thoughts or actions. The space in which we live or work can determine our language loyalties and discourse styles, as in the case of individuals crossing the Mexico-U.S. border who take on new languages and discourse styles in their new physical world. In sum, the modern learner must develop cognitive and linguistic flexibility as they adjust their language patterns to fit new situational contexts.

These organic, dynamic views of verbal expression should inform the way we conceive of speech not only in everyday life but, above all, in academic teaching and learning.

For example, in the classroom context teachers may find a lack of clarity or precision in arguments, uneven logic, or false starts in children's talk or writings. This book's view of language and discourse as a developmental and evolving process suggests that we cannot always expect the first expressions of a child to be definitive or even fully communicated. Nor can we know where a child or adolescent is headed (nor may they know) when they utter their first thoughts in a classroom. An utterance is a beginning leap of faith into learning. This, ultimately, leads to further expressions such as the gradual formation of new ideas or the abandonment of ill-formed ones. A first utterance is beginning input for an expert teacher who must decide how to take the discourse and the child so they can effectively compose instruction for this novice learner. Similarly, Northrop Frye (1964) conceived of the individual's connection to the literary world as the experience of "a world [filled with] imagination, a world of unborn or embryonic beliefs" waiting to find expression (p. 77).

Third, talk coexisting or combined with written text, when strategically planned, can have far reaching benefits. It can carry us over geographic space within a few decades, generations, or even centuries. Benjamin Franklin (1706–1790), one of the most remarkable figures in American history, is an example par excellence of someone who took financial planning, with official documentation, across physical space and time to an unusual extreme. In his will, Franklin (1789) gave 1,000 pounds sterling each to the cities of Boston and Philadelphia with directions for its use. He requested that this money be donated on the condition that part of it would not be touched for 100 years, at which time it should be used for city planning, including "fortifications, bridges, aqueducts, public buildings, baths, [and] pavements" (Codicil section, para. 8). The remaining funds were not to be used for 200 years, with its disposition left unspecified. In 1990, Philadelphia received the final funds and began to create a major renovation. But what seemed like an ordinary, simple, written transaction proved otherwise. *The New York Times* Current Events Edition (Butterfield, 1990) reported that oral disputes ensued over how to operationalize the gift. It has now matured into $6.5 million, creating more havoc and discussion about its use than Franklin may have ever imagined (Talbott, 2005; Wilcox, 1972).

Fourth, talk—as treated in this volume—extends beyond the traditional teaching of the rhetoric of public, formal speech-making to new styles and forms of discourse. At one time, the analysis of rhetorical theory, principles of argumentation, invention, and style were essential to speech training. Greek *topoi* (topics of study) were the vehicle for generating and building arguments in "law courts," "the public forum," or "in ceremonial addresses" (Corbett, 1971, p. 35). Style (a concept rhetoricians find worthy of study) was characterized by Quintilian as either plain, suited for *instruction*; middle, for *moving* an audience; or high, for *charming* an audience (see Corbett, 1971). At the turn of the twentieth century, elocution and articulation were the esteemed foundation of higher learning and literacy. Throughout the twentieth century, school speech practices led the way for composing processes in writing. From Aristotle to Leonard Bloomfield's (1933) philosophy of language, written sources were treated as a form of rhetoric, as "speech writ' down." With time, speech lost its prominence. Institutional leadership enforced an oral silencing in classrooms (or select language exercises) whereby written text came to be the primary learning tool, with particular functions associated with an effective classroom and civilized society. In contrast, in light of growing technologically based communication, today I believe there is a yearning for informal, authentic, face-to-face communicative styles in everyday life. There is also a yearning among many students for authentic talk with the adults they encounter in schools.

In this volume researchers and teachers show how *talking texts*—extended talk that is *text-like* (organized and cohesive) or written texts that are *talk-like* (with informal conversation-like features)—can draw students into learning. Moreover, "conversational" discourse, with a collective engagement, has become a communication style of great interest to researchers of classroom interaction.

However, it is not only in the classroom that informal styles of speaking are popular. Literacy and orality were once treated as dichotomous, with formal and definite boundaries that were touted in schools. In the last century, we have witnessed how talk and text boundaries have overlapped with a conversational, more everyday stylistic form observable through informal expressions, vocabulary, and phrases that are more appealing to students and the general public (Lakoff, 1982). In a recent analysis of inaugural addresses, which were once the bastion of formal, distanced rhetoric, there is now an interplay of the literate and the oral. Conversational texts have been delivered by Presidents such as Clinton and Bush (Kowal, O'Connell, Forbush, Higgins, Clarke, & D'Anna, 1997). Another example of conversational discourse in the formal arena is the January 2007 Madrid Conference of Middle-Eastern Leadership. Rhetoric and speeches were downplayed to be replaced by informal coffee conversations.

Deborah Tannen (1984) describes speech styles as "simply 'ways of speaking,'" or modes of "doing something" including pitch, amplitude, intonation, rate, and language choices that "determine the effect of an utterance in interaction and influence judgments … about what is said and about the speaker who says it" (p. 8). She gives no value to the concept of style (e.g., *fancy* is not better than *plain*, or vice versa). "Style is not something extra added on like frosting on a cake [but rather] it is the stuff of which the linguistic cake is made" (p. 8). In classrooms, a teacher's style may be evidenced by voice, eye contact, and body language. Linguists Wallace Chafe and Charles Fillmore have identified conversational talk as the baseline from which other discourse styles could be analyzed; this holds true for the analysis of classroom discourse.

School talk in this volume is approached as dialogic communication. It includes speech forms such as chats and discussions, private exchanges and public discourses, scientific or artistic collaborations, and also introspective metacognitive processes when conversations are used for self-reflection and -regulation during text processing. In the case of literacy lessons, students today are co-constructors of text and talk in one-on-one tutorials. Teachers have been encouraged to use oral scaffolding, reciprocal teaching, and verbal feedback sessions to help students internalize complex knowledge. Six-year-olds, amazingly, have been shown to be capable of leading small group discussions about writing and reading. Teachers are being trained to develop literacy circles, book clubs, communities of learners, and large-scale group discussions or talk-like lectures for adolescents that can be instructional and interactive at the same time. David Perkins (2003) cleverly promotes a King Arthur's style of round table collaborative conversations. Through sophisticated discourse analysis systems, researchers can trace the reasoning processes exercised in young students' interaction. There are also ethical and moral outcomes of talk styles for new scientific and humanistic understandings that have received heightened attention. In sum, the approach to school talk, evidenced here, is inter/ intra-personal and of a developmental-evolutionary nature that prides itself on being conversation-like and collaborative.

Fifth, conversational discourse shifts from a spontaneous and unconscious activity that is often taken for granted to a more consciously controlled activity depending on the age-grade and expertise of the learner. In their inquisitive preschool years, young children are unconsciously playful and inventive with spoken language as they spontaneously communicate and are propelled by the sound of their own and another's oral words. As they move along in the institution of schooling, writing becomes what Wallace Chafe (1994) calls language "worked over" (p. 43). "Creating a piece of written language is, or can be, like creating a piece of sculpture, revising, and reshaping a visual creation until its creator finds it adequate to display" (p. 43). Adults know when to be spontaneous and when they need to consciously control and transform their oral texts to written texts. This shift from oral to written language brings with it language consciousness and new metacognitive processes (Carter, 2004; Ong, 1977).

Astington and Baird (2005) show that language matters in cognitive shifts and is related to children's awareness of self and others' minds. Some research shows how language reflects and represents mental functions. Other research shows how language contributes to the development of a child's understanding of mind and cognitive growth. The present volume incorporates both perspectives.

Sixth, the study of the development of oral discourse, as a contributor to a learner's cognitive and social development, has taken on new theoretical perspectives with classroom applications. Contributions by Lev Vygotsky (1896–1936) and fellow Russian scholars were part of an emancipation associated with social interaction as fundamental for human growth. Their work has influenced the socio-cognitive and cultural discourse revolutions we witness today in educational research. It also has encouraged a *performance* (action) before *competence* (knowledge) view of learning with the idea that activities and events bring symbols and mental structures together, which results in constructivist thinking and learning.

More recently, Jack Goody (1987) elevated the role of speech in human development when he wrote, "The most significant moment in the course of a child's intellectual development is when speech and 'activities' converge" (p. 259). Opportunities to interact with others about school tasks allow the child to be creative and playful, to imagine and speculate, to find inspiration and reference objects and actions, and to relate everyday experiences that will ultimately form an identity to be connected to school learning. Through conversation, children perform a range of abstract thinking acts. These contribute to the child's theories of mind. Children grow in awareness of the intention of others' speech, the appropriation of speech with particular acts, and recognition of emotional states of others. They also grow in problem-solving skills, such as concept classification, procedural processes, and information organization—all of which are used in the building of new knowledge.

According to Goody (1987), "Before the coming of the transistorized tape recorder ... our knowledge of any except the shortest oral communication was confined to those produced ... when an outsider was usually involved as the audience and transcriber" (p. xi). Today, laptop and desktop computers, with voice and print functions, scoring systems for discourse analyses, and multiple media, such as video and digital cameras, have increased possible analyses of children's talk and meaning-making with classroom text.

In summary, with the above backdrop, this chapter sets the stage for the present book, one dedicated to the study of speech in schooling. It proceeds as follows: I discuss (a) the distinctive and overlapping nature of talk and text; (b) the historical and individual evolution of talking texts; (c) the co-occurrences, overlays, commingling, and commentaries of talk and text; (d) some of the institutional expectations that govern genres of talk; (e) oral discourse styles; and (f) developing talk in domains of knowledge taught in schools. Throughout the volume are illustrations of conversational discourse that may make for exemplary, advanced instruction. One may find commonalities and unique functions among the oral discourse styles presented across the chapters.

THE DISTINCTIVE AND OVERLAPPING NATURE
OF TALK AND TEXT

The conference paper, the quintessence of academic discourse, beautifully captures the distinctive and overlapping nature of talk and text, which, under most circumstances, is not so visible to the text reader or writer. Manuscripts undergo an evolution as they are produced from reflection that is written down and then read out loud to an audience. The conference paper is composed through small incremental steps based on the self-disciplined act of creative inquiry. This involves library research or computer searches with physical acts such as strokes of the pen or computer keys.[2] Its production depends on mental integration of ideas conveyed through oral and written-visual modes of expression. Ultimately, the reading aloud of the manuscript by the author or a designated representative may result in different outcomes. The oral presentation may vary by illocutionary force. The manuscript may be presented by a word- for-word reading, an outline, extemporaneous speaking guided by note cards, a dramatic oral performance, or a slide presentation. It has been characterized as "situated talk in action" (Rendle-Short, 2006).

At the other end, the audience interacts with the talk and the text. Audiences at a conference will process an oral presentation, an informal talk, and the written scholarly version of a conference presentation, or some combination of these, with their individual expectations and processing styles. Audiences will, undoubtedly, commingle and translate what initially appear to be independent systems of communication—the spoken with the written, the casual oral with the literate-written—until they reach a point of satisfaction and understanding.

As is commonly the case, one may find *listening* to a talk at a professional meeting a quite different experience from a later private, silent *reading* of that talk in a hotel room or at home—where the presenter's gestures and vocal intonations that were originally expressed at the conference are not synchronized with the talk (McNeill, 2004). Thus, the personal reading may generate a private voice, with interpretations quite different from the author's spoken public voice used in the original oral presentation (cf. Akinnaso, 1982; Chafe & Danielewicz, 1987;

Cornbleet & Carter, 2001; Coulmas, 1987, 1989; Elbow, 1985; Halliday, 1987; Horowitz, 1991a, b; Horowitz, 1998; 2004; 2006; Horowitz & Samuels, 1987; Raible, 1994; Schwanenflugel, Hamilton, Wisenbaker, Kuhn, & Stahl, 2004; Tottie & Bäcklund, 1986). Yet each mode and genre never operates entirely alone, but interfaces with the others depending on the professional event, society, or one's goals (Allen, 2000; Goody, 1987; Olson, 1997). Finally, an author's text comes alive, becomes a "talking text," with a reader's development (Clay, 2001), when the text is given a voice, rhythm, expressiveness, and audience (Beck, McKeown, & Worthy, 1995; Clay, 2001; Horowitz & Freeman, 1995; Horowitz & Norrick, 2006; Knoeller, 1998; Stahl & Kuhn, 2002; Wertsch, 1991). Texts come alive through the pedagogical practices and words of a teacher, who may be the guiding force and inspiration for a writer or reader (Johnston, 2004).

Through sustained dialoguing with others, and the self, an author may turn a manuscript into a publication with visible intertextual links. It is thereafter disseminated, sometimes through an array of media—from conference chatter to journals or proceedings, to books or documentaries or publisher advertisements—which convey its contributions to a reader-audience. In sum, this transforming process occurs through multiple oral and written sources. Often not considered, this transformation is highly influenced by the interlocutor and the discourse styles of particular disciplines, as well as the audiences the author wishes to target. Outcomes sought are influenced by distinct discourse communities and philosophies of constituencies in specified contexts.

Finally, a manuscript performs within a time frame in a cultural setting. If the manuscript becomes a book—a "Sefer" or a treatise—and has a life of its own. In the Judaic tradition, for "the People of the Book," it is a living, breathing document that is sacred (Horowitz, 2001). In the case of classical texts used over centuries or in the instance of the genres of liturgy or exegesis, when a book becomes tarnished and tattered, when it has reached its last bit of usefulness in everyday life, it is "Geniza." It is, ultimately, buried in the earth, as a once breathing-living document that has reached the culmination of its lifespan.

School Speaking and Writing

In school learning, speech and writing activities merge when one language system exerts an influence on the other, depending on how they are staged by the composer and received by the listener-reader. This influence of one language system of meaning "overlaying" another influences the impact of the message (e.g., it may increase the message valence and solidify meaning). One may imagine a statistical interaction for which the two events, objects, or variables are dynamic systems of meaning that mutually influence one another—until there is a blending of styles and content.

In school, the teachers' speech, for example, projects priorities. The words used interface with the priorities of written documents—such as textbooks, dictionaries, or maps—to clarify obtuse language or fill in gaps. This interaction is not only linguistically, but also cognitively, dependent on the rules of domains of knowledge. Further, reading about the brain in a science class and hearing about its evolution in a history class result in a different and deeper understanding than learning about it in just one discipline or setting.

Through computer functions such as e-mail, uses of the web and multiple media—compact discs, digital video discs, speaking and technological writing are changing in form and blending in style so that we have an informal discourse that is "rapid-fire" and more compact, with new conventions, and openly accessible to many (Harnad, 1995; Hunt, 1994; Finegan, 2002; 2006; Ong, 1992). The transfer of speech to writing (or vice versa) may be expressed by some children as a mere copy or imitation. For others, it may be expressed by a reconstruction of content that results in a new language expressed on the world of paper or the computer screen.

Theoretical Background for Speech and Writing Interactions

The interaction between speech and writing discussed here has been theoretically influenced by two publications. Jack Goody produced *The Interface Between the Written and the Oral* (1987) writing from the perspective of a linguist and anthropologist with appreciation for the historical. Goody argued it was a mistake to divide cultures into the oral and written—a dichotomy placing these in opposition—and to neglect the cultural-historical evolution and interconnectedness between talk and writing. He set the groundwork for study of the oral and written through fieldwork with the LoDagaa and Gonja in northern Ghana as they transitioned from the oral to the written and through his study of writing in India and China, by presenting not so much a theory but, as he describes it, "topics" worthy of further investigation.

Shortly thereafter, Deborah Tannen, ahead of her time, produced an essay in *American Speech* (1988) that piqued interest in academic discourse. Tannen proposed that the overlapping nature of talk and text in scholarly writing was essential to meaning-making and advancement of knowledge. In sum, following these lines of inquiry, it was evident that the evolution and interaction of talk and text warranted further exploration in a book-length manuscript with attention to schooling.

I found that despite the changing nature and overlays of formal talk and text in given cultural settings, these had been treated in the psychological and educational literature peripherally as static, disparate discourse forms. The present book is intended to broaden our perspectives about the creation and uses of this overlapping discourse. Some of the chapters set the stage for speech-reading interactions, others for speech-writing interactions; however, all are intended to add to our research, teaching, and policies on the primary, yet so often neglected, role of oral language in school literacy and learning.

While not sufficiently analyzed or scientifically studied, variations of teacher-student speech also interface with the school's institutional written documents. These documents can be binding and exert control on the student's daily life. Written documents include not only textbooks and encyclopedia-like sources—dictionaries and atlases in the classroom—but also standardized tests required by the United States federal government's *No Child Left Behind* mandate, children's cumulative records (e.g., report cards and attendance charts), contracts, health reports, and disciplinary pink slips. Expressions such as *"I will write you up," "This will go on your permanent record,"* and *"I'm sending you to the office!"* all communicate teacher-student text relationships and routines that are embedded within the macro-structures of institutional expectations. Teachers may write or speak as institutional managers of children. Some of the discourse becomes a source for determining reading and writing instruction. The words used establish policies that sort children into different tracks resulting in a child's affiliation with particular intellectual and social groups in school—not to mention cultural styles of behaving and learning (Ball, 2002; Olson, 2003).

Teacher-student interaction also contributes to the forming of a child's persona as a learner and communicator. As children move across group tasks and projects or teachers' rooms, they are continuously creating or re-establishing their in-school persona through discourse, whether they are the student leader or the class clown, a shy or an outgoing personality. Early on, children identify as at the top or bottom of the reading group, moreover, concomitantly as a science or a humanities student. Children pick up on the oral and body language of teachers to the point of imitation and voice rehearsals as they "study" a domain of knowledge. McPherson's research (2005) characterizes the evolution from "child to musician" during the beginning stages of learning an instrument and Bamberger (chap. 19, this volume) illustrates the conceptual change that occurs when children learn to think and talk about music. The evolution in understanding mathematical concepts can be abrupt or gradual. It can include expressions that communicate gesture-speech matches or mismatches to teachers. In turn, the teacher comes to understand child mathematical reasoning through utterances that are coupled with physical expressions (Alibali, 2005; Alibali & Goldin-Meadow, 1993; McNeill, 2004) in conjunction with texts.

To elaborate, in *Gesture and Thought*, David McNeill (2005) presents a conceptualization of gesture as imagery that is an integral part of the communication system, synchronized with language rather than simply a redundant attribute of speech. McNeill has examined how gesture and speech evolve and combine in real-time utterances following processing of visual representations such as videos. He proposes a theory which argues that evolution selected the ability to combine speech and gesture and proposes that different kinds of gestures may have different evolutions and trajectories. As we shall see in Philomena Donnelly and Kieran Egan's chapter in this volume, there are multiple biological dimensions of the speaker-writer that remain largely unexplored but are part of the child's evolution of talk and text.[3]

THE HISTORICAL EVOLUTION OF TALKING TEXTS

At the onset of *Comprehending Oral and Written Language* (1987), I proposed that written texts were becoming oral-like. Publishing shortly thereafter, Douglas Biber and Edward Finegan (1989) scientifically supported this claim. They developed an empirically based model of stylistic variation that illustrated dimensions of oral and literate varieties of English over time. Using that model, they empirically demonstrated that there has been a drift, across four centuries, from (a) detached, informational to involved production (where discourse is a more passionate, personal expression); (b) elaborated to situation-dependent reference; and (c) abstract to non-abstract style, resulting in more oral styles of written texts. They attribute this shift in written styles to an orality due to the rise in popular literacy, mass schooling, scientific purposes, and aesthetic preferences. A beautiful example of this shift in the sciences is reported by Scott Montgomery (2003). He provides samples in *Communicating Science* of the multi-modalities used to enhance cognition and learning through science texts.

The Bifurcation of the Oral and Written in Schools

The bifurcation of the oral and written in schools and educational research has been a result of the fractured state of affairs in language studies in higher education. In the United States, the oral and written have existed in separate departments, for historical, political, and economic reasons. Ultimately, this division has influenced undergraduate and graduate education and teacher training due to federal and state requirements for educators of the English language. Typically, speech development has been studied in linguistics departments, speech-communication programs, child language development courses, or as part of early childhood education in schools of education or institutes of child study. Of late, bicultural and bilingual programs and ethnic studies, along with anthropology programs, have taken up study of the way speaking and writing function in relation to one another in cultural contexts, with anthropologists examining the world's history of writing systems and texts.

Concomitantly, the written text and composing processes have been the subject of teaching and research in English department composition programs and English education programs. With the advent of the cognitive revolution, studies of speech have become part of the psychologist's study of identity and the mind.

Further, with the increasing attention to human language technology, the oral and written have been unified through scientific research on the use of the internet, the converting of acoustic signals to messaging, speaker-dependent dictation systems, or voice recognition software for dictating and composing or oral reading at the computer. These technological advancements have stimulated new multidisciplinary research on how the oral and written interface in machine-oriented social contexts (see Kelly & Chen, 1999; Mostow, et al., 2003).

While the oral and written have been brought together through technology, an alarmist rhetoric argues that conversational discourse is on the decline. If so, this has serious ramifications for school discourse. For example, in his 2006 *Conversation as a Declining Art*, Stephen Miller presents an historical account of the ways in which conversation has evolved, dating back to ancient times. He purports that conversations have been replaced by solitary ideas, television talk shows, interactive video games, multi-media communication, self-expression, and even emotional outbursts such as anger. Miller believes we live in an argument culture and one of "conversation avoidance." Similarly, a recent article distributed by the National Council of Teachers of English (Barker, 2006) promotes the idea that teenagers are speechless, "that text is the new talk" as "we are living in a 160-character nation, the maximum text message length" in a cell phone culture (p. 01D). Teenagers communicate via instant messaging, blogs, or social networks such as *MySpace* and *Facebook*. If face-to-face conversation is on the decline, an issue yet to be empirically and ethnographically investigated, students may not come to school with what have been thought of as the traditional tenets of everyday conversational skills (Dorval, 1990).

Speech in the Classroom

The history of speech in the classroom is missing from most historical accounts of speech-communication and rhetoric as a field of study. For instance, Herman Cohen's 1995 *The History of Speech Communication: The Emergence of a Discipline, 1914–1945* fails to include attention to the teacher as a communicator to and with students in a classroom, a situation that can be extended to the first 50 years of the 20th century.

However, the history of speech and national curricular accomplishments in schools has been studied extensively in the United Kingdom. A series of publications by Joan Tough of the University of Leeds (first published in 1979) outlines approaches to teacher talk, child talk, and assessment of children's talk with principles for curriculum and instruction. However, since then, exploration of the use of talk in U.K. classrooms appears to have declined due to political debates. Recently, Haworth (2001) and Barnes (1988) have addressed "oracy," noting "political tensions" over cross-cultural issues and teacher control. The United Kingdom has developed a *National Oracy Project* and *The National Literacy Strategy*. However, Haworth notes that similar to the United States, oral discourse continues to consist of teacher questions and response feedback such as in IREs (Initiate-Respond-Evaluate patterns) typical of large-group discussion in the United States. In contrast, Haworth provides an example of a discussion held by British seven year olds who have an understanding of the limits of IREs and the virtues of small-group interaction as a multi-voiced talk that evolves to convey a group's meaning-making. The students indicate, "We've all got different minds and … it's a bit like [supporting different] football teams" (p. 19).

Haworth concludes that "Oracy must be more than a subset of communication skills exercised by the resourceful teacher" (p. 22). Bakhtin (1986) compares "monologic talk with 'reciting by heart' and dialogic talk with the process of 'retelling in one's own words'" (p. 22) (see also chap. 2). Haworth argues that both have a place in the curriculum.

Close to home, the *Texas Essential Knowledge and Skills* (TEKS) provides guidelines for oral language development designed for Kindergarten through high school. However, the vision of oral language in the first grade is focused on the English phonology and orthography, with an emphasis on listening, responding appropriately, and receiving or retelling information rather than constructing or processing discourse. In second grade, there is more attention to purposes for speaking and listening across genres. However, the student is portrayed as practicing subskills of communication independently, rather than as an interlocutor engaged with peers and teachers in new idea generation. By third grade, there is more attention to discourse genres and writing but continued emphasis on reading for repeating, verbal and nonverbal talk, dramatic interpretations, and fluency for comprehension. Grades 4–8 show signs of increased attention to analyzing arguments, supporting evidence, elaborations in spoken ideas—reasoning skills that could be introduced in the earlier grades (chap. 7, this volume). By grade six, many important critical speaking and listening concepts are introduced, such as assessing speaker content, credibility, and delivery. The oral communication is presented by-and-large as public, official speaking. Nowhere did our graduate student group find attention to how the oral varies (from conversational talk to group literate-interactions, from narrative to informational exchange), how the oral is transformed to written discourse, or how the oral and written interact in daily or expert communication practices in different disciplines. This lack of curricular concern is an issue in grades 9–12. On a positive note, the curriculum does require attention to speech in groups, oral and written models of speeches as a basis for the development of speech skills, and oral and written critiques of formal speeches, but only in high school speech-communication electives.

Over the last half of the twentieth century, scholarly literature on the use of oral discourse and written texts in U.S. schools has grown substantially. Yet it lacks cohesion and unity. It requires organizing and inter-relating to a theory of school discourse if the research is to build substantial knowledge that can inform educational practices. While the present book does not purport to unify this literature, it does present some of the issues that we face in connecting talk and text processing in schools and understanding the commingling that occurs daily, for teacher and student alike. Table 1.1 is a 50-year timeline of theoretical books and reports, research methodologies, and significant research accomplishments. Many are classics. Most have influenced and will continue to influence the trajectory of our present thinking about oral and written instructional discourse as objects and speech and writing as creative processes.

TABLE 1.1
Classic Contributions to Classroom Talk and Text: A Fifty-Year Timeline

1956	Jerome Bruner, Jacqueline Goodnow, and George Austin produce *A Study of Thinking*, New York: Wiley.
1957	Lester Harrell produces *A Comparison of Oral and Written Languages in School Age Children*.
1962	Dell Hymes calls for an "Ethnography of Speaking" at a panel of the American Anthropology Association Conference.
1964	Dell Hymes produces "Toward Ethnographies of Communication," *The Ethnography of Communication*.
1966	Ronald Hyman, Arno Bellack, Herbert Kliebard, & Frank L. Smith develop an analysis of *The Language of the Classroom* that focuses on the teacher as the primary figure in communicating about concepts.
	Dell Hymes elaborates on "communicative competence."
1967	Roy O'Donnell, William Griffin, and Raymond Norris study children's oral and written language developmentally.
1968	Robert Rosenthal and Lenore Jacobson address *Pygmalion in the Classroom: Teacher Expectation and Pupils' Intellectual Development*. Teacher expectations are related to a pupils' intellectual development.
1970	Ned Flanders establishes The Flanders System of Talk that provides teacher question techniques; reported in *Analyzing Teaching Behavior*.
1971	Dell Hymes produces a paper on "Communicative Competence."
1972	John Gumperz & Dell Hymes establish the journal *Language in Society*.
	Courtney Cazden, Vera John, & Dell Hymes edit *Functions of Language in the Classroom*, designed to encourage teacher ethnography research.
1974	Ragnar Rommetveit presents *On Message Structure: A Framework for the Study of Language and Communication*.
	Aaron Cicourel produces the first classroom studies from sociology and ethnomethodology.
	Harvey Sacks, Emanuel Schegloff & Gail Jefferson's "A Simplest Systematics for the Organization of Turn-Taking in Conversation" is applied to classrooms.
	The National Institute of Education's (NIE) USA Report on Teaching as a "Linguistic Process" in a cultural setting in classrooms is released.

1975	Richard Bauman, & Joel Sherzer propose an "Ethnography of Speaking."
	John Sinclair & Malcolm Coulthard write *Towards an Analysis of Discourse: The English Used by Teachers and Pupils*, which provides approaches to discourse analysis.
	Michael Halliday produces *Learning How to Mean: Explorations in the Development of Language*, London: Edward Arnold.
1977	Frederic Erickson & Jeffrey Schultz ask: "When is a Context? Some issues and methods in the analysis of social competence."
	With Teun van Dijk's *Text and Context: Explorations in the Semantics and Pragmatics of Discourse*, context becomes an important factor in school text processing and comprehension.
	Roy Freedle, Founding Editor of *Discourse Processes*, produces a journal that is a major contribution to discourse studies.
1978	Elliott Mishler publishes "Meaning in context. Is there any other kind?" in the *Harvard Educational Review*.
1979	Anthropologist Clifford Geertz's examination of classrooms gains attention.
1980	James L. Kinneavy's *A Theory of Discourse* presents a historical approach to speech-writing bifurcations and a history of English departments and the teaching of composition at the secondary and college levels.
1981	Erving Goffman's *Forms of Talk* provides seminal essays on his conceptualization of talk—conversational dialogue that warrants "testing out."
	Judith Green & Cynthia Wallat map instructional conversations in *Ethnography and Language in Educational Settings*.
1982	Michael Halliday's work on what a text means gains attention.
	Jay Lemke's analysis of science talk in classrooms is one of the first analyses of science discourse in schools.
1987	Jack Goody, *The Interface between the Written and the Oral*, includes essays that address historical and philosophical perspectives about how writing and speaking interact.
	Rosalind Horowitz and S. Jay Samuels, *Comprehending Oral and Written Language*, examine similarities and differences in the production of spoken and written language, as objects—and listening and reading comprehension as processes essential for successful schooling.
1988	Judith Green & Judith Harker, *Multiple Perspective Analyses of Classroom Discourse*, address factors that must be examined when considering texts and broader discourse of the classroom.
	Douglas Biber, *Variation across Speech and Writing*, develops a linguistic, computerized system based on factor analysis contrasts of speech and writing.
	Deborah Tannen's "The commingling of orality and literacy in giving a paper at a scholarly conference" is published in *American Speech*.
1990	Ann Brown and Joseph Campione introduce and discuss the concept of "learning communities" in their chapter "Communities of Learning and Thinking, or a Context by Another Name" in Deanne Kuhn (Ed.) *Developmental Perspectives on Teaching and Learning Thinking Skills: Contributions in Human Development*.
	Jay Lemke's *Talking Science: Language, Learning and Values* is a linguistic analysis of school science talk.
1991	James Wertsch examines Vygotsky and Bakhtin's concept of "voice" in *Voices of the Mind: A Sociocultural Approach to Mediated Action*.

(continued)

TABLE 1.1   *(continued)*

1992	Rafael Diaz and Laura Berk's *Private Speech: From Social Organization to Self-Regulation* is produced.
1994	David Olson's *The World on Paper: The Conceptual and Cognitive Implications of Writing and Reading* examines how we come to know speech *after* the development in writing and knowledge of the world on paper. Ann Brown and Joseph Campione provide the chapter "Guided Discovery in a Community of Learners" in K. McGilly (Ed.) *Classroom Lessons: Integrating Cognitive Theory and Classroom Practice.*
1995	Charles Perfetti, Ann Britt, & Mara Georgia write *Text-Based Learning and Reasoning. Studies in History.*
1997	Martin Nystrand's *Opening Dialogue. Understanding the Dynamics of Language and Learning in the English Classroom* reports on a substantial study of upper-grade classroom interaction patterns. Nancy Spivey's *The Constructivist Metaphor: Reading, Writing, and the Making of Meaning* examines reading-writing relationships.
1998	Christian Knoeller, *Voicing Ourselves: Whose Words We Use When We Talk About Books.* Varieties of voicing used in high school student-led discussions.
1999	James Paul Gee produces *An Introduction to Discourse Analysis: Theory and Method.* Timothy Koschmann edits a special issue of *Discourse Processes, Meaning Making. Collaborating in problem-based discourse*, with CD-ROM. Gordon Wells writes *Dialogic Inquiry: Toward a Sociocultural Practice and Theory of Education.* Carnegie Mellon University's *Talk Bank* is established by Brian MacWhinney.
2000	Carol Lee and Peter Smagorinsky's *Vygotskian Perspectives on Literacy Research. Constructing Meaning through Collaborative Inquiry* is published. See Gordon Wells on *Dialogic Inquiry in Education*, which outlines the role of dialogue in knowledge building and different modes of knowing relevant to this book. Vera John-Steiner's *Creative Collaboration* examines scientific, artistic, feminist, "thought communities," and other creative collaborations. Brian MacWhinney creates *The CHILDES Project: Tools for Analyzing Talk. Transcription Format and Programs*, Third Edition, Vols. 1 & 2.
2001	James F. Voss is the guest editor of *Discourse Processes*. Special issue: Argumentation in Psychology, 32 (2&3).
2002	Otero, León, and Graesser edit *The Psychology of Science Text Comprehension*, a model analysis of discipline-specific text comprehension.
2003	Martin Nystrand and John Duffy edit *Towards a Rhetoric of Everyday Life.*
2004	Charles Bazerman and Paul Prior edit *What Writing Does and How it Does It.* Richard Bauman writes *A World of Others' Words: Cross-cultural Perspectives on Intertextuality*, which presents theoretical views of how texts evolve and are cross-linked as people make meaning out of them and life. Mary J. Schleppegrell's *The Language of Schooling* is a functional linguistics perspective to school language with attention to domains of knowledge.

2005	*Discourse Analysis & The Study of Classroom Language & Literacy Events—A Microethnographic Perspective* by David Bloome, et al., provides a sociolinguistic approach to classroom language, building on *New Literacy Studies*.
2006	Douglas Biber's *University Language: A Corpus-Based Study of Spoken and Written Registers* addresses the array of registers that university students process.

TALK AND TEXT: CO-OCCURRENCES, OVERLAPS, COMMINGLING, AND COMMENTARIES

Jack Goody's *The Interface Between the Written and the Oral* (1987) is a pivotal source for this volume. Goody considered talk-and-text among a range of individuals, cultures, and historical time periods. Listed below are six examples of talk-and-text relationships which have implications for classroom teaching that I generated following the reading of Goody's work.

Co-occurrences of Classroom Discourse Types

In classroom discourse, talk and written texts occur in relation to one another in specific pedagogical situations and contexts. They can be *concurrent*, where the text and speech are presented physically at the same time and are given equal psychological stature and weight. They can also be presented as *contiguous*, with one physically after another. Contiguous presentation may be *hierarchical*, such as when text is given precedence over what the teacher says or when a teacher's spoken instructions are superimposed on the written text in the everyday structure of school talk. Teachers determine oral-written relationships, given their instructional goals and children's instructional needs. Teachers convey which discourse should be given priority and why. In turn, students decipher the relationships intended between the talk and text (i.e., determine which is more relevant, will be needed in testing or for long-term recall). Students often remark, *"I don't understand the teacher, but I can get it from the book"* or, vice versa, *"I understand the teacher, not the book"* (see Aulls, 2002; Horowitz & Samuels, 1987; Poole, 2003; Schallert & Kleiman, 1979).

The *co-occurrence of talk and written sources* can be staged by a teacher to reflect some common classroom goal. For example, the move away from recitations by secondary students and monologues by teachers to the *"opening of dialogue"* and the use of discussion as a platform for instruction has been related to increased student motivation and achievement (Nystrand, 1997). It is quite conceivable that certain juxtapositions of talk with text influence the effort required in mental processing, e.g., ease of comprehension and interpretation, but will also increase learning and memory. These are questions that require research.

For example, in an eighth-grade history unit on ancient Egyptian society, the contributions of classroom discourse styles and communication patterns were examined as part of curriculum events and enactment on student content learning (Aulls, 1998). *Curriculum events* were defined as structured by clear beginnings and endings, clear patterns of teacher-student communication, and actions that functioned as part of a dynamic, ongoing learning process. Teachers and student participants, texts, other materials, and subject matter were all viewed as part of the lessons studied. The texts used in two classrooms were treated as embedded in a social cultural context. Content was processed through discourse patterns in separate-classroom events and as whole-classroom discourse.

The question posed was: *How does classroom discourse style correspond to the quantity and quality of student content learning in a history unit?* Classrooms were compared and contrasted over a 16-week period, using quantitative and qualitative discourse analysis measures. Conversations were categorized as academic or social conversations (managerial or other) using multiple measures as there were significant differences in the styles of the classrooms. What is important for the purposes of this chapter is that the classroom with the highest amount and better quality of learning contained the following attributes: This classroom spent more time on academic discourse in collaborative activities. It demonstrated the highest amount of learning as evidenced in higher recall of content and procedural knowledge. Students generated more questions than in the second class. The second class had more routine patterns of talk with more time focused on vocabulary definitions, no scaffolding, no teacher modeling and fewer teacher-roles, with the primary one as director or evaluator. It is important to highlight that the classroom with the highest learning included the teaching of history content as well as the methods of how to learn history; this classes' conversation is characterized by Aulls as "coherent," "sustained," and "collaborative." This is one of the first studies to link multiple features in teaching discourse style and classroom social culture with actual learning in a content field. Mark Aulls concludes:

> Learning is not a general state or an ability, separate from available opportunities arising from the teacher and class co-construction of curriculum events and from the type of instructional practices entailed within learning opportunities. As the teacher and students construct the curriculum as a text, they also establish social practices, define the focus of each event, and signal multiple textual relationships. [This study] ... points to the highly consistent correspondence of the content students recall to the quality of classroom discourse constructed during a curriculum event and to the emphasis and combinations of discourse forms that made up that event. (p. 65)

It is not only the connections of talk to printed textual sources that warrant our attention in learning, but also talk about the visual world—its images and artifacts that are part and parcel of the classroom. It has been shown how talk about visual representations of objects in real spatial arrangements *is* a "reading act" that will evolve and bear on other kinds of creative thinking (Ackerman, 2003; Paris, 2002; Perkins, 1977; Steiner, 2001). Further, conversations about art or museum objects represent a form of learning that stimulates high-level talk and high literacy (see Leinhardt, Crowley, & Knutson, 2002; Wilson, this volume). Sullivan (2005, p. 126) says "thinking in art and thinking about art, is language dependent." Further, "art talk is grounded in the sociocultural conventions of language." Talk can enhance perspective-taking, exercises in dramatic performance, and exegesis, resulting in creative levels of engagement and imagination (Greene, 2000; Perkins, 1992).

An example is given in David Hanauer's research (chap. 15, this volume) as he discusses the experiences of a Middle Eastern fourth-grade class in which children read the poem "The Lady with Baskets" (see pp. 374–376 in this volume). One of the teacher's strategies was to help the students focus on the repetition used in the poem, a strategy that can help to increase engagement with a text or create text cohesion. Repetition is also used in highly ritualized children's everyday speech to produce melodic text that enhances meaning (Horowitz & Cummings, 2000; Tannen, 1989; Bamberger, chap. 19). In some instances, repetition also is a holding pattern from which the reader will begin to imagine new associations.

The teacher-student dialogue about "The Lady with the Baskets" is dynamic, evolving, open-ended, reciprocal communication. While the context of the poem's creation is unclear and the language opaque, the listener-reader of Hanauer's poem makes associations to familiar contexts and dialogic expressions to interpret the poem. The poem is also explained based on associations within a given classroom context—what has transpired previously, the teacher's style of talk, what the teacher emphasizes or likes about poetry, and what the class has come to learn about what a poetic style does (see Elster & Hanauer, 2002, for further discussion of poetry as a literary tool for elaborated conversations).

The present volume includes two chapters on poetry because, although we often analyze stanzas, poetry is a unique genre of "talking text" that, much like a printed song, a musical symphony, or other art forms, cannot be broken down into parts if meaning is to be preserved. The physical presentation of poetry (and song) also conveys a unified meaning, as composers of music know too well (Zumthor, 1990).

To further explain "The Lady with Baskets," we turn to Voloshinov (1929/1986), who emphasizes that *reported speech*—one person's speech, reported by another person—is often separated from the context of origin. It thus appears as static and inert, borrowed language that is never quite the same as it originally was. Voloshinov states that what needs to be studied is "the dynamic interrelationship of … the speech being reported" (p. 119) (e.g., in Hanauer's poem (a) the woman's real speech on a bus, (b) the woman's speech as reported by the poem's narrator, and (c) the children's "reporting" through classroom talk of the woman's speech in the poem). After all, these three layers of sourcing function and take shape through their intertextual relationships and in relation to children's lives. See also Tannen (1989) for a discussion of repetition and imagery associated with another's words.

For many children, the original source and the words reported from that poetic source become the child's own personal possession, inner words of the child's psyche and context. Children also report and repeat linguistic elements of the written texts to which they are exposed. Pappas, Kiefer, and Levstik (1990) find that children's talk during joint reading actually matches the syntax of the texts read. Similarly, Eckhoff (1983) finds children's writing may incorporate the same kinds of discourse styles that they process in school basals.

Another type of *co-occurrences of source texts* may be found within children's new bilingual storybooks designed to promote biliteracy. These sources require specialized intertextual-cognitive and -linguistic processing. These books can have varied formats: English on one page and Spanish on the opposite page; English and Spanish presented contiguously, paragraph by paragraph, on the same page; and English-Spanish sentence-by-sentence translations. We have yet to know which of these bilingual designs are most effective for which English language learners (ELLs) and when. Nor do we know how children perceive these formats or if their perceptions may be commensurate or at odds with the teacher's expectations for bilingual reading.

Direction Giving: Common Co-occurrences of Spoken and Written Instructional Discourse

Direction giving is a referential communication practice that is used routinely in classrooms and occupational contexts to guide learning (Aijmer, 1996; Yule, 1997). In Chapter 2, Cynthia Kennedy, a middle school classroom teacher, gives directions to her students for reading and writing about camels in the desert.[4] In her oral directions, she refers to her written directions on the blackboard and to the tools the students will use in their writing. The oral directions are presented in a conversational style, very much in contrast to the formal style of the expository passage they will read on camels and the follow-up writing they will produce about camels for public consumption by their peers. Following children as they progress in talk and text processing, as they learn about the functions of camel types, can give teachers a lens for understanding how children tackle a new subject from different sources.

Overlays in Talk and Text

Instructional discourse often includes a variety of overlays in or between talk and text that the novice learner in a given content field will need to process. *Overlays (similar to the linguistic notion of overlaps that occur across sentences) may contain one or more sources of discourse, (e.g., oral and written directions) that are processed within or overlapping another source.*[5] These include speech contained within another sample of talk or text. Bilinguals, such as Hispanic Americans, Jewish Americans, and African Americans, use speech *in* writing consciously or unconsciously in distinct ways that reflect their social-cultural identity. By allowing these *overlays* or hybrids (e.g., Spanglish), school writing is richly influenced by personal expressions, rather than stripped of them, and the person is restored after a period of objectivity (Horowitz, 1995).

Overlays may include: (a) dialogue embedded within a text; (b) think-alouds, meta-cognitive monitoring about a text—produced during the reading or writing of a text; (c) marginalia or footnotes in a conversational style explicating meaning which the reader processes along with the text; or (d) one speaker's expression articulated over another speaker's words and sentences. The think-aloud processes or marginal explanations are another text in and of themselves, hybrids of talk and text such as found on the Internet. While oral genres in the everyday world and written-literate genres in school environs may seem like binary, competing discourse styles, exemplary instruction includes the ability to bring together oral and literate genres, what Moje, Ciechanowski, Kramer, Ellis, Carrillo, and Collazo (2004) call "working toward third space in content area literacy" (p. 38). The result is a new kind of conversation that reshapes academic content and literacy and could be conceived of as intersections of discourse types (see Fig. 1.1).

Overlays can be argumentative, opposing expressions or, in contrast, may also represent intense engagement with a source and serve as a sign of delicate cooperation and commitment to the dialogue or the interlocutor. It just de-

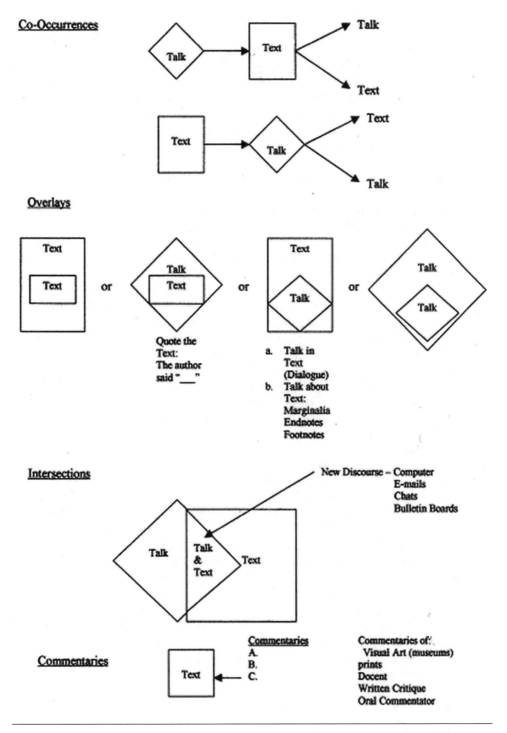

Figure 1.1   Instructional Decisions in Designing School Talk and Text Relationships

pends. Moerman (1988) astutely contends, "Every interruption, every overlap, every bit of talk is culturally—as well as socially, sequentially, and linguistically—constituted. Between speech communities, regions, and even individuals, the form, placement, and interpretation of overlaps may differ, often insidiously" (p. 28). When texts talk to readers, they become natural and self-reflective forms of communication. When talk becomes a written text (through cohesion devices, transcription, or translations), we distance ourselves from the discourse and analyze its meanings objectively. We place the discourse in the context of known texts as we seek connections between texts (Allen, 2000).

Overlays in Talk, Text, and Physical Task Manipulations

The historical image of reading is one of a person, usually a male, sitting alone beneath an oak tree with a book. But this is not true today. Experts at work engage in a different kind of reading, which has rarely been portrayed. In reality, experts maneuver talk, text, and tasks simultaneously and seldomly alone. In an exquisite study of pilot communication, Maurice Nevile (2004) presents schematizations of how talk, text, and non-talk activity overlay one another in a work setting, using audio and video equipment to study pilot discourse. He uses a discourse analysis system for the purpose of showing the relationships between pilots' moment-by-moment in-flight talk and physical actions. They manipulate the keyboard, interact orally to navigate the plane, and make notations on paper, almost simultaneously or in shifts of attention.

Another, more everyday, illustration of the overlays of talk, text, and task manipulations is the process of installing a computer modem. Directions may be given by a "live" person (on video, through the Internet, or by phone) speaking directly to the installer and by a written manual, both of which provide instructions about the physical actions and keyboard manipulations necessary to complete the installation. The interface of these three modes of learning (the talk, the text, and the touch of the keyboard) teaches the installer what to do. Human attention is shifted between the "live" oral directions, the written manual, and the physical manipulations. Thus, learning is not from the book alone.

When we turn to other physical tasks in everyday life that may be influenced by speech and writing, we find society may or may not value them. Physical activity at the workbench, with or without orality, is frequently given low prestige. Recently, Mike Rose (2004) asks that we rethink the hand-brain relationship. He argues that, typically, physical work such as carpentry or welding is regarded as "rudimentary, even primitive," those "neck down" (p. xix) performances that suggest these workers have low intelligence. Yet, they are often participants of highly technical oral discourse that guides their productivity. Furthermore, cognitive scientists associate the reading of technical manuals or thinking in procedural discourse patterns with high intelligence and high literacy.

Overlays of Talk, Text, and Cultures

Overlays also occur in the everyday language we speak that reflects one culture (e.g., an immigrant's culture, such as the Hmong) as it is related to another culture (e.g., the new culture encountered, such as English in Minnesota). An illustration of this is when immigrant women in Mexico City hire a scribe to complete their literacy acts so they can interact in everyday functions within and outside their neighborhoods (Kalman, 1999). Some of these women are more able than others to access the language and tools necessary to interface with their children's school. This ability contributes to the extent to which their children are successful in schooling. Intersections of talk and text from one culture may create a new discourse form or result in code-switching when introduced in a second culture.

Commentary: An Oral-Historical Perspective on Text

A commentary about text is an explanation or interpretation that clarifies a written text and relates it to another context (and text). Commentaries can be comments on vocabulary, etymology of lexical items, or concepts presented or comments about the structure of a sentence, stylistic matters, or rhetorical arguments of a text. They may address the context in which a passage is written, the perspective of the author or related sources, or the content. Goody (1987) asserts that "each literary work that is given high status … gives rise to commentaries only when they are written down" and become part of the corpus of written discourse (p. xiv).

In the case of ancient writings, words may take on different meanings in different historical periods (Nakanishi, 1980; Rabin, 1986). The commentator offers an explanation based on the time in which the commentator lives and the philosophy held. For example, the French Rabbi Rashi comments on the word choice of "land" in Genesis 13:6 from the Hebrew Bible, noting it is part of an elliptical phrase which translates as "pasturage," with all its eleventh-century connotations (Rabin, 1986, p. 220).

When a word or a phrase is not understood in everyday talk, the listener can simply call for another's clarification or check a dictionary. In ancient and modern texts, the commentator (who is the speaker) clarifies ambiguities through knowledge of the culture, text types, and historically and culturally based discourse conventions. We learn from historical texts through each generation's commentaries that overlay the previous generation's commentaries. In addition, study groups may comment on the commentaries and the original source and transmit their comments to still others—intragenerational groups.

In closing, the above six types of relationships between talk and text are not strictly an academic exercise. These six relationships can be applied to instruction to enhance children's construction of knowledge. Figure 1.1 illustrates instructional options teachers have in designing school talk and text relationships. Hybrid forms of communication can serve as a negotiation tool as teachers foster learning among culturally varied populations. Hybrid forms of talk (such as neighborhood and school talk) and forms of talk-text (such as stories combined with informational discourse) can provide teachers with discourse forms that will incorporate historical, communal, and individual perspectives on content processing and may bridge school learning across fields (Elster, 2005; Solsken, Willett, & Wilson-Keenan, 2000).

INSTITUTIONAL EXPECTATIONS AND GENRES OF TALK

Macro and Micro Structures of Discourse in Schooling

Concepts and principles in knowledge domains are learned through dialogues that modify our thinking. James Paul Gee (2001) illustrates this when he refers to antiquity. "For Plato, true knowledge comes about when one person makes a statement and another asks, *'What do you mean?'* [italics added] Such a request forces speakers to 're-say,' say in different words" what they mean. In this process they come to see more deeply what they mean as they respond to the perspective of another voice or viewpoint. Writing is also a "repeating" of what the text has said, or a peer validation that facilitates another level of critical analysis for an audience (Gee, 1996, p. 28). E-mail is often in the form of a statement-comment relationship whereby the receiver repeats and extends the sender's ideas.

Figure 1.2 depicts the range of macro and micro dialogues that could be applied to the theme *Invention and the Formation of Ideas*, an interdisciplinary unit that was used in a Toronto-based school I visited. After the visit, I identified the multiple discourses that could come to bear on a student's school encounter with the concept of invention and contemplation of the question *"Where do ideas come from?"* This boxology summarizes the social-psychological dimensions of discourse contexts outside the classroom—speech resources and references available within the broader institution of schooling, through libraries or computer labs (at a macrolevel)—and discourse within the classroom—school texts for problem-solving, academic disciplines, tasks, and speech as pre-text for the study of invention (at a micro-level).

George Steiner (2001) sees invention as time-bound and creation as timeless since "the Homeric poem, the Platonic dialogue, the Vermeer townscape, the Mozart sonata do not age and grow obsolescent as do the products of invention" (p. 262). Bruner (1979) sees creation as detachment, "a willingness to divorce oneself from the obvious" (p. 23). Similarly, Northrup Frye (1964) portrays the creative imagination as building tolerance through "the power of detachment, where things are removed just out of reach of belief and action" (p. 78).

ORAL DISCOURSE STYLES

The Peculiar and Unique Contributions of Classroom Discourse

In this section, we review the oral discourse styles that researchers and teachers in the present book have addressed. As a group, they convey the unique qualities of classroom discourse relative to conversations in other natural contexts, a contrast that needs further investigation. They also relate this specialized oral discourse to the documents used in school. This discourse and relevant documents mark the way for what will be an *advanced literacy* for the twenty-first century.

In Chapter 2 of this volume, Rosalind Horowitz and David R. Olson call for a *theory of discourse* that analyzes the kinds of intertextual relations and cross-referencing that occur among children, developmentally, as they become literate in schools. Children learn to incorporate multiple sources and to acknowledge those sources through linguistic devices that they, interestingly enough, invent. By way of *The Camel Study*, Horowitz and Olson show how 4th-, 7th-, and 8th-graders and university students progress in their ability to use and credit encyclopedic-like sources about the camel and avoid plagiarism. The writing samples, which were collected as part of a jigsaw method, demonstrate that without direct instruction, some more able learners may just naturally move through various stages in crediting oral and written sources. The texts to which they are exposed have a voice and talk to these learners in different ways as they mature through the grades. The stages of crediting sources proposed here show how use

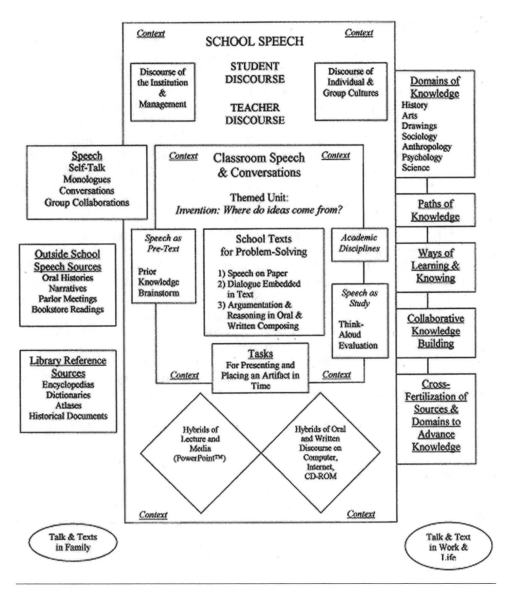

Figure 1.2.   School talk and text relationships.

of one's own words or that of another's words contribute to child and adolescent referencing. The skill of reference is a means of constructing organization and coherence as learners represent new content. In the past, referencing was primarily associated with children's speech that referenced another adult's or peer's words and later was studied in connection with referencing of narratives. Being able to manipulate informational sources one encounters, through embedding processes such as referencing, illustrates one kind of linguistic control that learners must acquire to advance in education and to attain expert-like status in the communication of disciplines.

Child, Adolescent, and Family Natural Conversations

Amy Sheldon, a linguist at the University of Minnesota and author of Chapter 3 in this volume, communicates a principle central to the entire volume: Talk *is* a text. Sheldon notes that the natural conversations children have "provide a transition and set the stage for entry into the mysteries and intricacies of written texts."

Children as young as three- to five-year-old girls in a daycare center use a persuasive strategy Sheldon calls "*double-voicing.*" They are voicing a stance, using "conflict mediation skills in which the speaker confronts the listener, gently without being confrontational" (p. 97, this volume). They are trying to win a point, but not lose face—nor do they wish to alienate or destroy friendships. Adult women know this. For example, an administrative assistant at my institution has a sign in her office that proclaims, "*It's better to be nice than right.*"

Sheldon shows how, in contrast to female discourse, pre-school male discourse is confrontational, more direct, and less tactful, all evidenced in male use of a "*single-voice discourse.*" They worry less about alienating another interlocutor. She finds that her female subjects, on the other hand, have the ability from an early age to use more than one voice within a brief segment of interaction, and they do so with great ease. Sheldon posits that the oral texts children produce at this age are far more complex than the written ones they are starting to read and write. Speech grammar may also be less regular than that of writing, especially during adolescence, as Anna-Brita Stenström (author of chap. 4 in this volume) illustrates, and more syntactically complex, as M. A. K. Halliday (1987) purports. Sheldon's proposition is consistent with Halliday's claim that natural speech is syntactically more complex than written language. Sheldon shows that young children, not yet in formal schooling, talk about talk—analyze their own and other's expressions as they negotiate access and sustain roles in pretend play.

Chats Versus Discussions

Although largely unresearched, adolescents use specialized oral discourse styles in their everyday lives *outside* of schools. *Chats*, common among teenagers, are open dialogues that ultimately evolve into other, more complex, forms of discourse such as discussions and debates. Teenagers develop skill with more complex discourses required in domains of knowledge in middle and high schools.

Anna-Brita Stenström, a linguist at The University of Bergen, Norway, investigated how teenage chats and discussions differ in natural contexts (chap. 4, this volume). Drawing from the famous Bergen Corpus of London Teenage Language (COLT), consisting of half a million words of spontaneous dialogue by 13–17 year olds, Stenström examined two conversations by 16-year-old females enrolled in a boarding school in outer London. The girls' first conversation, a *chat* about boys, evolved into a second conversation where they *discussed* smoking, drinking, and taking drugs. Stenström traced the speakers' use of *Initiating Moves, Responding Moves,* and *Follow-up Moves* (IRFs) to show how they modified their language according to topic and discourse.

The chats contained *Initiating* and *Responding Moves*, in the form of questions and answers, more affirmative expressions, and less planning than the discussions. They conveyed agreement and cooperation through use of "*and*" and "*so.*" In contrast, the discussions contained all three *moves*—consisting of speaker opinions, rhetorical questions, calls for clarifications—and contained more interruptions and overlaps, hesitations, repetitions, and complete constructions than the chats. They more often contained differences of opinion that were expressed through use of connectives *but* and *because* (cf. chap. 11 for further treatment of the development and use of these connectives). Stenström, Andersen, and Hasund's full report of teenage talk (2002) addresses reported speech, non-standard grammatical features, use of intensifiers, tags, and conflict talk that may be helpful for understanding adolescent classroom talk and writing styles (see also Calfee, Dunlap, & Wat, 1994; Horowitz, 1994; Rampton, 2006).

Dinner talk, analyzed by linguist Shoshana Blum-Kulka of The Hebrew University in Jerusalem (chap. 5, this volume), illustrates how out-of-school talk within the family can serve as a mediation strategy for in-school talk, enhance literacy development, and introduce children to the concept of participating in a democratic society. Middle-class Israeli and Jewish American families use dinner talk as a vehicle for intergenerational socialization discourse. This family activity consists of parents scaffolding communication through acknowledgments, explanations, clarification, and question-answer sequences not so different from teacher-child talk. Blum-Kulka emphasizes that the dinner talk is not random chitchat, but represents "culturally structured" discourse that is a precursor to development of adult discourse competencies. The ability to speak out ideas in decontextualized ways originates at the dinner table but also occurs in other everyday contexts, such as in car talk (Marvin, 1995), and is consistent with Basil Bernstein's (1971), by now quite famous, elaborate code characteristic of public discourse and its settings.

Interestingly enough, oral repetitions and conversational routines at family dinners may serve some of the same functions for children as repeated readings in school. They provide vocabulary and syntax rehearsals appropriate for a given task and context. Blum-Kulka finds that talk in families is culturally bound. In some middle-class families, it is an "open-ended" conversation, co-constructed with adults; in others, it is adult-defined and restrained. It is more formal in American Jewish families than Israeli families. She argues that (a) the regulation of the conversation, (b) the choices of topics, (c) the rules of turn-taking, (d) the modes of storytelling, and (e) the politeness and etiquette rules are culturally defined.

Most important for the purpose of the present book is that there is an ethos in middle-class families of child-centeredness. Children are equals in the table dialogue, with rights to speak. They are encouraged in American-Israeli families to argue, discuss, and be open. In sum, dinner talk may provide a first-of-its-kind context for decontextualized language and may be the first group communication children partake in that evolves through adult-guided thinking. In some instances, peer-guided interaction is developing simultaneously (Blum-Kulka, 1997, 2004, 2005; Blum-Kulka & Snow, 2002). This dinner talk is circumscribed by cultural styles of knowing.

Cultural Expectations in Parent-Child Talk and Literacy Development

Jerome Bruner (1996) characterizes culture as a "toolkit of techniques" (p. 98) for coping with life situations. Similarly, Lev Vygotsky argues one's culture provides the basic tools for human transactions and managing psychological daily dilemmas. Leila Monaghan and Jane Goodman's volume (2007) show how communication patterns about and in institutional settings are inseparable from culture. In this volume, Robert Bayley and Sandra Schecter (chap. 6) focus on four Spanish-speaking immigrant families' dilemmas and perceptions about instructional agendas in school tasks. Although these immigrant parents all continued to use Spanish at home, they enrolled their children in English classrooms with definite expectations that their children be taught English by the school. Bayley and Schecter find that: (a) the Spanish-speaking parents may not have enough English language skills to support their child's learning and, thus, rely on the school; (b) they may not be skilled in managing daily, routine decisions; and, (c) they may disagree with educators about parenting styles. Moreover, language minority and immigrant parents encounter challenges and experience shifts in their thinking that will influence their child's language, education, and identity formation over time. This research shows that on the one hand, they may wish to use their language to preserve a linguistic and cultural link to the past. On the other hand, they may wish that their American-born children become successful in school, fit into society, and develop the ability to speak, write, and read English for upward mobility in American society.

Chapter 6 conveys the ingenious strategies that primary caretakers use and the will power they have to resolve home-school differences in oral language and reading practices. Creative strategies arise as parental attitudes toward reading in Spanish and English change. Bayley and Schecter call for increased attention to parent-child home interactions and their relationships to school literacy learning (see also Bayley & Schecter, 2005 and Pease-Alvarez & Schecter, 2005).

EXEMPLARS OF FORMS OF TALK IN CLASSROOMS

The Forms of Talk, practiced in school can be explained through the theoretical work of Erving Goffman. In *Forms of Talk*, Goffman (1981) wrote about three elements of conversational dialogues relevant to chapters in the present volume. He explained (a) the ritualization of talk, (b) the participation framework, and (c) the embedding of talk.

First, in *The Presentation of Self in Everyday Life*, Goffman (1959) addresses the rituals of talk, that all speakers (and we should include teachers and students) are engaged in a theatrical performance of self, composed of familiar conversational rituals that are designed to control or manage the perceptions of the audience. The speaker expresses intentions and messages through rituals conveyed by multiple communication acts—vocal expressions, glares, physical appearance, "postural shifts" and tones of voice, updates, restarts, and pauses (Goffman, 1981, pp. 1–2).

> The listener who retells can fill in the gaps: In retelling events—an activity which occupies much of our speaking time … we are forced to sketch in these shadings a little …. Fiction writers and stage performers extend these everyday capacities …. But even here only sketching is found. (Goffman, 1981, p. 2)

Similarly, in schools, there is a range of talk rituals that children practice (e.g., expressed by the class clown or class cynic in the form of a dramatic performance) that can influence the instruction in a room.

Second, participant frameworks play a role in talk. Language occurs within the context of particular structural designs of classrooms. The students, their choice of vocabulary, sentence patterns, questions, replies, and responses result in a "participation status." Goffman conveys that the transcription used to study the discourse will depend upon the participants—in our case, whether remedial, gifted, or mainstream. Participant status also can be influenced by the physical arrangement throughout the school—e.g., the design of the library, the apparatus on the playground, and the school hallways with locker locations frequented by bullies (see Bloom, et al., 2005; Calfee, Dunlap, & Wat, 1994).

Third, familiar with the Russian psychologists, Goffman reiterates their views as he characterizes the embedding of talk—"the words we speak are often not our own" (p. 3). Goffman conveys that we may quote another (directly or indirectly, aware or unaware) with content (implied or explicit). This embedding of language can be thought of as citations, quotations, or commentaries—intertextual experiences. Goffman promises that "These markings can ... mimic, mime or reenact" (p. 4).

Children's Rhetorical Styles, Reasoning, and Argumentation Skills

In most classrooms, children have little opportunity to create rhetorical arguments or convey their claims, evidence, or reasoning in speech or writing (cf. Toulmin, 1958). However, at the same time, fourth-graders are increasingly faced with new facts and opinions in informational sources, making this an opportune time for study of rhetorical styles of arguments and their legitimacy. Although not solicited, the fourth grade was studied extensively in the research reported in this book. This fourth-grade focus is due to a desire to understand how children make the transition from oral to written discourse as they are exposed to varied combinations of oral-literate–like hybrid texts, work that I am pursuing with my colleague Amie Beckett. Some of the chapters in the present volume chronologically follow Palincsar and Magnusson (2001), who studied how fourth-grade classrooms function as a *community of inquiry* under "first-hand evaluation tasks" (when they actually see science experiments) and "second-hand evaluation tasks" (where they read about science tasks and experience them). Palincsar and Magnusson show that notebook texts—hybrid texts that contain a combination of narrative, expository, and argumentative discourse styles, and a clear voice—facilitate fourth-graders' investigation of arguments. As Hines (2001) conveys, and I have long held, controversy belongs in the science classroom (and in other fields as well) as it stimulates children to develop reasoning skills that may be applied to other domains beyond the study of science.

Talk as Collaborative Reasoning about Literature

How does a teacher change the patterns of classroom interaction in order to implement a reliable system of critical reading and thinking among elementary school children? Kim Nguyen-Jahiel, Richard C. Anderson, Martha Waggoner, and Betty Rowell (chap. 7, this volume) provide a model case study of a teacher's journey and evolution from direct instruction to a more open classroom participation. Nguyen-Jahiel et al. have strategically selected fourth-graders as their subjects and developed student reasoning about real-life dilemmas through class discussions. This is in keeping with attention to the fourth-grade in United States federal and corporate reports that provide assessment data that indicate substantial reading difficulties and usually a drop in performance, at fourth-grade—*The Nation's Report Card: Fourth-Grade Reading 2000* (Donahue, et al., 2001); The RAND (Research and Development Corporation) Report, *Reading for Understanding* (Snow, 2002); *The National Reading Panel Report* (2001); and the *NAEP* (National Assessment of Educational Progress) report (Dabbs & Block, 2002). In the present research approach to *Collaborative Reasoning*, the discussion topic often allows for multiple student perspectives. Narrative text and real student experiences are the basis for exploring the issues at hand. The teacher's emphasis is on understanding students' logical positions and how they arrived at them rather than on reaching a class consensus. With teachers as facilitators, students initiate control of the floor and regulate and direct the discussion. This method has been shown to be effective in building thinking and reasoning skills.

However, will the development of oral reasoning transfer to written reasoning? Extending this work, Reznitzkaya, Anderson, McNurlen, Nguyen-Jahiel, Archodidou, and Kim (2001) argue that supportive oral dialogical contexts can help develop well-reasoned writing so that essays contain acceptable reasons, counterarguments, rebuttals, and argument strategies. These have been taught in traditional rhetoric classes, but certainly not to children. The advantages of oral argumentation add to research on ways of developing speech and writing (Cazden, 2001a, b; Nystrand, 1997; Nystrand & Graff, 2001). Specific strategies referred to by Alma Reznitzkaya and colleagues include demonstrating reasoning processes through think alouds, challenging students with counter ideas, acknowledging good reasoning, summing up what has been said, and using the vocabulary of critical and reflective thinking (p. 158). Such discussion-based approaches are also rare in middle and high school classes where writing in content fields is needed (Applebee, Langer, Nystrand & Gamoran, 2003).

Research by Kim Nguyen-Jahiel and colleagues demonstrates that fourth-grade students exposed to *Collaborative Reasoning* produced significantly more "relevant arguments, counterarguments, rebuttals, formal argument devices, and uses of text information" in persuasive essays than those not exposed to collaborative reasoning. Several excellent articles follow Chapter 7 and support these claims. (See Anderson, et al., 2001; Anderson, Chinn, Waggoner, & Nguyen, 1997; Chinn, Anderson, & Waggoner, 2001; Reznitskaya, et al., 2001; Reznitskaya & Anderson, 2002.)

Teacher-Led Instructional Conversations

William Saunders and Claude Goldenberg (chap. 9, this volume) scientifically examine the effects of *Instructional Conversations* (ICs) in a teacher-led discussion, also with fourth-grade students, in this case in a transitional phase of a Spanish bilingual program. The *conversational elements* teachers incorporated included: (a) use of connected discourse; (b) use of fewer known answers; (c) teacher responsiveness to student contributions; (d) a challenging but non-threatening atmosphere; (e) self-selected turn-taking; and, (f) less teacher talk. The *instructional elements* teachers incorporated included: (a) a thematic focus; (b) the utilization of background knowledge; (c) the elicitation of complex, extended discourse; (d) promotion of bases for positions and statements; and, (e) direct teaching.

Using ICs, the researchers looked at 4th-grade Spanish-speaking English Language Learners (ELL) reading of a story about a mischievous friendship. The students participated in either ICs (experimental group) or conventional recitation-like reading (control group), which were followed by a writing activity. The researchers found that 63% of the IC students displayed a more complex concept of friendship than the control group. Through the use of IC principles, the minority students gained knowledge about the evolution of discourse, while at the same time learned how to work with open-ended questions about friendship. ICs promoted a high level of comprehension. Students also learned that friendship may result in disputes. Saunders and Goldenberg's use of the topic of friendship is noteworthy. Recent work by Pelligrini, Galda, and Flor (1997) shows that children's friendships may play an important role in literate language development and literacy. In addition, children may be attracted to these ICs because they are about texts on friendship.

Douglas Hacker and Arthur Graesser (chap. 10, this volume) assert there has not been research to show how the dialogue per se used in *Reciprocal Teaching* actually works in a natural tutoring context. *Reciprocal Teaching* is a form of "scaffolding" instruction that includes teacher-tutee questioning, summarizing, clarifying, and predicting, where the teacher moves from model to collaborator. Charles Goodwin and Alessandra Duranti (1992) define "scaffolding" as the difference between what the child can do on his or her own and what he or she can do under adult collaboration (p. 21). "For Vygotsky, what should be measured is not what the child knows before the test, but rather the ability of the child to interact with caretakers so as to extend one's present knowledge toward new frontiers" (p. 21).

Hacker and Graesser study collaboration in the teaching of research methods and algebra and the evolution of the tutor-tutee instruction relationship. Graduate school students tutored undergraduate students in a research methods course. High school students tutored 7th-graders in algebra. Thus, we have an expert student, a more capable peer and problem solver, tutoring a less knowledgeable novice student in reading in a social interactive situation where real reading problems are tackled. An elaborate transcript of 14 days of tutor-tutee dialogue was obtained. Hacker and Graesser focus on the collaborative aspects of the dialogue and the tutoring. They find that the collaborative tutoring resulted in a systematic conversational pattern and strategies, which entailed *pumping, prompting, splicing,* and *hinting,* that were used by the tutor in the collaboration. The teacher works to overcome obstacles and modify student thinking (Hacker & Tenent, 2002).

There are five steps that Hacker and Graesser propose that are based on the dialogue observed in their tutoring research, with Step 4 being singled out as critical. This is where the tutor extends and revises the dialogue during the collaboration. They conclude that this collaborative exchange is central to cognitive learning in the case of both their naturalistic tutoring and other work on reciprocal teaching. They demonstrate that "collaborative exchanges" contribute to what makes a high quality dialogue that influences learning.

Noteworthy is that in the cognitive apprenticeship of the tutee, the student is *not* learning regimented scripts, but rather strategies to be used *flexibly* in order to meet unique needs as a reader and problem solver.

Why is the collaborative exchange so important in tutoring? With a collaborative instructional style, there is a redefinition of power roles and a "reduction in asymmetry of power," with the teacher becoming more of an equal partner with the student in the dialogue. That is, the tutor and tutee are working together using language and their probing and problem-solving skills to reach a mutual understanding about a problem and its solution. One's question is an opportunity for the other's reply and yet another question, which then becomes an opportunity for the teacher to better understand where the student is cognitively and what next steps should be taken to help the student. Research on collaborative exchanges and, in particular, the Hacker-Graesser chapter is part of a growing trend in developing problem solving, self-regulation, and competent thinking in domains of learning (De Corte, Verschaffel, & Masui, 2004).

Children's Use of Conjunctions in Oral Language vs. Their Use In Processing Written Language

Esther Geva, of the University of Toronto and author of Chapter 11, shows how development and use of conjunctions in oral language relates to their use in processing written language as children transition from narrative to expository texts. Conjunctions explain logical relations essential to understanding domains of knowledge. While research on children's knowledge and use of conjunctions was conducted across a range of fields in the U.S. in the 1970s and 1980s, it began to taper off until European linguists and psychologists resumed these studies (see research in The Netherlands by Sanders, Spooren, & Noordman, 1992, 1993; Sanders & Gernsbacher, 2004). The multiple kinds of surface cues and their functions with content in conveying the tenor of text are evident in a special issue of *Discourse Processes* (Lagerwerf, Schober, Spooren, & Degand, 2006).

Geva shows that children use *and* frequently as an additive for cohesion. Knowledge of *because* and *although* present more difficulty and is followed by development in use of *when* and *if*. Moreover, familiarity with content resulted in more successful use and understanding of the conjunctions *because* and *and* while not so for *but*.

While children may use conjunctions in oral language, they may not process and comprehend them in decontextualized written contexts or when reading multiple texts in schools. In Geva's research, less skilled readers in grades 3 and 5 experienced difficulty with conjunctions in expository texts and did not make the proper inferences. The hardest task was the reading of text with adversative relationships and unfamiliar content. Joanna Williams (2006) found that children as young as the second grade could be taught adversative structures via signal words used in encyclopedia-sources and that this would enhance their comprehension of compare-contrast content. In her chapter, Geva argues that students with greater content knowledge will be more successful at using conjunctions to determine relationships between ideas than those students lacking content knowledge but possessing strategies.

Conjunctions are only one of many linguistic features that are used in literate-speech that will need to enter and ultimately be processed *within* literate-writing (i.e., when students are writers or readers). In addition to conjunctions, elaborated noun phrases, adverbs, and mental and linguistic verbs have also been identified as literate language features that occur in speech to increase explicitness and reduce ambiguity in decontextualized discourse. Curenton and Justice (2004) found the use of conjunctions and mental and linguistic verbs (e.g., *think, know, tell, call,* that provided information about the mental processes of story characters) were literate-like features that preschool-age children used in oral narratives. The use of these linguistic features increased with age, with three year olds using them less than four and five year olds. This research was undertaken with the intent that knowledge of uses of literate-speech features would enhance researchers' and clinicians' abilities to deliver prevention and intervention models for children requiring oral language support.

For Jerome Bruner (1979), intellectual activity is almost always a "continuation of dialogue," (p. vii) accompanied by a reconstruction of the conventional surprise, passion, and decorum. The right hand, according to Bruner, reflects logic and order—such as in geometry and engineering. The left hand is art and music. "While the poet, the mathematician, the scientist must each achieve detachment, they do it in the interest of commitment" (p. 24).

DEVELOPING TALK IN DOMAINS OF KNOWLEDGE

The ways in which talk and text are formed and interact depend on elements of domains of knowledge and academic disciplines that students encounter in the context of schooling.

Domains of knowledge are organized, rule-governed fields of study developed by experts outside of schools but also formulated and taught in schools as academic fields of study (e.g., history, science, music, art, mathematics, government). Talk and texts in different academic domains require a number of learned skills. These include: (a) the understanding of different epistemologies, the different intellectual requirements of the field; (b) the learner's ability to use different oral and written genres and registers germane to a given field; (c) the declarative concepts and principles (knowing *that* and *how*) represented by expository knowledge in the field; (d) the procedural knowledge including problem-solution and causal chains, cause-effect structures, and declarative and conditional knowledge; (e) the patterns of reasoning and questioning distinct to a field; (f) the field's evaluation procedures; (g) the new symbolic systems for expression of ideas, such as those found in mathematics, music, graphs, and geography; and, (h) the classroom's equipment or props and their use in domains of knowledge or cross-disciplinary fields (e.g., microscopes, algebra tiles, historical artifacts). Teachers, students, and textbook publishers each may have distinct conceptions of how domains of knowledge function and the way they should be taught.

Bazerman (1981, 1988) argues that the language of a field, such as science, and its use of references and symbols will influence the formation and expression of new knowledge in that field (see also Latour & Wilgoor, 1979). Once knowledge is created, it becomes autonomous and is separated from reality—an object rather than a subject of continued study and development. "The historical genius of the discipline is embodied in the development of its language" (Bazerman, 1981, p. 366; Bazerman, 1988). Arthur Applebee (2000) concurs that "Every field has its own special vocabularies and concepts, accepted forms of arguments, shared exemplars, and sense of which questions are interesting and which are not" (p. 1). Each field develops and uses specialized vocabulary, syntax, macro-structures, formats of presentations, and content unique to that field which students will need to learn. Effective arguments in one field of study such as science are formulated differently than arguments in another field such as history (Horowitz, 2005).

Attention to children's early cognitive competence in domains and theory-based knowledge provides amazing insights that may bear on use of talk and texts in schools. Rita Watson (1996) points out that children are now regarded as more cognitively competent than previously. A naive physics is visible as early as six months of age when children can tell figure-ground distinctions and possess knowledge of gravity. Watson cites research by Janet Astington and David R. Olson, that shows children as young as four years of age are able to infer another's beliefs and desires and recognize their own and others' minds as representational. Watson indicates that the school organization of curriculum into academic fields—geography, mathematics, and literature—is consistent with a domain-specific view of mind where there is movement from incidental principles to formal, explicit concepts, and abstract notions.

Finally, Michalene Chi finds that strategy use is intimately related to and determined by domain knowledge. Chi's research demonstrated that four to seven year olds who were highly knowledgeable about dinosaurs were able to produce complex hierarchical inferences, categories, and attributions beyond that of simple linear inferences produced by low knowledge children (Chi, Hutchison, & Robin, 1989b). But Chi continues to assert that it is not only quantity of knowledge that is important but the organization, identification, or representation of examples of knowledge (Chi & Koeske, 1983; Chi, Bassok, Lewis, Reimann, & Glaser, 1989a). Finally, in Alexander and Judy's review (1988) of the arguments for and literature on the interaction of domain-specific and strategic knowledge in academic performance, they unequivocally call for systematic examination of this interaction.

WHAT SHOULD OUR SCHOOLS TEACH THROUGH TALK AND TEXT?

In many classrooms, teachers teach domains of knowledge as academic fields through sterile, unconnected topics—such as dinosaurs, planets, addition and subtraction, or the Civil War—or through unconnected sources. Nel Noddings (2006), taking seriously the Socratic view of "know thyself," raises issues about the topics that should be used for reflective thinking in schools and society. She supports my belief that the topics used for talk and reading of texts are vital for quality learning. Not only are the topics used in schools problematic (due to textbook culture), the isolation of facts, figures, and sources is problematic. This isolation hinders the interconnectedness of spoken and written information.

In part, these problems associated with school topics also may be due to the separation of domains of knowledge, such as separating science from its philosophical approaches. In light of such obfuscation, a *Philosophy-Science Continuum* has been proposed by Howard Gardner (2001, p. B10). Gardner argues that the scientific approach to learning should be connected to humanistic approaches—which incorporate consciousness, ethics, values, beliefs, and affective factors. Furthermore, open-ended questions, such as *"Why is there hate in the world?"* or *"How can we create world cooperation and unity?"* can provide a structure for interdisciplinary study and teaching and the creation of authentic talk and texts (see also Gardner, 1971).

Talking History

The reading of history preserves and protects civilization. Yet research shows that children may avoid at all costs the reading of historical texts due to the content, gaps in text information, lack of cohesion, and student knowledge deficits. To overcome these obstacles, students will need exposure to multiple history sources and good instruction (Allen, 2000; Levstick & Barton, 2001; Stahl, Hynd, Britton, McNish, & Bosquet, 1996; Wineburg, 1991). History reading will require processing embedded texts such as inserted timelines and historical data, footnotes, or commentaries. In the upper grades, students will need to read primary and secondary sources with discourse structures such as causal-temporal relations characteristic of factual history and historical narratives or personal accounts, such as diaries (Jordan, 1984; Perfetti, Britt, & Georgi, 1995; Trabasso & van den Broek, 1985).

Given the topics and events reported in many history textbooks, children often do not understand the need to study history. When domains of knowledge "make the transition to school texts, an epistemological 'sameness' overtakes what are in fact distinct fields of study" (Paxton, 2002, p. 316). The issue the student and teacher face is how to take what is a voiceless text and distant time period and give it voice and life. Beck, McKeown, and Worthy (1995) show that giving a text voice can increase the text's comprehensibility.

Isabel Beck and Margaret McKeown (chap. 8, this volume) have been highly influential in helping educators rethink the basic role of questions in learning history. Excellent teaching and learning in democracies are driven by the premise that the author can be questioned and that the reader has the right to do so. Above all, students must recognize text is produced by another human being and learn to self-question in ways that are appropriate for a given source text. There is evidence that children as young as 6 years old can be taught to self-question as they listen to narratives in order to interpret and evaluate events in written stories (Carnes & Horowitz, 2006).

Beck and McKeown purport that the teacher can elevate and *move* the discussion forward by *marking* (calling attention to an idea through voice intonation or an affirmative word), *revoicing* (paraphrasing the student's ideas or saying it in other words), *turning back* (getting the student to think back on, or go back to, the text and determine if something makes sense), *annotating* (filling in the gap where background knowledge is missing), *modeling* thinking (through a think aloud of a difficult passage), or *recapping* (repeating or summarizing what the students have said about the text).

Talking Science and Mathematics

Joseph Polman and Roy Pea (chap. 12, this volume) report on *Project Science Learning Discourse.* They begin their chapter by asking: *"How can teachers help students learn when ... the students lack a pre-existing foundation of knowledge and experience that can be easily related to a science research project?"* and *"How do we get from a conceptually impoverished to a richer system of learning?"* For Piaget, learning is viewed as emanating from *within* the individual. For Polman and Pea, learning is appropriated through support and guidance from an expert *outside* the individual. Intelligence is characterized as being "distributed among persons" and the symbolic and physical world through tools and activity. By interacting with teachers, a student's performance, as Courtney Cazden (2001a) suggests, may precede competence (i.e., knowledge). Polman and Pea argue some aspects of cognitive achievement reside in the cultural and physical world, which may explain the learning paradox—how children might learn while yet limited in select prior knowledge and structures.

Rather than adopt a ritualistic model of learning, based on learning routines from a cultural base or a teacher as transmitter model, they present dialogue steps for science that are based on a teacher-student transformative communication model. Teacher and student, through verbalization, cooperatively create new meanings that each could not create alone (Chafe, 1977). Student-teacher dialogue transforms student intellectual progress from limited understanding to more sophisticated understanding that neither the teacher nor the student would have originally predicted, thus leading to mutual insights (see similarities to Bamberger's research in this volume; Horowitz, 1990).

Tools and symbols, as treated by Vygotsky and Luria (1994) are integrated with speech acts and can include the use of computers, graphs, tables, hand-held calculators, and portable digital assistants (PDAs). These artifacts are integral to learning and the building of knowledge in science and mathematics but also have implications for other domains as noted in this volume.

Talking Engineering

Cheryl Geisler and Barbara L. Lewis, Rensselaer Polytechnic Institute, established through their engineering case study (chap. 13, this volume) that the role of talk is significant in accomplishing creative engineering work. The process engineers use to design technical equipment (e.g., sewing machines) will change with the population being served, the time period, and situational uses of the equipment (see Geisler, 1994, 2004 for further discussion of time, texts, technology and the nature of expertise).

Geisler and Lewis emphasize that the act of design by engineers is highly collaborative. "Current design requires more knowledge than any single individual can bring to the table" (p. 319 in this volume). Like many experts operating from multiple domains of knowledge, Geisler and Lewis find engineers themselves are *not* fully conscious of the talk they use during design. They provide a longitudinal case study of a team of undergraduate engineering students at work. These engineering students designed a device to provide mobility for children handicapped with cerebral palsy. These engineers used social narratives, a conversational talk nested in other forms of talk. The teamwork included discussion of personal experiences as exemplars of exchange with the disabled and re-figured narratives as they imagined what new technology could do to aid a child. At the same time, the talk among the group members created cohesion for the team. But how do these stories work? What are described as folk wisdoms surprisingly enter into the storytelling of not only these engineers but also into other professions, such law, medicine, and education. Jerome Bruner (2002) shows that stories bring "a sudden reversal of circumstances," and help re-form our reality and hold details in memory.[6] Each social narrative is converted to an engineering design concept and process. Before the final product is produced, there must be negotiation and an environment which is conducive to establishing common definitions of the task and agreement on the priorities (see also Fejis, 2005).

Finally, Geisler and Lewis conclude that we make texts through talk and that these texts can serve us "outside of the textual borders." Talk overlays the technical texts that engineers use. Furthermore, determining how to proceed in this engineering design will require interaction with therapists, physicians, and special education teachers who have worked with cerebral palsy children and can provide input to the design process. As a result of this project, engineers are engaged in a "remaking of the world."

Talking Performing Arts

Talk about the arts deserves center stage in schools. Drama is a performance with layers of language—an extended dialogue—about real life dialogue. Following a performance, there is still another layer of dialogue where after-theatre talk becomes analytic observation.

Peter van Stapele of the University of Leiden, The Netherlands, studies the reading of dialogue in theatrical performances and the observation of these performances using discourse analysis procedures (chap. 14, this volume). Children as young as his four-year-old daughter, Miriam, may exhibit a remarkable ability to move across several levels of real and imaginary communicative contexts. This is a move from a consciousness of reality to a consciousness of play—where the imaginary is sustained. This is also a prerequisite, he posits, for participating in theatrical performances and the viewing and interpretation of theater. Drawing from semiotics, van Stapele examines the symbolism expressed through the uniqueness of theatrical dialogues that interface printed words, gestures, and space.

van Stapele's analysis calls attention to physical movement in dialogue. This is a feature of the evolution of oral discourse that is now gaining attention internationally because researchers are striving for a more complete picture of meaning-making across a range of fields (see Goodwin, 1981; Koschmann, 1999; MacWhinney, 1999). van Stapele alerts us that talk analysis must go beyond the study of words to incorporate those full-body gestures and the rhythms associated with movement like beats in music. Using speech act theory and semiotics, he stresses the value of analyzing the illocutionary force and motivations of dialogue expressed in theatrical gesture and body movement as part of a stage performance. Interestingly, children's movement in the form of dance as dialogue has been used as intervention to guide children who have difficulty communicating orally (Tortora, 2005).

More specifically, van Stapele (2005) studied the movement and evolution of action through dialogue as it runs parallel to the intended non-verbal physical action on stage. He focuses on the art of the *screenplay*. An example of a screenplay as defined by van Stapele is Arthur Miller's *Death of a Salesman*, which was eventually produced as a film. van Stapele describes how *indexicalization* (signs in the text) and characterization of *dramatic personae* (characterization of a personality) play a significant role in reading a screenplay and transforming the text into a performance using principles that formulate a poetics of screenplay. He advances a unique model of dramatic oral discourse that offers another avenue for school text processing—the production of re-enactment in a theatrical setting.

> The production in a drama-text can be made visible through segmenting a dialogue into beat. "Beats" are clear metrical units (segments of rhythm of movement in a dialogue…. The segmentation forms a basis of further interpretation of the intended creation of the performance. (van Stapele, 2005, p. 76)

Talking Poetic Texts

David Ian Hanauer (chap. 15, this volume) proposes that dialogue is central in the re-constructive process needed for reading poetry. The cognitive processing of poetry is influenced by *formal structural features of the language*, a matter addressed by the distinguished Russian linguist Roman Jakobson (1960). Jan Mukarovsky (1964), a Prague Formalist, indicates that poetry is different from the language of prose. It is this difference that draws the reader to an interpretation. Both linguists, however, focus on the hierarchically structured patterns of poetry, sound, and their symbols and view poetry reading as a bottom-up comprehension process.

Another perspective, what David Hanauer calls the *Conventionalist*, purports that poetry reading is more top-down—like schema theory in studies of text comprehension—and is contingent upon the reader's background knowledge. Stanley Fish (1980) proposes we function as groups of readers and writers within interpretive communities and common "interpretive strategies" (p. 331). It is possible that readers use one schema but then shift to additional schemata.

Hanauer raises an issue in literacy instruction seldom challenged. He points out that poetry is viewed as extremely difficult for children and, consequently, is rarely used as part of literacy education. He shows, on the contrary, that first-graders who read poetry are motivated to read other texts. Empirical studies of the development of poetry reading are needed to design curriculum and instruction using this genre across the grades (see Elster & Hanauer, 2002; Hanauer, 2004).

Above all, poetry is meant to be voiced. Hanauer reports that research shows the level of sensitivity that five- and six-year-old preschoolers demonstrate as they distinguish different text types by their musical features. Similarly, Georgia Green (1982) reports preschoolers' astute awareness of orally presented text styles when they were asked to distinguish authors of narrative texts. Peter Schreiber (1987) shows that seven-year-olds' sensitivity to oral syntax can exceed that of adults.

Philomena Donnelly and Kieran Egan (chap. 16, this volume) view speech and the mind as shaped and limited by our biological system, including the lips, tongue, and mouth (see also Fromkin, 1980). Donnelly and Egan show how talk about texts stimulates consciousness and reflection. Words emanate from the body in response to thought processes.

Kieran Egan poetically conveys this as part of *The Educated Mind* when he says:

> Language emerges from the body in the process of evolutionary and individual development …. Phrases and sentences, for example, are tied to the time we take to inhale and exhale … similarly, we use language to represent the world as it is disclosed by our … organs of perception. *In other words, the body is the most fundamental mediating tool that shapes our understanding* [italics added]. (1997, p. 7)

Using a Socratic talk structure in which there is discussion, justification, and clarification of thinking, 12- and 13-year-old students in Dublin, Ireland used classroom *Thinking Time* to explain how words live. The teacher posed profound questions: *Do words give us life? Does language evolve? Do you need a voice to think? Do we have too many words?* Teacher prompts kept the discussion evolving through a student-led dialogue. The philosophical nature of the questions suggests different viewpoints will be entertained.

So, then, *What is dialogue?* The persons here are "engaged in a joint search," which "builds community" and "conversation [that] is unpredictable." The teacher is flexible. Few remarks are made by the teacher to control the talk. "Children and teacher lose themselves in the dialogue and yet come out of it with a deeper understanding of themselves." The words here have a soul. From a 19-word poem by Emily Dickinson, these Irish children produce, to our astonishment, many hundreds of words.

Talking Ethics and Deeds

Jacob Neusner (chap. 17, this volume), a professor of theology, draws from 2,000 years of history to address written law (the *Talmud*) and an oral commentary of this law (the *Mishnah*), what Neusner calls "written-down talk." The *Talmud*, consists of 2.5 million words and 5,894 folio pages that were never intended to be read silently. Rather, it was intended to be orally discussed by multiple speakers and across generations living in multiple contexts and world locations.

Neusner presents a famous tractate to illustrate a dialectical argument. The example is well-known in Talmudic study groups. Two individuals fight over a garment, each claiming ownership of that garment. Questions posed are: *When two people claim ownership of a single object, is one of them necessarily lying? If so, how is a person who knowingly cheats to be treated?* This argument "forces us to address not the problem and the solution alone, but the problem and the various *ways* by which a solution may be reached" (p. 402 in this volume). Neusner highlights how important it is for one to follow the evolution and flow of an argument—its "forward motion." That is, each case provides a principle to be used in the next case. In the course of processing a dialectical argument, the reader-listener is responsible for not losing sight of the progression of ideas.

Neusner says, "Indeed, the Talmud treats coming generations the way composers treat unborn musicians: They provide the notes for the musicians to reconstruct the music" (p. 418 in this volume). He suggests that the *Talmud*, and its dialectical argumentation, serve as a model for framing classroom discourse.

Talking Art

Study of the arts has undergone a "quiet evolution" that is critical to the creation of mind (Eisner, 2002; Wilson, 1997). Discipline-based arts education (DBAE) in schools incorporates art history, art criticism, aesthetics, and the design of art forms. While processing art may seem far removed from processing texts, art can be approached as a "visual text" to be approached cognitively through different domains of knowledge and expert-novice perspectives.

In Chapter 18, Brent Wilson, Pennsylvania State University, reports on children's collaborative interpretations of artworks and the challenge children face when "writing" visual texts *within* the texts of their lives. His essay begins by noting that teachers were once prohibited from showing the works of artists out of fear that children might copy. Copy of visual art as verbal texts meant children might not become creative and expressive. In writing, copying is typically viewed as plagiarism. In the 1970s it was realized that children naturally create images that are "utterly filled with appropriations from the popular media and a myriad of other sources" (Wilson, this volume). This chapter suggests such representations of models may have a viable place in the visual arts.

Wilson shows, in keeping with the present book, that any given work of art may elicit different interpretations over a lifetime. Fourth-graders engaged in a discussion about a painting by James Cameron, produced in 1859 before the Civil War, talked about art as they addressed race relations issues. With increased emphasis on higher-order interpretations, the interpreters of art will change their perspective over time, resulting in the production of different inferences and meanings (Hoyt, 1992).

Wilson's chapter shows how cognitive psychology has influenced art study. DBAE and non-DBAE students were asked, *"What do you think the work means, and what evidence do you have to support your view?"* Wilson found DBAE students arrived at more effective and reassured interpretations of artworks' main ideas than non-DBAE learners. The DBAE students gave reasoned interpretations and provided evidence to support their interpretations. Teachers, not focusing on student claims and arguments, found DBAE students made reference in writing—to the sensory, formal, and expressive features of artworks—more often than non-DBAE students. Brent Wilson concludes that artwork, when addressed appropriately, can change lives—act on "the moral, ethical, artistic and aesthetic consequences of artworks."

Talking Music

Jeanne Bamberger of the Massachusetts Institute of Technology (chap. 19, this volume) examines the tensions between two kinds of meaning-making and their impact on how we learn. *Path-makers* make sense of the world through real-time activities—actions, repetitions, and corrections (Becker, 1984). According to this "theory," people make sense of the world through a set of prior texts accumulated through a lifetime (e.g., dialectical exchanges, memorized recitations, lecture quotations). In contrast, the *map-maker* uses temporal order qualities, logical procedures, and scientific inquiry. Bamberger characterizes these as "out of time" events, "a theory of approximation" functioning as symbols or representations of the physical world, such as maps.

Bamberger studies six eight and nine year olds attending an educational lab who were asked to use Cuisenaire rods to create instructions for teaching younger children how to clap the tune "Hot Cross Buns." Bamberger analyzes the instructional "text" of one child, Lucy, and her interactions with Mary, the lab teacher. Through a series of conversations, Mary attempts to understand why Lucy constructed her text with seemingly contradictory patterns.

Using a "mapping approach" Mary sees that Lucy has used a "fine-grained level of detail" in the first pattern, one that approximates the use of standard rhythm notation (SRN). Using this same approach on the second pattern, causes Mary to think Lucy has made a mistake, since her choice of rods does not match expectations for SRN. Mary, however, begins to see that Lucy uses both the mapping approach and the path-making approach. Her text is "an active invention," and Lucy is "learning in the real time."

The chapter shows how both the teacher and the student experience conceptual change for the task at hand as they attempt to understand one another. Bamberger suggests that we see the curriculum *not* as a "deliverable" but as a "selection" of possible teaching, content, and episodes that approximates knowledge that needs to be negotiated between teacher and child.

CONCLUSION

Talking texts elevates the role of speech in schooling as it interfaces with written texts. The speech that is used for study, problem solving, and knowledge building activities in classrooms—whether learning the alphabet, deciphering vocabulary in discussion of the disciplines, or composing and debating—is the foundation of learning. Talking texts raise personal and collective consciousness and, with time, become potentials for expression and appreciation of the self as learner.[7] Speech, as discussed in this volume, is tantamount to an act of creation.

To elaborate, George Steiner's *Grammars of Creation* (2001) raises issue with the limits of an education and a society that are focused strictly on scientific pursuits to the neglect of interaction with the humanities and arts—and individual creation. Drawing from his literary genius, the purpose of the discourse of schooling is to move students beyond the "understanding" of talking texts. The challenge schools face is to serve learners by teaching them to create discourse and their own minds in ways that will be useful in a range of disciplines for a lifetime of learning.

ACKNOWLEDGMENTS

This book is dedicated in memory of my beloved brother, Searle Seymour Horowitz (1947–87) (b. St. Paul, Minnesota and d. New York City) who loved the language of music and the lyrics of song. He was a composer of lyrics. Sy followed in the footsteps of our grandfather, who was a composer of music and our father who was a Cantor. Sy spread kindness and good deeds in his work in international travel and life. He was an advocate of social justice, respectful of community, and history, honorable, and utterly loyal to family and the individual lives he touched.

Chapter 1 is dedicated to the memory of Rabbi Nachmun Bulman (1925–2002), Jerusalem, Israel, former Professor, Yeshiva University, New York City and Dean, Ohr Someach, Jerusalem. We met at my presentation in 1991 on Zelig Pliskin's book, *The Power of Words*, which outlined the ways in which speech can elevate or diminish the self-esteem of a listener. Rabbi Bulman was a distinguished Talmud scholar, orator, teacher, and counselor and, above all, a compassionate human being who lived with utmost respect and dedication toward his fellow human beings. He truly put words into action.

Professor Karin Aijmer, English Department, Göteborg University, Göteborg, Sweden offered valuable insights to this chapter. I thank her for the meticulous input.

I am grateful to my graduate students Gayla Schill, Ruby Kainth, Anna Brown, Adriana Campos, Janet Flory, Terry Jones, Laura Mora, and Jean Wilbur and undergraduates Matthew Gueller and Keri Penman, who helped with the final copy of Chapter 1. I also thank reference librarian Charles Thurston at The University of Texas–San Antonio. Their devotion was beyond my expectations.

NOTES

1. I use the terms *talk* and *text* in the following ways: *Talk* refers to oral expressions, conversations, and discourse types that are spoken. *Text* is used by linguists and psychologists

to include extended oral and written or literate discourse that has structure and cohesion. *Speaking* and *writing* are language processes that are essential for creative learning in academic domains of knowledge.

See Horowitz and Samuels (1987) for further explanation of these terms. I use the term *writing* in a broad sense in the title of this volume, *Talking Texts: How Speech and Writing Interact in School Learning*, to refer to student processing or use of written language (while reading and interpreting text) and student production of written language (while in the role of composer of text).

Conversational discourse was introduced to educational researchers through Deborah Tannen's doctoral dissertation which was published as *Conversational Style: Analyzing Talk Among Friends* in 1984 and analyzed talk among friends at a Thanksgiving dinner. Written-text may contain oral-like features and spoken-text may contain written-like features.

In preparing this chapter, we found that 11,596 books containing the word "mind" as a title word or referenced as the subject were published from 2003–2005. However, this is only an approximate figure, since there are undoubtedly duplicate records in the Books in Print database. This may be indicative of the centrality of mind—in thinking, feeling, and the spiritual, cultural, and physical aspects of the human being—all of which are gaining attention in cognitive and linguistic research.

2. The nature of the research paper is receiving attention among composition theorists (see essay by Davis & Shadle, 2000). Research is changing rapidly in process, form, and functions in our society due to increased use of technologically oriented tools. There is interest in the rhetorical processes learners follow as they construct research reports.

   Richard Larson highlights the research paper's pervasiveness in spoken and written discourse:

   > Research can inform virtually any writing or speaking if the author wishes it to do so; there is nothing of substance or content that differentiates one paper that draws on data from outside the author's own self from another such paper—nothing that can enable one to say that this is a "research paper" and that paper is not .... I would assert therefore that the so-called "research paper" is a generic, cross-disciplinary term, has no conceptual or substantive identity .... Conceptually, the generic term "research paper" is for practical purposes meaningless. (p. 813)

3. The present book is one of the first attempts to characterize the current evolution and mingling of the oral and written in schooling and other educational contexts. Previous work by Rosalind Thomas (1992) traces the ways in which oral traditions and written documents have come together historically in classical Greece. Her volume is important because it highlights assumption that we make about the oral and written within a culture. We assume that when literate text becomes familiar and is regularly used, the oral is dismissed as a valuable means for preservation of ideas and memory. The oral and written are given particular roles in different places and for different purposes in classical Athens. Thomas highlights the greying of the oral and written as a space that needs further study in order to understand human activity and symbols, including the written and non-written. She accentuates that the oral transmission of information was essential to the democracy of Greece.

4. A transcript and video may be obtained through the *TalkBank* at Carnegie Mellon University under the auspices of Brian MacWhinney. See chapter 2, this volume, for a detailed discussion of the research that ensued.

5. Another form of overlays, called *overlaps* by the researcher, has been found to occur between sentences in conversations and has been studied by linguists and anthropologists to understand cultural differences in uses of language. Santamaria-Garcia (2001) points out that research has shown that *in English*, overlap of language in conversation occurs in agreeing to a statement whereas disagreeing results in pauses and hesitations rather than overlaps of language. However, she shows *in Spanish* that overlaps in communica-

tion occur in both agreement *and* disagreeing responses. This study of overlaps at the sentence level and across two languages is useful to help us understand that, at least in this case, the functions of overlaps in talk are influenced by the language and culture.

6. Stories contribute to the professional's discourse processes and thinking in law, literature, medicine, and other fields (see cf. Jerome Bruner's *Making Stories: Law, Literature, & Life* [Farrar, Straus, & Giroux, 2002]). Bruner argues that stories bring "a sudden reversal of circumstances," and help to form our reality and hold in memory details of people, events, and life circumstances. See also Rita Charon and Martha Montello (Eds.), *Stories Matter: The Role of Narrative in Medical Ethics* (2002).

7. Roy Harris addresses the way talk and texts overlap in his book on *Rethinking Writing* (2000). "What distinguishes a literate culture from a pre-literate culture is not so much the *addition* of quite separate mode of verbal communication as the *incorporation* of oral communication into a higher-order semiological synthesis involving the written sign. In that synthesis, however, it is increasingly the graphic element which dominates." (p. 212).

REFERENCES

Ackerman, J. (2003). The space for rhetoric in everyday life. In M. Nystrand & J. Duffy (Eds.), *Towards a rhetoric of everyday life: New directions in research on writing, text, and discourse* (pp. 84–117). Madison: University of Wisconsin Press.

Aijmer, K. (1996). *Conversational routines in English: Convention and creativity.* New York: Longman.

Akinnaso, F. N. (1982). On the differences between spoken and written language. *Language and Speech, 25*(2), 97–125.

Alexander, P. A., & Judy, J. E. (1988). The interaction of domain-specific and strategic knowledge in academic performance. *Review of Educational Research, 58,* 375–404.

Alibali, M. W. (2005). Mechanisms of change in the development of mathematical reasoning. In R.V. Kail (Ed.), *Advances in child development and behavior* (Vol. 33). New York: Academic Press.

Alibali, M. W., & Goldin-Meadow, S. (1993). Gesture-speech mismatch and mechanisms of learning: What the hands reveal about a child's state of mind. *Cognitive Psychology, 25,* 468–523.

Allen, G. (2000). *Intertextuality.* New York: Routledge.

Anderson, R. C., Chinn, C., Chang, J., Waggoner, M., & Yi, H. (1997). On the logical integrity of children's arguments. *Cognition and Instruction, 15,* 135–167.

Anderson, R. C., Nguyen-Jahiel, K., McNurlen, B., Archodidou, A., So-Young, K., Reznitskaya, A., Tillmanns, M., & Gilbert, L. (2001). The snowball phenomenon: Spread ways of talking and ways of thinking across groups of children. *Cognition and Instruction, 19*(1), 1–46.

Applebee, A. N. (2000). Engaging students in meaningful conversation leads to higher achievement. *English Update: A Newsletter from the Center for English Learning & Achievement (CELA), 1*(8). New York: University of Albany.

Applebee, A., Langer, J., Nystrand, M., & Gamoran, A. (2003). Discussion-based approaches to developing understanding: Classroom instruction and student performance in middle and high school English. *American Educational Research Journal, 40,* 685–730.

Astington, J. W., & Baird, J. A. (2005). *Why language matters for a theory of mind.* Oxford, England: Oxford University Press.

Aulls, M. (1998). Contributions of classroom discourse to what content students learn during curriculum enactment. *Journal of Educational Psychology, 90*(1), 56–69.

Aulls, M. (2002). The contributions of co-occurring forms of classroom discourse and academic activities to curriculum events and instruction. *Journal of Educational Psychology, 94,* 520–538.

Bakhtin, M. M. (1986). The problem of speech genres. In C. Emerson & M. Holquist (Eds.) & V. W. McGee (Trans.), *Speech genres and other late essays* (pp. 60–102). Austin: The University of Texas Press.

Ball, A. F. (2002). Three decades of research on classroom life: Illuminating the classroom communicative lives of America's at-risk students. In W. G. Secada (Ed.), *Review of Research in Education, 26*, 71–111. Washington, DC: American Educational Research Association.

Barnes, D. (1988). The politics of oracy. In M. McClure, T. Phillips, & A. Wilkinson (Eds.), *Oracy Matters*. Milton Keynes, England: Open University Press.

Barker, O. (2006, May 30). Technology leaves teens speechless. *USA Today*, pp. 01D.

Bauman, R. (2004). *A world of others' words: Cross-cultural perspectives on intertextuality*. London: Blackwell Publishers.

Bauman, R., & Sherzer, J. (1975). The ethnography of speaking. *Annual Review of Anthropology, 4*, 95–119.

Bayley, R., & Schecter, S. R. (2005). Language production across the bilingual continuum: Mexican-descent children's Spanish and English narratives. In K. E. Denham & A. Lobeck (Eds.), *Language in the schools: Integrating linguistic knowledge into K–12 teaching*. Mahwah, NJ: Lawrence Erlbaum Associates.

Bazerman, C. (1981). What written language does: Three examples of academic discourse. *Philosophy of the Social Sciences, 11*, 361–387.

Bazerman, C. (1988). *Shaping written language: The genre and activity of the experimental article in science*. Madison: University of Wisconsin Press.

Bazerman, C. (2004). Intertextuality: How texts rely on other texts. In C. Bazerman & P. Prior (Eds.), *What writing does and how it does it: An introduction to analyzing texts and textual practices* (pp. 83–96). Mahwah, NJ: Lawrence Erlbaum Associates.

Bazerman, C., & Prior, P. (Eds.). (2004). *What writing does and how it does it: An introduction to analyzing texts and textual practices*. Mahwah, NJ: Lawrence Erlbaum Associates.

Beck, I. L., & McKeown, M. G. (2001). Inviting students into the pursuit of meaning. *Educational Psychology Review, 13*, 225–241.

Beck, I. L., McKeown, M. G., & Worthy, J. (1995). Giving a text voice can improve students' understanding. *Reading Research Quarterly, 30*, 220–238.

Becker, A. L. (1984). Biography of a sentence: A Burmese proverb. In E. Bruner (Ed.), *Text, play, and story: The construction and reconstruction of self and society. The 1983 Proceedings of the American Ethnological Society* (pp. 135–154). Prospect Heights, IL: Waveland Press.

Bellack, A. A., Kliebard, H., Hymen, R., & Smith, F. (1966). *The language of the classroom*. New York: Teachers College Press.

Bernstein, B. (1971). On the classification and framing of educational knowledge. In *Class, codes, and control* (Vol. 1). Beverly Hills, CA: Sage.

Biber, D. (1988). *Variations across speech and writing*. Cambridge, England: Cambridge University Press.

Biber, D. (2006). *University language: A corpus-based study of spoken and written registers*. Amsterdam: John Benjamins.

Biber, D., & Finegan, E. (1989). Drift and the evolution of English style: A history of three genres. *Language, 65*, 487–517.

Bloome, D., Carter, S. P., Christian, B. M., Otto, S., & Shuart-Faris, N. (2005). *Discourse analysis and the study of classroom language and literacy events: A microethnographic perspective*. Mahwah, NJ: Lawrence Erlbaum Associates.

Bloomfield, L. (1933). *Language*. New York: Holt, Rinehart & Winston.

Blum-Kulka, S. (1997). *Dinner talk: Cultural patterns of sociability and socialization in family discourse*. Mahwah, NJ: Lawrence Erlbaum Associates.

Blum-Kulka, S. (2004). The role of peer interaction in later pragmatic development: The case of speech representation. In R. A. Berman (Ed.), *Language development across childhood and adolescence* (pp. 191–210). Amsterdam: John Benjamins Publishing.

Blum-Kulka, S. (2005). Modes of meaning making in young children's conversational storytelling. In J. Thornborrow & J. Coates (Eds.), *The sociolinguistics of narrative* (pp. 149–170). Amsterdam: John Benjamins Publishing.

Blum-Kulka, S., & Snow, C. (2002). *Talking to adults: The contribution of multiparty discourse to language acquisition.* Mahwah, NJ: Lawrence Erlbaum Associates.

Brown, A. L., & Campione, J. C. (1990). Communities of learning and thinking, or a context by any other name. In D. Kuhn (Ed.), *Developmental perspectives on teaching and learning thinking skills: Contributions to human development* (Vol. 21, pp. 108–126). Basel, Switzerland: S. Karger.

Brown, A. L., & Campione, J. C. (1994). Guided discovery in a community of learners. In K. McGilly (Ed.), *Classroom lessons: Integrating cognitive theory and classroom practice* (pp. 229–270). Cambridge, MA: MIT Press.

Bruner, J. S. (1979). The conditions of creativity. In *On knowing: Essays for the left hand* (pp. 17–30). Cambridge, MA: Harvard University Press.

Bruner, J. S. (1996). *The culture of education.* Cambridge, MA: Harvard University Press.

Bruner, J. S. (2002). *Making stories: Law, literature, & life.* New York: Farrar, Straus & Giroux.

Bruner, J. S., Goodnow, J., & Austin, G. (1956). *A study of thinking.* New York: Wiley.

Butterfield, F. (1990, April 21). Ben Franklin, a gift that's worth two fights. *The New York Times,* p. A1.

Calfee, R. C., Dunlap, K. L., & Wat, A. Y. (1994). Authentic discussion of texts in middle grade schooling: An analytic-narrative approach. In R. Horowitz (Ed.), *Classroom talk about text* [Special issue]. *The Journal of Reading, 37*(7), 18–28.

Carnes, P., & Horowitz, R. (2006). *Self-questioning using The Six Thinking Hats: An approach for scaffolding first-graders' analysis of text.* Unpublished manuscript.

Carter, R. (2004). *Language and creativity: The art of common talk.* London: Routledge.

Cazden, C. B. (2001a). *Classroom discourse: The language of teaching and learning.* Portsmouth, NH: Heinemann.

Cazden, C. B. (2001b). Research on classroom discourse. Paper presented at the National Academy of Education Proceedings, New York University, New York.

Cazden, C. B., John, V. P., & Hymes, D. (Eds.). (1972). *Functions of language in the classroom.* New York: Teachers College Press.

Chafe, W. (1977). Creativity in verbalization and its implications for the nature of stored knowledge. In R. Freedle (Ed.), *Discourse production and comprehension.* Norwood, NJ: Ablex.

Chafe, W., & Danielewicz, J. (1987). Properties of spoken and written language. In R. Horowitz & S. J. Samuels (Eds.), *Comprehending oral and written language* (pp. 83–113). San Diego, CA: Academic Press.

Charon, R., & Montello, M. (Eds.). (2002). *Stories matter: The role of narrative in medical ethics.* London: Routledge.

Chi, M. T. H., Bassok, M., Lewis, M., Reimann, P., & Glaser, R. (1989). Self-explanations: How students study and use examples in learning to solve problems. *Cognitive Science, 13,* 145–182.

Chi, M. T. H., Hutchison, J., & Robin, A. F. (1989). How inferences about novel domain-related concepts can be constrained by structured knowledge. *Merrill-Palmer Quarterly, 35,* 27–62.

Chi, M. T. H., & Koeske, R. (1983). Network representation of a child's dinosaur knowledge. *Developmental Psychology, 19,* 29–39.

Chinn, C. A., Anderson, R. C., & Waggoner, M. (2001). Patterns of discourse in two kinds of literature discussion. *Reading Research Quarterly, 36,* 378–411.

Cicourel, A. V. (1974). Language *use and school performance.* New York: Academic Press.

Clay, M. M. (2001). *Change over time in children's literacy development.* Westport, CT: Heinemann.

Cohen, H. (1994). *The history of speech communication: The emergence of a discipline, 1914–1945.* Washington, DC: National Communication Association.

Corbett, E. P. J. (1971). *Classical rhetoric for the modern student* (2nd ed.). Oxford, England: Oxford University Press.

Cornbleet, S., & Carter, R. (2001). *The language of speech and writing.* London: Routledge.

Coulmas, F. (1987). What writing can do to language. In S. Battestini (Ed.), *Georgetown University Roundtable on Languages and Linguistics 1986* (pp. 107–129). Washington, DC: Georgetown University Press.

Coulmas, F. (1989). *The writing systems of the world*. Oxford, England: Blackwell.

Curenton, S. M., & Justice, L. M. (2004). African American and Caucasian preschoolers' use of decontextualized language: Literate language features in oral narratives. *Language, speech, and hearing services in schools, 35*, 240–253.

Dabbs, P., & Block, H. (2002). *National Assessment of Educational Progess (NAEP) Year-at-a-Glance 2001: The nation's report card* (NCES 2002487). Retrieved June 27, 2006, from http://nces.ed.gov/pubs2002/2002487.pdf

Davis, R., & Shadle, M. (2000). "Building a mystery": Alternative research writing and the academic act of seeking. *College Composition and Communication, 51*, 417–446.

De Corte, E., Verschaffel, L., & Masui, C. (2004). The CLIA-Model: A framework for designing powerful learning environments for thinking and problem-solving. *European Journal of Psychology of Education, 19*, 365–384.

Diaz, R. M., & Berk, L. E. (Eds.). (1992). *Private speech: From social organization to self-regulation* (pp. 245–264). Hillsdale, NJ: Lawrence Erlbaum Associates.

Donahue, P. L., Finnegan, R. J., Lutkus, A. D., Allen, N. L., & Campbell, J. R. (2001). *The Nation's Report Card: Fourth-Grade Reading 2000* (NCES 2001499). Washington, DC: U.S. Department of Education and the Institute of Education Sciences.

Dorval, B. (Ed.). (1990). *Conversational organization and its development*. In R. O. Freedle (Series Ed.), *Advances in discourse processes* (Vol. 38). Norwood, NJ: Ablex Publishing Corporation.

Eckhoff, B. (1983). How reading affects children's writing. *Language Arts, 60*, 607–616.

Egan, K. (1997). *The educated mind: How cognitive tools shape our understanding*. Chicago: University of Chicago Press.

Eisner, E. (2002). *The arts and the creation of mind*. New Haven, CT: Yale University Press.

Elbow, P. (1985). The shifting relationships between speech and writing. *College Composition and Communication, 36*, 283–303.

Elster, C. A., & Hanauer, D. I. (2002). Voicing texts, voices around texts: Reading poems in elementary school classrooms. *Research in the Teaching of English, 37*(1), 89–134.

Elster, C. A. (2005). *Hybrid texts: Children's responses and creations*. Unpublished manuscript.

Erickson, F., & Schultz, J. (1977). When is a context? Some issues and methods in the analysis of social competence. *Quarterly Newsletter of the Institute for Comparative Human Development, 1*(2), 5–10. Also in J. Green & C. Wallat (Eds.), *Ethnography and language in educational settings*. Norwood, NJ: Ablex.

Fahnestock, J. (1999). *Rhetorical figures in science*. New York: Oxford.

Fejis, E. (2005). Constructing a learning environment that promotes reinvention. In R. Nemirovsky, A. S. Roseberry, J. Solomon, & B. Warren (Eds.), *Everyday matters in science and mathematics: Studies of complex classroom events* (pp. 241–266). Mahwah, NJ: Lawrence Erlbaum Associates.

Fillmore, C. (1974). Pragmatics and the description of discourse. *Berkeley Studies in Syntax and Semantics*. Berkeley, CA: University of California, Department of Linguistics.

Finnegan, R. (2002). *Communicating: The multiple modes of human understanding*. London: Routledge.

Finnegan, R. (2006). Not by words alone: Reclothing the "oral." In D. R. Olson & M. Cole (Eds.), *Technology, literacy, and evolution of society* (pp. 265–87). Mahwah, NJ: Lawrence Erlbaum Associates.

Fish, S. (1980). *Is there a text in this class?: The authority of interpretive communities*. Cambridge, MA: Harvard University Press.

Flanders, N. A. (1970). *Analyzing teacher behavior*. Reading, MA: Addison-Wesley.

Franklin, B. (1789). The last will and testament of Benjamin Franklin. *The Franklin Institute online*. Retrieved July 10, 2006, from http://www.fi.edu/franklin/family/lastwill.html

Fromkin, V. (Ed.). (1980). *Errors in linguistic performance: Slips of the tongue, ear, pen, and hand*. San Francisco: Academic Press.

Frye, N. (1964). *The educated imagination*. Bloomington: Indiana University.

Gage, N. L. (Ed) (1974). NIE Conference on studies in teaching: Panel 5. *Teaching as a linguistic process in a cultural setting*. (Eric Document No. ED111806)

Gardner, H. (1971). Problem solving in the arts and sciences. *Journal of Aesthetic Education,* 5(1), 93–113.

Gardner, H. (2001, March 9). The philosophy-science continuum. *The Chronicle of Higher Education,* B7–B10.

Gee, J. P. (1996). *Social linguistics and literacies: Ideology in discourses.* New York: Taylor & Francis.

Gee, J. P. (1999). *An introduction to discourse analysis: Theory and method.* London: Routledge.

Gee, J. P. (2001). Reading as situated language: A sociocognitive perspective. *Journal of Adolescent and Adult Literacy, 44,* 714–725.

Geisler, C. (1994). *Academic literacy and the nature of expertise: Reading, writing, and knowing in academic philosophy.* Hillsdale, NJ: Lawrence Erlbaum Associates.

Geisler, C. (2004, March). *Time, text, and technology.* Paper presented at the meeting of the Bahktin/Vygotsky Special Interest Group of the Conference on College Composition and Communication, San Antonio, TX.

Goffman, E. (1959). *The presentation of self in everyday life.* Garden City, NY: Doubleday.

Goffman, E. (1981). The lecture. In *Forms of talk* (pp. 162–195). Philadelphia: University of Pennsylvania Press.

Goodwin, C. (1981). *Conversational organization: Interaction between speakers and hearers.* New York: Academic Press.

Goodwin, C., & Duranti, A. (1992). Rethinking context: An introduction. In A. Duranti & C. Goodwin (Eds.), *Rethinking context: Language as an interactive phenomenon. Studies in the social and cultural foundations of language* (No. 11, pp. 1–42). Cambridge, England: Cambridge University Press.

Goody, J. (1987). *The interface between the written and the oral. (Studies in literacy, family, culture & the state).* Cambridge, England: Cambridge University Press.

Green, G. M. (1982). Competence for implicit text analysis: Literary style discrimination in five-year-olds. In D. Tannen (Ed.), *Analyzing discourse: Text and talk* (pp. 142–163). Washington, DC: Georgetown University Round Table on Languages and Linguistics.

Green, J., & Harker, J. (1991). *Multiple perspective analysis of classroom discourse.* Norwood, NJ: Ablex.

Green, J. L., & Wallat, C. (1981). Mapping instructional conversations: A sociolinguistic ethnography. In J. Green & C. Wallat (Eds.), *Ethnography and languages in educational settings* (pp. 161–195). Norwood, NJ: Ablex.

Greene, M. (2000). *Releasing the imagination. Essays on education, the arts, and social change.* San Francisco: Jossey-Bass.

Gumperz, J. J., & Hymes, D. (1972). *Directions in sociolinguistics: The ethnography of communication.* New York: Holt, Rinehart, & Winston.

Hacker, D. J., & Tenent, A. (2002). Implementing reciprocal teaching in the classroom: Overcoming obstacles and making modifications. *Journal of Educational Psychology, 94,* 699–718.

Halliday, M. A. K. (1975). *Learning how to mean: Explorations in the development of language.* London: Edward Arnold.

Halliday, M. A. K. (1987). Spoken and written modes of meaning. In R. Horowitz, & S. J. Samuels (Eds.), *Comprehending oral and written language* (pp. 55–113). London: Academic Press.

Hanauer, D. I. (2004). *Poetry and the meaning of life.* Toronto, Ontario, Canada: Pippin.

Harnad, S. (1995). Interactive cognition: Exploring the potential of electronic quote/commenting. In B. Gorayska & J. L. Mey (Eds.), *Cognitive technology: In search of a human interface* (pp. 397–414). Hong Kong, China: Elsevier.

Harrell, L. E., Jr. (1957). *A comparison of oral and written language in school-age children.* Lafayette, IN: Child Development Publications.

Harris, R. (2000). *Rethinking writing.* London: Continuum.

Havelock, E. A. (1988). *The muse learns to write: Reflections on orality and literacy from antiquity to the present.* New Haven, CT: Yale University Press.

Haworth, A. (2001). The re-positioning of oracy: A millennium project. *Cambridge Journal of Education 31*(1), 11–23.

Hines, P. J. (2001). Why controversy belongs in the science classroom. *Harvard Education Letter, 17*(5), 8–14.

Horowitz, R. (1990). Discourse structure in oral and written language: Critical contrasts for literacy and schooling. In J. H. A. L. de Jong & D. K. Stevenson (Eds.), *Individualizing the assessment of language abilities* (pp. 108–126). Clevedon Avon, England: Multilingual Matters.

Horowitz, R. (1991a). Orality and literacy and the design of schooling for the twenty-first century: Some introductory remarks. *Text, 11*(1), i–xvi.

Horowitz, R. (1991b). A reexamination of oral versus silent reading. *Text, 11*(1), 133–166.

Horowitz, R. (Ed.). (1994). Classroom talk about text: What teenagers and teachers come to know about the world through talk about text [Special themed issue]. *Journal of Reading, 37*(7), 4–10.

Horowitz, R. (1994). Written and oral English. In A. Purves (Ed.), *Encyclopedia of English studies and language arts* (pp. 1326–1328). Urbana, IL: National Council of Teachers of English.

Horowitz, R. (1995). Orality in literacy: The uses of speech in written language by bilingual and bicultural writers. In D. L. Rubin (Ed.), *Composing social identity in written language* (pp. 47–74). Hillsdale, NJ: Lawrence Erlbaum Associates.

Horowitz, R. (1998). The evolution of classroom talk: Contributions to text conceptualization and learning. In N. Ephraty & R. Lidor (Eds.), *Teacher education: Stability, evolution, and revolution* (pp. 921–932). Natanya, Israel: The Zinman College, Wingate Institute, Israel; in conjunction with the Ministry of Education and Mofett Institute.

Horowitz, R. (2001). *What's in a "Sefer"?* Paper presented at the symposium of *What's in a book? The creation and uses of books*. American Educational Research Association Conference, New Orleans, LA.

Horowitz, R. (2004, February). *Talk as a creative force in text comprehension and interpretation.* Keynote address presented at the mid-year conference of the Beginning Teacher Support and Assessment (BTSA) Program, Los Angeles Unified School District, Los Angeles, CA.

Horowitz, R. (2005). Book Review of Otero, J., León, J. A., & Graesser, A. C. (Eds.). (2002). The psychology of science text comprehension. *Discourse Studies, 7*(6), 763–768.

Horowitz, R. (2006, August). *Tracing how spoken language finds its way into written language.* Paper presented at the meeting of the International Conference on Speech, Writing, and Context, University of Alberta, Edmonton, Canada.

Horowitz, R., & Cummings, C. (2000). *Repetition in discourse: A linguistic strategy signifying involvement in children's conversational dialogues with a literary work.* Paper presented at the Society for Text and Discourse Conference, Lyon, France.

Horowitz, R., & Kincy-Freeman, S. H. (1995). Robots versus spaceships: The role of discussion in kindergartners' and second-graders' preference for science text. *The Reading Teacher, 49*(1), 30–40.

Horowitz, R., & Norrick, N. R. (2005, June). *Joke telling in the elementary school classroom: How teachers transform written jokes into oral performances.* Paper presented at The International Society for Humor Studies Conference, Youngstown, Ohio. Manuscript submitted for publication.

Horowitz, R., & Olson, D. R. (in press). Texts that talk: The special and peculiar nature of classroom discourse and the crediting of sources. In R. Horowitz (Ed.), *Talking Texts: How Speech and Writing Interact in School Learning*. Mahwah, NJ: Lawrence Erlbaum Associates.

Horowitz, R., & Samuels, S. J. (Eds.). (1987). *Comprehending oral and written language* (1st ed.). London: Academic Press.

Hoyt, L. (1992). Many ways of knowing: Using drama, oral interactions, and the visual arts to enhance reading comprehension. *The Reading Teacher, 45*, 580–584.

Hunt, R. A. (1994). Speech genres, writing genres, school genres, and computer genres. In A. Freedman & P. Medway (Eds.), *Learning and teaching genre* (pp. 243–262). Portsmouth, NJ: Heinemann.

Hymes, D. (1971). Competence and performance in linguistic theory. In R. Huxley & E. Ingram (Eds.), *Language acquisition: Models and methods* (pp. 3–28). New York: Academic Press.

Hymes, D. H. (1962). The ethnography of speaking. In T. Galdwin & W. Sturtevant (Eds.), *Anthropology and human behavior.* Washington, DC: Anthropological Society of Washington.

Hymes, D. H. (1964). Introduction: Toward ethnographies of communication. In J. J. Gumperz & D. H. Hymes (Eds.), *The Ethnography of communication. American Anthropologist, 66,* 1–34.

Hymes, D. H. (1966, June). *On communicative competence.* Paper presented at the Research planning conference on language development among disadvantaged children, Yeshiva University, New York.

Jakobson, R. (1960). Linguistics and poetics. In T. Sebeok (Ed.), *Style in language.* Cambridge, MA: MIT Press.

John-Steiner, V. (2000). *Creative collaboration.* Oxford, England: Oxford University Press.

Johnston, P. H. (2004). *Choice words: How our language affects children's learning.* Portland, ME: Stenhouse.

Jordan, M. P. (1984). *Rhetoric of everyday English texts.* St. Leonards, Australia: Allen & Unwin.

Kalman, J. (1999). *Writing on the plaza: Mediated practices of scribes and their clients in Mexico City.* Cresskill, NJ: Hampton Press.

Kelly, G. J., & Chen, C. (1999). The sound of music: Constructing science as sociocultural practices through oral and written discourse. *Journal of Research in Science Teaching, 36,* 883–915.

Kinneavy, J. L. (1980). *A theory of discourse: The aims of discourse.* London: W. W. Norton.

Knoeller, C. (1998). *Voicing ourselves: Whose words we use when we talk about books.* Albany, NY: State University of New York Press.

Koschmann, T. (Guest Ed.). (1999). Meaning Making. [Special issue]. *Discourse Processes, 27*(2), 103–240.

Kowal, S., O'Connell, D. C., Forbush, K., Higgins, M., Clarke, L., & D'Anna, K. (1997). Interplay of literacy and orality in inaugural rhetoric. *Journal of Psycholinguistic Research, 26*(1), 1–31.

Lagerwerf, L., Schober, M. F., Spooren, W., Degand, L. (Eds.). (2006). Surface cues of content and tenor in text [Special issue]. *Discourse Processes, 41*(2), 111–116.

Lakoff, R. (1982). Some of my favorite writers are literate: The mingling of oral and literate strategies in written communication. In D. Tannen (Ed.), *Spoken and written language: Exploring orality and literacy* (pp. 239–260). Norwood, NJ: Ablex.

Latour, B., & Wilgoor, S. (1979). *Laboratory life: The construction of scientific facts.* Beverly Hills, CA: Sage Publications.

Leander, K., & Prior, P. (2004). Speaking and writing: How talk and text interact in situated practices. In C. Bazerman & P. Prior (Eds.), *What writing does and how it does it: An introduction to analyzing texts and textual practices* (pp. 201–237). Mahwah, NJ: Lawrence Erlbaum Associates.

Lee, C. D., & Smagorinsky, P. (2000). *Vygotskian perspectives on literacy research: Constructing meaning through collaborative inquiry.* Cambridge, England: Cambridge University Press.

Leinhardt, G., Crowley, K., & Knutson, K. (Eds.). (2002). *Learning conversations in museums.* Mahwah, NJ: Lawrence Erlbaum Associates.

Lemke, J. L. (1983). *Classroom communication of science.* Final Report to the U.S. National Science Foundation. Arlington, VA: ERIC Documents Service (ED 222 346).

Lemke, J. L. (1990). *Talking science: Language, learning, and values.* Norwood, NJ: Ablex Publishing.

Levstick, L. S., & Barton, K. C. (2001). *Doing history: Investigating with children in elementary and middle schools* (2nd ed.). Mahwah, NJ: Lawrence Erlbaum Associates.

MacWhinney, B. (Ed.). (1999). *The emergence of language.* Mahwah, NJ: Lawrence Erlbaum Associates.

MacWhinney, B. (2000). *The CHILDES project: Tools for analyzing talk* (Vols. 1–2, 3rd ed.). Mahwah, NJ: Lawrence Erlbaum Associates.

Marvin, C. (1995). The family car as a "vehicle" for children's use of distant time referents. *Early Childhood Research, 10,* 185–202.

McNeill, D. (2004, August). *Convergence of gesture and discourse.* Paper presented at the annual meeting of the Society for Text and Discourse, Chicago, IL.

McNeill, D. (2005). *Gesture and thought.* Chicago: University of Chicago Press.

McPherson, G. E. (2005). From child to musician: Skill development during the beginning stages of learning an instrument. *Psychology of Music, 33*(1), 5–35.

Miller, S. (2006). *Conversation: A history of a declining art.* New Haven, CT: Yale University Press.

Mishler, E. G. (1979). Meaning in context: Is there any other kind? *Harvard Educational Review, 49,* 1–19.

Moerman, M. (1988). *Talking culture: Ethnography and conversation analysis.* Conduct and communicational series. Philadelphia: University of Pennsylvania Press.

Moje, E. B., Ciechanowski, K. M., Kramer, K., Ellis, L, Carrillo, R., & Collazo, T. (2004). Working toward third space in content area literacy: An examination of everyday funds of knowledge and discourse. *Reading Research Quarterly, 39*(1), 38–70.

Monaghan, L. F., & Goodman, J. E. (Eds.). (2007). *A cultural approach to international communication: Essential readings.* Malden, MA: Blackwell.

Montgomery, S. L. (2003). *The Chicago guide to communicating science.* Chicago: University of Chicago Press.

Mostow, J., Aist, G., Burkhead, P., Corbett, A., Cuneo, A., Eitelman, S., Huang, C., Junker, B., Sklar, M. B., & Tobin, B. (2003). Evaluation of an automated reading tutor that listens: Comparison to human tutoring and classroom instruction. *Journal of Educational Computing Research, 29*(1), 61–117.

Mukarovsky, J. (1964). Standard language and poetic language. In P. Garvin (Trans.), *A Prague school reader on aesthetics, literary structure, and style* (pp. 17–30). Washington, DC: Georgetown University Press.

Nakanishi, A. (1980). *Writing systems of the world.* Tokyo, Japan: Charles E. Tuttle.

National Institute of Child Health and Human Development. (2000). Report of the National Reading Panel. *Teaching Children to Read: An evidence-based Assessment of the Scientific Research Literature on Reading and its implications for Reading Instruction* (NIH Publication No. 00–4769). Washington, DC: U.S. Government Printing Office.

Nevile, M. (2004). Integrity in the airline cockpit: Embodying claims about progress for the conduct of an approach briefing. *Research on Language and Social Interaction, 37,* 447–480.

Noddings, N. (2006). *Critical lessons: What our schools should teach.* Cambridge, England: Cambridge University Press.

Nystrand, M. (1997). *Opening dialogue: Understanding the dynamics of language and learning in the English classroom.* New York: Teachers College Press.

Nystrand, M. (2006). Research on the role of classroom discourse as it affects reading comprehension. *Research in the Teaching of English, 40,* 392–412.

Nystrand, M., & Duffy, J. (Eds.). (2003). *Towards a rhetoric of everyday life. New directions in research on writing, text, and discourse.* Madison: University of Wisconsin Press.

Nystrand, M., & Graff, N. (2001). Report in argument's clothing: An ecological perspective on writing instruction in a seventh-grade classroom. *Elementary School Journal, 101,* 479–493.

O'Donnell, R., Griffin, W., & Norris, R. (1967). *Syntax of kindergarten and elementary school children: A transformational analysis.* Champaign, IL: National Council of Teachers of English.

Olson, D. R. (1977). From utterance to text: The bias of language in speech and writing. *Harvard Educational Review, 47,* 257–281.

Olson, D. R. (1994). *The world on paper: The conceptual and cognitive implications of writing and reading.* Cambridge, England: Cambridge University Press.

Olson, D. R. (1997). Critical thinking: Learning to talk about talk and text. In G. D. Phye (Ed.), *Handbook of academic learning: Construction of knowledge* (The Educational Psychology Series, pp. 493–510). San Diego, CA: Academic Press.

Olson, D. R. (2003). *Psychological theory and educational reform: How school remakes mind and society.* Cambridge, England: Cambridge University Press.

Olson, D. R., & Kamawar, D. (1999). The theory of ascriptions. In P. D. Zelazo, J. W. Astington, & D. R. Olson (Eds.), *Developing theories of intention: Social understanding and self-control* (pp. 153–166). Mahwah, NJ: Lawrence Erlbaum Associates.

Ong, W. J. (1977). *Interfaces of the world: Studies in the evolution of consciousness and culture.* Ithica, NY: Cornell University Press.

Ong, W. J. (1992). *Orality and literacy. The technologizing of the word.* London: Methuen.

Ong, W. J. (2002). *Orality and literacy: The technologizing of the word* (2nd ed.). London: Routledge.

Palincsar, A. S., & Magnusson, S. J. (2001). The interplay of first-hand and second-hand investigations to model and support the development of scientific knowledge and reasoning. In S. Carver & D. Klahr (Eds.), *Cognition and instruction: Twenty-five years of progress* (pp. 151–194). Mahwah, NJ: Lawrence Erlbaum Associates.

Paris, S. (Ed.). (2002). *Perspectives on object-centered learning in museums.* Mahwah, NJ: Lawrence Erlbaum Associates.

Pappas, C., Kiefer, B., & Levstik, L. (1990). *An integrated language perspective in the elementary school: Theory into action.* New York: Longman.

Paxton, R. J. (1999). A deafening silence: History textbooks and the students who read them. *Review of Educational Research, 69,* 315–339.

Paxton, R. J. (2002). The influence of author visibility on high school students solving a historical problem. *Cognition & Instruction, 20,* 197–248.

Pease-Alvarez, L., & Schecter, S. R. (Eds.). (2005). Learning, teaching, and community: Contributions of situated and participatory approaches to education innovation. Hillsdale, NJ: Lawrence Erlbaum Associates.

Pelligrini, A. D., Galda, L., & Flor, D. (1997). Relationships, individual differences, and children's use of literate language. *British Journal of Educational Psychology, 67,* 139–152.

Perfetti, C. A., Britt, M. A., & Georgi, M. C. (1995). *Text based learning and reasoning: Studies in history.* Hillsdale, NJ: Lawrence Erlbaum Associates.

Perinbanayagam, R. S. (1991). *Discursive acts: Communication and social order.* New York: Aldine de Gruyter.

Perkins, D. N. (1977). Talk about art. *Journal of Aesthetic Education, 11*(2), 87–116.

Perkins, D. N. (1992). *Smart schools: From training memories to educating minds.* New York: Free Press.

Perkins, D. N. (2003). *King Arthur's roundtable: How collaborative conversations create smart organizations.* Hoboken, NJ: John Wiley & Sons.

Pliskin, Z. (1988). *The power of words.* Brooklyn, NY: Benei Yakov Publications.

Poole, D. (2003). Linguistic connections between co-occurring speech and writing in a classroom literacy event. *Discourse Processes, 35*(2), 103–134.

Rabin, C. (1986). The discourse status of commentary. In C. R. Cooper & S. Greenbaum (Eds.), *Studying writing: Linguistic approaches* (pp. 215–225). Beverly Hills, CA: Sage.

Raible, W. (1994). Orality and literacy. In H. Gunther & O. Ludwig (Eds.), *Schrift und Schriftlichkeit. Writing and its use* (pp. 1–17). Berlin: Walter de Gruyter.

Rampton, B. (2006). *Language in late modernity: Interaction in an urban school* (Studies in Interactional Sociolinguistics, No. 22). Cambridge, England: Cambridge University Press.

Rendel-Short, J. (2006). *The academic presentation: Situated talk in action.* Aldershot, UK: Ashgate.

Reznitskaya, A., Anderson, R. C., McNurlen, B., Nguyen-Juhiel, K. Archodidou, A., & Kim, S. (2001). Influence of oral discussion on written argument [Special issue]. *Discourse Processes, 32,* 155–175.

Reznitskaya, A., & Anderson, R. C. (2002). *The argument schema and learning to reason.* In C. C. Block & M. Pressley (Eds.), *Comprehension Instruction* (pp. 319–334). New York: Guilford Press.

Rommetveit, R. (1974). *On message structure: A framework for the study of language and communication.* London: Wiley.

Rose, M. (2004). *The mind at work: Valuing the intelligence of the American worker.* New York: Viking.

Rosenthal, R., & Jacobson, L. (1968). *Pygmalion in the classroom: Teacher expectation and pupils' intellectual development.* New York: Holt, Rinehart, & Winston.

Rowe, S. (2004). Discourse in activity and activity as discourse. In R. Rogers (Ed.), *An introduction to critical discourse analysis in education* (pp. 79–96). Mahwah, NJ: Erlbaum.

Sacks, H., Scheploff, E. A., & Jefferson, G. (1974). A simplest systematics for the organization of turn-taking in conversation. *Language, 50,* 696–735.

Sanders, T. J. M., & Gernsbacher, M. A. (2004). Accessibility in text and discourse processing. [Special issue]. *Discourse Processes, 37*(2), 79–186.

Sanders, T. J. M., Spooren, W. P. M., & Noordman, L. G. M. (1992). Toward a taxonomy of coherence relations. *Discourse Processes, 15*(1), 1–35.

Sanders, T. J. M., Spooren, P. M., & Noordman, L. G. M. (1993). Coherence relations in a cognitive theory of discourse representation. *Cognitive Linguistics, 4*(2), 93–133.

Schallert, D. L., & Kleiman, G. M. (1979). *Some reasons why teachers are easier to understand
than textbooks* (Reading Education Technical Report, No. 9). Urbana: University of Illinois at Champaign-Urbana, Center for the Study of Reading.

Schleppegrell, M. J. (2004). *The language of schooling: A functional linguistics perspective.*
Mahwah, NJ: Lawrence Erlbaum Associates.

Schreiber, P. (1987). Prosody and structure in children's syntactic processing. In R.
Horowitz & S. J. Samuels (Eds.), *Comprehending oral and written language* (pp. 243–270).
San Diego: Academic Press.

Schwanenflugel, P. J., Hamilton, A. M., Wiesenbaker, J., Kuhn, M., & Stahl, S. (2004). Becoming a fluent reader: Reading skill and prosodic features in the oral reading of young readers. *Journal of Educational Psychology, 96*(1), 119–129.

Sinclair, J. M., & Coulthard, M. (1975). *Towards an analysis of discourse: The English used by
teachers and pupils.* London: Oxford University Press.

Snow, C. E. (1991). *Unfulfilled expectations: Home and school influences on literacy.* Cambridge,
MA: Harvard University Press.

Snow, C. (2002). *Reading for understanding: Toward a research and development program in reading comprehension.* Retrieved June 27, 2006, from the RAND Corporation, http://
www.rand.org/pubs/monograph_reports/MR1465/index.html

Solsken, J., Willett, J., & Wilson-Keenan, J. (2000). Cultivating hybrid texts in multicultural
classrooms: Promise and challenge. *Research in the Teaching of English, 35*(2), 179–212.

Spivey, N. (1997). *The constructivist metaphor: Reading, writing, and the making of meaning.* San
Diego: Academic Press.

Stahl, S., Hynd, C., Britton, B. K., McNish, M. M., & Bosquet, D. (1996). What happens when
students read multiple source documents in history? *Reading Research Quarterly, 31,*
430–457.

Stahl S. A., & Kuhn, M. R. (2002). Making it sound like language: Developing fluency. *The
Reading Teacher, 55,* 582–584.

Steiner, G. (2001). *Grammars of creation.* New Haven, CT: Yale University Press.

Stenström, A. B., Andersen, G., & Hasund, I. K. (2002). *Trends in teenage talk: Corpus compilation, analysis, and findings.* Amsterdam: John Benjamins.

Stenström, A. B., Andersen, G., & Hasund, I. K., Benjamins, J. (2005). Trends in teenage talk:
Corpus compilation. *Journal of Pragmatics, 37,* 589–593.

Sullivan, G. (2005). *Art practice as research: Inquiry in the visual arts.* Thousand Oaks, CA:
Sage.

Talbott, P. (Ed.). (2005). *Benjamin Franklin: In search of a better world.* New Haven, CT: Yale
University Press.

TalkBank. (n.d.). An international system for exchange of data on spoken interactions. *Child
Language Data Exchange System (CHILDES).* Available at http://www.talkbank.org/
data Retrieved July 13, 2006, from http://childes/psy.cmu.edu

Tannen, D. (1984). *Conversational style: Analyzing talk among friends.* Norwood, NJ: Ablex.

Tannen, D. (1988). The commingling of orality and literacy in giving a paper at a scholarly
conference. *American Speech, 63*(1), 34–43.

Tannen, D. (1989). *Talking voices: Repetition, dialogue, and imagery in conversational discourse.*
Cambridge, England: Cambridge University Press.

Thomas, R. (1991). *Oral tradition and written record in classical Athens.* Cambridge, England:
Cambridge University Press.

Tortora, S. (2005). *The dancing dialogue: Using the communicative power of movement with young children*. Baltimore, MD: Brookes Publishing.

Tottie, G., & Bäcklund, I. (Eds.). (1986). *English in speech and writing. A symposium*. Acta University, Uppsala, Sweden: Studia Anglistica Upsaliensta, Almqvist, and Wiksell International.

Toulmin, S. E. (1958). *The uses of argument*. Cambridge, England: Cambridge University Press.

Trabasso, T., & van den Broek, P. (1985). Causal thinking and the representation of narrative events. *Journal of Memory and Language, 24*, 612–630.

van Dijk, T. A. (1978). *Text and context: Explorations in the semantics and pragmatics of discourse*. London: Longman.

van Stapele, P. (2005). *Poetics of the screenplay as drama-text*. (Doctoral dissertation, University of Leiden). Wageningen, The Netherlands: Ponsen & Looijen, b.v.

Voloshinov, V. N. (1986). *Marxism and the philosophy of language*. (L. Matejka & I. R. Titunik, Trans.). Cambridge, MA: Harvard University Press. (Original work published 1929).

Voss, J. F. (Guest Ed.). (2001). Argumentation in psychology. [Special issue]. *Discourse Processes, 32*(2/3), 89–245.

Vygotsky, L., & Luria, A. (1994). Tool and symbol in child development. In R. Van der Veer & J. Valsiner (Eds.), *The Vygotsky Reader* (pp. 99–174). Oxford, England: Blackwell.

Watson, R. (1996). Rethinking readiness for learning. In D. R. Olson & N. Torrance (Eds.), *The handbook of education and human development* (pp. 148–172). Oxford, England: Blackwell.

Wells, G. C. (1999). *Dialogic inquiry: Towards a sociocultural theory and practice of education*. Cambridge, England: Cambridge University Press.

Wertsch, J. V. (1991). *Voices of the mind*. Cambridge, MA: Harvard University Press.

Willcox, W. B. (1972). *The papers of Benjamin Franklin* (Vol. 15). New Haven, CT: Yale University Press.

Wilson, B. (1997). *The quiet evolution: Changing the face of arts education*. Los Angeles: Getty Education Institute for the Arts.

Wineburg, S. (1991). On the reading of historical texts: Notes on the breach between school and academy. *American Educational Research Journal, 28*, 495–520.

Yule, G. (1997). *Referential communication tasks*. Mahwah, NJ: Lawrence Erlbaum Associates.

Zumthor, P. (1990). *Oral poetry: An introduction* (K. Murphy-Judy, Trans.). Theory and history of literature series (Vol. 70). Minneapolis, MN: University of Minnesota Press.

CHAPTER 2

Texts That Talk: The Special
and Peculiar Nature of Classroom
Discourse and the Crediting
of Sources

Rosalind Horowitz
David R. Olson

In the psychology of school learning there is a new confidence in the potential of discourse, the ongoing give and take of formal and informal discussion. Children's talk with teachers and peers enlarges the opportunities for integrating new information with pre-existing beliefs and knowledge with the prospect of improved learning and memory. The discourse of the school, however, has a so-to-say "silent partner," the school texts and reference books that provide the documentary base for schooling and have become, in a sense, texts that talk. Theories of discourse, then, have to accommodate to these texts and reference materials, allowing them to talk, to have their say. Just how texts come to have their say, how interaction with those silent partners relates to the oral discourse of the classroom, and how such talk is to be integrated into a theory of discourse is the concern of this chapter.

Three issues are at stake when examining the relation between the ongoing oral and written expressions of children and the written tasks they commonly encounter in school:

- How do the texts that children encounter in school become part of the speech and writing of students?
- How do children refer to and credit sources of information, whether oral or written, in their own speech and writing?
- How do these texts contribute to the formation of an awareness of self and of one's own point of view?

To address these questions, this chapter examines the nature of school texts, children's talk about texts, and the ways in which they refer to and acknowledge those texts.

THE NATURE OF SCHOOL TEXTS

Texts used in schools present unique challenges to and possibilities for learning that are notably different from the talk and storybooks children encounter everyday. During the course of the twentieth century, texts were classically defined as discourse that is fixed by writing (Ricoeur, 1967; Bloomfield, 1933). Although ever since the Enlightenment writing was treated as a privileged form of intellectual expression, in the present century, speech and oral discourse have come to be primary and writing has come to be seen as a derivative and secondary (Havelock, 1976; Hockett, 1958, 1960; Jakobson, 1978; Halliday, 1987). More recent research has suggested ways in which talk and text overlap (Horowitz, chap. 1 in this volume; Olson & Astington, 1993), but how texts become part of the students' speech and writing remains to be examined (Goody, 1987). Unlike the give-and-take that characterizes ordinary, conversational discourse, school discourse with a written document may be spectacularly one-sided. But a reader does more than simply memorize texts. The reader confronts a school text with a set of goals, interests, and beliefs, as well as a set of assumptions about the appropriate use of texts that influence how the text is "taken." For novices, texts tend to be taken as authoritative and autonomous and above criticism (Peskin, 1998). More expert readers may criticize an author's claims or, more likely, recognize what, if anything, warrants or justifies inclusion into the reader's viewpoint. In so doing, the reader's own personal viewpoint, *vis a vis* that of a text or the reader, may take shape. Hence, the reader's final writing now not only reflects the reader's spoken and written reconstruction of source ideas but also the clear distinction between the views expressed by a text and the subjectively held beliefs of the student. This synthesizing, extrapolating, articulating, negotiating, and integrating of a text's ideas with one's own ideas is basic to the reading and composing process.

How Children Read and Understand School Texts

In classrooms, reading is determined in large part by the mandated curriculum. Even if a text fails to "talk" to children in their language or address their ideas and interests, they are required to persist in the attempt to understand. But those attempts may be blocked by several different types of misunderstandings. Children or adolescents may not realize that writing serves specialized functions in different fields of study. They may not recognize that one must be well into a source before forming an opinion; they may not recognize that they have a right to their own opinion which they may then relate to a source text. They may not know how to selectively process a text to fit into their own beliefs and goals and to the overall purpose of their writing.

The difficulties of incorporating source ideas into one's own forms of reference or one's own rhetorical purpose may derive from the authoritative, sacrosanct stature of school texts. School texts—which include textbooks, library books, handbooks or encyclopedias, dictionaries or atlases, historical documents, or government-state prescribed curricula—are not mere texts but texts that carry a certain official authority in that they are selected by public agencies. They specify domains of information for which both teachers and students are held accountable. Consequently, these texts are regarded, consulted, and read in a particular way within the institutional context of schools; they provide the *normative* base for schooling. This is not to say that texts cannot be read ironically, or more informally, as some University of Toronto students frequently did when confronted with the high school English textbook entitled *Enduring Poetry*. They took it not as poetry that has endured but rather as poetry that they themselves had to endure. There are ways and modes of reading that characterize different historical periods, and there are ways of reading that children adopt when consulting different types of texts for different purposes such as preparing for a test or for composing an essay. These differences, although important, are pale in comparison to the difference between documentary texts as a whole and oral discourse, and it is that gulf that we shall explore in some detail in this chapter.

School texts, like any other authoritative document in a literate society, contain certain properties that are different from children's stories and are in some ways unique—not all of them conducive to children's reading and understanding. Sometimes elements of this discourse serve to mark off a domain of professional expertise in such a way as to be inaccessible to non-experts (Geisler, 1994). This is the case with medical, scientific, technological, theological, or legal talk and texts confronted in the adult world. For instance to lawyers, a torts text is a significant source because it falls within their rubrics of expertise and allows for communication in their professional networks; however, to one not versed in legalese, the writing seems peculiar and unnecessarily obtuse. Many school texts are halfway between children's stories and legal texts. They are designed to be accessible while retaining their authoritativeness. Some texts also have a technical dimension intended to enhance understanding of a specialized content domain but which may be a stumbling block for children just learning to read formal discourse. Teachers often play a mediating role between student and text.

Russian language theoreticians Alexander Luria (1976), Lev Vygotsky (1934/1986), and Mikhail Bakhtin (1986) propose that learning is a social activity linked to the speech act. Yet, the informational texts used in classrooms for writing are often arhetorical, devoid of a visible intentionality (Searle, 1983), lack the presence of a speaker/author's voice (cf. Wertsch, 1991), and are far removed from familiar social worlds (Fahnestock, 1986). They are often presented as a collection of authorless (Harris, 1986) or autonomous statements rather than as assertions by a speaker/writer. This special written form derives from the fact that texts are created as sources that teachers can treat as objective and against which student's knowledge and understanding are to be assessed. Through social interaction with teachers and peers, there is the possibility the text can advance from being frozen to being alive—turning the text into a third-party interlocutor in a series of conversations.

A further problem arises from cultural diversity. Children may find the text out of synchrony with their familiar dialogue patterns. The reader must experience a rapport with the written speech style and a formal content before engaging with a text. If a book does not match or make this cultural link for the learner, then the child may be at a loss. However, the more motivated reader will attempt to translate the text speech into their own language or the teacher will attempt to make the necessary connections. How this comes about is documented in the following section.

Finally, school texts present incomplete accounts of information—they rarely indicate to the reader who wrote them, the sources the author consulted or how they are intended to be used. Smith (1990) points out how official documents of the society

> drop away the traces of its making (references to evidence, research, researchers, the technical processes involved and so forth) and stand forth as an autonomous statement representing the actuality [what really is] of which it speaks. The account comes to stand in for the actuality it claims to represent. (p. 74)

Other social scientists (Latour & Woolgar, 1979) talk of this process as a *social construction of facts*. The process by which certain claims came to be treated as facts is lost, and the texts come to be seen as sources of authority. That is, whereas, once evidence provided the basis for a claim, now the written text *is* the evidence. And it is that evidence which children come to report and cite as facts. This was the case in the study to be reported—children never once inquired as to how we know that what the texts said about camels is true or who made the claims the text contained. They appear to treat texts *as* facts rather than as reports *about* facts.

Students not only confront curricular, mandated texts each new school year, but there are topics and content that are in vogue—sometimes due to the media—that become part of the formal and informal classroom curriculum and discourse. Such topics might include rainforests, endangered species, dinosaurs, oceans, space exploration, or the animals within a given terrain—for example, camels of the desert. These topics are chosen to play into the child's natural curiosity and perhaps to expose children, often for the first time, to the official documents of the society. This textual information is assumed to be readily integrated into what the child already knows, thereby expanding his or her world through texts.

A common source of information within school, and the one reported in this study, was the encyclopedia and other similar reference material. The encyclopedia represents the child's first serious encounter with a normative, authoritative source. The language of the encyclopedic text is, in many instances, more technical and expert oriented than that which children have previously encountered in the lower grades, perhaps still another reason for what Jeanne Chall (1990) has called "the fourth-grade slump."

There is little research that explicates how the encyclopedia is "entered" and "cited" in school reading and writing. Nancy Spivey (1983) investigated college students' "synthesis" writings. She selected passages from several encyclopedia sources (the *McGraw-Hill Encyclopedia of Science and Technology*, the *Encyclopedia Americana*, and *Collier's Encyclopedia*), all of which included descriptions of the armadillo. Spivey distributed these three text sources and asked university juniors and seniors to write a synthesis from these sources. She examined the selection of information from the original text structures and how students organized these sources in their own texts. There were differences between the less and more able comprehenders. The more able comprehenders produced texts with fewer themes and more elaboration while the less able comprehenders produced texts with multiple themes, little elaboration, and less detail. Further, Spivey points out that all of the students in her research were heavily "text-bound," conforming their writing to the content that was presented in the original three sources. We shall examine this "text-boundedness" in terms of student copying, quoting, and paraphrasing of texts.

Incidentally, not only is this new text source initially a "silent partner," this silence is sometimes extended by the silence of the school library. In writing from encyclopedic sources in the context of the library, children are not allowed to talk or to seek clarification or advice. The unsanctioned discourse which does occur in the library may be part of the learning process as much as the formal discourse of the classroom.

Documentary source materials include not only written texts but also maps, graphs, and illustrations, all of which may find their way into children's oral and written discourse. Fourth-graders in our study *chose* to sketch and map out the topography of the camels' habitat, e.g., dry land and palm trees, which conveyed the group's synthesis of visual ideas, without specific directions to do so (see Writing Example 1). Musical notations, too, may be used to represent knowledge of pitch, pauses, and rhythm of melodies (Bamberger, this volume).

What makes encyclopedic-like references difficult for children is that these references often contain complex maps and charts, symbols such as musical notations, and illustrations, which are both novel and contain more information than that which the student has encountered previously. On the positive side, the inclusion of multiple forms of representation invites the student to elaborate their own reports with maps, graphs, and drawings. Drawing, for many children, is a spontaneous act of notetaking, which is a precursor for composing and discourse synthesis. Drawings clearly play a role in such disciplines as mathematics, engineering, science, history, literature, architecture, psychology, or anthropology.

Your Own Words

An earlier study (Horowitz 1998a) found that beginning writers, when starting out to use written sources, slavishly copy them verbatim. Teachers attempt to modify this habit by exhorting their students to "say it in your own words." The distinction between simply copying and paraphrasing is such a subtle one that children are well into the middle school or beyond before they learn the difference. If asked, they may profess that they did not copy the language of a source but when a teacher examines their writing, the words of the original encyclopedia source stand out as repeated in the child's work. Or they may proclaim the ideas they wrote are *theirs* when in fact the ideas came from *an other* (Dillon, 1988; Jackson, Tway, & Frager, 1987). The problem of how to express ideas from another in "your own words" extends into special populations (Yoder, 2001), cultural groups (Goodwin, 1990), and adult writing. This is especially an issue for adults in higher education, as evidenced by reports in *The Chronicle of Higher Education* of plagiarism, particularly in the discipline of history where primary or secondary sources are used. Whereas repetition in talk following reading may be a step in learning or a sign of the speaker's engagement, in writing this tendency of repeating may indicate copying and a lack of authorial integrity. Gerhardt (2006) highlights that students do not know the rules of attribution. Moreover, given the large volume of constantly recycled popular culture and music, students do not understand the process and sometime complexities associated with copyright laws and scholarly

The Camel

A Camel can Survive longer than a Human—
In the Heat of the Desert.

HOW does the Camel keep Cool?
~~~~~~~~~~ the camel's body doesn't get hot
because It's long legs keeps it's body from the hot ground.

A camel has a fat Filled Hamp on it's back
that also keeps it cool.

How are Camels bad-Tempered?

Camels don't like everything and everybody.
Camels don't get along with other camels,

They spit, Bite, kick, For no Reason at all.
They kick with their Hind legs.
What they spit is called slimey cud.

By: Steve, Melissa, Mark, Russi.

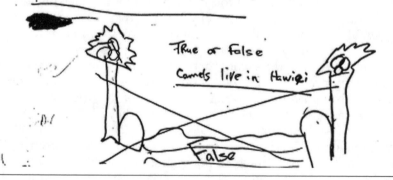

True or False
Camels live in Hawigi

False

Writing Example 1

communication. The *New York Times* goes so far as to label the United States "a nation of copiers" (Leland & La Feria, 2003).

When copying verbatim in writing, learners may not be comprehending. However, when they translate text into a paraphrase or as children engage in drawing, they *are* said to be comprehending that information. Graphics, like paraphrase, are an expression of the writer's integration of ideas and synthesis.

Referring to Oral Sources

How children cite and paraphrase written sources and information is foregrounded by their competence with referring to oral sources. How children talk about "what is said" appears first in their attempts at direct quotation (see also Bruner, 1999 for a discussion of the earliest forms of referring).

Children use quotation from a very early stage of language development. One of the first imperatives infants learn to respond to is, "Say 'Doggie'" where "Doggie" may be a pet, a toy, or a picture in a picture book. Indeed, it could be argued that before they learn any words at all, children have to learn what a word is, that it is different from the sound an animal makes. Thus, "Say Doggie" differs from "What does Doggie *say*?" McTear (1988) cites a pair of preschool siblings arguing thus: *"You said 'yes.'" "No, I said, 'no.' You said, 'yes.'"* Here both content cited and the source of the citations are clear. However, even preschool children report on speech using verbs such as *say, tell,* and *ask,* and by the early school years characterize their own and others' utterances as *secrets, lies, teases, or promises* (Olson & Astington, 1993). Marking their own stance to the material quoted through speech and verbs such as *explain, imply,* or *allege* may develop later, if at all.

A graduate student, Frances Frazier (personal communication), found that second-graders in her inner-city Texas school had a clear concept of quotation following her discussion of the concept. They interestingly enough described the quotation marks that surround the spoken words as lips surrounding the uttered language of another.

The origins of repeating oral sources are found in children's copycat games. For instance, children will repeat the words of adults and their peers to tease them.

Mom says: *"You can't go to the store."*
Child says: *"You can't go to the store."*
Mom says: *"Stop repeating what I'm saying."*
Child says: *"Stop repeating what I'm saying."*

Children have secrets that they appear to quote to one another to include or exclude others. A secret exists initially as either a direct quotation or as a reported idea that bonds children to one another and, through repetition and paraphrase, loses its status as a secret. It is unknown if secrets retain actual wording or merely preserve the central idea.

When a child "tattletales" about another child, they may use quoted speech.

Example 1:   "He took Mary's money and *said, 'You can't have it back.'"*

The phrase *"You can't have it back."* represents *quoted speech.*

Example 2:   Johnny said to his mother, "He crossed the street and *said* that *you told him he could."*

The latter phrase, *"you told him he could"* represents *indirect, quoted speech and paraphrasing*.

When children begin school they often cite the claims of teachers justifying its truth by saying, *"Teacher said."*

While children quote and report on what others have said, *extended quotation* is a more serious matter, and it is not clear that preschool children make any systematic distinction between direct quotation and indirect quotation, frequently reporting as what was said, what was in fact what they thought was meant (Robinson, Goelman, & Olson, 1983). Connie Meyer (personal communication) reports that deaf, signing children often cite others in sign, but have no means for distinguishing direct from indirect quotation. Indeed it may be argued that the distinction is a historically recent one, tied closely to the development of writing. Children's competence with direct and indirect quotation, while not widely studied, suggests that children are learning the rules for using their words (Hickman, 1993).

Unlike in writing, repetition may be acceptable and even valued in oral discourse. With an increasing number of teacher-led, group conversations about the novel, *Julie of the Wolves* (George, 1972), fifth-graders in San Antonio, Texas increased their use of repetition in classroom small group talk (Horowitz & Cummings, 2000). By the fourth or fifth conversation, children had repeated their main arguments and beliefs about Julie's assimilation and acculturation into the world of Alaskan wolves. (a) We viewed the repetitions as signs of student engagement and increasing involvement with the source and the classroom discussions. (b) The repetitions also conveyed emphasis and elaboration of points they were making in the dialogues. (c) Repetitions may be the first step or anchor for higher level referencing. However, such repetitions may or may not constitute quotations and while such repetition may be a part of oral discourse, Chafe and Danielewicz (1987) show how such repetition would not be acceptable in some formal written discourse.

Table 2.1 provides a listing of types of children's quoting and referencing of oral sources; the final two are the subject of the present study.

Referring to Written Sources

The study of cited texts provides a story of the history of the accumulation of human knowledge. Within different time periods, there have been different conventions for crediting sources and different purposes for doing so (Johns, 1998; Waugh, 1995).

The use of citations or references by a given writer serves several purposes. (a) The citation expresses a relationship between a writer-author and the original source that is quoted. (b) It allows the writer to trace the origin of the source-ideas so that the reader can trace the evolution of ideas across several authors, publications, social groups, or locations. (c) The reference placed in a writing sample shows the writer's care with the ideas and may be the beginning of expert-like expressiveness. (d) It avoids the charge of plagiarism.

Making Sense of a Child's Direct Quotation of Written Text Sources

Citation of written texts as reference material for a child's own speech and writing is additionally complicated by the peculiar nature of written texts in formal in-

TABLE 2.1
Children's Repetitions and Credit to Oral Sources

Meaning Based Repetitions

1. Secrets Told—Bonding. Gives structure and builds rapport.

2. Tattletales—Reporting the speech or actions to harm another child. It may include quotation but this remains unstudied.

3. Reported Lies—May involve incorrectly quoted speech but again this has not been studied.

Language Based Repetitions

4. Parroting—Mimic. No explicit referencing to source.

5. Copycat Games—Repeats without the other interlocutor's permission. It may include a quotation but this remains unstudied.

6. Quotation—Reported verbatim speech *with indication of sources* (e.g., "John said") or directly referring to another source without crediting the source.

7. Indirect Quotation—*Reported speech* with source (e.g., John said that *Mary was a leader*).

8. Citing—Use of a writing or speech convention to give credit to source of origin.

structional contexts. Although the discontinuities between speech and writing are obvious to everyone—the absence of a physically present author and/or reader to each other, the disappearance of a shared physical context, the evanescence of the utterance as opposed to the relative permanence of the written, and the like—deeper theories of their relation have been slow to develop.

Historically, writing at first was taken as the privileged form of expression with speech being seen as imperfect and derivative, while in much of the twentieth century the reverse has held—speech being seen as the fundamental endowment of the species with writing being seen as merely a recording device. Scinto (1986) reports on the ontogenesis and priority of speech over writing, which he shows places a primacy on the phonetic manifestations of language. Others have avoided the issue of the primacy of either oral or written language. Barthes (1982), for example, suggests that while speech is "heard," writing, and all literature, are "overheard," and in this sense distanced from the immediate context.

Olson (1999) has advanced a similar notion, arguing that writing bears a special relation to speech, that relation being characterized in terms of the properties of *direct quotation*. When confronted by a text, he argues, a modern reader takes the text as if it were in quotation marks. Technically speaking, the text is treated as *mentioned* (a symbol) rather than *used* (an object). As a consequence, the rules for interpreting text are just those rules that are appropriate to handling directly quoted speech. This view has some implications. First, it goes far toward explaining why writing has the metalinguistic implications well known in the literature; namely, that writing produced a kind of metalinguistic awareness. As a result of learning to read, children developing literacy come to think about not only the message conveyed by the text but also the properties of the text, including such notions as phoneme, word, sentence, paragraph, synonym, antonym, and the like.

Second, the theory helps explain why, in citing texts, rather precise rules for quoting and paraphrasing texts come into place. Specifically, in *direct quoting* no word changes are allowed, while in *indirect quoting* and *paraphrasing*, certain substitutions are not allowed. Thus, in what are called "opaque contexts" created by such verbs as *say, know,* and *think*, one cannot substitute terms even if the terms refer to the same object. An example: If John knows that a yellow ball is on the bed, and in fact, the yellow ball is the biggest ball in the room, it is not the case that John knows that the biggest ball in the room is on the bed. This is because he may not know that the yellow ball is the biggest ball (Olson & Kamawar, 1999; Kamawar & Olson, 2000).

Thus, in reading and interpreting a text, the reader is restricted in the substitutions they may make in paraphrasing a text to those substitutions the writer of that text may have been willing to agree to, not to those which the reader is willing to make. While the theory that writing is *not* like speech but rather is like *quoted speech* could be elaborated upon, it is sufficient here to indicate that confronting texts—especially those texts that are to be used as normative, authoritative reference materials—requires that students come to see them in a special way in the institution of schooling. That way will subsequently guide the reader/researcher in how they use texts in formulating their own beliefs and arguments in talking and writing about texts.

Plagiarism and the Crediting of Sources

In oral discourse, the use of a common vocabulary and common modes of referring and explaining are central to the achievement of productive, cooperative discourse. The problem of extended quotation and, ultimately, plagiarism does not arise in spoken discourse. Repetition does occur in the sense that children and adults do pick up words from their contexts of use and initially unfamiliar words regularly find their way into discussion. Paraphrase or repetition is called for when a quizzical look appears in the behavior of the listener or when requests for clarification are made. Under such circumstances, the speaker can't go on without being asked, "What do you mean?" and without explaining the sources to the listener who doesn't understand.

However, for written documents, such as study and reference materials, the use of verbatim quotation *does* create a problem. First, *quotation without acknowledgment* may ultimately lead to the charge of plagiarism, while even *quotation with acknowledgment* leaves the possibility that the quoter may not understand the information quoted. To steer between these alternatives, teachers not only require that the documents serve as reference material but that the information be reorganized into categories of thought provided by the learner. Indeed, in most important cases, the textual evidence may, for its interpretation, require that the learner revise their thinking in a fundamental way, a problem referred to as "conceptual change."

Children's Citations: How Children Reference Texts

Our interest in citation in this chapter is less with giving credit than in addressing the more general question of how children come to use textual information to elaborate their own knowledge. Just how children cite texts "in their own words" is an open and empirical question that has been examined only recently (Horowitz,

1995, 1996, 2000). First, children have to learn to distinguish the content from the expression, *what is said* from *what is meant* (Lee, Torrance, Olson, 1994, 2001). Of what is "said," they must distinguish direct from indirect quotation and paraphrase and master the use of punctuation to mark these relations. In so doing, they will also have to sort out the limits of lexical substitution in making a paraphrase and the ways of expressing anaphoric relationships. Second, children have to learn to carefully use language to distinguish the ideas they themselves hold from those they encounter in or attribute to a text. They may agree with a text and, by paraphrase, take it as their own view (Arrington, 1988), or they may quote it and either agree or disagree with it. But in either case, they, ultimately, have to learn to use textual information and credit sources in their writing. In many school-like texts the author is invisible or is anonymous thereby adding to the difficulty of recognizing the author's view (Paxton, 1999).

Skilled writers, we suggest, distance themselves from the text. They will mark their own stance vis-à-vis that of the authors they cite by means of such distancing speech act verbs as *claimed, alleged,* and *argued* or marking their agreement with authors cited by means of such verbs as *pointed out, showed,* or *proved.* To go beyond mere quoting or paraphrasing, the student must be in possession of a set of higher-order concepts in order to mark the attitude toward what they have quoted or cited. This set of concepts is extraordinarily large but includes such typical concepts as *assert, assume, claim, concede, conclude, confirm, contradict, criticize, declare, define, deny, discover, doubt, explain, hypothesize, imply, infer, interpret, observe, predict, prove, remember,* and *suggest.* This, we suspect, is the final stage of the development we analyze in this chapter. This stage was apparent in a task in which Horowitz and Cole (in progress) asked fifth-grade students to argue against or for a school dress code. These students distanced their own views from those advocated by the newspaper and the school principal by means of such speech act verbs as *claimed* and *argued,* thereby comparing and contrasting their own ideas with those of another—either a peer or instructor. The task given these fifth-graders was one which effectively elicited a position in their writing confirming how important the task selected and specific purpose for writing may be in eliciting writing with a position.

Hilkka Stötesbury (1999, 2002) asked Finnish university students, who were learning English as a second language for English Academic Purposes (EAP), to respond to two genres of text. Students were asked to produce (a) a report following the reading of a book review and (b) a critical summary following the reading of three source-texts. Stötesbury identifies the speech act verbs that subjects used in the writing following reading under each of these tasks. She argues that the task, genre, and context and the way the student perceived the writing task influenced the use of verbs and writing organization or macrostructures. The book report writing resulted in use of evaluation verbs including appraisals of the original author's writings or ideas (i.e. *quality*—good or bad, *moral judgment*—right or wrong) and reports of text impressions. On the other hand, the critical summary involved combining ideas from three source-texts, which resulted in higher-order speech act verbs such as *claimed* or *alleged* in addition to expressions such as *I believe* or *I agree.* The students displayed greater personal involvement with phrases such as *I think* or *in my opinion,* high visibility in their writing, and greater discussion of their views of the original source-texts. Stötesbury refers to this elaboration by the writer as *Discussion Proper.* This is parallel to what we describe in this chapter as *Commentary.*

We can summarize our theory of how writers cite or "source" documents in their own writing. These diverse ways, we propose, change with development from simply copying to quoting to *"saying it in your own words"* to formulating one's own perspective on a topic or a text through the use of speech act verbs or through evaluation and commentary. Table 2.2 identifies the forms of "sourcing" of discourse.

DEGREES AND TYPES OF COPYING

What kinds of copying do students produce? Why do they resort to copying?

Earlier than our work—but very related to it—James Britton and associates (1975) in the United Kingdom proposed a set of categories that represent what they call "a kind of scale" of "degrees of copying" (p. 46). This scale, discussed below, describes the use of printed sources in student writing.

- **The Writer Presents Others' Work**
  Mechanical copying may be based on a lack of realization (consciousness) that the student is copying or, if the student is conscious of copying, he or she just may not comprehend the text or may find copying to be the simplest way of completing a writing assignment.
  Copying with intention and *preferred copying* may occur because the student likes the way something is said, wants to preserve the original source for later use, or just wants to have it. Pamela, a 14-year-old student taught by Horowitz, copied poetry during her free time in an English class because she liked particular poems and wanted to remember the style of the poetry so she could reproduce it at a later point in her own writing.
  Teacher-required copying is when a teacher wants students to learn a passage "by heart" (p. 46). To aid their memory, the teacher may require the students to write out the passage verbatim.

None of the above is writing as an act of composing.

TABLE 2.2
Forms of "Sourcing" of Discourse

Copy—Repetition of a phrase or sentence or paragraph with no reference to the sources of this language.

Direct Quote—Repetition of original language of a text, with acknowledgment of the source usually with proper punctuation.

Indirect Quotation—Preserves the idea from the original sources while acknowledges the source (John said that), using a relative clause or embedded clause.

Paraphrase—Using one's own words with no acknowledgment or with acknowledgment of the source.

Speech Act Verbs—Commenting from the perspective of the reporter, distancing from the original source.

Commentary and Evaluation—Judging the source.

- **The Writer Presents Self**

  Summarization and expansion of ideas marks a significant step toward composing. At this time, the writer "tries to reproduce the ideas of the original" (p. 46) in one's own words and style.

  The writer presents the self and assimilates information to show the reader what he or she thinks is important. In the course of things, the writer is presenting self through choices being made about the sources.

  In the *apprentice-to-master relationship*, ... "element[s] of copying recede" (p. 46) but the writer draws heavily on other authors because he or she admires them or wishes to describe their ideas in order to elaborate on them.

  Using others' works, the writer seeks to *present his or her own synthesis*. This last step is a rarity in school writing but one that writing experts believe can be developed in schools.

The Britton system focuses on copying and the reasons for it. In advanced stages of reproducing content, the writer's self begins to emerge in order to find a synthesis of his or her own. Their system is particularly important given the large amount of copying that children naturally engage in and that was evident in the writing samples obtained in the present study to be reported below. Horowitz and Olson's forms of sourcing, outlined in Table 2.2, take the researcher or teacher of student sourcing a step further, beyond the sheer copying to still more advanced levels of "saying it in your own words." At this level, the self becomes strong enough and detached enough from the original sources to view them with a new perspective. This distanced perspective is necessary for the writer's original thinking to take shape and find expression.

THE CAMEL STUDY

Purposes of The Camel Study

In this section, we re-examine the three questions posed at the onset of this chapter and provide concrete examples of student writing from classroom sources. We show how students (a) consult, read, and interpret texts; (b) use texts by quoting or paraphrasing them in their speech and writing; and (c) refer to and credit the sources they use.

Participants in The Camel Study

The Camel Study took place in Toronto, Ontario, Canada and outside of San Antonio, Texas in the rural community of Natalia. Subjects included fourth-graders (N = 21) in a central urban district of Toronto; seventh-graders (N = 14) and eighth-graders (N = 46) in Natalia, Texas; and university students (N = 26) enrolled at The University of Texas–San Antonio.[1] There were a total of 107 subjects. Classrooms included in this research were volunteered by the classroom teacher who expressed an interest in research and the types of questions we were investigating.

The Toronto fourth-grade classroom that we studied was multicultural, including children that were Asian (students from Malaysia, Thailand, and China), Portuguese, Cuban, French-Canadian, and Jamaican. The teacher who volunteered her class for the research had established an excellent rapport with her students and was recommended by the district office as one having an outstanding classroom atmosphere. The fourth-grade was chosen because it is the grade where many teachers begin to include book reports, encyclopedic writing, and research projects in their curriculum. In the present fourth-grade classroom, children were routinely seated at tables in groups of six for cooperative activities, an arrangement that seemed perfectly consistent with the Jigsaw Method, primarily used in Social Studies, that we were to employ.

The Natalia sample involved seventh- and eighth-grade classrooms in a rural environment that was economically depressed. Approximately 75 percent of the seventh and eighth-graders were Mexican-American. The same procedures were followed in all classes, including the university classes.

Classroom Groups

There were five groups that were formed in each classroom. Each group received a one- to three-paragraph passage on the Camel. Group I, A Baggage Carrier, Some Things Never Change. Group II, Doesn't the Camel Ever Get Thirsty? ... Or Hungry? Group III, One-Humped Arabian Camel, Two-Humped Bactrian Camel; Group IV, Keeping Cool, Beware of Bad-Tempered Camels, and Group V, The Fold-Up Camel.

Passages and Jigsaw Method used in The Camel Study

The passages used in The Camel Study were extracted from a Toronto-based curriculum guide being used in the fourth-grade and were chosen by the classroom teacher as passages likely to be highly readable and thought provoking to her global, multicultural student population. It was also a topic deemed to be appealing to children in hot climates, including the southwestern United States.[2] "Getting to Know the Camel" by Judy Ross contained a four-page discussion of camels with headings followed by two to three paragraphs. A complete set of the camel passages are located in the Appendix. Line-drawings of the various types of camels were also included. The Toronto fourth-grade teachers frequently used the Jigsaw Method, following Aronson (1978).[3] This method is depicted in Figure 2.1. The Camel text was divided into one- or two-paragraph sections by subtopic. Headings, such as found in informational textbooks, preceded each of the sec-

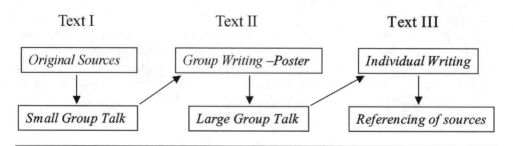

Figure 2.1.   Flow Chart for Classroom Sourcing. The Evolution of Camel Talk and Text.

tions. The heading and the one to two paragraphs that followed were cut into a unit that students would read at a given table. Each table received a different section and was instructed as follows:

> Silently read the passage that you have received. Then, discuss what you've learned with your group. Tell what you learned about the camel on a poster sheet that your group will display in the room on the blackboard. Be sure that you do not copy but say what was learned in your own words. Be sure to tell where you obtained your ideas.

This flow chart depicts movement of knowledge through student text processing, talk, and writing.

Once each poster was produced, the groups took turns reading their poster aloud to the entire class in the front of the room and then the posters were taped to the blackboards around the room. Finally, all the children were instructed to write what they had learned about camels using the information from the group posters. Although the reading and poster-making part of the lesson were group undertakings, the writing portion at the end was individual work. The students were permitted to use the original text and the posters as sources as they pursued their writings. The students were also instructed several times during the course of the activities to note on their papers where they obtained their information and were reminded again not to copy but to "say what they learned in their own words."

Scoring the Use and Crediting of Sources: Understanding How Students Express What They Have Learned

The student group posters and individual writings were scored by two graduate students for idea units—single thoughts expressed by a subject and verb—and for number and types of quotations and citations of sources produced in writing from the classroom oral presentations and written sources. Inter-rater reliability was .90.

The data was examined for changes across the grade levels studied to see how children develop in their ability to consult, use, and cite texts in their own writing.

We examined use of *Copying* (with and without punctuation and quotation marks), *Direct Quotations* (with and without acknowledgment of source, proper punctuation, and quotation marks), and *Indirect Quotations* (without the use of punctuation or quotation marks).

An *indirect quote* and *paraphrase* were distinguished in the following manner. When the writer used 70 percent or more of the original source language/text in their writing, it was scored as an *indirect quote*. When the writer used less than 70 percent of the original source language/text in their writing, assumed personal ownership, and conveyed their ideas using their own words and stance, it was scored as a *paraphrase*.

The children's written texts were analyzed using the following categories and definitions:

I. **Copying—Students may use the exact words of a written source as one's own or they may alter one or two words. More advanced writers may copy only phrases. There is no acknowledgment of the source.**

Original Source Text:
 Camels are used to haul heavy loads across the desert.

Students: fourth-grade, Toronto
 Camels are used for carrying loads across the desert.
 —Jeffrey, Tim, Te Xiu and Kevin (on group poster)

Original Source Text:
 They may bite a person or another animal for no reason and will kick out suddenly and viciously with their hind legs.

Student: eighth-grade, Texas
 They bite people and animals for no reason. Camels can suddenly and viciously kick something or someone.
 —Holly (individual essay)

II. Direct Quotation—Copying the language of a source using quotation marks to indicate that they have copied—with or without acknowledgment of the source.

Using Direct Quotation Without Acknowledgment of the Source:

Original Source Text:
 Because they carry baggage and people across the long stretches of sand—camels are sometimes called "ships of the desert."

Students: seventh-grade, Texas
 They are sometimes called "ships of the desert."
 —Janelle, Jamie, and Cynthia (on group poster)

Using Direct Quotation With Acknowledgment of the Source:

Original Source Text:
 Because they carry baggage and people across long stretches of sand—camels are sometimes called "ships of the desert."

Student: eighth-grade, Texas
 Their nickname is "ships of the desert."
 From: "A Baggage Carrier"
 —Sammi (individual essay)

Students: eighth-grade, Texas
 Camels nickname is "Ships of the desert" Cardina's (sic) Group
 —Jammie, Sue, and Tracy (on group poster)

III. Indirect Quotation—In indirect quotation, the writer may not use the exact words of the source but will acknowledge the source of the idea.

Students: fourth-grade, Canada
 Did not use the technical device of relative clauses to indicate the source of a quoted idea. Rather they expressed the idea, adding a separate sentence to indicate the source.

Student: fourth-grade, Toronto (see Writing Example 2)
 I learned that some camels have one hump and others have two humps.

I learned that from Adam, Mary, Diana, Yihan, and Jing.
—Kelley (individual essay)

Student: eighth-grade, Texas
It said that camels are used to pull plows and turn water wheels that irrigate farms.
—Leonard (individual essay)

IV. **Paraphrase—Preserving textual information through one's own words, with or without acknowledgment of the source.**
In our examination of fourth-, seventh-, and eighth-grade and adult writing, we found differences in the language unit used for paraphrasing. The younger subjects in our sample paraphrased sentence by sentence, while many of the eighth-graders and adult university students in this sample paraphrased using paragraphs as their basis for representing and rephrasing ideas.

Original Source Text:
Doesn't the camel ever get thirsty?
Because it can last for a long time without anything to eat or drink, the camel's body is perfect for life in the desert. It may have to live for months without water, but it can still survive because it gets moisture from its food, and from dew and rain. When offered water a thirsty camel can down well over a hundred liters in ten minutes.

... Or Hungry?
People used to believe that the camel's hump was a built-in storage tank for water, but it actually stores fat, not water. This fat is used for extra energy when food is scarce. Luckily the camel does not care what it drinks or eats. If fresh water isn't available, it will drink sea water. And it will eat almost anything if it gets hungry enough—even baskets, straw matting, or tents!

Student: eighth-grade, Texas
What I learned is that a camel can go far as it want and it doesn't get hungry or thirsty if it gets hungry it eats about anything like tents and other things and if it gets thirsty it will drink other water. A camel can last longer in the desert than a human. My information came from my own reading and from poster A Camel's Actions.
—Andrew (individual essay)

V. **Paraphrasing with Elaboration: Preserve textual information through one's own words and extend the concepts with inferences.**
Original Source Text:
Camels are used to haul heavy loads across the desert. They can carry up to 270 kg on their backs and cover as much as 50 km in one day. They also pull plows, turn water wheels to irrigate fields, and carry loads of grain to market. When walking, camels move the front and back legs of one side forward at the same time. This causes a swaying motion that makes some people feel sea-sick. Because of this—and because they carry baggage and people across long stretches of sand—camels are sometimes called "ships of the desert."

Students: seventh-grade, Texas

We learned that camels can carry up to 270 kg. Once they finish carrying the luggage they stop complaining. They are capable of carrying people and heavy loads across strechs of deserts.

—Janell, Jamie, and Cynthia (on group poster)

VI. Reconstruction and Elaboration of Text Ideas—Students begin to extrapolate from the text, reconstruct ideas, produce metaphors, and elaborate beyond text, adding their own perspective.

Original Source Text:

Camels seem to dislike everything and everybody—including other camels! They may bite a person or another animal for no reason, and will kick out suddenly and viciously with their hind legs. An angry camel may even spit a mouthful of slimy cud at someone passing by.

Student: fourth-grade, Toronto

I learned that camels don't like people and other camels. They kick, spit, and bite. *Their kick must hurt. They spit gooey discusting cud.* They must bite really hard.

—Melissa (individual essay) (italics is ours for emphasis)

VII. Commentator and Distancing—With development, writers learn to distance themselves from the source texts. They begin to comment on and give their opinions about what they have read. They may also use speech act verbs that express the student writer's voice and point of view about text ideas.

Commentary—remarks based on personal interpretation of the text:

University Student: Texas

Camels are the perfect desert animal for all these reasons.

—Kathy (individual essay)

VIII. Metacognitive commentary—Remarks about one's own thinking:

Student: fourth-grade, Toronto

The thing I don't understand is that they will do all this disgusting stuff for no reason at all … I really enjoyed reading about camels. I hope I have a chance to do a project on camels so I can read more about them. Maybe some day I will have a chance.

—Melissa (individual essay)

Student: fourth-grade, Toronto

I never knew that a camel can drink a hundred leters of water in ten minutes.

—Adam (individual essay)

University Student: Texas

There are numerous myths and misconceptions about camels but I have been *enlightened* to these by the class presentations on camels.

—Marco (individual essay)

By: Kellie

Monday, January 15.

I learned that some camels have one hump but other camels have two humps. I also learned that camels store fat not water.

I learned that from Adam, Mary, Diana, Yi han and Jing.

And I also learned that camels can carry upto 270 kg across the desert & that another name for camels is ships of the desert and they sway like a ship.

I learned that from a teacher groups story.

Portuguese/Canadian

Writing Example 2

University Student: Texas
Group 4 *explained* how a camel gets up and down.
Group 5 *informed me* of the way a camel walks.
—Author unknown

University Graduate Student: Texas
A second group *identified* several positive and negative facts about camels.

Group four *described* fold-up camels.
Group five *showed* the services that camels could perform.
—Alan (individual essay)

Developmental Changes in Citing Sources

We studied the different forms of individual student reporting of the discourse heard and read. We examined development in writing from sources by noting the degree of copying from the original sources and use of abstract devices for crediting or acknowledging sources—from paraphrasing, to evaluating, to expressing one's own ideas where there is a distancing from the original source and the beginnings of interpretation and criticism. For the first analysis of the data, we simply scored the incidence of verbatim repetition of the phrases or sentences from the source text, without noting whether these expressions were simply copies or were copied but acknowledged as quoted or paraphrased. Figure 2.2 indicates that the fourth-graders in Toronto individually copied nearly half, 43 percent, of the information they reported: eight percent of the ideas reported were copied from their own group's poster; two percent of the ideas reported were copied from the original text; and 33 percent were copied from another group's poster. Our seventh-graders from rural Texas performed much like the fourth-graders, with 48 percent of their writing being copied (see Fig. 2.3). In our sample of eighth-graders, there was an even larger incidence of copying, with 63 percent of the statements in the individual reports being copied (see Fig. 2.4). But these copied phrases were more often acknowledged or "sourced" than the fourth-grade writing. University students in teacher education, however, only copied nine percent of the information from the three sources. Copying included another group's poster (three percent), the original text (four percent), and their own group's poster (two percent) (see Fig. 2.5). In contrast, 85 percent of the ideas expressed by our university students consisted of paraphrases.

Across all grades there was greater use of information from another group's poster rather than one's own poster or than the original text source. This is de-

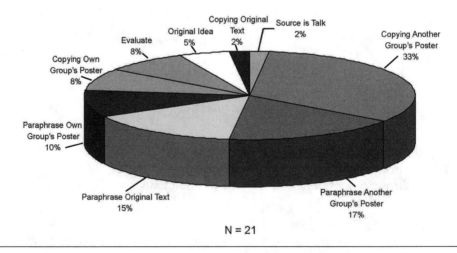

Figure 2.2. Use of Multiple Sources. Fourth Grade, Canada.

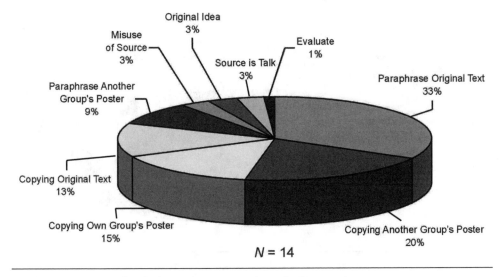

Figure 2.3.   Use of Multiple Sources. Seventh-grade, Texas.

picted in Figs. 2.2 through 2.5. For fourth-graders, 50 percent of the ideas conveyed came from another group; by eighth grade, 47 percent came from another group and by university level, 71 percent of the thoughts were from another group. It appears that the most recent text source was the more influential content to be incorporated in their writing rather than the first source read (the original source). It also appears that when we asked students to write what they learned, they preferred to report on learning from sources other than oneself, particularly the posters that were displayed on blackboards around the room.

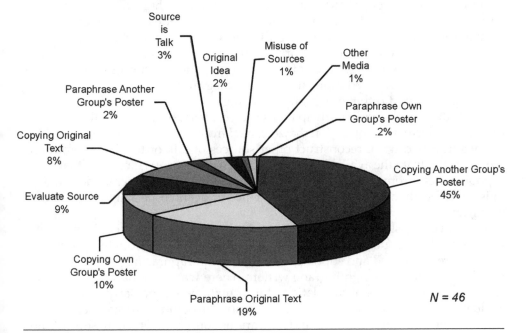

Figure 2.4.   Use of Multiple Sources. Eighth-grade, Texas.

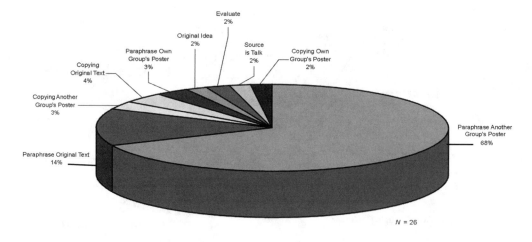

Figure 2.5.   Use of Multiple Sources. University Students, Texas.

The Canadian fourth-graders extracted information about equally from the original text sources and the posters. The writers showed preference for the information presented by students from groups other than their own. The students may have viewed this activity as one in which they were expected to reproduce information they gained from others, as they gave a lower priority to material from their own group's original text and poster. Many students used only one of the sources in a list structure format and did not integrate or attempt to organize ideas from more than one source. The seventh-graders, from an impoverished area in rural Texas, performed very much like the fourth-graders of inner-city Toronto; each group extensively copied, with over 40 idea units taken directly from the original sources. However, unlike the fourth-graders, the seventh-graders' first preference was for paraphrasing the original text read in the group in which they were working. Much of the writing by the seventh-graders was in a list structure, and showed more attempts at integration of ideas from the available sources than did the fourth-grade writings.

When the eighth-grade participants selected ideas to include in their essays, they gave priority to information they received from other groups over their own. Many students did not reconstruct other sources of talk or text but reproduced these directly from the available sources. There were over 200 idea units that came as copied ideas from other groups' posters, an average of 4.35 per student writer. This could be affected by the strong influence of peers (especially "high status" peers) among this age group.

The university students wrote longer essays with over 500 idea units that were paraphrased from another group's poster. The paraphrasing from this group was much more controlled and sophisticated than the paraphrasing produced by the fourth-, seventh-, and eighth-grade writers. There was more paraphrasing than copying or other forms of translation of information—particularly commentary, evaluation, or expression of new ideas. The university students organized and categorized the attributes of camels and the various sources in which these attributes were described. See the writing sample of the 30-year-old university student that appears later in this chapter on page 79.

Direct and Indirect Quotations from Source Texts

Each writer must decide how to *stage* the language and ideas that they are using from sources. The writer may convey the way a text (or talk) is to be "taken" and interpreted through speech act verbs ("said," "think," or "told") and mental state verbs (the reporter's view of what they read or heard "alleges," "believes," or "implies"). The distinction between the concept of *heard* (speech as heard) versus writing (text) as *overheard*, as one who is overhearing another's discourse (Olson, 1999) can be considered in the following sample.

Rena

I got this info off my group and Valire and Sandy
I <u>heard</u> that camels are diff. Camels also hates everyone and everything including ther own kind (I thought that was weird) Camels eat everything when they get hungry But the most thing's about camels is they can stay in the sun way way longer than a human can that's cool Well I thought that cool

---

This student uses the "I" to connect her thoughts to the classroom discourse and begins to decontextualize the events-discourse of the classroom (the presentations, the posters, and the texts) in a "peculiar way," so that the discourse becomes abstract and can be scrutinized and analyzed. The writer in our sample must decide how to *stage* the language and ideas that she has processed. Rena places her primary point in a location in the text to give it prominence. She begins: "I *heard* that camels are different." She underlines the word "heard" to emphasize that she is using an indirect quotation, a paraphrase of an original text attributed to a particular speaker. Rena concludes that camels hate everyone (an inference made and not directly stated in the classroom discourse) and offers her opinion, which is that this is "weird."

Working out the rules for representing speech on paper, conveying direct quotation and separating it from indirect quotation, and punctuating these quotations are conducted differently by culture and context. For instance, as Jacob Neusner, a scholar of Biblical and ancient Hebrew sources, shows in a chapter in the present volume, the Talmud is structured in a very particular way. The Talmud visually presents ancient Biblical text and separates it from the speech and dialogues (the oral, indirect questions, and commentaries) in the margins, below the text, or even between the text. These dialogues represent different schools of thought and talk, communicated by esteemed Rabbis, across several centuries and physical locations. Rashi (abbreviation for Rabbi Shelomoh Yitzchaqi of Troyes, Eastern France), for one, provides commentary that is the basis for study and deep analysis that strives to provide exegesis of the Bible of the eleventh century. As a commentator of Biblical passages, Rashi demonstrates skill at placing himself in the reader's position and imagining what might create difficulty, require special interpretation, or need to be asked that would clarify the text. He amazingly recognizes the needs of reader audiences of different historical time periods, schools of thought, and cultural contexts (Rabin, 1986).

In the case of the development of the child, there is a close relation between the child's treatment of quoted speech, notions of how to comment on text, and understanding of how to cite written texts. If so, it may be argued that it is experience with writing and teacher guidance that gives children the concepts and categories useful for thinking about their own and other's speech (Olson, 1994).

Conventions for engaging with textual materials in these ways requires that the learner adopt a new set of categories for handling information, categories such as "what I think" as opposed to "what a putative author thinks," categories of what the author "actually said" as opposed to what the "author argued or claimed more generally." Although many such categories may be relevant (see Olson & Astington, 1993; Olson, 1997), here we shall focus upon only two classifications: what the author of an authorized text actually said as opposed to conveyed (some will recognize this as the said/meant distinction) and what the author is taken as claiming or believing as opposed to what the reader or citer would like to claim or believe.

In The Camel Study, and across the grades studied, we found excessive verbatim quotation with few mental state verbs, which placed the readers at a distance from their sources. Certain limitations of the research are worth noting. First, the texts provided did not convey their origins. Hence, readers may have had little basis for citing or acknowledging them. Second, the students were given little prior information that would explain the stance of the original sources. Encyclopedic sources purport to be factual truth, and that is how students tend to take these institutional sources. Third, students may have perceived the intention of the task (and the teacher) to "report back" the information without changes, perhaps suspecting that any deviation would be considered incorrect and penalized.

Horowitz (1998b) found that students were more likely to express their own views if they believed the writing task to be "open-ended" and more likely to copy or paraphrase if they thought it to be a factual report (see also Dorhman, 1975). Provided in the following section are examples of the writings (in their original form) as produced by our students at specific age-grade levels included in the present study.*

Fourth-grader, Toronto, Canada

9-year old, female
What I learned about Camels.
I learned that camels don't like people and other Camels. They kick, spit, and bite. Their Kick must hurt. They spit gooey dusgusting cud. they must bit really hard. The thing I don't understand is that they do all this dusgusting stuff for no reason at all I learned this from a sheet of paper my teacher gave to my class with lots of information about camels. And the group I was in. I really enjoyed reading about camels. I hope I have a chance to do a project on camels. So I can ream more about them. Maybe some day I will have a chance.

---

*Note. Spelling and punctuation have been preserved as it appeared in each student's writing.

Eighth-grader, San Antonio, Texas

13-year old, male
Today I learned many things about camels never before did I realize that camels were so complex. In the passage I read, *A Baggage Carrier*, I learned that camels are very strong, hardy animals, for instance, did you know camels could carry up to 270 kg ont heir back? I knew they were strong, but not as strong as they are described to be. If I had 270 kg. on my back I don't thin I could travel 50 miles a day such as camels do. Aside from being immensely strong they are very useful. I is said that camels are used to pull ploughs and turn water wheels that irrigate farms. In a way camels could have once been horses but slowly evolved to a creature more suited for its environment. I also learned some interesting facts form a presentation another group in the class made. Sammi's group made it very clear that camels don't care what they eat or drink. When they get real hunger or thirsty they don't care where the urisment comes rom as long as they get it and it satisfies them. One of the fascinating facts that I learned from Sammi's group presentation was that a camel can drink 10 liters of water in 10 minutes. I guess camels get real thirsty. I never knew camels were so interesting. The presentations and passages were very informative.

University Student in Teacher Education

San Antonio, Texas
30-year old, male
Positive attributes of camels far out number the perceived negative aspects or characteristics. Negative characteristics include the notion that they dislike everybody and everything. They are also know to bite, kick with hind legs and on occasion spit its cud (all of these from group #2). Other negative aspects include the concepts of being both grump and whiney (group #5). Positive characteristics can be grouped into three distinct categories: Physical, environmental (temperature, etc.) and human significance.
Physical features that are very evident is that relatively speaking they have long legs (2,3) and a hump that stores fat (1,2). The act of kneeling or standing is constantly the same in that they kneel down on their front legs first and there hind legs (group 4). They can drink up to 100 liters in more than 10 minutes (1), will drink fresh H^2_O 1st (1) and they will eat anything if food is available (1) …

The ideas in the above eighth-grade sample of writing are extensions beyond what the original text they read *said*—to what they thought it *meant* for the student. Our eighth-grade student offered an explanation for the possible evolution of the camel as an animal that adapted to its desert environment. By college age, there is more attention to citing of references and one finds categorization of source information into an objective format that shows substantial reorganization from the original text. The following is one of the encyclopedia-like passages students read in this research, followed by student writing examples.

Doesn't the Camel Ever get Thirsty?

Because it can last for a long time without anything to eat or drink, the camel's body is perfect for life in the desert. It may have to live for months without water, but it can survive because it gets moisture from its food, and from dew and rain. When offered water a thirsty camel can down well over a hundred liters in ten minutes.

... Or Hungry?

People used to believe that the camel's hump was a built-in storage tank for water, but it actually stores fat, not water. This fat is used for extra energy when food is scarce. Luckily the camel does not care what it drinks or eats. If fresh water isn't available, it will drink sea water. And it will eat almost anything if it gets hungry enough—even baskets, straw matting, or tents!

The fourth-grade children in Group I (Adam, Mahy, Diana, Yi Han, and Jing), who were assigned the boxed passage, used a graphic-like form to present the concepts that they had learned about the camel. Although we never solicited this, Group I produced a list of facts that took on an artistic presentation in the form of a vertical design resembling a histogram.

The children produced a text structure referred to in the research literature as a "list-structure" consisting of seven fact-sentences. These sentences were sequentially numbered 1 to 7 and written in a sophisticated color-coded system which represented the concepts that were extracted from the original source (see Writing Example 3).

To elaborate, each child presented a fact on the list in a distinct color using their own handwritten script; they signed their names at the bottom of the sheet signifying they were a unified group by creating a circle around their names. Their "list-structure" followed the order of the sentences in the original source and the ideas and was in close proximity—precise and accurate. After each fact- sentence, they also used the first initial of their name perhaps as a means of proofreading and confirming their contribution to the whole. The presentation is symmetrical and creative.

This listing of facts constituted an initial step in the conceptualizing process. This may have been a first encounter with ideas about camels. As was the case with Group I, the posters from other groups also contained few insertions and references to the child's own portrayal of camels or their own point of view. When students copy heavily, verbatim, they are using a device very similar to what in speech would be called *direct quotation*. It was not just copying, however, as the children summarized by paraphrasing the text rather than copying.

We were impressed with the precision by which Group I students reported from the original written sources. The following box provides the three last points the students conveyed on their poster sheet (noted in Writing Example 3) and the original sentence that the students' paraphrase came from.

The Camel!!!!!

1. A camel can go with out water for month. A

2. It gets moisture from food and dew and rain. M

3. The camel can drink up to a hundred litres in ten min D

4. the Camels hump stores fat instead of water. A

5. The camel gets energy from the M fat in its hump!

6. the camel can drink any kind of water. Y

7. The camel can eat anything. J

by Adam
Maly &
Diana
yi Han   Mm. 37.
Jing

Writing Example 3: Poster produced by fourth-grade, group 1

The Camel!!!!!!

Source Text: People used to believe that the camel's hump was a built-in storage tank for water, but it actually stores fat, not water.
Sentence 4: The camel's hump stores fat instead of water. A

Source Text: This fat is used for extra energy when food is scarce.
Sentence 5: The camel gets energy from the fat in its hump. M

Source Text: Luckily the camel does not care what it drinks or eats.
Sentence 6: The camel can drink any kalimb of water. Y
Sentence 7: The camel can eat anything. J

**Forming and Transforming Concepts about the Camel—
Individual Writings**

Following the production of the poster and its presentation to the entire class, and after the students had listened to all of the presentations and seen all of the posters, they individually wrote what they had learned. The caveat they were given was that they say what they learned in their own words and be sure to give credit to their sources.

Adam in Group I produced the essay in Writing Example 4. Perhaps taken by the instructions to credit sources, his focus became crediting the sources so that he wrote very little about the content. It may be that attention limitations made it difficult to maneuver both tasks at once. He indicates that he learned the information about the camel *literally* "from the paper my teacher gave me" and "from the other groups" and "my own group." He concludes with a personal point of view, which separates the old (what he knew in the past) from the new (what he now knows), namely that camels can drink a hundred liters of water in ten minutes. Most striking is that he copyrights his text to ensure it is not stolen and serves as a model for the other children, who then follow his lead and also copyright their texts.

Writing Example 4

Group II solved the problem of how to say what they learned about camels by producing a poster that used rhetorical questions presented in expository block form as headings (see Writing Example 1). Unlike the first group, which produced single sentences in a vertical form with no cross-links, the second group conveyed the concepts that they learned in a text-like form, using language in a horizontal format, to be read left to right rather than from top to bottom, as with lists.

The texts available to the members of Group II are provided in the following box:

Keeping Cool

A camel can last ten times longer than a human being in the heat of the desert. Its long legs keep its body far from the hottest part of the desert, which is right at ground level. Its fat-filled hump also helps it to keep cool.

Beware of Bad-Tempered Camels!

Camels seem to dislike everything and everybody—including other camels! They may bite a person or another animal for no reason, and will kick out suddenly and viciously with their hind legs. An angry camel may even spit a mouthful of slimy cud at someone passing by.

Group II produced a text that resembled the informational references they may have already encountered in their earlier education. First, the essay has a title, "The Camel," and then there is a thesis or heading-like statement (note the use of capitalization) that introduces a comparison to humans, namely: "A Camel can Survive longer than a Human In the Heat of the Desert." They transformed the two original text headings into problem-questions and they were set apart from the resolution: (1) "How does the camel keep cool?" and (2) "How are camels bad tempered?" Finally, they conclude their poster with a drawing using horizontal lines, once again, which asks a true-false test question—such as typically found in questions at the end of the chapter in textbooks. The group text is an accurate paraphrase of the original text source in which the original ideas are reported back sentence by sentence.

Identifying Sources Of Information

Students tended to adopt one of three strategies.

Grade 4

Listing of Individual Names of Sources.   The instructions included: *"Be sure you tell where you obtained your ideas."* The children interpreted this literally. They listed the names of the voices they heard, those from whom they acquired their content knowledge, and what others had said individually and in a group during the oral presentations. Kelly, a Portuguese child, included a number of his classmates as his sources of information in his writing. He wrote: "I learned this from

Adam, Mary, Diana, Yi-han, and Jing." Another child, Tobi, from China, selectively placed the names of each child who provided information, the way references are integrated into expert academic prose. He attributed credit to each complete thought he wrote by referencing the peer who had expressed the idea.

Fourth-grader, Toronto, Canada
Tobi

I learn the one hump camel is called dromedary (just like in french), they can run for a long time or distance (Lisa, etc.), Camels are named twoship of the desert (Tia, etc.) the camel can drink hundred liters in ten minutes (Adam, etc.).

Somehow this child understands punctuation for quoting sources, that sources are placed in open parentheses in academic writing, that commas are inserted after a strand of information, followed by etc. and close parentheses, followed by another strand of information, with a string of these forming one paragraph.

   Crediting the Leader of a Given Group, Self or Headings of Text.   Another female child, Winnie, from China, wrote one paragraph about each group poster. At the end of each paragraph a female leader of the group was referenced. She concludes one paragraph with "I learned from Alice's group." For example, "I learned that the one humped camel is called a dromedary meaning the running camel. I also learned that the camel is worth a lot of money for its speed. I learned from Alice's group." Her next paragraph concludes with the following reference: "I learned this from Melissa's group." The last paragraph ends with, "I learned this from Mary's group."

   Still another child, Xiu, chose not to give credit to his peers, but gave himself credit for reading the passages assigned and said, "I learned that from reading myself." Children in The Camel Study also credited themselves for reading the sources and with the ultimate authorship for the synthesis of the ideas they produced in writing. Others pointed to prior resources on the camel, outside of the immediate context by referring to television or a sibling (e.g., a brother) as a source of knowledge.

Grade 8

   In the Texas writing samples, there is more detailed punctuation utilized as part of referencing. One subject used quotations to reference the exact text headings that appeared before the section of content that they read in their group. These headings or macrostructures, were directly quoted throughout their writing sample. An example of this citing system, drawing from a section of the student essay, follows:

   … They will drink water out of food, dew or rain. If they get really thirsty they can drink up to one hundred liters of water. (*Does a camel ever get thirsty?*) Camels can travel and carry at least 270 km. They can travel 50 km. a day with that much weight. They move from side to side which causes people to get seasick. (*A baggage carrier.*)

Another eighth-grader in Texas showed differential levels of cognition. Pauline skillfully separated what she *thought* to be *truth*, from what the essay *said*, from what she *surmises* people *believe* and *think*.

> I learned new things about camels that I never thought would be true about camels. For example, I didn't know that camels eat or drink any type of food or water when they are hungry or thirsty. I got that information another group; they were <u>Jammie</u>, <u>Maribel</u>, <u>Sammi</u>, and <u>Andrew</u>. And from their *poster* I also learned that the humps don't carry water like some people think that is stored fat. I think that was very interesting information that was presented.

She underlined the words to emphasize the sources she consulted. She concludes with a sentence telling her attitude to the information, thereby, separating or distancing herself from the sources and introducing her voice.

CONCLUSION

In learning to interact with texts, children seem to progress through at least three stages. At first they appear to simply adopt new information from a source into their own belief system focusing on ideas rather than the language in which those ideas are expressed. This, we believe, is typical of much of oral discourse. When confronted with written texts in the early grades, their attention is redirected from the ideas to the language in which the ideas are expressed. Consequently, the first obvious impact of text on their writing, talking, and thinking comes through simply copying those texts, whether as phrases or whole sentences. It is as if the ideas cannot be expressed in the child's own words or a paraphrase and further that the child lacks his/her own perspective on those ideas. What is important here is that there is no separation between the text and child. However, copying does have its benefits. It is a first step in contact with the text as an object from which the child will eventually distance themselves. The beginning of this distancing of self from the text first occurs with the use of quotation, then paraphrases, and later commentaries on the text (see Tang & Saganthi, 1999).

In quotation, one copies the language of the expression, but acknowledges that the source is not her or his own. This is further extended with indirect quotation in which the idea is preserved but again attributed to a source other than the self. In commentaries on the text, the distance between the source and the child is the greatest in that the child characterizes what the text says or means but also explicitly expresses their own stance, view, and "voice." Speech act verbs such as "identified" or "reported" are the vehicles for creating a distancing between the source and the self. Learning to work with text in this way is an important root to discovering one's own subjectivity.

APPENDIX I: ORIGINAL SOURCE TEXTS

Passages used in *The Camel Study*

Source Text #1

A Baggage Carrier.   Camels are used to haul heavy loads across the desert. They can carry up to 270 kg on their backs and cover as much as 50 km in one day.

They also pull ploughs, turn water wheels to irrigate fields, and carry loads of grain to market.

When walking, camels move the front and back legs of one side forward at the same time. This causes a swaying motion that makes some people feel seasick. Because of this—and because they carry baggage and people across the long stretches of sand—camels are sometimes called "ships of the desert."

Some Things Never Change.   Camels have worked for people for hundreds of years, but they still whine when a load is put on their backs and grunt loudly when they have to get to their feet. Once they are moving, however, they carry their loads without complaining.

Source Text #2

Doesn't the Camel Ever Get Thirsty?   Because it can last for a long time without anything to eat or drink, the camel's body is perfect for life in the desert. It may have to live for months without water, but it can still survive because it gets moisture from its food, and from dew and rain. When offered water a thirsty camel can down over a hundred liters in ten minutes.

... Or Hungry?   People used to believe that the camel's hump was a built-in storage tank for water, but it actually stores fat, not water. This fat is used for extra energy when food is scarce. Luckily the camel does not care what it drinks or eats. If fresh water isn't available, it will drink sea water. And it will eat almost anything if it gets hungry enough—even baskets, straw matting, or tents!

Source Text #3

Two-Humped Bactrian Camel.   The two-humped camel is a native of the ancient land of Bactria—now the high plains and mountains of Afghanistan and the southern Soviet Union. It is smaller, with shorter legs than the Arabian camel. Because the Bactrian camel lived in a cooler climate, its hair is thicker and more valued for making cloth.

One-Humped Arabian Camel.   Arabian camels are all domesticated. Their original range was in the Near East and Africa, but human beings later brought them to India and Australia. Most of the time these camels endure temperatures of 55°C.

The one-humped camel, called the dromedary (which means "running camel"), is used for riding. It can gallop for up to eighteen hours at a time, covering a distance of about 150 km a day. Because of its speed the dromedary is worth a lot of money, and often sells for thousands of dollars.

Source Text #4

Keeping Cool.   A camel can last ten times longer than a human being in the heat of the desert. Its long legs keep its body far from the hottest part of the desert, which is right at ground level. Its fat-filled hump also helps to keep it cool.

Beware of Bad-Tempered Camels!   Camels seem to dislike everything and everybody—including other camels! They may bite a person or another animal for no reason, and will kick out suddenly and viciously with their hind legs. An angry camel may even spit a mouthful of slimy cud at someone passing by.

Source Text #5

The Fold-up Camel.   Camels have an interesting way of kneeling down and standing up. When they are about to kneel, they bend their front legs and drop to their padded knees. Then they fold up their hind legs and fall to the ground. To get up again, they straighten their hind legs first and then jerk up onto their front legs.

ACKNOWLEDGMENTS

We are grateful to Cynthia Kennedy for her work on the extensive literature search, data collection in Texas middle school classrooms, and analysis of the written protocols. We appreciate her devoted work in completing the data analysis and the construction of diagrams presented in this chapter. Frances Frazier contributed in insightful ways to early drafts of the chapter. Mary Shaw assisted with the organization and retrieval of information. Jackie Magness contributed to the completion of diagrams. Gayla Schill was responsible for the final editing and for seeing this manuscript through to completion. Proofing and editing of this manuscript was done by Terry Jones with Tanya Figueroa, Anna Hernandez, and Nicole McLeod. The camel passages were produced by Judy Ross.

This chapter is based on work that began with a National Academy of Education Spencer Fellowship and was supported by a small grant from the University of Texas–San Antonio, to Rosalind Horowitz.

NOTES

1. The university students included upper-division undergraduate and post-baccalaureate students who were seeking certification in Elementary Education at The University of Texas—San Antonio.
2. This section on The Camel Study illustrates the importance of the topic and content in the evolution of instructional discourse. Not all topics and content are of equal value. Some topics have greater valence in reading and writing acts and result in finer tuning and detailed discussions than other topics. In selecting topics for research and instruction, we recommend paying heed to the choice of topics and the degree of attractiveness and mental stimulation that they hold for certain student groups.
3. The Jigsaw method has been used to enhance student collaboration and talk in classrooms. Students are typically assigned to small groups to read assigned segmented text materials. They become experts on what they have read and discuss what they have learned from the text with the entire class often through the presentation of a summary poster. See L. S. Walters. (May/June 2000). Four leading models. *Harvard Educational Letter, 16*(3), 5.

REFERENCES

Aronson, E. (1978). *The jigsaw classroom.* Beverly Hills, CA: Sage.

Arrington, P. (1988, May). A dramatistic approach to understanding and teaching the paraphrase. *College Composition and Communication, 39*(2), 185–197.

Bakhtin, M. M. (1986). The problem of speech genres. In C. Emerson & M. Holquist (Eds.) and V. W. McGee (Trans.), *Speech genres and other late essays* (pp. 60–102). Austin: University of Texas Press.

Bamberger, J. (in press). Changing musical perception through reflective conversation. In R. Horowitz (Ed.), *Talking Texts: How speech and writing interact in school learning.* Mahwah, NJ: Lawrence Erlbaum Associates.

Barthes, R. (1982). *Barthes reader.* (Edited, and with an introduction by Susan Sontag). New York: Hill & Wang.

Bloomfield, L. (1933). *Language.* New York: Allen & Unwin.

Britton, J., Burgess, T., Martin, N., McLeod, A., & Rosen, H. (1975). *The development of writing abilities* (pp. 11–18). London: Macmillan.

Bruner, J. (1999). The intentionality of referring. In P. D. Zelazo, J. W. Astington, & D. R. Olson (Eds.), *Developing theories of intention; Social understanding and self-control* (pp. 329–339). Mahwah, NJ: Lawrence Erlbaum Associates.

Chafe, W., & Danielewicz, J. (1987). Properties of spoken and written language. In R. Horowitz & S. J. Samuels, (Eds.), *Comprehending oral and written language* (pp. 83–113). San Diego: Academic Press.

Chall, J. S., Jacobs, V. A., & Baldwin, L. E. (1990). *The reading crisis: Why poor children fall behind.* Cambridge, MA: Harvard University Press.

Dillon, G. L. (1988). My words of another. *College English, 50*(1), 63–73.

Dorhman, M. H. (1975, May). Stopping "Copy-catting." *Elementary English, 52,* 651–652.

Fahnestock, J. (1986). Accommodating science: The rhetorical life of scientific facts. *Written Communication, 3,* 275–296.

Frazier, F. (1997). Personal communication at The University of Texas–San Antonio.

Geisler, C. (1994). *Academic literacy and the nature of expertise. Reading, writing, and knowing in academic philosophy.* Hillsdale, NJ: Lawrence Erlbaum Associates.

George, J. C. (1972). *Julie of the wolves.* New York: Harper Collins.

Gerhardt, D. R. (2006, May 26). The rules of attribution. *The Chronicle of Higher Education,* p. B20.

Goodwin, M. H. (1990). *He-Said-She-Said. Talk as social organization among Black children.* Bloomington: Indiana University Press.

Goody, J. (1987). *The interface between the written and the oral.* Cambridge, England: Cambridge University Press.

Halliday, M. A. K. (1987). Spoken and written modes of meaning. In R. Horowitz & S. J. Samuels (Eds.), *Comprehending oral and written language* (pp. 55–81). San Diego: Academic Press.

Harris, R. (1986). *The origin of writing.* London: Duckworth.

Havelock, E. A. (1976). *Origins of western literacy* (Monograph Series No. 14). Toronto: Ontario Institute for Studies in Education.

Hickmann, M. (1993). The boundaries of reported speech in narrative discourse: Some developmental aspects. In J. A. Lucy (Ed.), *Reflexive language: Reported speech and metapragmatics* (pp. 63–90). Cambridge, England: Cambridge University Press.

Hockett, C. F. (1958). *A course in modern linguistics.* New York: MacMillan.

Hockett, C. F. (1960). The origin of speech. *Scientific American, 203,* 89–96.

Horowitz, R. (1995). *How do developing writers reference speech or written language when they refer to these in school discussions or writing assignments?* Doctoral seminar presentation, Applied Cognitive Sciences, Ontario Institute for studies in Education (OISE), Toronto, Ontario, Canada.

Horowitz, R. (1996, July). *Combining multiple sources. When do students express genuine understanding and beliefs about oral and written discourse?* Invited address. Special Committee on Research in the Processing of Texts (SCRIPT). Eleventh Annual Meeting, Maaleh Hachamisha, Jerusalem, Israel. Organized by the Department of Education, Ben-Gurion University, Beersheva, Israel.

Horowitz, R. (1998a). The evolution of classroom talk: Contributions to text conceptualization and learning. In N. Ephraty & R. Lidor (Eds.), *Teacher education: Stability, evolution, and revolution* (pp. 921–932). Natanya, Israel: The Zinman College, Wingate Institute, Israel, in conjunction with the Ministry of Education and Mofet Institute.

Horowitz, R. (1998b, July). *Task and context impressions: Factors that contribute to expressing one's own ideas in multiple-source writing.* Paper presented at the International Conference on Speech, Writing, and Context: Literary and Linguistic Perspectives. University of Nottingham, England.

Horowitz, R. (2000, September). *The attribution of credit to multiple sources.* The Organizing Committee of the 12th World Congress of the International Association of Applied Linguistics (AILA). Based on a lecture delivered at Waseda University, Tokyo, Japan, August 2, 1999, CD-ROM.

Horowitz, R., & Cole, B. (in progress). Taking a stance in writing: Fifth-graders argue for or against a school dress code.

Horowitz, R., & Cummings, C. (2000, July 20). *Repetition in discourse: A linguistic strategy signifying involvement in children's conversational dialogues with a literary work.* Paper presented at the Society for Text and Discourse Conference, Lyon, France.

Jackson, L. A., Tway, E., & Frager, A. (1987, October). "Dear teacher, Johnny copied!" *The Reading Teacher, 1*(1) 151–159.

Jakobson, R. (1978). *Six lectures on sound and meaning.* Cambridge, MA: MIT Press.

Johns, A. (1998). *The nature of the book: Print and knowledge in the making.* Chicago, IL: University of Chicago Press.

Kamawar D., & Olson, D. R. (2000, October). Children's representational theory of language: The problem of opaque contexts. *Cognitive Development, 14*(4), 531–548.

Latour, B., & Woolgar, S. (1979). *Laboratory life: The social construction of scientific facts.* Beverly Hills, CA: Sage.

Lee, E. A., Torrance, N., & Olson, D. R. (1994, April). *The emerging concept of text: Can young children distinguish the exact words from a paraphrase.* Paper presented at the American Educational Research Association Conference, New Orleans, LA.

Lee, E. A., Torrance, N., & Olson, D. R. (2001, June). Young children and the say/mean distinction: Verbatim and paraphrase recognition in narrative and nursery rhyme contexts. *Journal of Child Language, 28*(2), 531–543.

Leland, J., & La Feria, R. (2003, September 14). Beyond file-sharing: A nation of copiers. *The New York Times*, p. ST1.

Luria, A. R. (1976). *Cognitive development: Its cultural and social foundations.* Cambridge, MA: Harvard University Press.

McTear, M. F. (1988). *Understanding cognitive science. Ellis Horwood Series in Cognitive Science* (pp. 191–209). Chichester, West Sussex, England: Ellis Horwood Ltd.

Meyer, C. (n.d.). Personal communication. University of Toronto.

Olson, D. R. (1994). *The world on paper.* Cambridge, MA: Cambridge University Press.

Olson, D. R. (1997). From utterance to text: The bias of language in speech and writing. *Harvard Educational Review, 47*, 257–281.

Olson, D. R. (1999, March 11). *The written word.* Inaugural lecture as University Professor, University of Toronto.

Olson, D. R., & Astington, J. W. (1993). Thinking about thinking: Learning how to take statements and hold beliefs. *Educational Psychologist, 28*, 7–23.

Olson, D. R., & Kamawar, D. (1999). The theory of ascriptions. In P. D. Zelazo, J. W. Astington, & D. R. Olson (Eds.), *Developing theories of intention. Social understanding and self-control* (pp. 153–166). Mahwah, NJ: Lawrence Erlbaum Associates.

Paxton, R. J. (1999, Fall). A deafening silence: History textbooks and the students who read them. *Review of Educational Research, 69*(3), 315–339.

Peskin, J. (1998). Constructing meaning when reading poetry: An expert-novice study. *Cognition and Instruction, 16*(3), 235–263.

Rabin, C. (1986). The discourse status of commentary. In C. R. Cooper & S. Greenbaum (Eds.), *Studying writing: Linguistic approaches* (pp. 215–225). Beverley Hills, CA: Sage.

Ricoeur, P. (1967, October). *Phenomenology and language.* Transcribed lecture given at the 14th Wheaton Philosophy Annual Conference, Wheaton College, Norton, MA.

Robinson, E., Goelman, H., & Olson, D. R. (1983). Children's relationship between expressions (what was said) and intentions (what was meant). *British Journal of Developmental Psychology, 1,* 75–86.

Ross, J. (n.d.). *Getting to know the camel.*

Scinto, L. F. M. (1986). *Written language and psychological development.* Orlando, FL: Academic Press.

Searle, J. R. (1983). *Intentionality.* Cambridge, MA: Cambridge University Press.

Smith, P. D. (1990). *An introduction to text processing.* Cambridge, MA: MIT.

Spivey, N. N. (1983, August). *Discourse synthesis: Constructing texts in reading and writing.* Doctoral Dissertation, the University of Texas—Austin.

Stötesbury, H. (1999). *Reporting, evaluation and discussion as exponents of interpretation in critical summarization.* Doctoral dissertation submitted to the Faculty of Arts of the University of Joensuu at the Savonlinna School of Translation Studies, Kuninkaankartanonkatu, Finland, and available as Joensuun Yliopiston Humanistisia Julkaisuja, University of Joensuu Publications in the Humanities, No. 23.

Stötesbury, H. (2002). A study of interpretation in critical writing. In G. Cortese & P. Riley (Eds.), *Domain-specific English. Textual practices across communities and classrooms: Vol. 2. Linguistic Insights* (pp. 325–343). Berlin & New York: Peter Lang.

Tang, R., & Saganthi, J. (1999). The 'I' in identity: Exploring writer identity in student academic writing through the first person pronoun [Special Issue]. *English for Specific Purposes, 18,* S23–S39.

Vygotsky, L. (1986). *Thought and language* (A. Kozulin, Trans. & Ed.). Cambridge, MA: MIT.

Waugh, L. (1995). Reported speech in journalistic discourse: The relation of function and text. *Text, 15*(1), 129–73.

Wertsch, J. V. (1991). *Voices of the mind: A sociocultural approach to mediated action.* Cambridge, MA: Harvard University Press.

Yoder, D. E. (2001, March). Having my say. *Augmentative & Alternative Communication, 17*(1), 2–10.

II

Child, Adolescent,
and Family Discourse:
Everyday Conversation as Text
Outside of Classroom Contexts

CHAPTER 3

Talk as Text: Gender and Children's Conversational Interaction

Amy Sheldon

This chapter discusses research on preschoolers' conversations. Conversations are a fundamental, yet mysterious, part of life. Preschool children are members of communities which are rich in conversations—communities such as families, neighborhoods, nursery schools, and daycare centers. Conversations are the medium in which, and through which, children have gotten to know others, have jointly explored objects, materials and events in their world, and have created and participated in various social activities. Preschoolers, like everyone else, construct oral (or signed)[1] texts that embody their everyday social interactions.

Children are sophisticated language users. By the time they reach elementary school, they already have extensive skills in oral text construction and processing. Unfortunately, a common view of young children, which is promoted in our culture and held by many teachers and parents, underestimates children's abilities with oral texts (orality). Then, because schools focus on teaching young children written language, that is, literacy skills, their conversational skills can be overlooked. This chapter puts the spotlight on the complex language expertise that children have acquired with oral texts before they even enter kindergarten—before they even begin to decode written texts. The acquisition of literacy is connected to children's skills with complex oral texts. They are built on them and in tandem with them.

When we bring the focus back to orality, we remind ourselves that children have been with playmates, friends, family members, and caregivers for years before entering kindergarten. These relationships are language relationships as much as any other kind. Children and their conversational partners have histories of creating and interpreting prior oral, or signed, texts. Some conversational histories are years in length, because they embody long-standing connections, such as family relationships.

CONVERSATIONS ARE TEXTS THAT CHILDREN ARE VERY GOOD AT PRODUCING AND UNDERSTANDING

A history of shared talk is a history of co-constructed *texts*. Conversations are texts—rule-governed and systematically organized. Children's prior conversational texts provide a transition and set the stage for their entry into the mysteries and intricacies of written texts. In addition, reading and writing are acquired in a social environment that is rich in conversations between teachers or parents and learners. Conversation, then, is the medium in which literacy is developed in school, as well as a complex skill that is the foundation for learning to read.

Conversational texts have some properties that differ from those of written texts. Conversational texts are dynamic; they continuously emerge but then immediately vanish. The study of preschool children's conversations reveals that they enter into the acquisition of literacy already knowing how to produce and interpret emergent oral texts that are far more complex than the written ones they will start to read or write.

This chapter provides some examples of ordinary conversations between preschoolers. It is hoped that by looking closely at these sorts of taken-for granted, mundane conversations, literacy educators might appreciate the complex textual skills that children bring to the task of learning how to read and write. This might also inspire educators to make strategic use of children's oral text skills as they teach reading and writing. The conversations discussed here emerged during these children's spontaneous play together. They were not guided or interfered with by an adult. In fact, adults were not visibly present when this talk was recorded.

These conversations come from a research project that is studying differences in how preschool girls and boys have conversations. These are oral texts that have been shaped by gender prescriptions and practices in their communities, in their families, and in their daycare centers. Even as young as 3 years of age, children's conversations show evidence of their acquisition of cultural information about gender. They are already talking as girls and boys are expected to in their community. Cultural prescriptions for gender are marked in their conversational interaction.

GENDER-MARKED LANGUAGE

One way that our attention has been brought to the connection between language, communication, and gender is in regard to sexist terminology in children's books and stories as well as in our own talk and writing. Sexist language practices can make females invisible. Examples are words such as *policeman* or *fireman*, or the use of *he* as a so-called generic pronoun when referring to females. New expressions have replaced many of these words, such as *police officer, fire fighter, she or he*, and sometimes the feminine pronoun *she* is used instead of the masculine (in some baby magazine articles written primarily for mothers or in some advertisements of products aimed at children).[2] Graham (1975) gives an eye-opening account of how the editors of *The American Heritage School Dictionary* discovered rampant sexism in children's books and how they set out to make a nonsexist dictionary as a result. Maggio (1991) also describes options for bias-free language use.

Educational inequities can also be inadvertently created in ways that teachers manage the discourse of classroom interaction. Boys often have greater access to teachers' attention, resources, encouragement, and feedback. Some research finds that boys get called on more, and teachers are often more responsive to boys than they are to girls. Such differences in the quality and quantity of classroom discourse and inadvertent messages about the value of girls' verbal contributions to large groups can have long-term consequences for girls' classroom performance, and can ultimately affect their career choices and educational satisfaction (e.g., American Association of University Women, 1991;[3] LeMaster & Hernandez-Katapodis, 2002; Sadker & Sadker, 1994; Swann, 1998).

It is often not obvious how language might be used in conversation in a gendered fashion, because we ordinarily take language for granted. We tend to look *through* language to something else in the communication event, such as the effects on the listener of what has been said. But sometimes we do notice ways in which language differentiates people along gender lines and how that relates to power. Children notice this too.

LEARNING ABOUT AND CONSTITUTING GENDER THROUGH LANGUAGE

When my daughter Nicole was 6 years old, she told me, "Mom, kings are royaler than queens." When I asked her why she thought that way, she replied, "Because on Mr. Rogers, when the trolley stops at the King and the Queen [in the Kingdom of Make-Believe], the King answers the questions the most." (see Sheldon, 1990a, for a discussion of this and other issues of language and sexism).[4] Nicole's insight into language was voiced at the time when she was still a novice reader but was hearing, remembering, and analyzing far more complex and lengthy oral texts than she could read by herself.

As it happened, a graduate student related Nicole's remark that kings were "royaler" than queens to her daughter who was also a young reader.[5] The daughter replied,

> I knew that. On Lamb Chops they said "the king got on his large horse, the queen got on her medium horse, and the princess got on her small horse." Also, the king is taller. So I already knew that, but I just pretend the queen is royaler, but if it would make you happy you can be king when daddy is out of town.

This anecdotal evidence gives us some insight into how conversation connects us to a larger social order and how everyday talk shapes what children are learning about gender and power. Not only can 6-year-olds notice how talk is constructed, they also have the ability to *talk about talk*. They are developing metalinguistic awareness and sociocognitive understanding of the conversations they hear around them at the same time they are learning to read and write. Children bring these skills in interpreting oral texts to the reading process, not only decoding linguistic meaning, but also extracting sociocultural subtexts that are conveyed through language. Perhaps the focus on teaching reading through phonetic decoding keeps us from seeing these *textual* aspects of talk and the prior textual skills that children have already developed via conversations before they dive into learning how to read. The parallels between oral and written texts and children's textual processing competence can elude us in the early stages of literacy acquisition, when attention is focused on teaching word attack skills and sound-symbol relationships, particularly when done out of context.

However, when we look at properties of a text beyond the sound-symbol level, we can explore the commonalities and differences between written texts and texts produced in conversations. This chapter gives a glimpse into children's sophistication in constructing and interpreting the oral texts that embody their daily world. These conversations reveal how culturally and linguistically/textually competent they have already become before entering kindergarten, how knowledgeable about gender prescriptions they are, and how their talk is gendered.

This work is part of a larger stream of research, relevant to literacy studies, examining children's oral texts, for example, research comparing the structure of children's narratives to adults' narratives (e.g., Bamberg, 1995; Stein, 1988) and research analyzing gender differences in the thematic and formal aspects of children's monologic and co-constructed stories (e.g., Davies, 1989; Kyratzis, 1992; Kyratzis & Ervin-Tripp, 1999; Kyratzis & Guo, 1996; Libby & Aries, 1989; Nicolopoulou, Scales, & Weintraub, 1994; Sheldon & Engstrom, 2005; Sheldon & Rohleder, 1996; Tarullo, 1994). Also related is research that reviews, and raises questions about, the significance of gender differences in language ability (e.g., Hyde & Linn, 1988). This work is set in the broader context of research into the interconnection between language and gender, discussed in an introduction by Eckert and McConnell-Ginet (2003). Pinker (1994) provides a general discussion of the nature of the human language capacity.

GENDER DIFFERENCES IN PRESCHOOLERS' CONVERSATIONS: VERBAL MANAGEMENT OF CONFLICT

Gender differences are often, and simplistically, framed in terms of polarities. Male groups and male conversations are often described in terms of *competition* and *hierarchy* (e.g., Goodwin, 1980; Maltz & Borker, 1982). Female groups and female conversations are often characterized as *cooperative* and *egalitarian* (Kalčik, 1975; Maltz & Borker, 1982). Although many aspects of children's conflicts have been studied (Shantz, 1987), descriptions of the verbal tactics children use in conflict talk are fairly new. A complicating factor is that much research has a male-centered bias. Boys' social behavior has been well studied, with the result that, as Maccoby (1986) points out, "we have a clearer picture of what girls' groups do *not* do than what they *do* do" (p. 271). Male bias can also be seen in our cultural assumption that the norm for conflict involves aggressive behaviors. However, when measured against that norm, girls' behaviors have been interpreted as less forceful (Miller, Danaher, & Forbes, 1986, p. 543) or less assertive (Sachs, 1987, pp. 185–188).

The implication is that girls are not as effective as boys at managing conflict. This is further reinforced by characterizations of girls' same-sex interaction as emphasizing an ethic of *harmony* and *collaboration* (Leaper, 1991, p. 796; Miller et al., 1986, p. 547). On the other hand, studies of girls in the early, middle, and teenage years leave no doubt about the importance of competition in girls' social interaction. Some of these studies emphasize that girls' competitive behaviors often co-occur with cooperation and mitigation (Eckert, 1990; Goodwin, 1980, 1995; Hughes, 1988; Sheldon, 1992).

The picture that emerges from this research is that competition, conflict, and the exercise of power are complex social behaviors and psychocultural issues that have not yet been well described and understood for females. Furthermore, if girls' conflict talk is described in the context of stereotypical masculine-related conflict behaviors, we run the risk of interpreting it as something "less" than the masculine mode, that is, less than dramatic instances of brute force.

This chapter questions stereotypical views that females are not effective at managing conflict, or that they lack a competitive dynamic, when compared to males. I analyze a vivid example of 4-year-old girls' negotiation of power and disagreement, which contradicts the stereotype. I show the extremely skillful verbal negotiation that preschool girls (and boys) are capable of, while at the same time they also maintain a degree of social equilibrium. This chapter extends the work of Goodwin and Goodwin (1987) and Sheldon (1992, 1993, 1996a, 1996b; Sheldon & Engstrom, 2005; Sheldon & Johnson, 1994). This research shows that feminine-related conflict talk can be linguistically more complicated than masculine-related conflict talk. Sheldon (1992a) describes this style of conflict talk as "double-voice discourse" (p. 99). As I show, girls and boys are not locked into "feminine-" or "masculine-related" conflict styles.

DOUBLE-VOICE DISCOURSE

Double-voice discourse embodies conflict mediation skills in which the speaker confronts without being confrontational, clarifies issues without backing down, and uses linguistic mitigators to soften the blow, while they act on their wishes and make their agenda matter. In double-voice discourse, the speaker is responsive to the companion's point of view even while pursuing his or her own agenda. Self-assertion is mitigated and contextualized, but nevertheless effective.

For example,[6] Lucy (4;9) and Karla (5;0) are playing. Lucy says, "Hey, I think I'll call a party. Now, 'tend you heard your telephone ring. Ding dong ding dong." Karla is busy driving her car and she doesn't want to cooperate. She says, "Pretend I wasn't there." Each girl invokes the pretend frame to control the other's behavior. Lucy's request is softer than a direct request to "pick up your phone." Lucy might also be anticipating Karla's resistance, because Karla is already doing something unrelated. Asking a companion to "pretend" may bring compliance and participation, but it also gives the person addressed a chance to cast her opposition in pretend terms as well. Karla resists Lucy's play suggestion. She cooperates in jointly imagining a pretend world in which the telephone is ringing, but she does not want to stop driving her car, either. She opposes Lucy's indirect request to answer the phone with a "yes-but" strategy, in which tacit agreement prefaces disagreement (see Pomerantz, 1984). Karla's opposition is just one example of how children do double-voice discourse. Karla mitigates her objection to Lucy's request and proposes an alternative that will allow her to continue her own play. She is responsive to Lucy's point of view and her wishes, while she pursues her own agenda.[7]

My theory of double-voice discourse reorients the debate about gender differences in talk from one described simplistically in terms of gendered polarities to one that reframes the issues and behaviors in a more complex way. Double-voice discourse reflects the active engagement of the speaker, often female, but not necessarily so, in verbal power plays and competition for social access and privilege.

GENDER AND CONFLICT

Conflict is a contest of wills. Gender ideology in many cultures gives males the license to argue, often ritualistically, in direct, demanding, and confrontational ways, with unmitigated rivalry. This is acceptable, even normal. When girls and women behave in this same way, it is considered threatening. Consequently, we risk being called, "bossy," "confrontational," "bitchy," "difficult," or worse for the same behaviors that boys and men are called "manly" or "assertive," when they do them. The gender ideology of middle-class, White America requires girls and women to "be nice." Sachs (1987) finds that preschool girls have already learned to "say it with a smile," pursuing their agenda and interests within the constraint that they not cause too much stress or jeopardize interpersonal harmony in their intimate groups.

METHOD

Subjects

The conversations to be analyzed here are from a study of 36 children, ages 3 to 5, in two preschool groups (from different rooms) at a daycare center in a large midwestern U.S. city. The children's parents are students, staff, or faculty at a large urban university. They are educationally and socially advantaged, middle-class children. The sample is predominantly White. The daycare providers are well trained. There is little staff turnover, and the adult-child ratio is good.

The children attended the daycare center for full days, year-round, and had played with each other daily for 1 to 3 years. I grouped the children into 12 same-sex triads after consultation with their teachers. Triads were made up of friends who were close in age. Six triads were female, and six were male. Before the study began, I had spent many hours at the center observing these children over a period of years.

Procedure

The participants were videotaped during their regular daycare hours in a playroom, separate from the room in which the rest of their group was playing. They were not supervised by an adult. A graduate assistant and the author sat somewhat out of sight in a play loft behind the play area, and although the children knew we were there, they ignored us. Each triad was videotaped on three different days at one of three activities, for approximately 25 minutes per session. The order of the activity sessions for each triad was counterbalanced across the 12 triads. The taping extended over a 5-week period.

For each session the room contained a different set of resources. One set was for housekeeping ("housekeeping session"), one for truck play ("truck session"), and the third was for an art activity ("art session"). The resources were chosen with gendered play preferences in mind (Connor & Serbin, 1977). (Art was the gender-neutral activity, but because none of the conversations reported here occurred in the art session, only the resources in the other two sessions will be described.) Each triad participated in each of the sessions. For the housekeeping session, an area of the room was set up with kitchen props: a toy stove and sink, a table and three chairs, a high chair, a basket of lifelike plastic food items, cooking pots, plastic eating utensils, paper plates, and cups. Nearby was a telephone next to a child-size easy chair. There was also a doll's bed with dolls and blankets. Close by was a doctor's kit. There was an area with dress-up clothes and a mirror.

For the truck session, the room was set up with three Fisher-Price trucks, three hard hats, small human figures, building blocks, and a tub full of plastic dinosaurs. There were three rideable wooden trucks; each had a removable seat that covered the truck's hollow body into which objects, like the dinosaurs, could be placed.

Recording

A camera operator in the doorway of the room videotaped the children; their voices were simultaneously recorded by an audio technician, who worked out of the children's sight. Each child wore a vest with a lavaliere microphone clipped to the lapel with a wire running to a wireless microphone transmitter (Freedomike), which was carried in a pocket on the back of the vest. The audio signals were fed from three receivers to a Tapco mixer. Each channel was fed to a corresponding analog tape recorder. The three channels were combined, fed to the camcorder, and recorded on the videotape sound track. This technique produced crisp and clear speech on the videotape. After recording more than 13 hours of interaction from the 12 triads, transcripts were made using both the audiotapes and videotapes.

Coding

The 24 housekeeping and truck sessions served as the basis of analysis. Half of the sessions were from the girls' triads and half from the boys'. They constitute approximately 9 hours of interaction. The transcripts were examined to find examples of double-voice discourse in episodes of mutual conflict (i.e., conflict that is expressed through mutual oppositions by the interactants). *Conflict* was defined as "a sequence which begins with an opposition and ends with a resolution or dissipation of conflict" (Eisenberg & Garvey, 1981, p. 150).

Training in coding for conflict and double-voice discourse was carried out by having two coders (a female research assistant and the author) independently examine a subset of the 24 transcripts. Once the coder identified a conflict episode, she looked within it for double-voice discourse—evidence of the voice of the self and the voice of the other, the latter often expressed through linguistic mitigation. It was necessary to view the videotapes to fully interpret the text. The coders met to compare coding. Discrepancies were resolved by discussion, and only those examples that both coders agreed on were retained for analysis.

Reliability Estimates and Distribution of Double-Voice Discourse

Inter-judge reliability on conflict episodes and double-voice discourse was determined for six different transcripts (25% of the total transcripts) that contained talk produced by half of the boys and half of the girls. Two housekeeping and one truck session were randomly chosen for each sex. Inter-rater agreement in identifying conflict episodes was 83.8%, which was counted before discussion. Inter-rater reliability was 86.9% for the boys' groups and 80% for the girls'.

The coders then identified whether each conflict displayed double-voice discourse. Conflicts that did not were negotiated through single-voice discourse. Inter-judge agreement in identifying double-voice discourse, counted before discussion, was 97%. The two cases of coding differences were each from conflicts in boys' groups, and they were resolved through discussion.

Sex Differences in Use of Double-Voice Discourse

The girls were 8 months younger, on average, than the boys. The nine girls ranged in age from 3;1 to 5;5 (*mean* = 3;9), and the nine boys ranged in age from 3;8 to 5;5 (*mean* = 4;5). Sixty-eight mutual conflicts were found. Thirty of those conflicts (44.1%) were in the girls' groups, and 38 (55.9%) were in the boys' groups. Although there were more conflicts among the boys, fewer of their conflicts (44.7%) were sites for double-voice discourse compared to the girls' conflicts (60%).

Additional coding by one of the coders established that there was a total of 147 conflicts in the housekeeping and trucks sessions of all 12 triads. Sixty-three were from the girls' groups, and 84 from the boys'. Of these, 50 of the girls' conflicts (79%) displayed double-voice discourse, whereas 30 of the boys' conflicts (36%) did.

In addition, in more than 13 hours of conversational interaction, no boys' conflict was found that comes close to matching the girls' for elaborateness or length of double-voice discourse. On the other hand, there are a number of similar complex examples of girls' conflicts, both long and short, which contain elaborate examples of double-voice discourse. Notably, however, *some* form of double-voice discourse occurred in the conversations of all 12 of the girls' and boys' triads. These results indicate that double-voice discourse is not a unique or uncommon event in children's conflicts and that independent coders can reliably identify it. The linguistic and pragmatic features of such discourse are described in the following examples.

RESULTS

Aggravated Conflict Talk

First, by way of contrast, consider an example of a dispute from a boys' triad that fits a familiar masculine-related cultural model of conflict, in which insistence and brute force can be acceptable strategies for trying to get what one wants. Linguistically aggravated and physically aggressive conflict exchanges of the sort in Example 1 have been found more *often* in boys' interaction than in girls' (see discussion in Goodwin, 1980; Leaper, 1991; Miller et al., 1986; Sheldon, 1990), although, as Goodwin (1980, 1995) demonstrates, girls have the same linguistic capacities as boys to argue in an aggravated manner. This conflict talk style uses direct, unmitigated, confrontational speech acts. Because the interactants have the single orientation of pursuing their own self-interest without orienting to the perspective of the partner or tempering their self-interest with mitigation, Sheldon (1992a) calls this dispute style "single-voice discourse" (p. 100). Examples follow.

Example 1. Boys' Single-Voice Discourse: "That's My Phone"

Charlie (4;0) and Tony (4;1) are together in a housekeeping session. Tony is sitting on a small foam chair/couch and is pushing the buttons on a touch-tone phone base that is on his lap. Charlie is nearby. (Emphasized words are capitalized.)

1. Tony: I pushed two squares (*giggles*), two squares like this. (*pushes phone buttons*)
2. Charlie: (*comes closer, puts his fist up to his ear and talks into an imaginary phone*) Hello!
3. Tony: (*puts his fist up to his ear and talks back*) Hello.
4. Charlie: (*picks up the receiver that is on Tony's chair*) No, that's my phone!
5. Tony: (*grabs the telephone cord and tries to pull the receiver away from Charlie*) No, tha–ah, it's on MY couch. It's on MY couch, Charlie. It's on MY couch. It's on MY couch.
6. Charlie: (*ignoring Tony, holding onto the receiver, and talking into the telephone now*) Hi. (*walks behind Tony's chair, the telephone base is still on Tony's lap*)
7. Tony: (*gets off the couch, sets the phone base on the floor*) I'll rock the couch like this. (*he turns the foam chair over on top of the telephone base and leans on it as Charlie tries to reach for it under the chair*) Don't! That's my phone!
8. Charlie: (*pushes the chair off the telephone and moves the telephone closer to himself, away from Tony*) I needa use it.
9. Tony: (*kneeling, sits back on his heels and watches Charlie playing with the phone*)

In this conflict, each child tries to physically overpower the other in order to use the telephone. Neither child negotiates or tries to persuade the other for a turn. No one voluntarily reconciles his wishes with the other. Insistence escalates rather than ends the opposition and leads to aggressive responses and a forceful resolution. Only a limited range of problem-solving strategies is tried here. The confrontational style left little opportunity for accommodative responses. This pattern of conflict management among boys is discussed further by Coie (1987) and Shantz (1986).

Example 2. Girls' Single-Voice Discourse: "I haven't had a turn"

In a truck session, Lisa (3;11), Mary (3;7), and Sue (3;3) are playing with blocks that they have put in a tall pile. They are pretending that the block at the top of the pile is a camera; one person stands behind the pile and pretends to take a picture of whoever is on the other side. Lisa has been taking longer turns taking pictures than the others. Now she is sitting in front of the camera in position to have her picture taken. Mary is standing behind the camera, and Sue is off to the side.

1. Mary: (*to Lisa*) No, Sue's turn 'spozed to be back there, okay Lisa?
2. Lisa: No, I–I–I can.

3. Mary: No, but Sue hasn't had a turn to be back there.
4. Lisa: I–I haven't had a turn to be back there. (*2-second pause*)
5. Mary: You did.
6. Lisa: No I didn't.
7. Mary: Yes you did. (*1.5-second pause*)
8. Lisa: No I didn't.
9. Mary: Yes you did, so-
10. Lisa: I can–I can go there.

The single-voice discourse in this example is composed of rounds of opposition aggravated by insistence. Self-assertion voiced in the oppositions after line 3 employs no mitigation, although the pauses might be interpreted as such. The talk lacks, however, the distancing and threatening moves that escalate and aggravate the boys' conflict in Example 1. After the rounds of insistence an accommodative solution is reached in 11:

11. Mary: No, (*to Sue*) you can get behind–you can get next to Lisa. Okay Sue, I'll come here (*she goes behind the camera*) too. (*Sue sits down next to Lisa in position to have her picture taken by Mary; the dispute ends*)

This resolution is inclusive and does not disrupt the interaction, like the foam chair overturning does in Example 1.

Double-Voice Discourse

The girls in this study also engaged in directly insistent confrontations. But in the more than 6 hours of girls' social play that were recorded, no oppositional exchanges were found in their groups that compared to the boys' in Example 1. On the other hand, similar examples of highly aggravated talk, insistence, or talk about threatened physical force occurred in other boys' examples. (For further discussion of gender differences, see Sheldon, 1997; Sheldon & Johnson, 1994.) Feminine-related conflict in the larger sample of children often involved the creation of complex oral texts of mediation and negotiation, which demonstrated a variety of verbal problem-solving strategies and showed an awareness of the other person's needs while trying to achieve one's own ends. Perhaps partly as a result of this, some of the girls' exchanges became very long and verbally complex. The complexity of the following conflict demonstrates the elaborate linguistic and interactional skills that these 4-year-olds can use and the difficult and artful verbal work they have learned to do in mediating opposition. It also shows the workings of a peer culture that contradicts cultural stereotypes that portray girls as passive, yielding, weak, or conflict-avoidant. It is instead a culture in which girls do resist and oppose one another in order to further their own wishes. The elaborate and long conflict described here is one of several found in girls' groups in this study.

As mentioned before, double-voice discourse *was* found in boys' disputes also, but less frequently and in less elaborate form. The differences discussed here are differences in linguistic choices. They reflect the fact that these children are aligning with their culture's interpretation of gender differences. That alignment results in girls and boys sometimes making different linguistic choices. But these choices are made with the same linguistic knowledge and skills that *both* groups have.

Example 3. Girls' Double-Voice Discourse: A Negotiation Tour De Force: "Nurses Getta Do Shots"

This conflict takes place between Arlene (4;9) and Elaine (4;6); Erica (4;2) is present briefly. They have been pretending that some dolls are sick children and they are nurses who are caring for them. A conflict develops over who will use some medical implements that are in the room. Elaine, who started enacting the role of nurse earlier than Arlene did, wants to keep control of the equipment. But Arlene wants to use something too. (Various techniques of double voicing are underlined, and loud speech is indicated by capital letters in the prevailing font size. Muted speech is presented n a smaller font size. In addition, there are various techniques of unmitigated self-assertion.)

1. Arlene: <u>Can I have that–that thing?</u> (*referring to the blood pressure gauge in Elaine's lap*) I'm going to take my baby's temperature.
2. Elaine: (*looking up from talking on the telephone*) You can use it–you can use my temperature. <u>Just</u> make sure you can't use anything else <u>unless</u> you can ask (*turns back to talking on the telephone*).

In 1, Arlene asks permission to use the blood pressure gauge. She gives a reason for her request. In 2, Elaine gives qualified agreement. She lets Arlene use the thermometer with restrictions, telling her to ask before she uses anything else. Although the girls are competing for goods here, there is an attempt to allow for a fair distribution. Elaine shows some flexibility by offering a concession, establishing "a middle ground which moves toward the other position but still opposes it" (Vuchinich, 1990, p. 126). However, a mutual opposition subsequently unfolds.

3. Arlene: (*picks up thermometer from a nearby table and takes her baby's temperature*) Eighty-three! She isn't sick. Yahoo! <u>May I?</u> (*she asks Elaine, who is still on the telephone, if she can use the needle-less hypodermic syringe*)
4. Elaine: No, <u>I'm gonna need to use the shot in a couple of minutes.</u>
5. Arlene: *But I–I need this <u>though.</u>* (*asks in a beseeching tone, picks up the hypodermic syringe*)
6. Elaine: (*firmly*) <u>Okay, just use it once.</u>

In 3, Arlene makes a polite request to use Elaine's syringe, "May I?" but in 4, Elaine denies the request with a flat "no" followed by a qualification of her refusal; she explains that she will need to use the shot soon. In 5, Arlene returns with an opposing move, adopting Elaine's reason, insisting that she also "needs" it, softening her demand with "though" while she picks up the contested syringe. In 6, Elaine reluctantly agrees to let her use it, again offering a concession that establishes a middle ground, but she firmly constrains the use to "just" one time.

7. Erica: (*whispers*) Arlene, let's play doctor.
8. Arlene: (*to Erica*) No, I'm gonna give her a shot on the–
9. Elaine: Hey, I'm the nurse. I'm the nurse. (*she puts down the phone and comes over to Arlene and the crib in which her doll is lying.*) <u>Arlene, remember, I'm the nurse, and the nurses getta do shots, remember?</u>
10. Arlene: *But* I get to do *some.*
11. Elaine: <u>Just a couple, okay?</u>

In 8, Arlene starts giving her baby a shot, but in 9, Elaine wants to be in control of the syringe. First she responds directly. She addresses Arlene by name and requests that Arlene "remember" Elaine's role. "I'm the nurse," Elaine asserts. She has adopted Arlene's pretend play frame of reference. Having a common frame of reference is a useful strategy for gaining entry to Arlene's play because it increases mutual involvement. This also provides a rationale for Elaine's access to the syringe: Nurses have a certain role to play, namely, they "getta do shots." She follows this justification with a tag question "remember?" which is intended to elicit agreement. It does elicit Arlene's token agreement and a request for another concession in 10 when Arlene says, "But I get to do some." This is a mitigating response, here called a *"yes-but" strategy*, in which agreement prefaces disagreement (discussed further in Sheldon, 1992; Pomerantz, 1984). It is a partial agreement and partial disagreement, in which Arlene backs off a bit, acknowledges that Elaine will use the syringe, yet still pursues her own agenda and states her intention to use it too. The *"yes-but" strategy* allows for an appearance of agreement, while the partners continue to negotiate their action plans. In 11, Elaine again offers a concession, telling Arlene that she can do "just a couple." She follows this directive with a tag question that solicits agreement, "ok?" although Arlene offers none.

All of Elaine's concessions-with-constraints allow her to hold on to her own agenda while accommodating her partner's agenda also. This is a form of double-voice discourse. However, although Elaine is accommodating Arlene's wishes, competition between the girls is actually escalating and intensifying because Arlene is pressing to keep control of the syringe for her own use and to administer to the doll in other nurse-like ways. The opposition over who has exclusive rights to administer to the doll grows. Whereas in 3, Arlene started out by asking permission to use the needle (May I?), she has now moved to directly asserting what she'll do, as in 12.

12. Arlene: I get to do some more things too. Now don't forget–now don't touch the baby until I get back, <u>because it IS MY BABY!</u> (*said to both of the other girls*) I'll check her ears, <u>ok</u>? (*puts down the syringe and picks up the ear scope*).
13. Elaine: Now I'll–and I'll give her–I'll have to give her (*the same doll*) a shot. (*picks up the syringe that Arlene has put down*)
14. Arlene: <u>There can only be</u> ONE thing that you–that–NO, she–*she only needs* one SHOT.
15. Elaine: <u>Well, let's pretend</u> it's <u>another</u> day that <u>we</u> have to look in her ears <u>together</u>.

At this point, Elaine wants to give the doll a shot, but in 12, Arlene has ordered her not to touch "her" baby. She announces she is not constrained in what she can do with the baby and that she will check the baby's ears. As Elaine has done previously, Arlene adds a tag question, "ok?" a marker that solicits agreement. Although Elaine does not directly respond to the tag question, she continues to act as a participant. In 13, she reannounces her plans to give a shot, "Now I'll—and I'll give her—I'll have to give her a shot." In two indirect statements in 14, in which no agent is mentioned and the responsibility for deciding who gives a shot is vaguely expressed, Arlene tries to cut Elaine out of the action by stating that "there can only be ONE thing …" and the baby "only needs one shot." Both girls are equally determined to have their own way. In 15, Elaine tries to get Arlene to consider an alternative in which they can both participate. She reframes the situation and responds in multiply mitigated ways. She opens with a delay, "well." She uses a joint directive "let's" and introduces a new pretend scenario: She displaces the time to "another day" and the medical problem to her "ears," in an effort to induce cooperation on a combined agenda—that "we" will work "together."

In 16, the conflict continues to heat up. In answer to Elaine's suggestion that they look in the doll's ears together, Arlene replies with a token agreement, "yeah but," and nevertheless continues to demand to examine the ears herself, directly ordering Elaine not to "shot her."

16. Arlene: No, no, <u>yeah but</u> I do the ear looking. Now don't SHOT–(<u>*lowering her voice* but still insisting</u>) DON'T SHOT HER! I'm the one who does all the shots, 'cause this is my baby!

17. Elaine: (*whispers*) <u>Well–I'm the nurse and nurses get to do the shots.</u>

18. Arlene: (*spoken very intensely*) An' me'–And men–<u>well, then men get to do the shots too even 'cause men can be nurses.</u> (*taunting, slightly sing-song*) <u>But you can't</u> shot her.

In 17, Elaine continues to mitigate by delaying, "well," and countering with a reason for why she should give a shot, "nurses get to do the shots." In 18, Arlene counters with a competing justification, that is intended to take some of the force out of Elaine's claim "… well, then men get to do the shots too even 'cause men can be nurses." Arlene indirectly questions whether Elaine, as a female, has an exclusive right to give shots. Arlene again orders her somewhat indirectly not to give a shot, "But you can't shot her."

19. Elaine: I'll have to shot her <u>after–after–after you listen–after you look in the ears.</u>

20. Erica: She (*Arlene*) already shot her even.

21. Elaine: We have–<u>she didn't do a shot on her finger.</u>

22. Arlene: But she did–she did–I DID TOO! Now don't shot her at all!

23. Elaine: We hafta do it–<u>Well,</u> I'm going to keep do it after she– this baby.

24. Arlene: (*intense <u>but lowered voice</u>*) "Now DON'T YOU DARE!"

In 19, Elaine insists, "I'll have to shot her," and also continues to offer a concession: that she will give the shot "after you look in her ears." When Erica says that Arlene "already shot her," Elaine assertively persists within the pretend frame, inventively countering (by noting a shortcoming in Arlene's procedure) in 21 that "she didn't do a shot on her finger"; that is, Arlene missed a spot and it needs to be done by Elaine. Thus, Elaine resists Arlene's attempts to exclude her and instead creatively offers alternatives in which she can share in the action too.

Although both girls are developing a complex negotiation in double-voice discourse, Arlene is gaining more in this struggle than Elaine is. In line 24, Arlene persists; she intensely, directly and threateningly orders Elaine to stop: "Now *DON'T YOU DARE!*" Arlene doesn't shout but instead mutes her voice by lowering it. As the confrontation reaches its peak of insistence, the girls' voices get lower and lower, not louder and louder with anger. In 25, Elaine directly orders Arlene, in an even lower voice:

25. Elaine: (*voice lowered more* than Arlene's but equally intense) STOP SAY-
                ING THAT! (*pause*) Well, then you can't come to my birthday!
26. Arlene: (*voice still lowered*) I DON'T WANT TO COME TO YOUR
                BIRTHDAY.

Finally, Elaine leaves Arlene at the crib and goes back to table.

As Elaine and Arlene escalate their dispute with words, instead of raising their voices in shouts or screams, which happens in the boys' example, their speaking voices paradoxically become more and more muted. There is a lack of consonance between the girls' angry words and their quieter and quieter tone. It is a dramatic example of the mitigation of the metaphorical "voice" of self-interest and self-assertion in their double-voice discourse. It seems that (literally) muting their speaking voice allows them to escalate the directness of their words and the confrontational nature of their demands and assertions. Notice also in 25, that the kind of threat that Elaine uses is one of social ostracism, "… you can't come to my birthday party," not the physical force that Tony used in Example 1, "I'll rock the couch like this."

DISCUSSION

Double-Voice Discourse as a Powerful Persuasion Mode

The negotiation of the conflict between Elaine and Arlene is an example of the linguistic and pragmatic complexity that is often involved in double-voice discourse. The girls used multiple argument strategies, which involve a variety of linguistic devices to soften conflict in order to be effective. In this example, Arlene was successful in getting what she wanted, in part, because Elaine was willing to negotiate numerous concessions. For the most part, the girls resist without being confrontational, justify themselves rather than give in, and use linguistic mitigators while trying to get what they want. Although both girls use double-voice discourse, the differences in how much they use and when they use it reflect differences in their ongoing successes in getting their way during the negotiation.

Double-voice discourse enabled the girls to construct an extensive oral text, which navigated them through a dispute. At the same time, it guided their play activity with resources in the housekeeping room. It actually developed their involvement with one another as they negotiated access to roles in order to play with the syringe and doll. At the same time, each is asserting her own interests.

CONCLUSION

This chapter provided some examples that elucidate children's skill with spoken language and knowledge of gender prescriptions reflected in their language use.

Language

Children ages 3 to 5 can be extremely sophisticated in producing and interpreting co-constructed oral texts with their friends, often strategically using language to their own social advantage. They have co-constructed conversational texts for years before coming to kindergarten, not only with caregivers but also in play sessions with friends. They are linguistic veterans who have already achieved a high level of communicative competence.

The achievement of equilibrium and the construction of reciprocality between Arlene and Elaine, for example, is a delicate and fluid use of language that proceeds with both self-assertion and mitigation simultaneously. The girls are skillfully using diverse language resources to mediate and overcome opposition. Their exchange demonstrates the challenge of self-assertion: staking out one's point of view or goal, stating it clearly, motivating it in an attempt to persuade or deflect the person who is opposing the speaker, and communicating this in clear verbal terms, without derailing play.

This verbal work requires attentiveness to discourse processes and memory for prior text in order to frame responses and to maintain thematic cohesion and relevance. Responses are produced to a partner's prior move and are framed to accommodate or distance the partner's next move.

Most of children's talk is with peers. Thus, children are language resources for each other, teaching and using language skills together in and out of the classroom.

Spoken language is a major medium through which school and nonschool activities are learned and accomplished. Because the quality and quantity of spoken language in the classroom, from both peer talk and teacher-student talk, is important, educators would be wise to create classroom contexts rich in spoken language.

Gender Inscription Through Language

Childhood is a time when children are learning how to become members of their family and community. Language is one of the most important tools for teaching these cultural novices how to *do* being a girl or a boy. Our language choices can align us with, and reflect, our gender, even early in childhood. Using language is one way we gender ourselves. By the time children reach kindergarten, their use of language reflects a growing understanding of what being a girl or a boy means in their community. That includes knowing how they are expected to talk to be socially normative. Learning language and culture usually takes place below the child's threshold of awareness, long before they are able to reflect on the implications. An analysis of oral texts, as demonstrated here, can reveal the complexity of everyday language practices that are involved in "doing gender."

Linguistic inscription of the sort shown here is extremely powerful and effective. The fact that children have learned so well to speak like a girl or boy by the age of 5 without having been explicitly taught to do so, makes these acquired gender differences, which are stylistic variations in talk, appear to be "natural," "normal," or "inevitable." In fact, people often assume that these linguistic differences in behavior must be consequences of our genetic makeup. But this is not the case.

An alternative explanation, which is often overlooked, is that these differences have been modeled by adults and peers for years in early childhood. In fact, research confirms that gender differences in language use are learned, transmitted by parents and caregivers, and practiced with peers well before children even reach kindergarten (e.g., Berko Gleason, 1983; Ely, Berko Gleason, & McCabe, 1996). Like most other kinds of socialization, language socialization is implicit and subtle. Language is usually a transparent medium. Systematic collection and analysis of spoken language are needed to make it visible.

Whether children's talk is gendered on any particular occasion is likely to depend on the context in which the talk occurs and the gender of the partner with whom the child is speaking. Context makes a difference. For example, few gender differences have been found so far in sibling talk (DeHart, 1996), but also few studies have observed talk between siblings so we have limited information about this context.

In addition, we are in need of many cross-class, cross-language, and cross-cultural comparisons to see whether, and to what extent, gender differences in communicative style vary across communities, languages, and cultures. We need to study more varied preschool communities, with different demographic features, in order to have more comprehensive information on how and when language in those particular communities is shaped by gender. Such research into possible variations in the interrelationship between language and gender is needed to evaluate the popular and unscientific belief that sexism is "normal" and that biological essentialism is the explanation for gender differences. Such folkloric beliefs perpetuate the presence of male-centered and misogynist educational material and classroom practices. Fortunately, antibias curricular materials are becoming more plentiful. They bring a richer mix of educational resources that more accurately reflect the rich diversity of human lives.

If further research upholds these findings that conversations can reflect cultural expectations of how girls and boys should behave and how their behavior should be reflected in talk, it might be fruitful to ask if the process and products of learning how to read and write also reflect gender stereotypes? Comparisons between children's oral text construction and interpretation, literacy acquisition, and literacy instruction can be a fruitful avenue for further research and exploration. An understanding of children's complex skills in constructing and interpreting oral texts is essential for practitioners who help them develop skills with written texts.

ACKNOWLEDGMENTS

Sections of this paper originally appeared in "Conflict Talk: Sociolinguistic Challenges to Self-Assertion and How Young Girls Meet Them," by A. Sheldon, 1992a, *Merrill-Palmer Quarterly, 38*(1), 95–117; and "Preschool Girls' Discourse Competence: Managing Conflict," by A. Sheldon, 1992b, in K. Hall, M. Bucholtz, & B. Moonwomon (Eds.), *Locating Power. Proceedings of the Second Berkeley Women and Language Conference* (Vol. 2, pp. 528–539), Berkeley, CA: Berkeley Women and Language Group. Reprinted with permission.

NOTES

1. My comments about talk as text pertain to both oral and signed texts, such as those produced in American Sign Language. Henceforth terms like *talk, spoken text, language, oral skills,* and *conversation(al)* will pertain to both spoken and signed modalities. Some suggestions for further reading about Deaf language and culture are Padden and Humphries (1988) and Solomon (1994).
2. For example, advertising on a Poptarts® box a few years ago used the pronoun "she," as a feminine generic when referring to a child.
3. The American Association of University Women has a number of resources on gender bias in education, available from AAUW Sales Office, PO Box 251, Annapolis Junction, MD 20701–0251; 800–225–9998, ext. 91.
4. Sheldon (1990) contains a list of resources discussing sexism and nonsexist resources in children's literature, in language, and in schools.
5. I am grateful to Rose Feehey for this example.
6. Data are from Garvey and Hogan (1973), and the longer transcript from which this excerpt comes is discussed in Sheldon (1992a). Numbers in parentheses indicate age and months: (4;9) indicates that the child is 4 years and 9 months of age.
7. Other examples of double-voice discourse conflict management strategies and further discussion can be found in Sheldon (1993, 1996a, 1996b, 1997) and Sheldon and Rohleder (1996). Sheldon (1990b) contains discussion of other gendered characteristics of preschoolers' disputes observed in the children's community described in this chapter.

REFERENCES

American Association of University Women. (1991). *Shortchanging girls, Shortchanging America, Report action guide,* and *Full data report: Shortchanging girls, Shortchanging America*. Available from the American Association of University Women, 1111 16th St. NW, Washington, DC 20036.

Bamberg, M. (1995). *Learning how to narrate: New directions in child development.* San Francisco: Jossey-Bass.

Berko Gleason, J., & Grief, E. (1983). Men's speech to young children. In B. Thorne, C. Kramarae, & N. Henley (Eds.), *Language, gender and society* (pp. 140–150). Rowley, MA: Newbury.

Coie, J. D. (1987). *An analysis of aggressive episodes: Age and peer status differences.* Paper presented at the biennial meeting of the Society for Research in Child Development, Baltimore, MD.

Connor, J. M., & Serbin, L. A. (1977). Behaviorally based masculine- and feminine-activity-preference scales for preschoolers: Correlates with other classroom behaviors and cognitive tests. *Child Development, 48,* 1411–1416.

Davies, B. (1989). *Frogs and snails and feminist tales.* Sydney, Australia: Allen & Unwin.

DeHart, G. B. (1996). Gender and mitigation in four-year-olds' pretend play talk with siblings. *Research on Language and Social Interaction, 29*(1), 81–96.

Eckert, P. (1990). Cooperative competition in adolescent "girl talk." *Discourse Processes, 13*(1), 91–122.

Eckert, P., & McConnell-Ginet, S. (2003). *Language and gender.* Cambridge, England: Cambridge University Press.

Eisenberg, A. R., & Garvey, C. (1981). Children's use of verbal strategies in resolving conflicts. *Discourse Processes, 4,* 149–170.

Ely, R., Berko Gleason, J., & McCabe, A. (1996). "Why didn't you talk to your Mommy, Honey?" Parents' and children's talk about talk. *Research on Language and Social Interaction, 29*(1), 7–25.

Garvey, C., & Hogan, R. (1973). Social speech and social interaction: Egocentrism revisited. *Child Development, 44,* 562–568.

Goodwin, M. H. (1980). Directive-response speech sequences in girls' and boys' task activities. In S. McConnell-Ginet, R. Borker, & N. Furman (Eds.), *Women and language in literature and society* (pp. 157–173). New York: Praeger.

Goodwin, M. H. (1995). Co-construction in girls' hopscotch. *Research on Language and Social Interaction, 28,* 261–281.

Goodwin, M. H., & Goodwin, C. (1987). Children's arguing. In S. U. Philips, S. Steele, & C. Tanz (Eds.), *Language, gender and sex in comparative perspective* (pp. 200–248). New York: Cambridge University Press.

Graham, A. (1975). The making of a nonsexist dictionary. In B. Thorne & N. Henley (Eds.), *Language and sex: Difference and dominance* (pp. 57–63). Rowley, MA: Newbury House. (Reprinted from *Ms., 2,* 12–16, 1973)

Hughes, L. (1988). "But that's not *really* mean": Competing in a cooperative mode. *Sex Roles, 19*(11–12), 669–687.

Hyde, J. S., & Linn, M. C. (1988). Gender differences in verbal ability: A meta-analysis. *Psychological Bulletin, 104,* 53–69.

Kalčik, S. (1975). "… like Ann's gynecologist or the time I was almost raped": Personal narratives in women's rap groups. *Journal of American Folklore, 88,* 3–11.

Kyratzis, A. (1992). Gender differences in the use of persuasive justification in children's pretend play. In R. Hall, M. Bucholtz, & B. Moonwomon (Eds.), *Locating power: Proceedings of the second Berkeley Women and Language Conference, 2* (pp. 326–337). Berkeley, CA: Berkeley Women and Language Group.

Kyratzis, A., & Ervin-Tripp, S. (1999). The development of discourse markers in peer interaction. *Journal of Pragmatics, 31,* 1321–1338.

Kyratzis, A., & Guo, J. (1996). "Separate worlds" for girls and boys?: Views from U.S. and Chinese mixed-sex friendship groups. In D. I. Slobin, J. Gerhardt, A. Kyratzis, & J. Guo (Eds.), *Social interaction, social context, and language: Essays in honor of Susan Ervin-Tripp* (pp. 555–578). Hillsdale, NJ: Lawrence Erlbaum Associates.

Leaper, C. (1991). Influence and involvement in children's discourse: Age, gender and partner effects. *Child Development, 62,* 797–811.

LeMaster, B., & Hernandez-Katapodis, M. M. (2002). In S. Benor, M. Rose, D. Sharma, J. Sweetland, & Q. Zhang (Eds.), *Gendered practices in language* (pp. 213–235). Stanford, CA: CSLI Publications.

Libby, M. N., & Aries, E. (1989). Gender differences in preschool children's narrative fantasy. *Psychology of Women Quarterly, 13,* 296–306.

Maccoby, E. (1986). Social groupings in childhood: Their relationship to pro-social and anti-social behavior in boys and girls. In D. Olweus, J. Block, & M. Radke-Yarrow (Eds.), *Development of antisocial and prosocial behavior* (pp. 263–284). San Diego: Academic Press.

Maggio, R. (1991). *The dictionary of bias-free usage.* Phoenix, AZ: Oryx Press.

Maltz, D., & Borker, R. (1982). A cultural approach to male-female miscommunication. In J. Gumperz (Ed.), *Language and social identity* (pp. 196–216). Cambridge, England: Cambridge University Press.

Miller, P., Danaher, D., & Forbes, D. (1986). Sex-related strategies for coping with interpersonal conflict in children aged five and seven. *Developmental Psychology, 22,* 543–548.

Nicolopoulou, A., Scales, B., & Weintraub, J. (1994). Gender differences and symbolic imagination in the stories of four-year-olds. In A. H. Dyson & C. Genishi (Eds.), *The need for story: Cultural diversity in classroom and community* (pp. 102–123). Urbana, IL: National Council of Teachers of English.

Padden, C., & Humphries, T. (1988). *Deaf in America.* Cambridge, MA: Harvard University Press.

Pinker, S. (1994). *The language instinct: How the mind creates language.* New York: Morrow.

Pomerantz, A. (1984). Agreeing and disagreeing with assessments: Some features of preferred/dispreferred turn shapes. In J. M. Atkinson & J. Heritage (Eds.), *Structures of social action: Studies in conversation analysis* (pp. 57–101). New York: Cambridge University Press.

Sachs, J. (1987). Preschool boys' and girls' language use in pretend play. In S. U. Philips, S. Steele, & C. Tanz (Eds.), *Language, gender and sex in comparative perspective* (pp. 178–188). New York: Cambridge University Press.

Sadker, M., & Sadker, D. (1994). *Failing at fairness: How America's schools cheat girls.* New York: Scribner.

Shantz, C. U. (1987). Conflicts between children. *Child Development, 58,* 283–305.

Shantz, D. W. (1986). Conflict, aggression and peer status: An observational study. *Child Development, 57,* 1322–1332.

Sheldon, A. (1990a). "Kings are royaler than queens": Language and socialization. *Young Children 45*(2), 4–9.

Sheldon, A. (1990b). Pickle fights: Gendered talk in preschool disputes. *Discourse Processes, 13*(1), 5–31. Reprinted in D. Tannen (Ed.). (1993). *Gender and conversational interaction* (pp. 83–109). Oxford, England: Oxford University Press.

Sheldon, A. (1992a). Conflict talk: Sociolinguistic challenges to self-assertion and how young girls meet them. *Merrill-Palmer Quarterly, 38*(1), 95–117.

Sheldon, A. (1992b). Preschool girls' discourse competence: Managing conflict. In K. Hall, M. Bucholtz, & B. Moonwomon (Eds.), *Locating power: Proceedings of the second Berkeley Women and Language Conference* (Vol. 2, pp. 258–539). Berkeley, CA: Berkeley Women and Language Group.

Sheldon, A. (1993). Saying it with a smile: Girls' conflict talk as double-voice discourse. In M. Eid & G. Iverson (Eds.), *Principles and prediction: The analysis of natural language* (pp. 215–232). Amsterdam: John Benjamins.

Sheldon, A. (1996a). Editor's introduction: Constituting gender through talk in childhood. *Research on Language and Social Interaction, 29*(1), 1–5.

Sheldon, A. (1996b). You can be the baby brother but you aren't born yet: Preschool girls' negotiation for power and access in pretend play. *Research on Language and Social Interaction, 29*(1), 57–80.

Sheldon, A. (1997). Talking power: Girls, gender enculturation and discourse. In R. Wodak (Ed.), *Gender and discourse* (pp. 225–244). London: Sage.

Sheldon, A., & Engstrom, H. (2005). Two styles of mutual engagement in preschool girls' and boys' dramatic play. In J. Coates & J. Thornborrow (Eds.), *The sociolinguistics of narrative, studies in narrative* (pp. 171–192). Amsterdam: John Benjamins.

Sheldon, A., & Johnson, D. (1994). Preschool negotiators: Gender differences in double-voice discourse as a conflict talk style in early childhood. In B. Sheppard, R. Lewicki, & R. Bies (Eds.), *Research on negotiation in organizations* (Vol. 4, pp. 27–57). Greenwich, CT: JAI Press. Reprinted in J. Cheshire & P. Trudgill (Eds.), (1998). *The sociolinguistics reader* (Vol. 2, pp. 76–98). London: Edward Arnold.

Sheldon, A., & Rohleder, L. (1996). Sharing the same world, telling different stories: Gender differences in co-constructed pretend narratives. In D. I. Slobin, J. Gerhardt, A. Kyratzis, & J. Guo (Eds.), *Social interaction, social context, and language. Essays in honor of Susan Ervin-Tripp* (pp. 613–632). Hillsdale, NJ: Lawrence Erlbaum Associates.

Solomon, A. (1994, August 24). Defiantly Deaf. *New York Times Magazine,* pp. 40–68.

Stein, N. (1988). The development of children's storytelling skill. In M. B. Franklin & S. Barten (Eds.), *Child language: A book of readings* (pp. 282–297). New York: Cambridge University Press.

Swann, J. (1998). Talk control: An illustration from the classroom of problems in analyzing male dominance of conversation. In J. Coates (Ed.), *Language and gender: A reader* (pp. 185–196). Oxford, England: Blackwell.

Tarullo, L. B. (1994). Windows on social worlds: Gender differences in children's play narratives. In A. Slade & D. P. Wolf (Eds.), *Children at play* (pp. 169–187). New York: Oxford University Press.

Vuchinich, S. (1990). The sequential organization of closing in verbal family conflict. In A. Grimshaw (Ed.), *Conflict talk* (pp. 118–138). New York: Cambridge University Press.

CHAPTER 4

Teenage Talk: A London-Based *Chat* and *Discussion* Compared

Anna-Brita Stenström

Spoken discourse changes through talk, in that speakers behave differently depending on what they are talking about. This study, which is based on data from the Bergen Corpus of London Teenage Language (COLT),[1] demonstrates how content shapes the form of spoken interaction by scrutinizing two different conversations between the same 16-year-old English school girls. Both conversations take place in a study at a boarding school in Outer London. In the first conversation, the girls chat about boys; in the second, they discuss smoking, drinking, and taking drugs. It appears that the change of topics affects not only the choice of vocabulary (from general to specific), the sentence structure (from simple to complex), and the speech processing (from effortless to hesitant), but also the speakers' overall interactional behavior (from more to less supportive).[2] The change of topics is also reflected in a marked change in conversational atmosphere (from light-hearted to sober).[3]

CHAT VERSUS DISCUSSION

A *chat*, according to *Collins Cobuild English Language Dictionary* (1987) is "an informal, friendly conversation, usually about things which are not serious or important" (p. 230), not to be mixed up with *gossip*, which involves "information about other people and their actions, often including unkind or disapproving comments about their private affairs" (p. 629), or which typically involves "details which are not confirmed as being true" (*New Oxford Dictionary of English*, 1998, p. 792). *Discussion*, in contrast, is defined as "a conversation, speech, or piece of writing in which a subject is considered in detail, from several points of view" (*Collins Cobuild Dictionary*, 1987, p. 401).

If we go to the Internet, we find that the word *chat* has acquired a much wider meaning, notably "a way people in different places can 'talk' to each other by typing their words into a computer" (Savage, n.d.), which involves "'talking' to people who are online at the same time you are." (Auburn University Office of

Information Technology, n.d.). Most chats are said to be "focused on a particular topic of interest," which implies that the borderline between a chat and a discussion in the traditional sense has suddenly become fuzzy: A chat is no longer typically about things that are "not serious or important" but very much like a discussion in its focus on a particular topic. In what follows, I deal with *chat* in the traditional sense, however, as an informal social activity, whereas I view *discussion* as varying from strictly businesslike to strongly personal.

TOPIC AND TOPIC DEVELOPMENT

According to Brown and Yule (1983), whose chapter "Topic and the Representation of Discourse Content" is probably the nearest we can get to a theory of topic in a model of discourse, "formal attempts to identify topics are doomed to failure" (p. 68). In their opinion, *topic* could be described as "the most frequently used, unexplained term in the analysis of discourse." (p. 70). This is supported by Clark (1996), who considers the notion of topic to be "notoriously vague." He argues further that, because conversation is both "opportunistic" and "under joint control," what is being talked about is not what the speaker is talking about but "what the *participants* are talking about," which he regards as an even "more slippery notion" (p. 342). In other words, because conversation is a joint activity, what is being talked about is common business. This is true especially for discussions, the purpose of which is to talk about a topic in some detail and perhaps come to a joint conclusion. Chats, on the other hand, are often unbalanced in that a speaker can take the opportunity to go on about her own experiences or interests, while the other participants act as attentive listeners by providing backchannels, but without taking an active part as co-speakers.

Because a topic cannot be formally defined, Brown and Yule (1983) argue that the interpretation should be based on the fact that "what a speaker is talking about is inevitably based on how he structures what he is saying" and, referring to Schank (1977) and Maynard (1980), that when defining *topic,* one should concentrate on the "topic shifts," which are generally formally marked, for instance, by intonational cues and/or pauses (p. 94; see also Stenström, 1990).

Brown and Yule (1983) emphasize that topics are not fixed beforehand but negotiated as the conversation proceeds, which leads to a gradual development of next topics (p. 89). Likewise, Coates (1998) shows how participants contribute to the development of topics by building on each other's contributions, which is facilitated by the use of minimal responses and epistemic modal forms (p. 246). The discussion sections of the talk in Coates's material were found to be more complex than the rest, and this is also where epistemic modal forms (including *just, kind of, sort of*) were most commonly used as facilitating devices. In these sections, speakers sometimes exposed their own feelings and sometimes discussed general points. (For topic development in different types of talk, see Stenström, 1994, pp. 169–198.)

THE CORPUS

COLT was compiled in the late spring of 1993 and consists of just under half a million words of spontaneous conversations between 13- to 17-year-old boys and girls from different parts of London and with varying socioeconomic backgrounds, ranging from lower-working to upper-middle class. London was chosen, as new linguistic trends tend to have their first appearance in a metropolis. To achieve the right social balance, we approached the Department of Education in London, who provided us with a list of schools in "socially different" parts of the city. The heads of the schools were then contacted and presented with a brief outline of the project and its aims and purposes and asked to help us find students who were willing to act as "recruits." Some headmasters and headmistresses were enthusiastic; others showed less enthusiasm. Schools with upper and upper-middle class students turned out to be least willing to cooperate, which is why we ended up with schools both in the inner city area and the greater London metropolitan area to get the right spread.

Altogether 33 students were willing to act as recruits and had their parent(s) sign a letter of consent. Being a recruit meant wearing a small Sony Walkman and a lapel microphone for a few days and recording all the conversations he or she took part in, preferably without anybody noticing that they were being recorded.

The COLT material has been orthographically transcribed by trained British transcribers and tagged for word classes. It is accessible on the Internet (http://torvald.aksis.uib.no/colt) and available on CD-ROM in an orthographically transcribed, word-class tagged version, accompanied by a sound file and a search program (for details, see Stenström, 2002).

The main aim of the COLT project was to make a reasonably large corpus of English teenage talk available for research. No such material was available, and we felt that far too little research had been done on teenage language, as opposed to child language and adult language. The importance of studying teenage language is obvious. For one thing, linguistic innovations often arise among teenagers, and for another, many new trends in the language of English teenagers tend to spread to teenagers of other nationalities. This should be of interest to both language experts and educators of teenagers.

A number of studies based on COLT have already been carried out at Bergen University, for instance, Andersen (1995) on auxiliary deletion, Stenström (1995) and Bynes (1998) on taboos, Andersen (1998) on functions of *like*, Hasund (1996) on conflict talk, Andersen (2000) on pragmatic markers, Berland (1997) on tags, Stenström (1997) on nonstandard grammatical features, Monstad (1998) on grammaticalization, Stenström (2000) on intensifiers, and Stenström et al. (2002) on general trends in teenage talk.

TOPIC DEVELOPMENT

Let us now consider the topic development in the two conversations under discussion. There is nothing surprising about the topics dealt with in the extracts that follow. Teenagers apparently love to talk about sex, drink, and drugs. School in general, sports, and school friends are other favorites. Girls' talk is typically about boys, looks, and how to be popular (cf. Eckert 1993). The first talk, which lasts 8 minutes, is characterized as a chat; the second, which lasts 15 minutes, is characterized as a discussion.

Chatting About Boys

Les and Judy have come to see Catie, whose study is a mess, judging by the warming-up talk, which goes on for a short while. When Les asks Catie if she is going home for the weekend and Catie answers that she is going to Freddy's, it turns out that Freddy used to be Les's boyfriend. Catie gets very curious:[4]

[1] Catie: You got off with Freddy?
     Les: Yeah I used to like, we used to see each other ... sort of ... [and I]
     Catie: [for a long time?]
     Les: No, no well the weird [part]
     Catie: [how long?]
     Les: It was like spaced ... it was just like, I dunno, not long at all [just a]
     Catie: [well roughly] how long?
     Les: couple of things ... we saw each other and then over a space of about two months we saw each other probably about three times.
     Catie: Oh.

A boy named Herb is also going, and this leads to the following sequence.

[2] Les: ... he he's fat, dark hair [<unclear>]
     Catie: [No not fat]
     Les: Is he good looking?
     Catie: Yeah quite.
     Les: Would I like him? Well what does he look like?
     Catie: Just a da= it's difficult to explain a bloke cos they're all, you know,
     Judy: <laughing> Short [brown </>]
     Les: [Do you know] Herb? In Upper six Leonard?

A minute later, the question of sending Valentine's cards is brought up.

[3] Les: Are you gonna to send any, Catie? I know it's a long way away but ...
     Catie: Yeah? But?
     Les: If you're still going out with Freddy ... would you send a Valentine's car to anybody else?
     Catie: Oh.
     Les: Yeah?
     Catie: I don't know cos there's no one else I'd really want to send a va oh <laughing> ...

Les's surprising and completely unexpected announcement that she has not received any pornographic mail causes a sudden shift and opens up for one daring suggestion after the other of how to trap boys.

[4] Judy: … We could charge the removes[5] for their first kiss.
      Catie: Yeah we're gonna start a little business. Up for it? Up for it, yeah. You just say, you know, five quid for a cuss behind the bushes.
      Les: And your first kiss. Really.

Apparently, the girls are not entirely innocent and inexperienced.

[5] Catie: … We, we'd given each other eyes over the bar in this pub and Genie goes well if you don't hurry up with him I'm gonna go and have him, if you don't hurry up, you know, and just like marched over [I said Charlotte give me a break]
      Les: [have you ever <unclear>]
      Catie: erm … no, no I haven't ever. But anyway she had, he had this nice cap so I said to him, you know, can I have it and he said no it's sentimental
      [and I said well I'll do anything]
      Les: [<unclear>]
      Catie: for it and he said … well, well er basically it just got down to well if you kiss me I'll give it to you …

And this goes on. At the end of the chat, when Judy leaves, Catie reveals that the entire conversation has been recorded.

[6] Catie: I recorded that conversation.
      Les: Did you?
      Catie: Mhm.
      Les: Really?
      Catie: A smile comes off of your face when you realize what we were what you were talking about at the beginning.

Then, there is a break in the recording, and the chat comes to an abrupt end.

Discussing Taboo Habits

The following talk involves Catie, Carla, Judy, and Les. A fifth girl, Kay, leaves the room right at the beginning. Judging by a casual comment on a break in the recording after a few minutes, the girls may have been aware of the recording from the very start. They might even have agreed on the topic beforehand, although there is no indication that this should be the case. Nor does anything in their language reflect that they know that they are being recorded.

   The first issue is smoking and the question of who has the responsibility to see to it that pupils do not smoke: the school or the parents.

[7] Kay: I don't know, it's not the parents' fault.
      Catie: Well I don't know anything about it [but I think you can't be responsible for what your children do.]

Carla: [No but some people think it is.]
Kay: Night.
Catie: Night.
Carla: Cos you don't [actually have that much <unclear>]
Les: [So therefore while he's] at school
Carla: No it's like   [guidance though]
Les: [so they're responsible] for what you're doing, [okay]
Carla: [if the school] didn't say don't smoke a lot more people would.
Catie: What?
Carla: They might.
Catie: If the school didn't say don't smoke?

According to Judy, there is not much either school or parents can do.

[8] Judy: No a lot, a lot of things to do with smoking, drugs and alcohol <nv>laugh</> is to do with your friends and, and who, who you go around with, it's got nothing to do with how much you're taught about it I don't think…. And it's got to do with the individual as well.
     Carla: Peer pressure it's called.
     Judy: What?
     Carla: Peer pressure, people do it cos it's sociable or something don't they?
     Judy: No.
     Catie: No some people do.

As far as the drug problem is concerned, Judy's father appears to have an extremely radical solution.

[9] Judy: My dad was once testing me on my biology and we came up to these films and the subject of drugs and I said just, you know, just as a joke and I thought he would just laugh it off, I said have you done any? And he said yes I've once done LSD and he said if you get the chance do it because you can't go through life, you know … and not do it, you know, it's something that you will do, you'll find that all your friends will when you get older … you know … just don't get addicted.
     Catie: [That's the thing]
     Judy: [And now he's said] that to me I'm not going to ….

Coming back to the school's responsibility, the girls discuss a recent incident when one of the boys was caught taking drugs.

[10] Carla: ... what do you think the school's responsibility is?

      Judy: Exactly what they've done, they saw him and they suspended him.

      Catie: Yeah what c= what more can they do? ...

      Judy: They can't put raiders on, radars on you, they just keep track of what you're doing every day

      Carla: No

      Judy: And do you think that's enough?

      Catie: To suspend [someone]

      Carla: [Yeah.]

      Judy: Mm.

      Catie: Yeah well if he gets caught again he'll be expelled ...

The conclusion, however, is that it is not just a matter of prohibition and being expelled.

[11] Judy: Do you seriously think that if you went to a school and it was like, you know, all cosy, you know, you had dealers and <unclear> weren't allowed to smoke, you weren't allowed to drink and you weren't allowed to take drugs do you seriously think anyone would go there? [<unclear>]

      Catie: [No they wouldn't and they'd all break the rules and it would be the biggest]

      Judy: and it'd be worse.

      Catie: cock up in, you know ... in Britain and it would just be the laughing stock, I mean you can't do that, you can't shelter everybody.

The discussion goes on for another couple of minutes and comes to an end when Judy realizes that she has to make a phone call.

Comparing the two previous sections, we notice at once the difference in "tenor" in the Hallidayan sense (Halliday & Hasan, 1976), which is reflected in the degree of formality as well as the choice of language. As appears, it also affects the speakers' interactional behavior—in terms of turn length and types of move.

INTERACTIONAL STRUCTURE

Each of the conversations will be seen as consisting of one transaction, that is, involving one topic, notably boys and forbidden habits, respectively. In my terminology (Stenström, 1994, following Sinclair & Coulthard, 1975), a transaction consists of one or more exchanges, defined as the smallest interactive units, whereas an exchange is made up of at least two moves by different speakers. The two basic exchange types consist of an Initiating move and a Responding move (IR) and of the Initiating and the Responding move followed by a Follow-up move (IRF).

[12] Catie: I think they should have phone numbers in there.
       Les: Mhm yeah exactly …

[13] Carla: What, can you die on half of one?
       Catie: Yeah. Depends on what's in it.
       Carla: Ooh

The Initiating move in conversation can be a statement, as in [12], or a question, as in [13], whereas the Responding move either replies to the statement or answers the question. Follow-up moves serve as Response "evaluators" in questioning exchanges. IRF exchanges, which typically occur in classroom talk, as demonstrated in Sinclair and Coulthard (1975), occurred only once in each conversation.

As much as 40% of the talk in the chat consisted of exchanges where the Initiating move was a question or of exchanges involving a questioning move later in the exchange, compared to a mere 10% in the first 8 minutes of the discussion, which means that the majority of the exchanges in both were of the statement-reply type.

Simple IR exchanges proved rare in both conversations but less so in the chat than in the discussion. The low number of basic patterns points to numerous irregular exchange patterns, such as when the question is responded to by another question, when the answer to a question is followed by a query, or when the Initiating statement is followed by a request for clarification.

[14] Catie: That's so awful she could've killed you.
       Les: What?
       Catie: She could have killed you.

The frequency of exchanges involving a question turned out to be exactly the same in the two talks, but considering that the discussion is twice as long as the chat, there is, of course, a considerable difference between the two.

Another difference is reflected in the type of statement. In the chat, the statements were mainly of the telling type, whereas the statements in the discussion involved expressing an opinion, suggesting, agreeing, objecting, and the like. In other words, the variety of "discourse acts" was greater in the discussion, and, unlike the chat, the discussion comprised a large portion of disagreement. The following sequence is typical of the chat, in which one questioning exchange follows the other and there is a great deal of laughter.

[15] Catie: **Herb Ross? [You sure? Upper six Leonard?]**
       Les: [Yeah that's right] yeah
       Judy: Herb Ross
       Les: <laughing><unclear> **his number quick</> where does he live?**
                <laugh>
       Catie: <laugh> … Camden

The questions here are pure requests for information. In [16] from the discussion, on the other hand, Catie's first question is a request for clarification, whereas the second questions what Judy just suggested.

16 Judy: If the school didn't say don't smoke a lot more people would.
    Catie: **What?**
    Judy: They might.
    Catie: **If the school didn't say don't smoke?**
    Judy: The c= school didn't, you know there wasn't a rule saying don't smoke and then you get busted and all that.
    Catie: Well exactly, **that's the [whole point!** If you're allowed to s= that's the, **that's the point]**
    Judy: [Yeah I know but if everyone were allow=, if you're allowed to]
    Catie: **That's the point!**
    Judy: Yeah I know if you're allowed to then everyone more people do it.
    Les: No.
    Catie: **Bullocks.** People might do it at first there might be like an epidemic of wow it's so cool we can smoke at school.

In sum, the basic exchange pattern IR(F) turned out to be fairly infrequent in both types of talk due to various irregular exchange patterns, and IR exchanges were less frequent in the discussion than in the chat. Moreover, IR moves were realized differently: Questions and responses dominated in the chat, and statements and replies dominated in the discussion. In addition, whereas the questions in the chat asked for information, they more often asked for clarification or constituted rhetorical questions in the discussion, while the statements in the chat were of the telling type and in the discussion expressed a speaker's opinion.

SPEAKER INTERACTION

Turn-Taking

The well-known observation by Sacks, Schegloss, and Jefferson (1974), with regard to turn-taking, that "overwhelmingly, one party talks at a time" (p. 700), is true for conversation in general and, by and large, also for the teenage conversations studied here. However, a comparison with the adult conversations in the London- Lund Corpus of Spoken English (cf. Svartvik & Quirk, 1980) shows that the teenage conversations are definitely much richer in overlaps and interruptions than those of the adult British English speakers.

The overall amount of overlapping speech is roughly the same in the chat and the discussion, but a closer look shows that the overlaps resulted in interruptions 5 times as often in the discussion as in the chat. This seems to indicate that the girls were so wrapped up in the topic that they forgot even the most basic turn-taking rules, but considering that Catie was responsible for all of the interruptions in the chat and nearly half of the interruptions in the discussion, the reason might simply be that she took her role as a recruit, responsible for the recording, too seriously or, alternatively, that she is one of those persons who simply cannot wait for her turn.

In general, turns are fairly short in both conversations. The exceptionally long turns, covering 10 or more lines in the transcripts, are more frequent in the discussion data and also somewhat longer than those in the chat data.

Interactional Signals

When we speak, we are helped by a set of speech-specific lexical items functioning as "interactional signals" to keep the conversation going (Stenström, 1994, pp. 206–209). They serve as minimal responses (*yes, no, right, OK*), backchannels (*mhm, oh, really*), uptakes (*well, yeah*), appealers (*OK, you know,* question tags), and so on (discourse markers are discussed later in this chapter).[6]

All of these items are multifunctional. For instance, *OK* and *right*, which are not only used as responses and appealers for feedback but also as backchannels providing feedback, and *you know* can serve as "empathizers" involving the listener (Stenström, 1994, pp. 126–128) and sometimes simply as a verbal "filler" (see Brown, 1977).

Judging by the London-Lund Corpus, *OK* and *right* abound in adult British English conversation. Yet, there were remarkably few examples of them in the teenage conversations studied here. This does not mean, of course, that appealers and feedback signals are lacking in teenage speech; it simply means that they are realized by other lexical items than *OK* and *right*, in this case, *yeah* and *you know*.

> [17]   Les: It's like this Bulger thing, **yeah**?
>   Judy: Yeah.

Yeah is an extremely frequent appealer (and empathizer) in some COLT speakers' talk, replacing both *you know* and traditional tag questions consisting of operator+subject plus/minus an enclitic negative particle (*isn't it, is it*). The girls studied here obviously preferred *you know*.

The fact that appealers were more frequent in the discussion shows that this is where speakers are most in need of understanding and support. Yet, backchannels, supporting the current speaker, occurred almost exclusively in the chat. This seems to indicate that, in the discussion, the girls were more interested in presenting their own opinions than in supporting anyone else's ideas, whereas, in the chat, they were very keen on knowing more.

> [18]   Catie: he was a real, real loud, **you know**
>   Judy: **Mm**?
>   Catie: but, yeah, but anyway erm Freddie said that you know he's not going and Herb is going, Herb is apparently really rude about everyone especially when he gets drunk

Judy's *Mm?* can be interpreted as a prompter, encouraging Catie to go on speaking, to tell more. In this case, the backchannel (*Mm?*) is preceded by an appealer (*you know*), which is by no means always the case.

In conversation in general, laughter is a common substitute for lexical backchannels. There is also a lot of laughter with a backchannelling effect in the chat, but the discussion has only three occurrences of laughter altogether in the entire 15 minutes, none of which seems to have a backchannelling function.

The tag *innit*, which is a frequent interactional device, usually an appealer, in a large number of COLT conversations—*They're at home* **innit** (aren't they) and *Should be in all day* **innit** (shouldn't they), did not occur at all in the conversations studied here. (The "invariant tag" *innit* is discussed in detail in Andersen, 2000.)

With regard to turntaking, this section has demonstrated that, although turns were generally fairly short in both conversations, the longest turns were found in the discussion. The fact that overlapping speech was as frequent in the chat as in the discussion but resulted in interruptions more frequently in the discussion is due partly to idiosyncratic behavior (Catie) and partly to conversational characteristics.

As for the use of interactional signals, it was pointed out that although *yeah* and *innit* are preferred as appealers and/or feedback signals by a great number of COLT speakers, *you know* dominated in these two conversations. Interestingly, support in the form of backchannels was much more common in the chat, despite the more frequent appealers for feedback in the discussion. Finally, the relative seriousness of the discussion compared to the chat is reflected in the complete lack of laughter.

SPEECH PROCESSING

Hesitation

Because conversation is produced on the spot, it usually contains a lot of hesitation in the form of silent pauses and filled pauses, verbal fillers (cf. Brown, 1977), repetitions, slips of the tongue, and new starts. These different types of hesitation phenomena tend to cluster, as in [19], from the discussion.

[19] Catie: What? [He thinks what?]
      Les: **[About the smo=]** about smoking.
      Catie: It should be made legal?
      Les: No.
      Catie: It shouldn't be made legal? He thinks the same as you, it should be banned and strictly **sort of ... [I don't]**
      Les: [No no]
          my dad thinks, he said ... he, he just said, he said cos when he was at Wellington he said there was this one boy and he used to go out under a bush *or something* and smoke and smoke and smoke all the time *and stuff* **and he knew and everyone knew** *you see* and he said that's fine, <u>you know</u>, you can go and do *things like that* as long as you don't get caught but **like** ... doing *things like that* in house **and, and** it's like you're ... the ideal for the removes and the younger people in the school, it's like they see all the upper, lower and upper sixth smoking and screwing and they think God **we want to go, we want to go** and try it out, <u>you know</u> cos that's them little sheep.

As appears, there may be more involved than what is usually referred to as markers of hesitation. Not only do we find new starts (*About the smo= about smoking; my dad thinks, he said; and he knew and everyone knew*), a verbal filler in combination with a long pause (*sort of ...*), and repetition (*he said ... he, he just said, he said; we want to go, we want to go*), but we also find vague expressions (*or something, and stuff, things like that*) and appealers (*you know, you see*), which often appear in combination with hesitation markers and add to the impression of hesitant behavior.

There was more hesitation overall in the discussion, which should be seen in relation to the generally longer turns. The most obvious difference was manifested in the occurrence of slips (*th= they smoke*), new starts (*I don't think they're even con= I don't think they're even* concerned), and reformulations (*that's the way that self= erm s= smoking is so selfish*), which were twice as frequent in the discussion as in the chat.

Discourse Markers

In addition to interactional signals, discourse markers help us carry on speaking. *Discourse markers,* which are used to organize and hold the turn and mark boundaries in the discourse, are "message oriented," whereas interactional signals, as we have seen, are "speaker oriented" (Stenström, 1994, pp. 206–209; cf. Schiffrin, 1987, for a somewhat different definition).[7] The difference between interactional signals and discourse markers is illustrated in [20] (which is partly a repetition of [18]).

[20]   Catie: but, **yeah, anyway** erm Freddy said that *you know* he's not going and Herb is going.

Catie's *yeah* is not a response but a step in the turn, indicating something like "enough of that," whereas *anyway* acts as a point of new departure. They both draw attention to the message itself. *You know*, on the other hand, which "involves" the other girls, is typically speaker oriented.

Discourse markers are typically realized by *right, OK, I mean, well, now,* and *anyway*. In these two conversations, discourse markers were exceptionally rare. The frequency was about the same for both, but the distribution was different. In the chat, where it was important to "move the story forward," *anyway, right,* and *well* served as boundary markers and topic resumers, as illustrated in [20]. In the discussion, where it was important to make one's meaning clear, *I mean* and *well* served as monitors (*Huge amounts of people have gone, **I mean** Andy ...*) or to emphasize a point (*Yeah no but **I mean** passive smoking is just ....*).

It is, of course, bewildering that the same lexical items are sometimes found as interactional signals and sometimes as discourse markers. Due to their multifunctionality, what they do depends on context and position in the discourse.

Although discourse markers help us go on speaking, speech processing generally involves a certain amount of hesitation. For obvious reasons, there was more hesitation in the discussion than in the chat, especially in the form of slips of the tongue, new starts, and reformulations. With regard to discourse markers, not only was there a different distribution in the two conversations but they were also used for different purposes: to move the story forward and to make one's point, respectively.

VOCABULARY

It goes without saying that the vocabulary we use is partly dependent on what we are talking about. Therefore, a serious discussion about smoke, drink, and drugs is likely to contain words and expressions that will not be found in a frivolous chat about boys. We do find in both conversations a large proportion of vague language.

Vague Language

Vagueness in language is reflected in the use of words with a generalized meaning or words that are void of meaning and need a contextual referent to be understood. Channell (1994, p. 18) discusses "vague additives" (*around* ten people) and "vague words" (*whatsit, loads of*). Extract [21[illustrates vague language in the chat.

> [21] Catie: … it was a Boss h= you know Boss the, the make the clothes and the perfume **and everything**? He had this really nice cap, and it was a really smart cap, I just really liked it and he was **a bit of** an ugly well he wasn't ugly he was just really gormless and I said erm he must have been **about** twenty **something** and I said to him, can I have your hat, he said no it's from a friend it's sentimental **or something**

Vague words are realized by "set-marking tags" (Dines, 1980) or "general extenders" (Overstreet, 1998), such as *and everything* and *or something*, and vague additives are realized by, for instance, *about* as in [21]. Other vague words and expressions used in the material are *a load of, and all that, things like that, all these things about things,* and *whatever.*

One might have expected that the more casual conversation, the chat, would have the largest proportion of vague expressions. However, vague expressions of the type referred to here occurred twice as often in the discussion as in the chat, often as a substitute for adequate vocabulary.

> [22] Judy: This is such a sexist comment, boys are taught about **all of this stuff** before we are, they've got **a lo= lot** more idea about drugs and **all that lot** than most girls are.

What strikes one when studying these conversations is not only the frequent use of vague words and expressions but also the heavy reliance on three particular lexical items: *just, like,* and *really.* They are definitely overused, and it is often difficult to establish exactly why they appear in the discourse. As demonstrated in [23], from the chat, *just* seems to have lost its original meaning of "only" to a great extent and serves merely as a kind of padding.

> [23] Judy: <nv>laugh</> I did laugh didn't I? I. I w= I was actually laughing my head off.
>
>   Catie: <laughing>Oh no</>
>
>   Judy: It was like a, it was like a sort of, she **just** [went (banging noise)] ?   [<nv>whistle</>]
>   <nv>laugh</nv>

Judy: and just fell over and I just saw this thing [in the corner of my
            eye <unclear>]

Catie: [<nv>laugh</>[

Judy: and she **just** lay there looking up going.

In the discussion, *just* seems to retain its original meaning in most of the cases. Examples are *Just because they're the youngest, cos they just haven't seen any,* and *Passive smoking is just as bad.* Notice that, in these cases, *just* is stressed.

   With regard to *like*, repeated instances tended to occur when the girls got excited, as in [24], from the chat.

[24]   Les: but it wasn't **like** a long thing but **like** … I, the time that I spent
            with him was **like** quite a long time, **like** the evening, whatever,
            so he'd get, and **like** it just used to be constant pauses, it used to
            be terrible and so we used to get off with each **like** you pause
            [for, for what]

       Catie: [And you, did you like] did you … were you attracted to him
            then?

Hedging—avoiding being straightforward for various reasons (Andersson & Trudgill, 1990; Coates, 1998)—is a highly frequent strategy in conversation, typically realized by *sort of* and (less often) *kind of,* in adult British English speech. In this material, *kind of* did not occur at all, and *sort of* was found only once in each conversation. Instead, *like* was used as a substitute for both. This was illustrated in [23], part of which is repeated here for the sake of convenience:

[23a] Les: <u>It was</u> **like** a, <u>it was</u> **like a sort of**, she <u>just</u> [went (banging
            noise)]

       ?:   [<nv>whistle</>]
            <nv>laugh</>

       Les: and <u>just</u> fell over ….

Or, considering the repetition of <u>like</u>, accompanied by "empty" *just*, should *like* simply be referred to as a verbal filler?

   The use of *really* is often easier to interpret. It is generally used as an intensifier.

[25]   Catie: … that was the night she was **really** pissed off because erm
            … people were paying more attention to me than they were
            to her, I don't know why, it's because I decide that I'm
            gonna be **really** outgoing and I **really** do and I was **really**
            loud and **really** boisterous and she's quite resigned like that
            and she thought I sh= bit shagged off with me <sniff> and
            then … like I was doing, there was this **really** good looking
            bloke and he was like … we, we'd given each other eyes
            over the bar in this pub and Lottie goes well if you don't
            hurry up with him I'm gonna go and have him, if you don't
            hurry up, you know, and just like marched over I said Char-
            lotte give me a break

However, in delicate situations, for which there is a need for the speaker to protect her face, it can be argued that it has the opposite function, namely as a hedge "to soften the force of what is said" (Coates, 1998, p. 164), as in [26].

[26] Judy: … I once got off with someone for some cigarettes. never felt so awful.

Catie: I got off with someone for his hat. He had this wicked in Geneva had this [amazing Boss hat]

Judy: [No he was **really**] he was **really** nice and I did actually [like him]

Catie: [and I] snogged him for it. And he goes to me, it was a Boss h= you know Boss the, the make the clothes and the perfume and everything? He had this **really** nice cap, and it was a **really** smart cap, I just really liked it and he was a bit of an ugly well he wasn't ugly he was just **really** gormless and I said erm he must have been about twenty something and I said to him, can I have your hat, he said no it's from a friend it's sentimental or something

The function of *really* as intensifier/hedge is dealt with in detail in Stenström (2002).

Just, like, and *really* were all more frequent in the chat. *Like* and *really* occurred more than twice as often and *just* somewhat less than twice as often in the chat as in the discussion.

Lexical Density

It will have become pretty obvious at this point that the teenage conversations discussed in this article are not exactly linguistically sophisticated, at least not if, by linguistic sophistication, we mean language that is lexically rich and varied.

The fact is that, when we speak, we use more grammatical than lexical words. The relative proportion of lexical words compared to grammatical words in written and spoken language has been discussed by Halliday (1989) under the heading "lexical density." Spoken language, Halliday says, is lexically sparse, as opposed to written language, which is lexically dense, the reason being that the nominalizations that are typical of written language are replaced by verb constructions in spoken language (see also Chafe & Danielewitz, 1987; Horowitz & Samuels, 1987).

A narrative passage chosen at random from the London-Lund Corpus (Text S2.7) showed that the adult speaker used fewer than 3 times as many grammatical words as lexical words, whereas the teenagers in this material used more than 3 times as many grammatical words as lexical words altogether. However, they used relatively more lexical words in the discussion than in the chat. (Notice that, in this calculation, interactional signals, discourse markers, and vague words were not regarded as lexical words.)

It appeared that only the discussion contained a fair number of words and expressions related to the topic, such as *get addicted, get busted, get high, get slaughtered, make legal, peer pressure, drug busting,* and *dealing.* The vocabulary in the chat is far more general, with very few topic-related expressions, such as *good-looking, get off with, kiss, snog,* and *sleep.*

Moreover, the discussion proved much richer in collocations and set expressions, such as *part of the fun is, find out the hard way, do you seriously think,* and *it was the last straw.*

The proportion of vague language differs depending on the speaking situation. In a chat, we do not have to, or are not expected to, be precise; when we take part in a discussion, on the other hand, where precision is a requirement, we often use vague words for lack of better terms. The fact that a discussion is more demanding than a chat is not only reflected in the greater amount of hesitation but also in the more frequent use of vague language. Yet, the lexical density was relatively higher in the discussion than in the chat, as it contained quite a large number of topic-related words and expressions.

GRAMMAR

Sentence Complexity

As most of the preceding examples have shown, the grammar of speech is far less "regular" than the grammar of writing. Halliday (1989) refers to the grammatical complexity of speech as "dynamic and intricate" as opposed to that of writing, which is "dense and static."

One might have expected the language of the teenage discussion to be somewhat more like writing than that of the chat and consequently somewhat less intricate. One way of measuring grammatical intricacy is to consider the amount of hesitation (including pauses, slips, repetitions, and new starts) and vague language (including vague words and expressions as well as the repeated use of *just, like,* and *really*). The fact that there was, indeed, more hesitation and more vagueness in the discussion points to a higher degree of grammatical intricacy in the discussion than in the chat, however.

We speak in clauses rather than sentences. Spoken "sentences" generally consist of a single clause or two or more coordinated clauses. Coordination dominated in both types of conversation, which is reflected in the high proportion of coordinating conjunctions, amounting to 65% in both.

And was by far the most common coordinator in the chat (6 times as frequent as *but*). Another common connector was *so.*

[27] Catie: .... I didn't love him **and** right *so, so* if I kissed him **and** met him the next day ... would I, would I snog, would, would he, he'd give me the hat *so* I said yeah sure, you know, whatever, *so* he goes okay **and** he like prepared himself and goes no I can't do it in here ... <nv>laugh</> <laughing> **and** *so* I had to go outside with him, snog him, got his hat **and** pissed off, never saw him again</>

But dominated in the discussion.

[28] Catie: [No **but** Carla, that's stupid.]
       Judy: [**But** everyone is, you've got an opinion] and you're gonna stick to it but everyone is totally different and everyone's got a, totally different view [on things]

Carla: [yeah **but** sometimes they [don't because]
Catie: [No **but**] Carla
          that's ridiculous ....

The repertoire of connectors as a whole was somewhat more varied in the discussion, where the most frequent connectors *and, but, cos,* and *so* were supplemented with subordinators such as *as long as* and *whether.*

Interestingly, *because* and *cos* had the same distribution in the discussion, whereas the reduced form *cos* was twice as frequent as the full form *because* in the chat. This was not entirely unexpected, however, considering the specific pragmatic function of *cos* in casual conversation, as a "take-off for further talk" (see Stenström, 1998), as exemplified in [29].

[29] Catie: .... if there's e= if there's ever like a pregnant pause then he's the one that like keeps it all going [<unclear>]
        Les: [<shouting>Really</>]
        Catie: Yeah.
        Les: **Cos** Freddy was the one that used to keep the <laughing> conversation</>

Because, by contrast, typically introduces a subordinate clause of reason.

[30] Catie: ... smoking is so selfish **because** you can't get away ...

Sentences involving clause subordination, complex clauses, were more common in the discussion than in the chat. Sentences involving embedded nonfinite clauses did not occur at all in the chat but added to the complexity of the sentences in the discussion (e.g., *I don't live my life looking up to other people, setting my life on the example of others*).

Noun Phrase Structure

Complex noun phrases were also more frequent in the discussion, that is, noun phrases involving both pre- and postmodification (e.g., *the younger people in the school; a lot more idea about drugs*); one in three was of this type, compared to one in ten in the chat. Noun phrases with an embedded clause did not occur at all in the chat, that is, noun phrases such as *all these things about things they don't really know much about*, where the postmodification consists of a prepositional phrase with the complement (*things*) postmodified by a relative clause with a zero relative.

The noun phrases in the chat were simpler. Four out of five were premodified, generally only by a determiner and an adjective (e.g., *a little business, this nice cap, this amazing Boss hat*). The same type of premodification occurred in the discussion, but not as often. Postmodification alone was the least common type in both conversations (e.g., *people outside school; rule for bringing up your child*).

In summary, the discussion proved to be more grammatically intricate (high degree of hesitation and vagueness) and more grammatically complex (finite and nonfinite subordination, complex noun phrases) than the chat. There was more coordination than subordination in both conversations, with *and* as the typical coordinator (which dominated in the chat) followed by *but* (which dominated in the discussion). The form *because* was typically used in the discussion, introducing a clause of reason, whereas the reduced form *cos* was typically used in the chat as a "take-off" signal.

CONCLUSION

This analysis of two pieces of talk produced on different topics by the same speakers has shown how spoken discourse executes changes depending on what is being talked about.

Typically, a chat is characterized by a congenial atmosphere where the participants agree with and support each other, whereas a discussion is characterized by differences of opinion, reflected in objections, queries, and statements of opinion. This difference is reflected in some of the features that were found to characterize the two pieces of talk.[8]

With regard to speaker interaction, for instance, the girls interrupted each other much more often in the discussion than in the chat, even though the amount of overlapping speech was the same. Moreover, the girl who held the turn appealed to the others for support much more frequently in the discussion. However, support in the form of backchannels, encouraging the current speaker to go on, was mainly given in the chat, and the frequent bursts of laughter in the chat were not repeated in the discussion. This shows that agreement and cooperation, which were dominant features in the chat (cf. Eckert, 1993), were less prominent in the discussion.

With respect to speech processing, the longer turns in the discussion gave rise to more hesitation in the form of pauses and fillers, slips, repetitions, new starts, and reformulations. Unfamiliarity with the right terminology was probably the reason for much of the vague language in the discussion. Although the use of discourse markers was restricted, it is interesting to notice the different distribution, which resulted in "move on" markers in the chat and monitoring and emphasizing markers in the discussion.

The chat turned out to have less densely packed vocabulary than did the discussion. The use of tags and set markers and the overuse of *just, like,* and *really* in the chat obviously contributed to the result. The topic in the discussion gave rise to a fairly specialized vocabulary, whereas the topic in the chat did not.

Finally, the grammar in the two conversations was similar in that clause coordination dominated in both. What distinguished them, however, was that the main coordinator in the chat was *and,* and the main coordinator in the discussion was *but.* As expected, the discussion turned out to be more complex in terms of clause subordination and complex noun phrases—noun phrases that were both pre- and postmodified. On the other hand, the lavish use of hesitation and vagueness devices also made the discussion more grammatically intricate.

The findings reported in this chapter, which are based on natural conversation, besides being a contribution to teenage language research in general and to sociolinguistics and stylistics, are directly applicable to language teaching and learning. McCarthy's *Discourse Analysis for Language Teachers* (1991) emphasizes the importance of studying genuine recordings to compensate for the lack of authentic dialogue in teaching materials. By using raw data, McCarthy argues, teachers should make students aware of what is typical of natural conversation as well as what features distinguish different types of talk. This is exactly what the findings reported in this chapter could be used for.

Finally, one intriguing question that arises is to what extent the results of this study match other studies of teenage talk. British English teenage talk—like teenage talk in general—has been comparatively little researched. Some notable exceptions include Cheshire (1982), Horowitz (1994), Sebba (1993), and Rampton (1995), but none of these studies reports on the types of data that have been discussed in the present study.[9] Hopefully, the availability of large corpora will soon make it possible for interested researchers to undertake large-scale studies of teenage talk to compensate for the present shortage.

KEY TO SYMBOLS

,	brief pause and/or end of clause
.	"regular" pause and/or end of sentence
...	long pause
....	speech precedes or follows
=	incomplete word
[ ]	overlapping speech
<cough>	nonverbal information
<nv>laugh</>	nonverbal beginning and end
<unclear>	one or more words left out

NOTES

1. For a description of the corpus, see Stenström, Andersen, and Hasund (2002).
2. With regard to the difference in general between teenage and adult language, Haslerud and Stenström (1994) found that "It is not just a matter of vocabulary, pronunciation, grammar and choice of topics but, perhaps first and foremost, overall interactive behaviour" (p. 64).
3. For a general description of discourse patterns in speech, see Aijmer and Stenström (2004).
4. The transcription was done by the Longman Group, London.
5. "Removes" are pupils who are put in a special class "before they are ready to go into the next higher one" (cf. *Longman Dictionary of Contemporary English*, 1987, p. 880).
6. The role of interactional signals and discourse markers, referred to as "pragmatic markers," is discussed in detail in Stenström (2004).
7. More about discourse markers and pragmatic particles in Fraser (1990) and Brinton (1996).
8. For more on female conversational style, see Holmes (1998).
9. The way gender identity is reflected in teenage talk is discussed in Stenström (2003).

REFERENCES

Aijmer, K., & Stenström, A.-B. (Eds.). (2004). *Discourse patterns in spoken and written corpora.* Amsterdam: Benjamins.

Aksis. (2001, September). Retrieved June 15, 2006, from Unifob AS, The Department of Culture, Language, and Information Technology Web site. http://www.aksis.uib.no/

Andersen, G. (1995). Omission of the primary verbs BE and HAVE in London teenage speech—A sociolinguistic study. Unpublished master's thesis, University of Bergen, Norway.

Andersen, G. (1998). The pragmatic marker *like* from a relevance-theoretic perspective. In A. Jucker Benjamins & Y. Ziv (Eds.), *Discourse markers: Descriptions and theory* (pp. 147–170). Amsterdam: John Benjamins.

Andersen, G. (2000). *Pragmatic markers and sociolinguistic variation. A relevance-theoretic approach to the language of adolescents.* Amsterdam: Rodopi.

Andersson, A., & Trudgill, P. (1990). *Bad language.* Oxford: Blackwell.

Auburn University, Office of Information Technology. (2006). *Office of Information Technology (OIT) Online Support Glossary.* Retrieved June 15, 2006, from the Auburn University Web site: http://www.auburn.edu/oit/glossary.php

Berland, U. (1997). Invariant tags: pragmatic functions of *innit, okay, right and yeah* in London teenage conversations. Unpublished master's thesis, University of Bergen, Norway.

Brinton, L. (1996). *Pragmatic markers in English. Grammaticalization and discourse functions.* Berlin: Mouton de Gruyter.

Brown, G. (1977). *Listening to spoken English.* London: Longman.

Brown, G., & Yule, G. (1983). Topic and the representation of discourse content. In G. Brown & G. Yule (Eds.), *Discourse analysis* (pp. 68–124). Cambridge: Cambridge University Press.

Bynes, A. (1998). Swearing in COLT: A corpus-based study of expletive use among London teenagers. Unpublished master's thesis, University of Bergen, Norway.

Chafe, W., & Danielewicz, J. (1987). Properties of spoken and written language. In R. Horowitz & S. J. Samuels (Eds.), *Comprehending oral and written language* (pp. 83–11). London: Academic Press.

Channell, J. (1994). *Vague language.* Oxford: Oxford University Press.

Cheshire, J. (1982). *Variation in an English dialect.* Cambridge: Cambridge University Press.

Clark, H. (1996). *Using language.* Cambridge: Cambridge University Press.

Coates, J. (1998). *Women talk.* Oxford: Blackwell.

Collins Cobuild English Language Dictionary. (1987). London: Collins.

Dines, E. (1980). Variation in discourse—and "stuff like that." *Language in Society 9,* 13–31.

Eckert, P. (1993). Cooperative competition in adolescent "girl talk." In D. Tannen (Ed.), *Gender and conversational interaction* (pp. 32–61). Oxford: Oxford University Press.

Fraser, B. (1990). An approach to discourse markers. *Journal of Pragmatics, 14,* 383–395.

Halliday, M. A. K. (1989). *Spoken and written language.* Oxford: Oxford University Press.

Halliday, M. A. K., & Hasan, R. (1976). *Cohesion in English.* London: Longman.

Haslerud, V., & Stenström, A.-B. (1994). COLT: Mark-up and trends. *HERMES, 13,* 55–70.

Hasund, I. K. (1996). COLT conflicts: Reflections of gender and class in the oppositional turn sequences of London teenage girls. Unpublished master's thesis, University of Bergen, Norway.

Holmes, J. (1998). Women's talk: The question of sociolinguistic universals. In J. Coates (Ed.), *Language and gender: A reader* (pp. 461–483). Oxford: Blackwell.

Horowitz, R. (1994). Adolescent beliefs about oral and written language. In R. Garner & P. Alexander (Eds.), *Beliefs about text and instruction with text* (pp. 1–24). Hillsdale, NJ: Lawrence Erlbaum Associates.

Horowitz, R., & Samuels, S. J. (Eds.). (1987). *Comprehending oral and written language* (pp. 83–113). London: Academic Press.

Maynard, D. W. (1980). Placement of topic changes in conversation. *Semiotica, 30,* 263–290.

McCarthy, M. (1991). *Discourse analysis for language teachers.* Cambridge, England: Cambridge University Press.

Monstad, H.-M. (1998). The grammaticalization of *sort of* and *kind of* in young and old Londoners' speech. Unpublished master's thesis, University of Bergen, Norway.

New Oxford Dictionary of English. (1998). Oxford: Clarendon Press.

Overstreet, M. (1998). The form and function of general extenders in English interactive discourse. Unpublished doctoral dissertation, University of Hawaii, Honolulu, HI.

Rampton, B. (1995). *Crossing. Language and ethnicity among adolescents*. London: Longman.

Sacks, H., Schegloff, E., & Jefferson, G. (1974). A simplest systematics for the organisation of turn-taking in conversation. *Language, 50*(4), 696–735.

Schank, R. C. (1977). Rules and topics in conversation. *Cognitive Science, 1,* 421–442.

Schiffrin, D. (1987). *Discourse markers*. Cambridge: Cambridge University Press.

Sebba, M. (1993). *London Jamaican*. London: Longman.

Sinclair, J., & Coulthard, M. (1975). *Towards an analysis of discourse: the English used by teachers and pupils*. Oxford: Oxford University Press.

Stenström, A.-B. (1990). Pauses in monologue and dialogue. In J. Svartvik (Ed.), *The London-Lund Corpus of Spoken English. Description and research* (pp. 253–266). Lund, Sweden: Lund University Press.

Stenström, A.-B. (1994). *An introduction to spoken interaction*. London: Longman.

Stenström, A.-B. (1995). Taboos in teenage talk. In G. Melchers & B. Warren (Eds.), *Studies in Anglistics* (pp. 71–80). Stockholm: Almqvist & Wiksell International.

Stenström, A.-B. (1997). *Can I have a chips please?—Just tell me what one you want:* Nonstandard grammatical features in London teenage talk. In J. Aarts, I. de Mönnink, & H. Wekker (Eds.), *Studies in English language learning* (pp. 141–151). Amsterdam: Rodopi.

Stenström, A.-B. (1998). From sentence to discourse: *Cos (because)* in teenage talk. In A. Jucker & Y. Ziv (Eds.), *Discourse markers* (pp. 127–146). Amsterdam: Benjamins.

Stenström, A.-B. (2000). *It's enough funny man*: Intensifiers in teenage talk. In J. Kirk (Ed.), *Corpora galore* (pp. 177–190). Amsterdam: Rodopi.

Stenström, A.-B. (2002). Taking another look at *really*. In S. Scholz, M. Klages, E. Hantson, & U. Römer (Eds.), *Language: Context and cognition. Papers in honour of Wolf-Dietrich Bald's 60th birthday* (pp. 301–308). München, Germany: Langenscheidt-Longman.

Stenström, A.-B. (2003). *It's not that I really care about him personally you know*: The construction of gender identity in London teenage talk. In J. Androutsopoulos & A. Georgakopoulou (Eds.), *Discourse constructions of youth identities* (pp. 93–117). Amsterdam: Benjamins.

Stenström, A.-B. (2004). What is going on between speakers. In A. Partington, J. Morley, & L. Haarman (Eds.), *Corpora and discourse* (pp. 259–283). Bern, Switzerland: Peter Lang.

Stenström, A.-B., Andersen, G., & Hasund, I. K. (2002). *Trends in teenage talk: Corpus compilation, analysis and findings*. Amsterdam: Benjamins.

Svartvik, J., & Quirk, R. (1980). *The London-Lund Corpus of Spoken English*. Lund, Sweden: Lund University Press.

CHAPTER 5

Dinner Talk: Gaining Cultural Membership in Modern Literate Societies

Shoshana Blum-Kulka

Children's modes of participation in cultural systems of practice vary with the degree of their embeddedness in the everyday life of adults. In traditional societies, children were (or are not) segregated from the work and social life of adults, and thus they learn to become members of their culture through nonverbal fostering of observation and engagement. In modern middle-class families, the emphasis shifts to interpersonal communication. Daily routines separate adults from children for most of the day, and dinnertime becomes one of the few opportunities for intergenerational gathering. This chapter analyzes the ways in which children's participation in the culturally structured activity of dinner, with the guidance, support, and challenge of adult companions, serves the development of discourse competencies related to membership in literate cultures.

Modern cultural practices foreground the primacy of talk as an agent of socialization. Talk serves as the major means for "guided participation" (Rogoff, 1990); development evolves through an emphasis on verbal, rather than nonverbal forms of mediation. In this essentially Vygotskyian approach to development, child development evolves through a child's active participation in culturally structured activities, with the guidance, support, and challenge of older companions. This theoretical perspective is particularly illuminating in interpreting the role of dinner talk for pragmatic socialization.

Our study of dinner talk in 34 Israeli and Jewish-American, middle-class families (Blum-Kulka, 1997)[1] revealed that in modern, middle-class families, dinners are an intergenerational, language-rich activity in which both the direct and indirect participation of children in family discourse serves as a primary mode of mediation in their developmental passage to the adult discourse world. The shared, "modern" principles of this process are apparent both with respect to the primary role of talk in socialization for pragmatic competencies and in the availability of parental facilitation for cognitive development along the lines of modern, analytic, and scientific ways of thinking.

DINNERTIME

Family dinnertime, in the families studied, is a communicative event bounded in time and space, delimited in its participants and—as will be shown—governed by its own rules of interaction. It occupies a particular place between mundane, day-to-day, "backstage" (Goffman, 1967) informal encounters and formal public events. There is an important element of replicability in these dinners: Provided the family regularly has dinner (or another meal) together, (with all the cultural, social, and individual variation in this domain), then it can be expected that these dinners will have certain features in common.

Family dinners are familial we events shared with children; as such, they may carry important *intentional* socialization functions, ranging from table manners to socialization for family values. But it is important to stress that, to varying degrees, children are also *ratified participants* (Goffman, 1981) in many layers of talk at dinner not specifically focused on their participation. Dinners, like ordinary conversation, allow members to enjoy conversation for social enjoyment only, with no visible outcome; such sociable talk also serves important socialization functions.

The nature of the activity affects certain layers of the talk. At all dinners, food has to be brought to the table and accessed by the participants. This activity, in turn, generates minimally the instrumental business talk of having dinner. The instrumental layer of dinner talk is replicated at all dinners, but it is also superimposed by other, more open-ended, conversational layers of talk. However, even when no guests are present, the presence of children may set certain criteria for what is doable and what is mentionable at dinner. In the families we recorded, almost no mention was made of three topics: money, sex, and politics. These unmentionables thus appear as a covert formal rule for topic selection; this rule is shared by all families, regardless of cultural background, though the interpretations attached to these avoidance practices may still vary by culture. Perceptions of formality for family dinners may, and do, vary overtly by culture; one of the interesting findings that emerged from comparing Israeli and Jewish-American dinners relates to this dimension. As witnessed by spatial arrangements, physical proximity at the dinner table, the presence or absence of tablecloth on the table, and especially in the mutual relationships developed with the observer from the research team, Jewish-American families enacted dinners in a comparatively more formal manner than Israeli families, and this difference, in turn, affected many dimensions of the talk.

When mealtime is shared physically and conversationally with children, it serves as a critical social context in which children become socialized to local cultural rules regulating conversation, such as the choice of topics, rules of turn-taking, modes of storytelling, and rules of politeness. Our study (Blum-Kulka, 1997) corroborates and expands previous findings that such cultural rules may be quite distinct, creating culturally defined discourse environments for all members present.[2] Yet all the dinner conversations analyzed in the study share a wide range of discourse practices we attribute to the quintessential modernity of these families. Differing from former generations and from other communities in the same countries, these urban, secular, middle-class families are modern in the way this concept was interpreted in the framework of Jewish history in the past century. Common to all is a physical and ideological distancing from the traditional Eastern European Jewish world historically shared by all. Among its many manifestations, this distancing finds its expression in current beliefs and practices of socialization for pragmatic competencies. Parents express such beliefs in the ways in which they describe, during interviews, the difference between their and their parents' parenting styles, and the manifestation of actual practices of socialization emerge from considering the dynamics of dinner talk in these families.

Asked during the interviews whether their parenting styles differ from those of their own parents, the adults in our study repeatedly mentioned discipline, children's status in the family, involvement, and talk. As the following extracts show, the topics are interwoven by their shared emphasis on socialization through interpersonal communication.

> We are more liberal with our children ... My parents just laid down the law and "pulled rank." No arguing or discussing. We are *more attentive and sharing* with our children. (American-Israeli family 8, Mother)

> I don't think we're the disciplinarians our parents were. I mean it was very black and white discipline with my father. We try to be more rational. And I'm much *more involved* than my parents. We try to do things together. (American-Israeli family 3, Father)

> I think [the children] are more coequal members of the family than I certainly was. I listen more. We will tend to *explain things longer* than my parents would to me as a kid. (Jewish-American family 4, Mother)

> The gap between me and my children is much smaller than between me and my parents. In all areas, there is much more *openness*. (Israeli family 5, Mother) [emphases added].

All the topics mentioned have their correlates in discourse practices, though the underlying messages do not always correspond in a simple manner to declared parenting ideologies. The comments seem to fall into three clusters of interwoven themes: an overall ethos of child-centeredness, expressed in terms like *involvement, attentiveness, sharing,* and *listening;* an egalitarian attitude to socialization that stresses the diminishing of intergenerational gaps; and finally the importance of language for socialization (children are co-equals, there is more openness, children get things explained to them and are encouraged to argue and discuss, parents are more rational).

The families manifest the hallmarks of child-centeredness that characterize white, middle-class, mainstream American families, differing from societies like the Kaluli or Samoan (e.g., Ochs & Schieffelin, 1984). A basic tenet of child-centeredness is the need for adult accommodation: The child is perceived as an incompetent member of society who has to have the situation adapted to his or her needs. The family dinner conversations we studied demonstrate how, through guided participation in multiparty, intergenerational talk, adults ease the passage of preschool and school-age children into adult discourse worlds, helping them to acquire the pragmatic skills needed to become communicatively fully competent.

At dinner, the most obvious expression of adaptation to children's needs is seen in the attention paid to the food needs of children of all ages. Parents take into account children's wishes and preferences, attribute intentionality to the utterances of even very young children, and thereby show respect for their personhood as autonomous beings. Parents' being more involved with and listening to their children more than their own parents listened to them as children is manifest in their tendency to grant center stage to children's topics at dinner and in the modes of facilitation through which adults help children participate and gain the skills needed for full and equal participation. As we shall see, adult-child co-constructed discourse sequences exemplify modes of easing children's passage to adult discourse worlds. But parental questions and responses to child contributions also set the criteria for norms of conversational coherence—exercising an indirect form of control—helping children acquire those norms and advance their skills as conversationalists and as capable of constructing extended stretches of discourse.

The status of children as coequals can be seen in the participatory roles of children at dinner conversations. Children of all ages are granted participatory rights as *ratified conversational partners:* They initiate topics of their own interest and are included in discussions of topics of general interest. Though discourse space in these families is undoubtedly more equally distributed than in traditional families within the same communities (see, e.g., Stahl, 1993, for descriptions of father-dominated Friday meals in traditional Sephardic families in Israel), in many ways adults still retain control. The topical agenda for the dinner conversation remains mostly adult dominated. Parents may occasionally delegitimize a child's topic and may sometimes frame the child as a side participant.

A central theme mentioned by parents is rationality. As a guiding principle, rationality penetrates several genres of family discourse. Rationality needs to be seen in the wider context of parental facilitation of cognitive development along the lines of modern analytic, scientific ways of thinking. This occurs as a by-product of several genres of talk, not necessarily of talk identifiable as explanatory or scientific. The emphasis on the need for rational explanations goes beyond reasons and justifications that accompany many requests; we also find it in the language of explanation and definitions provided in response to children's questions, where it is expected, and, most prominently, in the types of parental questions that guide parent-child co-construction of narratives.

Thus from the children's point of view, there is much to gain from talking to adults at dinner. My focus here is on the ways dinner conversations in these families promote discourse socialization along the lines of the decontextualized discourse worlds associated with Western literate traditions.

"I Never Talk. I Want to Talk": Why Participate?

The comment "I never talk. I want to talk," made by 5-year-old Joshua at dinner, hints at the meaning of talk as the symbolic representation of participatory rights in democratic societies. The comment expresses the child's subjective sense of frustration for "never" talking; namely, for not having a fair share, in his view, in the family discourse sphere constructed at dinners. Simultaneously, it serves as a bid for power: His declaration of intent "I want to talk" is his way of demanding entry into the family's discursive space, of gaining power by the right to talk.

The themes of talk as participation and talk as power are main concerns in Habermas's (1984, 1987) discussion of the public sphere. The public sphere in

Habermas's (1984) formulation is that realm of social life in which "something approaching public opinion can be formed" (p. 49). It is an essential component of democratic societies, representing a space where private individuals discuss public matters, a space that mediates between society and the state. In the ideal model of the public sphere, access is guaranteed to all citizens, and public opinions are formed through rational-critical discourse. For Habermas, families represent the private, rather than the public, domain of modern social life. Yet examination of family discourse shows that dinner talk in modern Western families plays an important role in giving children a voice in ways that can eventually prepare them for participation in the public discourse of literate democratic societies. Two interwoven facets of children's participation in dinner talk illustrate this point: (a) modes of parental facilitation in helping children gain access to talking space in different thematic frames at dinner and (b) modes of parental scaffolding in helping children hold the floor and construct extended stretches of discourse.

Gaining Access to the Floor: Developing Autonomy in Speaking Rights in Different Thematic Frames

One of the built-in paradoxes of dinner talk is that on the one hand, talk with children at dinner serves to enhance the status of children as children, indexing the power imbalance between them and the adults. On the other hand, the same talk serves to mediate between the two worlds of discourse, inviting and encouraging children to develop the discursive skills needed for participation in the adult world. To understand this paradox, we need to consider the various sources of parental power at dinner.

Family dinners represent unequal encounters between adults and children. Even in modern societies, parents and children are bound in an asymmetrical power relation (Queen, Habenstein, & Quadagno, 1985). This given structural asymmetry between parents and children is reconstructed in dinner talk in a variety of ways, including the language of control, metapragmatic comments on children's discourse, amount of talk, and topical control. Children's quantitative level of participation in the talk illustrates this point.

For example, in both Israeli and Jewish-American families, adults take up a significantly larger proportion of talking space than do children: In the Jewish-American families, children's participation reaches 38%, whereas in the two Israeli groups, it ranges from 22% to 34% of all on-topic talk. The mean number of utterances for an Israeli child is only 27, whereas for an American-Israeli child it rises to 34, and reaches 48 for the Jewish-American child. (Blum-Kulka, 1997).

Though adults remain basically in control of the talk, the discourse also manifests the egalitarian attitude to socialization expressed in the interviews. The quintessential expression of the egalitarian ideology is through the treatment of children at dinner as *ratified participants*. Being a ratified participant at any speech event carries with it rights of participation through talking, as well as participation through listening. The following example illustrates the degree of confidence young children may have in their participatory rights. With no preliminaries, Sandra, at some point in the middle of the dinner, turns to her mother and asks a question.

(1). Jewish-Americans 4; Jordan (8m); Sandra (4f).[3]
Sandra's initiation takes place half an hour into the dinner.
> 1 Sandra: Mommy to who will I tell how my day goes?
   2 Mother: Okay, let's hear your day.
   3 Sandra: Well # I xxx played puzzles xxx I made xxx
   [continued]

Sandra's question shows that she is already aware of her rights for taking part in the talk by displaying her day and, at this point, offers "her day" as a gift to be received. It is the duty of her family to appoint a receiver, and indeed, her mother acknowledges the gift, accepting it on behalf of all present ("Okay, let's hear your day"). Children thus have the right of self-nomination, and it is the obligation of recipients to display positive acceptance—not only yielding the floor for the speaker but also paying homage to the specific offering made. Children at the dinners we observed not only raised their own topics and participated in topics raised by adults but also sometimes listened to adult discussions and stories as a passive audience. Thus structural asymmetry is compensated for (at least partially) by the overall framing of dinners as a "we" event, where children have built-in participatory rights

A further asymmetry stems from the gap in pragmatic competencies. Young children are at an obvious disadvantage in an intergenerational gathering not specifically tailored to their needs. They may not be cognitively able to follow the topical development of the talk around them; even if they do, they still may lack the conversational skills needed for entering an ongoing conversation and engaging in orderly turn-taking. The gap in pragmatic competencies is compensated for in a rich array of scaffolding strategies that help Children Bridge the gap between the two discourse worlds. Modes of topic initiation by and with children illustrate these points.

Self-Nomination

To gain entry to the floor, initiating a new topic, the child needs to work conversationally harder than an adult. Whereas an adult can announce a new topic without naming the recipients (Father: "I had lunch with Miriam today"), a young child's entry into the conversation is typically explicitly targeted to specific recipients.

(2). Jewish-Americans 4; Jordan (8m); Sandra (4f).
   1 Jordan: Mommy you know what?
   2 Mother: Yes dear.
   3 Jordan: As um Snappy Smurf would say "I wish we didn't have to eat the vegetables." I just wish [/] I just wish we could et the little good things inside them.
   [continued]

The mother's response shows fine-tuning to the child's conversational needs. Instead of responding to the question literally, she interprets Jordan's move as a bid for a turn and responds by granting him the right to speak on the topic of his choice. This is not the response that would normally be given in adult-adult communication (to an adult, one would probably insert "what?" in this slot), but rather a clear indication to the child that his wish to take the floor has been understood and accepted. Subsequently, Jordan uses the speaking opportunity granted fully, expressing a wish to be excused from eating vegetables.

In the Jewish-American families, child topic initiation is often accompanied by reflexive attention to turn-taking rules. American children treat discourse space in the family as a public sphere where access needs to be guaranteed to all in a fair and equal manner and hence frequently engage in negotiations over floor space.

> (3). Jewish-Americans 2; Marvin (8m), Daniel (6m), Tina (4f).
>   [comments related to turn-taking are in italics]
> > 1 Marvin: Can I say something? Is it my turn?
> > 2 Mother: I don't know.
> > 3 Daniel: No! You have to wait until I finish!
> > 4 Marvin: (whining) You had a long turn, so there.
> > 5 Daniel: You had a longer one!
> > 6 Marvin: No, I didn't.
> > 7 Daniel: Yes, you did.
> > 8 Father: Daniel, are you finished saying what you were saying?
> >   9 Daniel: I am in the Polliwogs, but you know how high Adam is?
> >   [continued]

There is no corollary to the high level of meta-talk on turn-taking in the Israeli families. In gaining access to the floor, Israeli children tend to focus their attention on targeting an audience, using a preliminary move, as in (4), or launch into the narrative directly following the targeting, as in (5).

> (4). Israelis 2; Shlomit (12f); Riki (10f); Mira (5f).
> > 1 Mira: tishmeu mashehu   Listen to something.
> >   [15 turns omitted, while Mira gets no response]
> > 2 Mira: ima, ima.   Mommy, mommy.
> >   3 Mother: ma?   What?
> > 4 Mira: tishmeu bdixa.   Listen to a joke.
> >   5 Mother: nishma.   Let's hear it.

> (5). Israelis 6; Iris (6f); Lilax (6f).
> > 1 Iris: aba, ata yodea, halaxnu   Daddy, you know, we went
> >   la-giv'a ha-zot hayom   to that hill today.
> >   2 Father: eze? al yad malon holiland? Which one? The one near
> >   Holyland Hotel?

Elicitation

A second way for children to gain access to the floor is by responding to adult initiation. From the children's point of view, this may be problematic because both choice of speaker and topic are adult controlled, and the child may be held accountable for various aspects of his or her contribution. Adult efforts to give children a voice are particularly striking in cases where the child seems to resist the attempt to involve him or her in a dialogic exchange.

(6). Israelis 10; Daffi (12f); Noga (8f); Yaron (4m).

1 Mother:	Yaron, tesaper lanu ma	Yaron, tell us what you did in
	asita ha-yom ba-gan.	nursery school today.
2 Daffi:	ma, ex haya ba-gan?	What, how was school?
3 Yaron:	naim. Nice.	
> 4 Mother:	naim? ma haya naim?	Nice? What was nice?
	tesapper lanu ex haya naim.	

Tell us how was it nice.

5 Yaron:	sixaknu. We played.	
> 6 Mother:	be-ma sixaktem?	What did you play?
7 Yaron:	be-misxakim.	Games.
> 8 Mother:	eze? ba-xuc? ba-xacer?	What kind? Outside? In the yard?
[continued]		

Though the child's responses are minimal, the mother makes every effort to incorporate his responses as the basis for her clarification or expansion questions, framing the exchange as basically dialogic despite its inquisitive tone.

Elicitation can also serve as a form of participation-structure control. Adults at dinner frequently exercise nomination rights, using targeting as a subtle means for changing the participation structure, as, for instance, in shifting the speaking rights from one child to another.

(7). Jewish-Americans 4; Jordan (8m); Sandra (4f).

The question is raised after Jordan has given a lengthy account of a soccer game and Sandra has reported on her day.

> 1 Father:	So, are you done telling us about your day?
2 Sandra:	Yes.
> 3 Father:	Jordan, would you like to tell us something? Other than soccer, what happened today?
4 Jordan:	Well, we had a mean xxx for a teacher.

The father's question to Jordan (turn 3) invites the child to speak but also narrows Jordan's speaking rights by delegitimizing talk about soccer. The child's participation is doubly controlled: first, by being selected to take the floor, and second, by being told what *not* to speak about. But when Jordan complies, giving a lengthy account of the injustices he suffered that day from a substitute teacher, he is given ample support by both his parents for the full development of his narrative.

The topics raised by children and with children through elicitation and self-nomination tend to concern the immediate needs of dinner or the slightly less immediate concerns from the child's life, such as his or her day in school. These two clusters of topics represent three broad thematic frames: (1) the instrumental frame of serving and consuming dinner, (2) the "family news" frame within which all family members are entitled to tell their latest personal news, and (3) the broad category of talk about nonimmediate topics, including talk about spatio-temporally distant people or events. Whereas children's participation in the first two topical frames is closely controlled by adults, by entering the third frame, they achieve full conversational autonomy.

This happens when a child gains participatory rights by making a relevant contribution to an adult-initiated topic. This is the mode whereby children make a successful contribution to an exchange primarily sustained by adults. Participating in this mode carries a special bonus for child participants: Having your contribution seamlessly woven into the ongoing discourse is a powerful signal of being accepted as an equal, full-fledged conversational partner in the adult discourse world. In the following extract, conversational competence is expressed through the ability to collaborate in phatic talk (performing a topical shift) about the weather.

(8). Jewish-Americans 9; Andrew (9.5m); Ellen (7f).

	1 Mother:	We had no heat at my office today.
	2 Observer:	This is the <coldest day of the year> [>] +...
	3 Mother:	<That is the reason I cut> [<] it out early. I couldn't stand it there. I was absolutely freezing this morning.
>	4 Ellen:	Lisa our student teacher is always cold. She's always freezing.
	5 Father:	Speaking of Lisa, I think I saw her on the sidewalk today at Harvard Square.

Ellen's contribution ties in seamlessly with that of the others: It's both coherent ("on topic") and cohesive (through lexical reiteration, repeating both *cold* and *freezing* in a new context). The topical change subsequently accomplished by her father (turn 5) is based on her contribution, acknowledging it ("speaking of Lisa") as well as using it as the springboard for the shift in focus.

Older children may make meaningful contributions not only to phatic talk about the weather but also to the negotiation of meaning of topics concerning moral issues and cultural identities. A long stretch of conversation about Whoopie Goldberg includes the following extract:

(9). Jewish-Americans 1; Simon (13m); Jennifer (15f).

	1 Father:	It's set very good, um she did this thing on Anna Frank and +...
>	2 Simon:	It wasn't on, it was just a little bit about +/.
	3 Father:	Well, no# # it was really the central theme about # that thing with the junkie and +...
	% comment:	[6 turns omitted: Father is making sure Jennifer has seen the show].
	4 Father:	She was this junkie using all this foul language and also telling funny stuff, you know. People laughing and then she visits Anne Frank, the Anne Frank house in Amsterdam and the whole context of it xxx I mean, talk about a subject like that in the context of her performance, you know. I was ready to say "Oh my God, forget it, I'm not gonna watch this," but she does it. I mean she really pulls it off. She discusses, how do you discuss Anne Frank in a humorous context in a &co +/.
>	5 Jennifer:	But it wasn't humorous.
	6 Observer:	I don't think she was trying to be humorous.
	7 Father:	Well no, it's humor really in the best sense.
>	8 Simon:	On all her things she has like a moral for all of them.
	9 Father:	What was the moral of this?

> 10 Simon: Her, you know, her image # that she should appreciate her things more.
> 11 Jennifer: That anybody could +...
> 12 Simon: That her everyday problems are much less than # you know.
  13 Father: Yeah.
> 14 Jennifer: And then the thing with the Valley Girls.
  15 Mother: That was hysterical.
  16 Father: I think she's a genius, I think she's a genius.

The father seems deeply concerned about entitlement rights: Is a non-Jewish artist entitled to deal with a touchy subject like that in a humorous context? Can an outsider give a comic twist to "our" tragic story? The children play a significant role in negotiating the meaning of this conversation. Both children challenge the father's tendency to highlight the Jewish angle—first, by debating the centrality of Anna Frank in the show (turn 2) and then by contesting that it was humorous at all (Jennifer, backed by the observer, turn 5 and turn 6). Simon insists on the need to interpret Whoopie Goldberg in the wider context of her other shows, changing the debate's perspective and minimizing the importance of her dealing with Anna Frank in this specific one. It is eventually Simon with the assistance of Jennifer (turns 10–12) who formulates for all the coda of the specific Anna Frank episode. This justification of Whoopie Goldberg accepted (turn 13), the talk can move on to discussing yet another Whoopie Goldberg show.

We observed both Israeli and Jewish-American children relying on all three modes of conversational entry in gaining access to the floor. But despite the basic similarities in attitudes toward children, there is a cultural difference in modes of participation. The Jewish-American families seem to perceive of dinner as more child-centered than do the Israeli families. As a result, they initiate more conversations with children and encourage child initiations, resulting in a relatively higher proportion of overall child participation than in the Israeli families. But most of this participation tend to center around the two first frames, being focused on children's lives. In the Israeli families, adults take up more talking space, but children's participation is more equally distributed among the three thematic frames.

Adult-Child Co-Construction of Extended Discourse

Learning to Sustain the Floor

How do children learn the pragmatic skills needed for constructing conversationally relevant and internally coherent turns of talk? When young children obtain the right to speak at the dinner table, the adult-child conversation that subsequently ensues is often structured in a dialogic, question-answer format. Dialogic, question-answer sequences are a typical format of adult-child communication at the early stages of language acquisition. Bruner (1986) considers the adult's role in such dialogues as a support system provided by the social world for language acquisition. In dialogue with infants, adults give meaning and status to utterances that would be grammatically unacceptable in adult-adult communication, as when a child's mere vocalization is framed as a rightful turn of talk. From a pragmatic developmental perspective, the dialogic framework at dinner (as elsewhere) provides child respondents with practice in building coherence through question-answer sequences and in adhering to the demands of turn-taking rules. As discussed here, such exchanges also provide opportunities for learning how to construct autonomous, decontextualized texts (Blum-Kulka & Snow, 1992).

Scaffolding strategies associated with child-directed speech with young infants include acknowledgments, expansions, clarification questions, and recasting (Snow, 1984). The dinner-talk conversations with children of different ages show that adult support strategies also are used with children at an age where language acquisition is no longer the main concern.

(10). Jewish-Americans 4; Jordan (8m); Sandra (4f).
        The Father's question interrupts Jordan's lengthy account of soccer
        game.
        1 Father: Jordan would you like to tell us something? Other than
                     soccer what happened today?
        2 Jordan: Well + ...
        % comment: [simultaneously mother and Sandra engaged in
                     negotiating food.]
        3 Jordan: We had a mean xxx for a teacher.
        4 Father: <You what?> [>]
        % comment: [overlaps with Sandra softly singing to herself]
        5 Jordan: Our teacher got mean.
        6 Father: Your teacher # the substitute got mean?
        7 Jordan: Yes.
        8 Father: Why? What did you do to her today?
        9 Jordan: Nothing, but she Mrs. Yeaomans you know we have gym
                     today. Mrs. Yeomans always lets us go out but our
                     <substitute didn't> [>].
        % comment: [overlaps with Sandra's request for milk]
        10 Father: She didn't let you go out outside for gym?
        11 Jordan: She didn't let us go outside for recess!
        12 Father: Why not?
        13 Jordan: Right!
        14 Father: Why not?
        15 Jordan: Because she said we had gym. And ALL the kids protested
                     and said "but b- b- but Mrs. Yeomans always lets us"! But
                     she said "Mrs. Modden doesn't."
        16 Father: When is Mrs. Yeomans going to be back?
        17 Jordan: Well me and Darren are praying that it's going to be
                     tomorrow.
        18 Father: Because you you're tired of the substitute?
        19 Jordan: Yes. Mhmm. Very.
        20 Observer:What's wrong with your teacher?
        21 Father: Well, it's her kids they have the chicken pox.
        22 Observer:Ohuh!

Jordan's story emerges in response to a series of clarification questions from the father. The father also uses an expansion (turns 5 and 6) to make sure the information is explicit enough. Though each question might have appeared just as easily as in an adult-adult co-construction of a story, their accumulation gives the exchange the dialogic story co-construction format typical of adult-child communication. It is a format that might be a necessary condition for the story to emerge at all with younger children, but seems to be judged necessary by adults even when older children are involved. Not all of the father's questions to Jordan are supportive though; although the telling of the story is strongly supported by questions of clarification, its tale of complaint against the substitute teacher receives little support. Parental input to children's talk may focus on different dimensions of the talk (e.g., such the content or the speaking rights of the child), and the balance between support and challenge provided to these different dimensions may vary by the age of the child, the topic, family, and culture (Blum-Kulka, 1998).

The parental effort to elicit a "story" in this case highlights the relevance of his experience at school as a topic of conversation at dinner while simultaneously setting up criteria for the degree of informativeness that needs to be contained in the verbal recounting of such experiences. In other words, through this highly contextualized, dialogic mode of story co-construction, the child is invited to learn the requirements for eventually constructing decontextualized, autonomous accounts (Blum-Kulka & Snow, 1992). In this case, the events recounted are known to the teller only; however, similar probing is apparent in cases where attempts at co-construction relate to the retelling of shared events, as when a mother turns to a young child and asks him or her to recount a shared event to the father.

Learning to Speak in a Literate Mode

Bernstein's (1971) notion of elaborated code suffered much undue criticism since its original conceptualization in the 1970s. Recently it is becoming apparent that the distinction between elaborated and restricted codes captures, in essence, the possibility of variation in language use along a continuum of contextualization, rather than along a continuum of "richness" in vocabulary and syntactic structure. In this later interpretation, the notion of elaborated code is closely related to literacy: It is realized through the relatively decontextualized, autonomous mode of language use associated with certain genres of both written and spoken language. As Olson (1972), Wells (1981), and others have claimed, educating children in the use of this decontextualized, literate style is the ultimate goal of schooling. Different scholars stress different aspects of the competencies involved in the use of literate language. Both Scollon and Scollon (1981) and Snow and Tabors (1993) stress the capacity of the literate language user to take into account possible incongruencies in the information states of user and audience and structure the discourse's level of explicitness accordingly. Olson (1982) stresses the notion of verifiability: Because written texts carry a potential of verifiability absent from oral texts, their exact wording is of crucial importance. Children come to school with the pragmatic competence needed to infer indirect meanings in discourse, but they need to learn how to confine interpretations to the text, taking into account its specific cues. The need for verifiability is motivated by the overall high value placed in literate cultures on the search for factual truth. Heath (1983), for instance, considers the insistence on factuality as a discourse value a clear hallmark of literate traditions.

Intergenerational, especially multiparty, discourse can serve as a critical site in promoting the use of literate, elaborated codes. In their role as interlocutors in the presence of other children and adults, parents at dinner (as well as teachers in classrooms) facilitate the emergence of the child's discourse. Yet in the process of aiding and making it available for all present, they also assume the right to judge whether it meets their criteria of appropriateness. Such criteria of appropriateness may, of course, vary with culture, social class, or situation (home or school, for instance). In our sample of middle-class families, we found a common core of elaborated code-oriented criteria applied to children's discourse, with some cultural variation in the emphasis played on individual aspects.

These criteria are applied through metacomments. As Goffman (1967) notes, the articulation of norms often surfaces only when violations occur. The families attend metacommunicatively to perceived violations of the four conversational norms elaborated by Grice (1975), commenting on the apparent lack of *topical relevance* (the maxim of relevance), on *verbosity* or nonsatisfactory levels of *informativeness* (the maxim of quantity), *truth-value* (or facticity, the maxim of quality) and *clarity* (the maxim of manner). All four aspects are related to learning to construct coherent, decontextualized discourse of the type required in schools.

"Who, What Smells?": Learning to Adhere by the Maxim of Clarity.   Family discourse provides children with ample opportunities to develop the ability to construct autonomous, self-contained texts, texts that allow the audience to identify participants and events in the story world. Children learn to construct texts in the decontextualized mode, among other ways, through responsive comments pointing out problems with the comprehensibility of the text due to its lack of clarity. Parental reactions may transmit criteria for the degree of explicitness needed, such as in identifying characters in a story and in making clear the chronological order of the events related. The demand for clarity is particularly relevant in the case of personal experience stories. Such stories require a high degree of text-construction effort on the part of the child, because the information to be provided is known to the teller only, and hence he or she needs to balance between new and given information in a way that establishes reference networks clear to all (Blum-Kulka, 2005). The following example is typical of the way families in all groups show their concern with clarity of reference:

(11). Jewish-Americans 3; Samuel (10m); Jeffrey (6m).
	1 Jeffrey:	One day we stayed that much, all the way from xxx it's so smell.
>	2 Father:	What smells?
	3 Jeffrey:	It's xxx.
>	4 Father:	What smells?
>	5 Samuel:	We don't know what you're talking about. Who, what smells?
	6 Jeffrey:	The ice cream.
>	7 Father:	The ice cream?
	8 Jeffrey:	Yeah, it does.
>	9 Samuel:	Whose ice cream smells?
	10 Father:	I never smelled bad ice cream, Jeffrey.
	11 Jeffrey:	I smelled it.
	12 Father:	You did? Where?
	13 Jeffrey:	At school.
	14 Samuel:	Oh, at school.

15 Father: That's most unfortunate.
16 Jeffrey: Yeah, it stinks. That's the baddest in +...
17 Samuel: The best or the baddest?
18 Jeffrey: The baddest.
19 Father: Not the baddest, the worst.
20 Jeffrey: The worst.
@End.

The issue of clarity is best formulated by 10-year-old Samuel: "We don't know what you're talking about. Who, what smells?" As of turn 9, attention to clarity becomes confounded with concern about the truth value of the story, as the questions about the whereabouts of the "bad ice cream" ostensibly seek information but actually signal disbelief. By the end of the exchange, brother and father are concerned with correcting the child's language (turns 19 and 20). These repeated challenges address three different issues: clarity, truth, and grammar. Together they illustrate the role of family audiences as critics of child discourse, demanding accountability in trying to establish adult-discourse norms for the child.

"How Giant Is Giant?": Learning to Abide by the Maxim of Quality by Providing Verifiable Accounts.   True to their middle-class, modern, literate background, all families studied emphasize the importance of factuality, stressing verifiability in providing accounts. This emphasis is realized through questions challenging the accuracy of an account or by metapragmatic comments explicitly denying its truth value. A common practice in all families is to directly challenge a child's account if it seems illogical or counterfactual. In the following example, a child's report of her actions after school is challenged by both parents and her older brother:

(12). American-Israelis 6; Irit (13f); Noa (5f).
      Irit addresses the question to Noa.
         1 Irit: Did you have a good time at Leora's?
         2 Noa: I wasn't at Leora's.
      > 3 Father: Yes you were, this afternoon.
      > 4 Mother: You weren't? Where did you go from {gan} (nursery
                    school)?
         5 Noa: To a home.
      > 6 Mother: Not to this home. [laughs]
         7 Noa: Yes to this home.
      > 8 Mother: I wasn't here.
         9 Noa: Hm?
      > 10 David: You went to Nevo's Naomi? I mean to Leora's and then
                    from there to Nevo's?
      [Noa does not answer and family goes back to the previous topic]

In the next example, the issue of verifiability is elaborated to illustrate the principles of the scientific thinking in modern societies. The example is extraordinary in its highly didactic tone but not in the discourse values it represents, which underlie many of the adult-child interactions in these families.

(13). Jewish-Americans 3; Samuel (10m); Jeffrey (6m).

1 Samuel: Um Jacob # xxx and then they tipped over and there was this, ya know, a GIANT turtle, it was coming right at them.
2 Mother: Where? On the lake?
3 Samuel: On the lake.
4 Mother: They have giant turtles on the lake? I want to understand.
5 Samuel: Yeah. Four.
6 Father: In the lake like that a giant turtle? That's only six inches across.
7 Mother: Have you seen it?
8 Samuel: Oh, yeah.
9 Mother: How giant is giant?
10 Samuel: How giant is giant? About three feet.
11 Mother: Show me with your hands how big it is.
12 Samuel: I can't fit it. My arms aren't that big.
13 Mother: You really saw a giant turtle? In the lake?
14 Jeffrey: About this big? This big?
15 Mother: Were they like friendly?
16 Samuel: Its claws were like that long.
17 Father: xxx.
18 Jeffrey: xxx and its claws xxx I'm sure its fins are that big.
19 Father: xxx.
20 Mother: Did you see it, or did Jacob see it?
21 Samuel: Jacob saw it and I saw it too.
22 Mother: You saw a three-foot turtle?
23 Samuel: I didn't say it was exactly three foot, but approximately three feet.
24 Mother: Was it like this?
25 Samuel: No. Is that three feet?
26 Father: Was it bigger than the plate you're eating?
27 Samuel: Much.
28 Jeffrey: Bigger than a house? Bigger than a house?
29 Mother: I hope not. I wouldn't want to meet that turtle.
30 Jeffrey: Me either. Yuk. xxx! [making funny noises].
31 Father: I don't think xxx turtles grow that big.
32 Mother: xxx if Jacob says he saw it, it doesn't surprise me.
% comment: [There is a long pause]
33 Samuel: He didn't say it was three feet.
34 Mother: You said it was three feet.
35 Samuel: By the look of its head and tail it looked like three feet.
36 Father: By the look of its head, or did you see the body?
37 Samuel: I saw part of his body.
38 Father: But you didn't see its whole body.
39 Samuel: No.
40 Father: Now we have more of an understanding.
41 Mother: That's called an unconfirmed assumption. You know what that's worth?
42 Samuel: What?
43 Mother: Nothing.

44 Father: xxx.

45 Mother: Do you remember the story of the four blind men and the
             elephant? I was about to tell you a story as I tell you now
             xxx.[... tells the story, concluding]: And they all came to a
             different conclusion based on what area they were touching,
             because they didn't have the entire picture before them. Had
             they seen, which of course they couldn't do, that if you see
             the entire picture that's one thing, and if you see parts of it,
             you can't assume from that a whole picture if you only have
             certain parts of it. So, if you see a head of a turtle and a little
             bit of its body, you can't assume that it's three feet # #, if you
             didn't see the whole turtle.

@ End.

The parents put the burden of proof for the "giant turtle" on the child. Like a scientist announcing a new discovery, he is required to provide reliable evidence for his claim. As the exchange unfolds, the reliability of the evidence is challenged on several grounds, the challenge culminating not only in total dismissal of the claim but also in an explicit didactic statement defining the nature of scientific evidence in general.

As the exchange opens, Samuel's use of the word *giant* as a description of the turtle he saw on his trip to the lake immediately triggers doubt, which gradually and systematically builds up to the explicit expression of disbelief. For a while, Samuel holds his ground (turn 8), but with repeated questioning, his account begins to lose credibility. From the point he begins to admit doubt (turn 23), his mother's challenge gathers momentum, systematically undermining each of Samuel's claims, until the final collapse of his story in turns 37–39. Finally, the mother takes it on herself to dismiss the account in unequivocal terms, to formulate the scientific principle behind the dismissal in the elaborate code of literate language ("That's called an unconfirmed assumption") and to illustrate the result of the lack of critical thinking through the story of the four blind men and the elephant, concluding with yet another didactic exposition of the principles involved.

"Could You Begin to Tell Us in Words?": Learning to Provide Topically Relevant and Informative Turns of Talk.   In Grice's (1975) account, the maxim of informativeness (quantity) relates to the requirement to provide as much information as needed, relative to the general direction of the exchange and to the requirement not to provide more information than necessary. Because both requirements are subject to considerations of relevance in terms of the general goal of the exchange, the two maxims are interrelated. This interrelationship is particularly evident in family discourse, where negotiations over degree of informativeness are guided by considerations of situational and topical relevance.

The information requirement is only rarely implemented in family discourse through metapragmatic comments; the common practice is not to say "tell us more about that," but rather to pose information-seeking questions that shape both the amount and nature of the information required in connection with the topic at hand. With young children, the issue is to get the child to verbalize his or her experience in a manner that can be judged informative enough from the adult's point of view.

With younger children, a common practice is to try to elicit a coherent account for events known to both child and adult. Examples 6 and 11 illustrate such attempts. The "pop-up" mouse story (example 14) stands out because of its level of reflexivity. The mother is asking the child "to tell in words," namely to learn the principle of expressibility, namely to use the verbal mode for the rendering of personal experience in a way communicable to others.

(14). Jewish-Americans 4; Jordan (8m); Sandra (4f).
    1 Mother: Wait Sandra. Were you going to tell Elisabeth something about the pop-up mouse?
    2 Sandra: Okay. and xxx <whenever I go to sleep> [>], she pops up # I open my eyes!
    3 Jordan: <where in the refrigerator Mom?> [<]
    4 Sandra: Pops down # I close them. xxx she lives # I'll show you all where's. Just xxx where I am. Walk> [>] and I'll show where's, ok?
    5 Jordan: <xxxxxxxxxxxxxxxxxxxxxxxxx>
[<].
> 6 Mother: Could you begin to tell us in words?
    7 Jordan: xxx.
    8 Sandra: xxx he lives in +…
    9 Mother: He lives in a couch, the pop-up mouse. It's her explanation for waking up in the middle of the night.
    @End.

With older children, as among adults, negotiations over informativeness are more overtly linked to questions of relevance, namely to the types of information considered most relevant to the topic at hand. In the following extract (continued from talk initiated by one of the twins; see example 5), relevance is defined in terms of a specific type of scientific knowledge. The details required by the father foreground basic principles of the observational method in natural science: careful observation, attention to detail, and logical classification. Accordingly, the child is asked which flowers were seen, whether she learned to differentiate the various botanical parts of the flower, and whether she learned the names of these parts.

(15). Israelis 6; Lilax (6f); Iris, (6f).

1 Father:	ve-hayu eze xayot meyuxadot? macatem xargol lemashal?	And were there any special animals? Did you find a grasshopper for example?
2 Lilax:	ken, ani raiti xargol.	Yes, I saw a grasshopper.
3 Iris:	hem mac'u kalanit.	They found an anemone.
4 Father:	kalanit?	An anemone?
5 Lilax:	ani macati ve-karati La, La +	I found one and called the, the + …
6 Iris:	la-mora nili.	The teacher, Nili.
7 Lilax:	la-mora ve-hi amra le-kulam:	The teacher and she said to "everybody:

		Hebrew	English
		"tir'u, tir'u macanu kalanit.	"Look, look, we found an anemone."
8	Father:	ani od lo raiti ha-shana kalanit.	I haven't seen an anemone yet this year.
9	Lilax:	ani raiti. ani macati et ha-kalanit.	I have. I found the anemone.
10	Father:	kvar ptuxa?	Already open?
11	Lilax:	ma?	What?
> 12	Father:	ha-alim, ale ha-koteret.	The leaves, petals.
13	Lilax:	ken. ve-rainu afilu et ha-lavan shela.	Yes. And we even saw its white.
> 14	Father:	ma ze? eze lavan yesh la?	What? What white does it have?
> 15	Lilax:	et ha-lavan be-tox ha-ale koteret. yesh la lavan # im ha-adom.	The white inside its petals. It has white # with the red.
16	Iris:	LO, YESH GAM xx SHAXOR.	NO, IT ALSO HAS BLACK [shouting] xx. [shouting]
17	Lilax:	ken ha-avkanim hem shxorim.	Right the stamens are black.
18	Iris:	xashavti shaxor.	I thought black.
19	Lilax:	ha-lavan hu yaxad im ha-adom betox ha # le-yad ha + …	The white is together with the red in the # near the + …
> 20	Father:	az ulay ze &civ # hi amra she-ze kalanit?	So maybe it's a & tul # Did she say it was an anemone?
21	Mother:	yesh kvar kalaniyot ba-ir. lama lo?	There are already anemones in town. Why not?
> 22	Father:	ve-ma ha-madrixim hisbiru laxem?	And what did the guides tell you?
23	Lilax:	yesh li rak madrixa axat.	I have only one guide.
> 24	Father:	ma hi hisbira?	What did she say?
25	Lilax:	she-ze KALAnit!	That it's an ANEmone!
> 26	Father:	lo, ma hi hisbira bixlal?	No, what did she explain in general?
27	Lilax:	hi hisbira she-kalanit yod'im she-ze kalanit biglal ha-lavan shela. ve-pereg hu adom aval rak bli ha-lavan.	She explained that an anemone, you know it's an anemone by it's white and a poppy is also red but without the white.
30	Father:	xxx.	xxx.
31	Mother:	lo, aval +/.	No, but +/.
32	Iris:	ima, ma efshar od laxtox?	Mom, what else is there to cut?

% comment: [Iris is busy slicing cucumbers]

		Hebrew	English
33	Lilax:	kshe-nir'e parag az hi, hi tagid.	When we see a poppy she, she'll tell us.
> 34	Father:	hi tasbir.	She'll explain.
35	Lilax:	hi tasbir.	She'll explain.
> 36	Father:	et ha-hevdel?	The difference?
37	Lilax:	ken.	Yes.

> 38 Father: hi codeket.   She's right.
   @End

The particular rendition of an experience encouraged through parental questioning shows children which events are reportable, what components are worthy of elaboration, and what is important about them. Importance may be defined in terms of reportability, as in (1), specific observational detail, as in (13), or in terms of a causal explanation that seeks to provide motivations for the event(s) reported. In a joint account by two children of their visit to the science museum, as the story unfolds, the smallest child (Tina, 3) reports that the rat is placed in a small cage to play basketball, that he's very good at throwing the ball, and that when the rat gets the ball in the basket he receives food pellets. At this point the mother intervenes to ask: "Do you think that's why he was so eager to get it in the basket? So he could get something to eat?" encouraging the children to engage in logical, inferential thinking, to attribute to the rat the type of intentional goal-directed motivation that can explain human actions.

Such "why" questions may also relate to the overall significance of a story, demanding verbalization of its focal relevance. In co-constructing with 11-year-old Yoram (Israeli family 1) his experiences during a school trip to "a school for teachers or something like it," the adults not only pose clarifying questions ("Who organized it?, Did you go with your teacher?"), which signal to the child the shortcomings of his account in terms of the maxim of informativeness, but also ask questions that direct him to think about the overall significance of the event ("Did they explain to you what the goal was? Why did they take you there and what are they trying to find in this?").

But children also have to learn how to define the amount of information required relevant to a given topic, not saying more than necessary. Censoring forthcoming information, in line with this second part of the informativeness requirement may be implemented on the grounds of redundancy ("we already heard that") or be subject to considerations of relevance. The following exchange exemplifies how adults model the requirement for novelty, when the father indirectly apologizes ("Oh, right. You told me. I forgot all about it" (turn 6)) for having asked the same question twice.

(16). Israeli 6; Lilax (6f); Iris (6f).
   1 Father: ma at asit be-shiur   What did you do in your last
              xonxut ha-axaron shelax?   tutoring lesson?
   2 Lilax: ehm ani asiti ani ose ehm +...Ehm, I did, I'm making ehm +...
   3 Lilax: od lo gamarti et ze.   I haven't finished it yet.
   4 Father: ma ze?   What?
   5 Lilax: aval ani osa # simaniya.   But I'm making a book mark.
 > 6 Father: ah naxon, amart li.   Oh right. You told me. I forgot
              shaxaxti legamre.   all about it.
   @End

Censorship may be also self-imposed, implying conversationally that the topic raised is not relevant to the occasion, possibly due to the presence of the children at the dinner table.

(17). Jewish-Americans 1; Jennifer (15f); Simon (13m).
    1 Father: I won't say in detail what Nancy Black told me. Just let me
                      say there's verification.
    2 Simon: For what?
    3 Father: Never mind.
    @End.

Both adults and siblings engage in curtailing forthcoming information on the grounds of irrelevance in terms of the interests of one or some of the participants present at dinner.

(18). Jewish-Americans 2; Marvin (8m); Daniel (6m). Marvin and Daniel are
    telling the story of "The Flight of the Navigator."
    1 Daniel: And the alien says: "I told you that turnpike would be
                      hectic. Then they stopped xxx. They didn't find on the way,
                      you know, # and, well, first they ask +/.
    2 Marvin: Hey leave that! xxx He escapes in that +/.
> 3 Mother: You know what, Susan might want to see this movie. Don't
                      tell us every detail.
    [continued]

(19). Jewish-Americans 1; Jennifer (15f); Simon (13m).
    Simon is telling what's going to happen in future episodes of some soap
    opera.
    1 Simon: What happens is that she and Patrick, you know, they got
                      drunk and they, and then +/.
> 2 Jennifer: Shut up, Simon!
    3 Simon: She walks out.
> 4 Jennifer: Simon, shut up! Forget it!
    @ End

Israeli and Jewish-American families do not differ much in the relative importance attached to adherence to any of the four conversational maxims. The cultural difference in attitudes to discourse emerges in comparing the degree of attention paid to conversational maxims with the degree of attention paid to discourse management and metalinguistic talk. In the Jewish-American families, discourse management is a central topic of talk, taking up twice the discourse space devoted to it in the Israeli families. This concern seems to reflect underlying American cultural values of individualism and "fairness," expressed in dinner talk in a highly reflexive manner. The situation is reversed in relation to topicalizing issues of language: probably for historical reasons connected with the revival of Hebrew, Israeli families are highly concerned with matters of etymology, grammaticality, and bilingual practices, a domain of marginal importance for the Jewish-Americans.

CONCLUSION

The modern consciousness shared by all of the families studied is reflected in expressed attitudes to child-socialization as well as in their discursive practices.

Children are encouraged to have a voice in the family, are helped to sustain the floor and develop their turns, and learn discursive norms by being held account-able for various aspects of their discursive performance. Thus dinner talk is seen as playing a primary role in helping children gain membership in a literate soci-ety. There are two theoretical underpinnings to this argument. First, it assumes a broad view of literacy not only as a modality (e.g., written vs. oral language) but foremost as a discursive repertoire to what Bernstein (1990) calls "an elaborated orientation to meaning." Second, it adopts a social interactionist position with regard to pragmatic development, granting dyadic and multiparty, intergenerational, and peer discursive practices a central role in mediating learn-ing (Blum-Kulka & Snow, 2002, 2004; Ninio & Snow, 1996). In the study of this in-herently dialogic process, the main emphasis in former research has been on the contribution of dyadic, mother-child interactions. The study of dinner talk ques-tions the implicit assumption of the primacy of one speaker–one hearer interac-tion for development, showing the complexity of participant structures and multiplicity of discourse genres children participate in at the multiparty, intergenerational, speech event of family dinners. From a different perspective, the intergenerational one-to-one model has also been challenged by ethnographic studies of children's natural peer talk. Though family meals repre-sent a speech event deeply embedded in cultural matrixes (e.g., Blum-Kulka, 1997), this chapter has attempted to show that they may share across cultures un-derlying attitudes to literate discourse, facilitating for children the process of learning autonomous, literate ways of using language.

NOTES

1. The study involved three groups of middle-class, college-educated families: two Israeli groups (native Israelis and American-born Israelis) and a group of American-born Jew-ish Americans. All families came from an Eastern European background and had, at the time of the research, two to three school-aged children. Families were observed at their homes in Israel and the United States. An observer from the research team participated at three dinners, taped the conversation (twice by audio and once by video), and con-ducted in-depth ethnographic interviews with the families on a separate occasion (see Blum-Kulka, 1997).

2. Findings that point in these directions come from psychological studies in pragmatic de-velopment (Ninio & Snow, 1996), sociolinguistic, analytical studies of family discourse in American-Italian and Swiss families (Erickson, 1990; Keppler & Luckman, 1991; Watts, 1991), and anthropologically oriented studies of family discourse (e.g., Ochs, Smith, & Taylor, 1989; Ochs, Taylor, Rudolps, & Smith, 1992; Varenne, 1992).

3. Transcription follows the CHAT (MacWhinney, 1991) format for the following conven-tions:
   < > = overlap;
   [>] = overlap follows;
   [<] = overlap precedes;
   # = noticeable pause longer than one second;
   each subsequent second is marked by additional # signs);
   [/] = retracing without correction;
   [//] = retracing with correction;
   +/. = interrupted utterance;
   +... = trailing off, (incompletion);

+^ = quick uptake (latching);

+, = self-completion;

++ = other completion;

& = an incomplete word;

[text] = paralinguistic material;

[%com] = contextual information;

xxx = inaudible utterance (s);

    number of xs stands for length of inaudible utterance in seconds.

In addition, punctuation symbols indicate intonation contours, italics = emphatic stress;

    CAPS = very emphatic stress.

    > = used at left-hand margin of the transcript point to a feature of interest;

    @End = marks end of topical segment.

REFERENCES

Bernstein, B. (1971). *Class, codes and control* (Vol. 1). London: Routledge & Kegan Paul.

Bernstein, B. (1990). *The structure of pedagogic discourse*. London: Routledge.

Blum-Kulka, S. (1997). *Dinner talk: Cultural patterns of sociability and socialization in family discourse*. Mahwah, NJ: Lawrence Erlbaum Associates.

Blum-Kulka, S. (1998). Involvement in narrative practice: Audience response in child-adult conversational story telling. In A. Aksu-Koc, E. Erguvanti-Taylor, S. Ozsoy, & A. Kuntay (Eds.), *Perspectives on language acquisition: Selected papers from the 7th International Congress for the Study of Child Language* (pp. 221–236). Mahwah, NJ: Lawrence Erlbaum Associates.

Blum-Kulka, S., & Snow, C. (1992). Developing autonomy for tellers, tales and telling in family narrative-events. *Journal of Narrative and Life History, 2,* 187–217.

Blum-Kulka, S., & Snow, C. (Eds.). (2002). *Talking to adults: The contribution of multiparty discourse to language acquisition*. Mahwah, NJ: Lawrence Erlbaum Associates.

Blum-Kulka, S. (2005). Modes of meaning making in young children's conversational storytelling. In J. Thornborrow & J. Coates (Eds.), *The Sociolinguistics of Narrative* (pp. 149–170). Philadelphia: John Benjamins.

Bruner, J. (1986). *Actual minds, possible words*. Cambridge, MA: Harvard University Press.

Erickson, F. (1990). The social construction of discourse coherence in a family dinner table conversation. In B. Dorval (Ed.), *Conversation organization and its development* (pp. 207–239). Norwood, NJ: Ablex.

Goffman, E. (1967). *Interaction ritual: Essays on face to face behavior*. New York: Doubleday.

Goffman, E. (1981). *Forms of talk*. Philadelphia: University of Pennsylvania Press.

Grice, H. P. (1975). Logic and conversation. In P. Cole & J. Morgan (Eds.), *Syntax and semantics 3: Speech acts* (pp. 41–58). New York: Academic Press.

Habermas, J. (1984). The public sphere: An encyclopedia article (1964). *New German Critique, 3,* 49–55.

Habermas, J. (1987). *The theory of communicative action: Vol. 2. Lifeworld and system: A critique of functionalist reason*. Boston: Beacon.

Heath, S. B. (1983). *Ways with words: Language, life and work in communities and Classrooms*. Cambridge: Cambridge University, Press.

Keppler, A., & Luckman, T. (1991). "Teaching": Conversational transmission of knowledge. In I. Markova & K. Foppa (Eds.), *Asymmetries in dialogue* (pp. 143–166). Savage, MD: Barnes & Noble.

MacWhinney, B. (1991). *The CHILDES Project: Tools for analyzing talk*. Hillsdale, NJ: Lawrence Erlbaum Associates.

Ninio, A., & Snow, C. (1996). *Pragmatic development*. Boulder, CO: Westview Press.

Ochs, E., & Schieffelin, B. (1984). Language acquisition and socialization: Three developmental stories and their application. In R. Sweder & R. A. Levine (Eds.), *Culture theory* (pp. 276–323). Cambridge: Cambridge University Press.

Ochs, E., Smith, R., & Taylor, C. (1989). Detective stories at dinnertime: Problem solving through co-narration. *Cultural Dynamics, 2*, 238–257.

Ochs, E., Taylor, C., Rudolph, D., & Smith, R. (1992). Storytelling as a theory-building activity. *Discourse Processes, 15*, 37–72.

Olson, D. (1982). Consequences of schooling. *The Quarterly Newsletter of Comparative Human Condition, 4*, 75–78.

Queen, A. S., Habenstein, W. R., & Quadagno, S. J. (1985). *The family in various cultures.* New York: Harper & Row.

Rogoff, B. (1990). *Apprenticeship in thinking: Cognitive development in social context.* New York: Oxford University Press.

Scollon, R., & Scollon, S. (1981). *Narrative, literacy and face in interethnic communication.* Norwood, NJ: Ablex.

Snow, C. (1984). Parent-child interaction and the development of communicative ability. In R. Schiefelbush & J. Pickar (Eds.), *Communicative competence: Acquisition and intervention* (pp. 69–107). Baltimore: University Park Press.

Snow, C. E., & Tabors, P. O. (1993). Language skills that relate to literacy development. In B. Spodek & O. Saracho (Eds.), *Language and literacy in early childhood education* (pp. 1–20). New York: Teachers College Press.

Stahl, A. (1993). *Family and child-rearing in Oriental Jewry.* Jerusalem: Academon.

Varenne, H. (1992). *Ambiguous harmony: Family talk in America.* Norwood, NJ: Ablex.

Watts, R. J. (1991). *Power in family discourse.* Berlin: Mouton de Gruyter.

Wells, G. (1981). *Learning through interaction.* London: Cambridge University Press.

CHAPTER 6

Doing School at Home: Mexican Immigrant Families Interpret Texts and Instructional Agendas*

Robert J. Bayley
Sandra R. Schecter

In the United States, complex decisions confront language minority parents. Many wish to transmit their language and culture to their children. At the same time, they wish to assist them to succeed in a school system in which immigrant bilingualism is frequently viewed as a transitional stage on the way to a desirable monolingual English norm (Bayley, 2004; Hakuta, 1986). Moreover, although numerous social, cultural, and demographic factors have been shown to contribute to minority language retention or loss, recent research suggests that minority languages cannot be maintained across generations without a strong commitment on the part of the home (Bayley, Schecter, & Torres-Ayala, 1996; Crago, Chen, Genesee, & Allen, 1998; Fishman, 1991; Hakuta & D'Andrea, 1992; Hakuta & Pease-Alvarez, 1994; Schecter & Bayley, 1997, 2002). In addition, research indicates that language minority children, particularly those who attend schools where they make the transition from the home language to English at an early age, are in greater danger of losing their mother tongue than they are of failing to acquire English (Portes & Schauffler, 1996; Wong Fillmore, 1991).

This chapter explores the ways language minority parents attempt to resolve the contradictions arising from their desire to preserve linguistic and cultural continuity while preparing their children to succeed in a school system which often evaluates children solely on the basis of their English performance (Valdés & Figueroa, 1994). Specifically, we examine how language minority parents organize their parenting in relation to their perceptions of the role of schooling, and their views of their own and other family members' roles in children's linguistic and academic development. Our focus is on parent-child and sibling-sibling interactions in typical school and literacy tasks such as assistance with homework and reading to a preschool child. However, our discussion is not confined to these examples. By attending to family interactions around texts, we also examine the ways in which cultural practice informs the pedagogical stances assumed by language minority parents in their role as primary organizers of their children's participation in schooling (Griffith & Schecter, 1998). For a number of reasons, these stances do not always coordinate with the agendas of schools. First, language minority parents may not possess the necessary proficiency in the dominant language to be able to support the school's agenda in a manner professional educators deem beneficial for children's development. Second, for language minority families, the ordinary work of parents in constructing the relationship between their family and school is embedded in another equally ordinary process, which, on a daily basis, entails thousands of routine decisions concerning language choice (Griffith & Schecter, 1998; Schecter & Bayley, 1997). This process may problematize the relationship between home caregiving and schooling by introducing the additional important element of language maintenance or loss into the determination of educational priorities. Third, parents and professional educators may disagree in their strategies for addressing crucial concerns about children's development as well as over rights and prerogatives of the various stakeholders with regard to the education of children (Griffith & Schecter, 1998; Pacini, 1998).

The following analysis draws from a sample of 40 Mexican immigrant and Mexican American families who participated in a study of the relationship between home language socialization and the development of bilingual and biliterate abilities by children of Mexican background in California and Texas. In this chapter, we examine four immigrant families: three in northern California and one in south Texas.[1] The four families represent a range of decisions regarding home language practices, as well as socioeconomic class and life modes. Participants include two urban working-class families in northern California, a rural working-class family in south Texas, and a northern California middle-class professional family.

The chapter is organized as follows. First, we briefly review recent work in language socialization, the research perspective that informs our analysis. We suggest that this research tradition, despite the many insights it has provided into children's development, has not attended sufficiently to the dynamic nature of language socialization in language minority families. Second, we outline our methods of data collection, reduction, and analysis. The main section presents the findings, organized as portraits of families' experiences with literacy and schooling. Finally, we discuss the implications of the study, with emphasis on the effects of change and continuity in home language practices on children's linguistic and literacy development.

A LANGUAGE SOCIALIZATION PERSPECTIVE

Much of the research on language acquisition has focused on children's acquisition of structures judged important from the point of view of linguistic theory, whether in Chomskyan (e.g., Chomsky, 1981; Jaeggli & Safir, 1989; Meisel, 1995; Pinker, 1984) or connectionist frameworks (e.g., Plunkett, 1995; Rumelhart & McClelland, 1986). Language socialization research, in contrast to work in formal linguistics, has conceptualized the process of language acquisition more broadly. Researchers in language socialization have tended to view language acquisition as a composite phenomenon of cognitive-linguistic and sociocultural factors

(Gaskins, Miller, & Corsaro, 1992; Heath, 1982; Ochs, 1988; Ochs & Schieffelin, 1995; Schieffelin, 1990; Schieffelin & Ochs, 1986). The process by which children become socialized into the interpretative frameworks of their culture, moreover, includes not only the period of primary language acquisition, that is, from infancy to age 5; it extends throughout childhood and into adolescence and beyond (Bayley & Schecter, 2003; Goodwin, 1990; Heath, 1983). Researchers working within this framework see both the context of interaction and the culturally sanctioned roles of the participants as major determinants of language forms and strategies used in given situations.

Recently, a number of scholars have extended the tradition of language socialization research to study the linguistic development of children in bilingual and multilingual communities. In general, this research has documented the difficulties of maintaining minority languages, whether Inuktitut in the far north of Québec (Crago et al., 1998; Patrick, 2003), Taiap in the isolation of rural New Guinea (Kulick, 1992), or Spanish in U.S. cities (Bayley et al., 1996; Pease-Alvarez, 2002; Pease-Alvarez & Vasquez, 1994; Schecter & Bayley, 1997, 2002; Schecter, Sharken-Taboada, & Bayley, 1996; Vasquez, Pease-Alvarez, & Shannon, 1994; Zentella, 1997, 2005). In U.S. Latino communities, language socialization research has examined children's developing competence in various speech and literacy events, such as teasing and other forms of verbal play (Eisenberg, 1986), reading Spanish-language advertising flyers (Bayley et al., 1996), or simultaneous translation (Pease-Alvarez & Vasquez, 1994). This line of research has also documented the wide range of linguistic resources available to children in bilingual communities and the ways children learn to choose among these resources for their symbolic value. For example, standard Puerto Rican Spanish, popular Puerto Rican Spanish, English-dominant Spanish, Puerto Rican English, African American Vernacular English, standard New York English, and Hispanized English were all spoken by various residents of the New York *barrio* block studied by Zentella (1997, pp. 41–48). Moreover, a speaker's choice of one or another variety represented not only a linguistic decision, but, perhaps more importantly, a choice of identity. Indeed, Zentella's 14-year longitudinal study shows how, for children and adolescents of a community such as *el bloque,* language socialization includes becoming competent in many of the varieties spoken in the community and learning to switch from one variety to another according to the image of herself that the speaker wishes to present.

Research in bilingual and multilingual communities has begun to focus on the dynamic nature of language socialization practices, particularly in societal or situational contexts where individuals have choice with regard to the use of the minority versus dominant language. The long-term perspective afforded by the methodology used in conjunction with our research on family language environment and bilingual development, for example, revealed a significant number of shifts in minority language maintenance strategies. Many families reported changes over time in their patterns of language use in the home (Schecter & Bayley, 2002). These shifts tended to co-occur with either of the following sets of circumstances: a crucial juncture in the child's formal education (e.g., transition from home to preschool); or a time of flux on the home front, causing changes in enabling or constraining forces (e.g., change of geographic locale occasioned by a move; separation or divorce of parents; arrival of a new sibling). These circumstances, experienced frequently as traumas by both adults and children, caused respondents to reevaluate their goals and attitudes with regard to language use in the home (Schecter & Bayley, 1997; Schecter et al., 1996).

Thus, recent research in the language socialization of children in bilingual and multilingual communities, in addition to evaluating children's developing competencies in various speech and literacy events, has helped to elucidate changes in the symbolic associations of the use of different language varieties in speech and literacy performances. In addition, research has documented changes in family and community ideologies concerning the importance of different languages. This chapter seeks to contribute to this growing body of work that explores choice of language practices in fluid social contexts. Special attention is given to the issues that arise among parents, children, and schools when a minority language plays a significant role in language socialization.

METHODS

This chapter is based on a multifaceted study of the relationship between home language socialization and the development of bilingual and biliterate abilities by Mexican-descent children (Bayley, Alvarez-Calderón, & Schecter, 1998; Bayley et al., 1996; Schecter & Bayley, 1997, 1998, 2002, 2004). The larger inquiry sought to redress the lack of basic information about Mexican-origin children's home language use and linguistic development by examining family language practices in two different communities, San Antonio, Texas, and the San Francisco Bay Area, California, located in the two states that contain the largest Mexican-background populations in the United States. The project aimed to provide practitioners and policymakers with a deeper understanding of the adaptive and interpretive learning strategies that children from bilingual families bring to the classroom. The results offer detailed information about the ecology of bilingual homes that can be used to develop successful home-school collaborations.

Forty families participated in the larger study: 20 in California and 20 in Texas. Participating families had at least one parent or primary caretaker of Mexican origin and at least one fourth-, fifth-, or sixth-grade child who served as the focal child for the study. Our focus on the role of home language practices in facilitating or impeding Spanish maintenance led to the decision to select families with children in the fourth- to sixth-grades. By the time they reach fourth- or fifth-grade, children in bilingual education programs are normally transitioned to all-English classrooms. Support for Spanish maintenance and literacy development, therefore, must come from sources outside the school, primarily the home.

Data from the each of the 40 families consist of two interviews with a parent (usually the mother) or other primary caretaker(s), two interviews with the focal child, and samples of the focal child's writing in English. We also collected Spanish writing samples from children who were literate in Spanish. In addition, as one measure of language proficiency, we collected English and Spanish oral narratives based on two wordless picture books. Finally, because siblings often play a key role in language minority children's adaptation to the linguistic and cultural requirements of schooling, where possible, we interviewed the focal children's siblings.

From the original sample of 40 families, 4 families at each site were selected for intensive case study. Selection was based on the representativeness of the family language use profiles distilled from interviews and preliminary observations of the 40 families. For the case study families, the primary focus of attention was on patterns of communication in the home (e.g., who spoke which language to whom) and on the relationships among language choice and dimensions of language use such as topic, register, mode, and speaker age. To capture a range of family interactions in the case study families, including those focusing on school and literacy activities, at least 12 home observations were conducted at four different times during 3 separate weeks when school was in session. Observation periods, which normally extended over several months, included at least three afternoons, beginning shortly after the children returned from school, three early morning periods from the time the children awoke until they left for school, three weekend mornings, and three Sunday evenings from the time the family returned from their weekend activities until the children's bedtime. During home observations, focal children wore belts designed for joggers containing small professional-quality tape recorders. They also wore lapel microphones. Although recorders were occasionally turned off accidentally when children engaged in vigorous physical activity, the combination generally worked well and enabled us to access a great deal of relatively unmonitored speech. Microphones picked up all utterances of the focal children, including *sotto voce* self-regulatory remarks, as well as nearly all the speech of others in the immediate vicinity.

To prepare the data, audio recordings of interviews with family members were transcribed in full. Selected portions of the home observations, containing informal interactions between focal children and siblings, parents, and other relatives, were also transcribed, as were conversations concerning schoolwork and other aspects of literacy. Standard procedures for analyzing qualitative data were employed (e.g., Bogdan & Biklen, 1992; Miles & Huberman, 1984; Spindler & Spindler, 1987). That is, all data relating to the same family were grouped to yield case studies of different families' experiences with bilingualism. Behaviors and responses of individual family members were compared, and a second comparison was made across families.

In this chapter, we examine family interactions focused on school-related or school-like literacy activities in three of the eight families selected for intensive case study—two in the San Francisco Bay Area and one in San Antonio—as well as one San Francisco area family from the larger sample. The families selected, in addition to representing different geographical regions, represent different life modes, different areas of origin in Mexico, and different socioeconomic strata. They also represent different approaches to defining the pedagogical work of families in relation to school-based learning.

FINDINGS

Inventive Adaptations

The Esparza Family: An Early Focus on English Literacy

Our first family account focuses on early literacy and adaptation to mainstream educational expectations. Teresa Esparza[2] immigrated to northern California as a young adult, after a highly mobile childhood during which she spent varying periods of time in four different central and northern Mexican states. In Mexico, she completed 6 years of schooling. After immigrating, she settled in the largely working-class Mexican immigrant community of Lincoln City, approximately 20 miles south of San Francisco. Teresa later obtained a general equivalency diploma (GED) and completed a beauty course while working as a domestic and caring for her daughter Marcella. A single mother, Teresa, who at the time of Marcella's birth spoke virtually no English, radically modified her lifestyle to prepare her daughter for a school program that she felt would allow the child to obtain the social opportunities that she had lacked.

Early on, Teresa, influenced in some degree by an educator whose house she cleaned, determined that Marcella would attend an English-medium school. She believed that it was her responsibility to prepare her child for a school environment where she would be expected to compete with native speakers of English. In our first interview with her, Teresa remarked, "*Yo quería cuando ella fuera a la escuela que se sintiera cómoda ... con poder leer y escribir en inglés*" (I wanted her to feel comfortable when she went to school ... with the ability to read and to write in English). However, she faced an obvious quandary. Her English proficiency fell far short of what she believed was necessary to give Marcella the head start she desired for her daughter. Moreover, during her daughter's early years, she lived with her Spanish monolingual mother and other relatives in a Spanish-speaking environment. Teresa, however, devised an ingenious strategy to compensate for her own limited English and to prepare her daughter for the type of school she wished her to attend:

> *Cuando Marcella era baby, yo no hablaba inglés pero yo tenía cassettes y compraba los libros. Yo nunca le leí en español. Yo tenía los cassettes, [y] yo me acostaba en la alfombra y ponía el cassette y como si yo me estuviera leyendo con ella ... hasta que yo aprendí a leer ... libros de baby pero yo siempre le leí en inglés.*

> (When Marcella was a baby, I didn't speak English, but I had cassettes and I bought books. I never read in Spanish. I had the cassettes and I used to lie down on the rug and put on the cassette as if I were reading with her ... until I learned to read baby books, but I always read in English.)[3]

Teresa, whose English proficiency had improved considerably in the years since Marcella was a baby, concluded the narrative of this simultaneous language and literacy acquisition odyssey in English: "And I learned a lot that way."

Apparently Marcella, aged 11 at the beginning of our study, learned a lot as well. During our first interview with her, she also recalled listening to recordings of English books and later recited from memory one of the Dr. Seuss books that she had listened to as a young child:

> *Como ella* [Mrs. Esparza] *no sabía cómo leer en inglés entonces me compró esos, esos* tapes y los libros ... you can read along you know. So that's pretty much how I learned ... *me enseñaron el Dr. Seuss*. Oh, I loved those books.

> (Since she [Mrs. Esparza] didn't know how to read in English she bought me those, those tapes and books ... they taught me Dr. Seuss ....)

When it came time to enroll her daughter in school, Teresa considered a neighborhood public school but opted instead to send Marcella to St. Mary's Academy (a pseudonym), a Catholic school located in the adjacent, affluent town of Oak Grove, where the language of instruction was English. She explained this decision by pointing to *"el nivel educativo bien bajo"* (the very low educational level) in the public system, especially in the schools serving Latino children. At the time of our study, the decision seemed a successful one, and Teresa was satisfied with her daughter's academic achievement, although the appearance of several Bs in math and science on her report card, rather than the usual As, were of concern. Both Teresa and her daughter attributed the drop in grades to the fact that the academic subject matter had, by that time, surpassed the mother's abilities, and consequently, she could no longer assist Marcella with homework. Marcella explained the situation as follows:

Interviewer: *¿y te ayuda tu mami con tu tarea?* (And does your mom help you with your homework?)

Marcella: *A veces sí cuando estaba más chiquita sí pero como ya voy a grados más altos y ya no me ayuda porque ella no- no fue a la escuela mucho porque ella vivía en ranchos.* (Sometimes yes when I was littler yes, but since now I go to higher grades and now she doesn't help me because she didn't, didn't go to school much because she lived on ranches.)

Although Marcella's English literacy had developed to the point where the appearance of an occasional B on her report card was a cause of concern, predictably, her Spanish literacy, which was never reinforced at school, lagged considerably behind. When asked about her favorite books and her current reading, she named a number of well-known children's books and provided detailed plot summaries of several. However, although she voiced a strong preference for reading in English, she regretted her inability to read age-appropriate books in Spanish, despite her evident ability to speak the language:

Yo no puedo leer mucho [en español] pero ... me gustaría aprender cómo hacerlo más porque a mí me gusta leer los libros como más grandes, más de las niñas de mi año, pero como no puedo leer muy bien entonces tengo que leer como a los chiquitos libros ... no sé, me, me hace un poquito raro ....

(I can't read much [in Spanish] but ... I'd like to learn how to do it better because I like to read, like, more mature books, more for girls my age, but since I can't read very well then I have to read like little kids' books ... I don't know, it seems a little strange to me ....)

Thus, Teresa's inventive adaptation to the requirements of her daughter's schooling and to perceived societal requirements was not without cost. However, Marcella has at least maintained sufficient oral proficiency to serve as a foundation for her to develop Spanish literacy later should she so desire. Moreover, as we ended our study, Spanish had acquired increased prominence in the Esparza household because Teresa's new partner was a monolingual speaker of Spanish. This change in the household linguistic environment did not, however, lead to a change in the language of sibling interactions. Marcella continued to use only English with her new baby sister, Kimberly.

The Villegas Family: Accommodating Conflicting School and Family Agendas

Mariana and Enrique Villegas and their daughter, Diana (age 11), and son, Luis (age 5), rent a small, detached house, also in Lincoln City. The Villegas residence, on the fringe of a middle-class neighborhood and within short walking distance from commercial activity, is located about a half mile west of the *barrio* which contains Lincoln City's majority Mexican-origin population. Both Mariana and Enrique are from Guadalajara. Their families, most of whom have remained in Mexico, belong to the small, well-educated, *profesionista* (professional) stratum.[4] The couple moved to northern California when Diana was 2 years old so that Enrique could pursue a degree in business. Mariana, a Spanish-English bilingual who learned to speak, read, and write both languages at the American School in Guadalajara, planned to profit from her U.S. stay by taking courses to qualify as a medical assistant.

During their early years in the United States, both Mariana and Enrique worked full time in addition to attending classes. During the day, preschooler Diana was placed in professional daycare. The couple selected an "all-English" facility since they wished to take advantage of their limited time in the United States for their daughter to acquire a good base in the language. Around the time Diana was ready to start primary school, Mariana and Enrique made the important decision to remain permanently in the United States, where Enrique planned to start his own business after completing his studies.

The decision to immigrate changed the Villegases' orientation toward schooling for their daughter. The selection of a primary and middle school now had long-term consequences for Diana's future. Mariana and Enrique were primarily concerned with identifying a school with high academic standards that would provide a solid foundation for high school and college. After researching the schools within close driving distance, they decided that the wisest choice would be St. Mary's Academy, the same school attended by Marcella Esparza.

The issues of home language choice and mother tongue literacy came up early in the Villegases' relations with the school. In her first meeting with Diana's kindergarten teacher, Mariana was firmly advised against teaching her daughter to read in Spanish. The teacher also urged the parents to alter their usual practice of speaking Spanish at home and to speak English whenever possible so as not to "create a conflict" that would cause the child to experience problems in school. The Villegases saw no reason to question this advice. In the words of Mariana, *"queremos … que la niña se adapte lo más pronto posible al sistema"* (we wanted the child to adapt to the system as quickly as possible).

Mariana and Enrique's attempt to comply with the advice of their daughter's school, however, changed abruptly a year or two later during a visit from Mexico by Diana's maternal grandmother. Mrs. Villegas was alarmed at the degree of Spanish language loss her granddaughter exhibited. Ensuing discussions provoked a major change in Diana's parents' attitude. To halt the language attrition that so alarmed Mrs. Villegas, they briefly considered enrolling their daughter in a bilingual program in a local public school. However, as speakers of the cultivated standard of the Mexican elite, they were disturbed by what they regarded as the poor quality of the Spanish they observed in the neighborhood schools and quickly rejected the idea of transferring their daughter to a public school.

Mariana reported, "*Los niños eran de tercer grado y: leyeron un cuento ... y tenían que escribir una pequeña composición de lo que habían entendido ... y no había coherencia ... usaban cosas en español ... 'voy pa' 'trás ....'*"[5] (The children were third-graders and they read a story ... and they had to write a little composition about what they had understood ... and there was no coherence ... they used things in Spanish ... *'voy pa' 'trás ....'*).

Given their profound concerns about their daughter's mother tongue attrition and all that it entailed for cultural loss, as well as their reservations concerning bilingual programs in the local schools, the Villegases decided that their only option was to require the exclusive use of the Spanish in the home. From the time Diana entered third grade, a Spanish-only policy prevailed in the household: Diana's parents initiated interaction with their daughter in Spanish and required the use of Spanish in return. In addition, Mariana, with the help of books sent from Mexico by her mother-in-law, began a formal program of teaching her daughter to read and write in Spanish. As Diana described it, "*[mi mamá] me pone a leer libros que tenemos en español y me pone a hacer ejercicios*" (my mom set me to reading books that we have in Spanish and set me to doing exercises).

Despite the official, Spanish-only policy that governed the Villegas household, Diana used a fair amount of English, although not normally with her parents or her teenage cousin Leticia, who arrived from Mexico midway through the observation period. With her school friends, however, she spoke exclusively English, even though her two closest friends were also Latinas who spoke fluent Spanish. Diana agreed with her mother's explanation that given the monolingual context of St. Mary's, the girls found communication in their native language awkward, even outside of the school environment. Like her parents, she also spoke a great deal of English with her younger brother, Luis, who had been rejected for admission by St. Mary's kindergarten because he was unable to write his name in English.[6] As a consequence of this rejection, the household language policy was relaxed for Luis, as illustrated in the following exchange. Here Diana, seated at the family computer, is pretending to be a receptionist in a medical office, while Luis, who is less than fully engaged, plays the role of a new patient. In the exchange, revealing initiation-response sequences representative of formal schooling environments, Luis speaks entirely in English. Diana uses mostly English as well, with only a few formulaic Spanish phrases:

Diana:	Hold on, yes? O.K. U:rm, we need you to fill out this form, your name is Luis what?
Luis:	Villegas.
Diana:	Luis Villegas. Let's put you on the computer. Er Villegas?
Luis:	Uhhum (he makes engine noise while she types).
Diana:	Villegas, O.K. ¿*Cuántos años tienes?* (How old are you?)
Luis:	Five years.
Diana:	Your age is five. Erm, ¿*dónde vives?* (Where do you live?)
Luis:	Five, five, five.
Diana:	No
Luis:	fifty, fifty, six, six.
Diana:	Ma- di- son (reads as types). O:h, Lincoln City?

Luis: Aha.

Diana: Lincoln- City?

Luis: Uhhum.

Diana: Lincoln City, California, what is your zip code? Nine, four, 1, 2, 3. O.K. well, we just want you to fill out this form, er, I want you to put your name, er, where you live, erm, the problem you're having ....[7]

Diana also spoke a considerable amount of English with her parents when the topic was school related, a practice to which Mariana had no objection. Indeed, she reasoned that she would defeat her own purpose of promoting her daughter's academic success in an all-English school environment if she required Diana to use Spanish in discussions of her academic work. The following example from a tutorial session focusing on a homework assignment with which Diana was having difficulty, was recorded during a weekday afternoon observation.

Diana: Um, O.K. I didn't get that one /Mariana: O.K./ I had trouble.

Mariana: O.K. What does it—the Wulf family uses an average of three hundred, ninety-one, point four kilowatt hours each month, so they pay this each month. What could you do—what's the equation, *¿qué- qué ecuación hiciste ahí?* (what- what equation did you write here?)

Diana: XX multiply this XX.

Mariana: *No, ¿por qué multiplicas? Si ellos pagan esto al mes, es lo que ellos pagan al mes, digo, e:r por hora, por cada* kilowatt, *déjame tú mi calculadora.* (No, why do you multiply? If they pay this much a month, it's what they pay each month, say, er, per hour, for each kilowatt, give me my calculator.) [Diana returns with the calculator. Mariana starts making the calculation] *trescientos noventa y uno, punto cuatro, cero punto dieciocho, mamita, sí multiplicaste,* (three hundred and one point four, zero point eighteen, my little one, yes, you multiplied) it's absolutely right. *¿Te acuerdas que te dije?* (Remember what I told you?), when you see these words "per" /Diana: uhhum/ it's the same as saying "times," remember? How come, when you multiply this by this, gives you this? No way! The answer is seventy point forty-five!

Diana: How did you get that?

Mariana: I multiplied three ninety-one, point fi- er four, times—*¡a ver!* (Let's see!) Do it! *¡Hazlo!* (Do it!)

Diana: Three ninety-one- *¡No! ¡Yo lo sé, yo lo sé!* (No! I've got it, I've got it!) Oops! Three ninety-one.

As illustrated by the preceding excerpt, in some cases Spanish was used for emphasis, as in Mariana's repetition of the question, "what's the equation?" first in English and then in Spanish. A similar emphatic use of Spanish can be observed in Mariana's command to Diana to perform the required calculation, "Do it! *¡Hazlo!*" In these examples, as in her command to her daughter to fetch a calculator, Mariana appears to use Spanish to emphasize the seriousness of the directives.

Moreover, the commands themselves provide Diana with no relevant information that is not already available in English or they are extraneous to the solution of the math problem on which mother and daughter are working. However, Mariana also uses Spanish for explanations that are crucial to the solution of the problem, for example, *Si ellos pagan esto al mes* …. (If they pay this much a month ….). This explanation of the relationship between the monthly utility bill and the amount per kilowatt hour was not repeated in English elsewhere in the discourse, and, judging from her comment (*¡Yo lo sé!*, I've got it!), Diana's understanding was not impeded by her mother's code alternation.

Tutorial sessions of the type illustrated occurred frequently in the Villegas household, where "doing school," as Diana put it, was an integral part of family routine. Moreover, the participants were not confined to members of the immediate family. Because her level of education and her English proficiency were considerably higher than most of the parents of Diana's closest school friends, Mariana often took an active role in instructing these children. These informal pair or group tutoring sessions, normally conducted in English, involved a range of school subjects. During our observations, we recorded Mariana preparing Diana and a close friend for spelling and math tests. Mariana sat at the kitchen table with the two girls and quizzed them on spelling words, providing corrections and rule explanations, or guided them to the solutions to word problems assigned as math homework.

Mariana's role as academic mentor to her daughter's friends was valued in the community, although it often seemed to entail heavy responsibilities. Thus, during one visit, Mariana complained about a call she had recently received from Teresa Esparza, Marcella's mother. Marcella had been less successful than her mother believed she should have been on a math test for which Mariana had been helping her to prepare, and Teresa held the tutor accountable.

In general, Diana was able to navigate the changes in the language environment that characterized her life at home and at school. Before her family moved to California, she was well on the way to full acquisition of Spanish as her primary language. After the move, she adjusted to the new environment of an all-English daycare program. During her preschool years in Lincoln City, however, Spanish remained the language of home interactions. As we have seen, the home language environment changed abruptly to English when Diana entered St. Mary's, and then just as abruptly changed back to Spanish a few years later as the parents attempted to avert cultural loss and to satisfy the expectations of the grandparents. Throughout these changes, Diana developed native-like command of English without losing oral proficiency in Spanish. Her private speech was characterized by frequent code alternation, and she developed appropriate sociolinguistic rules for dealing with interlocutors. Specifically, in conversations about school or school-like texts, she used English primarily, both with her parents and when she assumed an adult role with her younger brother. However, she did not experience problems when her parents used Spanish in explanations of school-related tasks.

Continuity in Minority Language Use

We turn now to two families who have remained consistent in their home language practices, the Hernández family in northern California and the Gómez family in south Texas. In both families, intergenerational transmission of Spanish is dictated by the pragmatic requirements of parent-child communication. Three of the four parents are monolingual Spanish speakers, and, in both families, instructional discourse takes place in Spanish. Despite these commonalties, however, the families are characterized by very different patterns of sibling interaction, and, in the Gómez family, sibling interactions frequently focus on school-related tasks.

The Hernández Family: Spanish for Serious Matters

Raul and María Carmen Hernández and their three sons, Eduardo (age 10, the focal child), Francisco (age 9), and Tomás (age 6), live in a small bungalow in the East Bay community of San Ignacio, California. Although the economy of San Ignacio, populated largely by working-class and economically marginalized families, has received a boost as a result of the two recently opened casinos, this good fortune does not appear to have mitigated the notoriety associated with the town's name. San Ignacio's streets are still considered unsafe, and the city has made a number of unfortunate choices with regard to senior school personnel, resulting in the insolvency of its schools.

Because of the generally unsafe nature of the area, the Hernández brothers spend much of their outdoor time either in the street in front of their house or in their backyard. The boys play baseball or football, rollerblade, or plain horse around, while their music (Selena, Boys II Men) blasts from a boom box strategically positioned on the front stoop. The three brothers are frequently joined in their outdoor activity by their next door neighbor, Jacobo, age 13. Typically, their conversation takes place in a mixture of Spanish and English. Following is an excerpt from a conversation between Eduardo and Jacobo (with an interruption by Tomás), as twilight brought closure to their football practice. The conversation, which contains several typical examples of the type of codeswitching common among the youth of the neighborhood, concerns their schedule for the following day, which was also Halloween. Jacobo informs his friend that his plans have been curtailed because he has to serve a detention for arriving late to school.

Jacobo:	Yeah, *eso es que* if you go late … if you go late to school, if you get three
Eduardo:	uh huh
Jacobo:	you er
Eduardo:	you get suspended
Jacobo:	mm mm
Tomás:	Eduardo, *¡que vengas!* (come on!)
Jacobo:	Wait a little bit, either you get a work detail and you get a hum er sweep the hall or sharpen pencils
Eduardo:	a:h hah
Jacobo:	=or clean the school for one hour *y si no,* (and if not) if you don't go, you get suspended for one day … *y yo tengo que- y te dan* (and I have to- they give you) work detail *y luego yo tengo que ir en* (and then I have to go on) Halloween.

Inside their house, the brothers' conversations with one another are also characterized by frequent codeswitching, a strategy that Eduardo refers to as *"los dos"* (both). The boys' running commentaries during one evening of English-language television watching yield examples such as "*Mataron muchos* ducks" (They killed a lot of ducks) and "*¿Qué pasó?* (What happened?) It crashed?"

With his parents, Eduardo speaks primarily Spanish, a strategy dictated both by the requirements of communication with his monolingual Spanish-speaking mother and his parents' ideological stance toward Spanish maintenance. Raul begins in English to explain his and his wife's position—"I think that's the only way to keep a little bit of what we used to have," then switches to Spanish—"*el único modo de mantener algo de la cultura que tenemos=*" (the only way to maintain something of our culture). The conclusion to his sentence is anticipated by his wife, as the two rejoin "*=hablando el idioma*" ([by] speaking the language).

Both Raul and María Carmen are from the central Mexican city of Guanajuato. Although Raul speaks, reads, and writes Spanish fluently, he claims English as his primary language. His parents immigrated to the United States when he was 5 years old, and for 7 years, he attended an all-English elementary school in San Francisco. Raul reports that during his formative years, he came into contact with few Latinos, so that eventually he actually had to "learn" Spanish. His motive for such learning was decidedly affective: While on vacation in his birth town of Guanajuato, he met and fell in love with then 17-year-old María Carmen, who confirmed that Raul was strongly English dominant when she met him, "*Cuando yo lo conocí a él, bueno cuando ya nos casamos, no hablaba casi español*" (When I first knew him, well, when we were already married, he hardly spoke Spanish.) After 10 years of residence in the United States, María Carmen still spoke only Spanish: "*Yo, nada más español*" (I [speak] only Spanish).

Because of María Carmen's limited receptive capability in English, like the immigrant children described by Malakoff and Hakuta (1991) and Pease-Alvarez and Vasquez (1994), Eduardo is often called on by his mother to translate important documents or to act as a broker between her and the outside world. An instance of the latter occurred one intemperate Monday morning after the family had passed the weekend without electricity, as a result of a particularly brutal rainstorm that wreaked havoc in the area. María Carmen asked her son to phone his school in order to find out if there would be classes that day:

Eduardo: [looking for telephone number to phone school] Mom, *¿esto es un* six *o un* zero? (is this a six or a zero?)

María Carmen: *U:n* six.

Eduardo: Yes, erm are we gonna- are we gonna go- have school today? OK. Thank you. Bye. [to Mother] *Dijo que sí.* (S/he said yes.)

Eduardo's father speaks English fluently, and he has no objection when the boys use a fair amount of English with him when they are horsing around; however, Raul is firm that "as soon as they finish playing, having their fun, it's back to, to the serious, uh to Spanish." He adds that sometimes the boys need to be reminded to speak Spanish: "… *y muchas veces se les puede olvidar, pero lo más tarde que uno les diga no: hijo háblame en español, tu- tu idioma es español, me gustaría que supieras el idioma de origen tuyo*" (… and many times they can forget, but then later I tell them "no: son speak to me in Spanish, your—your language is Spanish, I'd like for you to know the language of your origin").

Outside of the proximity of his mother and father, Eduardo spoke Spanish with some interlocutors (his grandmother, who came to visit from Mexico, a "new" boy on the block, from Peru); English with others (his aunt, several cousins); Spanish, with some codeswitching to English, with others (his younger brother, Tomás, who prefers Spanish), and English, with some codeswitching into Spanish with still others (his middle brother, Francisco, who prefers English).[8] His language choices illustrated the principle of accommodation (Giles & Smith, 1979). Asked how he made decisions about which language to use with whom when, Eduardo responded: *"Hablo el inglés cuando cuando no- alguien no sabe hablar en español y en español cuando alguien no sabe hablar en inglés"* (I speak English when when no-someone doesn't know Spanish and Spanish when someone doesn't know English).

All three boys attended the same neighborhood elementary school, and all three were enrolled in English-only classes. When the time came for Eduardo to start kindergarten, his parents were advised that their son would be placed in a bilingual program. Despite his strong belief in Spanish maintenance, Raul was not happy. From his observations of the school experiences of friends and their children in the area, he was convinced that if his son were placed in the bilingual strand, he would not learn English. He went to speak with the school principal:

> *Les dije yo que no, que si le iban a poner en el salón bilingüe yo lo sacaba de la escuela y lo ponía en otra escuela, porque el español estoy yo pa' enseñárselos … yo los mando a la escuela a enseñarles el inglés, no el español, si yo quisiera que supieran el español me los llevo a México, verdad.*

> (I told them no, that if they were going to put him in the bilingual classroom that I would take him out of school and put him in another school, because I'm the one who teaches them Spanish … I send them to school to learn English, not Spanish, if I wanted them to know Spanish I'd take them to Mexico, right?)

Raul and María Carmen were satisfied with the quality of their son's public school education, although they attributed much of the credit for his success to Eduardo himself. From an early age, they informed us, their son was studious, *"un muy buen muchacho"* (a very good boy). Neither Eduardo nor his parents remember reading to him when he was younger. However, according to Raul and María Carmen, the child always showed a strong interest in learning and, before entering school, had taught himself to read in both Spanish and English. From their favorable comments, Eduardo's parents knew that their son's efforts in school were appreciated by his teachers. Notwithstanding the good rapport that Eduardo enjoyed with school personnel, in the course of the observation period, the child started to have difficulty with school math and was frequently stumped when attempting to complete his math homework. María Carmen was concerned and expressed the view to her husband that they should get her son some outside, school-recommended assistance. Raul, however, made the decision to tutor the boy himself, although later he modified this initial strategy to one that combined tutoring with material incentive. ("I told him if he pulled up his grades, I would take him to Disneyland.") However, because school learning was a serious topic, he conducted these tutoring sessions in Spanish, as the following example makes clear:

¿Y y no agarraste la regla y contaste los inches? *Es que por eso ... cuando dice* three feet *y no eres familiar tienes que ir a a a los* (Eduardo: uhhuh) XXXX *y te fijas que son* feet *y por qué se dividen en todo y sacas lo que es, cúantos* inches *hay en* three feet *y qué necesitas para determinar eso.*

(And and you didn't get the ruler and count the inches? For this ... when it says three feet and you don't know you have to go to the /Eduardo: uh huh/ XXXXX and realize that they are feet and why they are divided and you take what is, how many inches there are in three feet and what you need to determine this.)

After Eduardo completes middle school, his parents plan for him to attend high school in Mexico, where he will reside with his maternal grandmother. Eduardo was looking forward to living with his grandmother; he spoke warmly about the stories she told about her childhood, and appreciated the books in Spanish that she sent from Mexico, artifacts that facilitated his transition to school-based literacy.

The Gómez Family: Adapting School Agendas to a Strategy of Aggressive Spanish Maintenance

Esteban and María Gómez and their three sons, Ernesto (age 12), Carlos (age 10), and Antonio (age 5), live on a cattle ranch in the southwest quadrant of San Antonio, where Esteban has worked for more than 10 years. Although the ranch is within the city limits, the environment is rural. Only two other families, also immigrants from northern Mexico, live within easy walking distance. Both Esteban and María were raised in northern Mexico, Esteban on a cattle ranch and María in a small border city. Both completed 9 years of schooling in Mexico. Over the course of several interviews, María, who also completed a secretarial course and later worked as a secretary, evidenced considerable pride in her own proper use of Spanish, as well as concern that her children acquire standard Mexican Spanish, as distinct from the local Texas variety.

Of the families profiled here, the Gómezes maintained the closest ties to Mexico. Nearly all of their relatives lived in a neighboring Mexican state, and most members of María's large family have continued to live in the border city where she grew up. During the period of our case study, the family made the short journey to the border approximately twice a month to spend the weekend with family members. The Gómez children, who also regularly spent parts of their school vacations with their father's family on a Mexican ranch, had ample occasions to use Spanish with their non-English speaking relatives.

Unlike Raul Hernández or Mariana and Enrique Villegas, neither Esteban nor María Gómez had sufficient proficiency in English to choose whether to raise their children with Spanish, English, or both languages. Most of Esteban's working days at the ranch were spent performing tasks alone or with other Spanish-dominant workers. María had taken English classes in the local adult school and achieved the basic proficiency necessary to obtain a part-time position in a school cafeteria. However, she never gained sufficient proficiency to be able to engage in sustained English conversation.

Despite the fact that they did not have a choice as to which language their children would acquire first, the Gómezes did have a clearly articulated vision of the language proficiencies that they desired for their children and a clearly developed strategy for achieving that goal. After considerable discussion, they had decided that their children would have ample opportunity to learn English at school; their role as parents would be to ensure that their sons did not lose Spanish. In our first interview with her, María outlined the family's language decisions,

> *Mi esposo y yo siempre hemos platicado de eso y queremos que aquí en la casa sea el español. Y queremos aprender inglés para cuando salimos. Pero aquí en casa primero- lo primero queremos que los niños aprendan bien el español.*

> (My husband and I have talked a great deal about this and we want Spanish to be the language of the home. And we want to learn English for when we go out. But here at home the first- the first thing we want is for the children to learn Spanish well.)

Somewhat later in the same interview, María clarified her idea of the conditions necessary for her children to become proficient bilinguals. She had no doubt that the children would acquire English. Both of the school-age children had been enrolled in all-English classes since the first grade. Her role in helping her sons to become bilingual was to make sure that they kept up with their Spanish. As she put it: *[los niños] van a ser bilingües porque el español aquí lo van a tener* (they [the boys] are going to be bilingual because they are going to have Spanish here [at home]).

María and Esteban's decision, constantly reaffirmed, to insist on Spanish in family interactions proved effective for minority language maintenance. Indeed, although the two older boys were both fluent in English and the youngest had attended a predominantly English-speaking preschool for 2 years, the Gómez children were among the few in the study who regularly used Spanish in their conversations with one another. Moreover, the Gómez brothers' use of Spanish was not restricted to informal activities but extended to their discussions about school assignments. Among the many responsibilities he exercised as the oldest son, Ernesto, who was very successful in his school work, was often charged with assisting his younger brother with homework. In the following excerpt, recorded during one of the after school observations, Ernesto volunteers to help Carlos to review his assigned spelling words. Note that although the subject, English spelling, is one that would seem most likely to favor the use of English, the main language of the interaction is Spanish.

Ernesto: *Te ayudo con la, para para que estudies diciéndote las palabras, a Carlos.* (I'm helping you with the [word list] so, so that you can study while I read you the words, ok Carlos?)

Carlos: *¿Cuáles palabras?* (What words?)

Ernesto: *Pos las palabras que tienes para* Mrs. Lamar … *las palabras aquí están. A ver. ¿Las palabras que tienen estrella?* (Well the words that you have for Mrs. Lamar … the words are here [points to a sheet of paper with spelling words]. Let's see. The words that have an asterisk?)

Carlos: Yeah.

Ernesto: *A ver. Listo a ver* … bargain. (Let's see. Ready, let's see …)

Carlos: b-a-g-a-i-n.

Ernesto: *Carlos mira, fíjate, dijiste … Ok. bien nomás que te faltó una letra b-a-r. No* b-a-g-a-i-n. (Carlos look, pay attention, you said … Ok. well, the only thing that's missing is a letter.)

Although Ernesto often assumed the role of tutor for his younger brothers, María was also heavily involved with her children's school work, despite the fact that she did not speak the language of the school. Frequently, her participation involved the two older boys' preparation for spelling tests. During several of our visits, she drilled the boys on word lists and checked the correctness of their written answers by orthographic matching with a master list from their school. Moreover, as illustrated by the following exchange between María and Ernesto, recorded during a weekday afternoon observation, she also monitored their progress closely.

María: *No me dijiste cuanto te sacaste ....* (You didn't tell me how you did.)

Ernesto: *Un treinta y dos.* (A thirty two.)

María: *¿Por qué?* (Why?)

Ernesto: *porque eran treinta y tres palabras, treinta y tres cosas. Y cada uno valía un punto y nada más me faltó una palabra.* (because there were thirty three words, thirty three things. And each one was worth a point, and I only missed one word.)

María: *o sea te equivocasté en una ....* (so you were wrong on one ....)

Ernesto: *De todo el examen nada más me saque una mala.* (On the whole exam I only got one wrong.)

María: *¿De todo el examen qué?* (Of the whole exam, what?)

Ernesto: *Nada más me saqué una mal. Una.* (I didn't get any more wrong. Just one.)

María saw her role in her sons' schooling, however, as going beyond monitoring their progress as measured by test scores, or making sure that they were prepared for tasks like spelling quizzes that were accomplished primarily by rote memorization. Although her lack of proficiency in English prevented her from playing an active role in some curricular areas such as writing, she was a highly involved participant in many of the boys' school projects. For example, Ernesto, the oldest brother, spent the greater part of one weekday afternoon observation working on an assignment to construct a rather large and elaborate floor plan, with metric measurements, based loosely on the Gómezes' very modest residence. María was quickly enlisted in the activity. Throughout the process, during which she pointed out the need to include various objects of furniture and commented on her son's choice of colors, María engaged in an extended series of questions in an effort to focus Ernesto's attention on missing details (e.g., an entrance to a bathroom) or to clarify the function of the various rooms:

María: *Bueno, espérame, por ejemplo esta recámara—* (Good, wait a minute, for example, this bedroom—)

Ernesto: Hmm *¿cuál?* (which?)

María: *Uno y dos. Yo no veo baño.* (One and two. I don't see a bathroom.)

Ernesto: *Es el que está con la recámara tres, fíjate aquí en se- en seguida.* (It's the one that's with bedroom three, look right here.)

María: *A que bue—entonces hay que entrar por el pasillo.* (Ah good—then you have to enter from the hallway.)

Ernesto:	*Tienes que salir de la recámara uno y dos, y: entras.* (You have to leave bedroom one and two, and enter [the bathroom].)
María:	*¿De dónde? O sí sí sí.* (From where. O yes, yes, yes.)
Ernesto:	*Eso tiene aquí.* (This has it here.)
María:	*Falta una recámara Ernesto.* (It's missing a bedroom, Ernesto.)
Ernesto:	*¿La de quién?* (Whose?)
María:	*¿Tú con quién vas a dormir?* (Who are you going to sleep with?)
Ernesto:	*Recámara uno.* (Bedroom one.)
María:	*¿Y en la dos?* (And in the second?)
Ernesto:	*Papá y mamá.* (Father and mother.)
María:	*¿Y en la tres?* (And in the third?)
Ernesto:	*Es la recámara de invitados.* (It's the guest bedroom.)
María:	*¿Y Carlos y Antonio?* (And Carlos and Antonio?)
Ernesto:	*Ellos quedan cada quien en su casa.* (Each of them can stay in their own house.)

As the previous excerpt suggests, María's questions, although brief and requiring equally brief responses, are genuine requests for clarification and information. For example, María has no way of knowing that her oldest son intends to evict his younger brothers from his idealized version of the family's living quarters. In this respect, they are typical of the discourse patterns observed in elsewhere in Latino and other minority communities (Heath, 1983; Pease-Alvarez & Vasquez, 1994; Philips, 1983). Indeed, as concerns this family's interactions, aside from instances in which parents or older siblings were quizzing children about rote tasks such as memorizing lists of spelling words, we seldom observed instances of the initiation, response, evaluation pattern that remains the most common sequence of teacher-student interaction in mainstream classrooms (Cazden, 1988; Mehan, 1979; Tharp & Gallimore, 1989).

Esteban and María's strategy, reinforced by the relative isolation of the ranch, by frequent and sometimes prolonged visits to Mexico, and by close ties with monolingual Spanish-speaking relatives, was successful for Spanish maintenance. In contrast to many of the children studied by Wong Fillmore (1991), Ernesto had retained native speaker proficiency in Spanish and, in large measure due to his mother's efforts, had learned to read and write in Spanish as well. Nor did his English suffer as a result. Rather, as indicated by his superior performance in all-English classes, by his writing sample, and by his performance in an extended English interview with one of the English-dominant members of the research team, he developed native-like proficiency in English.

However, Carlos, the middle child in the family, although he also retained native proficiency in Spanish and near-native proficiency in English, experienced frequent difficulties in his schoolwork. María was willing to expend a great deal of time and energy to ensure that her sons met school requirements and, as illustrated in the previous excerpt, she often enlisted her oldest child, Ernesto, in her efforts to provide the additional help that her middle child sometimes required. The primary concern of both María and Esteban, however, was that their children maintain Spanish, which they viewed as a prerequisite for maintaining their own parental authority and for participation in extended and easily accessible family networks in Mexico.

DISCUSSION

Parents in the families profiled here were all intensely involved with their children's literacy development and schooling, and they often developed ingenious strategies to compensate for their own limitations. Parents differed, however, in their ability and willingness to alter their home language practices to match those of the schools their children attended. In two families, parents modified their home language practices repeatedly in order to fulfill the often conflicting requirements of school success for the children, the expectations of relatives who wished to see Spanish transmitted to the next generation, and the pragmatic requirements of communication with Spanish monolingual members of the household. Teresa Esparza relied on recordings of English children's books to prepare her preschool daughter for a private, English-medium school. When her daughter reached the upper elementary grades where the curriculum surpassed her own limited educational background, Teresa enlisted the aid of Mariana Villegas, the most highly educated of the parents of Marcella's friends. Like Teresa Esparza, Mariana and Enrique Villegas altered their own home language practices, in their case, at the express urging of their daughter's teacher. The Villegases possessed far greater linguistic and educational capital than did Teresa, in English proficiency, particularly on the part of Mariana, and in access to Spanish literacy in the form of books and a Spanish-language encyclopedia sent from Mexico by Enrique's mother. Thus, they had greater ability to meet the conflicting demands that they perceived from the school and their own families and to alter their home language practices accordingly.

For both the Esparza and the Villegas families, however, the changes in home language practices involved some cost. Teresa, for example, concerned with providing her daughter with access to the dominant language and the educational advantages associated with such access, focused exclusively on teaching the then preschooler Marcella to read in English. Marcella was never taught to read in Spanish, and, as we have seen, she regretted her inability to read age-appropriate books in the language that occupied such an important place in her home. Although Marcella will be able to develop her Spanish literacy later should she so desire, to the extent that the neglect of mother tongue literacy seen in her case is typical of children in immigrant families, the long-term consequences for language maintenance and cultural continuity can be predicted.

The linguistic losses occasioned by shifts in home language practices in the Villegas family did not appear to affect Diana Villegas's general progress in school or Spanish proficiency. However, the changes in family language policy did exact a toll. For example, Enrique Villegas initially welcomed the opportunity to improve his own English provided by his and Mariana's effort to use English in home interactions, a practice strongly advocated by their daughter's kindergarten teacher at St. Mary's. Before long, however, all members of the household came to view these interactions as disorienting. Mariana and Enrique also had to deal with the consequences of their decision to resume the use of Spanish at home and to insist that their children use the language as well. Their anguish in this regard was particularly evident after Luis Villegas was refused entry to St. Mary's kindergarten midway through the study. The couple wrestled with their feelings of guilt over the possibility that their decision to return to using Spanish at home with their children in an effort to avert Diana's language attrition had interfered with their younger child's development. Mariana's decision to teach Luis how to write again brought the issue of language choice to the fore:

> *Ahora con Luis el problema es … yo le empecé a enseñar de escribir, porque en la escuela me dijeron que … no pudo entrar porque no sabe hacer nada. Entonces yo empecé a enseñarle a escribir su nombre, y ahora mi problema es qué hago, le enseño en inglés o le enseño en español, y no sé.*

> (Now with Luis the problem is … I began to teach him how to write, because in the school [Saint Mary's] they told me that … he couldn't enter [kindergarten] because he didn't know how to do anything. Then I began to teach him to write his name, and now my problem is what to do, teach him in English or teach him in Spanish, and I don't know.)

The Villegas and the Esparza families illustrate the dilemmas faced by parents who attempt to alter patterns of home language use to meet what they perceive to be the expectations of the schools. The Hernández and Gómez families demonstrate the persistence required by parents who wish to maintain a minority language as the language of the home while fostering their children's academic development in English. Raul Hernández reported that he frequently needed to remind his sons to speak Spanish when speaking of serious topics, including schoolwork. Moreover, although the use of Spanish by a bilingual parent to supervise and assist with English homework assignments might seem counterproductive, the practice had a basis in the life trajectories Raul and María Carmen envisioned for their children, which included attending high school in Mexico. It also conformed to Raul's language ideology, which held that Spanish was worthy of being used for serious matters, including school learning.

Like the Hernández family, the Gómez family remained consistent in their home language practices. María and Esteban's insistence that their children use only Spanish at home, including in sibling-sibling interactions, was facilitated by the relative isolation of the ranch on which they lived as well as by their frequent visits with the Mexican relatives who formed their primary social networks, factors that have been identified as favoring minority language maintenance (Fishman, 1991; Ortiz, 1975). Insistence on the use of Spanish in home interactions, however, did not preclude parental involvement in the school's activities. María Gómez's lack of proficiency in the language of the school prevented her from working with her sons in some areas of the curriculum. Nevertheless, she was actively engaged in areas where she could be of help and closely monitored her children's progress in other areas as well.

CONCLUSION

Parents in this study, whose strongest or only language differed from that of the school, adopted a wide range of strategies in order to assist their children with school-related tasks. These strategies included using audio recordings of children's books to teach a child to read in English, using the cooperative social networks that characterize Latino immigrant communities to find assistance for a child when the level of schoolwork had surpassed the mother's educational attainment, and providing at-home tutorial and review sessions in English, Spanish, or both when children experienced difficulty with particular subjects. These strategies, moreover, were not devised ad hoc to deal with problems as they arose. Rather, they were expressions of well-formed ideologies—about Spanish maintenance and its relationship to cultural identity and about factors that parents believed fostered language learning.

Along with this first set of ideologies concerning issues of minority language maintenance and dominant language acquisition, however, parents provided evidence of another set of beliefs concerning the respective roles and responsibilities of different societal institutions, notably schools and homes, in child development. Here, although differences among the families were observed with regard to perception of issues of power and inequality, the families we worked with acquiesced to the ideological framing through which professional educators—teachers, administrators, and policymakers—understood and sought to practice the family-school relationship. Specifically with regard to their engagement in literacy activities, their primary concern was with how the pedagogical work that they did at home, involving interactions with texts, fit with and supported the work of the classroom in promoting school literacy—that is, literacy for literacy's sake. Although our data contain some examples of home literacy activities for instrumental purposes (e.g., deciphering the information on promotional coupons), we found that, overwhelmingly, the school literacy agenda dominated home literacy activities (cf. McDermott, Goldman, & Varenne, 1984). This finding is understandable, especially given an absence of encouraging large-scale evidence concerning the success of Latino students in North American schools. Nevertheless, we view as troubling the increasing tendency on the part of contemporary schooling to link parents' performance of activities that support and extend the school's agenda to children's educability. Such expectations, in addition to contributing to the stressful nature of language socialization decisions for language minority parents, do little to address the gaps and disjunctures in the complex relationship between parents, education, and schooling.

We suggest that the gaps and disjunctures in the perspectives of educators and language minority parents might be better addressed if educators attended more closely to parental aspirations for their children's schooling. As illustrated by the families profiled here, language minority parents are likely to have clearly developed visions, which many educators share, of the academic language proficiencies they desire for their children. Many have also developed a variety of inventive strategies for achieving the linguistic and literacy goals they envision for their children. In a similar spirit, educators who are mindful of the resources language minority parents contribute to their children's education will be in an advantageous position to develop successful home-school partnerships based on a more fundamentally democratic relationship between schools and families than is currently the norm.

NOTES

*This research was supported by a U.S. Department of Education Field-Initiated Studies Grant (R117E40326–94) and a Spencer Foundation Grant to both authors, and by a National Academy of Education Spencer Fellowship and a University of Texas at San Antonio faculty development leave to the first author. Adriana Boogerman, Martha López-Durkin, Johanna Meighan, Elvia Ornelos-García, Rose Mary Reyna, and Buenaventura Torres-Ayala assisted with observations, interviews, and transcriptions. Special thanks to the families who allowed us to share a portion of their lives and trusted us to tell their stories from our perspectives.

1. The preponderance of California immigrant families reflects our overall sample, which sought to mirror the overall Mexican-background population of the two states. In California, approximately 70% of Mexican-background adults were born in Mexico. In Texas, approximately 70% were born in Texas (Solé, 1995).

2. Teresa Esparza and all other participant names are pseudonyms, as are the names of the northern California towns. The population structure of San Antonio, with more than 500,000 inhabitants of Mexican origin, made it unnecessary to use a pseudonym for the city.

3. We have kept transcription conventions to a minimum for the sake of readability. The following conventions have been retained: all uppercase letters indicate strong emphasis; a colon following a vowel (e.g., *e*:) indicates an elongated vowel; an equal sign (=) indicates an overlap; X indicates inaudible text, with each X indicating a syllable; translations are in parentheses and comments are in brackets.

4. It is difficult to estimate the percentage of the Mexican population that belongs to this stratum, particularly in the period following the collapse of the peso in December, 1994. However, Nolasco and Acevedo (1985, cited in Valdés, 1996, pp. 175–176), who studied social stratification in Ciudad Juárez and Tijuana, estimated that 8% of the population belonged to this stratum, which also included middle-level executives and business people.

5. The expression *ir pa' 'trás* (lit. to go back), a socially salient variant which is common in popular dialects of U.S. Spanish, is most likely an English calque. *Regresar* (to return) is the standard form.

6. The rejection of their son by St. Mary's resulted in considerable consternation in the Villegas household. Mariana and Enrique's initial feelings of guilt over the consequences of their household language policy eventually turned to anger against a system in which the fate of their children was determined more by overt descriptors such as ethnicity and language than by less visible ones such as class. See Schecter and Bayley (2002) for a more detailed account of the Villegases' journey from Mexican elite to U.S. minority status.

7. The address given here is, of course, fictitious.

8. The issue of what is the base language in any conversation involving extensive codeswitching is admittedly complex. For the purposes of this study, we adopt Myers-Scotton's (1993) matrix language frame model. According to this model, in a mixed language conversation, the language that supplies the majority of system morphemes is the base language. The base language can (and does) change as new interlocutors enter into a conversation or as the topic shifts.

REFERENCES

Bayley, R. (2004). Linguistic diversity and English language acquisition. In E. Finegan & J. R. Rickford (Eds.), *Language in the USA: Themes for the 21st century* (pp. 268–286). Cambridge: Cambridge University Press.

Bayley, R., Alvarez-Calderón, A., & Schecter, S. R. (1998). Tense and aspect in Mexican-descent children's Spanish narratives. In E. V. Clark (Ed.), *The proceedings of the twenty-ninth annual Child Language Research Forum* (pp. 221–230). Stanford, CA: Center for the Study of Language and Information.

Bayley, R., & Schecter, S. R. (Eds.). (2003). *Language socialization in bilingual and multilingual societies*. Clevedon, England: Multilingual Matters.

Bayley, R., Schecter, S. R., & Torres-Ayala, B. (1996). Strategies for bilingual maintenance: Case studies of Mexican-origin families in Texas. *Linguistics and Education, 8,* 389–408.

Bogdan, R. C., & Biklen, S. K. (1992). *Qualitative research for education: An introduction to theory and methods.* Boston: Allyn & Bacon.

Cazden, C. (1988). *Classroom discourse: The language of teaching and learning.* Portsmouth, NH: Heinemann.

Chomsky, N. (1981). *Lectures on government and binding.* Dordrecht: Foris.

Crago, M. B., Chen, C., Genesee, F., & Allen, S. E. M. (1998). Power and deference: Bilingual decision making in Inuit homes. *Journal for a Just and Caring Education, 4,* 78–95.

Eisenberg, A. (1986). Teasing: Verbal play in two Mexicano homes. In B. B. Schieffelin & E. Ochs (Eds.), *Language socialization across cultures* (pp. 182–108). Cambridge: Cambridge University Press.

Fishman, J. A. (1991). *Reversing language shift: Theoretical and empirical foundations of assistance to threatened languages.* Clevedon, England: Multilingual Matters.

Gaskins, S., Miller, P. J., & Corsaro, W. A. (1992). Theoretical and methodological perspectives in the interpretative study of children. In W. A. Corsaro & P. J. Miller (Eds.), *Interpretative approaches to children's socialization* (pp. 5–23). San Francisco: Jossey-Bass.

Giles, H., & Smith, P. (1979). Accommodation theory: Optimal levels of convergence. In H. Giles & R. St. Clair (Eds.), *Language and social psychology* (pp. 45–65). Oxford: Blackwell.

Goodwin, M. H. (1990). *He-said-she-said: Talk as social organization among Black children.* Bloomington: Indiana University Press.

Griffith, A., & Schecter, S. R. (1998). Introduction to the special issue: Mothering, educating, and schooling. *Journal for a Just and Caring Education, 4,* 5–10.

Hakuta, K. (1986). *Mirror of language: The debate on bilingualism.* New York: Basic Books.

Hakuta, K., & D'Andrea, D. (1992). Some properties of bilingual maintenance and loss in Mexican background high-school students. *Applied Linguistics, 13,* 72–99.

Hakuta, K., & Pease-Alvarez, L. (1994). Proficiency, choice and attitudes in bilingual Mexican-American children. In G. Extra & L. Verhoeven (Eds.), *The cross-linguistic study of bilingual development* (pp. 145–164). Amsterdam: The Netherlands Academy of Arts and Sciences.

Heath, S. B. (1982). What no bedtime story means: Narrative skills at home and at school. *Language in Society, 11,* 49–76.

Heath, S. B. (1983). *Ways with words: Language, life, and work in communities and classrooms.* Cambridge: Cambridge University Press.

Jaeggli, O. A., & Safir, K. (Eds.). (1989). *The null subject parameter.* Dordrecht: Kluwer.

Kulick, D. (1992). *Language shift and cultural reproduction: Socialization, self, and syncretism in a Papua New Guinean village.* Cambridge: Cambridge University Press.

Malakoff, M., & Hakuta, K. (1991). Translation skill and metalinguistic awareness in bilinguals. In E. Bialystok (Ed.), *Language processing in bilingual children* (pp. 141–166). Cambridge: Cambridge University Press.

McDermott, R. P., Goldman, S., & Varenne, H. (1984). When school goes home: Some problems in the organization of homework. *Teachers College Record, 85,* 381–409.

Mehan, H. (1979). What time is it, Denise?: Asking known information questions in classroom discourse. *Theory into Practice, 18,* 285–294.

Meisel, J. M. (1995). Parameters in acquisition. In P. Fletcher & B. MacWhinney (Eds.), *The handbook of child language* (pp. 10–35). Oxford: Blackwell.

Miles, M. B., & Huberman, A. M. (1984). *Qualitative data analysis: A sourcebook of new methods.* Beverly Hills, CA: Sage.

Myers-Scotton, C. (1993). *Duelling languages: Grammatical structure in codeswitching.* Oxford: Oxford University Press.

Nolasco, M., & Acevedo, M. L. (1985). *Los niños de la frontera* [Border children]. Mexico City: Centro de Ecodesarrollo, Ediciones Oceano, S. A.

Ochs, E. (1988). *Culture and language development: Language acquisition and language socialization in a Samoan village.* Cambridge: Cambridge University Press.

Ochs, E., & Schieffelin, B. B. (1995). The impact of language socialization on grammatical development. In P. Fletcher & B. MacWhinney (Eds.), *The handbook of child language* (pp. 73–94). Oxford: Blackwell.

Ortiz, L. I. (1975). *A sociolinguistic study of language maintenance in the northern New Mexico community of Arroyo Seco.* Unpublished doctoral dissertation, University of New Mexico.

Pacini, M. V. (1998). *The language of power: Interactions between Latino parents and the Canadian school system.* Unpublished master's thesis, York University, Ontario.

Patrick, D. (2003). Language socialization and second language acquisition in a multilingual arctic Québec community. In R. Bayley & S. R. Schecter (Eds.), *Language socialization in bilingual and multilingual societies* (pp. 165–181). Clevedon, England: Multilingual Matters.

Pease-Alvarez, L. (2002). Moving beyond linear trajectories of language shift and bilingual language socialization. *Hispanic Journal of Behavioral Sciences, 24,* 114–137.

Pease-Alvarez, L., & Vasquez, O. (1994). Language socialization in ethnic minority communities. In F. Genesee (Ed.), *Educating second language children: The whole child, the whole curriculum, the whole community* (pp. 82–102). New York: Cambridge University Press.

Philips, S. U. (1983). *The invisible culture: Communication in classroom and community on the Warm Springs Indian Reservation.* New York: Longman.

Pinker, S. (1984). *Language learnability and language development.* Cambridge, MA: Harvard University Press.

Plunkett, K. (1995). Connectionism and language acquisition. In P. Fletcher & B. MacWhinney (Eds.), *The handbook of child language* (pp. 36–72). Oxford: Blackwell.

Portes, A., & Schauffler, R. (1996). Language and the second generation: Bilingualism yesterday and today. In A. Portes (Ed.), *The new second generation* (pp. 8–29). New York: Russell Sage Foundation.

Rumelhart, D. E., & McClelland, J. L. (1986). On learning the past tense of English verbs. In J. L. McClelland, D. E. Rumelhart, & the PDP Research Group (Eds.), *Parallel distributed processing: Explorations in the microstructure of cognition: Vol. 2. Psychological and biological models* (pp. 216–271). Cambridge, MA: MIT Press.

Schecter, S. R., & Bayley, R. (1997). Language socialization practices and cultural identity: Case studies of Mexican-descent families in California and Texas. *TESOL Quarterly, 31,* 513–541.

Schecter, S. R., & Bayley, R. (1998). Concurrence and complementarity: Mexican-background parents' decisions about language and schooling. *Journal for a Just and Caring Education, 4,* 47–64.

Schecter, S. R., & Bayley, R. (2002). *Language as cultural practice: Mexicanos en el norte.* Mahwah, NJ: Lawrence Erlbaum Associates.

Schecter, S. R., & Bayley, R. (2004). Language socialization in theory and practice. *International Journal of Qualitative Studies in Education, 17,* 606–625.

Schecter, S. R., Sharken-Taboada, D., & Bayley, R. (1996). Bilingual by choice: Latino parents' rationales and strategies for raising children with two languages. *Bilingual Research Journal, 20,* 261–281.

Schieffelin, B. B. (1990). *The give and take of everyday life: Language socialization of Kaluli children.* Cambridge: Cambridge University Press.

Schieffelin, B. B., & Ochs, E. (1986). Language socialization. *Annual Review of Anthropology, 15,* 163–191.

Solé, Y. R. (1995). Language, nationalism, and ethnicity in the Americas. *International Journal of the Sociology of Language, 116,* 111–138.

Spindler, G., & Spindler, L. (Eds.). (1987). *Interpretative ethnography of education: At home and abroad.* Hillsdale, NJ: Lawrence Erlbaum Associates.

Tharp, R., & Gallimore, R. (1989). *Rousing minds to life: Teaching, learning, and schooling in social context.* New York: Cambridge University Press.

Valdés, G. (1996). *Con respeto: Bridging the distances between culturally diverse families and schools.* New York: Teachers College Press.

Valdés, G., & Figueroa, R. (1994). *Bilingualism and testing: A special case of bias.* Norwood, NJ: Ablex.

Vasquez, O., Pease-Alvarez, L., & Shannon, S. (1994). *Pushing boundaries: Language and culture in a Mexicano community.* Cambridge: Cambridge University Press.

Wong Fillmore, L. (1991). When learning a second language means losing the first. *Early Childhood Research Quarterly, 6,* 323–346.

Zentella, A. C. (1997). *Growing up bilingual: Puerto Rican children in New York.* Oxford: Blackwell.

Zentella, A. C. (Ed.). (2005). *Building on strength: Language and literacy in Latino families and communities.* New York: Teachers College Press.

III

Exemplars of Forms of Talk
and Their Evolution
Inside of School Contexts

CHAPTER 7

Using Literature Discussions to Reason Through Real-Life Dilemmas: A Journey Taken by One Teacher and Her Fourth-Grade Students

Kim T. Nguyen-Jahiel
Richard C. Anderson
Martha Waggoner
Betty Rowell

This chapter traces one veteran teacher's implementation of a new discussion method called Collaborative Reasoning (CR) in her classroom. It is a case study from a larger research program at the University of Illinois which uses microanalyses to explore the use of reasoned discourse as a means of stimulating critical reading and thinking skills in elementary school students (Anderson, Chinn, Waggoner, & Nguyen, 1998; Anderson, Chinn, Chang, Waggoner, & Yi, 1997; Chinn, Anderson, & Waggoner, 2001; Clark et al., 2003; Reznitskaya et al., 2001; Waggoner, Chinn, Anderson, & Yi, 1995). We will see how this teacher—whom we will call Shirley Rogers—and a group of her fourth-grade students were able to meet the challenges of using this new method. We first describe a typical language arts session in Mrs. Rogers's classroom, followed by a synopsis of the CR model. We then look at Mrs. Rogers's implementation of this model with her group of students. After looking at the changes in Mrs. Rogers's practice, we examine the transformations that occurred both in the focus of the discussion and in the patterns of interactions in the group. Finally, we conclude with some reflections on the process of negotiation and renegotiation of roles that took place as Mrs. Rogers and her group adopted the model.

The elementary school in which we found Mrs. Rogers and her students is located in a midsized midwestern U.S. town. Its student body comes from an ethnically mixed neighborhood. Over 50% of the students are African American, about 30% are Caucasian, and the remainder are from Latina/o, Asian, and other minority cultures. Over 90% of these students are eligible for subsidized breakfast and lunch programs. Mrs. Rogers's fourth-grade classroom had 24 students: 15 boys and 9 girls. She considered 8 of these students to be accelerated, 8 average, 3 borderline low-average, and 5 below average for their grade level. The students featured in this chapter belonged to the average ability reading group. Mrs. Rogers had approximately 20 years of teaching and had taught in the current school for about 10 years. Considered by the school district and her colleagues to be a master teacher, Mrs. Rogers is often asked to conduct workshops for other teachers.

Our research team collaborated with Mrs. Rogers over a period of 3 months to implement CR in group discussions in her classroom. Group discussions were approximately 20 minutes in length, and took place twice a week for 2½ months. The analysis at the heart of this chapter is based on videotapes taken of 20 of these group discussions, post-project interviews with Mrs. Rogers, and field notes taken by a research team member. Mrs. Rogers volunteered to take part in this semester-long study of CR after she participated in a workshop for the faculty at her school. The workshop contrasted conventional direct instruction with the responsive teaching expected in CR. Mrs. Rogers forewarned us, "You know that direct instruction teacher you were talking about? That's me!"

To appreciate the transformation that occurred in Mrs. Rogers's group discussions during their use of CR, it is helpful to visualize a typical language arts session in her classroom prior to the implementation of this new approach. Before this project, if one were to walk into Mrs. Rogers's room during language arts period, one would almost always see teacher-directed, whole-class discussion. The objectives of the discussion would be to ensure that the students knew the main points in the selected story and were able to make personal connections to the characters and events. Mrs. Rogers closely guided students' thinking about the day's selection, often punctuating the discussion with colorful personal anecdotes and inviting students to draw parallels to their lives. She set the parameters within which the students would interpret the selection, as in her introduction of the poem, "We Never Get to Do Anything" (Alexander, 1970):

Mrs. Rogers: What we're doing today is talk about vocabulary words, today, as well as a poem that I found rather amusing. I had fun reading it and I hope you had fun.

[Several lines omitted]

Mrs. Rogers: Listen to this humorous poem. The reason it's called humorous is because it should be a little bit funny. It should tickle your innards a little bit. Think about it as I read it. The title of the poem is "I'm Never Allowed to Do Anything" [sic].

Thus, she set the stage for how the students should receive the poem. From her introduction, the students learned that they, too, should find the poem amusing.

The discussion of this poem, depicting a battle of wills between a boy and his mother, consisted primarily of students reflecting on remarks or questions that Mrs. Rogers initiated. The students were not given the space to propose their own interpretations of, or responses to, the poem.

This was consistent with the typical Initiation Response Evaluation (IRE) pattern of interaction—teacher question, student response, teacher evaluation (Sinclair & Coulthard, 1975)—which characterized Mrs. Rogers's classroom discussions at the time that the project began. Mrs. Rogers dominated the discussions and posed almost all of the questions. Some of her questions assessed whether students knew vocabulary words or specific details of a story. Other questions, such as "How many of you are a part of a family where your mom lives in one place and your dad lives in another?" were to elicit choral responses from the entire class (students responded by raising their hands) rather than response from an individual student. She posed many rhetorical questions such as "did you think about x ?" to get the students to reflect on the themes in the stories.

COLLABORATIVE REASONING: AN ALTERNATIVE FORMAT FOR LITERATURE DISCUSSION

Collaborative Reasoning is one approach to story discussion that allows students greater expressive latitude than typical recitations (Commeyras, 1994; Eeds & Wells, 1989; Raphael & McMahon, 1994; Short & Pierce, 1990). The overarching goal of CR is "inculcating the values and habits of mind to use reasoned discourse as a means for choosing among competing ideas" (Anderson et al., 1998). The immediate goal is to help students reason through complex issues as revealed by a piece of literature. Through the process of group reasoning, literature is brought to life in the classroom. Literature discussion thus becomes a process of teasing out and working through "big" issues; handling ambiguity and opposing viewpoints; reasoning, exploring, and building arguments; and holding one's own or letting go within a social context. The stories have to matter to the students, and the structure of the discussions must promote open dialogue. With this in mind, our stories are carefully selected such that they raise real issues and problems: race relations, marriage, filial obligations, injustice, inequality, honesty, integrity, and winning and losing. These problems are multilayered, morally ambiguous, and often controversial. For each story, we find a "central question" to be used as a springboard for discussion. One of the prominent features of CR is the open participation structure, encouraging a free and natural dialogue among group members. Students orchestrate their discussions by managing the turntaking and topical flow with little control or direction from the teacher. Students decide when to talk and when to shift topics without being acknowledged by the teacher. The teacher plays a secondary role by providing support to the group.

A typical CR discussion begins with students reading silently at their seats. They then gather in a small group to discuss the story. The dialogue begins with the teacher posing the central question that addresses the complex issues in the story. Students express their positions on the issue and are expected to provide reasons and supporting evidence for their positions. They are also expected to carefully listen and evaluate one another's arguments. Students come to the discussion not just to present their arguments or challenge the positions of others but, in a cooperative effort, to explore alternative perspectives. The role of the teacher is to promote a thoughtful discussion by offering challenging viewpoints. In addition, the teacher provides scaffolding for good thinking strategies by asking students for clarification, prompting for evidence to support a position, challenging a reason, or offering counterarguments. Eventually the teacher relinquishes her role as expert and joins the group as an equal discussant—one who is also wrestling with the big issues.

Mrs. Rogers's Implementation of Collaborative Reasoning

The CR approach was so different from Mrs. Rogers's regular language arts lessons that both teacher and students had to learn new ways of talking and thinking. Mrs. Rogers had a powerful presence in her classroom and commanded a great deal of respect from her students. The clearly defined roles in her room, based on traditional notions of teacher as the giver of knowledge and students as receivers, made it difficult, at first, for Mrs. Rogers to take off her cloak of authority and for her students to assume responsibility for their own thinking.

During the first several CR discussions, Mrs. Rogers wrote the reasons students gave for their positions on the chalkboard. While she was writing, the children would sit quietly waiting for her to finish instead of continuing to discuss the central question. Several times she had to urge the children to continue talking. Finally, as the children began whispered conversations about the question, Mrs. Rogers turned from the board to hear a child ask another child the reasons for her position. Mrs. Rogers exclaimed that asking others for their reasons and evidence was exactly what she wanted them to do. This turned out to be a pivotal moment for the group. Subsequently, the children began to assume more and more responsibility for inviting others into the discussion and probing their arguments. Eventually, Mrs. Rogers gave up listing reasons on the chalkboard, as it became apparent that this practice slowed down the discussion.

Mrs. Rogers had students use cards with a "yes" on one side and a "no" on the other side to indicate their positions on the discussion question. Introducing the position cards, she said, "Turn your card so I can see your position." All the students then faced their cards toward Mrs. Rogers and waited for her to manage the discussion. Two days later, after realizing that in CR students are supposed to engage one another, she changed her direction to "Turn your card so others in the group can see your position." This change brought more spontaneity into the discussion as the children began to prompt and challenge one another without relying on Mrs. Rogers.

Coached by a research team member [M. W.] who was a participant observer in the classroom, Mrs. Rogers employed several CR instructional moves (see Waggoner, Chinn, Yi, & Anderson, 1995) to facilitate the group discussions. These included *prompting* students to give evidence and support for their positions, *modeling* the reasoning process, *asking for clarification* of students' meaning, *challenging* students with alternative perspectives, *encouraging* students, *summing up* what students have said, and *fostering independence*. These are similar to the strategies in reciprocal teaching, articulated by Hacker and Graesser (chap. 10, this vol.) and Palincsar and Brown (1985). In addition to using the aforementioned instructional moves developed by the research team, Mrs. Rogers invented her own, such as the position cards already described, as well as students' argument outlines and debriefing sessions following the discussions (described later in this chapter).

Which instructional move is appropriate at a given moment in a discussion depends on the degree of control that students have over reasoning and rhetorical strategies and their level of independence. In the beginning, when they were learning how to engage in reasoned argumentation, Mrs. Rogers relied on instructional moves that provided a great deal of support to the students. Also, it seemed that she preferred to use some moves more than others simply because they were more consistent with her personal style.

Prompting

Mrs. Rogers prompted frequently during the first few discussion sessions because students were not spontaneously giving reasons and supporting evidence for their positions. To help students develop their reasoning, she asked many prompting questions, such as, "Can you tell me why?" "What makes you think that …?" and "Is there any proof in the story?" Also, just as the students were learning to answer questions like these, Mrs. Rogers was learning how to ask them. We see this in an excerpt of the first discussion session. The group was talking about a story titled "Fishing All Day" (Dobrin, 1973). In the story, a boy named Nikki had to decide whether to go to Moscow to live with a childless couple who had befriended him or stay home and take care of his sick aunt. The central question was "Should Nikki go to Moscow with Simon and his wife?"

Mrs. Rogers:	… What makes you think that his aunt needs him so much?
Kenny:	Um, he care he cares about his aunt.
Mrs. Rogers:	Where does it say that?
Kenny:	Um, where it says, "But, what about my aunt?"
Mrs. Rogers:	Okay. Is that on the, uh, back page then? Which paragraphs? Which number? Do you see the numbers on the side?
Kenny:	Ten.
Mrs. Rogers:	Okay. Paragraph ten. Read that please.
Kenny:	'But what about my aunt?' asked Nikki."
Mrs. Rogers:	Okay. That's proof that his aunt needs him. He considers her. What else, uh, which paragraph would you refer to let us know that his aunt truly needs him? Most of you, three of you are talking about his relationship with his aunt and how she needs him, and that's why he should not go. Do you have any other proof that she needs him?

Kenny made an assertion about Nikki's relationship with his aunt without backing it up. Mrs. Rogers then asked him to provide proof from the text. Not only did she ask him for evidence, but she insisted that he quote specific sections in the story. In later discussions, her prompts were more open ended. Rather than asking students for the specific page and paragraph number, Mrs. Rogers would simply ask students if they had any proof for their statements. Students sometimes provided specific citations in later discussions without being asked (see Anderson et al., 2001).

Modeling

In response to suggestions from the research team member in her room, Mrs. Rogers attempted to model aspects of reflective thinking, but seldom carried it through. In a couple of discussions, Mrs. Rogers began, "When I think of …," but then immediately became more direct. When students failed to make a particular move, such as challenging or rebutting one another, Mrs. Rogers would explicitly tell them what they should have done rather than modeling the moves. We see her direct approach in an excerpt from an earlier discussion session when the group talked about the book *The Gold Cadillac* (Taylor, 1987). In this story, a Black Ohio man took his family in his brand new Cadillac to the South to visit his extended family. If set in today's time period, there might or might not be much to the story. But, this story was set in the pre–civil rights South. The question to be dealt with, from his daughters' perspective, was "Should Father have taken the Cadillac to the South?"

Tamika:	'cuz they're mad because, I guess they're mad because they won and so if they can't have slavery they're going to treat them mean in a different way.
Student:	Can I ask everybody a question? Um, would you guys like to live in a, would you guys like a like, Mississippi to be like that?
All students:	No!
Mrs. Rogers:	Why not is what you should be asking your classmates.

During this discussion, the students generated ideas about life in the South. Tamika insightfully pointed out that even though slavery had formally ended, injustice and inequality continued in other forms. One student wondered if anyone in the group would even want to live in Mississippi. When this student failed to follow up on the resounding "No!" response from his peers, Mrs. Rogers instructed him to ask them why.

Although Mrs. Rogers rarely modeled the thinking process, she frequently used the vocabulary of critical and reflective thinking. At first, when the students neglected to use these terms and instead would say, "I feel the same as [name]," Mrs. Rogers immediately would reword their statements with "OK. So, you agree with [name]." After only a few sessions, the students began to use these terms with ease. The most common of these were "I challenge [name]" and "I agree/disagree with [name]."

Asking for Clarification

During the first few sessions, the students had difficulty being clear in their references to the characters and events in the story. Consequently, their arguments were elliptical and difficult to follow. To help them be more precise about their references, Mrs. Rogers frequently directed them to identify the characters by name. The following excerpt, taken from a discussion about *The Gold Cadillac*, illustrates how she guided the students to be more lucid in their statements.

John:	What if they, what if they don't send the letters, send the letters to, to his, uh his parents?

Tamika:	They have a right to do that, to mail the letters //
John:	What if they don't?
Joshua:	If they write them, then how //
Mrs. Rogers:	What do you mean *they*? "What if *they* don't," who's *they*?
John:	The people who sent the letters.
Joshua:	The post office people.
John:	The post office people.
Mrs. Rogers:	OK. The post office people
Joshua:	Then writing letters wouldn't help.

All of the students used the pronoun *they*, but each referred to different people. In the beginning, John used *they* to refer to the postal workers when he asked, "What if they don't send the letters to his parents?" But Tamika used *they* to designate somebody else entirely in her response, "They have the right to do that, to mail the letters." Here, *they* might refer to the families—the families have the right to send each other mail. Though the students were trying to challenge one another, their talk was muddled. John even got lost in his own argument, at first referring to the postal workers but later switching to the "people who send the letters" when Mrs. Rogers asked him to clarify, "What if they don't, who's *they*?" Once the group agreed on a common referent of *they* (to mean the postal workers), Joshua concluded that "writing letters wouldn't help" the family.

Challenging

In CR, when students all line up on one side of an issue, the teacher is supposed to play the devil's advocate to challenge students to consider other perspectives. At first, Mrs. Rogers would express another side of an issue so forcefully that by the time she had finished speaking, all of the students had switched their position cards. With coaching from the research team member, she began to problematize her talk, introducing alternate perspectives with such phrases as, "Some people might say that ..." By the end of the year, although Mrs. Rogers still sometimes stated alternative positions more strongly than the research team would have preferred, students were defending their positions even when their teacher expressed an opposing view.

This can be seen in one of the later discussion sessions on logging. In this discussion, two opposing perspectives were presented. The first perspective, that of Mrs. Morgan and the loggers, supported the logging of Oak Grove Forest. The second perspective, that taken by Mr. Held and the environmentalists, opposed the logging of the forest. The central question in this story was, "Should logging on Oak Grove Forest be stopped?"

| Mrs. Rogers: | ... I really think, and I think a lot of people that aren't in this room with us today would agree that, uh, we better look out for the people and think about the loggers first because people are more important than these animals, plants, and trees ... We're number one. Then, we can worry about the plants, trees, and the animals after we take care of ourselves and make sure we have |

our tissue paper, our paper for school, our books, pages for our books ...

Kenny: I want to challenge Mrs. Rogers because, um, you don't have to kill, they don't have to chop down all the trees because you could stop using so much toilet paper and, um, and you don't and you, um ... Teachers like take lots of paper and copy it and they could like, um, stop copying all the papers.

Mrs. Rogers: What am I going to do, just talk all day, Kenny?

[Several turns deleted]

Mrs. Rogers: No books to read from, no paper to write on, we just talk.

Kenny: No, you could just like, still keep things, just make it littler and, um, stop using so much wood for like houses and chairs. You could make 'em like the plastic chairs that we have.

Prior to this excerpt, Kenny had maintained that logging in Oak Grove Forest should be stopped. Playing the role of the devil's advocate, Mrs. Rogers went to great length to present the perspective of the loggers, but Kenny did not back down. He asserted that one could look out for the well-being of people and, at the same time, respect the environment. In fact, he even upped the ante by challenging Mrs. Rogers personally. He singled out teachers as an example of a group of people that contributed to the destruction of the forest through their wasteful use "of lots of paper." He boldly stated, "stop copying all the papers." Despite her persistent challenging, "What am I going to do, just talk all day?" and "No books to read from, no paper to write on, we just talk," Kenny held fast to his position, pointing out that one "could still keep things" but "just stop using so much."

Encouraging

Mrs. Rogers had a special knack for encouraging students. She would sing the praises of students who displayed new reasoning and discussion skills, often talking at considerable length about exactly what a student had done that was praiseworthy, why it was praiseworthy, and when others might consider following the example in the future. Particularly in the early discussions, Mrs. Rogers used praise to encourage students to express reasons and back arguments with supporting evidence from the text. She would often say that she liked the way that they "looked for proof" when students were searching the story or "That's a great question!" when a student asked a good question.

Fostering Independence

Actively promoting student independence or, at the beginning, even allowing student independence was, in her own words, "very difficult" for Mrs. Rogers. She would urge students to work things out for themselves but then would jump in to rescue them at the slightest sign of trouble. Toward the end, however, she was able to transfer a considerable amount of responsibility for turntaking, control of discussion topic, and interpretation to her students. She began to realize that when students were given the freedom to work independently, they were capable of excellent thinking. In fact, she regarded this to be her most valuable insight from participating in the project:

> The most important thing, in my mind, that I learned about all of my students is that they really have some great ideas. And all of the things that they try and nudge at you, and tap on your shoulders for, and call your name for, all day long. The things that they really want to talk about and don't have an opportunity to talk about, they get an opportunity to talk about some real important issues. And they get to understand how they feel about things, that perhaps no one has ever had time to ask them about or to talk to them about.

Argument Outlines

Mrs. Rogers was always introducing strategies of her own, never content just to follow the strategies suggested by the research team. Asking students to prepare argument outlines was one of her innovations. Before the students gathered to discuss the stories, Mrs. Rogers had them write outlines, laying out the arguments to their positions on the central question. To ensure that students considered different viewpoints, at first Mrs. Rogers had the students list arguments on both sides of the central question. Later, as they became more competent with the process, she allowed them to concentrate on their own positions. During the discussions, the students would refer to their argument outlines while articulating their views. The outlines were especially helpful to timid members of the group who found it hard to express their viewpoints fluently. The argument outlines also gave Mrs. Rogers something concrete with which to track the students' development.

Debriefing

While the students were debating among themselves, Mrs. Rogers took elaborate notes detailing their positions and the manner in which these were presented, as well as how often the students participated. At the end of the discussion, she would review her notes with the students, evaluating their performance and providing them with concrete goals toward which they could work. For instance, when a shy student worked up the courage to participate even a little, Mrs. Rogers would praise him or her during the debriefing period; then she would follow up by encouraging the student to participate more in upcoming discussions. In addition to giving individual reviews, Mrs. Rogers gave feedback on the group's performance as a whole, applauding the students especially when the discussions were animated. Because debriefing proved to be so useful, this instructional move has been incorporated into the CR model and shared with other teachers.

From Knowing the Story to Understanding the Issues

In the first few discussions, Mrs. Rogers still began with a recitation. Evidently, before she would permit students to discuss the central issue, she felt the need to make sure that they knew the story. From an excerpt of an early discussion about the story "Fishing All Day," we see Mrs. Rogers leading a review of the main points in the story.

Mrs. Rogers:	We needed to refresh our memory or review what the story was all about. So, can you please share with me what the story, um, "Fishing All Day" was about?
Kenny:	It's about a boy that fishes all day and … uh … a wife and her husband comes and wants to take him back to the, um, back where they live, and doesn't know if h-, he should go or not.
Mrs. Rogers:	Okay.
Tony:	Um, he fish and take the fish to his aunt's sometimes.
Mrs. Rogers:	Good. That definitely happened. That was an important part of the story … what else do you remember : that we should
Tony:	They, that, um, they, um, went to take to take, um, it was the neighbors lived next door to him, and they wanted to take him to Moscow with.
Tamika:	His mother died.
Mrs. Rogers:	Okay. That's important to know and understand. Who did he live with?
Tamika:	His aunt.

In the preceding excerpt, Mrs. Rogers asked students to summarize events in the story. Kenny proceeded to recount the basic plot but neglected to include another aspect of Nikki's dilemma—that he might have an obligation to take care of his sick aunt with whom he lived. When Tony added that Nikki "take the fish to his aunt's," Mrs. Rogers acknowledged this point. Still, she was not satisfied that all of the important aspects of the story were covered and prompted the group further by asking, "what else do you remember?" Tony and Tamika added more detail, but there were additional points that Mrs. Rogers wanted the group recognize. Students took several more turns, not included in the excerpt, reviewing salient details of the story. It was not until Mrs. Rogers felt that all the important points had been covered that the students began tackling the big question.

Once she realized that the main points and specific details in the stories would be brought out spontaneously by students as they wrestled with the bigger, more complex issues, Mrs. Rogers dropped the reviewing and dove right into the central question. However, she continued to be concerned with the "right" reading of the story. If a student had a misreading, Mrs. Rogers was quick to point out the contradiction without allowing students the chance to notice the contradiction on their own. For instance, during the discussion of *The Gold Cadillac*, Kenny thought that in the South, White people still owned slaves.

Kenny:	What if their owners, like, well they get their letters. Like, like all of the mail goes to like, their owners and they, he doesn't give them the letters.
Mrs. Rogers:	Wait, say that again. What if the letters what?
Kenny:	Went to their like, their owners and he didn't give them to them.
Mrs. Rogers:	Oh, I see what Kenny is thinking. Can some one correct his thinking? He's thinking that the members of the family are owned by White people. Are you thinking about slavery time here? Is that accurate?

In this segment, Mrs. Rogers first gave Kenny the chance to clarify what he meant by his notion that the "owners" might receive the father's mail. When it became clear that he literally meant that the members of the family were owned by White people, Mrs. Rogers immediately pointed out that Kenny was mistaken.

Although she encouraged other members of the group to "correct his thinking," before they could do so, Mrs. Rogers corrected him herself.

Ensuring that students knew the main points in the stories remained crucial to Mrs. Rogers throughout the year; however, the discussions began to revolve more around *understanding* the central issues rather than on the specifics of the stories. Mrs. Rogers loosened her grip and allowed students greater freedom to talk about their own interpretations of the events and issues in stories, even when, on the surface, the talk could have been considered a digression. We see this in an excerpt from a discussion of a book titled *Grandma's Secret* (Bourgeois, 1989). The central question was "Does grandma enjoy life as much as the children?" Instead of concentrating on the central question, the students began exploring whether Grandma wanted to be a kid again. Mrs. Rogers not only gave them room to pursue this topic (the students talked about this for most of the discussion), but she actually encouraged it.

Angelique:	She probably wanted to be a kid again if she wanted to be around a lot of kids.
Mrs. Rogers:	I'd like to stop for a minute and uh, talk about what Angelique said. Does anyone remember what she just said?
All students:	She said she wanted to be a kid again.
Mrs. Rogers:	Okay.
Monique:	Tamika, what did you say?
Teacher:	I'd like to stop and talk about what Angelique just said about Grandma liking to be a kid again.
Joanna:	Angelique, why do you think she wants to be a kid?
Angelique:	Because she like to swim and she likes to be around a lot of kids.

As they genuinely tried to work through the controversies, students began to display advanced discussion skills and began to generate more complex webs of argument. Both points are illustrated in the following extract from a discussion of *The Friendship* (Taylor, 1987), a complicated story set in Pre–World War II South about a friendship between a Black man, Tom Bee, and a White man, John Wallace. Bee and Wallace became friends after Bee saved Wallace's life, at which time Wallace promised Bee that he could always call him by his first name. Later, however, Wallace asked Bee to stop calling him John. When Bee insisted on addressing Wallace by his first name, Wallace shot him in the leg. The central question was "Should Mr. Tom Bee have called Mr. John Wallace by his first name?"

Joanna:	Tamika, what do you think, why do you think that he shouldn't have called him John?
Tamika:	Because he knew that he wasn't supposed to call him John. He was supposed to call him Mr. Wallace and I think that he knew, he knew he would get killed if he called him by his first name.

> Joanna: But don't you think in the story when he said that he promised
> him, he gave him his word that nobody would have to call him
> Mr. Wallace. They would have to call him John.
>
> Tamika: Do you think a promise or your life is more important?

When inviting Tamika to state her views, Joanna begins with the vague "what do you think" but, monitoring her own talk, corrected to the more precise "why do you think he shouldn't have called him John?" Tamika responded that Bee knew he could get killed if he called Wallace by his first name. Joanna then argued that Wallace had given his word that Bee could call him John. The extract ends with Tamika countering Joanna's argument with a sophisticated conversational gambit, a rhetorical question, "Do you think a promise or your life is more important?" The episode shows children who were managing turntaking and topic, expressing their arguments clearly and aptly, without any assistance from the teacher. These were serious arguments about serious topics: Black and White, a promise made and a promise broken, and life and death.

From Teacher-Student Interactions to Student-Student Exchanges

Despite her avowed intention to enable free-flowing, student-centered discussion, Mrs. Rogers unwittingly continued to control the topic and turntaking in the first few CR discussions. She did this by asking a string of questions. She held on to interpretive authority by providing an evaluation after each student's response. Discussions were marked by volleys of turns between Mrs. Rogers and an individual student while the rest of the students were left out of the conversation. The students' responses tended to be short and unconnected to previous points. In the following excerpt from an early discussion of the story "Fishing All Day," we see Mrs. Rogers taking every other turn. No doubt unintentionally, she kept her hands on the reigns by revoicing (O'Connor & Michaels, 1993) what Angelique said.

> Angelique: Um, the reason why I think he should go back, I mean, the rea-
> son why I think he should go to Moscow with his neighbors is
> because he can be a manager, and he can work.
>
> Mrs. Rogers: Okay. He can be a manager and work.
>
> Angelique: He can earn some money.
>
> Mrs. Rogers: And he can earn some money. How will he use the money?
> What do you think he'd use the money for?
>
> Angelique: He can send it to his aunt.

When Mrs. Rogers tried to release control by moving to the chalkboard and encouraging the students to talk without her direction, there were awkward silences, the students were flustered, and did not seem to know what was expected of them. Neither teacher nor students were able to shake the teacher-dominated pattern until the fourth session. In the beginning, the students had waited for Mrs. Rogers to select a person to start off the discussion and relied on her to rescue them if the discussion stalled. However, once she introduced the position cards, the students dove into the discussion.

Another key to the shift in control was a discussion led by one of the researchers who was a participant observer in the classroom. After a lackluster discussion, Mrs. Rogers turned to the researcher and said in exasperation, "All right, you do the next one." The discussion the researcher led proved to be more fluid and conversational than those before. Mrs. Rogers's next discussion was more natural and open, with many student-student interactions.

As the students needed less of her support, Mrs. Rogers began to pull herself out of the discussion. Rather than immediately jumping in, Mrs. Rogers allowed the students space to correct and challenge one another. There were then more student-student turns in which students asked one another why they held certain positions. At this point, the students were going around the group taking turns presenting their positions and challenging one another. These exchanges began to involve *countering, elaboration, clarification,* and *concession.* This is illustrated in the excerpt of the discussion of the story *Grandma's Secret.*

Joanna:	Angelique, why do you think she wants to be a kid?
Angelique:	Because she likes to swim and she likes to be around a lot of kids
Tamika:	And she likes playing a lot, with the kids and stuff?
Angelique:	Yes.
Joshua:	And I agree because if she wasn't swimming she'd probably be sitting back in a rocking chair ... She's having a lot of fun, some fun like (the) children.
Joanna:	I think the same thing as Angelique was saying that she'd probably like to be a kid again and um, probably she had a good life because she did a lot of stuff and you know how we, um, how we are now ...

[Several turns deleted]

Brian:	I disagree. I disagree with Angelique ... 'Cuz my grandma, she cleans up the house, she goes swimming and everything else, but I don't think she'd like to be a kid again.
Angelique:	Brian, that's different, but she still probably wants to be a kid again, this grandma in the story.
Brian:	Because if I was that age, I wouldn't want to be a kid again because I'd have to go through all that, getting my license again, getting more money to get the house, then I've got to go get a job again, and everything over and over.
Angelique:	But that's probably what she wanted to do. It doesn't mean trying to be a kid again.

This sequence begins with Joanna probing Angelique on why she thought that Grandma wanted to be a kid again. Angelique responded that Grandma enjoyed being around a lot of kids. Tamika, Joshua, and Joanna then elaborated on her point; that not only did Grandma like being around kids, but she also had a lot of fun participating in the same activities as the kids. So, they concluded, Grandma must want to be a kid again. Brian dissented and challenged this line of argument. Using his own grandmother as an example, he pointed out that the reasons given were not sufficient enough to conclude that Grandma necessarily wanted to be a kid again. One could enjoy life, doing all of the fun things in life that kids enjoy, without wanting to be a kid. Angelique rejected Brian's challenge, asserting that the two situations, that of his own grandmother and that of Grandma in the story, were different. Brian then counterchallenged, stating that Grandma would have to relive her other experiences, such as getting her license; saving money for her house; and getting a job, all over again. The excerpt ends with Angelique switching to Brian's side, "It doesn't mean trying to be a kid again." This segment demonstrates children assuming responsibility for their own discussion, exploring the central question in depth, and building arguments to convey their viewpoints. Given the opportunity, they chose to seriously and reflectively discuss complex issues regarding the value of life—what it means to enjoy life, being young, and being old. All of this was accomplished with little guidance from Mrs. Rogers.

From Individual Student Performances to Multiple Student Collaborations

A consequence of the teacher-student interaction typical during the first few discussion sessions was a lack of collaboration among the students. Individual students gave constrained one-line responses to Mrs. Rogers's questions as others watched from the sidelines. Even when a student espoused a commonly shared opinion, unless prompted by Mrs. Rogers, no one took the initiative to elaborate on what was being said.

An excerpt from a discussion of the story "a Bit of Detective Work" (Bauer, 1989) illustrates how one student was left to "hold his own" with Mrs. Rogers. In this story, a boy named Jason bore witness to some "strange" events and activities while visiting his great uncle Glad. Jason found the Uncle's house in disarray and was bewildered when he saw this elderly Uncle Glad talking to and setting out a bowl of food for the ashes of a dead dog. He had apprehensions about the uncle's sanity until he found the bowl of food, sitting exactly where the uncle had left it, mysteriously all cleaned out. The question the students had to address was "What should Jason tell his parents about his uncle?"

Mrs. Rogers: Okay, what do you think Kenny?
Kenny: Um, I think he, um, Jason should tell his parents that um maybe that he could live with them or something or live at a home instead of living by himself. Because he's acting weird and he's not taking care of him or the house.
Mrs. Rogers: How's he acting weird? Prove it.
Kenny: Not acting weird, but eating weird stuff.

[All the students flip through the pages]

Mrs. Rogers: Where does it say he's eating weird stuff?
Kenny: When he has um//
Mrs. Rogers: Which page?
Kenny: Sixty-seven.

Mrs. Rogers:	Bottom of 66–67? Which paragraph?
Kenny:	Um, the last one.
Mrs. Rogers:	All right.

This segment begins with Mrs. Rogers calling on Kenny to present his position. He expressed that Jason should tell his parents to have his uncle live with them because he was "acting weird." Mrs. Rogers pressed Kenny to provide evidence that the uncle was acting weird, at which point he clarified that the uncle was only "eating weird stuff." Once again, she insisted that he back his argument with information from the story. Kenny began to fumble, unable to readily locate the information he needed. Based on what many students later said, we realize they shared Kenny's view that the uncle was "weird." However, while Kenny was being grilled by Mrs. Rogers, no one came to his aid to provide the evidence even though they were all looking through the story. It was not until 17 turns later that another student, Tamika, suggested to Kenny where he might find the evidence.

As the group evolved, the students relied less on Mrs. Rogers and became more animated as they interacted with one another. Often there was verbal jousting between students, who proved quite adept at defending their own points of view. Eventually, extended student-student exchanges involving two or more students became commonplace. Students would come to one another's defense by chiming in their support when someone with whom they agreed was being challenged.

A passage from the discussion of a story titled "What Should Kelly Do?" depicted an alliance emerging as two students formed a united front in the face of challenges from other group members. In this story, a girl named Kelly saw a painting that was to be entered into the school art contest, propped outside, about to get rained on. This painting was made by her friend Evelyn, who was the best artist in the school. Kelly had just entered what she considered her best painting into this contest and really wanted to win. Kelly believed that the painting Evelyn had carelessly left on the playground was much better than hers. Now Kelly had to decide whether to rescue Evelyn's painting—and most likely lose the art contest— or do nothing, leaving the painting outside where it would be ruined by the rain (Weiner, 1980).

Kenny:	I think she *should* get it because everyone would be hurt if um, if her painting was ruined by the rain.
Tamika:	I wanna challenge you because, did it seem like when she was propped up there and she went on the swings did it seem like she really cared about it?
Kenny:	Well, not really cared about it, but wouldn't you be sad if *your* painting got ruined by the rain?
Tamika:	Yes, but I wouldn't be sad because it got ruined so I couldn't enter the contest.
Sonia:	I agree with Tamika.
Tamika:	Why?
Sonia:	That um, because, if I left my painting out there, and, and I didn't really care about it, I wouldn't be sad if I wasn't in the contest, or if I didn't get first place.

Tamika: Yeah, um, I agree with Sonia and because um, there's no reason for her to be sad. Sh- she propped it against there and went to go swing and forgot about it. She shouldn't (have) been in the first place so she has no reason to be mad. She should be mad at *herself*.

Sonia: For example, if I was, if I was a good drawer, and um, there was somebody better than me, and, if they won, the um, first place, um, I think, it doesn't matter because everybody's not perfect.

Kenny: But wouldn't, but would you be sad if your painting was ruined by the rain?

Sonia: I would be sad but, I wouldn't, be mad that I wouldn't be in the contest.

Kenny: But wouldn't you be glad if someone's um, saved it for you, so you could um, keep it?

Sonia: [nods]

Tamika: Um, uh, I would be glad too but, if they didn't I have no reason to be mad at them if they didn't tell me before because it wasn't their, it wasn't their fault so, it was the person who left it out there, it was Evelyn's fault, so if Kelly were to tell her, um (and) her painting was already ruined, she'd have no reason to be mad.

At the outset of this episode, Kenny argued that Kelly should rescue the painting because not doing so would hurt "everyone," implying that Evelyn would be hurt. Tamika disputed this on the grounds that there was no indication from Evelyn that she cared about her painting. Kenny conceded that Evelyn may not have cared about the painting, but he challenged Tamika by forcing her to place herself in the story world. He did this by asking Tamika how *she* would feel if her painting got ruined by the rain. On the surface, Tamika's response was a bit ambiguous. Earlier in the discussion, however, Tamika had stated that Evelyn "didn't really care if she entered it (the contest) or not." Her current response to Kenny seemed to indicate that although she would be sad if the painting got ruined, her sadness would not be due to the fact that she could no longer enter the contest. Sonia voiced support for Tamika's position, to which Tamika responded by challenging her, "why?" We see that Tamika did not accept Sonia's alliance blindly; rather, she had to first make sure that Sonia, indeed, shared her perspective. Once sure, she then articulated agreement with Sonia and elaborated on her own initial argument. Sonia then built on Tamika's point by providing an example for the group. Kenny was not quite persuaded, so he reiterated his argument. Finally, he directed his challenge at Sonia. She replied with a simple nod, and it was Tamika who gave a more elaborate response. This piece depicts children, left to their own devices, collaborating in depth to explore a difficult dilemma—where notions of up-holding one's integrity and being responsible and accountable for one's own actions are dealt with.

REFLECTION ON TEACHER AND STUDENT CHANGE

This story began with a typical scene from a language arts lesson. We saw Mrs. Rogers doing most of the talking with seldom as much as a peep out of her students except when they were responding to questions. Two and a half months later, the scene is different. We see the students gathered in a small group, engaged in animated talk with one another as they explore the central issue in a story; it is Mrs. Rogers who is listening while the students do most of the talking.

In the end, Mrs. Rogers and her students had become confident participants in open, student-centered discussion. However, the journey to reach this point was anything but smooth. Mrs. Rogers had developed her own directive teaching style over her 20 years as a teacher, and similar to the teachers described by Alvermann and Hayes (1989), Afflerbach (1996), and Hamilton and Richardson (1995), modifying this style was not a simple task for her. Nor was it a simple matter for her students to assume independent control of the social aspects of discussion. When Mrs. Rogers was ready to extend control to her students, they dared not let go of her support. Both she and her students had to adjust their respective roles and acquire new ways of managing their discourse.

Although Mrs. Rogers's command of direct instruction seemed to stifle independence in the early CR discussions, we believe that it also allowed her to make the characteristics of a well-reasoned argument and good discussion participation unmistakably clear to her students. The objectives and ground rules of the discussions were clearly explicated by Mrs. Rogers at the beginning, and she took care to ensure that these were understood and met by her students throughout the course of the 3-month period. She vigilantly prompted students for specific evidence and insisted on clarity in their dialogues. Furthermore, by taking elaborate notes on the students' participation and presentation of arguments and challenges, and using these notes to provide detailed and relevant feedback following the discussions, Mrs. Rogers was, as she put it, "providing the tools" for eventual student control. Thus, we saw students eventually building arguments, listening to each other, responding to each other's arguments, and inviting quiet classmates into the discussion.

By the end of the year, Mrs. Rogers had completely transferred the management of turntaking and choice of topic to her students. Her students had become more independent thinkers who were able to articulate their points of view, support them with evidence, challenge one another, and decide when to change or maintain their positions—all without much guidance. Literature discussion, in Mrs. Rogers's class, was no longer simply about knowing the stories, but became a process wherein students were challenged to deal with "big" real-life issues through reasoning, exploring, and building arguments. They had begun honing their skills to participate in the Discourse (Gee, 1992) that is so commonly used— in congressional chambers, courts of law, research groups, executive suites, and union halls.

We judge that several factors contributed to the success of Mrs. Rogers and her students. The parameters of CR were well defined, offering a structure that could be readily understood and adopted by Mrs. Rogers and her students. Without this structure, developed over years of work by the research group, it would have been extremely hard to both make Mrs. Rogers see the value of the CR approach as well as scaffold her attempts to integrate it into her classroom. It is also important to note that this structure, though well defined, was also flexible enough to allow Mrs. Rogers to modify the model to fit her unique classroom setting. She was able to modify the approach according the to strength and weaknesses of her students and her personal preferences. Moreover, she could do this gradually—moving from her standard, teacher-directed classroom participation structure toward a more free-flowing, student-controlled one, through small but very significant steps. The presence of a participant observer, who was herself an experienced and successful teacher, in the classroom offering suggestions, helping to solve problems, and occasionally modeling the CR approach also helped. Every discussion was videotaped and viewed by the research group, who gave feedback to the participant observer, who, in turn, passed on this information to Mrs. Rogers. In essence, Mrs. Rogers received consultation from the whole team. Finally, and most important, were Mrs. Rogers's excellence as a teacher, professionalism, self-knowledge, ability to be self-critical, and determination to master a new approach that made for a successful integration of the CR approach.

REFLECTIONS ON OUR RESEARCH

Keeping in mind our more immediate goal for literature discussions—that is, to help students think through complex issues on their own—we found that CR literature discussions are themselves more stimulating and engaging for the students (Anderson et al., 1998). Rather than relying on the teacher, students are generating their own questions to be explored by the group (Anderson et al., 2001). Furthermore, through the expression, elaboration, challenging, and defense of opinions and viewpoints that take place in CR, we have seen students as young as Grade 4 construct logical and complex arguments in group discussions (Anderson et al., 1997). The reasoning and communication skills honed in the collaborative oral discussions also proved to be useful in helping students write better persuasive essays (Reznitskaya et al., 2001). Collaboratively, students are making connections to each other's thinking and helping one another build more elaborate and complex arguments (Chinn, Anderson, & Waggoner, 2001). This format provides opportunities for social learning, as students both pick up and appropriate effective argument stratagems used by one another (Anderson et al., 2001). Lastly, the release of teacher control can allow for student leadership to develop and evolve, a rarely occurring occasion in typical classroom settings. In fact CR provides a forum in which girls thrive as leaders (Li et al., 2007).

Though our examination and use of CR has yielded promising results, other areas still need to be explored. Some of our preliminary analyses have indicated that rates of participation between girls and boys are equalized under the CR approach (Archodidou & Nguyen-Jahiel, 2002). In addition, we would like to investigate whether the appearance of rhetorical forms is more a matter of individual dispositions and competencies or immediate social context. Finally, we still need to demonstrate the degree to which young students can indeed reach a deeper understanding of others' viewpoints through discussions.

REFERENCES

Afflerbach, P. (1996, Winter). *Barriers to the implementation of a statewide performance program: School personnel perspectives* (Reading Research Report No. 51). Athens, GA: National Reading Research Center.

Alvermann, D. E., & Hayes, D. A. (1989). Classroom discussion of content area reading assignments: An intervention study. *Reading Research Quarterly, 24*(3), 305–335.

Alexander, M. (1970). *We never get to do anything.* New York: Dial Press.

Anderson, R., Chinn, C., Chang, J., Waggoner, M., & Yi, H. (1997). The logical integrity of children's arguments. *Cognition and Instruction, 15*(2), 135–167.

Anderson, R., Chinn, C., Waggoner, M., & Nguyen, K. (1998). Intellectually stimulating story discussions. In R. C. Anderson, J. Osborn, & F. Lehr (Eds.), *Literacy for all.* New York: Guild.

Anderson, R., Nguyen-Jahiel, K., McNurlen, B., Archodidou, A., Kim, S., Reznitskaya, A., et al. (2001). The snowball phenomenon: Spread of ways of talking and ways of thinking across groups of children. *Cognition and Instruction, 19*(1), 1–46.

Archodidou, A., & Nguyen-Jahiel, K. (2002). *Influences on gender and ethnicity on small group discussions.* Paper presented at the annual meeting of the American Educational Research Association, New Orleans.

Bourgeois, P. (1989). *Grandma's secret* (M. Kovalski, Illus.). Toronto: Kids Can Press.

Chinn, C., Anderson, R., & Waggoner, M. (2001). Patterns of participation in two kinds of literature discussions. *Reading Research Quarterly, 36*(4), 378–411.

Clark, A.-M., Anderson, R., Kuo, L., Kim, I.-L., Archodidou, A., & Nguyen-Jahiel, K. (2003). Collaborative reasoning: Expanding ways for children to talk and think in school. *Educational Psychology Review, 15*(2), 181–198.

Commeyras, M. (1994). Promoting critical thinking through dialogical thinking reading lessons. *The Reading Teacher, 46,* 486–494.

Dobrin, A. (1973). Fishing all day (Adapted from *Going to Moscow and other stories*). New York: Four Winds Press.

Eeds, M., & Wells, D. (1989). Grand conversations: An explanation of meaning construction in literature study groups. *Research in the Teaching of English, 23*(1), 4–29.

Gee, J. P. (1992). *The social mind: Language , ideology, and social practice.* New York: Bergin & Garvey.

Li, Y., Anderson, R. C., Nguyen-Jahiel, K., Dong, T., Archodidou, A., Kim, I.-H., et al. (2007). Emergent leadership in children's discussion groups. *Cognition and Instruction, 25*(1), 75–110..

O'Connor, M. C., & Michaels, S. (1993). Aligning academic task and participation status through revoicing: Analysis of a classroom discourse strategy. *Anthropology and Education Quarterly, 24*(4), 318–335.

Palincsar, A. S., & Brown, A. L. (1985). Reciprocal teaching: A means to a meaningful end. In J. Osborn, P. T. Wilson, & R. C. Anderson (Eds.), *Reading education: Foundations for a literate America* (pp. 229–310). Lexington, MA: D.C. Heath.

Raphael, T. E., & McMahon, S. I. (1994). Book Club: An alternative framework for reading instruction. *Reading Teacher, 48,* 102–116.

Reznitskaya, A., Anderson, R., McNurlen, B., Nguyen-Jahiel, K., Archodidou, A., & Kim, S. (2001). Influence of oral discussion on written argument. *Discourse Processes, 32*(2–3), 155–175.

Short, K. G., & Pierce, K. M. (1990). *Talking about books: Creating literate communities.* Portsmouth, NH: Heinemann.

Sinclair, J. M., & Coulthard, R. M. (1975). *Towards an analysis of discourse: The English used by teachers and pupils.* London: Oxford University Press.

Taylor, M. D. (1987). *The friendship* (M. Ginsburg, Illus.). New York: Dial Books for Young Readers.

Taylor, M. D. (1987). *The gold Cadillac* (M. Ginsburg, Illus.). New York: Dial Books for Young Readers.

Waggoner, M., Chinn, C., Anderson, R., & Yi, H. (1995). Collaborative reasoning about stories. *Language Arts, 72,* 582–588.

Weiner, E. H. (1980). What should Kelly do? In *Unfinished stories: For facilitating decision making in the elementary classroom.* Washington, D.C.: National Education Association.

CHAPTER 8

How Teachers Can Support Productive Classroom Talk: Move the Thinking to the Students

Isabel L. Beck
Margaret G. McKeown

Classroom talk about text ranges from very brief student responses to teachers' questions, exemplified in the traditional initiation-response-evaluation (IRE) pattern (Cazden, 1988), to an open floor in which students are free to express their ideas and views. The goal of the former is to get the facts from a text established. The goal of the latter is to provide the opportunity for students to express their ideas. In these two extremes, which have been described by Roby (1988), the role of the teacher and the responsibility of the students are quite different. In the IRE, students are responsible to the text, to be faithful to what the text says, and the teacher's role is to match what the students say to what the text says. In the other extreme, students do not have to be faithful to any source; rather, their responsibilities are to express their notions. In this open floor situation, the teacher's role is to do as little as possible, so as to allow students to control the content and flow of the discourse. The reduction or limitation of the teacher's role in classroom discussions is viewed as positive (Almasi, 1995; Goldenberg, 1993; O'Flahaven, Stein, Weincek, & Marks, 1992).

Although there are certainly topics and occasions in which it is appropriate that the teacher take a passive role, it is our position that in a discussion about text, especially difficult text, it is appropriate that the teacher take a very active role. However, the teacher's activity should be directed toward enabling students to construct meaning through prompting, guiding, challenging, focusing, and the like.

In this chapter, we present extended excerpts from three lessons that focus on class discussion of a text being read. Each excerpt reveals a very different teacher role, ranging from teacher domination of the talk to sharing the floor, and from the teacher doing the work of connecting ideas and creating a meaningful picture to the teacher prompting students to develop meaning. We then characterize actions teachers take that seem effective in fostering productive discussion in which students work to construct meaning. The examples and characterizations are based on our work with Questioning the Author, an instructional approach to engaging students in discussion of text toward building meaning.

BACKGROUND TO THE APPROACH

We developed Questioning the Author in response to observations of how students dealt with their textbooks. In studies in which we gave students textbook passages to read and recall, we often found that students gave jumbled and inaccurate accounts of what they had read, and seemed to do so based on rather cursory readings of the text. It was as if students gleaned whatever information they could from a quick pass through the text and formulated a recall based on that, giving little reflection as to its fidelity to the ideas expressed. Our goal became to develop an approach to text that would encourage students to dig in and grapple with ideas toward making sense of them.

Questioning the Author is thus designed around a constellation of four features: (a) It addresses text as the product of a fallible author, as "someone's ideas written down," so that the reason for needing effort to figure out ideas in a text is shifted from a reader's inadequacies to an author's vulnerability; (b) it deals with text through teacher-posed queries such as "What is the author trying to say?" and "What do you think the author means by that?"; (c) it takes place online, in the context of reading as it initially occurs, by going back and forth between reading portions of text and discussing the ideas encountered; and (d) it encourages collaborative discussion in which students are urged to grapple with ideas in the service of constructing meaning.

Across 3 years of work with five teachers, Questioning the Author succeeded in changing classroom discourse patterns from a focus on retrieving information to one of collaborative querying, building, and elaborating ideas. The work included about 120 fourth- and fifth-grade students in two schools: one an urban private school with a mainly African American student population, and the other in a town with high unemployment and a mainly white student population. Teachers ranged in experience from their first classroom assignment to 20 years of teaching. Results, based on transcripts of lessons across the school year compared to baseline lessons taught before teacher began implementing Questioning the Author, show that teachers' questions and students' responses changed from focusing on retrieving information to the meaning and integration of ideas. Teacher talk greatly diminished with a concomitant increase in student participation (Beck, McKeown, Worthy, Sandora, & Kucan, 1996; McKeown, Beck, & Sandora, 1996).

Another study compared Questioning the Author to the Junior Great Books discussion approach for sixth and seventh-graders. The texts used in the study were complex narratives, and the results show that Questioning the Author promoted both greater student recall and richer interpretation of text ideas (Sandora, 1994).

Questioning the Author is strongly based on constructivist theory, which holds that understanding something requires actively grappling with ideas (Bruer, 1993). Constructing meaning from text involves putting together pieces of information, in contrast to simply retrieving text or offering one's view of what's in a text (Beck & Carpenter, 1986; Beck & McKeown, 2001, 2002; McKeown & Beck, 1998, 2006; Palincsar & Brown, 1989). Certainly, a reader's personal views play a role in understanding what is read, but the key is how that knowledge is used to create meaning, not simply that it's brought to a discussion. (See also Kucan & Beck, 1997, 2003; McKeown & Beck, 1999, 2004).

THE TEACHER'S ROLE IN FOSTERING STUDENTS' CONSTRUCTION OF MEANING

The point of discussion in Questioning the Author is to engage students' cognitive efforts toward making text information meaningful, and the teacher plays an enormously important role in making that happen. Dealing with students' comments toward developing productive discussion creates a sizable task for the teacher. The complexity of the task has been captured in an analogy to a symphony conductor in Shulman's (1987) description of an expert teacher leading a discussion.

Although the symphony conductor analogy captures some of the inherent complexity of classroom discussion, the analogy falls somewhat short in capturing the role of the teacher. That is, members of a symphony orchestra are assumed to already understand the meanings of their respective parts and possess the technical expertise to express that meaning. The conductor's job is to bring the individual sounds into harmony. The teacher, on the other hand, must deal with a wide range of individual performances, including less-than-expert reading and some discordant responses. Added to the teacher's task, then, is the need to focus or reformulate some responses before they can play a productive role in meaning building.

FACILITATION OF CLASSROOM TALK IN SERVICE OF STUDENTS' CONSTRUCTING MEANING

The first excerpt, presented in Table 8.1, shows a teacher facilitating and focusing discussion by continually prompting students to figure out the ideas encountered in the text. The transcript from which this excerpt is taken is of a fifth-grade Questioning the Author social studies lesson. The students were working with a chapter about European settlements in North America. The previous lesson focused on the Roanoke colony and the losses that Sir Walter Raleigh sustained in that venture. The current lesson begins with reading a paragraph of text that introduces the idea of a joint-stock company as a way to raise money to start a colony. The point is that joint ownership allows English merchants to share the costs and risks of development in the New World. Key to developing understanding here are the notion of pooling resources to share ownership and why developing a colony was a risk venture.

As the transcript suggests, the teacher was very active in managing the discussion, but his management was directed toward scaffolding the students to do the cognitive work of building meaning. Note how he probes students' comments by asking "What do you mean share the cost?" "What kind of expenses would they have to share?" "Why would a colony be at risk for losing money?" and "Can you think of an example?" His role was to engage and extend students' cognitive efforts toward grappling with ideas.

TABLE 8.1
Transcript and Commentary From a Fifth-Grade Discussion Illustrating a Teacher's Active Role in Encouraging Students to Construct Meaning

	Transcript	*Commentary*
Teacher	What is this [the text passage just read] about? Um, joint-stock company and sharing and what is that about?	The teacher initiates the discussion by marking some important text concepts.
Shirley	Okay there are these English people, right? Ah and they are um, they all have the idea, they decide, yeah, they decided to start a um English colony. They decided to share the cost of a um, to put together an English colony.	Shirley's comments indicate that she is thinking, but her ideas are not well formed.
Teacher	Share the cost? What do you mean by share the cost?	The teacher picks up on Shirley's comment about sharing the cost, but turns responsibility back to the students for clarifying the idea.
Shirley	By forming um a joint-stock company, you know how when they share the um expenses? Like if one merchant makes money and like it all goes together.	
Teacher	Wait. First, I was with you when you said form a company. Okay, these people are going to form a company. And they're going to share expenses. What kind of expense would they have to share?	The teacher maintains the sharing expenses focus and probes for elaboration.
Wayne	Money. And the reason, the reason, you know how like they pitch in for pizza? Like people pitch in for pizza.	Wayne's analogy suggests he is constructing meaning.
Teacher	Okay.	
Wayne	They'd kind of, well, gather up enough money to—like the wood builders. They will not work for free.	
Teacher	Oh, I see. So you mean the wood builders were going to build the ship?	The teacher clarifies what he thinks Wayne is trying to say.
Wayne	Yes.	
Teacher	So since they won't work for free, a bunch of people gather up all their money and say, "Okay, we'll pay you to build the ship?"	The teacher elaborates what Wayne has been trying to express.

DOMINATION OF CLASSROOM TALK IN SERVICE OF GETTING THE "FACTS" OUT

In contrast to Table 8.1, the transcript in Table 8.2 shows how little cognitive effort was required from students in a fourth-grade language arts lesson. The transcript is from a baseline lesson of a teacher before her experience with Questioning the Author. The students were reading an excerpt of a story from a basal reader titled *The Best Bad Thing* (Uchida, 1983). The story is about a girl who spends the summer with her aunt and cousins on their farm. The characters include the girl (Rinko), her aunt and cousins, and an old man who makes beautiful kites. In the excerpt the class is reading, the old man has appeared with two new kites. The text hints at some unhappiness of Rinko's and that she has been left out of kite-flying activities in the past. The discussion follows the initial section of the excerpt in which the characters are introduced, and the old man takes the children, including Rinko—to her surprise—out to fly the kites.

TABLE 8.2
Transcript and Commentary From a Discussion Illustrating a Teacher who Tends to Do the Cognitive Work Herself

	Transcript	*Commentary*
Teacher	Okay. So we have Zenny, we have Rinko, we have the aunt, and we have the old man, right? Now, what are they going to do? Zenny's doing her supper dishes. The old man walks in, and he says he wants to do something. What does he want to do?	Teacher establishes characters, sets up the scene, and asks a "retrieve answer [RA] from text question."
Tiera	He wants to play with the kids and asks them if they want to fly the kites.	
Teacher	Alright. He asks if anyone wants to fly this kite. Now what did this old man do with kites to begin with? Do you remember, from the very beginning of the story?	Teacher repeats the part of Tiera's response that relates to her question and asks an RA question.
Jamal	Makes them.	
Teacher	He makes beautiful kites. And Rinko has seen them. So he brings two kites. Do you remember what were on the kites, what pictures?	Teacher elaborates Jamal's brief response, adds additional text information, and asks an RA question.
Charles	There's a samurai.	
Teacher	A samurai. What's a samurai?	
Students	A warrior.	
Teacher	A warrior, a fighter. So Japan's soldiers were called samurai and they were very, very good fighters. So there's a picture of a really big warrior on one of the kites. Now what is the picture of the other kite?	Teacher repeats, elaborates, and asks an RA question.
Temika	A butterfly.	

(continued)

TABLE 8.2 *(continued)*

	Transcript	Commentary
Teacher	A butterfly. Right. Okay. Now, after he comes in and says he wants to fly two kites, and he wants to know who wants to fly, she knows that there are two kites. So what does she think automatically, because there are only two kites?	Teacher repeats, elaborates, and asks an RA question.
Brandy	That the old man wants to fly one and the little boy …	Teacher doesn't let Brandy complete her idea.
Teacher	Okay. She thinks the old man's going to fly one and the little boy Zenny is going to fly one. So where does that leave her?	Teacher paraphrases Brandy's comment and completes her thought, which Brandy might have been able to do herself, and asks an RA question.
Roberta	Out of it.	
Teacher	Out of it. So she's kind of disappointed. She's thinking that she's not going to get a chance. But what does the old man do to surprise her? What does he do?	Teacher repeats, elaborates, and asks an RA question.
April	He lets her fly a butterfly kite.	
Teacher	He lets her fly a butterfly kite and she's excited. So they go outside. And now, can anyone explain to me what happens outside? What does the old man do?	The teacher asks students to "explain," which seems to invite more thinking and a more elaborate student response.
Shanelle	Um, he helps, he helps them um, to try to fly the …	Shanelle seems tentative, so notice what the teacher does next.
Teacher	Alright. He helps them. He must be pretty good at flying the kites, right? Why did you think that? Why would he be good at flying kites? Why would I say that?	The teacher jumps in, completes Shanelle's thought, and moves on. Note that the question she asks has potential to break the "and then what happened" pattern.
Darleen	'Cause if he wasn't if he wasn't interested or if he wasn't good at flying kites, he probably wouldn't be making them.	Darleen's response goes beyond surface features of events and begins to explore the old man's character.
Teacher	Alright. So how do you think he feels about kites?	And the teacher responds to Darleen in kind.
Jamal	He loves them.	
Teacher	He loves them. He thinks they're fantastic. Okay. So we have two kids and two kites and he's teaching them how to fly them, and he throwing them up in the air. He's shouting up. Now what is connected to a kite at all times?	But now, rather than pursuing the character issue, the teacher summarizes the literal event sequence and asks a question that continues toward establishing that sequence.

As indicated in the transcript on Table 8.2, the teacher uses a version of the IRE format in which she essentially retells the story the class has read—giving the students the role of filling in some blanks in her retelling. Notice that students' responses are rarely more than three or four words long. The discussion excerpt clearly demonstrates that, in such classroom discourse, students scarcely need to think about, and deal with, ideas. The teacher was doing virtually all the work, and if there was any thinking going on, it was in the teacher's head. Relatedly, she is extremely directive; her agenda, and only her agenda, was considered.

COLLECTING STUDENTS' COMMENTS
WITH LITTLE FOCUSING OF IDEAS

In contrast to the excessively directive approach demonstrated by the teacher in the *The Best Bad Thing* lesson, Table 8.3 presents a transcript of a lesson at the other extreme. The teacher was excessively nondirective, and, as such, the discussion did not move toward constructing meaning and exploring ideas. The transcript comes from a teacher who has been introduced to Questioning the Author but who, as of the time the lesson was videotaped, had little experience with the approach. The lesson is from a fourth-grade discussion about a section of a novel, *Be a Perfect Person in Just Three Days* (Manes, 1982), which students were reading. The book is about a boy, Milo, who has become engaged in a quest for perfection after finding a book that prescribes how to become perfect in three days. Milo has been dutifully following instructions from the book, including such things as wearing broccoli around his neck all day. In the excerpt presented in Table 8.3, the students had just completed reading the current instructions from the book, which told Milo that his next step toward perfection was to do absolutely nothing for 24 hours. This is turning out to be much more difficult for Milo than it sounded.

As the transcript indicates, the teacher initiated good probing questions at several points in the lesson, but when a student responded to her question, she did not continue to pursue the issues the student raised. She made no attempt to draw students' comments together, to highlight the meaning or significance of doing nothing and how it might affect the character's view of achieving perfection. She simply seemed to collect student responses.

THE TEACHERS' ROLES IN THE THREE LESSONS VIS-À-VIS
STUDENTS' COGNITIVE EFFORT

The teacher's role in the second excerpt, *The Best Bad Thing*, was to get the events of the story established. She did so by retelling the story and allowing the students to fill in some blanks in her retelling. Further evidence of the teacher's dominance of the lesson is that the proportion of teacher-to-student talk (determined by number of lines in the transcript) was 82 to 18. The students not only did very little talking, they did very little thinking. Whatever cognitive effort and thinking that was going on, it was being done by the teacher.

Whereas *The Best Bad Thing* teacher had a definite preestablished agenda, the *Be a Perfect Person* teacher seemed to have no agenda. In the "Perfect Person" discussion, the teacher's role seemed to be to collect and accept students' comments but not to use them toward building a coherent representation. Students had more opportunity to talk in the *Be a Perfect Person* lesson, which had a ratio of teacher-

TABLE 8.3
Transcript and Commentary From a Fourth-Grade Discussion Illustrating a Teacher Who Tends to Collect Students' Ideas With Little Focusing

	Transcript	Commentary
Teacher	How are things looking for Milo right now?	
Kelly	Very bad.	
Teacher	Why do you say they're bad?	The teacher is giving the student an opportunity to elaborate.
Kelly	Because he can't do nothing. And he's wishing that, um, he could build model planes and play with cards, and that.	
Teacher	Okay, and you're saying that having nothing to do isn't very much fun, right? It's not very much fun. Amber.	Teacher characterizes what Kelly has said, calls on another student, whose hand is raised, but does not invite that student to link up to what's already been said.
Amber	Um, maybe sometimes he wishes that um, he thinks that other kids are lucky 'cause they get to do something.	
Teacher	He thinks the other kids are lucky 'cause they get to do something.	Repeats Amber's comment.
Amber	Well, it's like other kids that are um, playing, he probably thinks they're lucky.	Amber's comment is similar to her previous comment.
Teacher	Is there something in the book that makes you think that he is thinking about other kids?	Teacher does a nice job of probing for the root of Amber's idea.
Amber	Um, that's just what I think.	
		Why Amber thinks what she thinks is good grist for discussion, but the teacher simply accepts Amber's comment and calls on another student.
Teacher	That's just what you're thinking about, that's an idea in your head. Annie?	
Annie	He thinks he's just doing this for nothing, and he's never gonna be perfect.	Annie's comment that the character won't reach his goal could be excellent grist for discussion.
Teacher	You don't think he's ever going to be perfect.	The teacher does not pursue why Annie thinks what she thinks.
Annie	That's what he thinks, he just said that.	
Teacher	He just said that.	Again, the teacher gives a flat response, just echoing what Annie said.
Michelle	He's beginning to get drowsy and everything. And he's just sitting there and then he still has the whole night and day to go.	

Teacher	Alright, Michelle just said that he's getting drowsy, that he still has the whole night ahead. Is there something here that, that doesn't look real good for Milo since he's getting drowsy and he still has the whole night ahead? Could this mean something?	The teacher seems to be trying to focus the discussion productively by getting back to Milo's problem, which is his drowsiness and the long night ahead.
Mike	It means that he's going to fall asleep pretty good.	
Teacher	You think he's going to fall asleep. Zack?	The teacher doesn't probe how Josh's literal answer "he's going to fall asleep" connects to Milo's problem; she just goes on to the next student.
Zack	Um, I … wouldn't care if I was perfect or not. He shouldn't be still all the whole day. You could just picture all your friends playing football, riding bikes, going to school …	Zack's response is rich with potential to explore what doing nothing has to do with being perfect and whether perfection is even a desirable goal.
Teacher	So what you're saying is it's not worth doing this.	Teacher doesn't pick up on the possibilities of Zack's response, but rather summarizes it in a flat way.
Zack	Yeah, I'd quit. I wouldn't do it.	Zack then merely paraphrases the teacher's response rather than continuing his line of thinking.
Teacher	Alright, you're going to quit and you don't think it's going to be worth it. Okay.	The teacher seems to close off the potential line of discussion by again echoing Zack's response rather than pursuing the ideas.

to-student talk of 52 to 48. However, what students said was not taken advantage of to promote thinking. That is, the teacher didn't connect students' comments to each other or to text content, nor did she give students much encouragement to explain their ideas. In 8 of the 11 responses to student comments, the teacher merely echoed what students said, which did not facilitate or move the discussion. As such, students had little opportunity to grapple with the ideas. In fact, the underlying message to students in this kind of discourse may be that "all ideas are equal" and "whatever you say is fine."

In the lesson about the joint-stock company, as in the *Be a Perfect Person* lesson, the proportion of teacher-to-student talk was nearly even (48 to 52); however, the nature of the teacher's talk in the two lessons was quite different. In the joint-stock company discussion, the teacher took an active role in making student comments productive. When he echoed a student's comment, he used it to continue the discussion, for example, by probing students to clarify or elaborate the ideas expressed. Such probes helped students focus on meaningful information, prompted connections, and set up information so it could be productively grappled with.

The teacher was very active, but in contrast to the activity the teacher showed in *The Best Bad Thing* lesson, this teacher's activity was directed toward responding to students and asking questions that required the students to put cognitive effort into making the information meaningful. He made students responsible for pursuing ideas that were brought up in the discussion.

TEACHERS ACTIONS TO FACILITATE DISCUSSION IN THE SERVICE OF CONSTRUCTING MEANING

The purpose of classroom talk in Questioning the Author is to have students discuss ideas in order to construct meaning—not simply to state the facts from a text or express their ideas, but to do those things toward making sense of what they read. From analyses of classroom transcripts, we have discerned certain teacher actions that seem to promote meaning-oriented discussion in that they foster student thinking while not taking over the job of thinking.

We have conceptualized these teacher actions as six *Discussion Moves*.[1] The first Discussion Move is *Marking*. Teachers use Marking in the course of a discussion to draw attention to, and emphasize the importance of, an idea that a student has raised. This is usually done subtly, sometimes simply with voice intonation or an affirmative word. An example of Marking is seen in Table 8.1, following Kristen's reintroduction of an important concept into the discussion by saying, "But this risky thing." The teacher marked that idea by responding "Yes, this risky thing, Kristen …" and then by posing a question to address the issue. There are a variety of other ways in which teachers mark students' comments in a discussion, such as by explicitly acknowledging an idea's importance with something like: "Good point. It's important to know that."

Another Discussion Move, *Revoicing*, involves interpreting what students are struggling to express and rephrasing the ideas so that they can become part of the discussion. Revoicing is a kind of "in other words" mechanism to assist students in expressing their own ideas and distilling from their comments the most important information or implicit ideas. For example, in the transcript in Table 8.1, as William tried to explain what sharing the cost meant, he said, "They'd kind of, well, gather up enough money—like the wood builders. They will not work for free." The teacher revoiced what he thought William meant, saying, "Oh, I see. So you mean the wood builders were going to build the ship?" And when William agreed that that was his point, the teacher revoiced it further, so it could become part of a productive discussion. The teacher's "in other words" phrasing was "… a bunch of people gather up all their money and say, 'Okay, we'll pay you to build the ship.'"

The Revoicing and Marking moves have similar functions. In both cases, the "thinking" work has already been done by students and the moves are used to emphasize and focus ideas, making them easier for other students to react to. In this way, relevant ideas readily become the building blocks of productive discussion.

A third Discussion Move, the *Turning back* move, is associated with two kinds of teacher actions. First, Turning back refers to the teacher's turning responsibility back to students for their reconsideration or elaboration. Second, Turning back can also refer to turning students' attention back to the text as a source for clarifying their thinking. The transcript in Table 8.1 contains several instances of turning back responsibility to the students. One example follows Kristen's first comment that included the statement "... They decided to share the cost of a um, to put together an English colony." The teacher turned the response back to the students for explanation, responding, "Share the cost? What do you mean share the cost?"

Other ways we have seen teachers use Turning-back responsibility includes encouraging students to connect their ideas with the ideas of other students. For example, consider a Questioning the Author teacher's query about an event in a story: "How does Karen's idea about the situation connect to what Lisa said about his feelings towards his friends?"

The other form of the Turning-back move is Turning-back to text. In some cases, the move of Turning-back to text is a quick way to clear up confusion. For instance, in a discussion of a story, a student commented, "Maybe the mouse could just drive his motorcycle to find a new place." Yet that comment was in conflict with the text information about the condition of the motorcycle. So the teacher said, "Wait, go back and see what the author told us about his motorcycle."

Turning-back to text is also a useful move when students introduce unrelated ideas and argue points that have little to do with the major content under consideration or when they debate an issue that can be easily clarified by what the author has explicitly presented. Directing students back to the text can forestall young students' tendency to go off on tangents and introduce irrelevant information.

In addition to the three Discussion Moves just presented—Marking, Revoicing, and Turning-back to students and to text—there is another set of Discussion Moves in which teachers bring themselves into the interaction more directly than in the previous moves. The three additional moves are Recapping, Modeling, and Annotating.

Recapping is a Discussion Move that is useful when students have come to a place in their construction of ideas that indicates they are ready to move on, either because it appears that students have grasped the essential ideas or because they perseverate in repetitive discussion of the same point. The teacher in the joint-stock company lesson used Recapping for the latter purpose by trying to wrap up an issue the students kept coming back to: the sharing costs issue. As indicated in Table 8.1, the teacher said, "Okay, so I think we all agree that having lots of people chip in money is a lot better than having one person pay for everything."

The fifth Discussion Move is *Modeling*. Modeling refers to a teacher's thinking aloud as she reads to show students how her mind is actively interacting with the ideas in a text. One way in which Modeling can be used effectively is to identify confusing portions of text and show how one might work through them. In the case of Questioning the Author, calling attention to text that is not clear is especially useful because it reinforces an underlying notion of Questioning the Author, that of a fallible author—someone who is trying to communicate a message that may not be clear or complete.

In the example that follows, a teacher models how a reader might handle a text that seemed to present too many details:

> When I first read all this description about the features of the land, I thought what's going on here? What's the author want me to remember from all the information? So I went back and read it again and decided that the big idea was that this was a good place to build a town because it was close to a river and protected by forests on the other side. That's what I think the author was trying to get at.

A teacher's modeling of grappling with portions of text that were somewhat contradictory went like this:

> Okay, now, when I was reading this, I understood that in the first sentence, the author said most people in developing countries make a living by farming. But later on the author said, "However, there is a shortage of food." Well, if everyone makes their living by farming, why would there be a shortage of food? What's going on here? Let's think this through.

It has been our experience that when Modeling is briefly folded into ongoing discussions over time, it is a powerful way for students to encounter a range of expert reading behaviors. Moreover, Modeling is particularly important in a Questioning the Author discussion because it reinforces for the students the teacher's role as a participant collaborator in constructing meaning.

The last discussion move is *Annotating,* which involves those instances during a discussion when a teacher provides information. This is needed because sometimes authors simply do not provide enough content for students to be able to construct meaning from the text alone. There are gaps in information, holes in lines of reasoning, and assumptions about background knowledge that readers do not have. For example, in a fourth-grade social studies class, students read the textbook's rather cursory account of the Whiskey Rebellion. As discussion of the text proceeded, it became clear that the text did not offer students adequate information to build an understanding of why the Whiskey Rebellion was significant in U.S. history. The teacher's subsequent contribution to the discussion provided a good example of Annotating: "The author didn't tell us, but the Whiskey Rebellion was a real test for the new government. President Washington's decision to send troops to put down the rebellion was a message to the entire country."

The Discussion Moves are actions that we have seen Questioning the Author teachers take to keep discussion focused and productive. The moves are not a prescription for creating a discussion; they are simply resources teachers can draw on to keep students engaged in the constructive work of building understanding.

A FINAL WORD

In Questioning the Author, the discourse between students and teacher and among students is the substance from which meaning is built. Yet group talk will not necessarily lead to meaning building. Discourse that leads to meaning building needs direction, focus, and movement toward a goal. To effectively foster such discourse, a teacher must not only attend to the content of what is being read and the ideas important for building meaning from that content, but also monitor where students are in the construction process and then pull from that combination of factors ways of directing the dialogue to promote understanding. As Cazden (1988) says, "It is easy to imagine talk in which ideas are explored rather than answers to teachers' text questions provided and evaluated .... Easy to imagine, but not easy to do" (p. 54).

Initially our research interest was in tracking how students respond to an environment that promotes collaborative meaning building. However, the complexity of the teacher's task in such an environment emerged as a new focus. The complexity became apparent as we observed the extent to which the approach upset the apple cart of the traditional lesson. The Questioning the Author framework meant that lessons no longer consisted of reading straight through a text, followed by questions aimed at retrieving text information. Rather, teachers needed to develop strategies to foster meaningful classroom discourse.

We have come to understand very clearly how much effort and attention it takes to change one's teaching practices to a more constructivist orientation and to engage and use classroom talk toward developing understanding. Our current efforts are directed toward taking advantage of all we have learned in working with our collaborating teachers and transforming that knowledge into forms that other teachers can use. We believe that the key is to develop ways to support teachers as they attempt to change their teaching practices day by day.

The development of effective support materials calls for understanding and anticipating pitfalls that teachers encounter as they move toward constructivist practices and the design of resources to help teachers address those situations. Toward addressing that need, we have developed resources we call *accessibles*. Each accessible describes an issue that concerned teachers during implementation and offers examples of the issue and how to deal with it. The examples are based on actual classroom interactions from the Questioning the Author database of more than 120 videotaped lessons. An accessible presents excerpts of classroom discussion that set up a problem or issue, accompanied by explanatory annotations that illustrate how the issue developed, why it might arise, and how it can be addressed. We are currently exploring the effectiveness of the accessibles by closely following teachers as they implement Questioning the Author using the accessibles as support materials.

ACKNOWLEDGMENTS

The research described in this paper was supported by a grant to the authors from the Spencer Foundation and by funds from the Office of Educational Research and Improvement (OERI), U.S. Department of Education. The opinions expressed do not necessarily reflect the position or policy of the Spencer Foundation or OERI, and no official endorsement should be inferred.

NOTE

1. The joint-stock company teacher used four of the six moves, and we draw examples of those moves from the transcript in Table 8.1. Examples of the other two moves are drawn from other Questioning the Author transcripts.

REFERENCES

Almasi, J. F. (1995). The nature of fourth-graders' sociocognitive conflicts in peer-led and teacher-led discussion of literature. *Reading Research Quarterly, 30*(3), 314–351.

Beck, I. L., & Carpenter, P. A. (1986). Cognitive approaches to understanding reading: Implications for instructional practice. *American Psychologist, 41*(10), 1098–1105.

Beck, I. L., & McKeown, M. G. (2001). Inviting students into the pursuit of meaning. *Educational Psychology Review, 13*, 225–241.

Beck, I. L., & McKeown, M. G. (2002). Questioning the author: Making sense of social studies. *Educational Leadership, 60*(3), 44–47.

Beck, I. L., McKeown, M. G., Worthy, J., Sandora, C. A., & Kucan, L. (1996). Questioning the author: A year-long classroom implementation to engage students with text. *The Elementary School Journal, 96*(4), 385–414.

Bruer, J. T. (1993). *Schools for thought: A science of learning in the classroom.* Cambridge, MA: MIT Press.

Cazden, C. B. (1988). *Classroom discourse: The language of teaching and learning.* Portsmouth, NH: Heinemann.

Goldenberg, C. (1993). Instructional conversations: Promoting comprehension through discussion. *The Reading Teacher, 46,* 316–326.

Kucan, L., & Beck, I. L. (1997). Thinking aloud and reading comprehension research: Inquiry, instruction, and social interaction. *Review of Educational Research, 67,* 271–299.

Kucan, L., & Beck, I. L. (2003). Inviting students to talk about expository texts: A comparison of two discourse environments and their effects on comprehension. *Reading Research and Instruction, 42*(3), 1–31.

Manes, S. (1982). *Be a perfect person in just three days.* New York: Bantam.

McKeown, M. G., & Beck, I. L. (1998). Talking to an author: Readers taking charge of the reading process. *Yearbook of the National Society for the Study of Education, 97,* 112–130.

McKeown, M. G., & Beck, I. L. (1999). Getting the discussion started. *Educational Leadership, 57*(3), 25–28.

McKeown, M. G., & Beck, I. L. (2004). Transforming knowledge into professional development resources: Six teachers implement a model of teaching for understanding text. *The Elementary School Journal, 104,* 391–408.

McKeown, M. G., & Beck, I. L. (2006). Encouraging young children's language interactions with stories. In D. Dickenson & S. Neuman (Eds.), *Handbook of early literacy research: Volume 2* (pp. 281–294). New York: Guilford.

McKeown, M. G., Beck, I. L., & Sandora, C. A. (1996). Questioning the author: An approach to developing meaningful classroom discourse. In M. G. Graves, M. M. Taylor, & P. van den Broek (Eds.), *The first R: A right of all children* (pp. 97–119). New York: Teacher's College Press.

O'Flahavan, J. F., Stein, C., Wiencek, J., & Marks, T. (1992). *Interpretive development in peer discussion about literature: An exploration of the teacher's role.* Paper presented at the 42nd annual meeting of the National Reading Conference, San Antonio, TX.

Palincsar, A. S., & Brown, A. L. (1989). Instruction for self-regulated reading. In L. Resnick & L. Klopfer (Eds.), *Toward the thinking curriculum: Current cognitive research* (pp. 19–39). Alexandria, VA: Association for Curriculum & Supervision Development.

Roby, T. W. (1988). Models of discussion. In J. T. Dillon (Ed.), *Questioning and discussion: A multidisciplinary study* (pp. 163–191). Norwood, NJ: Ablex.

Sandora, C. A. (1994). *A comparison of two discussion techniques: Great Books (post-reading) and Questioning the Author (on-line) on students' comprehension and interpretation of narrative texts.* Unpublished doctoral dissertation, University of Pittsburgh, Pennsylvania.

Shulman, L. (1987). Knowledge and teaching: Foundations of the new reform. *Harvard Educational Review, 57*(1), 1–22.

Uchida, Y. (1983). *The best bad thing.* New York: Atheneum.

CHAPTER 9

The Effects of an Instructional Conversation on English Language Learners' Concepts of Friendship and Story Comprehension[1]

William M. Saunders
Claude Goldenberg

A recent review of research involving English language learners (ELLs) conducted in the United States over the past 20 years found that both direct instruction and more interactive approaches to instruction (singly or together) are successful with ELLs (Genesee, Lindholm-Leary, Saunders, & Christian, 2006). Although the U.S. empirical literature on the effects of these instructional approaches on ELLs remains relatively small, this finding represents a new synthesis.

As recently as 20 years ago, researchers and educators often had to extrapolate from non-ELL research to identify instructional approaches that might be effective with ELLs. Because of the persistent underachievement among language minority populations (e.g., Committee for Economic Development, 1991), findings derived from studies of low-achieving non-ELL students were often presumed to apply to ELLs. For the most part, this resulted in an emphasis on direct instruction and explicit teaching of specific skills:

> Low-achieving students need more control and structuring from their teachers: more active instruction and feedback, more redundancy, and smaller steps with higher success rates. This will mean more review, drill, and practice, and thus more lower-level questions. (Brophy & Good, 1986, p. 365)

No doubt there is a broad literature demonstrating that direct instruction is effective when done well. Modeling, demonstrations, clear explanations, lectures, feedback, correctives, and practice all promote learning (Gage, 1978; Gage & Berliner, 1988; Rosenshine & Stevens, 1986; Walberg, 1990).

At the same time, second-language acquisition theories (Cummins, 1989; Krashen, 1987) emphasize the importance of social interaction in the language acquisition process. Indeed, several studies document the paucity of interaction in ELL classrooms (Arreaga-Mayer & Perdomo-Rivera, 1996; Berman et al., 1992; Ramirez, 1992) and/or the tendency to weight ELL instruction toward lower level skills lessons and factually oriented lessons (see, e.g., Barrera, 1983; Goldenberg, 1989b; Hiebert, 1983; Knapp & Shields, 1990). Such findings, as well the emergence of newer studies documenting the potential value of interactive instruction (Palinscar & Brown, 1985; Tharp & Gallimore, 1988), served to stimulate and justify increasing interest in interactive approaches (Dalton, 1998; Tharp, 1997) and the promise of programs specifically for ELLs that utilized both direct instruction and interactive approaches (August & Hakuta, 1998; Calderón, Hertz-Lazarowitz, & Slavin, 1998; García, 1992; Gersten, 1996, Goldenberg, 1996; Saunders, 1999).

Much of the research conducted in the United States over the last 20 years has focused on the comparative effects of specific language-of-instruction programs, such as English immersion, transition bilingual education, maintenance bilingual education, and two-way bilingual education (Genesee et al., 2006). As such, the emergence of research on specific instructional approaches, including the singular and combined effects of different approaches like direct and interactive instruction, represents an important advance in ELL research.

At this point, however, existing research constitutes just a beginning. There remains an urgent need to continue conceptualizing and studying instructional approaches that assist ELLs in acquiring knowledge, skills, and higher level concepts, both in their primary language and in English. Over the past 15 years, we have been researching and developing a middle to upper elementary grades language arts program for ELLs applicable to both transitional bilingual and English immersion contexts: Opportunities through Language Arts (OLA; Saunders & Goldenberg, 2001, 2003). The program incorporates direct instruction for some areas of literacy instruction (e.g., reading comprehension strategies, writing conventions) and interactive instruction for other areas (e.g., studying literature, writing process). At the heart of the OLA program is Instructional Conversation (IC), an interactive approach to the study of literature. For us, and for the many teachers with whom we have worked, IC is a way to capitalize on the teaching and learning potential of "talk about text."

In this chapter, first we overview and provide background on the concept and practice of IC and review some of our previous research on IC. Next we describe the methods and report the results of a study we conducted to examine the effects of an IC lesson on fourth-grade ELLs' conceptual understandings and literal comprehension of a story about friendship. We also analyze the content and sociolinguistic properties of IC lessons in contrast to more conventional approaches to story discussions. Finally, we discuss the implications of the study's results and additional questions that need to be pursued to more fully assess and understand the potential of IC as an interactive instructional approach.

BACKGROUND ON INSTRUCTIONAL CONVERSATION AND THE STUDY

Turning a Good but Elusive Idea Into a Concrete Model

The idea of instructional conversation is by no means a new one. Since the time of Socrates, philosophers and educators have talked about and encouraged teachers to engage students in substantive interactions (Goldenberg, 1991). From the early part of the 20th century up through today, researchers have promoted the value of discussions for developing critical thinking, productive social interaction, intellectual risk taking, and academic engagement (Thayer, 1928; Wilen, 1990). At the same time, the past two decades have produced the first body of actual research on the status and nature of classroom talk or discourse. Contrary to what we might assume, good discussions rarely occur in American classrooms. Elementary and secondary students generally spend less than 5% of class time participating in "real" discussions (Goodlad, 1984; Nystrand & Gamoran, 1991). More often than not, classroom interactions conform to a predictable pattern of "recitation," with the teacher asking a question, a student responding, and the teacher evaluating the response and then moving on to another question (Cazden, 1988; Mehan, 1979, 1991).

Recitation has a number of well-documented strengths, including promoting active participation (Wang, Haertel, & Walberg, 1993) and effective review and practice (Stodolsky, Ferguson, & Wimpelberg, 1981). But because it is characterized by known-answer questions, short student responses, and minimal continuity from one question to the next, recitation does not allow for the exploration and development of ideas that characterize "real" discussions. Researchers have put forth a variety of explanations for the paucity of discussion and the predominance of recitation. Some argue that recitation is deeply rooted in Western belief systems about teaching (Tharp & Gallimore, 1988). Others suggest that it is extremely difficult for teachers to give up the familiar and traditional role of knowledge giver and enter into new, more collaborative relationships and interactions with their students (Langer, 1987).

Our work with teachers, however, has led us to a different assessment. Many teachers are eager to engage in meaningful and productive discussions with their students, but they are uncertain about how to do it well and have few concrete models to inform their efforts (Saunders & Goldenberg, 1996). Our work on instructional conversation (or good classroom discussions) arose out of this identified need. Building on research conducted at the Kamehameha Early Education Program (e.g., Au, 1979; Tharp & Gallimore, 1988), we have been working in language-minority schools over the past 15 years to elaborate the concept of IC, to specify its elements in clear and plain terms, and help teachers instantiate ICs in their classrooms (Goldenberg, 1992–1993; Goldenberg & Gallimore, 1991; Saunders & Goldenberg, 2000; Saunders, Goldenberg, & Hamann, 1992; Saunders, O'Brien, Lennon, & McLean,1998).

What is an Instructional Conversation?

At present, we have identified 10 elements that seem to define the essence of instructional conversation. They are presented, in abbreviated form, in Table 9.1 (see Goldenberg, 1991, 1992–1993, for more extensive descriptions).

TABLE 9.1
Elements of the Instructional Conversation

INSTRUCTIONAL ELEMENTS

1. Thematic focus. The teacher selects a theme or idea to serve as a starting point for focusing the discussion and has a general plan for how the theme will unfold, including how to "chunk" the text to permit optimal exploration of the theme.

2. Activation and use of background and relevant schemata. The teacher either "hooks into" or provides students with pertinent background knowledge and relevant schemata necessary for understanding a text. Background knowledge and schemata are then woven into the discussion that follows.

3. Direct teaching. When necessary, the teacher provides direct teaching of a skill or concept.

4. Promotion of more complex language and expression. The teacher elicits more extended student contributions by using a variety of elicitation techniques—invitations to expand (e.g., "Tell me more about that"), questions (e.g., "What do you mean?"), restatements (e.g., "In other words,"), and pauses.

5. Elicitation of bases for statements or positions. The teacher promotes students' use of text, pictures, and reasoning to support an argument or position. Without overwhelming students, the teacher probes for the bases of students' statements, for example. "How do you know?" "What makes you think that?" "Show us where it says __."

CONVERSATIONAL ELEMENTS

6. Fewer "known-answer" questions. Much of the discussion centers on questions and answers for which there might be more than one correct answer.

7. Responsivity to student contributions. In addition to having an initial plan and maintaining the focus and coherence of the discussion, the teacher is also responsive to students' statements and the opportunities they provide.

8. Connected discourse. The discussion is characterized by multiple, interactive, connected turns; succeeding utterances build on and extend previous ones.

9. A challenging but nonthreatening atmosphere. The teacher creates a "zone of proximal development," where a challenging atmosphere is balanced by a positive affective climate. The teacher is more collaborator than evaluator and creates an atmosphere that challenges students and allows them to negotiate and construct the meaning of the text.

10. General participation, including self-selected turns. The teacher encourages general participation among students. The teacher does not hold exclusive right to determine who talks, and students are encouraged to volunteer or otherwise influence the selection of speaking turns.

Successfully addressed, the 10 elements combine to produce what might appear as an excellent discussion conducted by a teacher and a group of students.

"Instructional conversation" is, first, interesting and engaging. Is is about an idea or a concept that has meaning and relevance for students. It has a focus that, while it might shift as the discussion evolves, remains discernible throughout. There is a high level of participation, without undue domination by any one individual, particularly the teacher ... Teachers and students are responsive to what others say, so that each statement or contribution builds upon, challenges, or extends pervious ones. Topics are picked up, developed, elaborated…. Strategically, the teacher (or discussion leader) questions, prods, challenges, coaxes—or keeps quiet. He or she clarifies and instructs when necessary, but does so efficiently, without wasting time or words. The teacher assures that the discussion proceeds at an appropriate pace—neither too fast to prohibit the development of ideas, nor too slowly to maintain interest and momentum. The teacher knows when to bear down and draw out a student's ideas and when to ease up, allowing thought and reflection to take over. Perhaps most important, the teacher manages to keep everyone engaged in a substantive and extended conversation, weaving individual participants' comments into a larger tapestry of meaning. (Goldenberg, 1991, pp. 3–4)

In the following section, we provide short examples to illustrate the differences between IC and recitation (additional IC excerpts are introduced later in the chapter). In the IC example, the teacher's questions are open-ended, calling for interpretations of the story; students' contributions are longer, and their turns are often prompted and followed by those of other students. In the recitation example, the teacher's questions are less open-ended and concern the facts of the story; student responses tend to be shorter, and their turns are uniformly prompted and followed by the teacher's. The IC example is identifiable as a segment taken from a larger discussion in which the events of the story are under analysis and debate. The recitation is a series of questions across which the events in the story are being reviewed and rehearsed. Each has a place in the curriculum, but IC and recitation are clearly different forms of interaction that produce very different kinds of talk about text.

Instructional Conversation	*Recitation*
Tchr: What should Rob have decided?	Tchr: What was the problem in the story?
Karla: Oh, he should have told his friend not to do that.	Maria: The haircut.
	Tchr: The haircut. Okay. Albert.
Rosa: But he said that he wanted to go into the barbershop. He wanted to go and he [Soup] said no I'll cut your hair free. And he goes, FREE.	Al: They wasted their money on candy.
	Tchr: Wasted money?
	Ricky: Rob wanted a haircut, but he wanted candy more.
Karla: No that didn't happen.	Tchr: Good. Was Soup involved?
Tchr: So he-	Ricky: Soup tricked him.
Char: It said he said, IF I had a barbershop I would cut your hair free.	Tchr: Oh. Soup was tricky.
	Marta: Yeah, he told 'em, I'll cut you hair for free.
Tchr: Now was that a good friend?	Tchr: Okay. And then what happens?

Instructional Conversation in Previous Studies

As part of our efforts to define and implement IC, our research team has conducted several studies to formally advance the idea and practice. In a series of sociolinguistic analyses, we found that ICs differ from more common forms of classroom lessons. For example, in comparison to directed lessons, during ICs teachers talk significantly less, students talk significantly more, and the actual content of lessons is more likely to be mutually shaped and defined by student and teacher understandings (Goldenberg & Patthey-Chavez, 1994). Over time (one school year), upper elementary school students' participation in ICs improves: They learn to follow up on each other's comments and maintain topics for longer stretches of conversation (Patthey-Chavez & Goldenberg, 1992). ICs can have a broader effect on the classroom environment, contributing to a greater sense of community and scholarship among students and teacher (Patthey-Chavez, Clare, & Gallimore, 1995). We also know that ICs help both ELLs and non-ELLs arrive at higher levels of story comprehension and thematic understanding than they attain when reading stories and completing study exercises on their own (Saunders & Goldenberg, 1999). Moreover, we know that IC can be implemented in other content areas and with older students, for example, middle school mathematics classes (Dalton & Sison, 1995), and successfully adapted to special education settings (Echevarria, 1995; Echevarria & McDonough, 1995).

Given sufficient time and assistance to learn about and implement IC, teachers continue to use it several years after training and assistance ends; they report that IC allows them to more successfully address higher level thinking and comprehension goals than previous approaches they had used (Saunders & Goldenberg, 1996). In fact, in the seminal project in which we successfully tested the effects of the OLA program, which includes several components (literature units, literature logs, writing-as-a-process, comprehension strategies, pleasure reading, and dictation), teachers rated IC as *the* most important component for promoting students' literacy development (Saunders & Goldenberg, 1997). We also know that it takes at least a year of fairly intensive effort and assistance to be able to implement ICs effectively (at least as defined by the elements listed in Table 9.1). In our most effective training settings, teachers conduct ICs on a regular basis, videotape their lessons, and then in weekly meetings led by a teacher or researcher with substantial IC experience, they view, analyze, and discuss each other's lessons (Saunders et al., 1992).

Study Objective

Despite its strong theoretical basis, the prominence teachers afford IC, and the evidence suggesting that ICs engender deeper story understandings than students achieve on their own, we know nothing about the effects of IC in contrast to other modes of literature instruction. Discussions tend to be more effective than lectures for college students (Gall & Gall, 1990). Middle school students score higher on measures of literature achievement and evidence higher levels of engagement in English classes where discussions are more rather than less frequent (Nystrand & Gamoran, 1991). To the best of our knowledge, however, there is virtually no research about the effects of discussions—or ICs—in the lower grades or in comparison to other teaching methods commonly used at the elementary level, such as recitation (Hoetker & Ahlbrand, 1969). Previous research on "higher order questions" serves as a reminder of the need to demonstrate the effectiveness of proposed teaching procedures, no matter how logical it might appear that these procedures should prove beneficial to students. Gage (1978) has noted that research of the early 1970s failed to demonstrate any benefits of higher order questions, that is, questions asking for critical thinking and problem solving. Indeed, the reverse seemed to be the case—lower order questions stressing factual recall were often associated with higher levels of student achievement. Although ICs involve far more than asking "higher order questions," the results of this research remind us that we can never take for granted the effectiveness of particular procedures or approaches. The study reported in this chapter addresses four questions:

1. Does IC develop students' understandings of complex concepts?
2. Does IC support literal comprehension of stories?
3. Can English language learners transitioning from Spanish to English instruction successfully participate in IC s conducted in English about English texts?
4. What do teachers do within IC s that might contribute to students' understandings of complex concepts and support their literal comprehension of stories?

First, a good IC (or series of them) focuses on a substantive theme(s) relevant to the story. Substantive themes are usually complex and multifaceted concepts, such as friendship, sacrifice, justice, commitment, or legacy. We have assumed that students come away from successful ICs with a better understanding of the theme/concept, as well as the story itself, because a good IC should challenge and assist students to articulate, reflect on, and expand their understandings of concepts being discussed. In this study, we wanted to formally test that assumption (question 1).

Second, in comparison to other kinds of literature discussions (e.g., like those recommended in basal readers), when they conduct ICs, teachers spend much less time explicitly reviewing the literal details of the story (sequence of events, information about the characters, descriptions of settings). More time is devoted to analysis and interpretation of story content and the potential meanings of the story and theme. We have assumed that given a well-chosen story (generally appropriate readability level but good thematic potential), students need only minimal explicit review and clarification of literal details: A good IC allows students to solidify their understanding of literal details through the process of analyzing and interpreting story content. This is the second assumption we wanted to test (question 2).

Third, when ELLs in transitional bilingual programs demonstrate sufficient first language (L1) literacy skills and second language (L2) oral skills, they usually begin a 6- to 18-month program of transitional language arts, wherein formal English reading and writing are introduced. Transition is the one phase in bilingual programs in which L2 students are least likely to receive higher level curricula and most likely to receive large amounts of lower level skill instruction (Berman et al., 1992). We have assumed that experienced IC teachers can make it possible for transition students to participate successfully in ICs—promoting high levels of participation, drawing out more elaborated language, articulating and clarifying issues, and ultimately helping students develop deeper understandings of the story and theme. This is the third assumption we wanted to test (question 3).

Fourth, a good IC should bring forth interaction that reveals both a high degree of verbal participation on the part of the students and also responsiveness and instructional purposefulness on the part of the teacher. We have assumed that experienced IC teachers successfully negotiate a dual role as conversation facilitator and instructor, promoting productive and spontaneous conversation but shaping and directing that conversation toward instructional ends. This is the fourth assumption we wanted to test (question 4).

METHODS

Setting and Population

The student body at the urban K–5 elementary school where this study was conducted is 93% Hispanic and 88% limited English-proficient; 80% of students qualify for the federal free meal program; an additional 15% qualify for reduced-price meals. A large majority of parents, both at this particular school and around the district (which is located in the metropolitan Los Angeles area), work in skilled, semi-skilled, or unskilled occupations and have received an average 6 to 7 years of formal schooling (Gallimore, Reese, Balzano, Benson, & Goldenberg, 1991; Goldenberg, 1989a).

At the time of the study, 75% of the children at the school were below grade level in mathematics and reading. Based on state tests, students' achievement in reading, writing, and mathematics placed the school at the 15th percentile among California schools. The school's achievement level was not atypical, given its socioeconomic characteristics. Although scores were in the lower percentile ranges statewide, in comparison to schools with similar socioeconomic characteristics, the school's scores were in the middle percentile rankings—30th for writing, 40th for math, and 58th for reading. (See Goldenberg, 2004, and Goldenberg & Sullivan, 1994, for results of the larger, long-term project to improve achievement at the school.)

Classroom Context

The study was conducted in the fourth-grade classroom of one of our project teachers, Mrs. Fiske, a veteran instructor in her first year as a participant in the IC project. Of the 31 students in the class, 27 were in their first year of transition from Spanish to English instruction; 4 students were native English speakers. All or most of the 27 students qualified to transition at the end of third or the beginning of fourth grade because they tested on or close to grade level in Spanish reading (3.2, end of book tests for the Spanish reading series) and had demonstrated the ability to generally converse in English (Bilingual Syntax Measure, Level 4 or speech emergence). Of the four native English speakers, one was Anglo, another was Hispanic, and two were African American. Two were very proficient readers, and two were substantially below grade level. The class provided a unique research opportunity: Mrs. Fiske was a willing and helpful collaborator, her ICs were becoming highly successful, and we were interested in examining the effects of IC specifically on transition students. (All students, with the exception of a special education student and three students absent for a major portion of the study, are included in the analysis; N = 27.)

The study was conducted near the end of the school year, as the class was completing a month-long unit on *Charlotte's Web* (White, 1952). Throughout the unit, the teacher and students had discussed a variety of themes, the most prominent of which was the concept of friendship. The teacher had observed that students, perhaps not unlike many 9- and 10-year-olds, generally expressed absolute notions of friendship—for example, friends *never* fight, friends *always* get along, friends *always* share. On the basis of her observations, Mrs. Fiske decided to pursue in her ICs a more differentiated and complex conception of friendship—for example, that friendship can be problematic, friends don't always like each other, sometimes they disagree, friendship often requires tolerance and patience. The study was thus built around the instructional goal of helping students develop a more subtle, complex, and differentiated view of "friendship."

Together with the authors, the teacher developed an adjunct lesson (interjected into the larger *Charlotte's Web* unit) on a short story that seemed particularly suited to pursuing this differentiated concept of friendship. The story, "Quarter for a Haircut" (Peck, 1989), is about two friends, Soup and Rob. Soup convinces Rob to let him cut his hair so they can use the haircut money to buy bubble gum. Soup's haircut is terrible, and Rob must then face an angry mother, who had given him a quarter for the expressed purpose of going to the barber shop.

Half the students participated in an IC lesson; the other half served as the control group and participated in a "recitation" lesson in which the teacher reviewed with the students the literal details of the story (a more conventional "basal-like" literature lesson). So as not to deprive the students in the control group, the same instructional goal was pursued in subsequent lessons as part of the *Charlotte's Web* unit.

Procedures

Students with fall test scores on the Spanish Assessment of Basic Skills (CTB/McGraw Hill, 1987) were matched by quartile, then randomly assigned either to an IC or control group. In the case of missing test scores (n = 11), students were randomly assigned to one of the two conditions. To keep the instructional groups small, students were divided into four groups of seven or eight each—2 IC subgroups and two control subgroups. Based on the teacher's judgments of students' proficiency and achievement in English reading and speaking across the year, within each condition, we made the two subgroups heterogeneous and comparable (i.e., roughly the same composition of high, medium, and low).

Four days prior to the experiment, the teacher asked the entire class to write an essay about friendship in response to the following prompt: *Explain what friendship is. Pick a friend of yours, describe that person, and tell why that person is your friend.* Students were given as much time as they needed, and all finished within 40 minutes. Such a writing assignment was not uncommon in the classroom, as students often completed "drafts" or "quickwrites" as a way of initiating a coming lesson in reading, science, or social studies.

Papers were collected and analyzed by the teacher and the authors as a "pre-test" to determine if there was any evidence of a more differentiated concept of friendship. The vast majority of papers confirmed what the students had maintained in previous discussions: Friends never fight, friends always get along, and that is why they are friends. Only three students demonstrated any understanding of more complex aspects of friendship.

Before beginning the small-group lessons, the teacher spent 10 minutes with the entire class introducing the short story, providing background she felt would facilitate their reading of the story (e.g., about the anthology from which the story was taken, about the time period—when haircuts cost a quarter at the local barbershop, and about the setting—a small rural town). She also read aloud the first two pages of the 11-page story (1,590 words, 3.2 grade level). Students then spent 15 minutes reading the rest of the story independently and silently. When all students had finished reading the story, the teacher began her small-group lessons. Children who were not involved in the lesson went to another room with the instructional aide to review other material.

The order of the lessons was counterbalanced across conditions:

Group 1:   Instructional conversation
Group 2:   Control
Group 3:   Control
Group 4:   Instructional conversation

To verify that the two groups of lessons provided a suitable contrast between IC and non-IC, the four lessons were videotaped, then scored using a rating scale developed by Rueda, Goldenberg, and Gallimore (1991). Scores revealed a very large difference—experimental lessons demonstrated all or virtually all IC elements, whereas the control lessons demonstrated very few (see Rueda et al., 1991, for details regarding scale development, reliability, and validity).

Lesson Content

Prior to the experiment, the teacher and the authors developed a lesson plan for each of the two conditions. The plan for the IC was consistent with what the teacher had been doing for the whole year: (a) Establish the important factual details of the story, capitalizing on opportunities to initiate discussion on the theme of friendship; (b) focus on friendship and try to build a more differentiated conceptualization of friendship; then (c) relate the conceptualization back to the text.

The plan for the control group lesson was based on what the teacher did in previous years when teaching a literature lesson from the basal text. The control lessons contained more elements of what has been referred to as "recitation" instruction, where the primary focus is to make certain that the students have understood the literal details of the story: (a) Pose a series of factual questions about the setting, characters, and events in the story; (b) plot the sequence of events in the story; (c) share teacher and student experiences related to the story; (d) discuss an inference question (e.g., what will happen to the two boys); and (e) ask students about their favorite part(s) of the story. (Descriptions and transcript excerpts for IC and control lessons are provided in the results section.)

Post-Lesson Data

After all groups participated in their lessons, the entire class convened in the classroom to complete two assignments: an essay and a set of 10 comprehension questions. The prompt for the essay was identical to the one administered 4 days prior. As with the initial essay, all students completed their essays within 40 minutes. After the essays had been collected, students completed a 10-question, short-answer comprehension test. Nine of the questions addressed the literal details of the story (e.g., how one boy gets the other to spend his quarter on something else). The final question asked the students to make an inference: Would the two boys remain friends? Why? The administration of the essay and comprehension test was videotaped to provide a record of all procedures.

Analysis of the Lessons

Videotaped lessons were transcribed, read, and the segments within each lesson were identified (e.g., reviewing factual details, sequencing, charting words to define friendship, discussing whether Soup was a good friend). Then for each lesson, the number of teacher and student turns and utterances was tabulated. A turn is the occurrence of someone speaking. An utterance is a unit of meaning within the turn. An utterance can be as short as a word (e.g., Uh huh or What?) and as long as a independent clause (e.g., He wanted to get a haircut). A turn can have any number of utterances. Next, each turn was coded for length—for the nature and number of utterances within the turn: A turn with one utterance less than an independent clause in length was coded as 0 (e.g., Yes., What?, From the store.); a turn with an utterance one independent clause in length was coded as 1 (e.g., "Oh, he should have told his friend not to do that."); a turn with two independent clauses was designated with 2 (e.g., "Rob wanted a haircut, but he wanted candy more."); a turn with three was assigned a 3; and a turn with four or more independent clauses received a 4. The utterance data allow us to quantify the proportion of student versus teacher talk in a lesson (i.e., who produces most of the talk in the lesson?). The turn-length data allow us to quantify the level of elaboration in student versus teacher talk during the lesson (i.e., how much are the parties allowed to elaborate when they talk in the lesson?).

Analysis of Tests and Essays

Both the pre- and post-essays were entered on a word processor. To eliminate the influence of handwriting, spelling, and punctuation on the independent coding of the essays, simple misspellings and omissions of end-marks were corrected. The content was unchanged. Comprehension tests were not modified in any way.

Two blind raters coded the essays and the comprehension test. For the essays, the raters assigned a 1 to the texts that included any language concerning the difficulty or problematic aspects of friendships—for example, sometimes friends don't get along; they have to talk things out when there are problems; friendship sometimes requires tolerance, patience, and so on. (Henceforth we refer to such language as "the tracer" [Newman, Griffin, & Cole, 1989][2] because it provides a trace in the students' essays of the differentiated conceptualization in which we were interested.) Raters assigned a 0 to texts containing no such language.

For the comprehension tests, a key of possible acceptable answers was developed by the second author. Raters scored each answer on a 3-point scale: 0, incorrect—inconsistent with the story; .5, partially correct—consistent with the story but not a complete answer; 1, correct, consistent with story and a complete answer. Raters also coded the last question on the comprehension test (Will they still be friends? Why?) for any evidence of the "tracer" in the students' justifications. Interrater reliability (percent agreement) for the essays was 94%; for the total comprehension, 94%; and for the last question on the comprehension test, 92%.

In addition, descriptive statistics were also generated for the essays: total number of words, number of T-units, and average T-unit length (an estimation of syntactical maturity; Hunt, 1977). These statistics were used to check the comparability of the different groups with regard to their writing development.

Data Analysis

A t test was performed on each of the descriptive statistics to assess comparability of the four groups. We collapsed the subgroups for each condition and performed chi-squares for the essay data. A 2×3 Analysis of Variance (IC vs. Control; High, Medium, Low proficiency and achievement in English reading during the year) was conducted on the scores from the comprehension test. Due to absences, not all of the 27 students included in the study completed all assignments—two students did not write pre-essays; three students did not complete the comprehension test.

RESULTS

First, we report results on the comparability of the IC and control groups. Next, we report results specific to our four research questions: (1) Does IC develop students' understanding of complex concepts? (2) Does IC support literal comprehension? (3) Can transition students successfully participate in ICs in English? and (4) What do teachers do within ICs that might contribute to students' understandings of complex concepts and support their literal comprehension of stories?

Were the Instructional Conversation and Control Groups Comparable?

On fall standardized Spanish-language tests, students in the two groups who had taken the test were nearly identical: Mean scale score = 631 for both groups, $SD = 29$ ($n = 9$) and 21 ($n = 8$) for experimental and control groups, respectively ($p = .95$, 2-tailed t test). The median national percentile for all students who took the test was 46.

With respect to students' writing competence, as evidenced by their written performance for the experiment, the two groups continued to be equivalent. As Table 9.2 shows, no significant differences were found between the two groups for any of the descriptive statistics tested. Students in both groups generated more writing in their post-lesson essays than in their pre-lesson essays. However, the two groups were virtually identical in terms of the quantity and general syntactic maturity of their writing at both occasions.

TABLE 9.2
Length and Syntactical Maturity of Pre-and Post-Lesson Student Essays

Pre-lesson essays	IC Mean/SD (pre-lesson n = 12)	Control Mean/SD (pre-lesson n = 13)	t*
Total words	49.3 (14.3)	58.9 (27.2)	−1.2
No. of T-units	6.2 (1.5)	7.8 (3.2)	−1.6
T-unit length	7.8 (.95)	7.7 (1.7)	.22
Post-lesson essays	(post-lesson n = 13)	(post-lesson n = 14)	
Total words	79.5 (33.1)	83.1 (24.6)	−.32
No. of T-units	10.3 (4.6)	10.7 (3.6)	−.26
T-unit length	8.0 (1.6)	8.0 (1.5)	.11

*All *t* tests (1-tailed) not significant at .05.

Does Instructional Conversation Develop Students' Understandings of Complex Concepts?

Yes. The "tracer" (evidence of a more differentiated view of friendship) was evident in the post lesson writings (essays and question 10 responses) for a majority of the IC students but in very few of the post-lesson writings of the control students.

Essays

As Figure 9.1 shows, the students in the IC lessons were more than 4 times as likely (62% vs. 14%) to mention more subtle, problematic, or differentiated aspects of friendship, for example, that friendship is not always perfect or that friends

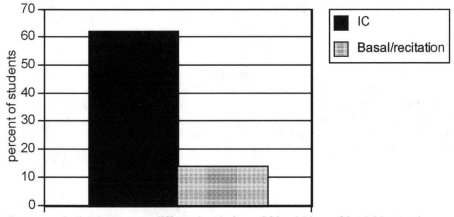

*Language indicating a more differentiated view of friendship — friendship not always perfect; friends sometimes have problems; they have to work at solving problems.

Figure 9.1.   Presence of Tracer* in Student Essays Following Lesson.

sometimes have problems they have to work at solving.[3] The difference between the two groups is statistically significant, $p = .01$ (chi^2 = 6.45; df = 1).

Pre- and post-essays from three students[4] provide an illustration of the data and the differences between the two treatment conditions (underscored portions were coded as "tracer").

Karla: Before IC Lesson	Karla: After IC Lesson
To me my example of a friend is loyal, a companion, nice and some love for each other. To me my friends are best friends. Their names are … Marta, Nellie and Michelle. They are fun loyal and very good companions. They are there when I am happy or when I am sad. Thanks to them for being my friends.	My friends are Marta and Nellie. Actually they are my best friends. To me my friends are colleagues, affectionate. They are my best friends. And we play together and we walk, talk and have great times together. When we fight we try to work things over and we do what we have to do to keep our friendship together. They feel like sisters.

Karla's pre IC essay reveals no language concerning the problematic nature of friendships. She lists a set of positive attributes, names her friends, applies those attributes to her friends, characterizes her friends' loyalty and stability, and closes with a statement of appreciation. She notes that her friends—best friends—"are there when I am happy or when I am sad." Thus, she recognizes that friends tolerate changes in mood, and perhaps as other students suggested, they help you when you have problems—when you're troubled. In contrast, the essay she wrote after her participation in the IC lesson reveals a more differentiated conception of friendship because she acknowledges that conflicts enter into friendship: "When we fight …" She also describes the actions she and her friends take to resolve conflicts and preserve the friendship: "try to work things over." Both Karla's pre- and post-essays provide a tribute to her friends. The post-essay, however, does so on new grounds: They are best friends—like sisters—because they overcome conflicts.

Luis—another student from the IC condition—also showed an increasingly differentiated conception of friendship in his post-essay as compared to his pre essay:

Luis: Before IC Lesso	Luis: After IC Lessonn
I am going to tell you how I met my friends. My first friend was Michael. I met Michael in Mrs. Tiara's class. Then they move me to Mrs Fiskes class and Michael too and my first friend here was Gilbert and then I met Freddy then Hector so then the whole class. So now I have good friends.	Friends is something that you could play with like you have to never fight or have problems. I am going to tell you a story but real one. When I was in 1st or 2nd grade I met a friend. So we played and when we got in a fight I showed kindness and I always trust him and sometimes I got mad but I forgave him and we spent time together and I would help him. But one day we got in a fight and since that day we always fight and he was one of my best friend.

In his pre-essay, Luis names his friends and describes how he met them. In fact, he seems to characterize everyone as his friend: "… then I met Freddy then Hector so then the whole class. So now I have good friends." In the opening line of his post-essay, Luis says that friends *"never* fight." But then he provides an account of a friendship that did indeed involve conflict: "when we got in a fight … sometimes I got mad." Like Karla, Luis lists the actions he took as a friend to deal with the conflict: "I showed kindness … always trust[ed] him … but I forgave him." The contradiction between the opening line and the account suggests that Luis is grappling with the concept of friendship: "Friends never fight," but in fact, he had a friend with whom he *did* fight. It is not clear whether Luis still considers this person a friend: "He *was* one of my best friend[s]." In fact, he may be trying to suggest that in some instances, conflicts cannot be resolved, and some friendships end. Though he makes a different point than Karla, his post-essay indicates that he was able to apply this more differentiated view of friendship (friendships can be problematic) to his own experiences.

With the exception of two students, the pre- and post-essays from the students in the control group contained no evidence of a change in conceptualization. Erika's essays are representative. Erika's pre-essay provides two positive attributes—loving and caring. She also lists categories for those who are capable of having friends—youngsters, grown-ups, and really everybody—though she adds and then repeats at the end, "If you have a friend you are lucky." She also names two friends and says they will play together after school. In her post-essay, Erika adds more detail about her friends, but, there is no evidence of a more differentiated view of friendship.

Erika: Before Control Lesson	Erika: After Control Lesson
A new friend is a loving caring person who cares for you a lot. Youngsters have many friends. If you have a friend you are lucky to have that person. Grownups have friends too! So every body has a friend. You can be a friend by caring. Michelle is my friend. So is Yvonne. We are going to play at her house after school. So if you have a friend you are lucky!	A friend is a loveable caring friend that helps you and cares for you. My first friend is Yvonne Saldivar. She is a friend by playing with me and caring. My second friend is Angelica Aguirre because she plays at my house. And my final friend is Michelle Bailey because she makes me laugh and she cares. Actually every body is my friend. But if you have a friend you are lucky!!!!! If you care for someone you are a special person because you are a best friend to that person!

Question 10 From the Comprehension Test

The results from the essays are corroborated by the students' responses to the inference question on the comprehension test: "Do you think Rob and Soup will remain friends? Why?"

As indicated in Figure 9.2, what the students chose to include as their substantiation varied by condition. Seventy-three percent (73%, 8/11) of the students in the IC condition[5] made some reference to actions the characters would take to resolve their conflict and repair their friendship (e.g., talk it out, they will forgive each other). Only 15% (2/13) of the students in the control group made similar references (chi^2 = 8.061, df = 1; $p < .005$). Responses from four students from each condition illustrate the differences between the IC and control groups.

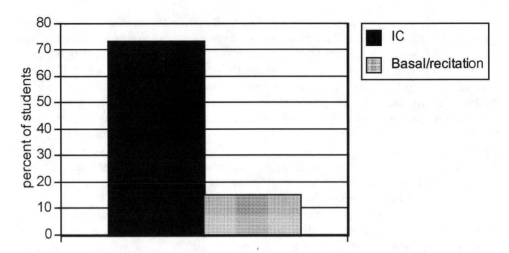

*Language indicating a more differentiated view of friendship — friendship not always perfect; friends sometimes have problems; they have to work at solving problems.

Figure 9.2.   Presence of Tracer* in Question 10 of Comprehension Test Following Lesson.

IC	Control
—Yes, because they will talk it over and they will be friends again	—I think they will be friends because there just kids
—I think Rob and Soup will still be friends because I think Rob will forgive him	—Yes, they will be friends because they're good friends
—Yes, because Soup tried to help him near the end	—I think they're still friends because it was an accident
—Yes, because they could forgive each other	—Yes, because they're still kids

In Sum

As gauged by the post-lesson writings (essays and question 10), the instructional conversation helped a majority of students further develop their understandings of friendship. We can reasonably attribute the pre-to-post changes to the IC lesson—as opposed to the story, itself—because there was no similar pattern of change for students in the control group who read and reviewed with the teacher the same story. If the story itself and reviewing the literal details of the story could have produced these conceptual changes, then we would have found the tracer in the post-lesson writings of a larger number of control students.

Does Instructional Conversation Support Literal Comprehension of Stories?

Yes. IC students scored as well or better than students in the control group on the 10-item literal comprehension test (see Table 9.3). We compared comprehension test results for the two groups and across the three levels of achievement in English

TABLE 9.3
Comprehension Test Results

| | Relative standing in terms of progress in English proficiency and achievement | | | Combined |
	High n = 4, 4	Medium n = 2, 4	Low n = 5, 5	n = 11, 13
Instructional Conversation	Mean 9.12**	9.25*	6.30	7.86
	SD 0.63	0.35	0.27	1.55
Control/Recitation	Mean 7.25	7.38	7.60	7.42
	SD 0.50	0.95	2.68	1.64

**Difference significant at .05; * difference significant at .1.

reading and speaking (IC vs. Control; High, Medium, Low). The 2 × 3 analysis of variance on scores from the comprehension test revealed a significant interaction $F(2, 18) = 3.84$, $p < .05$ (main effects for group and achievement level were not significant). Because of the presence of the interaction, analyses of simple effects were conducted. This revealed a significant difference between groups for high achievers, $F(1,6) = 21.77$, $p < .01$ (means and SDs are: IC: 9.12, .63; Control: 7.25, .50). Middle achieving students in the IC condition also outscored controls, but the difference was not significant (IC: 9.25, .35; Control: 7.38, .95; $p < .1$). Lower achieving students in the control condition performed slightly better than lower achieving IC students, but this difference was also not statistically significant (IC: 6.30, .27; Control: 7.60, 2.68; $p > .3$).

Can "Transition" Students Successfully Participate in Instructional Conversations Conducted in English About English Texts?

Yes. Results presented thus far indicate that transition students can successfully participate in ICs in English about English texts. In fact, whether students were identified by the teacher as high, medium, or low in terms of their relative progress and achievement in English across the year had no bearing on students' participation in the IC lesson or any of the measures reported, except for comprehension (see Table 9.4). The more verbal participants (above the median number of student utterances) were just as likely to come from the lower group (2 of 5) as the middle and high groups (2 of 4, and 2 of 4). The tracer was detected in the essays of at least 50% of the students at each achievement level (low: 3 of 5; middle: 2 of 4; high: 3 of 4), and the same held true for detecting the tracer in students' responses to comprehension question 10 (low: 4 of 5; middle, 2 of 2; high: 2 of 4). The one exception to this pattern, however, was the comprehension test, where both the high and middle students scored significantly better than lower achieving students in the IC condition (low: 6.30; middle: 9.25; high: 9.12; Scheffe post-hocs, $p < .05$ for each comparison). We address this matter in the conclusion.

TABLE 9.4
Participation and Post-Lesson Results for IC Students of Different Levels of English
Proficiency and Achievement

Measures	Relative standing in terms of progress in English proficiency and achievement		
	High n = 4	Medium n = 4	Low n = 5
Comprehension test	Mean 9.12	9.25*	6.30
	SD 0.63	0.35	0.27
Tracer detected in post-lesson essay	3 of 4	2 of 4	3 of 5
Tracer detected in comprehension question 10	2 of 4	2 of 2*	4 of 5
Above median** participation in the IC lesson	2 of 4	2 of 4	2 of 5

*n = 2. **Median participation indexed by median number of utterances produced by students in the IC lesson.

What Do Teachers Do Within Instructional Conversations That Might Contribute to Students' Understandings of Complex Concepts and Support Their Literal Comprehension of Stories?

Table 9.5 combines two forms of information about the IC and control group lessons: the focus of the various segments in the lessons and descriptive statistics about student and teacher talk in the lessons. (Data in Table 9.5 are based on the first IC lesson and the first control group lesson, which are representative of what transpired in each condition.) We focus on the broad differences between the IC and control lessons and then examine the features of the IC that might have made it successful. How was time and talk spent in each lesson? In the control group, the majority of time and talk was spent reviewing and rehearsing the literal details of the story (segments 1 and 2 accounting for a combined 67% of all utterances in the lesson). In the IC, the vast majority of talk (89% of all utterances in the lesson) was evenly split between review and discussion of the concept of friendship (segments 2, 3, 4, and 8 = 44%) and then applying that concept to the story (segments 5, 6, and 7 = 45%). Only 11% of the IC was devoted to explicitly reviewing the literal details of the story (segment 1).

Based on this information, then, we can formulate the following synthesis of results: According to the comprehension test results, students in the IC condition understood the literal details as well or better than students who explicitly reviewed and rehearsed then substantially more. Moreover, the large proportion of talk devoted to the concept of friendship and its relationship to the story helped at least 63% of the students in the IC condition arrive at an understanding of friendship they likely would not have developed on their own just as a result of reading the story. What was it about the IC lesson that made this possible?

The answer has to do with instruction, conversation, and the potential that co-mes in the successful combination of the two. As we would expect, students had the opportunity to do a lot of talking in the IC (see Table 9.5): They produced 55% of all utterances in the IC lesson; their turns at talk were, on average, almost as long as the teacher's, 1.5 and 1.9, respectively; and they produced a fairly substantial

TABLE 9.5
Focus of the Talk and Descriptive Statistics for an IC and Control Lesson

Focus of Lesson Segments	Initiating Speaker	Percentage of lesson utterances	Percentage of segment utterances		Mean utterances per turn		Percentage of lengthier turns*	
INSTRUCTIONAL CONVERSATION			%T	%S	T	S	%T	%S
1—Reviewing literal details of story	Teacher	11	42	58	1.6	1.4	45	55
2—What do we know about friendship? charting	Teacher	10	71	29	3.3	1.1	100	0
3—Debating—Do friends sometimes fight?	Student	23	39	61	1.9	2.1	58	42
4—Adding to friendship chart	Teacher	8	53	47	1.5	1.0	100	0
5—Is Soup a good friend?	Teacher	20	37	63	1.6	1.8	57	43
6—Should Rob have trusted Soup?	Student	18	45	55	2.0	1.3	56	44
7—What will happen to Rob and Soup?	Teacher	7	42	58	1.7	1.8	50	50
8—Wrap: What do we know about friendship?	Teacher	3	56	44	1.5	1.0	100	0
Lesson means			45	55	1.9	1.5	61	39
CONTROL: RECITATION								
1—Reviewing literal details of story	Teacher	27	56	44	2.0	1.3	63	33
2—Sequencing events in the story	Teacher	40	72	28	3.4	1.1	94	6
3—Sharing experiences related to story	Teacher	23	74	26	11.0	3.8	67	33
4—What will happen to Rob and Soup?	Teacher	5	65	35	1.8	1.0	100	0
5—What was your favorite part of the story?	Teacher	5	70	30	2.8	1.2	80	20
Lesson means			68	32	3.3	1.3	78	22

Note. Data are based on the first IC and Control lessons and are comparable to data for the second lesson for each condition. The IC lasted 20 minutes, included 330 total speaking turns and 550 total utterances; Control: 18 minutes, 217 turns, 484 utterances.
    *A "lengthier" turn is a turn with two or more independent clauses; for the IC, 25% of the turns in the lesson (84/330) had two or more independent clauses; Control: 30% (65/217).

proportion, 39%, of the lengthier turns in the lesson (more elaborated turns at least two independent clauses in length). In comparison, students in the control lessons produced only 32% of all utterances; their turns were much shorter than the teachers, 1.3 and 3.3, respectively; and they produced just 22% of the lengthier turns in the lesson.

But it is also evident in the lesson data (Table 9.5) that the talk and its distribution between students and teacher in the IC varied across the lesson segments. Across segments 1–5, for example, the percentage of student utterances fluctuated considerably (58, 29, 61, 47, and 63), as did the average length of student turns (1.4, 1.1, 2.1, 1.0, and 1.8) and the percentage of lengthier turns produced by students (55, 0, 42, 0, and 43). In the IC, the teacher was carefully utilizing talk differently at different points in the lesson: in certain segments prompting and driving for single words and phrases to define the concept of friendship, and in others promoting and allowing for more elaborated responses so students could articulate, substantiate, and develop their ideas of friendship and interpretations of the story. Over the course of the lesson, she was using talk as a means to consecutive instructional ends, as opposed to treating talk and necessarily more student talk as an end in itself. We can illustrate this process with a few transcript excerpts from the same IC lesson described quantitatively in Table 9.5. (Note: Double slashes indicate the onset of overlap; uppercase means a language spoken with emphasis; equal signs indicate turns produced without hesitation or interruption; numbers represent the consecutive number each turn was given in the lesson; referents for ambiguous words are provided in brackets to facilitate reading.)

Excerpts From One of the Instruction Conversation Lessons

The teacher began the IC with an invitation for students to summarize or gist the story (segment 1), allowing students to challenge each other in order to build an accurate account of the story's plot, but also using their talk to gauge students' grasp of the literal details. For example,

1	Tchr:	Okay, somebody, tell me what this story is all about that we just read. Rosa,
2	Rosa:	mm, it's about a haircut, Um Rob wants a haircut and his mother sent him to a town, and he had just only a quarter for the haircut, //for the haircut.
3	Tchr:	Okay, did he want a haircut you said?
4	Ss:	Yeah.
5	Tchr:	He wants a haircut? Everybody agree with that? He wants a haircut.
6	Karla:	No, because he wanted to buy some candy,
7	Tchr:	He wants to buy some candy. Anybody else add to what she told us about? Good ideas. What else happened in the story?

Within a few minutes, the teacher determined that students had a reasonable grasp of the story's facts, so she began activating the friendship schema she had been working on with the class in previous lessons:

42	Tchr:	Let's go back and think about friendship, and we'll- maybe we can get some new ideas about friendship from this um, story. What are some of the THINGS from *Charlotte's Web* and the other stories that we've talked about? Ideas about friendship, hm?
43	Luis:	Help each other.
44	Tchr:	Helping, okay and why did you pick helping to go in there this morning.
45	Vic:	Because um Soup helped umm, Rob to- to cut his hair.

In this part of the lesson (segment 2: What do we know about friendship?), the teacher was drawing out and clustering (or word webbing) on a chart single words and phrases students associated with the idea of friendship. The discourse moved swiftly with the teacher prompting and students providing short responses (students produced 29% of utterances, with 1.1 utterances per turn and 0% of the lengthier turns in the segment). But she was also looking for a hook, an opportunity to begin working on the theme (friendship can be problematic). The opportunity came as one student nominated the word "patience" for the cluster and another immediately linked the idea of patience to the story (see turns 65 and 66, Lidia and Karla).

61	Ger:	Kindness
62	Tchr:	Kindness. ((writes on chart))
63	Lidia:	Patient.
64	Karla:	Happiness, happiness,
65	Lidia:	//Patience.
66	Karla:	Yeap, patience because, he [Rob] didn't get mad when //they cut the hair.
67	Char:	Yeah.
68	Tchr:	Who didn't get mad when they cut the hair?
69	Karla:	Rob
70	Tchr:	Rob didn't get mad. So you think he fits in here [the friendship cluster]?
71	Ss:	Yes.
72	Tchr:	He was patient, but how patient should you be with a friend?

The teacher took advantage of the opening with a gentle challenge, "how patient should you be with a friend" (turn 72). Her challenge invites students to begin exploring a less rosy and more differentiated concept of friendship. In fact, students took up the invitation and the IC advanced to segment 3 (Debating: Do friends sometimes fight?), the longest segment in the lesson (23%), and a segment with substantial student talk (61% of utterances, 2.1 utterances per turn, 42% of lengthier turns). It started with one girl's declaration that perhaps Rob (the haircut victim) should have displayed some anger. (She explained that, according to her mother, an aunt would be much happier if she allowed herself to get mad sometimes.) This provided the teacher with the opportunity to bring the theme (friendship can be problematic) explicitly into the discussion.

88	Tchr:	Oh. Well, do we sometimes //get mad at our friends?
89	Karla:	You have to forgive them, too, but-
90	Tchr:	Do we sometimes get mad at our friends?
91	Char:	Yes
92	Karla:	Yes, o'course.
93	Tchr:	When- Why d'you say "course," like of course? What happens when you get mad at your friends.
94	Karla:	They get mad at you,
95	Tchr:	Oh, you get mad back at each other
		((laughter))

As the discussion progressed, the concept of what might occur within a friendship expanded. On the teacher's urging, students explained that friends do get mad at each other, sometimes they don't share, sometimes friends have problems, and in some cases they even fight. The introduction of the word "fighting," however, brought about a difference of opinion among the students (118–121) and a series of elaborated examples (Lidia, turn 124).

117	Tchr:	And I even heard a word bigger than problems, fighting. Can friends fight?
118	Vic:	Yes.
119	Char:	No
120	Ss:	YES!
121	Luis:	//Yes. So?
122	Tchr:	Okay someone that said yes. Tell me how friends can fight.
123	Karla:	//My friend my friend one day, we were out of order and uh-
124	Lidia:	Like, umm, yesterday! I was playing with my sister, and I told her, let me see that for a second, and she said "no you always get it," and we started fighting! And then we went with my mom and then, we [both] said she doesn't wanna give me that, she doesn't wanna give me this, and //I started crying=
125	Char:	That's not a true friend.

Charisse (turn 125) adds a wrinkle: the distinction between casual and true friends. Like the teacher was doing earlier, she is challenging narrow definitions of friendship and advancing the discussion toward greater differentiation (*true* friends). In fact, this led to an articulation of the kinds of things friends do to preserve friendships, like talking things out (see turns 134–135).

131	Tchr:	They all said that true friends can fight, but you say no. Tell me more about it.
132	Char:	If, true friends fight, then that's not true friends! It just, it just doesn't work out. It's not true friends.
133	Tchr:	So, if you are a true friend you would never have a fight. But how would true friends solve problems?
134	Ger:	//Talking.
135	Char:	By talking, not fighting.

136		Tchr:	By talking not fighting. //Aha,
137	Rosa:		Ms. Fiske, so many times that um, like friends when, when they talk to you, you make friends again

At this point, the teacher challenged the students to weigh the views expressed in the discussion in concrete terms: Should "fighting" be added to the cluster (recall thus far the cluster was filled with terms like helping each other, playing together, sharing, happiness, and patience). Like her earlier challenge, this one prompted substantiation, elaborated turns in defense of a position.

138	Tchr:	Okay, so you're saying you can have a friend that can count it cool even with a problem, maybe even fighting each other. Should I put fighting up here?
139	Karla:	I say yes, because, my friend, she always plays with us. And, we were playing and she gets mad because she wants to be this, or she wants to be that, and they don't let her. So then I told her, uhm, you don't- if you don't want to be that you don't have to. And she screamed and said, "Yes, I wanna be that. But you can change if you WANT to," she said, "I can change if I want to and you be something [else]. You are gonna have to um, do that!" So then okay cause we were both doing the same thing and then, she, she started, winning the others. My friends and I started fighting with her and, she said that she wasn't gonna be her friend again, and then she was her friend again! She was talking to her later.
140	Tchr:	Okay. So should I put fighting up here?
141	Ss:	Yeah.

Shortly thereafter, the IC advanced to segment 4 (adding to the friendship chart), with the teacher probing and students supplying single words and phrases: fighting, not sharing, problems, tolerate, and talking it over. Like segment 2, the first pass at the cluster about friendship, in segment 4 the teacher plays a more prominent role (percentage of student utterances reduces to 47%, their average turn length drops to 1.0 utterances, and they produce 0% of the lengthier turns in the segment). In fact, at one point the teacher takes the opportunity to introduce a word of her own for the friendship cluster:

161	Tchr:	You know something, sometimes I have a fight with my friend, but we make up, and sometimes she makes me really ANGRY, but I have to do something. Maybe you know this word. ((writes on chart))
162	Ss:	Tolerate
163	Tchr:	Tolerate. What does tolerate mean?
164	Char:	Deal //with it
165	Ger:	Like deal with it.
166	Tchr:	Deal with it. Put up with it. What happened in the story that somewhat-
167	Luis:	He had to,

168   Ger: Have patience!
169   Tchr: Have patience. That's- that's a good word here patience
              ((writes)) and put up with.

With a more developed and differentiating cluster of terms to define friendship
completed, the teacher then returned to the story to discuss the trials of Rob and
Soup as a case of friendship. The major issue was whether or not Soup—having
persuaded Rob to spend the haircut money on gum and then butchering Rob's
hair—was a good friend (segment 5: Is Soup a good friend?). Like segment 3, this
fifth segment involved substantial student talk (63% of the segments utterances,
1.8 utterances per turn, and 43% of the lengthier turns). In segment 3, students'
turns became more elaborated because they were developing their views of
friendship and, in some cases, citing personal experiences to substantiate their
points. In segment 5, their turns became more elaborated because they were developing interpretations of events in the story and sometimes citing the text to
substantiate their claims. For example,

237   Tchr: So what do you say about this Soup. Is he a good friend or
              isn't he?
238   Ss: //No
239   Lidia: No. Ms. Fiske. I,
240   Luis: No, no.
241   Tchr: He's not a good friend. Okay Lidia tell us.
242   Lidia: Right here it said that if he had a barber shop, but he didn't.
              So he told I cut my cousin's hair once for free, it says. And
              then, the words just repeated all over his head or something
              like that. And then, uh, he said, "Will you cut MY hair for
              free?" Rob said, "Will you cut my hair for free?"
243   Tchr: So you say that Rob had something to do in- in that too,
              right?
244   Luis: Yeah.
245   Tchr: Rob should take a little responsibility //for what happened?
246   Luis: But his mom said go straight to the barber shop to cut his
              hair.
247   Char: Does he do that with (inaudible)?

Using the text as her source, Lidia (turn 242) advances an idea that had been playing itself out over several turns preceding this excerpt: Rob asked Soup to cut his
hair. In other words, he went along with mischief when he could or should have,
"Got a haircut like his mother told him," as Charisse said earlier. This line of analysis led to a discussion of whether or not Soup should have trusted Rob (segment 6),
which was another opportunity for students to search, examine, and ultimately
reference the text to support their interpretations. For example,

273   Vic: Three-THIRTY-one.
274   Tchr: What happens at- starts happening on 331?
275   Rosa: Ms. Fiske, I know, Ms. Fiske //he was scared [when Soup
              was cutting his hair].

276	Char:	Hey Soup. //Hey Soup. ((role playing Rob in fearful voice))
277	Tchr:	He was a little scared. Why was he scared?
278	Rosa:	Cause he- because Soup said that he made a mistake on his hair.
279	T & Ss:	//Wouw!
280	Rosa:	And he make um holes, and then he then he, Soup say, //"Winter's coming=
281	Karla:	That's no big problem.
282	Rosa:	=and he [Rob] say it's still //August=
283	Ger:	August
284	Rosa:	=it's hot".
285	Tchr:	So he- He got a little bit worried? He wasn't sure he trusted him, huh.

Here students were developing the idea that Rob quickly realized he had mistakenly trusted Soup as soon as Soup started cutting his hair. Shortly thereafter, the discussion focused on the end of the story to test one student's claim that if Soup were really a good, trustworthy friend, he would be there for Rob when he had to face his mother.

293	Tchr:	But, what you were talking about, Karla, and you said that they [Soup and Rob] have to face it. Where do you think uh, Soup was when he had to face the mother?
294	Ger:	OOOh. He was FAR from there. He is, uh, if-
295	Tchr:	Would a good friend //be far from there?
296	Ss:	//No!
297	Karla:	I don't think so.
298	Tchr:	Where would a good //friend be?
299	Vic:	//He would go.
300	Luis:	In his house.
301	Tchr:	With him?
302	Luis:	No, in ROB's house.
303	Rosa:	He didn't want to be in trouble. In the last page, he like, he said that the gum sticks on the head, and then what about if you stick [it] back.
304	Tchr:	Well that's what happens.
305	Char:	It says, ((reads)) "Under the hands of my mother, the hair and the pink awful did come off when my head was held under the pump."

Although this chapter does not allow for an analysis of the entire IC lesson (and the slight but interesting differences that were evident between the first and second IC lessons), these short excerpts help illuminate the results of the study. Students spent a good deal of time actually studying the concept of friendship, starting with the teacher drawing out students' initial terms to define friendship (segment 2), expanding into a robust debate about the potential problematic aspects of friendship (segment 3), and then converging on new terms to flesh out a more differentiated concept of friendship. Students also spent a good deal of time studying the

story as a interesting case of friendship, developing interpretations of the characters and using the text itself to confirm or revise their interpretation (segments 5
and 6). As a result, all of the students grasped the more differentiated concept of
friendship well enough to introduce it in their post-lesson essays or in question 10
of the comprehension test, and all of the students displayed at least a modest (for
most, a very thorough) understanding of the story's literal details on the post-
lesson comprehension test.

Excerpts From One of the Control/Recitation Lessons

By design, the majority of talk in the control lessons sustained a review or recitation of the story's literal details. For example, in the following excerpt, the teacher
is trying to establish a description of the story's setting.

32	Tchr:	Where are they at? Where did the story happen?
33	Mich:	At main street.
34	Jov:	Noo
35	Alb:	In the ba- in the candy shop!
36	Maria:	//In the town.
37	Tchr:	Main street, okay. Where do you find main street?
38	Maria:	In town!
39	Tchr:	In a little town,
40	Jov:	Right here! ((reads)) On a little dirt road.
41	Tchr:	Okay. Okay he's telling us that they,=
42	Ricky:	=near the mountains.
43	Tchr:	Okay they're down a dusty dirt road, so it's kind of out in the country!
44	Ricky:	Yeah.
45	Tchr:	Okay, so they get on the main street of the little town.

In the next excerpt, the teacher is helping students sequence the events in the story.

67	Tchr:	Yeah. Well let's look at the sequence of this story. What happened first.
68	Maria:	He had to get a haircut,
69	Tchr:	Okay, get a haircut. Then what happened?
70	Jov:	They went to buy candy,
71	Tchr:	Okay, they bought //candy
72	Marta:	They didn't- They didn't cut the hair to buy candy.
73	Tchr:	Okay, did they just walk directly to the candy store?
74	Ss:	No.
75	Tchr:	How did it happen?
76	Ricky:	They went to the town.
77	Tchr:	They went to town. Okay, then what happened?
78	Mitch:	They stopped at the barber shop,
79	Tchr:	Did they go to the barber shop?
80	Marta:	Yeah to get- after, after they went to the candy shop.
81	Ricky:	They went to the barber shop to get scissors.
82	Tchr:	Did they ever go inside the barber shop?

83   Ss: No.

On some occasions, the talk in the control lessons expanded somewhat as the review of literal details prompted more substantive interpretations of the story's events. For example, the following excerpt is taken from the sequencing exercise (segment 2), when the teacher asked students which event is most important for the rest of the story.

121   Ricky: Ms. Fiske, right here! It says—um, the word is free, the main word is free.
122   Tchr: How's free an important word?=
123   Ricky: =the secret word is free.
124   Tchr: So he thinks he's gonna get something free. Who's gonna get something free.
125   Ss: Rob.
126   Ricky: Rob! //he gets the haircut free,
127   Tchr: Rob, //So if Rob gets something free, then they have the quarter to spend! Okay. So maybe a part of that is when they make that decision! What was that- the decision?
128   Maria: The decision was, to, to go the barber shop and, waste all the money or,=
129   Tchr: =to the barber shop?
130   Maria: uh or, go to the candy store.
131   Tchr: Okay well maybe the- maybe the important point is when they make that decision,
132   Ricky: Ms. Fiske it says right here. ((reads)) It says "Yes, he said. Someday, I'll have my own barbershop. Honest, I already gave my cousin a haircut. You did? [said] Soup? For free! That was the magic word. free, it rang"=
133   Tchr: =How did free become such a magical word there Ricky?
134   Ricky: Cause he didn't have to waste the quarters=
135   Tchr: Aha! //so if it's free!
136   Ricky: =For the haircut.
137   Tchr: Then we can make a decision to go and get?
138   Jov: Gum ((faint))
139   Ricky: //The candy.
140   Tchr: Gum! Yeah.

Although this series of exchanges helps establish perhaps the critical juncture in the story, because the lesson has no guiding theme (like the IC), the teacher uses Ricky's analysis only to clarify the events in the story (with the free haircut, they could go and get gum). In an excerpt presented earlier from the IC, Lidia (turn 247) used the exact same portion of the text as evidence that Rob shared some responsibility for the mischief that transpired during the discussion of whether Soup was a good friend. This contrast helps illustrate the fundamental difference between the control/recitation and IC lessons. In the control lessons, the talk focused almost exclusively on the facts and details of the text itself; in the IC, the talk focused predominantly on the text in relationship to a larger theme, the concept of friendship.

Do the Conceptual Effects of Instructional Conversation Endure Over Time?

Did the students hold onto this differentiated concepts of friendship? The study design made no a priori provision for assessing the durability of the IC effects. Our primary goal was to address the four main research questions. In conducting our analysis, however, we uncovered two sources of evidence that suggest that for many of the students, the conceptualization endured for at least a few weeks. In the 5 weeks that followed the experiment (the last 5 weeks of the school year), two writing assignments related to the friendship unit were completed.

First, students were given the opportunity to revise and edit the essays they wrote after the experiment. Of the IC students who originally included language about the problematic nature of friendship, 63% (5/8) went on to elaborate on that point in their revision of the essay. Thus, more than a week after they originally composed that content, many of the IC students found it still important enough to warrant further articulation and clarification.

Second, as a culminating activity for the friendship unit, all students in the class developed an original short story that was supposed to *show* what they thought was most important about friendship. Twenty-eight students completed the short story assignment, of which 64% focused on one of the two themes that emerged from the series of IC lessons in the friendship unit.[6] Half of those (32%) exemplified the theme, "Friends help each other in times of need," and the other half (32%) illustrated the theme, "Friendship can sometimes be problematic."[6] As such, for at least two thirds of the class the themes from the IC lessons were understood well enough and deemed important enough such that students could produce a work of fiction around them. Moreover, 5 weeks after the lessons from the experiment, a third of the class was still working with the theme featured in the IC condition.

DISCUSSION AND CONCLUSION

Instructional Conversation promotes higher level understandings of significant concepts without sacrificing literal comprehension. In the lessons used for this study, identifying details about characters, plot, setting, and main ideas—commonly the focus of standard textbook-driven literature instruction—were successfully embedded in discussions where higher levels of thinking about themes, concepts, and the related experiences of the students emerged. These higher level discussions, then, produced more sophisticated and differentiated understandings of a complex concept, in this case, friendship.

ICs provide a means for accomplishing some of the important, but difficult, goals educators have long strived for and that have recently begun to receive renewed attention—engaging students in meaningful, complex, and challenging interactions around important and relevant ideas and concepts. These goals appear to be particularly important and clearly appropriate for English language learners. Our data suggest that such students can perform successfully, given opportunities to engage with teacher and peers in linguistically and conceptually rich interactions.

There are some caveats, however, and our results are limited in four respects. First, they speak only to short-term effects. At this point, we do not know if the differentiated concept of friendship remained durable for these students beyond the 5 weeks our data address.

Second, we also do not know why the effects never surfaced at all for a small number of students. It is conceivable that some students in the IC condition were simply unable to capture in writing cognitions they might have experienced. Oral interviews would have provided a way to test this hypothesis. It is also possible that unlike a majority of their peers, some students might not have been influenced by their participation in the IC.

Third, we are not absolutely sure how to interpret the differences across English achievement levels on the comprehension test. Without a comprehension measure taken immediately after reading and prior to the lesson, we do not know the exact impact on literal comprehension of the lessons. It seems, however, that high and middle achieving students benefitted from the IC (scoring significantly higher than controls) more than lower achieving students (scoring about the same or slightly lower than controls). Perhaps the less proficient students had more difficulty using interpretative discussions of the story to firm up their understanding of literal details, and they may have needed a slightly longer explicit review of the story at the beginning of the IC.

Fourth, we have not demonstrated that IC is the only mode of teaching through which complex concepts like friendship might be addressed. As Gall and Gall (1990) have pointed out, one of the challenges we face is to compare the effects of ICs (or discussions) *in relation* to other viable teaching modes, such as a lecture or a directed lesson. The lack of effect in the control group simply demonstrates the obvious: Instruction that does not focus on concepts is unlikely to yield conceptual change. What we can say, however, is that in comparison to a more typical "basal/recitation" lesson, children not only understood the story as well or better (at a literal level), but in addition, a significant majority of them were able to articulate a more sophisticated understanding of an important concept.

NOTES

1. This research was made possible by grants from the Linguistic Minority Research project, University of California, and the Office of Educational Research and Improvement, U.S. Department of Education. No endorsement by either is implied nor should be inferred. Sincerest thanks to Wanda Fuler, Genevieve Patthey-Chavez, Ronald Gallimore, and "Mrs. Fiske's" fourth-grade class.

2. Our thanks to Genevieve Patthey-Chavez for suggesting the idea of a "tracer."

3. Three students in the control condition, but none of the students in the experimental condition, wrote pre-essays containing evidence of the tracer. Interestingly, the tracer did not appear in the post-essays of two of the three control students.

4. All names used in the following are pseudonyms.

5. If we consider the presence of the tracer in *either* the essays *or* comprehension question 10, 100% of the IC students gave evidence of the tracer, whereas only 38% of the control students did.

6. Of the remaining essays, 11% showed friends in the midst of fantastical adventures; 7% were romance sagas; and 18% had no controlling theme.

REFERENCES

Arreaga-Mayer, C., & Perdomo-Rivera, C. (1996). Ecobehavioral analysis of instruction for at-risk language-minority students. *Elementary School Journal, 96*, 245–258.

Au, K. H. (1979). Using the experience-text-relationship method with minority children. *Reading Teacher, 32*, 677–679.

August, D., & Hakuta, K. (1998). *Educating language-minority children*. Washington, DC: National Academy Press.

Barrera, R. B. (1983). Bilingual reading in the primary grades: Some questions about questionable views and practices. In T. A. Escobedo (Ed.), *Early childhood bilingual education: A Hispanic perspective* (pp. 164–184). New York: Teachers College Press.

Berman, P., Chambers, J., Gandara, P., McLaughlin, B., Minicucci, C., Nelson, B., et al. (1992). *Meeting the challenge of language diversity: An evaluation of programs for pupils with limited English proficiency* (Executive summary, Vol. 1). Berkeley, CA: BW Associates.

Brophy, J., & Good, T. (1986). Teacher behavior and student achievement. In M. Wittrock (Ed.), *Handbook of research on teaching* (3rd ed., pp. 328–375). New York: Macmillan.

Calderón, M., Hertz-Lazarowitz, R., & Slavin, R. (1998). Effects of bilingual cooperative integrated reading and composition on students making the transition from Spanish to English reading. *Elementary School Journal, 99*(2), 153–165.

Cazden, C. (1988). *Classroom discourse: The language of teaching and learning*. Portsmouth, NH: Heinemann.

Committee for Economic Development. (1991). *The unfinished agenda: A new vision for child development and education*. New York: Author

CTB/McGraw-Hill. (1987). *SABE: Spanish Assessment of Basic Education*. Monterey, CA: Author.

Cummins, J. (1989). *Empowering minority students*. Sacramento, CA: California Association for Bilingual Education.

Dalton, S. (1998). *Pedagogy matters: Standards for effective teaching practice* (Research Report No. 4). Santa Cruz, CA: Center for Research on Education, Diversity & Excellence.

Dalton, S., & Sison, J. (1995). *Enacting instructional conversation with Spanish-speaking students in middle school mathematics* (Research Report No. 12). Washington, DC: Center for Applied Linguistics/National Center for Research on Cultural Diversity and Second Language Learning.

Echevarria, J. (1995). Interactive reading instruction: A comparison of proximal and distal effects of instructional conversations. *Exceptional Children, 61*(6), 536–552.

Echevarria, J., & McDonough, R. (1995). An alternative reading approach: Instructional Conversations in bilingual special education settings. *Learning Disabilities: Research and Practice, 10*(2), 108–119.

Gage, N. L. (1978). *The scientific basis of the art of teaching*. New York: Teachers College Press, Columbia University.

Gage, N., & Berliner, D. (1988). *Educational psychology* (4th ed.). Boston: Houghton Mifflin.

Gall, M., & Gall, J. (1990). Outcomes of classroom discussion. In W. Wilen (Ed.), *Teaching and learning through discussion* (pp. 25–44). Springfield, IL: Charles C Thomas.

Gallimore, R., Reese, L., Balzano, S., Benson, C., & Goldenberg, C. (1991, April). *Ecocultural sources of early literacy experiences: Job-required literacy, home literacy environments, and school reading*. Paper presented at the annual meeting of American Educational Research Association, Chicago, IL.

García, E. (1992). Effective instruction for language minority students: The teacher. *Journal of Education, 173*(2), 130–141.

Genesee, F., Lindholm-Leary, K., Saunders, W., & Christian, D. (2006). *Educating English language learners: A synthesis of research evidence*. Cambridge: Cambridge University Press.

Gersten, R. (1996). Literacy instruction for language-minority students: The transition years. *Elementary School Journal, 96*, 227–244.

Goldenberg, C. (1989a). *The home literacy experiences of low-income Hispanic kindergarten children*. Paper presented at the annual meeting of the American Educational Research Association, San Francisco, CA.

Goldenberg, C. (1989b). Making success a more common occurrence for children at risk for failure: Lessons from Hispanic first-graders learning to read. In J. Allen & J. M. Mason (Eds.), *Risk makers, risk takers, risk breakers: Reducing the risks for young literacy learners* (pp. 48–78). Portsmouth, NH: Heinemann.

Goldenberg, C. (1991). *Instructional conversations and their classroom application*. Washington, DC: Center for Applied Linguistics/National Center for Research on Cultural Diversity and Second Language Learning.

Goldenberg, C. (1992–1993). Instructional conversations: Promoting comprehension through discussion. *The Reading Teacher, 46,* 316–326.

Goldenberg, C. (1996). The education of language-minority students: Where are we, and where do we need to go? *Elementary School Journal, 96,* 227–244.

Goldenberg, C. (2004). *Successful school change: Creating settings to improve teaching and learning.* New York: Teachers College Press.

Goldenberg, C., & Gallimore, R. (1991, April). *Teaching and learning in a new key: The instructional conversation.* Paper presented at the annual meeting of the American Educational Research Association, Chicago, IL.

Goldenberg, C., & Patthey-Chavez, G. (1995). Discourse processes in instructional conversations: Interactions between teachers and transition readers. *Discourse Processes, 19,* 57–73.

Goldenberg, C., & Sullivan, J. (1994). *Making change happen in a language-minority school: A search for coherence* (Educational Practice Report No. 13). Washington, DC: Center for Applied Linguistics.

Goodlad, J. (1984). *A place called school.* New York: McGraw-Hill.

Hiebert, E. (1983). An examination of ability grouping for reading instruction. *Reading Research Quarterly, 18,* 231–255.

Hoetker, J., & Ahlbrand, W. (1969). The persistence of recitation. *American Educational Research Journal, 6,* 145–167.

Hunt, K. W. (1977). Early blooming and late blooming syntactic structures. In C. R. Cooper & L. Odell (Eds.), *Evaluating writing: describing, measuring, judging* (pp. 107–134). Urbana, IL: National Council of Teachers of English.

Knapp, M., & Shields, P. (1990). Reconceiving academic instruction for the children of poverty. *Phi Delta Kappan, 71*(10), 753–758.

Krashen, S. (1987). *Principles and practice in second language acquisition.* New York: Prentice-Hall.

Langer, J. A. (1987). The sociocognitive perspective on literacy. In J. A. Langer (Ed.), *Language, literacy, and culture: Issues of society and schooling* (pp. 1–20). Norwood, NJ: Ablex.

Mehan, H. (1979). Learning lessons. Cambridge, MA: Harvard University Press.

Mehan, H. (1991). *Sociolinguistic foundations supporting the study of cultural diversity.* Working paper #1, Center for Cultural Diversity and Second Language Learning, University of California, Santa Cruz.

Newman, D., Griffin, P., & Cole, M. (1989). *The construction zone: Working for cognitive change in school.* Cambridge: Cambridge University Press.

Nystrand, M., & Gamoran, A. (1991). Instructional discourse, student engagement, and literature achievement. *Research in the Teaching of English, 25*(3), 261–290.

Palinscar, A., & Brown, A. (1985). Reciprocal teaching: A means to a meaningful end. In J. Osborn, P. Wilson, & R. C. Anderson (Eds.), *Reading education: Foundations for a literate America* (pp. 299–310). Lexington, MA: Heath.

Patthey-Chavez, G., Clare, L., & Gallimore, R. (1995). *Creating a community of scholarship with Instructional Conversation in a transitional bilingual classroom* (Educational Practice Report No. 15). Washington, DC: Center for Applied Linguistics/National Center for Research on Cultural Diversity and Second Language Learning.

Patthey-Chavez, G., & Goldenberg, C. (1992). *Topical cohesion in Instructional Conversations.* Unpublished manuscript, National Center for Research in Cultural Diversity and Second Language Learning, University of California, Santa Cruz.

Peck, R. (1989). Quarter for a haircut. (Excerpted from *Soup and me,* Random House, 1975). In *Never a worm this long* (pp. 323–336). Lexington, MA: Heath.

Ramirez, J. D. (1992). Executive summary. *Bilingual Research Journal, 16,* 1–62.

Rosenshine, B., & Stevens, R. (1986). Teaching functions. In M. Wittrock (Ed.), *Handbook of research on teaching* (3rd ed., pp. 376–391). New York: Macmillan.

Rueda, R., Goldenberg, C., & Gallimore, R. (1991, April). *When is an instructional conversation?* Paper presented at the annual meeting of the American Educational Research Association, Chicago, IL.

Saunders, W. (1999). Improving literacy achievement for English learners in transitional bilingual programs. *Educational Research and Evaluation, 5*(4), 345–381.

Saunders, W., & Goldenberg, C. (1996). Four elementary school teachers working to define constructivism and teacher directed-learning: Implications for teacher assessment. *Elementary School Journal, 97,* 139–161.

Saunders, W., & Goldenberg, C. (1997). *Identifying salient elements of a successful transition program for English language learners.* Paper presented at the annual meeting of the American Educational Research Association, Chicago, IL.

Saunders, W., & Goldenberg, C. (1999). The effects of instructional conversations and literature logs on limited- and fluent-English proficient students' story comprehension and thematic understanding. *The Elementary School Journal, 99*(4), 277–301.

Saunders, W., & Goldenberg, C. (2000). *The effects of a comprehensive Language Arts/Transition Program on the literacy development of English learners.* Paper presented at the annual meeting of the American Educational Research Association, April, New Orleans, LA.

Saunders, W., & Goldenberg, C. (2001). Strengthening the transition in transitional bilingual education. In D. Christian & F. Genesee (Eds.), *Bilingual education* (pp. 41–56). Alexandria, VA: Teachers of English to Speakers of Other Languages.

Saunders, W., & Goldenberg, C. (2003). Opportunities through Language Arts: Video and Program Manual [DVD series and unpublished manuscript]. Long Beach: California State University.

Saunders, W., Goldenberg, G., & Hamann, J. (1992). Instructional conversations beget instructional conversations. *Teaching and Teacher Education, 8,* 199–218.

Saunders, W., O'Brien, G., Lennon, D., & McLean, J. (1998). Making the transition to English literacy successful: Effective strategies for studying literature with transition students. In R. Gersten & R. Jiménez (Eds.), *Promoting learning for culturally and linguistically diverse students: Classroom applications from contemporary research* (pp. 99–132). Monterey, CA: Brooks/Cole.

Stodolsky, S., Ferguson, T., & Wimpelberg, K. (1981). The recitation persists, but what does it look like? *Journal of Curriculum Studies, 13,* 121–130.

Tharp, R. (1997). *From at-risk to excellence: Research, theory, and principles for practice* (Research Report No. 1). Santa Cruz, CA: Center for Research on Education, Diversity & Excellence.

Tharp, R., & Gallimore, R. (1988). *Rousing minds to life: Teaching, learning and schooling in social context.* Cambridge: Cambridge University Press.

Thayer, V. (1928). The passing of the recitation. Boston, MA: D.C. Heath.

Walberg, H. (1990). Productive teaching and instruction: Assessing the knowledge base. *Phi Delta Kappan, 71,* 470–478.

Wang, M., Haertel, G., & Walberg, H. (1993). Toward a knowledge base for school learning. *Review of Educational Research, 63,* 249–294.

White, E. B. (1952). *Charlotte's web.* New York: Harper & Row.

Wilen, W. (1990). Forms and phases of discussion. In W. Wilen (Ed.), *Teaching and learning through discussion* (pp. 3–24). Springfield, IL: Charles C Thomas.

CHAPTER 10

The Role of Dialogue in Reciprocal Teaching and Naturalistic Tutoring

Douglas J. Hacker
Arthur C. Graesser

In an article entitled *The Role of Dialogue in Providing Scaffolded Instruction,* Palincsar (1986) examined the critical role dialogue plays in promoting scaffolded instruction of the reading comprehension strategies contained in reciprocal teaching (Palincsar & Brown, 1984). The importance of dialogue, Palincsar noted, was made evident by certain features of the dialogues of students who were functioning more independently of their teachers at the end of instruction. These features included the following: (a) Students' contributions were encouraged at the idea level as opposed to the word level, (b) students' ideas were linked to new knowledge, (c) the dialogues were focused and directed by the teachers, (d) the point of instruction was made explicit to the student, and (e) evaluative statements were made that changed the complexion of student responses from negative to constructive (Palincsar, 1986). Palincsar's hope at that time was for further serious examinations of these features and the critical role classroom dialogue plays in facilitating scaffolded instruction. For her, and for many others, one of the central questions for the future of reading instruction was whether there were other fundamental ways that teachers and students engaged in dialogue during reading.

Unfortunately, since Palincsar's important work, there has been surprisingly little research on dialogue in reciprocal teaching (Rosenshine & Meister, 1994). Researchers have not systematically examined how learning is affected by the quality of dialogue among teachers and students during reciprocal teaching. They have neglected investigations of how the quality of dialogue can be improved. Until more work is done in these critical areas, researchers and practitioners of reciprocal teaching are left little choice but to rely on empirical work that has focused more generally on the role of dialogue in instruction or, as we argue here, on empirical work that has focused on dialogue in other contexts of learning, specifically, naturalistic tutoring.

This chapter focuses on the characteristics of dialogue in reciprocal teaching. We discuss changes in reciprocal teaching strategies over time and how dialogue can facilitate change. With this groundwork having been laid, we will explore whether the work by Graesser and his associates on dialogue in naturalistic tutoring (Graesser, Bowers, Hacker, & Person, 1997; Graesser, Person, & Magliano, 1995) might inform researchers and practitioners on how to improve dialogue in reciprocal teaching.

RECIPROCAL TEACHING

Reciprocal teaching is a method of instruction in which small groups of students learn to improve their reading comprehension through "scaffolded instruction" of comprehension-fostering and comprehension-monitoring strategies (Brown & Palincsar, 1989; Palincsar & Brown, 1984). These strategies are generating questions, summarizing, clarifying word meanings or clarifying confusing text, and predicting what might appear in the next paragraph. By engaging in these strategies, students increase their interaction with the text and become more cognizant of whether they understand what they are reading (Taylor & Frye, 1992). The scaffolded nature of the instruction provides students ample opportunities to observe teachers modeling the strategies and to assume control of the strategies as they gain greater and greater proficiency.

Instruction of the strategies occurs through an ongoing dialogue between students and the teacher (i.e., the dialogue leader). An example of the kind of dialogue that occurs and how the four strategies are used is provided in the following transcript of reciprocal teaching, which has been borrowed from Palincsar (1986, pp. 90–91, 93). The transcript is of a first-grade teacher reading expository text to a group of six students, four of whom were identified as at risk for academic difficulty. The first transcript is from Day 4 of instruction, and the second is of the same teacher and students from Day 19.

Teacher D, Day 4

18	T:	Do you remember what this paragraph is telling you, A_____? What did you learn? (pause) Did it move, or talk in some way? Who was the cat talking to?
19	S5:	To the mother.
20	T:	When the cat was talking to its mother, do you remember what it did? (pause) How does a cat talk to its mother? Does it make sounds? Do you remember what kind of sound it makes? Shall we let some of the others help us out?
21	S1:	It sometimes rubs against you on your arms.
22	T:	What rubs against you on your arms?
23	S1:	Cats do.
24	T:	All right. So you would summarize that the kitten rubs against your arms. Why? Can you give us a little more information?
25	S5:	Because it wants some love.

26	T:	So, it is trying to get your attention. It is wanting to talk, to communicate, right?
27	S1:	Baby kittens find their mother from the sounds.
28	T:	So you might want to ask a question from that information. You might ask how … does the kitten know where its mother is if it cannot see, if its eyes are closed?
29	S2:	They hear the sounds. But, it may be a different cat. They might have a cat next door, and they might think that it's their mother and they might be wrong.
30	T:	That's an interesting idea. If they all have their eyes closed, they wouldn't be able to tell the difference. If you had your eyes closed at the table, would you be able to tell who was who?
31	S2:	Yes.
32	T:	How would you be able to tell, C_____?
33	S2:	From their voice.
34	T:	Okay. Now, what do you think this story is going to tell next? Do you think that we have learned all about how they communicate?
35	S3:	No.
36	T:	Then what is your prediction?
37	S3:	That they communicate …
38	T:	Let's see if you're right. (reads paragraph)

Teacher D, Day 19

1	S6:	(question) What does the daddy longlegs do when something comes around it? J_____?
2	S1:	Use that odor and … (not audible)
3	S6:	Yeah. C_____.
4	S2:	When an animal comes along, he puts out his odor and they get too sick to catch him.
5	S6:	Yeah. M_____.
6	S4:	Or too weak.
7	S3:	They feel too weak and too sick.
8	S6:	Everybody gave me good answers.
9	T:	Very good.
10	S6:	(summary) I will summarize. When an animal comes around, it gives out its bad smell, and they get weak and too old to catch it.
11	S1:	(clarification) Who does?
12	S6:	That's the daddy longlegs.
13	S1:	(clarification) Who does?
14	S3:	The animals.
15	S1:	(clarification) Which animals?
16	S3:	All kinds of animals.
17	S6:	Yeah, different kinds.
18	S1:	Different kinds of animals put out a spray?

19	S3:	(clarification) Um, it might be the same kind of animal as tries to catch the daddy longlegs.
20	T:	Okay, I think you are talking about two different things. He's talking about the animals that come around to the spider and he's trying to get you to say who puts out the odor. Is it all animals?
21	S1:	No, the daddy longlegs.

On Day 4, the teacher (i.e., the dialogue leader) initially dominates the dialogue by asking questions about specific portions of the text and encouraging students to ask questions (lines 18, 20, 22, and 28). *Question generation,* which requires students to identify key information and frame that information in the form of a question (Palincsar, 1986), has been shown to be an effective method for improving comprehension (Graesser & McMahen, 1993; Graesser & Olde, 2003; King, 1994). The dialogue leader then *summarizes* the gist of the text (line 24) and encourages discussion of the summaries (Palincsar, 1986). Summarization encourages students to integrate information across sentences, paragraphs, and pages. As is the case for question generation, summarization also has been shown to be an effective way to increase comprehension (Armbruster, Anderson, & Ostertag, 1987). *Clarifications* are provided by the dialogue leader whenever a misunderstanding or unfamiliar information is encountered (lines 18, 22, 24, 26, 30, and 32). Through clarification, students note comprehension failures, identify the source of the failure, and take steps to rectify the failures (Palincsar, 1986). As a final step, the dialogue leader encourages students to make *predictions* about upcoming text information (lines 34 and 36). Such predictions help students to activate relevant background knowledge (Palincsar, 1986).

As illustrated in the Day 19 transcript, over time more and more responsibility for the four strategies shifts to the students, and the teacher gradually fades from his or her involvement by having students take turns as dialogue leader. The overall goal of the instruction is not so much the mastery of specific strategies as it is to create through collaboration flexible strategy use in response to the kind of text and the needs of the reader (Palincsar, David, Winn, & Stevens, 1991). The ultimate goal, of course, is for students to derive greater meaning from the text.

Key to learning and applying the four strategies is the collaboration that occurs between teacher and students (Hacker & Tenent, 2002; King & Johnson, 1999). Collaborative processes have been identified as crucial to facilitating learning (e.g., Daiute & Dalton, 1993). In some forms of collaboration, a cognitive apprenticeship is encouraged between teacher and student. In these apprenticeships, the student (a) actively constructs his or her knowledge through culturally meaningful activities, (b) observes expert modeling of strategies in which strategies are used flexibly or generated anew to meet the unique needs of the moment, (c) is taught how to generate questions designed to guide comprehension, (d) is encouraged to reflect on his or her progress through the learning event, and (e) is provided with immediate feedback as he or she is assessed dynamically throughout the learning event (Daiute & Dalton, 1993).

There is nothing new about instructing students to use strategies to improve reading comprehension (Taylor & Frye, 1992). Moreover, the four strategies in reciprocal teaching have been used in other reading programs (Palincsar & Klenk,

1992). Reading programs such as Informed Strategies for Learning (Paris, Cross, & Lipson, 1984), Strategies Intervention Model (Deshler & Schumaker, 1986), and SQ3R-Survey, Question, Read, Recite, and Review (Robinson, 1961) have used one or more of the four strategies that are used in reciprocal teaching.

What is new about reciprocal teaching, and what is perhaps more promising, is the context in which instruction occurs. Instruction occurs in social, interactive, and holistic dialogues (Palincsar & Klenk, 1992) between novice problems solvers and an expert teacher or more capable peer (Palincsar, 2003). Novice and expert work together to solve real problems in real reading contexts (Garner, 1992) rather than through contrived worksheets or reading workbooks. This kind of scaffolded context for learning has received support not only from reading researchers but from proponents of situativity theory who argue that "cognitive activities should be understood primarily as interactions between agents and physical systems and with other people" (Greeno & Moore, 1993, p. 49). This context for learning provides students ample opportunities to use the skills being taught under the direction of an expert who can provide feedback for students to learn how to calibrate the level of difficulty of specific tasks, recognize when additional support is needed, and understand what has led to correct comprehension (Palincsar, 1986).

As instruction progresses in reciprocal teaching, there is a gradual reduction in the distinction between novice student and expert teacher. Garner (1992) has identified this reduction in the "asymmetry of power" between teacher and student as an important component in developing "true" conversation, in which students can verbalize their thoughts and share their expertise with other students. With a reduction in the asymmetry of power, the role of teacher changes from model to collaborator. The role of student changes from a passive receptor of knowledge to an active constructor of knowledge. The student becomes one who can self-regulate his or her management and planning of reading and who can reflect not only on what has been read but on how it has been read (Hacker & Tenent, 2002). Learning becomes intentional, that is, purposeful, effortful, self-regulated, and active (Bereiter & Scardamalia, 1989). And with an increase in intentionality, the reader begins to acquire the skills (e.g., summarizing, questioning, predicting) that good readers seem to employ spontaneously (Dole & Pearson, 1987).

Many studies since Palincsar and Brown's (1984) seminal work have been performed to replicate their results. There have been investigations using at-risk readers; remedial readers; good, average, and poor comprehenders; and readers who were poor comprehenders but good decoders (Rosenshine & Meister, 1994). Participants in these investigations have ranged in age from 7 years to older adults. Even though results differ according to the kinds of measures used to evaluate instructional effectiveness, comprehension skills have consistently increased through reciprocal teaching.

Palincsar's own program of research has documented the benefits of reciprocal teaching. In particular, reciprocal teaching (a) contributes markedly to students' ability to summarize, question, clarify, and predict; (b) produces comprehension improvements that are large, reliable, and durable; (c) generalizes to classroom settings; and (d) transfers to tasks that are similar but distinct from the training tasks (Palincsar, 1986). Palincsar reports that attempts to isolate the essential features of reciprocal teaching have identified the scaffolded dialogue between expert and novice as contributing to greater gains in comprehension skills.

SHIFTS IN STRATEGIES AND DIALOGUE OVER TIME

Experienced readers approach reading flexibly. They modify their reading according to the nature of the text and the task, the structure of the text, and the knowledge they can bring to bear on the text topic. Experienced readers spontaneously plan and evaluate their reading (Dole & Pearson, 1987). They use specific reading strategies to perform specific reading tasks, and they have an awareness of how their strategy use is progressing over time (Daiute & Dalton, 1993). When a comprehension failure is noted, they have an understanding of what fix-up strategy is most likely to resolve the failure, and they have a greater number and variety of fix-up strategies from which to choose (Hacker, 2004; Palincsar & Brown, 1984). Moreover, as a consequence of monitoring their reading, experienced readers modify existing strategies or invent new ones to meet the novel and specific demands of the moment (Pressley, Forrest-Pressley, Elliott-Faust, & Miller, 1985; Wong, 1989).

Given these characteristics of a proficient reader, how can we help less proficient readers become more proficient? Reading instruction that purports to do so must teach students to (a) plan and evaluate their reading, (b) use reading strategies and monitor and control their use, (c) deal with comprehension failures, and (d) modify existing reading strategies or create new ones (Hacker, 2004). Examinations of reciprocal teaching have shown that many kinds of readers (e.g., poor to good, young to old) learn (a), (b), and (c) and thereby become more proficient at reading. However, what remains to be examined is whether reciprocal teaching encourages shifts in strategy use through modification of existing strategies or the creation of new ones (Hacker & Tenent, 2002). Moreover, does dialogue facilitate these shifts? "Shifts" in strategy use are as important as all the other components of reciprocal teaching (Garner, 1992). There is some evidence to suggest that students do make them. However, a stronger empirical examination is necessary to determine the adaptive and maladaptive modifications that readers make to their reading strategies as they attempt to resolve problems in their reading (Garner, 1992).

The transcripts of reciprocal teaching dialogue provided earlier in this chapter (Palincsar, 1986, pp. 90–91, 93) illustrate how teacher-student dialogue supports scaffolded instruction and how strategy use can change with time. Perhaps the most apparent change in the dialogues from Day 4 to Day 19 is the decrease in teacher input (Palincsar, 1986). On Day 4, the teacher was clearly dialogue leader of the discussion: The teacher asked questions for the students to consider, provided summaries of text information, prompted clarifications of uncertain or confusing information, and asked students to predict upcoming text information. Thus, like more traditional classroom interactions in which teachers provide approximately 80% of the reacting statements to their own questions and soliciting statements (Palincsar, 1986), the teacher in this transcript dominated the dialogue with more traditional direct instruction of the strategies. However, on Day 19, the students were clearly dominating the dialogue. They were actively involved in true conversation with one another, and they moved their strategy use from other-regulation to self-regulation (Garner, 1992). The few teacher comments on Day 19 served mainly to praise student efforts and arbitrate student disagreements.

Also readily apparent in these transcripts is how the formal labeling of strategies was discontinued by Day 19. On Day 4, the teacher explicitly named each strategy as it was being used, and, although not shown in this particular transcript, the students mimicked these teacher verbalizations. On Day 19, students were still using the strategies; however, their explicit labeling of them had nearly ended. Thus, the highly scaffolded structure of reciprocal teaching that had been established at the beginning of instruction had been removed, in part, by Day 19, and as it was removed, the dialogue that had occurred earlier between students and teacher became internalized in the students' own thinking (cf. Vygotsky, 1978).

The transcripts from the two days of instruction also show a difference in the general progression of dialogue. The dialogue on Day 4 progressed linearly. The discussion between teacher and students first focused on cats rubbing against one's arms, then moved on to cats wanting love, and finally focused on the sounds a mother cats makes. In contrast, the dialogue on Day 19 was more repetitive, focusing repeatedly on the role of odor. Teacher and students first discussed the odor produced by daddy longlegs. They then discussed the weak sensation caused by the odor. Finally, they discussed the odors that different kinds of animals put out. By encouraging multiple repetitions of information, teachers often help students advance to new levels of cognitive complexity (Daiute & Dalton, 1993). Relatedly, Horowitz (1998) reports that in a study with fifth-grade students, repetition was used as an important way to sustain student involvement with the text. Allowing students to engage in oftentimes time-consuming repetitions is a difficult choice that teachers must make. However, if internalization of strategy use is desired, allowing repetitions of information appears to be a critical element in collaboration.

Although not evident in the Day 4 and Day 19 transcripts, Palincsar (1986; Palincsar & Klenk, 1992) noted other significant changes in dialogue over time. Student questions changed from verbatim phrases taken from the text to paraphrases of main points. Questions changed from simple and literal to questions that asked for multiple, diverse, and more complex responses. Student summaries changed from being detailed oriented to including main ideas. Students who initially waited for teacher questions and comments before responding began to interrupt the teacher to interject their predictions, comments, and questions. Students' use of strategies changed from ritualized and mechanical to thoughtful and discriminating. The use of strategies began to be driven by the unique content and discourse itself. Finally, the amount of playfulness among students increased with time. In a related area, Daiute and Dalton (1993) have shown that children who balance planning and revising of writing tasks with implicit playful strategies are those who benefit the most from collaborating. What needs to be examined is whether playfulness has similar effects on reading tasks during reciprocal teaching. Palincsar and Klenk (1992) have observed that playfulness can assume an important role in facilitating student engagement in discussions of text.

DIALOGUE IN NATURALISTIC TUTORING

The superiority of one-to-one tutoring over traditional classroom instruction has been well documented (Bloom, 1984; Cohen, Kulik, & Kulik, 1982; Mohan, 1972). However, the identification of exactly what aspects of one-to-one tutoring contribute to this superiority has received little attention. In an effort to identify these aspects, Graesser and his associates (Graesser et al., 1995, 1997) examined two samples of tutors. In one sample, graduate students from the Psychology Department at The University of Memphis tutored undergraduate students on trouble-some topics in a research methods course. In the other sample, high school students tutored seventh graders on troublesome topics in algebra.

A content analysis of the tutor-student dialogues from both samples indicated that of the many learning components emphasized in contemporary pedagogical theories and intelligent tutoring systems (Graesser, Hu, & McNamara, 2005), the ones that surfaced as prime candidates for explaining the superiority of tutoring over classroom instruction were (a) collaborative problem solving and question answering, (b) extensive use of example problems, and (c) deep explanatory reasoning. Of course, all three of these are germane to instruction. However, given our current focus on dialogue, we examine more closely only the collaborative aspects of tutoring.

The Evolution of Systematic Collaborative Conversation

The analysis of our tutor-student dialogues shows that as tutor and student collaboratively solved problems and answered questions, a systematic pattern of collaborative conversation evolved that gradually imposed a structure onto the dialogues. As discussed earlier, many educational theorists and practitioners have emphasized the important role that collaboration plays in many contexts of learning. What is unique to tutoring, however, is the way in which the systematic pattern of collaboration evolves. In this section, we first describe this pattern. We then argue that this pattern can serve (a) as a tool to aid in the analysis of dialogue quality during scaffolded instruction of reciprocal teaching and (b) as a way to improve dialogue quality and facilitate change of strategy use over time.

In contrast to the typical three-step dialogue exchanges established in traditional classroom instruction—initiation, response, feedback (Mehan, 1979)—the dialogue pattern observed in our tutoring sessions evolved into a five-step framework:

Step 1:   Tutor asks question.
Step 2:   Student answers question.
Step 3:   Tutor gives short feedback on the quality of the answer.
Step 4:   Tutor and student collaboratively improve the quality of the answer.
Step 5:   Tutor assesses student's understanding of the answer.

The first three steps correspond to the three steps of the typical classroom pattern: (a) Teacher initiates a question, (b) student provides a response, and (c) teacher evaluates the response. With the addition of the last two steps, particularly Step 4 during which a collaborative exchange of ideas occurs, the potency of the learning event is greatly increased. It is precisely this collaborative exchange of ideas through dialogue that has been identified as key to cognitive development and learning (Goodwin & Heritage, 1990; Greeno, 1991; Lave & Wenger, 1987; Roschelle, 1992; Suchman, 1987, Vygotsky, 1978).

An example of the five-step pattern taken from our college sample is given here (Graesser et al., 1995):

Step 1.   Tutor: Now what is a factorial design?

Step 2.	Student:	The design has two variables.
Step 3.	Tutor:	Uh-huh.
Step 4.	Tutor:	So there are two or more independent variables and one (pause)
	Student:	dependent variable.
Step 5.	Tutor:	Do you see that?
	Student:	Uh-huh.

It is important to keep in mind that the dialogue occurring in Step 4 is rarely ever limited to the simple exchange illustrated in this example. In most cases, the number of conversational turns can be extensive and, depending on the nature of the tutor's question, can extend upwards from 10 to 19 turns.

The collaborative exchange of ideas between tutor and student occurring in Step 4 can be singled out as perhaps the most critical component of tutor-student dialogue. During these exchanges, tutors improved the quality of students' responses by relying on a wide variety of strategies. These strategies served to encourage, extend, elaborate, revise, and redirect the dialogue. Of the many strategies tutors relied on, five specific kinds appeared to be used more frequently than others: pumping, prompting, splicing, hinting, and summarizing.

Pumping

Tutors periodically needed to pump students to encourage them to share more of their knowledge and elaborate on their answers. A typical example of pumping in which the tutor provides continual neutral feedback to encourage the student's responses is given in the following example.

Tutor:	Why would a researcher even want to use more than two levels of an independent variable in an experiment?
Student:	More than two levels?
Tutor:	Mmm-hmm.
Student:	They would, um, it'd be real accurate 'cause it would show if there's a curvilinear
Tutor:	Mmm-hmm.
Student:	Uh, let's see … um, they like show partial effects and, um, correlational effects?
Tutor:	Mmm-hmm.
Student:	I think …
Tutor:	Yeah. Okay. And what's meant by a factorial design?

Prompting

Frequently, tutors prompted students to contribute more information. This was done by first providing the student a rich discourse and then, by pausing or using intonation, prompting the student to fill in a missing word or phrase. An example of this is given in the following exchange.

Tutor: As you know by now, correlation does not mean … (pause)
Student: causation

Splicing

When a student provided an error-ridden response to a question, the tutor quickly jumped in with a correct answer. The metaphor "splicing" is used to indicate that during these exchanges the tutor and student often jointly constructed a connected structure of ideas. An example of splicing is given in the following example.

Tutor: According to the graph, how should memory be affected by imagery?
Student: It should get worse because …
Tutor: (interrupts) It should get better because …

Hinting

Students sometimes failed to give responses, or their responses were sometimes vague. When this occurred, tutors were reluctant to take responsibility from students by simply providing the correct answers. Instead, the tutors often provided a partially correct answer, revised the question, or elaborated the context to support students in their responses. In other words, tutors provided hints to students, an example of which is given in the following exchange.

Tutor: What type of scale would that be?
Student: Oh, let me think, which one. I don't know.
Tutor: Try to think. Nominal or (pause)?
Student: Ordinal, yeah.
Tutor: It would be. Why would it be an ordinal scale?

Summarizing

Because answers typically evolved over many conversational turns, it was often necessary for tutors to provide summaries of answers at the end of exchanges. Ideally, such summaries would be the responsibility of students; however, it may be difficult for students to sift through several minutes of correct and incorrect responses and then provide concise summaries of the salient points. Additionally, because summarizing provides tutors one more opportunity to emphasize salient points, it may be more beneficial to allow them to do so.

ENHANCEMENT OF DIALOGUE IN RECIPROCAL TEACHING: RESEARCH AND PRACTICE

The critical collaborative exchanges that occur in Step 4 of the five-step tutor-student dialogues occur as a logical consequence of the questions and answers exchanged during Steps 1, 2, and 3 and the assessment of the student's understanding in Step 5. This last step then leads back to a reiteration of the original question-and-answer exchange or to the statement of another question at which point Step 1 is once again initiated. Sharing meaning and actively constructing new meaning with a more capable tutor, peer, or teacher in a collaborative exchange are aspects of instruction that have been identified as essential to student learning. This collaborative exchange of ideas is what naturalistic tutoring and reciprocal teaching have in common.

We believe that this commonality between naturalistic tutoring and reciprocal teaching can be exploited to benefit both research and practice of reciprocal teaching. We propose that the five-step pattern identified in our examinations of naturalistic tutoring can serve as a tool in the examination of dialogue quality in reciprocal teaching. We further propose that the collaborative strategies used by our tutors to improve the quality of student responses can be used in reciprocal teaching. It remains for future research to determine the utility of our proposed research tool and the effectiveness of our strategies. Our intent here is not to make empirical claims but rather to suggest avenues that we believe hold promise as ways to understand further the role of dialogue in reciprocal teaching and to enhance its effectiveness.

The Examination of Dialogue Quality

To demonstrate how the five-step pattern can be used as a tool in the analysis of dialogue quality, we first describe how dialogues can be dissected into the five steps. By dissecting the dialogues into five steps, each identifying a unique and specific aspect of dialogue, a more detailed analysis of the dialogues is possible. We then describe ways in which the dialogue in each of the five steps can be analyzed for specific measures of quality, and in so doing, we make suggestions for possible dependent variables.

Because the collaborative exchanges that occur in both naturalistic tutoring and reciprocal teaching involve turn-taking interactions between students and a teacher, tutor, or more capable peer, the five-step pattern observed in naturalistic tutoring is readily observable in reciprocal teaching. To illustrate this, consider how the two sample transcripts that were discussed earlier in this chapter (Palincsar, 1986, pp. 90–91, 93), particularly lines 20–34 from Day 4 and lines 1–9 from Day 19, can be dissected into the five-step pattern.

In Table 10.1, line 20 from the first transcript clearly illustrates Step 1, Tutor asks a question. Step 2, Student answers question, is performed by Student S1 in line 21. Step 3, Tutor gives short feedback by asking for clarification from Student S1 in lines 22–23. Lines 24–33 illustrate Step 4, in which the teacher and three of the students engage in a collaborative exchange to improve the quality of the response. Line 34 completes the five-step pattern as the Tutor assesses the students' understanding, provides the feedback "Okay," and then begins the five-step pattern again.

Similarly, line 1 of the second example illustrates Step 1, Tutor asks a question (Table 10.2), although in this example, the question is being asked by a student who is acting as dialogue leader. Step 2, Student answers question, is performed by Student S1 in line 2. Step 3, the student dialogue leader provides short feedback in lines 3 and 5. Step 4, the collaborative exchange to improve the quality of the response occurs in lines 4–7. Finally, the student dialogue leader assesses students'

TABLE 10.1
Transcript of Teacher D, Day 4 Dissected Into Five-Step Pattern

Step 2: Student answers question.		
21	S1:	It sometimes rubs against you on your arms.
Step 3: Tutor (teacher) gives short feedback on the quality of the answer.		
22	T:	What rubs against you on your arms?
23	S1:	Cats do.
Step 4: Tutor (teacher) and students collaboratively improve the quality of the answer.		
24	T:	All right. So you would summarize that the kitten rubs against your arms. Why? Can you give us a little more information?
25	S5:	Because it wants some love.
26	T:	So, it is trying to get your attention. It is wanting to talk, to communicate, right?
27	S1:	Baby kittens find their mother from the sounds.
28	T:	So you might want to ask a question from that information. You might ask how … does the kitten know where its mother is if it cannot see, if its eyes are closed?
29	S2:	They hear the sounds. But, it may be a different cat. They might have a cat next door, and they might think that it's their mother and they might be wrong.
30	T:	That's an interesting idea. If they all have their eyes closed, they wouldn't be able to tell the difference. If you had your eyes closed at the table, would you be able to tell who was who?
31	S2:	Yes.
32	T:	How would you be able to tell, C?
33	S2:	From their voice.
Step 5: Tutor (teacher) assesses students' understanding of the answer.		
34	T:	Okay. Now, what do you think this story is going to tell next? Do you think that we have learned all about how they communicate?

understanding in line 8, and the teacher provides his or her assessment in line 9. Line 10 then begins a new five-step pattern.

Once all of the dialogue has been dissected into the five steps, the steps can be analyzed for specific measures of quality. There are many measures of quality that could be used, so the ones we suggested are not meant to be exhaustive. However, given the scaffolded nature of reciprocal teaching and its goal to teach comprehension strategies, we believe that an analysis of dialogue quality should include at least the following four measures: (a) number of student contributions to the total dialogues, (b) number of student collaborations, (c) number of student collaborations independent of the teacher; and (d) number of times students use comprehension strategies independently of the teacher.

Because of the scaffolded nature of reciprocal teaching, students are expected to assume more and more responsibility for the dialogues as teacher support is grad-

TABLE 10.2
Transcript of Teacher D, Day 19 Dissected Into Five-Step Pattern

Step 2: Student answers question.		
2	S1:	Use that odor and ... (not audible)
Step 3: Tutor (student dialogue leader) gives short feedback on the quality of the answer.		
3	S6:	Yeah. C
Step 4: Tutor (student dialogue leader) and students collaboratively improve the quality of the answer.		
4	S2:	When an animal comes along, he puts out his odor and they get too sick to catch him.
5	S6:	Yeah. M
6	S4:	Or too weak.
7	S3:	They feel too weak and too sick.
Step 5: Tutor (student dialogue leader) assesses students' understanding of the answer.		
8	S6:	Everybody gave me good answers.
9	T:	Very good.

ually removed. Thus, if dialogue is progressing effectively, the number of student contributions to the dialogue will gradually increase as the number of teacher contributions decrease. Dialogue quality, therefore, would be evident in the relative amounts of teacher and student contributions throughout instruction. This could be determined by calculating the proportion of either teacher or student dialogue turns to total number of turns occurring in each identified five-step pattern and then examining the change in the proportions over time. For example, in the Day 4 transcript, the teacher contributed 8 of the 15 turns within the identified five-step pattern, for a proportion of .53, and on Day 19 contributed only 1 of the 9 turns, for a proportion of .11. On the basis of this limited example, the change in the proportions on these two days suggests that scaffolded instruction was supporting greater student contributions.

Dialogue quality will be reflected in the extent to which students are actively engaged in dialogue and whether their engagement increases with time. As discussed earlier, it appears that the critical collaborative exchanges occur in Step 4 of the five-step pattern. Therefore, the greater number of conversational turns that occur during these exchanges would indicate greater engagement on the part of students. A simple measure of this would be a count of the number of conversational turns occurring during Step 4 of each identified five-step pattern. Examining how this number changes across the dialogues over time would indicate either increases or decreases in engagement. Furthermore, important information about how to facilitate student engagement could be obtained by performing a content analysis of the Step 4 exchanges to identify the kind of interactions that consistently lead to increases in collaboration.

Dialogue quality also would be reflected in the extent to which student collaborations during Step 4 become independent of teacher support. The ultimate goal of scaffolded instruction is to achieve unassisted student learning. Whether this goal is being achieved would be reflected in the number of student collaborations occurring without teacher assistance. A measure of independent student collaborations could be derived by calculating the proportion of student dialogue turns to total number of turns occurring in Step 4 of each identified five-step pattern. An increase over time in these proportions would indicate that the dialogue is of sufficient quality to promote independent student collaboration.

Finally, the quality of dialogue would be reflected in the extent to which the dialogue supports not only student strategy use but also students' independent use of the strategies. In reciprocal teaching, students learn to apply the four comprehension strategies to their reading through a dialogue with the teacher. The teacher first explains the strategies and models their use, and over time, students are to internalize the dialogue and apply the strategies independently of the teacher. Therefore, examining the number of times students use strategies in each of the identified five-step patterns across all identified five-step patterns would indicate how well the dialogue has progressed. Perhaps more importantly, comparing the number of times students use strategies independent of teacher assistance compared to the total number of times strategies are used would indicate how well the dialogue has encouraged the internalization of strategies.

The Use of Collaborative Strategies

In our analyses of naturalistic tutoring in research methods and algebra, we found that our graduate school and high school tutors used a variety of collaborative strategies to improve the quality of student responses. Of these strategies, five appeared to be used more frequently than others: summarizing, pumping, splicing, hinting, and prompting. However, we are uncertain how our observed tutors learned to use these strategies or whether they were even aware that they were using them. Despite these uncertainties, however, our analyses of the dialogues indicated that the strategies served as aids to the collaborative exchanges occurring between tutor and student. Whether instruction of these strategies would further increase the effectiveness of collaboration is something for future research to determine. In the meantime, it is reasonable to assume that because collaboration is not often used in classrooms and few opportunities to practice it are provided (Hacker & Tenent, 2002; Marks, Pressley, Coley, Craig, Gardner, DePinto, & Rose, 1993; Palincsar, 1986), students likely lack collaborative skills. Thus, preliminary to the instruction of strategies to facilitate reading comprehension, students may benefit greatly from the instruction of strategies to facilitate peer collaboration. Certainly, the collaborative strategies found in naturalistic tutoring would be a good place to start.

Of the five most prevalent strategies found in naturalistic tutoring, summarizing is one that is already incorporated in reciprocal teaching. For example, line 24 of the Day 4 transcript provided in Table 10–1 illustrates the teacher's modeling of it, "All right. So you would summarize that the kitten rubs against your arms." By Day 19, some of the students became proficient users of the strategy, which is evident in Student S6's statement on line 10, "I will summarize. When an animal comes around, it gives out its bad smell, and they get weak and too old to catch it." Encouraging students as often as possible to generate their own summaries makes them more active in their reading and more attentive to the ongoing dialogue.

Pumping was a strategy used in tutoring as a way to encourage students to share more of their knowledge with one another and to elaborate on their answers. The teacher on line 24 of Day 4 provides an illustration of its use in reciprocal teaching, "Can you give us a little more information?" to which Student S5 replies, "Because it wants some love." Whether students are aware of the subtleties of such teacher encouragement is uncertain; however, on line 17 of Day 19, Student S6 missed an opportunity to pump for more information that quickly led to confusion among the students concerning which animals put out an odor. In addition to having provided the statement, "Yeah, different kinds," had Student S6 pumped students for more information about other animals that put out a spray, this additional information may have resolved the ensuing confusion. Moreover, pumping students to share more of their knowledge and to elaborate on their knowledge increases the chances that students will link their ideas to the new knowledge being read (Palincsar, 1986). The more often these links can be made, the more likely the new knowledge will become a student's own.

Splicing occurs when a student quickly jumps in to correct an error-ridden response of another student. The confusion that arose among the students on Day 19 also may have been avoided had someone quickly corrected Student S6's incorrect statement on line 12. On line 11, Student S1 asked for clarification regarding who gets too weak and old to catch it? To this Student S6 replied incorrectly, "That's the daddy longlegs." Student S6 should have said that it was the animal trying to attack the daddy longlegs who gets sick and old. Unfortunately, no one corrected this misstatement so there was confusion on lines 13–21.

Palincsar (1986) reported that the effectiveness of dialogue was supported by the teacher's evaluative comments that changed the complexion of student responses from negative to constructive. Splicing could be used for a similar purpose. Rather than focusing on the negativity of corrective responses, students could be encouraged to use splices that support the collaborative goal of constructing a common meaning from the text.

Hinting also was used as an effective strategy to facilitate collaboration in tutoring. When students failed to give responses or when responses were vague, tutors provided partially correct answers, asked revised questions, or elaborated the context to encourage student responses. As illustrated on line 20 of Day 4, hinting was a strategy used by the teacher in reciprocal teaching. Here the teacher first elaborated the notion that the young cat communicates with its mother and then supported student responses by hinting at the ways in which this communication occurs.

Finally, tutors prompted students to share more of their knowledge first by providing a rich discourse and then by pausing or using intonation in an effort to prompt them to fill in a missing word or phrase. The teacher's dialogue on line 26 of Day 4 indicates that prompting also is used in reciprocal teaching: First, the teacher explains more completely why the cat is trying to get someone's attention and then ends with a questioning "Right?" to prompt student responses. It is likely that students also use hinting and prompting to some extent during reciprocal teaching; however, more thorough instruction in the use of these two collaborative strategies and greater awareness of their effectiveness would certainly lead to greater gains in dialogue quality. Moreover, following on Palincsar's (1986) findings, hinting and prompting at "idea" levels rather than "word" levels could add considerably to the effectiveness of instruction. Instead of prompting students to fill in missing words or hinting at single phrases, dialogue leaders who ask students to provide concepts or elaborate at conceptual levels would likely encourage deeper processing of the text.

Areas that are ripe for investigation concern whether teachers spontaneously use these collaborative strategies to enhance collaboration in reciprocal teaching and whether students learn them through modeling and use them in their interactions with one another. Likely, the same kinds of content analyses performed by Graesser and his associates on the dialogues during naturalistic tutoring would reveal similar use during reciprocal teaching. Furthermore, whether explicit instruction in their use would increase the quality of dialogue in reciprocal teaching and facilitate the shift in strategy use from other-regulation to self-regulation also remains to be tested. Until such investigations are completed, however, we have only the evidence provided by the examinations of naturalistic tutoring to show that use of these strategies does contribute to collaboration and learning.

SUMMARY

Student-teacher dialogue occurring in a wide variety of instructional contexts has been shown to play a critical role in learning and development. It is now time to examine the common features of dialogue that are responsible for enhancing learning regardless of the instructional context. In 1986, Palincsar asked, "What features would characterize such dialogue?" (p. 95). Only by examining dialogue in a wide variety of contexts and finding the common features can this question be answered. We have attempted to do so here by bringing tutoring, a commonly employed and effective teaching strategy, and reciprocal teaching, also an effective teaching strategy, closer together. Our examination has revealed certain key features shared by both and has suggested several avenues that research can take to examine further the presence of these key features and how they contribute to the quality and utility of dialogue as a tool for learning. Finally, we ended our examinations of reciprocal teaching and naturalistic tutoring with suggestions about how the quality of dialogue can be improved to make reciprocal teaching an even more effective instructional method for increasing students' ability to read.

REFERENCES

Armbruster, B. B., Anderson, T. H., & Ostertag, J. (1987). Does text structured/summarization instruction facilitate learning from expository text? *Reading Research Quarterly, 22,* 331–346.

Bereiter, C., & Scardamalia, M. (1989). Intentional learning. In L. B. Resnick (Ed.), *Knowing, learning, and instruction: Essays in honor of Robert Glaser* (pp. 361–392). Hillsdale, NJ: Lawrence Erlbaum Associates.

Bloom, B. S. (1984). The 2 sigma problem: The search for methods of group instruction as effective as one-to-one tutoring. *Educational Researcher, 13,* 4–16.

Brown, A. L., & Palincsar, A. S. (1989). Guided cooperative learning and individual knowledge acquisition. In L. B. Resnick (Ed.), *Knowing, learning, and instruction: Essays in honor of Robert Glaser* (pp. 393–451). Hillsdale, NJ: Lawrence Erlbaum Associates.

Cohen, P. A., Kulik, J. A., & Kulik, C. C. (1982). Educational outcomes of tutoring: A meta-analysis of findings. *American Educational Research Journal, 19,* 237–248.

Daiute, C., & Dalton, B. (1993). Collaboration between children learning to write: Can novices be masters? *Cognition and Instruction, 10,* 281–333.

Deshler, D. D., & Schumaker, J. B. (1986). Learning strategies: An instructional alternative for low-achieving adolescents. *Exceptional Children, 52,* 583–590.

Dole, E., & Pearson, P. D. (1987). Explicit comprehension instruction: A review of research and a new conceptualization of instruction. *The Elementary School Journal, 88,* 151–165.

Garner, R. (1992). Self-regulated learning, strategy shifts, and shared expertise: Reactions to Palincsar and Klenk. *Journal of Learning Disabilities, 25,* 226–229.

Goodwin, C., & Heritage, J. (1990). Conversational analysis. *Annual Review of Anthropology, 19,* 283–307.

Graesser, A. C., Bowers, C., Hacker, D. J., & Person, N. (1997). An anatomy of naturalistic tutoring. In K. Hogan & M. Pressley (Eds.), *Scaffolding student learning: Instructional approaches and issues* (pp. 145–184). Cambridge, MA: Brookline Books.

Graesser, A. C., Hu, X., & McNamara, D. S. (2005). Computerized learning environments that incorporate research in discourse psychology, cognitive science, and computational linguistics. In A. F. Healy (Ed.), *Experimental cognitive psychology and its applications* (pp. 183–194). Washington, DC: American Psychological Association.

Graesser, A. C., & McMahen, C. L. (1993). Anomalous information triggers questions when adults solve quantitative problems and comprehend stories. *Journal of Educational Psychology, 85,* 136–151.

Graesser, A. C., & Olde, B. A. (2003). How does one know whether a person understands a device? The quality of the questions the person asks when the device breaks down. *Journal of Educational Psychology, 95,* 524–536.

Graesser, A. C., Person, N. K., & Magliano, J. P. (1995). Collaborative dialogue patterns in naturalistic one-to-one tutoring. *Applied Cognitive Psychology, 9,* 1–28.

Greeno, J. G. (1991). Number sense as situated knowing in a conceptual domain. *Journal for Research in Mathematics Teaching, 22,* 170–218.

Greeno, J. G., & Moore, J. L. (1993). Situativity and symbols: Response to Vera and Simon. *Cognitive Science, 17,* 49–59.

Hacker, D. J. (2004). Self-regulated comprehension during normal reading. In R. B. Ruddell & N. Unrau (Eds.), *Theoretical models and processes of reading* (5th ed., pp. 775–779). Newark, DE: International Reading Association.

Hacker, D. J., & Tenent, A. (2002). Implementing reciprocal teaching in the classroom: Overcoming obstacles and making modifications. *Journal of Educational Psychology, 94,* 699–718.

Horowitz, R. (1998). The evolution of classroom talk: Contributions to text conceptualization and learning. In N. Ephraty & R. Lidor (Eds.), *Teacher education: Stability, evolution, and revolution* (pp. 921–932). Natanya, Israel: The Zinman College, Wingate Institute, Israel in conjunction with the Ministry of Education and Mofet Institute.

King, A. (1994). Guiding knowledge construction in the classroom: Effects of teaching children how to question and how to explain. *American Educational Research Journal, 31,* 338–368.

King, C. M., & Johnson, L. M. P. (1999). Constructing meaning via reciprocal teaching. *Reading Research & Instruction, 38,* 169–186.

Lave, J., & Wenger, E. (1987). *Situated learning: Legitimate peripheral participation.* Cambridge, MA: Cambridge University Press.

Marks, M., Pressley, M., Coley, J. D., Craig, S., Gardner, R., DePinto, W., et al. (1993). Three teachers' adaptations of reciprocal teaching in comparison to traditional reciprocal teaching. *The Elementary School Journal, 94,* 267–283.

Mehan, H. (1979). *Learning lessons: Social organization in the classroom.* Cambridge, MA: Harvard University Press.

Mohan, M. (1972). *Peer tutoring as a technique for teaching the unmotivated.* Fredonia: State University of New York, Teacher Education Research Center. (ERIC Document Reproduction Service No. ED061154)

Palincsar, A. S. (2003). Ann L. Brown: Advancing a theoretical model of learning and instruction. In B. J. Zimmerman & D. H. Schunk (Eds.), *Educational psychology: A century of contributions* (pp. 459–475). Mahwah, NJ: Lawrence Erlbaum Associates.

Palincsar, A. S., & Brown, A. L. (1984). Reciprocal teaching of comprehension-fostering and comprehension-monitoring activities. *Cognition and Instruction, 1,* 117–175.

Palincsar, A. S., David, Y. M., Winn, J. A., & Stevens, D. D. (1991). Examining the context of strategy instruction. *Remedial and Special Education, 12,* 43–53.

Palincsar, A. S., & Klenk, L. (1992). Fostering literacy learning in supportive contexts. *Journal of Learning Disabilities, 25,* 211–225.

Paris, S. G., Cross, D. R., & Lipson, M. Y. (1984). Informal strategies for learning: A program to improve children's reading awareness and comprehension. *Journal of Educational Psychology, 76,* 1239–1252.

Pressley, M., Forrest-Pressley, D. L., Elliott-Faust, D., & Miller, G. (1985). Children's use of cognitive strategies, how to teach strategies, and what to do if they can't be taught. In M. Pressley & C. J. Brainerd (Eds.), *Cognitive learning and memory in children* (pp. 1–47). New York: Springer-Verlag.

Robinson, F. P. (1961). *Effective study* (rev. ed.). New York: Harper & Row.

Roschelle, J. (1992). Learning by collaboration: Convergent conceptual change. *Journal of the Learning Sciences, 2,* 235–276.

Rosenshine, B., & Meister, C. (1994). Reciprocal teaching: A review of the research. *Review of Educational Research, 64,* 479–530.

Suchman, L. A. (1987). *Plans and situated actions: The problem of human-machine communication.* Cambridge, MA: Cambridge University Press.

Taylor, B. M., & Frye, B. J. (1992). Comprehension strategy instruction in the intermediate grades. *Reading Research and Instruction, 32,* 39–48.

Vygotsky, L. S. (1978). *Mind in society.* Cambridge, MA: Harvard University Press.

Wong, B. Y. L. (1989). Musing about cognitive strategy training. *Intelligence, 13,* 1–4.

CHAPTER 11

Conjunction Use in School Children's Oral Language and Reading*

Esther Geva

INTRODUCTION

Why devote a chapter to conjunctions in a book concerned with the relationships and interactions between oral and written language? The simple answer is that conjunctions make explicit the logical relations between propositions (Crothers, 1978; Kintsch & Van Dijk , 1978), they help readers in integrating the texts they link (Guzman, 2004), evoke inter-clause integration (Millis & Just, 1994), constitute a cognitive-linguistic category that is relatively easy to isolate (Sanders & Noordman, 1997), occur in oral and written language, and reflect cognitive and linguistic development. Numerous studies focusing on language development suggest that the acquisition of the logical implications of conjunctions continues to develop through the school years, that it is related to cognitive growth, and that certain conjunctions are acquired earlier than others. Studies concerned with reading comprehension indicate that skilled readers can infer logical relations such as cause-effect, contrast, additivity, and conditionality even when they are not made explicit in the text. On the other hand, there is evidence that less skilled readers rely on the use of conjunctions to understand the text. However, the use of connectives by less skilled readers depends on several conditions (see Cain, 2003).

In an oft-cited article describing the psycholinguistic correlates of the transition from oral to written expression, Olson (1977; see also Olson, 1994) pointed out that "schooling, particularly learning to read, is the critical process in the transformation of children's language from utterance to text" (p. 278). Learning to read and learn from expository texts is one of the major goals of schooling. This is so because school curricula rely heavily on the transmission of knowledge through written language which is "formal, academic and planned" (Horowitz & Samuels, 1987). Those readers who can read texts carefully and have learned to attend to explicit linguistic clues in text learn more from them. Growth in knowledge about the logical implications of conjunctions in texts, and a concomitant growth in the repertoire of signaling devices learners can recognize and use, constitute one of the components of this transition from "utterance to text." It seems, however, that the relations between utterance and text is not unidirectional, as might be implied by Olson. Rather, with schooling and enhanced reading skills, children's language is transformed. This transformation is fostered by reading, and in turn, it enhances reading comprehension further (Chall, 1991; Cunningham & Stanovich, 1991; Vellutino, Scanlon, Small, & Tanzman, 1991).

From the perspective of development in oral language, numerous studies in the 1970s and 1980s explored comprehension and use of connectives such as *and, but, because, then,* and *if* (see following sections). Research interest has focused primarily on how adults use coherence markers such as conjunctions in reading and writing continues to this day (e.g., Sanders, Janssen, van der Pool, Schilperoord, & van Wijk, 1996). Less is known, however, about how young school children come to understand and use conjunctions when they read texts. This chapter focuses on a critical period in school children's literacy development, a period where they shift from "learning to read" to "reading to learn" (Chall, 1996).

The remainder of this chapter consists of five sections. The first section, which revolves around school children's oral language, provides an overview of developmental research showing that with schooling, children's understanding of the logical implications of conjunctions continues to grow; cognitive factors associated with this growth are also discussed. The second section describes a study concerned with how the conclusions we draw about children's comprehension of logical relations might differ as a function of content familiarity and reading level. The chapter then shifts, in the third section, to an overview of research on comprehension of logical relationships in texts. This is followed, in the fourth section, with a detailed account of a study involving comprehension of logical relationships in narrative and expository texts, where the familiarity theme is tackled again. The concluding section offers a discussion of some theoretical and applied implications of the body of research addressed.

CONJUNCTIONS IN CHILDREN'S ORAL LANGUAGE

Conclusions that can be drawn from the research on children's comprehension and use of conjunctions in their oral language are that this development is not random, that it continues to develop throughout the school years, and that semantic and structural complexity may determine this developmental course. For example, there is evidence of conjunction use in the spoken language of 3- and 4-year-old children (Johansson and Sjolin, 1975; Miller, 1973). Yet, Inhelder and Piaget (1974) argued that appropriate conjunction use requires the ability to logically manipulate several terms, a skill that is clearly not developed yet at the age of 4. Neimark and Slotnik (1970) brought evidence to support this latter argument. They reported that only in Grade 4 could the majority of students understand *and* as expressing class interaction, and only in college the meaning of *or* as expressing class union. Katz and Brent (1968) found that *and* appears earlier and is more accurately used at all ages than is *but,* which is described by Halliday and Hasan (1976) as incorporating the logical meaning of *and* and an "adversative" meaning.

More recently studies have been conducted with preschool children at 3, 4, and 5 years of age that examine the use of coordinating conjunctions (e.g., *and, but*, or *so*) and subordinating conjunctions (e.g., *because, since, until, when*) regarded as literate language features in oral narratives. Work by Curenton and Justice (2004) shows how African American and Caucasian preschoolers have already acquired a decontextualized language characteristic of the development of literacy and indicates an age effect for children's use of conjunctions. Greenhalgh and Strong (2001) also look at literate language features in spoken narratives. They also find these features in the speech of 7- and 10-year-olds and identified conjunctions as a significant measure that differentiates school-age children with typical language from those with language impairments. In another still more recent study, Cain, Patson, and Andrews (2005) found the understanding of conjunctions to express additive, temporal, causal adversative relationships "is still developing long after these terms are used correctly in children's speech" (p. 877)—as children make the transition to text processing.

There is evidence that the more semantically complex a lexical item is, the later it is acquired. A case in point is a study by McClure and Steffenson (1980), who tested children in Grades 4, 6, and 8, and found that the positive conjunctions *and* and *because* were acquired before their correspondingly negative counterparts *but* and *even though*. Likewise, Schdnick and Wing (1982) found in a developmental study of 9-, 11-, and 19-year-olds that, in general, the more positive the beliefs the conjunction embodied, the easier its comprehension was. For example, they found that *because* and *although* were mastered before *unless* and *if*.

Additional evidence showing that one of the factors that determines the order of acquisition of conjunctions involves the semantic complexity of these linguistic-cognitive markers comes from Carole's (1986) study, which examined the use of *but* in the narratives told by 4- to 9-year-old children. The youngest children were much more likely to make errors such as mistakenly using *but* when causal or precausal relations exist. Furthermore, although all children used *but* to signal semantic opposition or violation of expectation, the oldest children used *but* proportionately more often to encode more complex contrasts. However, children at all ages used *but* for pragmatic functions such as interrupting the flow of their narrative in order to insert relevant comments and monitor the listener's attention or change the topic. Carole concluded that *but* signals a change in discourse level within a speaker's turn.

The semantic complexity principle is also implicated in children's use of *and*. In everyday language, *and* is often used as a "neutral filler" to relate sequential and causal propositions as well as for additive purposes. It is often used by young children as an "all-purpose" connective to indicate a relationship, without being specific about the exact nature of the logical relationship. This is especially noticeable in oral language but has been observed also in reading and writing tasks with everyday concepts. For example, McClure and Geva (1983) found that children in Grades 3 and 4 will often insert *and* rather than the linguistically more accurate *since* or *but* between two related propositions. Children of this age may understand the meaning of *since* and *but* when they are signaled by oral language devices and contextual cues (Collins & Michaels, 1980; Hirsch, 1977; Widdowson, 1978). What they have to learn is that *and* is used primarily for additive purposes; that languages such as English provide more accurate lexical devices for marking additive, causal, temporal and adversative logical relations; and that such markers are especially important in written language.

Peterson and McCabe (1987) examined the assumption that with development, children should use *and* less to express logical relationships for which more specific connectives exist and that it should be increasingly reserved for simple coordination. For this purpose, they examined narratives produced by 4- to 9-year-old children. Contrary to expectations, *and* was not used differently by 9-year-olds than by 4-year-olds, and simple coordination constituted no more than 20% of the relationships. Peterson and McCabe concluded that within this age range, *and* is used to indicate cohesion between sentences, without regard to semantic relationship.

Several studies suggest that knowledge of conjunctions develops in two phases: First, conjunctions such as *but, because,* and *although* come to be understood as marking the relation between clauses in terms of a logical relations independent of order of mention. Later, they come to be understood as marking the focus or topical relations between sentences. Evidence for the characteristics of the first stage comes from studies focusing on children's oral language, as well as studies focusing on comprehension of orally presented information. For instance, Bullock and Gelman (1978) found that preschool children rely on temporal ordering as a cue to causality (i.e., cause before effect), though their verbal explanations lag behind their nonverbal behavior. Seven-year-old children, on the other hand, are also able to articulate their beliefs regarding an assumption of unidirectional order in reasoning about causality. In a related study, Bebout, Segalowitz, and White (1980) reported that 5-year-old children have no difficulty in comprehending sentences where order of mention of the surface form corresponds to order in the real world (e.g., "I pushed Sarah *so* she fell"). Yet, only by Grade 4 is there a near-perfect comprehension of sentences where the surface form does not fit the order of events (e.g., "Sarah fell *because* I pushed her"). Relatedly, French (1985b) assessed children's comprehension of *because* and *so* on enactment and sentence completion of causal connectives. It appears then that understanding of such relational terms is initially context dependent and that with accompanying linguistic and literacy development, children learn to understand these relations in context independent situations.

The second phase in conjunction use concerns the understanding that conjunctions mark the focus or topical relations between sentences. It was explored by McClure and Geva (1983) in a study focusing on the ability of Grade 4, Grade 6, and highly literate adults to attend to and handle the differential role played by *but* and *although* in marking focus and coherence in two-clause sentences. Consider for instance:

(1) The box was light but it was large.

(2) The box was light although it was large.

(a) So it was hard to hold.

(b) So it was easy to lift.

Participants were asked to read different combinations of two-proposition sentences such as (1) and (2), conjoined by either *but* or *although,* and to choose one of two options to continue each sentence (consider [a] and [b] above). Grade 4 children often ignored altogether the nature of the conjunctions used and chose a continuation on the basis of salience of one of the two propositions, regardless of order of mention and the conjunction used. By Grade 6, children paid more attention to form and cohesion, but for them cohesion was determined mainly on the basis of semantic proximity. For instance, in the previous example, they would choose option (a) as a continuation to sentence (1) and (2) alike. Only participants in the highly literate adult group showed that they considered jointly coherence and focus marking requirements. That is, they considered simultaneously two implicit linguistic rules, namely, that typically one elaborates on what was stated last, but that in addition, one should elaborate on the main clause. In other words, they concurred with the younger children regarding sentence (1), but they preferred option (b) as a continuation of sentence (2). This pattern revealed that concomitant with highly developed reading and writing skills, one becomes sensitive to differential focus marking (e.g., that *but* is a coordinating conjunction, and *although* is a subordinating conjunction) and to subtle rules governing how coherence can be achieved (e.g., that typically one elaborates on what was stated last; however, in the case of subordination, the main clause should be elaborated on, regardless of position). Given this background, the next section describes a study that probed the role of background knowledge and reading skills in children's comprehension of conjunctions that often occur in children's oral language.

COMPREHENDING *AND*, *BUT*, AND *BECAUSE* IN WRITTEN SENTENCES—A STUDY

This section describes a study that focused on young, school-age children's comprehension of familiar and unfamiliar logical relationships. The focus was on high-frequency conjunctions that occur in oral as well as written language. To probe children's "deep" comprehension of causal (*because*), adversative (*but*), and additive (*and*) relationships, a two-step task was employed. Children had to first read a two-clause sentence and choose a conjunction that best completes it (see, e.g., 3a and 4a). They were then asked to read and choose one of two paraphrases that would best fit the sentence they had just completed (see 3b and 4b). It was assumed that this metalinguistic task would provide a stringent measure of children's comprehension of logical relationships. That is, those children who would be able to select an elaboration that was congruent with their initial choice of a conjunction in (a) would display more advanced comprehension of the logical implications of conjunctions than children who would be unable to select a continuation in (b), whose meaning was congruent with the meaning of the first (completed) sentence. This procedure was designed to alleviate the criticism that children can more accurately handle conjunctions with familiar materials just because they can apply "unanalyzed routines" (Bialystok & Ryan, 1986; Vygotsky, 1962) or what has also been called a "good-enough approach" (Fereira, Bailey, & Farrero, 2002; Sanford, 2002). By requiring children to reflect on the extent to which the meaning created in the first step was mirrored in the elaboration in the second step, we assumed that an application of unanalyzed routines across the board was restricted, thus reflecting more accurately children's deep concepts of logical relationships.

Method

Forty children attending public school in a working-class neighborhood in a small industrial town in Ontario, Canada, participated in the study. The majority of people in this town are employed in car manufacturing plants, the prime employers in the town. Ten boys and 10 girls were randomly selected from each of three Grade 3 classrooms and one Grade 5 classroom, in one school. All children spoke English as their first language. Prior to the application of the random sampling procedure, teachers were asked to indicate whether any of the children in their respective classrooms had a known exceptionality which would seriously hinder their ability to read independently. Three such children were identified in the Grade 3 cohort and one in the Grade 5 cohort. These children were not included in the study. The Gates-MacGinitie Reading Comprehension Test (Gates & MacGinitie, 1978) was administered on a group basis to differentiate skilled from less-skilled readers.

Altogether, each child had to complete 48 sentences (24 familiar and 24 unfamiliar). Twenty-four of the sentences were based on *familiar* content. That is, the content and the relations in the sentences would be familiar to Grade 3 and Grade 5 children alike (see 3a). The 24 familiar items were common to the Grade 3 and Grade 5 children. An additional 24 items were composed of *unfamiliar* content; that is, the information presented in these sentences was new to the children (see illustration in example 4a). The material for these sentences was taken from Grade 4 and Grade 6 science curricula for the Grade 3 and Grade 5 groups, respectively. The 24 unfamiliar items were different for Grade 3 and Grade 5 children. The familiar and unfamiliar sentences were organized into booklets—two for Grade 3 and two for Grade 5. In each familiarity condition, four sentences could be correctly completed with the conjunctions *and*, *but*, and *because*, respectively. In each grade level, children were tested individually, in two testing sessions. In each session, they completed randomly ordered familiar and unfamiliar items (12 of each).

Familiar (common to Grade 3 and 5)

3(a) The painting of flowers was given first prize (*because, and, but*) all the judges thought the painting was beautiful. (*because* correct response)

3(b) (I) Does this sentence tell you that some people didn't think the painting was beautiful? (i.e., adversative interpretation), or

(ii) Does this sentence tell you that the judges gave the prize to the most beautiful picture? (i.e., causal interpretation)

Unfamiliar (Grade 6)

4(a) There is stored plant energy in trees (*and, because, but*) when we burn wood we release the plant energy. (*and* correct response)

4(b) (I) Does this sentence tell you that we burn wood to use up plant energy? (i.e., causal interpretation), or

(ii) Does this sentence tell you that after we burn trees we won't have plant energy? (i.e., additive interpretation)

The frequency of correct conjunction choice and the number of times that the selection of an elaboration was congruent with the choice of a conjunction were the dependent variables. In what follows, the first measure will be referred to as *Choice* scores and the second as *Congruence* scores. The analyses examined the effects of content familiarity (familiar/unfamiliar), developmental level (Grade 3/Grade 5) and reading level (High/Low) on performances on Choice and Congruence scores. In addition, the effects of familiarity and reading level on performance on each of the three conjunction types was analyzed in order to examine the extent to which reading level and familiarity interacted differently with mastery of each of these linguistic-cognitive markers.

Results

The first area of interest concerns the effects of developmental level (i.e., grade), familiarity, and type of logical relationship on Choice scores. Statistical analyses (3-way ANOVA) of Choice scores indicated that Grade 5 children could more accurately insert conjunctions than Grade 3 children ($p < .05$). Furthermore, children could more accurately insert correct conjunctions in items drawn from familiar domains than in items drawn from unfamiliar domains ($p < .05$) (see Fig. 11.1).

Of high interest is the finding that in the unfamiliar condition, the difference between the two grade levels was not significant. In other words, the difference between grades was apparent only with familiar items taken from everyday events. Recall that the familiar items were common to the two age groups. These results show that even when the content is familiar, Grade 5 children can more accurately insert the correct "connecting word." However, when the content of the statements is unfamiliar, 8- to 10-year-old children are equally challenged. In other words, it would be inaccurate to conclude that just because 8- to 10-year-old children use words such as *and, but,* and *because* in their oral language, they can fully contemplate the logical aspects of logical relations. It appears that when the task involves less familiar content, task demands are increased.

Figure 11.2 presents graphically the significant relationships between familiarity condition and type of logical relationships for Choice (and Congruence) scores. As can be noted, in the familiar condition, the means for *and, but,* and *because* were almost identical. However, *because* was more often chosen correctly than *but* and *and* in the unfamiliar condition ($p < .05$). That is, the relative difficulty of *but* and *and* over *because* was revealed when item content was unfamiliar, but not when content was familiar. The fact that children do better in unfamiliar contexts on *be-*

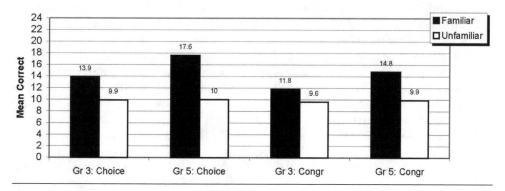

Figure 11.1. Effects of Grade and Familiarity on Choice and Congruence Scores.

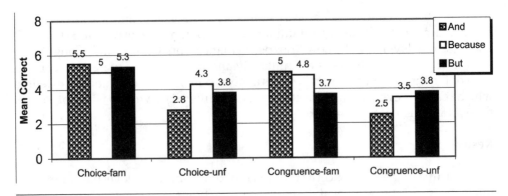

Figure 11.2.   Effects of Familiarity on Comprehension of *and, because,* and *but* in Choice and Congruence Tasks.

cause than on *but* and *and* and suggests that by the time they reach middle school, linguistic knowledge associated with *because* is more advanced than that for *and* and *but*, presumably because it is cognitively less demanding (Fabian, 1982). In the fourth section of this chapter, this theme is examined further in relation to the processing of logical relationships in connected discourse.

The discussion turns now to a description of the effects of developmental level (i.e., grade), familiarity, and type of logical relationship on Congruence scores. In general, these effects mirror those noted for the Choice scores. The (three-way) ANOVA for Congruence scores yielded also significant main effects for grade ($p <$ .05) and familiarity ($p < .01$). Grade 5 children could choose congruent elaborations more accurately than Grade 3 children. Furthermore, as can be seen in Figure 11.1, Congruence scores were higher with familiar items than with unfamiliar items, a result mirroring the pattern noted with Choice scores.

Further analyses explored the source of the significant interaction between familiarity and logical relationship. Congruence scores were higher when children dealt with *and* and *because* taken from familiar domains, than when these relationships were embedded in an unfamiliar domain ($p < .05$). However, Congruence scores for *but* were similar in both the familiar and unfamiliar condition. Indeed, as can be seen in Figure 11.2 the facilitating effect of domain familiarity was noted for *and* and *because* but less so for *but* relationships, which seemed to be equally difficult to the target group regardless of the extent to which item content was familiar or unfamiliar ($p < .05$).

To examine the role played by reading level, participants were divided into two groups according to their scores on the reading comprehension test: Lower than the 50th percentile (low/less-skilled) and higher than the 50th percentile (high/skilled). The ANOVA on number of correct Choice scores yielded a significant main effect for reading level ($p < .05$). That is, in each grade skilled readers achieved higher Choice scores than children in the less-skilled group.

The ANOVA involving the effect of reading level on Congruence scores yielded somewhat more complex results. As was the case with Choice scores, skilled readers outperformed less-skilled readers in each grade level ($p < .05$). Furthermore, there was a significant interaction of reading level by familiarity ($p < .05$), and a triple interaction of grade by reading level by logical relationship ($p < .05$). In addition, there was a significant difference between skilled and less-skilled readers in the familiar condition ($p < .05$) but not in the unfamiliar condition. As can be noted in Figure 11.3, in Grade 3, the Congruence scores for *and*, *but*, and *because* items within each reading level did not differ significantly from each other, even though the reading level advantage was maintained. In Grade 5, there was more differentiation—the older, Grade 5, skilled readers could handle additive items as well as causal ones. The performance of Grade 5 children who were less-skilled readers, however, indicated that they had not mastered the additive relationships. At the same time, regardless of reading level, even in grade 5 children continued to have difficulty with adversative relationships signaled by *but*.

Discussion

The purpose of this study was to examine a number of variables which might contribute to school children's comprehension of logical relationships and the linguistic means used to express such relationships. This study has demonstrated that familiarity with content is an important contributing factor. When comprehension of logical relationships is tested with simple sentences, based on common everyday experience, 8- to 10-year-old children are much more accurate in demonstrating their ability to use productively logical connectives, than when they face materials which draw on academic and unfamiliar content. In the latter case, children have to first analyze the meaning of each sentence and then infer a possible logical relationship that might hold between sentences. This is presumably carried out on the basis of this analysis and on the basis of linguistic or other relevant content knowledge that they may have. This cognitive-linguistic task puts heavy demands on their processing resources. With novel materials and no prior factual knowledge about the content of the basic propositions or about the logical relationships between sets of propositions, the performance of children in both age groups is taxed.

The relative advantage that children have with familiar materials cannot be attributed simply to the application of unanalyzed routines, since the facilitating effect of familiar content was noted also with the more stringent Congruence scores.

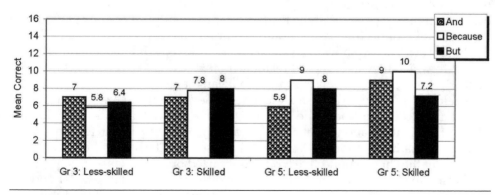

Figure 11.3. Effects of Grade and Reading Level on *and*, *because*, and *but* Congruence Scores.

To succeed in choosing a paraphrase congruent with the logical relationships expressed through the choice of a conjunction is a demanding task which cannot be performed without reflection by simply applying "automatic" routines. French (1985a) maintains that 3- to 5-year-old children first manifest comprehension of *before, after, because, so, if, but,* and *or* when they function to express a relationship which is already known. With development they gradually come to use relational terms as the basis for establishing representations of previously unknown connections (see also Nelson & Gruendel, 1981). The present study supports French's contextual model and extends it to middle-school children. It is significant in that it shows that the comprehension of high frequency lexical items such as *but, because,* and *and,* which are so common in children's oral language, is not complete even when children are eight to ten years old. Moreover, growth in the ability to fully understand and use successfully these connecting words progresses in a piecemeal fashion, and is related to reading and developmental level. This observation implies that children's ability to determine logical relationships in tasks involving connected discourse might also depend on familiarity with content and reading level. This latter point is the focus of the study described in the next section.

CHILDREN'S USE OF CONJUNCTIONS IN TEXTS

The previous section was concerned with issues pertaining to the semantic complexity of various logical connectives, and described is some detail a study demonstrating that certain aspects of logical connectives are mastered later in children's oral language. Mastery of specific semantic and syntactic considerations (e.g., focus and subordination; causality and order) are acquired gradually, and it is possible to differentiate between children by increasing task demands. One way of increasing task demands is achieved by observing linguistic performance in decontextualized contexts and by controlling for degree of familiarity. In this section the focus of the discussion shifts to an examination of how school children comprehend logical relationships in the texts they read, and what might be some intra-child and text factors which constrain or enhance the comprehension of logical relationships in text.[1]

In written discourse (as well as in oral language) logical relations are not always made explicit by the use of conjunctions or other specialized linguistic markers (Chafe, 1985; Geva & Olson, 1983; Kress, 1982). What happens when various logical relations are implicit? Will the readers infer these implicit relations in order to perform "text connecting" as part of the comprehension process?

There is evidence to show that skilled and less-skilled adult readers differ in the degree to which they infer logical relations in text (Geva, 1983). There is also evidence that university students who are second language learners find it more taxing to infer logical relations in expository texts (e.g., Geva, 1993).[2] Likewise, Sanders and Noordman (2000) and Noord and Vonk (1998) have shown that texts that reflect explicitly causal information enhance the processing of information in text. In a study with undergraduate students, Maury and Teisserenc (2005) found evidence that presence of the causal connective *because* optimized online text readings.

Turning to children, Irwin (1980) examined the effects of clause order and explicitness of causal conjunctions on the comprehension of reversible causal relationships by fifth-grade and college students. She reported that fifth-grade students achieved higher comprehension scores when causal relationships were explicitly marked in the texts than did students who read the same texts but with the conjunctions removed. She also found that when the causal relationships appeared in the text in a reversed order, explicitness of causal relationships facilitated comprehension even for adults. Complementary results were also reported by Geva and Ryan (1985); Horowitz (1982, 1987); Marshall and Glock (1978–1979); Meyer, Brandt and Bluth (1980); Meyer (2003); and Pretorius (1996). In general, it seems that explicitly marked logical relations facilitate text comprehension for young school children, for less-skilled readers and for second language learners. As a corollary, one finds that older learners, good readers and highly proficient second language learners can infer logical relations in texts with less difficulty (e.g., Degand & Sanders, 2002; McClure & Geva, 1983; Pretorius, 1996; Sanders & Noordman, 2000).

Disentangling Prior Knowledge From Knowledge of Conjunctions

The degree to which comprehension may be enhanced by noticing and processing the logical-cohesive properties of conjunctions in text may depend on the availability of relevant prior knowledge in a given domain. There is evidence from adult-based research that presence of relational markers in text enhances text comprehension when background knowledge is controlled (Degand & Sanders, 2002).

When texts deal with familiar events, it should be easier to infer implicit logical relations than when no such familiarity can be assumed. Consider the three examples in the following section. In (5) the causal relations may be inferred without too much effort: Being hungry caused John to prepare a sandwich.

(5) John was hungry. He made himself a sandwich.

(6) John was hungry. He went to bed.

(7) The rat was hungry. It pressed the lever.

Even for (6) one may be able to construct a logical temporal-causal framework: John was poor, he had no money to buy food so he tried to pass the time by sleeping, or perhaps, John was too weak to stay awake. However, unless one knows something about learning theories, one is unlikely to infer the causal relations implied in (7) between being hungry and pressing a lever, even if there is a parallel between order of mention and order of events in the statement.

Flores D'Arcais (1978) makes a similar distinction between familiar ("real life") and unfamiliar events. In discussing studies which claim that children notice causation within a story framework (Brown & French, 1976; Stein, 1978) Flores D'Arcais argues that children probably respond on the basis of familiarity with content rather than on the basis of an explicit analysis of the logical relations involved. He maintains that complete comprehension of causation is reached when children can perform metalinguistic tasks in decontextualized situations (see also Vygotsky, 1962).

Theories of cognitive development suggest that the development of cognitive abilities may be characterized as a process of "gradual decontextualization" (e.g., Brown, Bransford, Ferrara, & Campione, 1983; Gee, 1999; Heath, 1983; Karmiloff-Smith, 1992; Olson, 1994). In general, the argument is that the child gradually becomes able to separate competence developed in particular contexts and apply it more widely. It follows from this analysis that even if children use and comprehend in a more or less age-appropriate manner conjunctions in their oral language, they may continue to experience difficulties in comprehending logical relationships in texts, especially when the content of the text is unfamiliar and de-contextualized. When the conjunctions are not explicitly marked, and the child has to infer the relationships in order to comprehend and learn from text the task may become too difficult. This argument extends a notion proposed in the context of oral language development to written language contexts. In the context of examining the development of conjunction use in oral language it has been argued that it is not only lexical knowledge which needs to develop, but also the ability of the child to coordinate available lexical knowledge with cognitive demands associated with the task (Fabian, 1982; French, 1985a, 1985b; Geva, 1986). Indeed, it is safe to assume that normally achieving school children are familiar with *because* and *but* and use them appropriately in their oral language. It is also clear that with exposure to expository materials in reading and writing assignments learners might expand their repertoire to include synonyms to *because* and *but* such as *due to*, and *nevertheless*. Their word schemata (Nagy & Scott, 1990) might expand to include the knowledge that unlike *because* and *but*, *due to*, and *nevertheless* occur more frequently in expository texts than in narratives or informal oral language contexts (Geva, 1986, 1987). Such trends may have important implications for what learners at different developmental levels and with varying degrees of reading proficiency can be expected to learn from less than perfect authentic texts, that is, in texts where logical relationships are sometimes implied rather than stated explicitly. This difficulty may be exacerbated by the challenges of shifting form the reading of narratives to the reading of expository texts in middle school.

Text Genres

A number of studies have focused on the importance of causal reasoning during comprehension (e.g., Sanders & Noordman, 2000; Trabasso, Secco, & van den Broek, 1984; van den Broek & Trabasso, 1986). What we learn from these studies is that readers can infer logical relations when they read unfamiliar narratives. Narratives usually deal with familiar and meaningful events. One may assume therefore that it is relatively easy to infer logical relations that are implicit in narratives, even when these narratives are unfamiliar to the reader. What is less clear is the extent to which the same readers can infer logical relations when they read unfamiliar texts about unfamiliar facts. In particular, when school children read expository texts dealing with unfamiliar content, they may be less able to infer implicit logical relations, because prior relevant knowledge is less likely to be available.

This analysis suggests that a child's ability to comprehend logical relationships and to infer them when such relationships are not explicitly signaled may vary as a function of text genre. This may be so because the middle-school child has less experience with expository text processing, limited domain-relevant knowledge and, as shown in the previous section, less developed analyzed routines (Bialystok & Ryan, 1986) for texts which are not of the narrative type. It follows that even if children show that they are able to comprehend and infer logical relationships under less onerous conditions, they may not be as successful when they have to read and learn from expository texts. This view is supported by Singer and O'Connell (2003) in their study that examined the impact of the presence of connectives in the inference processes involved in the comprehension of expository texts. They found that successful inference of meaning was dependent on causal connectives. This difficulty may illustrate the challenges facing children as the focus of literacy programs shifts from "learning to read," a prominent target in the primary grades to "reading to learn" in middle-school and beyond (Chall, 1996; Vellutino, 1991).

CONSTRAINTS ON THE COMPREHENSION OF LOGICAL RELATIONS IN TEXTS—A STUDY

Previous sections reviewed studies showing that even though children use conjunctions spontaneously in their oral language, they are challenged when asked to consider and evaluate the meaning of such relationships in metalinguistic, decontextualized contexts. What happens when children read naturally occurring texts? Do they perform more successfully when context is available? Or is the task just as challenging? Would their comprehension be enhanced with the more familiar narrative genre than with expository texts? Is it an all-or-none phenomenon or does it matter what type of logical relationship is the target? Do skilled and less-skilled readers respond differentially to these conditions? To address these questions, I provide in this section an overview of a study concerned with children's comprehension of logical relationships in authentic texts. The objective was to tease apart linguistic and developmental determinants of knowledge of conjunctions from prior knowledge and reading proficiency, by studying the comprehension of additive (*and*), causal (*because*) and adversative (*but*) relations in narrative and expository texts of Grade 3 and 5 children.

Method

Participants were 45 Grade 3 and 42 Grade 5 students from two schools in a working-class, small industrial town in Ontario, Canada. Both schools were located in the same neighborhood, and all the children spoke English as their first or best language. At each grade level students were randomly sampled from two classes per school. An equal number of boys and girls were sampled from each class. Prior to the application of the sampling procedure in each class home-room teachers were asked to identify children with a known exceptionality (e.g., reading disability, hearing impairment) which might hinder their ability to work independently on reading comprehension tasks. Altogether, one such child was identified in Grade 3 and 2 in Grade 5. These children were not included in the participant pool to which the random sampling procedure was applied. The Gates-MacGinitie Reading Comprehension Test (Gates & MacGinitie, 1978) was administered on a group basis within each grade level in order to differentiate skilled from less-skilled readers.

For each grade level, 4 expository (social studies; sciences) and 4 narrative, one-page texts were selected. Within each text type the topic of two texts was assumed to be familiar to students at that particular grade level (e.g., "Sleeping beauty wakes up" for a Grade 3 narrative; "City Neighborhoods" for a Grade 3 expository, descriptive text) and the topic of two texts was assumed to be unfamiliar (e.g., "The Dog Gellert" for a Grade 3 narrative; "The Hare Indians" for a Grade 3 expository, descriptive text). Familiarity was determined by consulting school teachers and the curriculum guidelines in these schools.

Each text could appear in an *explicit* condition (i.e., all conjunctions available in the text) or *implicit* condition (i.e., all conjunctions removed). Following each text students had to answer three multiple-choice, comprehension questions focusing on causal and adversative relations. The relations were either implied or explicitly marked in the texts, and children were to answer the questions without looking back at the text. It was expected that in the implicit condition children would have to infer the logical relationship in order to answer correctly the comprehension questions, whereas in the explicit condition children could rely on explicit linguistic markers to aid them in forming a representation of the relationships between specific text segments in the course of reading. Each participant read four texts which were either familiar or unfamiliar. Regardless of familiarity condition, each participant read two narratives and two expository texts. Furthermore, within each text type each child read one text with the conjunctions intact (explicit) and one from which the conjunctions were removed (implicit). Order of texts was counterbalanced and different children were assigned on a random basis to a particular combination of texts. The Gates MacGinitie Reading Test (Gates & MacGinitie, 1978) was administered to Grade 3 and 5 students to obtain an independent evaluation of children's reading comprehension skills. Children who read below the 50th percentile were considered as less-skilled readers, and children who read above the 50th percentile were considered as skilled readers.

Results

ANOVAs indicated that, as might be expected, in general, Grade 5 students and skilled readers had higher comprehension scores than Grade 3 students and students in the less-skilled reading group ($p < .01$). Furthermore, as predicted, students had higher comprehension scores on narratives than on expository texts.

As can be seen in Figure 11.4, the effect of text was not consistent; rather, on familiar topics (which were different for each grade level) the comprehension level was significantly higher in Grade 5 than it was in Grade 3 ($p < .05$). On the other hand, on unfamiliar topics (which were also different for each grade level) there was no difference between the two grade levels. In other words, the two grade levels differed from each other in the predicted direction on familiar topics but not on unfamiliar topics. These results suggest that when confronted with familiar topics Grade 5 children are better able to utilize their prior knowledge than Grade 3 children. However, when content is novel, in both age groups children are challenged by the need to note and process logical relationships. It is important to note that these results emulate the pattern described in the previous section where performance on discrete items was targeted.

Statistical analyses designed to explore the nature of the significant interaction between reading level, text genre, and text manipulation are summarized graphically in Figure 11.5. These analyses revealed that skilled readers had higher comprehension scores than less-skilled readers ($p < .05$) when they read narrative-explicit or expository-implicit texts. Furthermore, less-skilled readers had significantly higher scores when they read expository-explicit texts than when they read expository-implicit texts ($p < .05$). Notably, when less-skilled readers read narrative-implicit or narrative-explicit texts their scores were higher than

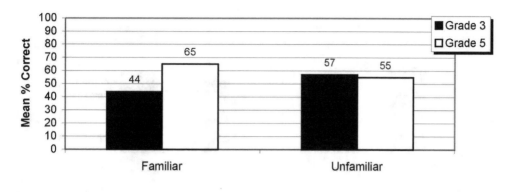

Figure 11.4.   Effects of Familiarity on Comprehension of Logical Relationships in Text.

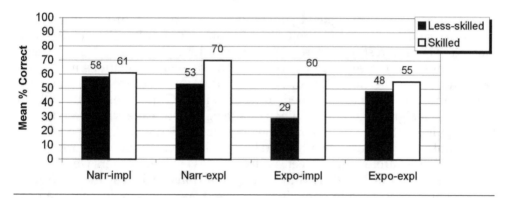

Figure 11.5.   Effects of Reading Level, Genre, and Conjunction Manipulation on Text Comprehension.

when they read expository-implicit texts ($p < .05$). In sum, the comprehension of logical relations was drastically impaired when less-skilled readers tackled expository texts from which conjunctions were removed. Such drastic differences were not noted however among skilled readers, whose performance did not fluctuate as much in response to conjunction manipulation or text genre.

Results of the analysis exploring the comprehension of causal and adversative relationships within genre and familiarity conditions are presented graphically in Figure 11.6. As can be seen in Figure 11.6, when children read unfamiliar expository materials, causal relationships were comprehended significantly better than adversative relationships ($p < .05$). Moreover, the advantage in comprehending narratives over expository texts was noticeable when the comprehension questions focused on causal relationships ($p < .05$), with familiar content ($p < .05$), as well as when comprehension questions dealt with adversative relationships in unfamiliar domains ($p < .05$). In short, text comprehension was particularly impaired when the questions addressed adversative relationships and the texts were of the unfamiliar expository type.

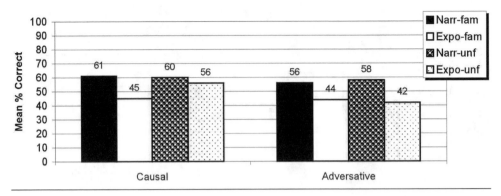

Figure 11.6. Comprehension of Causal and Adversative Relationships as a Function of Genre and Familiarity.

Statistical analyses designed to untangle the significant four-way interaction between grade, reading level, conjunction manipulation and logical relationship yielded some interesting differences (see Fig. 11.7). First, causal relationships were comprehended significantly better than adversative relationships under two conditions: when less-skilled, Grade 5 readers read texts in which logical relationships were explicitly signaled, or when skilled, Grade 5 read texts without such explicit signaling. Second, when Grade 5, skilled readers answered questions dealing with adversative relationships in implicit texts their scores were significantly lower than when these relationships were explicitly marked ($p < .05$). Third, the differences between skilled and less-skilled readers were significant when Grade 3 children had to answer questions dealing with adversative relationships embedded in implicit texts, as well as when Grade 5 children answered such questions embedded in explicit texts ($p < .05$). Finally, Grade 5 children in the low reading level had higher comprehension scores than Grade 3 children in the low reading level only when they had to answer causal questions in explicit texts.

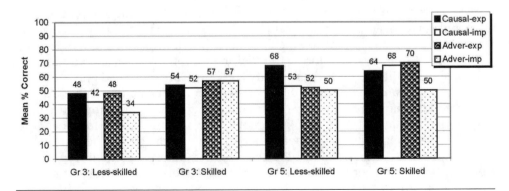

Figure 11.7. Interaction of Grade, Reading Level, Conjunction, Manipulation, and Conjunction Type With Reading Comprehension.

Discussion

This study provides ample support for the hypothesis regarding text genre; children could more easily comprehend logical relationships in narrative texts than in expository texts. Furthermore, while good readers could infer implicit relationships in narratives and in expository texts equally well, this was not the case for less-skilled readers; their comprehension was especially affected when they had to infer logical relationships in expository texts.

Geva and Ryan (1985) report that Grade 5 and 7 children who were good readers were more likely to infer logical relationships in expository texts than were less-skilled readers. In the present study we found that on expository-implicit texts skilled readers in Grade 3 and 5 had higher scores than less-skilled readers. These results support the Geva and Ryan (1985) findings and extend them to younger school-age children. By the time they start to read expository texts in order to learn, children who are more proficient readers are more likely to attend to logical relationships between text segments and to infer relationships that are not explicitly marked. Furthermore, the fact that less-skilled readers are more likely to infer logical relationships in narratives than in expository texts suggests that less-skilled readers *can* infer logical relationships in texts, provided that they deal with a well rehearsed text genre in which meaningful and familiar events have to be interpreted. What they do not do readily is perform "text connecting" when textual prompts are not available and the content is unfamiliar. Additional research is needed to find out why it is that less-skilled readers infer logical relationships embedded in narratives but are less likely to do so with expository, school-like texts. It is possible that in narratives logical relationships are denser so that several nodes are causally linked. As a result, even less-skilled readers have enough instances to build a mental representation of interrelationship between events. This notion has been suggested by van den Broek and Trabasso (1986) to explain story recall. These authors have shown that when the number of causal connections increased, the likelihood of these statements being included in summaries was increased.

One of the questions posed at the onset of the study reviewed here was whether the propensity to infer specific logical relations interacts with text genre, or whether a general strategy determined by age and reading skill explains the ability to use conjunctions in a text, to notice focus, to comprehend logical concepts and to learn from text. The significant interaction involving text genre, topic familiarity and logical relationships, as well as the significant four-way interaction involving grade, reading level, type of logical relationship, and conjunction manipulations, suggest that the answer to this question is not a straightforward one. The first of these two interactions points to the fact that not only do children have, on the whole, more problems in comprehending logical relationships in expository texts, but they find it especially difficult to comprehend adversative relationships in these texts when the topics discussed are unfamiliar to them. A complementary finding was noted in the previous section. Taken together these results suggests that well-developed understanding of adversativeness, as expressing negation of an expected result, is not mastered completely even by Grade 5 children. The fact that children use *but* in their oral language does not mean that they have mastered the linguistic constraints guiding its usage, nor the ability to infer it successfully in text.

Less-skilled Grade 5 readers notice and process causal relationships that are explicitly marked in the text. However, they have difficulties in comprehending adversative relationships even when these are explicitly signaled. The picture for the Grade 5 skilled readers is different. These children can notice and comprehend causal relationships, as well as adversative relationships, as long as the text includes explicit signals which point to these relationships. However, when these relations are implied, and the child has to notice without textual prompts that "text connecting" has to be performed, the task becomes more difficult. Under these circumstances skilled readers can infer causal relationships but fail to accurately infer adversative relationships.

Are less-skilled readers in the younger age group similar to their older counterparts? Our results indicate that a developmental advantage is present in children's ability to note and utilize explicitly marked causal relations in text. However, regardless of age, less-skilled readers' performance was below chance level even when they had to deal with adversative relationships that were explicitly signaled in the texts. Likewise, regardless of age, less-skilled readers did not succeed in answering comprehension questions that focused on implied causal relations.

This study has shown that children's ability to monitor their comprehension by noticing and inferring logical relations in texts varies to some extent as a function of age and reading skill. It has also confirmed the conjecture that, in general, logical relationships in narratives are more likely to be noted and inferred correctly than in expository texts. Most importantly, it has shown that less-skilled readers' comprehension declines especially when logical relationships are not marked explicitly in expository texts. One of the points made in the review of the literature presented in the first section was that in spontaneous language, and under controlled conditions younger children appear to comprehend causal relations before adversative relations. The results of the two studies described here show that this phenomenon continues to exist even once children have begun to expand their repertoire of reading and writing skills. Reading skills, maturational factors, text genre as well as the nature of the specific logical concepts discussed in the text, combine and influence the reading comprehension process in a complex fashion.

CONCLUSIONS

A complex set of interacting variables contributes to children's developing comprehension of logical relationships even when they are expressed by means of highly frequent lexical items which are present often in informal communicative contexts. Children who are proficient readers have an advantage over children whose reading comprehension skills are less developed. The child for whom reading is automatized and the child who can more efficiently perform logical operations involving relations between propositions (Case, 1985) is at an advantage when the reading task involves a complex series of logical operations. Older children appear to be more accurate in noting explicitly expressed logical relations, and more consistent in seeking congruence between the words used to mark linguistic markers and their logical/semantic implications. However, this developmental advantage does not occur in an all-or-none fashion; The linguistic knowledge of conjunctions possessed by 8- to 10-year-old children is not complete. They can demonstrate command of logical relationships expressed by the conjunctions *and, but,* and *because,* provided that contextual scaffolding in the form of domain familiarity and general prior knowledge is available. They are less successful when such scaffolding is unavailable.

Children's command of specific logical relationships continues to develop gradually throughout the school years. A more advanced performance involving the ability to recognize logical relationships and analyze their implications in unfamiliar or arbitrary contexts is first instantiated for causal relationships, and is presumably mastered only later with additive and adversative logical relationships. This observation is valid across tasks varying in the amount of context and analyzed knowledge required—it has been noted in the performance of reading disabled children in oral informal contexts (Geva & Wade-Woolley, 1993), when their attention is explicitly drawn to these relations in sentence combining reading tasks, and even when the task may be characterized as involving incidental attention to logical relationships, as was the case in the text comprehension study.

Clearly, comprehension of logical relationships continues to develop in middle school. It appears that by Grade 5 children have a better understanding and awareness of logical relationships. Their analyzed knowledge of possible relationships between familiar events and the linguistic means of expressing these relationships is more accurate and more differentiated than that of their younger counterparts. In addition, the older children seem to be better able to exercise more control in performing linguistic tasks. This developmental advantage is evident in the familiar domain but is not strong enough yet to be extended across the board with unfamiliar content.

The complexity of the process whereby young school children gradually learn to fully comprehend logical relationships and to take advantage of this comprehension in written language is further illustrated by the interactions between categories of logical relationships, reading level, and developmental level. A more complete command of logical relationships, one that involves an ability to note a particular logical relationship and recognize its alternative reformulation independently of content familiarity, emerges first for causal relationships somewhere between the child's eighth and tenth year. Within this age range however, similar command over adversative and additive relationships has not emerged yet. Instead we see that the ability to choose *but* or *and* accurately is facilitated by domain familiarity. It seems that a more complete concept of additivity, involving the ability to choose a paraphrase compatible with *and* comes to be understood next. This is followed presumably in subsequent years, as a result of exposure and learning and the cumulative effects of reading and writing, by a more complete comprehension of adversative relationships and of the linguistic means for signaling them.

The relationships between reading comprehension and linguistic development are difficult to tease apart, but it is reasonable to assume that they are mutually facilitating, and that over time, the relationships between these two components is mutually facilitating. The more proficient reader has better developed linguistic skills needed for attending to logical relationships and inferring them when necessary. In turn, comprehension of logical relationships, and semantic knowledge of conjunctions promotes comprehension and knowledge acquisition.

The research reviewed here suggests that the child who is beginning to "read in order to learn" from texts is initially more successful in handling logical relations embedded in narratives. At the same time, the child's ability to handle causal and adversative relationships in texts is limited by developmental constraints: causal relationships come to be well understood before adversative relationships, and the child who is a fluent reader is better able to notice and process these relationships when the relationships are explicitly marked, and to infer them when necessary. The less-skilled reader and the younger child need textual supports in the form of explicit conjunctions or other linguistic markers of logical relationships to facilitate comprehension.

Geva (1986) has shown that adversative and causal relations are often only implied in school texts. Relatedly, Davison et al. (1980) compared adult versions of expository texts with simplified versions adapted for younger readers. They argued that one of the results of rigidly applying readability formula is that texts become more difficult, since readers have to infer many of those relations that are considered complex, because the critical conjunctions have been deleted from the text. A similar argument has been made recently by Meyer (2003), who points out that while explicit signaling makes readability ratios higher, it makes reading easier since it is easier to understand coherent texts. It is clear from the research reviewed here that the assumption that these relationships can be easily and automatically inferred by the young child in the course of reading is unwarranted; even skilled readers are not always accurate when they are asked to infer logical relationships in texts. Moreover, as noted above, it is inaccurate to assume that children who use in their oral language words which might be used to signal logical relationships in written language can necessarily comprehend and infer logical relationships in narratives, or that they can automatically extend this knowledge to other, more demanding text genres.

A developmental trend seems to emerge whereby logical relationships are best understood in narrative texts in which logical relationships are explicitly marked, followed by narrative texts in which logical relationships have to be inferred. Expository texts with logical relationships explicitly marked come to be understood next followed by expository texts in which logical relationships have to be inferred.

Implications

One implication of the research reviewed here is that logical relationships in expository texts should be marked explicitly to enhance comprehension. Furthermore, young students, and poor readers, should be explicitly taught to attend to conjunctions in expository texts in order to perform text connecting, and to infer logical relationships when explicit signaling is unavailable.

Typically, school curricula do not provide guidance and suggestions regarding the explicit teaching of logical relationships and "text connecting" techniques. The focus in Grades 1–2 is mainly on "learning how to read," using narratives as the main vehicle of instruction. Once social studies and science become an integral part of the curriculum, the hidden assumption shared by educators is that children already know how to read. The text then becomes a medium for transmitting knowledge. However, texts do not always make explicit logical relationships, and in such cases the child carries the prime responsibility of inferring relationships and performing "text connecting." This may be especially onerous for the learning disabled child or the second language learner. The research reviewed here shows that children do not always engage on their own in seeking the relationships between text segments. Even when they are explicitly asked to determine logical relationships between text segments, children are not always successful. Teachers might use this knowledge to give children opportunities to practice explicitly their comprehension of logical relationships in various oral and written contexts, and to expand their repertoire of useful linguistic markers they may require in reading and writing. Indeed, this recommendation is pertinent to the language and literacy enhancement of English as a second language (ESL) or limited English proficiency (LEP) learners, and to the assessment of children who are at risk of failure because of other debilitating factors such as learning disabilities. Indeed, this recommendation is pertinent to the language and literacy enhancement of English as a second language (ESL) or limited English proficiency (LEP) learners, and to children who are at risk of failure because of other debilitating factors such as learning disabilities. Furthermore, knowledge of connectives may have implications on the assessment of language and speech difficulties. Gillam, Pena, and Miller (1999) describe an alternative assessment tool used by speech language pathologists used to evaluate children's narrative and expository literacy skills. The tool's analysis of narrative literacy was based on oral narratives provided by the student based on a picture/scene shown to the student. Although Dynamic Assessment's analysis of the narratives is wide ranging (e.g., it examines episodic structure, creativity, complexity of ideas), the tool measures Story Productivity (total number of words and total number of clauses). In the analysis of expository discourse, students were shown pictures that a problematic situation. Responses were analyzed (among a wide range of other analyses) to determine the student's understanding of cause and consequence, and to determine grammatical complexity. Grammatical complexity was determined by counting the number and type of clauses. The authors found that when student responses were higher in syntactic complexity, semantic complexity was also heightened (Gillam, Pena, & Miller, 1999).

NOTES

*The research reported in this chapter was partially funded by a grant from the Social Sciences and Humanities Research Council of Canada (Grant # 810-83-0356).
1. Due to space limitations this chapter does not address research pertaining to the use of connectives in writing or to different discourse genres.
2. Note that much of the research in this area has focused on adults.

REFERENCES

Bebout, L. J., Segalowitz, S. J., & White, G. J. (1980). Children's comprehension of casual constructions with "because" and "so." *Child Development, 51,* 565–568.

Bialystok, E., & Ryan, E. B. (1986). Toward a definition of metalinguistic skills. *Merrill-Palmer Quarterly, 31,* 229–264.

Brown, A. & French, L. (1976). Construction and regeneration of logical sequences using cases or consequences as the point of departure. *Child Development, 47,* 930–940.

Brown, A. L., Bransford, J. D., Ferrara, R. A., & Campione, J. C. (1983). Learning, remembering and understanding. In J. H. Flavell & E. M. Markman (Eds.), *Cognitive Development* (pp. 77–166). New York: Wiley.

Bullock, M., & Gelman, R. (1978). Preschool children's assumptions about cause and effect: Temporal ordering. *Child Development, 50,* 89–96.

Cain, K. (2003). Text comprehension and its relation to coherence and cohesion in children's fictional narratives. *British Journal of Developmental Psychology, 21,* 335–351.

Cain, K., Patson, N., & Andrews, L. (2005). Age- and ability-related differences in young readers' use of conjunctions. *Journal of Child Language, 32,* 877–892.

Case, R. (1985). *Intellectual development: Birth to adulthood.* Orlando: Academic Press.

Chafe, W. L. (1985). Linguistic differences produced by differences between speaking and writing. In D. R. Olson, N. Torrance, & A. Hildyard (Eds.), *Literacy, Language and learning* (pp. 105–123). Cambridge: Cambridge University Press.

Chall, J. S., Baldwin, L. E., & Jacobs, V. A. (1990). *The reading crisis: Why poor children fall behind.* Cambridge, MA: Harvard University Press.

Chall, J. S. (1996). *Learning to read: The great debate* (revised ed.). New York: McGraw-Hill.

Clark, E. V. (1971). On the acquisition of the meaning of before and after. *Journal of Verbal Learning and Verbal Behaviour, 10,* 266–275.

Collins, J., & Michaels, S. (1980). The importance of conversational discourse strategies in the acquisition of literacy. In *Proceedings of the Sixth Annual Meeting of the Berkeley Linguistics Society,* Berkeley, CA.

Crothers, E. J. (1978). Inference and coherence. *Discourse Processes, 1,* 51–71.

Cunningham, A. E., & Stanovich, K. E. (1991). Tracking the unique effects of print exposure in children: Associations with vocabulary, general knowledge, and spelling. *Journal of Educational Psychology, 83,* 264–274.

Curenton, S., & Justice, L. (2004). African American and Caucasian preschoolers' use of decontextualized language: Literate language features in oral narratives. *Language, Speech & Hearing Services in Schools, 35*(3), 240–253.

Davison, A., Kantor, R. N., Hannah, J., Hermand, G., Lutz, R., & Salzillo, R. (1980). *Limitations of readability of formulas in guiding adaptations of texts* (Tech. Rep. No. 162). Urbana: University of Illinois, Center for the Study of Reading.

Degand, L., & Sanders, T. (2002). The impact of relational markers on expository text comprehension in L1 and L2. *Reading and Writing: An Interdisciplinary Journal, 15,* 739–757.

Fabian, V. (1982). *Language development after 5: A neo-Piagetian investigation of subordinate conjunctions.* Unpublished doctoral dissertation, University of California, Berkeley.

Ferreira, F., Bailey, K., & Ferraro, V. (2002). Good-enough representations in language comprehension. *Current Directions in Psychological Science, 11,* 11–15.

French, L. A. (1985a). Acquiring and using words to express logical relationships. In S. A. Kuczaj & M. D. Barrett (Eds.), *Development of word meaning* (pp. 303–338). New York: Springer-Verlag.

French, L. A. (1988). The development of children's understanding of "because and "so." *Journal of Experimental Child Psychology, 45*(2), 262–279.

Flores D'Arcais, G. B. (1978). Levels of semantic knowledge in children's use of connectives. In A. Sinclair, R. J. Jarvella, & W. J. M. Levelt (Eds.), *The child's conception of language* (pp. 133–153). New York: Springer-Verlag.

Gates, A. J., & MacGinitie, W. H. (1978). *Gates-MacGinitie Reading Test.* New York: Teacher's College Press.

Gee, J. P. (1999). Critical issues: Reading and the new literacy studies: Reframing the National Academy of Sciences report on reading. *Journal of Literacy Research, 31,* 355–374.

Geva, E. (1983). Facilitating reading comprehension through flowcharting, *Reading Research Quarterly, 18,* 384–405.

Geva, E. (1986). *Knowledge of conjunctions and its role in comprehension.* Final Report submitted to the Social Sciences and Humanities Research Council of Canada.

Geva, E. (1987). *Conjunctions: Their role in facilitating reading expository texts by adult L2 learners.* Final Report submitted to the Social Sciences and Humanities Research Council of Canada.

Geva, E. (1992). The role of conjunctions in L2 text comprehension. *TESOL Quarterly, 26,* 731–747.

Geva, E., & Olson, D. R. (1983). Children's story retelling. *First Language, 4,* 85–110.

Geva, E., & Ryan, E. B. (1985). Use of conjunctions in expository texts by skilled and less skilled readers. *Journal of Reading Behavior, 17,* 331–346.

Geva, E., & Wade-Woolley, L. (1993, December). *Examining the comprehension and expression of logical relationships between propositions in reading disabled and normally-achieving children*. Presented at the annual meeting of the National Reading Conference, Charleston, South Carolina.

Gillam, R., Pena, E., & Miller, L. (1999). Dynamic Assessment of narrative and expository discourse. *Topics in Language Disorders, 20*(1), 33–47.

Greenhalgh, K., & Strong, C. (2001). Literate language features in spoken narratives of children with typical language and children with language impairments. *Language, Speech & Hearing Services in Schools, 32*(2), 114–125.

Guzman, A. (2004). The role of connectives in written discourse. Dissertation Abstracts International, 65, 08B.

Halliday, M. A. K., & Hasan, R. (1977). *Cohesion in English*. London: Longman.

Heath, S. B. (1983). *Ways with words*. Cambridge, England: Cambridge University Press.

Hirsch, E. (1977). *The philosophy of composition*. Chicago: University of Chicago Press.

Horowitz, R. (1982). *The limitations of contrasted rhetorical predicates on reader recall of expository English prose*. Unpublished doctoral dissertation, University of Minnesota.

Horowitz, R., & Samuels, S. J. (1987). Rhetorical structure in discourse processing. In R. Horowitz & S. J. Samuels (Eds.), *Comprehending oral and written language* (pp. 117–155). London: Academic Press, 1–52.

Horowitz, R., & Samuels, S. J. (1987). Comprehending oral and written language: Critical contrasts for literacy and schooling. In R. Horowitz & S. J. Samuels (Eds.), *Comprehending oral and written language* (pp. 1–52). London: Academic Press.

Irwin, W. J. (1980). The effects of explicitness and clause order on the comprehension of reversible casual relationships. *Reading Research Quarterly, 15*, 477–488.

Johansson, B. S., & Sjolin, B. (1975). Preschool children's understanding of the coordinators *and* and *or*. *Journal of Experimental Child Psychology, 19*, 233–240.

Karmiloff-Smith, A. (1992). *Beyond modularity: A developmental perspective on cognitive science*. Cambridge, MA: Bradford Books, MIT press.

Katz, E. W., & Brent, S. B. (1968). Understanding connective. *Journal of Verbal Learning and Verbal Behavior, 7*, 501–509.

Kintsch, W., & Van Dijk, T. A. (1978). Toward a model of text comprehension and production. *Psychological Review, 85*, 363–394.

Kress, G. (1982). *Learning to write*. London: Routledge & Kegan Paul.

Marshall, N., & Glock, M. D. (1978–1979). Comprehension of connected discourse: A study into the relationship between the structure of text and information recalled. *Reading Research Quarterly, 14*, 10–56.

Maury, P., & Teisserenc, _. (2005). The role of connectives in science text comprehension and memory. *Language and Cognitive Processes, 20*(3), 489–512.

McClure, E., & Geva, E. (1983). The development of the cohesive use of adversative conjunctions in discourse. *Discourse Processes, 6*, 411–432.

McClure, E., & Steffensen, M. S. (1980, January). *A study of the use of conjunctions across grades and ethnic groups* (Tech. Rep. No. 158). Urbana: University of Illinois, Center for the Study of Reading. (ERIC Document No. ED182688)

Meyer, B. J. F. (2003). Text coherence and readability. *Topics in Language Disorder, 23*, 204–224.

Meyer, B. F. J., Brandt, D. N., & Bluth, G. J. (1980). Use of author's textual schema: Key for ninth-graders' comprehension. *Reading Research Quarterly, 16*, 72–103.

Miller, W. (1973). The acquisition of grammatical rules by children. In C. A. Ferguson and D. I. Slobin (Eds.), *Studies of child language development*. New York: Holt, Rinehart & Winston.

Millis, K. K., & Just, M. A. (1994). The influence of connectives on sentence comprehension. *Journal of Memory and Language, 33*, 128–147.

Nagy, W. E., & Scott, J. A. (1990). Word Schemas: Expectations about the form and meaning of new words. *Cognition and Instruction, 7*, 105–127.

Neimark, E. D., & Slotnick, N. S. (1970). Development of the understanding of logical connectives. *Journal of Educational Psychology, 61*, 451–460.

Nelson, K., & Gruendel, J. M. (1981). Generalized event representations: Basic building blocks of cognitive development. In M. Lamb & A. L. Brown (Eds.), *Advances in developmental psychology* (Vol. 1). Hillsdale, NJ: Lawrence Erlbaum Associates.

Noord, L. G. M., & Vonk, W. (1998). Memory-based processing in understanding causal information. *Discourse Processes, 26,* 191–212.

Olson, D. R. (1977). From utterance to test: The bias of language in speech and writing. *Harvard Educational Review, 47,* 257–281.

Olson, R. D. (1994). *The world on paper.* New York: Cambridge University Press.

Peterson, C., & McCabe, A. (1987). The connective "and": Do older children use it less as they learn other connectives? *Journal of Child Language, 14,* 375–381.

Pretorius, E. J. (1996). A profile of causal development among ten-year olds: Implications for reading and writing. *Reading and Writing: An Interdisciplinary Journal, 8,* 385–406.

Sanders, T., Janssen, D., van der Pool, E., Schilperoord, J., & van Wijk, C. (1996). Hierarchical text structure in writing products and writing processes. In G. Rijlaarsdam, H. van den Bergh, & Michel Cousijn (Eds.), *Theories, models and methodology in writing research* (pp. 472–493). Amsterdam: Amsterdam University Press.

Sanders, T. J. M., & Noordman, L. G. M. (2000). The role or coherence relations and their linguistic markers in text processing. *Discourse Processes, 29,* 37–60.

Sanford, A. (2002). Context, attention, and depth for processing during interpretation. *Mind & Learning, 17,* 188–206.

Schdnick, E. K., & Wing, C. S. (1982). The pragmatics of subordinating conjunctions: A second look. *Journal of Child Language, 9,* 461–479.

Singer, M., & O'Connell, G. (2003). Robust inference processes in expository text comprehension. *European Journal of Cognitive Psychology, 15*(4), 607–631.

Stein, N. L. (1978). *How children understand stories: A developmental analysis* (Tech. Rep. No. 69). Urbana: University of Illinois. (ERIC Document Reproduction Source No. ED1532-5)

Trabasso, T., Secco, T., & van den Broek, P. (1984). Casual Cohesion and Story Coherence. In H. Mandler, N. L. Stein, & T. Trabasso (Eds.), *Learning and comprehension of text.* Hillsdale, NJ: Lawrence Erlbaum Associates.

Van den Broek, P., & Trabasso, T. (1986). Casual networks versus goal hierarchies in summarizing texts. *Discourse Processes, 9,* 1–15.

Vellutino, F. R., Scanlon, D., Small, S., & Tanzman, M. (1991). The linguistic bases of reading disability: Converting written to oral language. *Text, 11,* 99–133.

Vygotsky, L. S. (1962). *Thought and language.* Cambridge, MA: MIT Press.

Widdowson, H. C. (1978). *Teaching language as communication.* Oxford: University of Oxford Press.

IV

Developing Talk That Interacts With
Text in Domains of Knowledge

CHAPTER 12

Transformative Communication in Project Science Learning Discourse

Joseph L. Polman
Roy D. Pea

TEACHING CHALLENGES AND THE CONSTRUCTIVIST LEARNING PARADOX

How can teachers help their students learn ideas and strategies that are almost completely foreign to the students' experiences? This problem is faced daily by teachers who are trying to help their students learn complex subject matter and tasks such as scientific or historical inquiry. Traditional wisdom would have the teachers simply *tell* their students what they need to know. However, constructivist theory and research, including Piagetian, information-processing, and social constructivist approaches, has done much to emphasize that telling students is not enough to ensure that they have learned something. Instead, the students must construct their own knowledge, perhaps with the teachers' help. Say a teacher is trying to help students learn how to use data from an analysis as evidence to support a claim in scientific inquiry, in a way that seems much different from anything the students have been challenged to do in the past. Popular wisdom, rooted in the work of Dewey (e.g., 1902), would have the teacher ask the students to "learn by doing" within the context of a science research project. Still, if students lack a preexisting foundation of knowledge and experience that can be easily related to the science research project, the teacher's invitation to "do a project" will fall on uncomprehending ears. How can students build this new knowledge when there is seemingly no foundation and few raw materials in their mental toolkit with which to build the desired cognitive structures?

This question is related to a problem sometimes referred to as the "learning paradox." As numerous theoreticians and researchers have pointed out (e.g., Bereiter, 1985; Fodor, 1975, 1980), the commonly held view that knowledge is actively constructed by learners encounters a paradox at a fundamental level. How learners can process information so as to construct new cognitive structures that are more complex than their already existing cognitive structures is unclear. As Fodor (1980) forcefully put it:

> There literally isn't such a thing as the notion of learning a conceptual system richer than the one that one already has; we simply have no idea of what it would be like to get from a conceptually impoverished to a conceptually richer system by anything like a process of learning. (p. 149, cited in Bereiter, 1985)

In this chapter, we argue that a solution to the learning paradox as well as teachers' everyday dilemmas lies in a neo-Vygotskian theory of distributed intelligence and transformative communication. After laying out the theoretical background, we illustrate the use of a specific discourse strategy for transformative communication that has proven particularly useful in teaching-learning situations such as project-based science.

DISTRIBUTED INTELLIGENCE AND THE LEARNING PARADOX

In previous works, Pea (1993b, 2002) has argued that intelligence is more realistically conceived as distributed among persons and the symbolic and physical environment rather than within individual, isolated minds. In addition, intelligence is more aptly viewed as manifest in the dynamics of activity, rather than as static. The distribution of intelligence among persons is often evident in collaborative activity (e.g., Barron, 2003; Roschelle, 1992) and dialogue in parent-child dyads (e.g., Rogoff, 1990)—in many such instances no individual can be said to be the one who has solved a problem or accomplished an activity. One of the most evident examples of this co-constructive activity lies in early language development—the transitional time following the single-word utterance period, and before the regular use of syntactic, multiword utterances, is marked by the collaborative development of full sentences, over speaker turns and across speakers (Ochs, Schieffelin, & Platt, 1979). Consider an example described by Wertsch (1991): A child has lost a toy, and she approaches her father for help. The father does not know where the toy is but asks the child a series of questions that help her structure her search. Did she have it in her room? No. In the yard? No. In the car? That could be. They check and find the toy in the car. It is the child-parent *system* that solved the problem, with unique contributions from both persons that the other did not supply. Numerous researchers and theorists following in the footsteps of Russian sociocultural research (e.g., Leont'ev, 1981; Vygotsky, 1978) have been refining the vision of intelligent action carried out between persons, in what Wertsch (1991) terms the *intermental* realm.

As Pea has recounted in more detail elsewhere (1993b), he was struck by the fact that although many were recognizing the distribution of intelligence across persons, the contribution of designed objects such as physical tools, computer programs, or inscriptional systems such as x-y coordinate graphing to intelligent action was often neglected. Vygotsky (1978) had emphasized the importance of cultural tools in mediating human action, but he had focused on language as a tool. Ironically, given the concreteness of the "tool" metaphor, concrete physical tools and nonverbal but semantically rich representational systems had often been neglected in analyses of distributed cognitive activity. But the integral use of arti-facts such as pencils and lists in everyday cognitive achievements highlights the ubiquity of tools in our surroundings, which have certain sorts of intelligence "built in." Some of our work has focused on how educational designers can build in more effective affordances for cognitive tools such as software designed to sup-port science inquiry (e.g., Edelson, Gordin, & Pea, 1999; Gordin, Polman, & Pea, 1994; Pea, 1993a, 1998) in the geosciences.

In this chapter, and other recent work, we are more directly concerned with the ways in which intelligence is distributed in social arrangements and activity struc-tures that support human learning through "guided participation" (Polman, 2000, in press; Polman & Pea, 2001; Rogoff, 1990). Examples of such arrangements in-clude Palincsar and Brown's (1984) influential model of "reciprocal teaching," in which the teacher places students in roles that divide important aspects of the reading task, supports the accomplishment of those roles, and through repeated activity involving role shifts for students brings the group as a whole to more expert performance.

Strategies such as reciprocal teaching are based on Vygotsky's (1978) "general genetic law of cultural development." Vygotsky held that learners accomplish ac-tivities with the help of more expert others in a social setting—on the intermental (Wertsch, 1991) plane between minds—that the learners could not achieve on their own. This sort of intermental action is for the individual learner what Courtney Cazden (1981) aptly calls "performance before competence." After such perfor-mance, learners can advance their own understanding, on what Wertsch terms the *intramental* plane (i.e., within an individual's mind). The student-and-teacher-act-ing-together-in-the-world thus provides a structure, which the student can then internalize so that the student can later act in a similar fashion without the teacher's help (Cole, 1996). Related considerations apply to the conditions under which an individual may elect to use external representations or tools in the envi-ronment to serve as scaffolds of their own activity, because of the stressful de-mands of the task situation—"internalization" is thus not a trait that an individual develops for a task but a state of the situation (Pea, 2004; also see Glick, 1983), as when an adult uses "egocentric speech" to help plan a complex activity in a noisy situation.

This would seem to provide a solution to the learning paradox: the building blocks for new conceptual structures are not just an individual's concepts in the head but also the sociocultural world and actions in it that can be internalized. As Bereiter (1985) has pointed out, however, there is a catch in the use of the term *in-ternalized*, which Vygotsky's research group also recognized. If the more complex cognitive structures end up being completely "in the head," then their building blocks must also be located there. To some degree, this problem is mitigated by the idea that the memories of action sequences carried out with the support of others could serve as the building blocks themselves, provided the actions are designed in such a way as to scaffold for future "fading" of support (for an exam-ple with reading strategies, see Cole, 1996, pp. 272–280). Researchers rooted in the tradition of computational cognitive modeling of individual minds have been exploring this sort of learning for some time, under the rubric of case-based reasoning (e.g., Kolodner, Gray, & Fasse, 2003; Schank, 1990); they have devel-oped information-processing paradigms whereby the memories of event sequences can be stored, retrieved, and adapted in reasoning about possible future actions.

Regardless of the adequacy of such approaches, we would join others in emphasizing that not all forms of distributed intelligence can reasonably be described as eventually or ideally "internalized" (e.g., Hutchins, 1993, 1995; Pea, 1993b, 2004; Wertsch, 1998). To take Hutchins's oft-cited example, the idea that the navigation of a large naval vessel is or should be meaningfully located in one individual's head verges on nonsensical: The carrying out of navigation is always and always should be embedded within a distributed social and material-technical system. In the social realm, many persons playing complementary roles are necessary, and in the material realm, a great deal of specialized equipment with embedded intelligence of various sorts is necessary. Exploitation in the real-time achievement of intelligent activity is also required.

Due to consideration of cases such as navigation, and the ongoing importance of context and tools for much intelligent action, many researchers have come to prefer terms such as *appropriation* (Brown et al., 1993; Pea, 1992; Rogoff, 1990) and/or *mastery* (Wertsch, 1998) rather than *internalization*. Unlike internalization, the terms *appropriation* and *mastery* do not imply that residuals "in the head" are unsupported by tools in the world. Some sort of mental representations are appropriated by individuals intramentally and can be applied across multiple contexts, but the mental representations do not do the work of cognition alone. Because much of the complexity of cognitive achievements *always* remains in the cultural and material world, the learning paradox is not necessarily a problem. There are continually dialectical processes in which the "internal uses" of cognitive structure are complemented by the affordances of external tools, representations and features of the physical as well as social environments in which the learner operates. The tools that an individual needs to carry out actions may not be available in all settings, but part of what humans do is create or arrange their environments so that not all the work to be done requires mental gymnastics (Pea, 1993b). Further, it is important to note that the individual mental representation involved in mastery of a tool does *not* require a full description of a tool's complexity. In other words, the understanding of how tools work is not necessary for their mastery. For example, we do not have to understand how our computers work at the electronics level or even the programming level to use our word processors in an expert way. Recalling Cazden's (1981) phrase "performance before competence," we are emphasizing that "competence" does not always imply complete understanding of all aspects of the performance; rather, the person's contribution to intelligent action must "dovetail" (Clark, 1997) with the tool's affordances. Dovetailing effectively with tools in the world does not require that we have complete copies of tools and how they work in our heads (Clark, 1997). We may have to understand a good deal of how the computer and software works to *invent* the word processor from scratch, but as James Burke's *Connections* series (1995) remind us, even inventions often involve the combination of existing ideas and devices in new ways, with or without an understanding of the parts' origins and operation. The re-usability of intelligent tools designed for certain purposes is the great insight of object-oriented programming: Code that performs certain operations does not have to constantly be reinvented but instead can be invoked from within multiple contexts.

TRANSFORMATIVE COMMUNICATION IN GUIDED PARTICIPATION

Although the learning paradox may not be a philosophical problem given this neo-Vygotskian viewpoint, how to support learners so that they can appropriate some valued aspects of activity is a constant dilemma for teachers. In Vygotsky's (1978) terminology, the *zone of proximal development* (ZPD) describes the limit of actions that learners can meaningfully participate in intermentally, and subsequently appropriate intramentally. Beyond the ZPD, learners cannot relate actions to their current understandings.

How teachers and students can accomplish learning and activity in the ZPD is not at all straightforward. To be most effective, teachers must diagnose where students are developmentally and figure out, in each case, what it would look like for the students to perform meaningfully, if not yet fully competently. For teachers, like experts in a domain, it may be quite difficult to avoid inadvertently acting outside a novice's ZPD. In our work within the CoVis project (Pea, 1993a), we were faced with these issues in a realm where students appeared to be facing somewhat of a "bootstrapping" dilemma: They had few experiences that helped them to know how to carry out certain aspects of science inquiry, much less use the Internet and scientific visualization tools in the context of that higher-order activity (Polman, 1996). Thus, if the teacher just gives them a clearly circumscribed path, as is done in many traditional labs, the meaning of the actions students carry out will not necessarily relate to the teacher's goal of students learning about experimental design (because the students are not required to *participate* in the design). This problem is also too often manifest in various forms of student-scientist partnerships in education (Cohen, 1997). In studies such as the multinational precollege GLOBE Project (Global Learning through Observations to Benefit the Environment, n.d.), students collect data around the world. They do so according to protocols that are designed by scientists to ensure data quality and reliability, and without care, in designs such as these, learners may be relegated to the role of "databots," collecting data without an understanding of the designs that render the data meaningful (Pea et al., 1997). Teachers cannot just give the students the steps to follow by rote, nor can they leave the students unguided to recapitulate the development of all science knowledge. What is needed is some kind of interactive process of guided participation, which allows the student to be an active inquirer and the teacher to be an active guide. "Transformative communication" is one such process for guiding participation (Pea, 1994); we came to see that it provides some explanation of why certain incidents prove productive for teaching and learning in a project-based science classroom.

The view of communication as *transformative* can be contrasted with common views of communication as *ritual* and as *transmission* (Pea, 1994). The view of communication as ritual tends to encourage active participation by all parties, but in activities with already shared meanings. The ritual nature of much cultural activity helps to explain how it is successfully carried out: for instance, telephone greetings rely on a highly specific series of key words, pauses, and intonations to get a great deal of information across quickly (Schegloff, 1979). Despite the obvious importance of ritual communication in cultural activity, it does not involve the sort of generativity at fostering new development that is needed for education.

The dominant view of communication in learning settings as *transmission* of knowledge from the teacher to the student (Cohen, 1988; Pea, 1994; Polman, 2000) is associated with entirely teacher-directed pedagogy such as lectures (Rogoff, 1994). In lecture-based classrooms, the teacher is an active presenter of knowledge and the students are passive receivers of knowledge. In part because of the recognition already discussed that knowledge is actively constructed (e.g., Bransford, Brown, & Cocking, 1999), educational reform efforts such as project-based learning are often designed in hopes of changing the students' passivity. When implemented as *unguided discovery*, however, project-based learning demands that students become active in the acquisition of knowledge, but it leaves *teachers* passive. Rather than either of these extremes, educational researchers have come to recommend the model of *"community of learners,"* in which "learning occurs as people participate in shared endeavors with others, with all playing active but asymmetrical roles" (Rogoff, 1994, p. 209; see also Brown & Campione, 1994). Teachers interested in supporting inquiry learning, rather than just "letting their students go" to see if learning will occur, would thus do well to try to create a "community of learners" atmosphere in their classes. This implies that they must play a unique role of structuring and guiding student activities without taking away the students' active role. Some researchers refer to this middle ground as "guided discovery" or "guided learning," but note that the role of guide is difficult to master. Ann Brown (1992) notes,

> Guided learning is easier to talk about than do. It takes clinical judgment to know when to intervene. Successful teachers must engage continually in on-line diagnosis of student understanding. They must be sensitive to overlapping zones of proximal development, where students are ripe for new learning. Guided discovery places a great deal of responsibility in the hands of teachers, who must model, foster, and guide the "discovery" process into forms of disciplined inquiry that would not be reached without expert guidance. (p. 169)

As Brown points out, the complexity of structuring and guiding students in project work is increased because different students in a class need different levels and kinds of support; because their existing knowledge bases are different, the individuals in a class end up interpreting whatever support they get, even if it is a statement by a teacher to the whole class, differently as well. Matching the kind and level of support students need with what a teacher provides them is a difficult balance to maintain, though. Consequently, as one teacher put it, a teacher trying to support students can "feel sort of like a tree swaying between two extremes of providing students with structure and allowing them to do it all themselves." One way to conceptualize teachers' new role in such classrooms is by *scaffolding* student work (Collins, Brown, & Newman, 1989). Scaffolding can occur either by modeling, by structuring activity, or by coaching—supporting and guiding students' work along the way. In this chapter, we are most concerned with the use of one powerful form of coaching, transformative communication, in a project-based science class. So what is transformative communication? Pea (1994) has described it as follows:

> The initiate in new ways of thinking and knowing in education and learning practices is transformed by the process of communication with the cultural messages of others, but so, too, is the other (whether teacher or peer) in what is learned about the unique

voice and understanding of the initiate. Each participant potentially provides creative resources for transforming existing practice. (p. 288)

Transformative communication is achieved through mutual appropriation (Newman, Griffin, & Cole, 1984; Pea, 1993b) by participants in social interaction to create meanings that neither participant alone brought to the interaction. In some project-based science classrooms—ones designed to support students in carrying out their own original research—it involves transforming students' actions into more successful "moves" in the "language game" of science (Wittgenstein, 1967). Put another way, it allows students to participate in a new way in "talking science" (Lemke, 1990; Pea, 1992).

GETTING TO SPECIFICS: METHODS, DATA SOURCES, AND FRAMEWORKS

All this discussion will only be meaningful insofar as it can be related to specific learning environments and conversations. For the balance of this chapter, we discuss episodes involving transformative communication in one classroom.

The episodes related in this chapter are part of a larger interpretive case study (Polman, 2000) conducted from 1994 through 1996 in Rory Wagner's[1] class, one of many participating in the CoVis Project. One of the central features of the class was that students conduct Earth Science projects *of their own design*. What this meant in practice is that they participated in the formulation of a research question, the gathering of data to provide empirical evidence for addressing the question, analysis of those data, and reporting in both written and oral formats.

Polman was a participant observer in Wagner's classroom for 3 years—1½ years acting as a technical assistant and 1½ years conducting the formal study (1994–1995 through winter 1995–1996). Data were collected in field notes and videotapes of classroom observation at each project phase, artifacts created by the teacher and students, and formal and informal interviews with the teacher and selected students. Formal interviews were recorded with audiotape and transcribed, whereas informal interviews were recorded with handwritten notes. For this chapter, we use these data to illustrate ways transformative communication was used in specific episodes to scaffold students' accomplishment of science inquiry.

Our interest in these episodes began with a vague recognition that they seemed to involve some sort of "ah ha" quality among participants and played a key role in the subsequent success of the projects of which they were a part. We thought that a better understanding of the episodes might enable researchers and teachers involved in our project to foster more widespread success, for the challenges of project-based science learning are many. We came to recognize that part of the power of the episodes was due to the fact that they involved mutual appropriation and transformative communication. We surmised that an adequate description of what was unique about them could provide elements of a prescription for future effective action. Table 12.1 provides our general description of the episodes in the form of a dialogue sequence that transformative communication followed.

We do not intend to imply that all communication that results in learning is transformative in the manner described here. Nor do we mean to imply that all communication that could reasonably be termed transformative follows this sequence in strict stepwise order; the sequence is intended to describe the general

TABLE 12.1
Dialogue Sequence for Transformative Communication

(1)	Students make a move in the research process with certain intentions, guided as well as limited by their current knowledge.
(2)	The teacher does not expect the students' move, given a sense of their competencies, but understands how the move, if pursued, can have additional implications in the research process that the students may not have intended.
(3)	The teacher reinterprets the students' move, and together students and teacher reach mutual insights about the students' research project through questions, suggestions, and/or reference to artifacts.
(4)	The meaning of the original action is transformed, and learning takes place in the students' zone of proximal development, as the teacher's interpretation and reappraisal (i.e., appropriation) of the students' move is taken up by the student.

trajectory of some key dialogues, which inevitably involve a great deal of interactive give-and-take that we are not going to examine at the level of detail afforded by, for instance, conversation analysis (as in Polman, in press). What we hope to accomplish with analyzing this dialogue sequence is twofold: (1) to describe important features of dialogue that have proved productive in transformative teaching-learning episodes, and (2) to provide a discourse strategy that teachers may productively use as a cultural tool in future episodes with their students. In summarizing these cases, we focus on how student groups conducting projects arrived at an incident of transformative communication, their interaction with the teacher going through the steps of the dialogue sequence, and the subsequent impact of the transformative communication event on the progress of their project.

PLESIOSAURS: TRANSFORMING A QUEST FOR "THE FACTS" INTO A RESEARCH QUESTION

As detailed elsewhere (Polman, 2000, in press), Wagner guided his students through open-ended projects through a project unit activity structure (Doyle, 1979; Lemke, 1990; Mehan, 1978) consisting of several parts, each leading to the next, with "milestone" deliverable artifacts due from the students at many of them. The complete series of milestones was (1) select group and topic, (2) write up background information, (3) provide research question/proposal, (4) collect data, (5) analyze data, (6) complete research report modeled on the scientific research article genre, (7) revise research report, and (8) present to the class. Somewhat akin to inscriptions made by professional scientists (Latour, 1988; Gordin, Polman, & Pea, 1994), the written milestone artifacts are "shared, critiquable externalizations of student knowledge" (Blumenfeld et al., 1991; Guzdial, 1995) that become useful as occasions for feedback and transformative communication.

Three 11th-grade young women named Beth, Laura, and Cindy teamed up for their first project in Wagner's class. Beth emerged as their leader, with Laura making frequent contributions and Cindy mostly remaining quiet in the background. Cindy and Laura decided one day when Beth was not present that their project topic should be an extinct sea creature called a "plesiosaur." Part of the creature's appeal was its long neck, somewhat like that of a brontosaurus, which made it look in artists' renderings like the fabled Loch Ness monster. Beth, Laura, and Cindy initially had a great deal of trouble locating any specific details on the plesiosaur for the "background information" phase, but with Wagner's assistance they located World Wide Web resources related to the creature. They used the information from the Web and library books to write up their background information report. During the following week, the Plesiosaur group had to complete their focused research proposal. After a whole-class, teacher-led discussion on research questions, students began working in their groups generating potential questions about their topics. The next day, Beth and Cindy approached Wagner to announce they had a research question: "Are accumulations of plesiosaurs associated with areas of high marine productivity?" Wagner was pleased that they followed his advice on choosing a question examinable with empirical data, but he feared the spotty plesiosaur fossil record would prevent the students from coming to valid conclusions about locations in which they thrived; in essence, some locations where plesiosaurs dwelled might have been conducive to fossil formation and discovery, and others not, leading to spurious trends. To avoid these pitfalls, Wagner asked them to reconsider what attracted them to plesiosaurs as a topic in the first place. In response, Cindy mentioned their long necks, and Beth how they swam with large flippers. That reminded Wagner of a comment Beth had made while looking at library books 2 weeks earlier. She had announced, "This [book] says they flew through the water like sea turtles, and sea turtles swim very quickly ... This [book] says they didn't swim very quickly." Wagner had not followed up on the comment at the time, perhaps because he was interrupted by a question from another student. The group had not mentioned swimming speed in their background information milestone report, but the teacher recalled it. Referring to these books, he asked, "Didn't you read a debate about whether [plesiosaurs] were fast or slow swimmers?" Beth confirmed, "Some of them said they were fast and some said slow."

In this exchange, it is notable that Wagner interpreted and recalled the conflicting accounts of plesiosaur swimming speed as a scientific debate, which he understood in terms of the scientific community of scholars attempting to reach consensus. The student, on the other hand, had simply noted that the accounts related different ideas but did not understand those ideas within the frame of "scientific debate." Based on his assumption that there was a debate about swimming motion, Wagner suggested they could do an "analysis of swimming motion ... like how fast they go. You would need to know how animals move and how they swim." Thus, Wagner "revoiced" (O'Connor & Michaels, 1996) the information Beth had originally stated, with a reconceptualization (Cazden, 2001) to include the notion of scientific debate. Beth and the other members of her group liked the idea and decided to run with it. As Beth said, it reminded her "of the reanalysis of dinosaurs that they did and whether they were slow or fast—Jurassic Park was more accurate than the old picture of lumbering dinosaurs." With this reference to a popular culture notion that helped her understand scientific debates about the speed of extinct creatures, Beth began to better understand the process of science inquiry.

Following this discussion, during which they decided to focus on the swimming motion of plesiosaurs, the group members reviewed the relevant sections in the library books they had gathered, and Beth returned a few days later saying incredulously, "Mr. Wagner! Do you know whether the plesiosaur moved by rowing its flippers or flapping them like wings?" One of her library books reported that Plesiosaurs swam with a rowing motion, and another book mentioned that they swam by underwater flight, flapping their flippers like wings straight up and down in the water. Again, neither book mentioned a controversy. As Beth reported later, she "thought he was like all-knowing." She appeared to be looking for her teacher to provide *the answer,* the kind needed for what he called "traditional library research." Wagner was determined to have her do more extensive inquiry, however. Beth, by her own admission, "had never done a project where there [wasn't] really an answer, or someone who's already found the answer." Wagner showed Beth that her question about the swimming method could be more than a quest for the accepted fact; it could be *their research question—they* could assemble evidence to support their own claim of how plesiosaurs swam.

This interaction enabled Wagner to support Beth in accomplishing an activity with which she was unfamiliar, by means of the sort of "transformative communication" described earlier. We can see a concrete enactment of the 4-stage dialogue sequence shown in Table 12.1: (1) Beth approached her teacher looking for *the answer* to two fact-based questions that she expected her "all-knowing" teacher to provide: Did plesiosaurs swim fast or slow, and did they swim by "underwater flight" or a rowing motion? If she could get the answers, she would include them in her report on plesiosaurs, which she may have been seeing still as a library research project like she had done in other classes, with established facts about a topic synthesized and described. (2) Wagner did not know the fact Beth was looking for, nor was he sure there was a debate about plesiosaur swimming motion, but he did know that part of the game of science involves marshaling evidence to support one of several competing claims such as the ones in the books Beth had found. (3) The teacher reconceptualized Beth's move, admitting he did not know the answer but pointing out that an interesting project could use this as a research question. They talked about how she and the other group members could contribute new evidence to a scientific debate rather than just report others' findings. (4) Beth's fact question has been transformed into a research question, as evidenced in her subsequent practice. The student group framed their data collection and analysis in terms of this debate and marshaled the evidence they could to support the theory of a slow rowing motion.

UFO SIGHTINGS: TRANSFORMING A CITATION INTO AN OPPORTUNITY FOR CONFIRMING RESEARCH

Researchers on tutoring and project-based learning have pointed out that motivational benefits can be reaped when students are given *control* over decisions about what they do—as Wagner gave Beth and her project partners—and when they are given the opportunity to work on problems and projects that *interest* them (Blumenfeld et al., 1991; Lepper, Woolverton, Mumme, & Gurtner, 1993). Bruce, Sylvia, and Cheryl's project shows how a project built on students' interests that might seem dubious at first from a scientific standpoint can be transformed into tractable empirical research. Through transformative communication, their project went from being a project about "whether UFOs are alien space ships" to a project about confirming or falsifying natural explanations of UFO sightings.

Along with the other groups, the UFO Sightings group began their project by collecting and synthesizing background research on the topic, before deciding on a specific research question. In their interim report of background research, they mentioned the so-called Condon report (Condon & Gillmor, 1968), an official study put out by the U.S. government, in which UFO sightings were explained by meteor showers, rocket launches, and other known phenomena. Two days after he got the milestone background information reports from students, Wagner mentioned to Polman before class that Cheryl, Bruce, and Sylvia might need extra support on their project given the problematic nature of the UFO topic in the previous classes. He was pleased with the potential in the group's description of the Condon report, as the government's analysis took an empirical approach based on supportable or refutable claims about alternate explanations for UFO sightings—essentially taking a scientific approach to a problem usually approached through mere hearsay. So during class that day, Wagner initiated a discussion with the UFO Sightings group about potential research questions. The interaction with the UFO Sightings group proved a pivotal incident of transformative communication resulting in the formulation of a specific research question.

Shortly after completing attendance and answering some procedural questions from various students about the research proposal assignment, Wagner sat down with Cheryl, Bruce and Sylvia. The following interaction took place:

> Rory: OK, what do you want to do?
>
> Bruce: We want to show UFOs are alien space ships.
>
> Rory: [doubtfully] Any ideas on how?
>
> Bruce: I don't think there's any way to prove it unless they saw the alien in there and they waved at them. That's the only evidence there is.
>
> Rory: Right. That's the problem.
>
> Cheryl: I don't see why we can't write a report on it if people have written whole books on it. [Cheryl interpreted the project at this point as essentially the same as an extensive report for an English class. As time went on, she began to grasp the importance of using empirical data to support a claim.]
>
> Rory: [does not directly address Cheryl's confusion at this time] You know, Joe [Polman] and I were talking about the analysis Condon did that you wrote about in your background information [report]. It was interesting because Condon claimed to have explained the sightings with known phenomena. [For your project] you could verify what somebody like Condon has done. That's another thing people do in science …

He described the example of the cold fusion debate a few years ago, pointing to how it could be applied in their project:

These guys said they had created cold fusion in the lab. But when other people tried it, they couldn't duplicate what they said … In science, once someone says they've proved something, others check it … The idea [here] is to verify the government's explanations. Say they said it was a meteor shower. You could look at the date, where the meteor shower was, and when and where people saw the UFO. Does it match the same spot? If the sighting was here [points one direction] and the meteor shower there [points another direction], the government's explanation could be wrong.

The students decided to run with the idea. In this example, the students originally presented the Condon report as relevant to the history of the UFO debate and thus something to be cited in a review of literature but otherwise not used. Through their interaction, the teacher and students created a new meaning for the citation: the seeds of a study intended to provide independent confirmation or falsification. Thus, this sequence of interactions, starting with the submission of the report by the students and continuing with the discussion in class, can be seen as another instance of transformative communication. The students referred to some research in their background information report, intending it as an example of what is known and has been reported about their subject. Based on his greater understanding of the scientific process of verification, Wagner showed the students they could use the study as the seeds for the next phase of the activity structure: a research proposal to independently confirm or falsify the previous research.

After this interaction, the group's research formulation proved fruitful. For their final research report, the group chose four UFO sightings from the 1960s, described in the Condon report, and tried to independently confirm or falsify Condon and Gillmor's explanations. Their independent confirmation was based on printed data sources found in library searches, such as NASA launch records (Stanford, 1990) that confirmed a scheduled re-entry of satellite Agena into the Earth's atmosphere occurred at the time an airplane crew reported a UFO over Mexico and could have been seen in that location.

Rory Wagner has found the "beginning of the project and the end of the project" to be the most difficult for students. Specifically, the early phase requires that students formulate a research question and proposal, and the later phase requires that they use data analysis to reach an empirically supported conclusion. The UFO Sightings project and the Plesiosaur project (described earlier) provide examples of transformative communication in the form of "action negotiation dialogues" (Polman, in press) around the formulation of research questions. The Hurricanes and the Moons projects provide examples of transformative communication at the data analysis phase.

HURRICANES: TRANSFORMING AN INTUITION INTO A CODING SCHEME

Dave and TJ became interested in hurricanes because of the destruction they cause. Through conversations with Wagner and a scientist "telementor" (O'Neill & Polman, 2004; O'Neill & Scardamalia, 2000) Wagner put them in contact with by e-mail, the students settled on the research question "Is there a preferred pattern of hurricane movement in the Northern Hemisphere?" Over the 2-week data collection period, TJ and Dave worked diligently to gather image data showing hurricane paths off a Web site they found linked from a page their telementor had directed them to. They began their data analysis by combining the hurricane paths onto one image, which gave them an impression of the shapes those paths could take. In an interview outside of class, Dave noted that many of the hurricanes made "a little semicircle" on the southeast edge of the United States.

However, figuring out how to turn this general impression into an analysis of data supporting their conclusions proved difficult for Dave and TJ, as it did for most of their peers in Wagner's class. They turned in an initial stab at an analysis of 4 seemingly random years and got some advice from their teacher about choosing a larger sample of continuous years. With a day to go before their research report was due, Dave and TJ had a long conversation with Wagner trying to solidify data analysis techniques. Their teacher asked them what the general pattern of hurricanes was, and TJ showed him the semicircle or "C" shape Dave had described previously. Wagner made a few suggestions for ways to systematically describe many hurricane shapes, while they continued to look over the composite image of hurricane paths. Then Wagner noticed that *not* all the hurricanes followed the C-shaped path Dave and TJ had described. Some were straighter than the standard C, and others appeared erratic. He then suggested they could devise a categorization scheme for the shapes of paths. They could go back to each year and put a categorical label on each hurricane path shape, count up the frequencies of each shape, and calculate the percentages.

The conversation about data analysis was productive from Wagner's standpoint and nearly constituted a complete sequence of transformative communication. But because Dave and TJ did not effectively take up the jointly developed idea about categories of path shapes in the day remaining for the preparation of their written project report, it was not complete.

In his extensive commentaries written on Dave and TJ's report, Wagner tried to be encouraging and concretely helpful to move them forward. He wrote that they had "made statements in this analysis section *without* referring to the data once. You *can't* do that." He pointed out specific examples. TJ and Dave had written, "We found that most of the recorded storms began in the Atlantic Ocean, east of the Caribbean and made a C-like shape towards the United States and finished back east of the northern United States." He pushed them to "show/prove this [was] true" by showing "how many (and then, what %) of the storms had this 'C-shape' path." He pointed out how they could classify each storm in the time period as having one of a set of path shapes, such as the C-shape they mentioned.

For their revised report, the boys took up many of their teacher's suggestions, thus completing the transformative communication sequence. They categorized each storm as having one of three path shapes and gave the number of storms within each category from among the 83 storms over the period. They also produced a pie chart showing that 51% of the storms followed the C-shape, 22% a "straight-C," and 27% "irregular." The Hurricane group's revised report was a significant improvement over their first draft, with conclusions supported specifically by data analysis.

As with the group who did the project on plesiosaurs, Dave and TJ needed two tries at the third and fourth step in the transformative communication sequence, negotiating the meaning of the teacher's transformation of their idea and putting it into practice, before they could effectively appropriate the idea. In Dave and TJ's case, the second attempts at Step 3 took place in the form of an "action feedback dialogue" (Polman, in press) on their previously written-up analysis, and in Step 4 was implemented in their revised report. In addition, the transformative communication took place through a combination of written and oral verbal exchanges. In addition to the repetition in the second try and Wagner's greater specificity, the stability of Wagner's written comments as compared to his oral suggestions may have been necessary for the students to glean his intended meaning given their lack of expertise at these scientific practices.

MOONS: TRANSFORMING AN UNSUPPORTED CLAIM INTO A GRAPH OF TWO VARIABLES

For their project, Rich and Steve compared and contrasted moons in our solar system. They gathered data on various characteristics of moons, such as density, size, mass, and orbital period, and meticulously organized the data in tables and graphs—a separate graph for each variable. In numerous conversations and comments on interim milestones, Wagner pushed them to think about questions their data could illuminate, such as why the moons were different from one another or what the connections were between variables. But the students had difficulty in finding patterns.

The crucial exchange began when Rory received Rich and Steve's final research report. The students had included only graphs of single variables and then listed each graph's interpretation separately. For instance, they included a line graph showing each of the moon's orbital time period and a bar graph of each moon's density. In the text, the students wrote, "The graph [of orbital period] shows that Earth's moon has the longest orbital period, 27.32 days, while Miranda has the shortest orbital period, 1.4 days." Similar graphs in different styles were included for mass, surface temperature, and distance from planet. In the Data Analysis section of the paper, Steve and Rich did not describe any relationships between variables, except in the statement that "Titan has a short orbital period in relation to its mass"—a statement they did not choose to elaborate. But at the very end of the paper, buried in the Conclusion, they wrote something more like a testable claim: "We have come [to] the conclusion that both Titan and Earth's moon [have] a much greater mass and density than Miranda, and that this could be why both Titan and Earth's moon have longer orbiting time periods." Wagner seized this claim about how mass and density could be related to the orbital period of the moons and showed Rich and Steve how they could directly test it by graphing, for instance, density on the y-axis and time period on the x-axis.

Once again, Wagner perceived that the students' work could be transformed to a more successful move in the game of science than they themselves were originally aware. Like the group who did the Hurricanes project, Rich and Steve had developed a sense that a relationship existed in the data—that is why they put the comment in the conclusion—but they did not know how to present their data to back up a claim. In both cases, a clear analysis technique may be difficult to find even after a general impression has been reached by working with the data. Wagner's greater experience enabled him to see that a graph of one variable against the other would enable the students to directly check their claim that the two variables covaried. When graphed, it appeared that in the students' data, a relationship between density and orbital period, but not between mass and time period, was supported. Using similar methods, Wagner suggested that the students could create combination graphs for all the possible pairs of variables from their separate graphs. In this way, another apparent linear relationship was revealed—between the mass of a moon and its distance from the planet.

When Steve and Rich got the final version of the paper back, they were excited, because, as Steve put it, they "finally saw, you know, what [we] were trying to find, with the patterns." Although there was no provision for revising their paper again, the students got a chance to use the insight in their presentation to the class the following week. Steve and Rich created graphs of their own using Wagner's sketches as a model. In their presentation, they used the line graphs of two variables to support their claims, such as the one that "if a moon has a greater mass, that might affect its distance from the planet that it comes from." With statements about one factor "contributing to" or being "affected by" another, Rich and Steve had finally moved into the realm of making empirically warranted causal arguments, albeit tentative and somewhat awkwardly stated ones. As in the scientific community, they were making their claims with the aid of particular types of inscriptions—in this case, somewhat crude graphs. The graphs made their claim more compelling and understandable (Gordin et al., 1994; Latour, 1988). Steve and Rich had a great deal to learn about analyzing data, but transformative communication helped them to begin making progress.

MUTUAL INSIGHTS THROUGH CONVERSATION WITH ONE ANOTHER AND THE SITUATION

For effective teaching and learning, it is not enough for teachers to simply tell students what to do. Wagner wanted to ensure that students participated in research design and the selection of analysis techniques so that they could learn about research design and analysis strategies. This contrasts to traditional "cookbook" labs, which take such decisions out of the hands of students and consequently preclude opportunities for deeper learning likely to lead to autonomous action in the future. But involving students can be time consuming and difficult. The difficulty and pitfalls of student participation in the *whole* process of research has been recognized by a number of student-scientist collaborative efforts, but even though it is often messy from scientists' perspective to have students involved in the whole process, it is educationally significant (Pea et al., 1997). Transformative communication can prove useful in maintaining this balance between student ownership and the teacher finding ways to guide students in potentially promising directions, as *both* parties make crucial contributions. As Rory described it,

> Sometimes [students] come up with things that are really creative that I would have never thought about, which then leads me to think of other things that might be do-able. And sometimes—[and] this gets in to the negotiating thing—sometimes they get real close to something, or have a neat idea, but it's not do-able, so then, how do you turn that into something that is do-able? Sometimes they do it, [and] sometimes I can do it.

And in some cases like those detailed earlier, the students and teacher can truly do it together. In the interactions described, the teacher helped the students transform the moves they made in the research process into more sophisticated moves that neither he nor the students would have originally predicted, thus leading to *mutual insights*. The interactions can take place over an extended period of time, in real-time or written discussions, but the important thing is that *both* teacher and student participation contributes. To borrow a phrase from Donald Schön (1982), the process of transformative communication enables both Rory and his students to "engage in a conversation with the situation which they are shaping" (p. 103). In this case, it also allows them to engage in a conversation with each other. Whereas Schön was talking about reflective practitioners of design, such as architects, working alone, the process is remarkably analogous in these social interactions between teacher and student. Like architects who find "new and unexpected meanings" in drawings they create, Wagner and his students sometimes found new and unexpected meanings in the changes they produced *in one another's interpretations* and *the situation*. As Wagner stressed to his students, they *did* know important and useful things about their topic and data as they conducted their inquiry, but he often needed to help them conceptualize how what they knew could be used to accomplish scientific inquiry.

In these cases, the "project unit activity structure," with its set of interim milestones that Wagner designed for conducting projects and "verbal exchange activity structures" such as action negotiation dialogues and action feedback dialogues (Polman, 2000, in press), helped him to support students through transformative communication. The project unit activity structure set up the students' desire to formulate a researchable question or an analysis strategy that would help them to answer their question, and Rory made suggestions in verbal exchanges that helped students see how the work they had done and knowledge they had gained could help them get to the next stage in the project. As Wagner observed, students learn in projects on a need-to-know basis: "They won't care [about data analysis strategies] until they have to do it." But when faced with taking their project to the next step, they more readily recognized the value of Wagner's insights.

CONCLUSION

Project-based science teaching and learning involve complex role changes for teachers and students. Too often, the complex work teachers perform as facilitators and guides for project-based student work is left mysterious. In this chapter, we described a dialogue sequence for transformative communication, one productive discourse strategy teachers can use in the role of facilitator. We also elaborated concrete cases in which this strategy was used successfully to help students accomplish science inquiry with more sophistication than they could originally conceive. When teachers set up project activities that challenge and scaffold students in carrying out authentic elements of science practice (National Research Council, 2000; O'Neill & Polman, 2004), the students will develop numerous seeds of scientifically interesting and rigorous inquiry. But as the learning paradox teaches us, the seeds alone do not have what is needed to enable the production of new knowledge. The environment the seeds are planted in must be fertile. The seeds need the sunlight of teacher's more expert vision to reveal their potential, and the soil and water of interaction between teacher and students, before they will sprout to reach their full potential.

ACKNOWLEDGMENT

The authors are grateful to the National Science Foundation, which supported this research of the CoVis Project (archived at: http://www.covis.nwu.edu/) under grants RED-9454729 and MDR88-55582. A grant from the James S. McDonnell Foundation supported the first author's completion of this chapter.

NOTE

1. At his request, Rory Wagner's real name is used. All students' names are pseudonyms.

REFERENCES

Barron, B. (2003). When smart groups fail. *Journal of the Learning Sciences, 12,* 307–359.

Bereiter, C. (1985). Toward a solution of the learning paradox. *Review of educational research,* 55(2), 201–226.

Blumenfeld, P. C., Soloway, E., Marx, R. W., Krajcik, J. S., Guzdial, M., & Palincsar, A. (1991). Motivating project-based learning: Sustaining the doing, supporting the learning. *Educational Psychologist, 26*(3), 369–398.

Bransford, J. D., Brown, A. L. & Cocking, R. R. (1999). *How people learn: Brain, mind, experience, and school.* Washington, DC: National Academy Press.

Brown, A., Ash, D., Rutherford, M., Nakagawa, K., Gordon, A., & Campione, J. (1993). Distributed expertise in the classroom. In G. Salomon (Ed.), *Distributed cognitions: Psychological and educational considerations* (pp. 188–228). New York: Cambridge University Press.

Brown, A. L. (1992). Design experiments: Theoretical and methodological challenges in creating complex interventions in classroom settings. *Journal of the Learning Sciences, 2*(2), 141–178.

Brown, A. L., & Campione, J. C. (1994). Guided discovery in a community of learners. In K. McGilly (Ed.), *Classroom lessons: Integrating cognitive theory and classroom practice* (pp. 229–270). Cambridge, MA: MIT Press.

Burke, J. (1995). *Connections.* Boston: Little, Brown, and Company.

Cazden, C. (1981). Performance before competence: Assistance to child discourse in the zone of proximal development. *Quarterly Newsletter of the Laboratory of Comparative Human Cognition, 3,* 5–8.

Cazden, C. B. (2001). *Classroom discourse: The language of teaching and learning* (2nd Edition). Portsmouth, NH: Heinemann.

Clark, A. (1997). *Being there: Putting brain, body, and world together again.* Cambridge, MA: MIT Press.

Cohen, D. K. (1988). Teaching practice: Plus ça change …. In P. Jackson (Ed.), *Contributing to educational change: Perspectives on research and practice.* Berkeley, CA: McCutchan.

Cohen, K. (Ed.). (1997). *Internet links for science education: Student-scientist partnerships.* New York: Plenum Press.

Cole, M. (1996). *Cultural psychology: A once and future discipline.* Cambridge, MA: Harvard University Press.

Collins, A., Brown, J. S., & Newman, S. E. (1989). Cognitive apprenticeship: Teaching the craft of reading, writing, and mathematics. In L. B. Resnick (Ed.), *Knowing, learning, and instruction: Essays in honor of Robert Glaser* (pp. 453–494). Hillsdale, NJ: Lawrence Erlbaum Associates.

Condon, E. U., & Gillmor, D. S. (1968). *Final report of the scientific study of unidentified flying objects.* New York: Bantam Books.

Dewey, J. (1902). The child and the curriculum. In J. J. McDermott (Ed.), *The philosophy of John Dewey,:Vol. II. The lived experience* (pp. 467–483). New York: Putnam.

Doyle, W. (1979). Classroom tasks and students' abilities. In P. L. Peterson & H. L. Walberg (Eds.), *Research on teaching: Concepts, findings, and implications* (pp. 183–205). Berkeley, CA: McCutchan.

Edelson, D. C., Gordin, D. N., & Pea, R. D. (1999). Addressing the challenges of inquiry-based learning through technology and curriculum design. *Journal of the Learning Sciences, 8*(3–4), 391–450.

Fodor, J. A. (1975). *The language of thought.* New York: Crowell.

Fodor, J. A. (1980). Fixation of belief and concept acquisition. In M. Piattelli-Palmerini (Ed.), *Language and learning: The debate between Jean Piaget and Noam Chomsky* (pp. 142–149). Cambridge, MA: Harvard University Press.

Glick. J. A. (1983). Piaget, Vygotsky and Werner. In S. Wapner & B. Kaplan (Eds.), *Toward a holistic developmental psychology* (pp. 35–52). Hillsdale, NJ: Lawrence Erlbaum Associates.

GLOBE Program. (n.d.). The GLOBE Program. Retrieved January 8, 2007 from http://www.globe.gov

Gordin, D., Polman, J. L., & Pea, R. D. (1994). The Climate Visualizer: Sense-making through scientific visualization. *Journal of Science Education and Technology, 3*(4), 203–226.

Guzdial, M. (1995, April). *Artifacts of learning: A perspective on students' learning processes and strategies through their learning products.* Paper presented at the annual meeting of the American Educational Research Association, San Francisco, CA.

Hutchins, E. (1993). Learning to navigate. In S. Chaiklin & J. Lave (Eds.), *Understanding practice: Perspectives on activity and context* (pp. 35–63). Cambridge: Cambridge University Press.

Hutchins, E. (1995). *Cognition in the wild.* Cambridge, MA: MIT Press.

Kolodner, J. L., Gray, J. T, & Fasse, B. B. (2003). Promoting transfer through case-based reasoning: Rituals and practices in Learning by Design™ Classrooms. *Cognitive Science Quarterly, 3*(2), 119–170.

Latour, B. (1988). Drawing things together. In M. Lynch & S. Woolgar (Eds.), *Representation in scientific practice* (pp. 19–68). Cambridge, MA: MIT Press.

Lemke, J. L. (1990). *Talking science: Language, learning, and values.* Norwood, NJ: Ablex.

Leont'ev, A. N. (1981). The problem of activity in psychology. In J. V. Wertsch (Ed.), *The concept of activity in Soviet psychology* (pp. 37–71). Armonk, NY: Sharpe.

Lepper, M. R., Woolverton, M., Mumme, D. L., & Gurtner, J.-L. (1993). Motivational techniques of expert human tutors: Lessons for the design of computer-based tutors. In S. P. Lajoie & S. J. Derry (Eds.), *Computers as cognitive tools* (pp. 75–105). Hillsdale, NJ: Lawrence Erlbaum Associates.

Mehan, H. (1978). Structuring school structure. *Harvard Educational Review, 48*(1), 32–64.

National Research Council. (2000). *Inquiry and the National Science Education Standards.* Washington, DC: National Academy Press.

Newman, D., Griffin, P., & Cole, M. (1984). Social constraints in laboratory and classroom tasks. In B. Rogoff & J. Lave (Eds.), *Everyday cognition: Its development in social context* (pp. 172–193). Cambridge, MA: Harvard University Press.

Ochs, E., Schieffelin, B., & Platt, M. (1979). Propositions across utterances and speakers. In E. Ochs & B. Schieffelin (Eds.), *Developmental pragmatics* (pp. 251–268). New York: Academic Press.

O'Connor, M., & Michaels, S. (1996). Shifting participant frameworks: Orchestrating thinking practices in group discussions. In D. Hicks (Ed.), *Discourse, learning, and schooling* (pp. 63–103). New York: Cambridge University Press.

O'Neill, D. K., & Polman, J. L. (2004). Why educate "little scientists?" Examining the potential of practice-based scientific literacy. *Journal of Research in Science Teaching, 41*(3), 234–266.

O'Neill, D. K., & Scardamalia, M. (2000). Mentoring in the open: A strategy for supporting human development in the knowledge society. In B. J. Fishman & S. F. O'Connor-Divelbiss (Eds.), *Proceedings of the International Conference of the Learning Sciences, 2000.* Mahwah, NJ: Lawrence Erlbaum Associates.

Palincsar, A. S., & Brown, A. L. (1984). Reciprocal teaching of comprehension-fostering and comprehension monitoring activities. *Cognition and Instruction, 1*, 117–175.

Pea, R. D. (1992). Augmenting the discourse of learning with computer-based learning environments. In E. de Corte, M. Linn, H. Mandl, & L. Verschaffel (Eds.), *Computer-based learning environments and problem-solving* (pp. 313–344). New York: Springer-Verlag.

Pea, R. D. (1993a). The collaborative visualization project. *Communications of the ACM, 36*(5), 60–63.

Pea, R. D. (1993b). Practices of distributed intelligence and designs for education. In G. Salomon (Ed.), *Distributed cognitions: Psychological and educational considerations* (pp.

47–87). New York: Cambridge University Press. (Abridged version to appear in Japanese, 1998, in Y. Sayeki (Ed.), *Joho to media*. Tokyo: Iwanami-Shoten)

Pea, R. D. (1994). Seeing what we build together: Distributed multimedia learning environments for transformative communications. *Journal of the Learning Sciences, 3*(3), 285–299.

Pea, R. D. (1998). Distributed intelligence and the growth of virtual learning communities over the global Internet (Keynote Address). In H. Nikada (Ed.), *Proceedings of PC97*. Kyoto, Japan, Council for Improving Educational Computing. (Translation in Japanese)

Pea, R. D. (2002). Learning science through collaborative visualization over the Internet. In N. Ringertz (Ed.), *Nobel Symposium: Virtual museums and public understanding of science and culture*. Stockholm, Sweden: Nobel Academy Press. Retrieved June 14, 2004, from http://www.nobel.se/nobel/nobelfoundation/symposia/interdisciplinary/ns120/lectures/pea.pdf

Pea, R. D. (2004). The social and technological dimensions of scaffolding and related theoretical concepts for learning, education, and human activity. *Journal of the Learning Sciences, 13*(3), 423–451.

Pea, R. D., Gomez, L. M., Edelson, D. C., Fishman, B. J., Gordin, D. N., & O'Neill, D. K. (1997). Science education as a driver of cyberspace technology development. In K. C. Cohen (Ed.), *Internet links for science education: Student-scientist partnerships* (pp. 189–220). New York: Plenum Press.

Polman, J. L. (1996). Bootstrapping a community of practice: Learning science by doing projects in a high school classroom. In D. C. Edelson & E. A. Domeshek (Eds.), *Proceedings of the International Conference on the Learning Sciences, 1996* (pp. 474–479). Charlottesville, VA: AACE.

Polman, J. (2000). *Designing project-based science: Connecting learners through guided inquiry.* New York: Teachers College Press.

Polman, J. L. (in press). Dialogic activity structures for project-based learning environments. *Cognition and Instruction.*

Polman, J. L., & Pea, R. D. (2001). Transformative communication as a cultural tool for guiding inquiry science. *Science Education, 85,* 223–238.

Rogoff, B. (1990). *Apprenticeship in thinking: Cognitive development in social context.* New York: Oxford University Press.

Rogoff, B. (1994). Developing understanding of the idea of communities of learners. *Mind, Culture, and Activity, 1*(4), 209–229.

Roschelle, J. (1992). Learning by collaborating: Convergent conceptual change. *Journal of the Learning Sciences, 2*(3), 235–276.

Schank, R. C. (1990). *Tell me a story: A new look at real and artificial memory.* New York: Scribner.

Schegloff, E. A. (1979). Identification and recognition in telephone conversation openings. In G. Psathas (Ed.), *Everyday language: Studies in ethnomethodology* (pp. 23–78). New York: Irvington.

Schön, D. A. (1982). *The reflective practitioner: How professionals think in action.* New York: Basic Books.

Stanford, R. (1990). *NASA launch bulletin.* New York: Norton.

Vygotsky, L. S. (1978). *Mind in society.* Cambridge, MA: Harvard University Press.

Wertsch, J. V. (1991). *Voices of the mind: A sociocultural approach to mediated action.* Cambridge, MA: Harvard University Press.

Wertsch, J. V. (1998). *Mind as action.* New York: Oxford University Press.

Wittgenstein, L. (1967). *Philosophical investigations.* Oxford: Blackwell.

CHAPTER 13

Remaking the World Through Talk and Text: What We Should Learn From How Engineers Use Language to Design

Cheryl Geisler
Barbara Lewis

Although the work of design engineers is all around us—in the cars we drive, in the bridges we cross, in the coffee makers we rely on in the morning—most of us know little about the engineering design process. Who makes the technological artifacts that surround us? How do they do it? What motivates their work? And, most important for our present purposes, what role can language arts educators play in preparing students to participate in this process?

Despite the plethora of technological artifacts that surround us, many of us find the technical detail of engineering design to be a barrier to understanding what turns out to be a very human process. As a consequence, we may be missing opportunities to help students learn important language practices. As humans, engineers use creativity, capacity for imagination, tools, and materials to make new things to make our lives better, more interesting, and more fun. Engineers' success at "remaking the world" is important not only to their success as individuals in the world of work, but also to society as a whole. As language arts educators, we need to realize that the students we teach today will become the designers of the technological artifacts that surround us tomorrow.

In this chapter, we draw on 10 years of work watching engineers design. Our aim has been to see through the technical detail—just as engineers so often see through language—in order to appreciate the role that language plays in the process of remaking the world. This watching has convinced us that language is crucial to engineering design. Talk and texts are fundamental tools with which engineers bring technological artifacts from the realm of the unthought into the realm of the everyday. By better understanding the role talk and text play, we can do a better job of preparing students to participate in this process. We, as language arts teachers, can, in other words, have real and continuing impact on the quality of life in a technological society by helping students learn how to remake the world through words.

REMAKING THE WORLD THROUGH ENGINEERING DESIGN

Whenever we find ourselves dissatisfied with our current situation, reflect on the source of that dissatisfaction, and develop and carry out plans to make improvements, we act as *designers* in the broadest sense of the word. The natural and social sciences, with which we are more familiar, are not like design: They aim at certain knowledge, facts that can remain true or universal despite changes in the perspectives from which we as humans view those facts. Design, by contrast, can never remain detached from the human perspective because it is always concerned with improving the current human situation, making things better using what we know right now.

Good design *now* will not be good design in 20 years, in 50 years, in 100 years—not just because we will know more, have better materials, and have a better understanding of how things work, but also because the human situation will have changed and what we seek and hope for to make our lives better will have changed. One hundred and fifty years ago, for example, new household technologies like the sewing machine, washing machine, and vacuum cleaner were regarded as major innovations in the design of household technologies. Without a doubt, they made life better for many people, but the definition of *better* depended on human perspectives that, at the close of the 20th century, we now recognize as altered.

In the second half of the 19th century, for example, the sewing machine enabled women to take responsibility for the clothing needs of the entire family, and it enabled the family to aspire to a more varied wardrobe. The prior custom had been to have only one new outfit per season and to hire seamstresses to help in their construction (Cowan, 1983). Such customs had become increasingly burdensome to women in the early 20th century because women had to compete with factories for good household help and because those same factories made the production of cheaper and more varied cloth possible. The sewing machine, an advance in engineering design enabled by the development of a lock-stitch mechanism, by which a top thread encircled and locked down a bottom or bobbin thread (Brandon, 1996), made it possible for women to fill these needs, providing their families with more clothing options on their own.

Today we still have home sewing machines, but they do not make our lives "better" in the same way they did 75 years ago. Now women generally do not have the time to sew to meet all of their family's clothing needs, and retail clothing stores now offer low-priced clothing that makes the effort of sewing unnecessary. The sewing machine has instead evolved into a hobbyist tool: Those who sew no longer sew because they have to but because they want to. In response to these social changes, the sewing machine has developed from a single, multifunctional mechanical device into a room full of specialized computerized machines—sewing machines, sergers, embroidery machines, and so on. Addressing women's changing social roles, they offer both time-saving techniques that can produce quick returns ("Make it today; wear it tonight") and advanced techniques like machine quilting and embroidery, which require large investments in both time and technical competence. Good engineers respond to such social changes, imagining ways in which advances like computerization can be used in the context of changing social conditions to address ever-changing notions of "better."

As this example from household technology illustrates, engineering design is "the strategy for causing the best change in a poorly understood or uncertain situation within the available resources" (Koen, 1987). What counts as "best" (more clothes or more time?) and what the available resources are (household servants? computers? a room of one's own?) is always changing, making the "best design" an impossible ideal. Design is always making do, weighing competing constraints, and getting inspired.

Increasingly, design is also collaborative. Replacing the ideal of the single inspired inventor working in the garage, current design requires more knowledge than any single individual can bring to the table. Innovations in household technologies like the computerized sewing machine are increasingly driven by developments in a hybrid of mechanical engineering and electronics that did not exist a decade ago. In the future, our students will be faced with ever more varied collaborations, many of which we cannot begin to imagine.

SEEING THE LANGUAGE IN DESIGN

For a variety of complex reasons, the traditional language arts curriculum has done a poor job of providing students with the strategies for talk and text that will enable them to participate in the design of a technological future. Engineers tend to see through the texts they write and the talk they talk and therefore have limited consciousness of the role language plays in their work. Sharing widely held cultural assumptions, they tend to believe that the best language is language that is transparently clear: language that shows where to tighten the bolt on the new grill, how to install the latest release of a word processor, or how to avoid meltdown at Three Mile Island. Under ideal circumstances, that is, language should serve as a clear *reflection* of an external world. For this reason, most textbooks about engineering design relegate language to a "mop up" process of documenting artifacts and processes that have been developed by other, more technical means.

As language arts educators, we should be wary of taking at face value engineers' discounting of language. It is human to take for granted and lose consciousness of the tools one is using (Collins, 1985; Polyani, 1958): We don't think through the 150 years of innovation behind the vacuum cleaner when we decide to clean the house. Engineers, however, need this awareness when they make the vacuum cleaner the object of their design work. In a parallel fashion, engineers are not aware of the talk and text they use to design. As language arts specialists, however, we need this awareness when we make these language practices the object of our research and teaching.

REMAKING THE WORLD FOR CHILDREN WITH CEREBRAL PALSY

In the rest of this chapter, we illustrate the purposes to which language is put in engineering design by drawing on a detailed case study of a team of four undergraduate engineering students—Sam, Paul, Tim, and Jack[1]—who worked together for more than 15 weeks to develop a design for a motorized device that would provide mobility for children with cerebral palsy. The team was given this assignment by their professor, George, as part of their "capstone" experience in mechanical engineering design, an experience required of students graduating with engineering degrees by the Accreditation Board of Engineering and Technology (ABET). The assignment George gave the students told them that children with cerebral palsy needed to experience independent movement through their environment and observe its effects, an experience that was currently expensive and hard to provide.

As shown in Figure 13.1, the device the students designed looked a bit like the walkers babies use, but slightly larger. The walker's frame included a horseshoe-shaped, molded plastic base, which rode on four castor wheels: the "horseshoe" was closed by a bar holding a toy filled with balls that popped when the child walked. Instead of a plastic tray surrounding the child, on which baby walkers rely, the students designed a plastic tube, curving up in front of the child, to serve as a handlebar. A series of pads and straps secured the child to a backboard, which was supported on an arm rising up from the back of the frame. The backboard was able to slide up and down, allowing children to squat, and it could be adjusted for height. Underneath, instead of a seat, the walker provided hip support pads that could be rotated a specific number of degrees by a motorized move-

FINAL CONCEPT

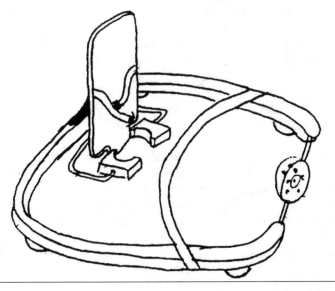

Figure 13.1.   Students' Final Design for a Powered Mobility Device for Children With Cerebral Palsy.

ment mechanism at the bottom and rear of the backboard. The timing of the movement mechanism was controlled by a timing prompter, which could be set to prompt the child to move one leg or the other at intervals appropriate for the child.

At the end of the course, George judged the students' design to be a very good one because of its combination of an adjustable frame with innovative ideas for prompting children with cerebral palsy to walk. These innovations, in both the movement mechanism and the timing prompter took Sam, Paul, Tim, and Jack beyond simply providing powered mobility—as George had originally assigned them—to provide a kind of technologically assisted therapy. In the next three sections, we examine the role that talk and text played in enabling the student designers to make this design transformation.

REMAKING THE WORLD THROUGH NARRATIVE TALK

Because engineers design to improve some current situation, the technological artifacts they produce always refigure an existing social narrative. For this reason, one of the most significant ways talk enters into the process of engineering design is in the construction of existing and refigured social narratives. After the fact, and simply looking at the design artifact, we might assume that the construction and refiguring of such social narratives are a relatively straightforward process; indeed, their role is seldom recognized by engineering designers. But, as the talk of Sam, Paul, Tim, and Jack reveals, narratives, and the talk in which they are embedded, shape the design of technological artifacts in complex ways.

Social narratives of the existing situation emerged in the earliest talk among Sam, Paul, Tim, and Jack as they recalled personal experiences with the disabled. Sam initiated this process with a narrative of a sixth-grade classmate in a powered wheelchair:

> I knew a guy in my class in sixth-grade, up through high school. He was in a powered wheelchair, and I don't know what he had, but he could move his right hand and his head and that was it. I mean, he could move his left arm a little bit, but it was an extreme effort just for him to kind of go like that [gesture] ... And he had a little joy stick to move the wheelchair around, but that's all he could do. And his legs, I guess he couldn't move them. That's why he never got any exercise. They were really small.... (Team meeting on 9/11)

With this narrative of an existing situation, Sam began to personify for himself and his teammates the social situation they would try to improve. This story provided them with a concrete image of one kind of powered mobility device—the powered wheelchair—and it yoked together the assigned goal of providing mobility for the disabled with the more complex goal of providing them with exercise appropriate to their abilities. As we shall see, ability-appropriate exercise became a central feature of their eventual design.

The second kind of narrative that shapes the process of engineering is a reconfigured narrative of the design in use. Engineers produce refigured narratives by imagining how an existing social situation might be improved with technology. Two days after Sam told the story of his grade-school classmate who controlled his powered wheelchair with a joystick, Pete produced a refigured narrative of an amplified mobility device controlled by an adjustable wheel:

This is just what I thought of: Maybe some kind of wheel with two handles that a child could be turning with their finger, with their hand, whatever the ... For example, the child could move his hands, both hands, not to a great degree, but he could do something. Well, I'm saying that, you know, you could put a sensor in the ... in a wheel and detect how fast the wheel is turning. We don't have to use that wheel to move, you know, to move the whole thing, but we could ... sense the motion, and from there, we could, from the motion and how fast the wheel's turning, we could use that. (Team meeting on 9/16)

Social narratives like these have a powerful influence on the course of an engineering design process. They provide designers with a concrete understanding of the social situation they are trying to address, an understanding that they explore and elaborate on throughout the design process.

Over the first two weeks of their project, two social narratives appeared in the talk of our team: each associated with a possible design concept and each competing for the allegiance of our student designers. The first, as we have just seen, was an amplified mobility device suggested by the narrative of the classmate in the powered wheelchair. Paul was an early and strong advocate of this approach, imagining children with cerebral palsy moving about in powered Ninja Turtle cars. A second, competing narrative that emerged in this early stage involved assisting the child not just with mobility but also with the process of learning to walk. Sam was an early advocate of this baby-walker approach, which he described in their first team meeting:

> S: The first thing I thought of was one of those little things you get for kids where they sit down in a little chair, and they kind of walk themselves around ... and they have little things to play with and it has four ... not really roller, but something so they can ... walk themselves around. Something like that, only they sit in it, and there's a little motor that moves them around. (Team meeting on 9/11)

Talk helped Sam, Paul, Tim, and Jack create these competing social narratives. In the next two sections, we look at how they analyzed and synthesized these narratives through a combination of talk and text.

REMAKING THE WORLD THROUGH TALK FROM TEXT

In the language arts classroom, shaped by the culture of literary interpretation, we often think of talk and text as distinct realms of activity: talk as something we do together and text as something—ideally at least—we do alone. We need to recognize, however, that in engineering design, as in many other workplace settings, texts and talk do not exist in isolation but are almost always linked to one another. In their work on the mobility device, for example, Sam, Paul, Tim, and Jack used talk to make nearly 1,300 separate proposals about the frame, but over 70% of those proposals were made using some kind of text. In this section, we examine the reasons behind this heavy reliance on text mediation.

Design assignments, like most design texts, have an inherent ambiguity that often serves the purpose of richly affording, but not forcing, design choices. The original design assignment George gave his students, for example, spoke of the need to train children with cerebral palsy "in independent movement." This ambiguous phrase can be interpreted in many ways. One interpretation—which George himself provided the students with in an early meeting—was "training in the sensation of movement":

> G: You know how flight simulators work, basically? They don't really move much, but they give you the whole sensation that you're making large motions by simulating some small changes of acceleration and movement and things and giving you a visual effect. So if what you're trying to do was provide somebody ... if the purpose was to allow them to learn what it was like to have independent movement, then something like a flight simulator could be the answer.

A second interpretation, preferred by the team, identified "independent movement" with "walking" and thus made "training in independent movement" synonymous with "training children to walk." Their interpretation, though clearly different than the one George originally had in mind, had a validity that allowed the team to adopt the concept of the baby walker, a crucial milestone in the development of their design concept. By affording multiple interpretations such as these, design texts gives students important tools with which to define design goals.

Another kind of text that plays a significant role in moving students' design work forward are source texts that enable researchers to understand the *state of the art* in their design. Researching the state of the art in cerebral palsy mobility devices, for example, Sam, Paul, Tim, and Jack went to the library, to works like Scherzer and Tscharnuter's *Early Diagnosis and Therapy in Cerebral Palsy* (1990), Levitt's *Treatment of Cerebral Palsy and Motor Delay* (1982), and Wolf's *The Results of Treatment in Cerebral Palsy* (1969).

One major function these source texts played was to inculcate students into the values and norms of the professional therapists toward whom they would eventually aim their device. In particular, the assumption that cerebral children learn to walk as a result of therapeutic intervention rather than as a result of solitary effort was deeply embedded in the community of professional therapists represented by the charts and descriptions these students consulted (see Fig. 13.2):

> S: [studying Semans, Phillips, Romanoli, Miller, & Skillen, 1969, p. 268, in Wolf, 1969, shown in Fig. 13.2]
> Um, we could probably start to help them in [stage] 9:
> 9. Sitting erect. Soles of feet together, hips flexed and externally rotated to at least forty-five degrees.
> T: Um-hmm. I might have another chart, I think.
> S: Or maybe at [stage] 11 [reading from Semans et al., 1969, p. 269]:
> 11. Legs hanging over edge of table.
> Then start to move their legs. (Team meeting on 9/29)

The stage descriptions the students here consulted communicated the community's assumption that learning to walk was, for children with cerebral palsy, a sit-

Cerebral Palsy Assessment Chart Basic Motor Control

Name:_____ Birthdate: _____ Diagnosis:_____

Test Postures and Movements	Examiner:	Name:		Name:		Name:	
		Date	Remarks	Date	Remarks	Date	Remarks
Sitting Erect 9. Soles of feet together, hips flexed and externally rotated to at least 45°							
10. Knees extended and legs abducted; hips 90°-100°							
11. Legs hanging over edge of table. (a) Extend right knee (b) Extend left knee							

Figure 13.2.   Chart Consulted by Students From Semans et. al. (1969).

uation including both a child struggling to walk and a therapist helping her—placing her on a table, rotating her feet, and moving her legs. This assumption of a therapeutic dyad was important for Sam, Paul, Tim, and Jack because it eventually distinguished the technology of the basic baby walker, the concept with which Sam had started, from the assisted therapy device, the concept to which the team finally moved.

Source texts like these do not, however, operate in isolation from the talk and observation that inevitably accompany design work. The therapeutic dyad described by Semans et al. (1969), Levitt (1982), and other authors was also the situation the students observed. In fact, the actual function of the timing prompter that the students eventually included in their design was suggested by observations of a real therapist interacting with a child in a baby walker, observations that Sam and Jack later reviewed in a design meeting:

> J: The suggestions were that we do something [to show them] how to take a step.
>
> S: There was a lot of take one step and stop. And they'd be like, "Okay, come on! Take another step!" (Team meeting on 10/23)

In this way—building on the assumption of the therapeutic dyad that they found in source texts and elaborated on through observations—the students inched closer to the design of a timing prompter, which would replace the therapist's repetitive encouragement with a device that would mechanically prompt the child to take step after step. Through such text and talk, then, designers instantiate technologically what they first observe socially.

In addition to conveying the existing norms and values of a community, source texts also play an important role in providing students with an analytic framework in which to design. To design, students must move away from thinking narratively about the technology they are designing—as something that acts over time—to thinking of it as something in space. Through the process of analysis, designers take the first step toward considering the design as an object in and of itself; once again, talk and text play important roles in this accomplishment.

Sam, Paul, Tim, and Jack began the analysis of their design as object by surveying the existing technologies they encountered in source texts:

> S: [looking at the Amesbury Walker in Levitt, 1982, shown in Fig. 13.3]
>   I don't know what this thing is, but this is pretty good.
> P: That looks good. Maybe [I'll] sketch it.
>   [20-second pause]
> S: [reading from Levitt]
>   It says, uh … It says,
>> With trunk support given by a padded support to chest or by chest slings attached to overhead. The Amesbury Walker is shown with an adjustable and chest to waist support as the child improves his control.
>
>   Right there [Pointing to Fig. 13.3].
>   [pause]
>   I mean, hell, that's what we've got here. You know, throw a motor in there and a platform on the bottom, there you go. [laughs a bit]
> T: Uh-hmm.
>   [10-second pause]
>   And the seat? We can have it so the kid could sit?
> S: Yeah, well …
> T: With the motor. And maybe take the chair away and make it a standing support.
> S: Yeah.

Constructing a state-of-the-art review of existing technologies helps students to analyze the features they might want to create. As the previous excerpt illustrates, looking at the Amesbury Walker helped Sam, Paul, Tim, and Jack to understand which features might be critical to their own design: padded support? adjustability? a motor? a platform? a seat?

Source texts additionally provide students with categories for what design engineers call a *functional analysis,* an analysis that lays out what the design object must accomplish. In this regard, the source text by Levitt once again served our team by providing them with an analysis of the main functions that any therapy for walking would need to address:

> T: [reading from Levitt, 1982, page 135]:
>   Development of Standing and Walking

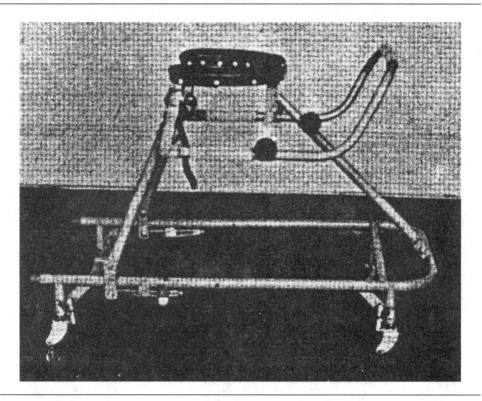

Figure 13.3.   A Picture of the Amesbury Walker Consulted by Students. See Levitt (1982, p. 247).

The following main aspects should be developed:
And there's a list.

Antigravity support or weight bearing on feet ....
Postural fixation of the head and trunk and on the pelvis in the vertical ....
Postural fixation ....
Tilt reactions ....
Saving from falling ....

As with their social narratives, the students did not use source texts to develop their analysis in isolation from the talk and observation that made up design work. Instead, they went back and forth between information supplied by source texts, information supplied by talks with the therapist, and their own developing beliefs about the design. Paul, for instance, began by advocating an analytic scheme provided by the therapist's talk:

P: Well, basically what we found out is that there's no one stage of walking that's, you know, especially difficult ... All the stages are difficult. That's what she told us. And, well, some of the problems that she told us was that there are like four main problems. Tone control is one. Two is weight shifting. Three is disassociation. Four is isolation.

Tim, however, felt this analysis left out the problems that children with cerebral palsy have with balance. Instead of using talk with the therapist to argue his point, he used a source text:

> T: Here [reading from Scherzer & Tscharnuter, 1990, p. 124]
>
> > The major problem with the patient with cerebral palsy is not caused by a dysfunction of individual muscles or muscle groups but by a lack of coordination of muscle action.
>
> It's the coordination I think that we should concentrate on. [skipping to p. 125]:
>
> > Some of the most important automatic postural reactions are righting and equilibrium reactions. The development of these motor patterns is crucial for the development of antigravity posture and efficient, controlled movement patterns.
>
> So before they can move correctly they need to [be] equalized in balance.[continuing from p. 125]
>
> > Equilibrium reactions provide postural control and balance.
>
> So what I'm saying is I think we can concentrate on teaching the child to develop their equilibrium reactions, which is muscle coordination, or part of muscle coordination. (Team meeting on 10/7)

The difference between the analytic scheme suggested by the therapist's talk and an alternative analysis offered by a source text posed a synthesis problem for our students that is characteristic of design: How to explore the possible relationships among conflicting concepts? How do we synthesize apparent divergences into a analytic framework stable enough to support subsequent work? Answering these questions requires designers to confront the inherent ambiguity of language, and, for this purpose, they almost always turn to writing, which we examine in the next section.

REMAKING THE WORLD THROUGH TALK TO TEXT

The texts students write to design represent a range of genres far beyond those we traditionally teach in language arts. Not only are many of these texts written collaboratively, but they also include more than the linear, discursive prose most of us think of when we think of "text." For example, Sam, Paul, Tim, and Jack spent most of three or four early meetings constructing the diagram shown in Figure 13.4, an *objectives tree* to display the relationships among their design objectives.

Seeing such diagrams as texts enables us to better understand how designers negotiate the inherent ambiguity of language. In particular, our observations suggest that such diagrammatic texts place a system on the process of argumentation which is characteristic of design. In the following excerpt, for example, the team was stuck composing at the top of their objectives tree, trying to decide on their

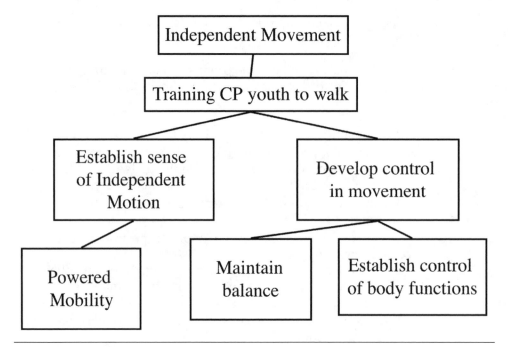

Figure 13.4.   Students' Developing Objectives Tree.

main objective and its relationship to other objectives. In the very lengthy argument that ensued, the team, driven by the need to compose the objectives tree, analyzed the relationship among the objectives they had previously constructed for their design:

> T: But the whole … Why are we training? For mobility, right? So that's what goes on top, is mobility.
>
> P: Yeah. But the purpose of mobility is to train.
>
> T & S: Yeah.
>
> P: The purpose of … the powered mobility is to train them for independent mobility.
>
> T & S: Right. That's right.
>
> P: So the main point is to … train them to be independent.
>
> J: Whether it's powered or ….
>
> P: So everything goes around that, revolves around that …. And powered mobility goes around that.
>
> T: That's the tip of the tree.
> [pause]
>
> J: Mobility is independence, right?
>
> P: Yeah. But you're training them to be independent … by providing them with ….
>
> T: Independent means you can move by yourself.

P: Yeah. But you had to train them … the process of training them to be independent.

T: How are we gonna have independent movement? We're gonna have it by mobility. How are we gonna give them mobility? We're gonna do it through physical training … teaching them to walk.

P: Yeah. I guess. If you put it that way, then …. (Team meeting on 9/26)

As this example indicates, composing nonlinear texts is not that different from composing more traditional discursive texts. As they are drafted and redrafted, both kinds of texts help members of a team to develop shared understanding, to see each other's intentions, and to clarify the relationships among those intentions.

Because of its collaborative nature, however, design requires going beyond these simple shared understandings. In fact, good design results when team members synthesize competing ideas, not just choose among them. And once again, texts have a major role to play in achieving this design purpose. In particular, the process by which Sam, Paul, Tim, and Jack composed illustrates how talk to text can move designers from a competing analytic schemes to a shared design.

As we noted in the last section, our team had drawn on a variety of sources—source texts from the library, interviews with a therapist, and observations of children with cerebral palsy—to analyze the design problem they faced. By their October 7 meeting, they were faced with two competing functional analyses: one, the therapist's scheme, which identified four distinct problems affecting children with cerebral palsy; the other, suggested by the source text by Scherzer and Tscharnuter (1990) and championed by Tim, which emphasized overall coordination and balance.

Midway through the meeting, Paul was finally convinced by Tim's oral argument that their design should help children develop a sense of balance. But this conviction still left the team with the problem of integrating this new function (sense of balance) into the four-part functional analysis that the therapist had proposed (tone control, weight shifting, disassociation, and isolation). To address this challenge, Paul worked through the scheme aloud, using talk to check that the others agreed with his synthesis. He asked if sense of balance "followed" from tone control, and he accepted Tim's suggestion that tone control "helps to develop" a sense of balance. Jack added that balance "also would help the dissociation," because more muscle tone would allow children to move their feet more accurately.

When Paul finally summarized what he understood to be true, Jack pointed out that they had redrafted their problem statement, a short statement they had originally composed to express their shared understanding of the design problem. This new draft now read:

Design a device that will aid in the development of balance, weight shifting, and control of limbs, in order to enable children with c.p. to develop walking skills.

Adding the concept of "sense of balance" from Tim's source text, the team not only kept the concept of "weight shifting" proposed by the therapist, but they also redefined the more technical concepts of "dissociation" and "isolation" with a new phrase, "control of the limbs." In doing so, the students used writing to perform a synthesis task characteristic of good design, blending an existing analytic scheme with an original idea in a way that better addressed the design situation.

THE TEXT-MAKING OF WORLD-MAKING

This brief glimpse of the work of Sam, Paul, Tim, and Jack only begins to suggest the complex interaction of talk and text in the process of engineering design. Thus far, we have used specific excerpts of talk and text to show how texts not only were present during most of the students' design work but also played a crucial role in stimulating and enabling that work. At the beginning, the ambiguities of design texts afforded the team many possibilities for design. Source texts then helped to introduce them to the values and knowledge of the community targeted by their design. Next, composing nonlinear texts pushed them to develop shared understanding. And finally, composing texts led them to synthesize a common analytic framework and generate new design concepts. Methods have been needed for analyzing talk and text and their interactions. *Analyzing Streams of Language: Twelve Steps to the Systematic Coding of Text, Talk, and Other Verbal Data* (Geisler, 2004) provides a step-by-step methodology for analyzing and describing a stream of continuous verbal data that may be oral, written, or electronic interactions. This system is designed to help researchers across disciplines to use language as a basis for formulating research questions.

As a way of emphasizing the text-making intensity of engineering design, the chart in Figure 13.5 shows graphically how the students' production of design ideas about the movement mechanism of their design was directly related, in every case, to the requirement to produce text:

- The first small peak, on September 18, came as the students drafted the initial problem statement for their adviser.

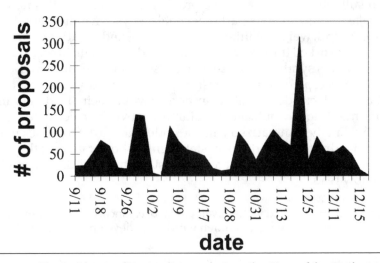

Figure 13.5. The Incidence of Design Proposals Over the Time of the Students' Design Work.

- The second peak, on September 26 and 29, came as the team planned and wrote their state-of-the-art review.
- The third peak, between October 7 and October 17, found the team composing a design matrix.
- The fourth peak, at October 30, arose as they prepared their mid-term reports.
- The final series of peaks, from November 7 through December 9, occurred as they drafted the final report originally due on December 6 and finally delivered on December 9.

Through the course of their work, then, each time that our students faced a design task, they were both impelled by and supported by the need for text-making.

WHAT WE SHOULD LEARN FROM HOW ENGINEERS USE LANGUAGE TO DESIGN

In no small measure, in engineering design, the task of world-making through design is the task of text-making through talk. Unlike simple talk, which is not generally designed by its interlocutors, texts can be understood as designs in themselves, material artifacts of paper and ink, with their own functions and features, addressing their own problematic situations. In engineering, what appears to happen is that designers capitalize on the designed nature of text, making design choices by making text choices. The result is a synergy for design innovation from which we, as language arts instructors, have much to learn.

Engineering design is only one of the most obvious processes of cultural production by which citizens attempt to remake the world. As many have noted before us, the traditional language arts classroom has tended to present talk and text as the handmaidens of the society's justified concern with the transmission of a world already made. From design engineers, however, we can begin to understand talk and text as also useful for remaking that world.

What are the lessons we, as language arts educators, might take from the analysis presented in this chapter for how talk and text might enable all of our students—not just those few who will become design engineers—to have this opportunity?

A Different Kind of Text Consulting

Research in the reading classroom suggests that students have often been presented with a view of reading as a process of "text-consulting" (Heap, 1985), a process by which free-standing text worlds are constructed and explored (Baker & Freebody, 1989). Our analysis of the work of Sam, Paul, Tim, and Jack shows, however, that texts can also be read in juxtaposition to worlds outside of their textual borders. This second kind of reading, which we might think of as a different kind of text consulting, juxtaposes the representation of the world proposed by one text against representations proposed other texts, nontextual sources, and the reader's own experience. Sam, for example, used this kind of reading to compare the Amesbury Walker described by Levitt with his own developing design ideas ("throw a motor in there and a platform on the bottom, there you go").

Unlike traditional notions of text consulting, however, the juxtaposition process in which students engage during the process of design is not primarily aimed at answering questions such as "Is this text right?" or "Should I trust this text?" Instead, in engineering design, questions of textual veracity are generally set aside in favor of a different question, "Is this text useful?" When Tim, for example, used the text by Scherzer and Tscharnuter (1990) to argue that their design should address the problems that children with cerebral palsy have with balance, he did not need to show that the alternative four-part analysis presented by the therapist was wrong and that Scherzer and Tscharnuter were right. He only needed to establish that Scherzer and Tscharnuter pointed to something useful for their design work.

A Different Kind of Critical Reading

In the traditional language arts classroom, the synthesis task of bringing together multiple sources of information to produce a new interpretation has often been conceived only in terms of textual sources. Through research papers and other synthesis tasks, we teach students the useful skills of shifting, comparing, and combining (Kaufer, Geisler, & Neuwirth, 1988). We seldom, however, ask students to synthesize textual and nontextual sources.

The analysis we have presented in this chapter, suggests, however, that such synthesis is not only common but also presents its own interesting issues of authority and purpose. When Tim, for example, assumed the rhetorical burden of persuading his teammates to synthesize the analytic category, "sense of balance," into the four-part scheme proposed by the therapist, he did not simply have to address the question we have already noted, that is, "Is this useful?" He also had to contend with the team's justified concern with the acceptability of the resulting synthesis to the therapist who had proposed something else. The question that had to be asked, in other words, was "Is this acceptable?"

The point here is that all representations of the world, whether originating from textual or nontextual sources, come *valanced*, marked with the authority of their originators; some are inevitably more significant than others to the purpose at hand. In teaching students to evaluate sources for a research paper, we do not often teach them the critical reading skills necessary to deal with such valances. We may ask students to compare dates of publication, or we may push them to use more than popular magazines, but we seldom ask them to evaluate their sources in relationship to their own purposes for writing and acting.

The work of design engineers helps us to understand how students in any situation in which they adopt the purpose to persuade others to action must treat sources as valanced by the purposes at hand. Trying to convince a city council member to adopt your proposal? Better consider what he wrote on the issue during last year's election. Trying to persuade the school to adopt a different approach to reading instruction? Better become familiar with the state guidelines. Critical reading skills in such situations involve developing a set of contextually-defined criteria to identify what, in the current state of thinking, should be built on as we remake the world.

A Different Kind of Teacher Role

In the late 19th and early 20th centuries, when the foundational assumptions for this country's educational system were being developed, the best thinkers assumed that knowledge would be made by experts in a variety of specializations and disseminated through the educational system to a broad band of citizenry (McGrath et al., 1948). The role of the good citizen was to *know,* that is, to understand the emerging concepts from the sciences, social sciences, and humanities well enough to make informed civic choices. But it was left to the experts to *do,* to engage in the specialized processes of cultural production required to generate the choices with which the general public would be presented.

The teacher roles with which many of us are familiar developed in this culture of expertise. Participating in the education of good citizens, language arts teachers set their sights on teaching students the text-consulting practices necessary to understand the texts written by experts and the critical reading skills necessary to distinguish those experts from those without the appropriate credentials.

In the late 20th and early 21st centuries, many have come to reconsider the great divide between expert and layperson (Geisler, 1994) and to reclaim for the general citizen an active role in the production of culture. It is in this context that what we as language arts teachers can learn from how engineers use language to design takes on broader significance:

- Present talk and text as part of the *doing* of an active citizenship.
- Teach text consulting as part of an active citizen's *remaking the world.*
- Show students how choices are *valanced* by the civic purposes at hand.

As we teach these lessons critical to a more active citizenry, we will find that our role as teacher becomes more like the role George assumed in working with Sam, Paul, Tim, and Jack. In his weekly meetings with them, George listened to the students, and he used his own talk to clarify their choices and support their goals. Here is how he did it early in the design process we've already detailed:

> G: There's potentially two focuses that could evolve here. One could be something that tries to do the same kinds of functions that a wheelchair would do: provide the independent movement and ability to go where wheelchairs can go, okay? The other might be more of a training or therapy device, okay?
>
> P: Couldn't we have something in a combination of both?
>
> G: Could you have a comb … Yes, perhaps you could. That would be outstanding. (Meeting with instructor on 9/18)

As this interchange illustrates, a teacher's role in supporting students' language for active citizenship involves carefully listening to and reflecting back the choices inherent in what students say. George posed the students with a choice; the students pushed back with an alternative George hadn't thought of; George saw the promise of that alternative and encouraged them to go forward. Like George, good teachers will never use talk to impose decisions on students. To do so would be to take away the choices that they as citizens must learn to make. The most important lesson that we can learn from how engineers use language to design, then, may be the most simple: The world is ours to remake. The resources of talk and text are here to help us in that task.

NOTES

*This paper is written in sincere appreciation of the engineering design students and their teachers who have so graciously allowed us to watch them work.

1. The names of these students and their instructor have been changed to protect their privacy.

REFERENCES

Brandon, R. (1996). *Singer and the sewing machine*. New York: Kodansha International.

Collins, H. (1985). *Changing order: Replication and induction in scientific practice*. Beverly Hills, CA: Sage.

Geisler, C. (1995). *Academic literacy and the nature of expertise: Reading, writing, and knowing in academic philosophy*. Hillsdale, NJ: Lawrence Erlbaum Associates.

Geisler, C. (2004). *Analyzing streams of language: Twelve steps to the systematic coding of text, talk, and other verbal data*. New York: Pearson Education.

Levitt, S. (1982). *Treatment of cerebral palsy and motor delay*. London: Blackwell.

McGrath, E. J., Bloomers, P. J., Gerber, J. C., Goetsch, W. R., Jacobs, J. A., Longman, L. D., et al. (1948). *Toward general education*. New York: Macmillan.

Polanyi, M. (1958). *Personal knowledge: Towards a post-critical philosophy*. Chicago: University of Chicago Press.

Scherzer, A. L., & Tscharnuter, I. (1990). *Early diagnosis and therapy in cerebral palsy: A primer on infant developmental problems*. New York: Marcel Dekker.

Semans, S., Phillips, R., Romanoli, M., Miller, R., & Skillen, M. (1969). A cerebral palsy assessment chart: Instructions for administration of the test. In J. M. Wolf (Ed.), *The results of treatment in cerebral palsy* (pp. 267–275). Springfield, IL: Charles C Thomas.

Wolf, J. M. (1969). *The results of treatment in cerebral palsy*. Springfield, IL: Charles C Thomas.

CHAPTER 14

The Use of Dialogue in Drama: Reading Dialogue and Observing Performance

Peter van Stapele

CREATING DIALOGUE AND STORIES THROUGH PLAY

About five years ago my 4-year-old daughter Miriam and I were playing with two toy bears. The bear Miriam was playing with was actually a panda, which she called Pandabear Pebbles; my little bear was supposed to be a dog named Doggy Fun. Doggy Fun lived in a house on my knees. Pandabear Pebbles rings the doorbell. Doggy Fun opens the door. "Hello Pandabear Pebbles, nice to see you. Come in, let's play together."

That is what Miriam makes me say, because I am the player who makes Doggy Fun act. Miriam creates the characters, the situation, and the dialogues, which are the main vehicles with which she develops the plot of the story of our play. And she coaches me in the process of creating the story we play, especially through the use of dialogue.

The play and its development are based on contrasts–conflicts between the characters and on the principle that all important events have a cause. The contrasts between the characters are not necessarily very big (e.g., a possible disagreement about revealing a little secret to another character), but they are necessary to forward the story's plot.

By playacting with Miriam, I learned that very young children are able to create and to direct the stories that emerge during their play and that most stories have a dramatic character. In a natural way, children are conscious of the distinction between different realities while they are playing. Miriam, for instance, was conscious of the distinction between (1) the realities she and I were acting in, (2) the reality of being Miriam and Daddy, (3) the reality of being players, and (4) the reality of the characters, Pandabear Pebbles and Doggy Fun. It is fascinating to observe that children are able to create such realities and to take control of the working process, which is essential to their development (see Horowitz, 1990).

During this play there was one event that has affected the way I think about the concept of "realities" and has influenced the way I work as a teacher. At a certain moment, I made Doggy Fun speak to Miriam: "Say, Miriam, where are Bert and Ernie?" Miriam then put down Pandabear Pebbles, looked at me, and told me in all seriousness: "No, that is not possible. Doggy Fun cannot talk to me. I don't play in the play, and neither do you." I withdrew Doggy Fun and said: "But Doggy Fun wants to know where Bert and Ernie are." Miriam said, "Then he must ask Pandabear Pebbles. Children … you … grown-up people … don't play in the play, like the animals and the dolls." I understood. We played on. Later, I accidentally said something to Pandabear Pebbles, and Miriam became very impatient: "No, you were not in the play."

Children engage in dramatic play with siblings and peers every day. They place themselves in another reality, another world—the world of characters like Pandabear Pebbles and Doggy Fun, for example, pretending they have a puppy living with them all the time. They create such realities and everything that occurs in them, and they have the power to feel what characters feel, to let them talk, to create dialogues. Pellegrini (1997) writes, "Pretend play is a vital part of children's everyday life which they delve in and out to learn and practice all sorts of new behaviors" (p. 488). Together, children are producers of the creative process through which they learn to take into account each other's feelings and desires and each other's possibilities and powers, as well as those of the characters in their play.

Realities

Through the medium of playing, young children learn the art of understanding and telling stories, which forms the basis of the development of their knowledge and abilities and of their character and mental powers. Learning the art means learning to create a structured account of real or imaginary events in a certain situation. These events and situations I call *realities:*

R1   a part of the reality in which we and our ancestors and descendants live (e.g., people we tell or write about); R1 is a reality in *the reality we live in*

R2   a specific situation of *communication in R1* (e.g., playing, reading, performing a play before an audience, writing a letter to someone, a talk about "what will happen next"); R2 is a reality of communication

R3   a reality that comes into being in R2 by our *creating a story*, which can be any structured account of events in a certain situation, either fiction or fact, and which is based on a clear *premise* (the underlying idea of the story) and on interesting and fundamental contrasts and the principle of causality.

Young children learn the fundamentals of creating stories by playing, not by performing. This distinction between children playing stories—being naturally creative—and children learning to make and perform stories—being culturally and socially creative—is important. In the first period of their life, children should have the opportunity and the time to develop their art of playing before they learn to perform in the broad sense of the word. Then they are able to develop a broad and solid basis on which they are able to learn to perform skillfully, learning the ways of the world without losing their natural simplicity.

Stories (R3) have dramatic qualities because they tell about action, which is based on contrasts and on the principle of causality. Therefore, by making stories—also when we observe, read, or listen to them—we create the workings of contrasts as well as the relation between cause and effect. The principle that everything important happens for a reason is the way in which we make sense of different situations in different realities or create new ones. Especially with words, images, and sounds, we form new realities related to existing ones in a process of interaction with other human beings. This is a continual process, for each individual as well as for any group in society. It is mainly through creating stories with dramatic qualities that we make sense of the world. The result of this *making sense of the world* is the making—or the speaking and writing about interpretations and valuations—of fantasies, ideas, concepts, opinions, myths, texts, paintings, pictures, television programs, exhibitions, and so on.

Learning the art of understanding and telling stories is the basis of education (van Stapele, 1988, 1989a). Learning to understand and to tell stories, especially through the use of dialogue, has a natural basis, as children playing stories show us.

Objective of This Chapter

The objective is to enable students to create and use a *metalanguage* (toolbox) that enables them to develop the way they feel, think, and communicate about observing, listening to, reading, talking about, and writing about certain situations (R3, as well as R1 and R2). The basic idea is that students are able to learn or to develop listening and observing, talking, reading, and writing skills by transforming the nature of their ability to play into the culture of their ability to perform. The heart of creativity is the ability to *play*.

DIALOGUE

The reality of characters (R3) in a performance in theatre (R2) takes shape through the use of signs—words, gestures, movements, and so on—which actors (R1/2) in the performance transmit to spectators (R1/2). In drama for the stage, which is based on dramatic texts, the use of those signs by actors is based on the interpretation of the written dialogue. *Dialogue between characters in a dramatic text, therefore, forms the basis of communication between actors and audience in the performing of a play at the theater.*

Dialogue in drama (R3) is different from dialogue in everyday life (R1). In dialogue in drama, every word counts because it is the main vehicle of the plot, which creates a complete story within a relatively short time of performance and enables readers and spectators to create stories in their mind (interpretants). Looking at dialogue in drama, therefore, requires looking at aspects and elements of the creation of the following:

- Space (including stage settings and props)
- A dramatic situation of characters in that space, which is a situation of contrast(s) and (possible) conflict(s)
- The characters in that situation and their relation to one another

- The development of dramatic action, which is the interrelation of the acts of the characters (including speaking) in a process of action-and-reaction in which emotions play an important part and which is based on contrasts—related to motivation and objectives—and on the principle of causality

In this chapter, the matter of developing a plot is treated only on the level of dialogue itself, not on the level of the genre of drama as a whole (see Beckerman, 1979; Kennedy, 1983; Pavis, 1987; Pfister, 1991).

Information Through Stage Directions

"Like the look of him?" This is the first sentence of Samuel Beckett's play *Catastrophe*. The mind of the reader must become acquainted with enough information to interpret that sentence. The writer gives the reader the requested information before the dialogue of the play begins:

Director (D).

His female assistant (A).

Protagonist (P).

Luke, in charge of the lighting, offstage (L).

Rehearsal. Final touches to the last scene. Bare stage. A and L have just set the lighting. D has just arrived.

D   in an armchair downstairs audience left. Fur coat. Fur toque to match. Age and physique unimportant.

A   standing beside him. White overall. Bare head. Pencil on ear. Age and physique unimportant.

P   midstage standing on a black block 18 inches high. Black wide-brimmed hat. Black dressing-gown to ankles. Barefoot. Head bowed. Hands in pocket. Age and physique unimportant.

D and A contemplate P. Long pause.

(Beckett, 1990)

When *A* speaks the first sentence, "Like the look of him?" the mind of the reader is acquainted with enough information to interpret the beginning of the play. Each dramatic text may be considered to be a potential fact, which can be interpreted. The interpreting mind of a reader of a dramatic text cannot become acquainted with the reality the text in question denotes—the reality of characters (R3)—unless it creates that reality in his or her mind.

The interpretation takes place in the context of the part of the play the reader has read so far, as we can see in the example of the beginning of *Catastrophe* by Samuel Beckett: "Like the look of him?" We have read that "him" is the Protagonist and that "the look of him" is related to "P midstage standing on a black block 18 inches high. Black wide-brimmed hat. Black dressing-gown to ankles. Barefoot. Head bowed. Hands in pocket. Age and physique unimportant," on which the Director and his female Assistant are contemplating. The line "Like the look of him?" is spoken by *A* to *D*, which we learn when we read that he answers her question. All this information is the basis for making decisions about staging the play and about the use of theater-space during the performance.

This information is written in the text as *stage directions*. The function of these instructions is to provide the interpreting mind of the reader with information about space and setting, and about the characters, their situation, and some of their acts. Stage directions give information necessary to enable the reader to interpret (the relevant part of) the dramatic story in which the dialogue occurs. Stage directions give information on the surface of the plot as well as about what is hidden in and underneath the text (*subtext*, which otherwise could not be interpreted). An understanding of the subtext is as critical for readers as it is for actors:

> Leaning on the work of Constantin Stanislavski, actor and artistic director of the Moscow Art Theatre, Vygotsky (1986) suggests that underneath the written or spoken text lies the subtext of thought and emotion. An understanding of the subtext or the "inner life" of the text is critical to actors in the theaters (Stanislavski, 1961). (Wolf, Edmiston, & Encico, 1997, p. 496)

Stage directions are not a part of the dialogue. They give the minimal information necessary to interpret the story. The interpreting mind of a reader will add information, which is also based on what the reader reads in the dialogue and on his or her cultural background, character and emotions, knowledge, and personal experiences. To describe it as a metaphor, a sophisticated reader of dramatic dialogue creates, consciously or not, a performance of the dialogue in her or his mind. Many playwrights are careful not to use stage directions unnecessarily. In many cases, through intensive reading and studying dialogue, readers are able to create in their mind what in a performance on the stage can be seen and heard. Dramatic dialogue gives form to imagining space, and the use or the possible use of that space, through information within dialogue and through the way movement in dialogue is constructed.

Information Within Dialogue

Learning to read a dialogue is learning to see and hear in which situation characters say what they say and how they are saying it. The situation in which the characters act, their use of space, space itself (including settings), and the springs of their actions take shape in the mind of the reader through interpreting what is partially hidden in and underneath the text (subtext). Frequently characters, for one reason or another, do not say plainly what they feel or think. This is illustrated by an excerpt from the first scene of a performance by Eugene O'Neill's *Long Day's Journey Into Night*, an adaptation of the stage performance by the National Theatre (UK) to television by Michael Blakemore and Peter Wood, with James Tyrone played by Laurence Olivier and Mary Tyrone by Constance Cummings:

1   Tyrone: You're a fine armful now, Mary, with those twenty pounds you've gained.
2   Mary: I've gotten too fat, you mean, dear. I really ought to reduce.
3   Tyrone: None of that, my lady! You're just right. We'll have no talk of reducing. Is that why you ate so little breakfast?

4	Mary:	So little? I thought I ate a lot.
5	Tyrone:	You didn't. Not as much as I'd like to see, anyway.
6	Mary:	Oh, you! You expect everyone to eat the enormous breakfast you do. Nobody in the world could without dying of indigestion.
7	Tyrone:	I hope I'm not as big a glutton as that sounds. But thank God, I've kept my appetite and I've the digestion of a young man of twenty, if I am sixty-five.
8	Mary:	You surely have, James. No one could deny that. Why did the boys stay in the dining-room I wonder? Cathleen must be waiting to clear the table.
9	Tyrone:	Some secret confab they don't want me to hear, I suppose. I'll bet they're cooking up some new scheme to touch the Old Man. Oh, by the way, dear, McGuire has said he'll phone me around lunchtime.
10	Mary:	I hope he didn't put you on to any new piece of property. His real-estate bargains don't work out so well.
11	Tyrone:	I wouldn't say that, Mary. After all, he was the one who advised me to buy the place on Chestnut Street and I made a quick turnover on it for a fine profit.
12	Mary:	I know dear. The famous one stroke of good luck. I'm sure McGuire never dreamed that … that—. Oh well, never mind, James. I know it's a waste of breath trying to convince you you're not a cunning real-estate speculator.
13	Tyrone:	I've no such idea. But land is land, and it's safer than the stocks and bonds of Wall Street swindlers. Let's not argue about business this early in the morning.
14	Mary:	James, it's Edmund you should scold for not eating enough. He hardly touched anything except coffee. He needs to eat to keep up his strength. I keep telling him that but he simply says he has not any appetite. Of course, nothing takes away your appetite like a bad summer cold.
15	Tyrone:	No no no, it's only natural. So don't let yourself get worried—.
16	Mary:	Oh, I'm not. I know he'll be all right in a few days if he takes care of himself. It just seems a pity he should have to be sick right now.
17	Tyrone:	Oh yes, it is bad luck. But you mustn't let it upset you, Mary. You remember, you got yourself to take care of, too.
18	Mary:	Oh, I'm not upset. There's nothing to be upset about. What makes you think I'm upset?
19	Tyrone:	Why, nothing, except you've seemed a bit high-strung these past few days.
20	Mary:	I have? Oh, nonsense, dear. It's your imagination. You really must not watch me all the time, James. I mean, it makes me self-conscious.
21	Tyrone:	Now, Mary. That's your imagination. If I've watched you it was to admire how fat and beautiful you become. I can't tell you the deep happiness it gives me, darling, to see you as

you've been since you came back to us, your dear sweet old
self again. So keep up the good work, Mary.

22   Mary: Oh, I will, dear. Thank heavens, the fog is gone…. I do feel
out of sorts this morning. I wasn't able to get much sleep
with that awful foghorn going all night long.

Through reading the fragment, we already are able to see the complicated character Tyrone is, the situation he lives in, his relation with Mary and with his sons, and
his problems and anxieties. All this is solely created by the way he speaks and reacts, the themes he discusses or does not want to speak about, his choice of words
and his grammar, the things he repeats, and so on. And we also learn to know
Tyrone by the way Mary speaks to him and the way she reacts to what he is saying
and doing.

Mary must be severely ill. We learn that she does not want to speak about her
condition and that she contradicts Tyrone's anxieties. She wants to convince him
that there is no ground for the fear and uncertainty he is showing. She tries to tease
Tyrone, and she knows that he is a bit self-satisfied and self-conscious. She does
not like Tyrone's real-estate bargains, but she seems to have no say in matters of
business.

As we analyze Mary this way, we begin to see her situation and problems, her
relation with Tyrone, and we see the growing tension between the two characters.
This tension already exists in Tyrone's first speech, because he makes, consciously
or not, an introductory remark to give a reaction, not a reaction to what has happened during breakfast but to what he feels could be the cause of Mary eating so
little breakfast. In the beginning of the dialogue, the first signs of tension that exist
in the subtext come to the surface. It concerns the energy that drives the movement
of action and reaction in the dialogue, which is discussed in the next section.

Information Through Movement in Dialogue

This section describes why and in which way the most important information in
dramatic texts comes from the structure of the rhythm of movement in dramatic
dialogue. The analysis and interpretation of a dramatic text on this level consider
the structure of the rhythm of movement as a pattern of actions and reactions—also within each separate speech. An experienced reader will, consciously
or not, feel that rhythm and relate it to imagining how it is expressed through the
way characters act.

Interpreting and discussing movement in dialogue concern the interpretation
of interaction (of actions and reactions) of the characters in the text, especially with
regard to the interchangeability of I and you (Elam, 1980, p. 143). Such an interpretation defines the dramatic world in very major aspect: characters, conflict and
emotions, and arrangement and movement of interaction in a certain space.

The rhythm in a dramatic dialogue can be made visible through segmenting the
text into beats, marking the rhythm of the text, like phrases in music (Lewis, 1958,
p. 33). This rhythm is produced by changes in the direction of a discourse, made by
one character and taken over by the partner. This may run parallel with change in
discourse topics. Close reading of the turns at the beginning of the dialogue between Mary and Tyrone make it apparent how we know that Tyrone wants to
speak about Mary's condition and that Mary wants to avoid the subject. She wants

to speak about Edmund's condition, which is brushed aside by Tyrone. Both characters change the subject several times. When they speak about Mary's condition the first time (speeches 1–5), Tyrone makes references to time (*now; breakfast*). When they speak about Mary condition for the third time (17–22), both are referring to time, but Tyrone refers to the past (*remember; these past few days; since you came back*) whereas Mary does not react on this and speaks only about time in general in the present (*all the time*) and about very recent time (*this morning; all night long*). These references to time create the relationship between action and time frame. Features like these show the development of suspense in drama, which is slowly built up, generating questions and wonder in the readers or the spectators.

Most dramatic situations come into existence through the interaction between the characters. The direct context-of-utterance can be represented as speak (*I*), listening (*you*), time of utterance (*now*), locations of utterance (*here*), and the utterance itself (Elam, 1980, p. 138). In speech 5 of the dialogue between Tyrone and Mary, Tyrone changes from focusing on "you" into focusing on "I" by mentioning himself in the second part of his speech. This immediately is taken up by Mary, who, in her reaction in speech 6, concentrates on "you" instead of on herself. "O *you! You* expect ..."

This example illustrates that the dramatic text is characterized by a succession of acts based on speeches which, at the same time, are divided from and related to one another as well as to the dramatic context in the making.

The interrelation of the different speeches (of actions and reactions) takes shape through the relationship between smaller units within the speeches. These units are called *deictic units* because they refer to the dramatic context in creation. They can be used to actually *show* the beats of the rhythm of the pattern of actions and reactions in a dramatic text. This method of analyzing the dramatic dialogue is discussed in the next section.

Deictic Analysis of Movement in Dialogue

The method of deictic analysis used in this chapter is based on previous work by various scholars (Benveniste, 1970; Elam, 1980; Honzl, 1943/1976; Kowzan, 1976; Lyons, 1977; Rauh, 1983; Serpieri, Elam, Publiatti, Kemeny, & Rutelli, 1981).

A deictic analysis shows the structure of the rhythm of movement in the use of language in a dramatic dialogue. As we have seen in the previous sections, the term *drama* in general means the development of situation(s) of conflict between characters, mainly through the interrelation of their acts in a process of action-and-reaction. Criteria for choosing *deictic units* in a character's speeches, therefore, is based on the feature relation-between-characters. Deictic analysis is focused on the protagonists, especially the *I* and *you* in their dramatic discourse.

The pattern of actions and reactions of the characters—also within each separate speech—can be embodied in the description of the results of the analysis, which can be described in a well-organized and comprehensible way. An example is the analysis of the following part of a dialogue (A = she; B = he):

1A: *You* are not looking at *me*.
2B: That's not true, otherwise *I* could not have noticed that *you* are blushing.

3A: *I* am not. *You* are trying to change the subject. *You* were not looking at *me*.

1A: You / me.

2B: ... / *I* /, *you*

3A: *I* / You, You / me.

Changes of focus occur within all three speeches, and in speech 2, character B ends his speech by focusing on "you," followed by A's "I" in speech 3. In this example, a clear deictic turn occurs, related to a change of subject. The changes of focus and the clear deictic turn that starts in speech 2 are signs showing what happens inside and between the characters, related to the change of subject. We then see that A seems to realize what B is doing, and she repeats the subject of he first speech. Three speeches and already the drama is developing, with changes in the direction of the discourse that make drama possible. There are no big contrasts yet, but the fact that the characters are in disagreement with each other could, depending on the subtext, grow into something big.

This method of analyzing and describing movement in dialogue can be considered a part of the toolbox, which, for example, can be used in going deeper into interpreting difficult parts of texts. With respect to the beginning of the dialogue between Mary and Tyrone in the beginning of *Long Day's Journey Into Night*, it is easy to determine, and to check, that the following units of speeches are the beats of the rhythm of movement of action and reaction between the partners in that dialogue: 1–5 / 5–8 / 8-9 / 9–12 / 12–14 / 14–15 / 15–16 / 16–17 / 17–22.

The results of the analysis of the pattern of movement in the dialogue can be put in a diagram showing the beats, parallel with expressions of: /space / time / the main subjects of the discourse /:

1–5:   / ... / now, breakfast / Mary's condition

5–8:   / ... / (sixty-five) / Tyrone's condition

8–9:   / dining-room / stay, waiting / the boys, scheme

9–12:   / the place on Chestnut Street / around lunchtime / McGuire, real-estate bargains, profit

12–13:   / Wall Street / this early in the morning / Tyrone's capacity for speculating, swindlers, arguing

14–15:   / (breakfast) / summer cold / Edmund's health

15–16:   / ... / ... / Mary's condition

16–17:   / ... / in a few days, right now / Edmund's health

17–22:   / (night) / remember, these past few days, all the time, since you came back, again, this morning, (sleep), all night long / Mary's condition, (fog, foghorn)

We should be aware of the fact that the beats are signs of the subtext that also is expressed through nonverbal action of the characters. Therefore, to examine the value of the results of such an analysis, it is worthwhile to compare them with the results of studying a performance of the dialogue, describing carefully how the rhythm in the dialogue has been transformed into the rhythm of acting in space.

Through learning to read text and subtext based on what has been described here, students will be able to enter into the characters' minds and understand and feel their emotions and the motivations of their acts, even without performing the dialogue—although this would intensify the emotional dimension of their interpretation. Transforming dialogue into performance becomes part of the inner life of trained readers, as it does of the inner life of actors and actresses as readers—and then on stage—because everything "must be real in the imaginary life of the an actor" (Stanislavski, 1989, p. 157).

Like actors, students could learn to interpret the text as a reality, really spoken in a certain situation in time and space, in which the characters move and use that rhythm in the way they speak and use their bodies, creating signs of the tension and the dynamic of drama.

Through studying body language and body code (Birdwhistell, 1971; Lamb & Watson, 1979), students will better understand how processes of life and their rhythm are expressed in the dramatic text and how the text in this way gives form to subtext:

> [The] printed words do not contain the full meaning, as in purely literary forms. They depend on what lies beneath them, on the subtext. The script ceases to be an art-form based on verbal organization, like a poem or a novel, and becomes the pretext and context for an activity. (Benedetti, 1982, p. 44)

Subtext is, for example, related to the springs of Tyrone's and Mary's words in the beginning of *Long Day's Journey Into Night,* which they surely will show in their spatial behavior because *characters (R3), like people in reality (R1), will not be able to hide some of the information they do not want to speak about. Text and subtext together form a basis for transforming text into performance.*

The Study of Performance

Although not everything that occurs in a performance needs to be the result of conscious acting, every performance (R2) consists of signs that are communicated among sign users (players and audience) and can, therefore, be described by means of semiotics (Aston & Savona, 1991; Counsell, 1996; De Marinis, 1993; Elam, 1980; Hogendoorn, 1976; Kowzan, 1968, 1976; Melrose, 1994; van Kesteren, 1981; Van Stapele, 1985).

It is not easy to observe, describe, and analyze performances in theater or on television. As soon as we take a closer look at a performance and try to describe what happens in it, we might lose our grip of what we see. Often the biggest problem is that in a performance, many different kinds of sign systems are used simultaneously, including language, voice, movement, makeup, and props (Hogendoorn, 1976; Kowzan, 1968, 1976; Van Stapele, 1985). The observer, looking at a certain situation (R3), has to choose to analyze the use of certain kinds of signs, related to the questions he or she has, because he or she will not be able to observe all that characters actually do when they speak their speeches and listen to their partners in the dialogue.

The main question we have about the performance at the beginning of *Long Day's Journey Into Night* is how the nonverbal behavior of the actors playing Mary and Tyrone will show something of the tension that exists within and between the characters and how that behavior relates to the spoken text. While analyzing the behavior, we must observe whether it is complementary to, identical, or in contradiction with what the characters are saying. Our question is related to the fact that it is easier to lie about emotions or to conceal them through the use of words than through nonverbal action (van Stapele, Halliday, Gibbons, & Nicholas, 1990), which is also related to the use of voice and other sounds (Martin, 1991; Weis, 1982). As Wolf, Edmiston, & Enciso (1997) argue, "It is the vocal shaping of the context which provides the sense, not simply the meaning (Vygotsky, 1986)" (p. 499).

To answer our question, we look at postures, gestures, distance, touch, and movement through space. In this way, it is possible to describe and to make plain and clear the use of different sign systems by which the actress and the actor, consciously or not, crate the performance as a sign system on which spectators base their interpretation, "reading" how actors have interpreted the text.

We have seen that Mary is contradicting Tyrone from the very first line she speaks and that he is aware of her shying away from the apparently unpleasant subject he wants to speak about. At the beginning of the play, Tyrone and Mary enter the living room and remain close to one another. In the performance, after the clear deictic turn in speech 5, Tyrone is starting to increase the distance between Mary and him (R3). Tyrone's words and closeness have been ineffectual, and he senses that he is making Mary act on the defensive. She is uncomfortable, which is shown by the fact that she hardly moves at all. By distancing himself from Mary, Tyrone is trying to relax the atmosphere and the dynamic of their interaction. But the subject he wants to speak about is not forgotten.

In this way, interpretations can be understood because they are based on a clear insight in what is occurring in text and performance and because they are able to account for what occurs in a performance or what might occur in the mind of a reader or a spectator.

Another example of how we can compare text with performance is that during speech 14, the posture of both Tyrone and Mary is changing. Tyrone's posture changes from vertical/sagittal (an oblique position) into complete vertical as if he is listening very carefully. Mary's posture is changing for a very short time from vertical into vertical/slightly sagittal. Especially this small change in Mary's nonverbal behavior is remarkable. Her posture during a great part of the dialogue is almost rigidly vertical, which expresses her state of mind far more clearly than her words. Together with other signs—she hardly makes any gesture, does not look at Tyrone, and she is speaking with a slightly high-pitched voice—Mary's nonverbal behavior contradicts her nimble talk in the beginning of the performance. She is only jesting there to shy away from the unpleasant subject Tyrone wants to speak about. The very short interruption of her posture during speech 14 indicates that she has an important point to make, and as we have seen earlier, Tyrone is responding to her, also in a nonverbal way.

In the performance, another important turn in the nonverbal behavior of both characters during speech 21 can be noticed. Tyrone's posture here changes from vertical into vertical/sagittal when he speaks the words "I can't tell you the deep happiness it gives me darling ...." His changing posture, while he touches Mary tenderly, underlines his reassuring words. But Mary seems not to be soothed. She hardly changes her vertical posture; she only moves a very short moment at the end of Tyrone's reassuring sentences.

Then Tyrone's posture is changing again and becomes vertical while he says, "So keep up the good work, Mary." At the same time, he is distancing himself from her. His nonverbal behavior is expressing his real, unspoken message. The audience could sense that Tyrone feels fear of what has happened in the past and that he is reading signs that "it" is happening again. He wants to caution Mary against it. It can be seen that Tyrone wants to allay his fear, without being able to speak about it explicitly. Mary does not want to respond to that. For one reason or another, she seems to be locked up in herself.

Tyrone's nonverbal behavior reveals his emotions more than his kind and cautious words do. Mary is not soothed or misled as to the intention of Tyrone's words, which she above all "tells" with her nonverbal behavior. She hardly moves at all, in contrast to Tyrone, who is moving almost all the time. We may conclude that Tyrone's acts in this fragment fail, partly because Mary is not cooperative, which can been *seen*. At this moment in the performance (speech 22), spectators who do not know the play do not know why. They may begin to sense that Tyrone and Mary are not well related to each other, that both are not very informative, that they are not saying to each other what they really mean, and that they are "showing" this. In this way, subtext is beginning to come to the surface. Especially their nonverbal interaction tells that Mary and Tyrone live in a dramatic situation in terms of (the history of) their relationship.

In this section, we have seen how we can study movement in nonverbal action related to movement in dialogue, which makes it possible to see how *subtext breaks through the surface of text.* Rhythm of movement in dialogue means rhythm in space: the rhythm of action that gives form to what lives in and underneath the text. For that reason, the most important information about characters and their acts, about their situation, and about space and the possible use of it in the dramatic text comes from the structure of rhythm of movement in the dialogues. A deictic analysis of the text shows that structure, as a pattern of actions and reactions, which is also within each separate speech.

As has been said earlier, a sophisticated reader will experience the beats of the rhythm in a dramatic dialogue and relate it, consciously or not, to imagining how the rhythm is expressed in the action of the characters within a certain space. The key to understanding this process is that without creating in our mind, consciously or not, the nonverbal aspects and elements of the situation and of the action of the characters, we cannot really understand the meaning of their utterances. We should be fully conscious of the fact that speaking means acting and that acting dialogue will bring aspects and elements of subtext to the surface. This process is related to the speech acts of the different speeches within the dialogue.

The Study of Illocution

"It is the 'illocution' which constitutes the speech act proper," which concerns "the act performed *in* saying something, such as asking a question, ordering someone to do something, promising, asserting the truth of a proposition, etc." (Elam, 1980, p. 158).

A speech act can be expressed clearly and exactly in one or more words. When someone says "Close the window," in a certain situation, the speech act is "I ask you" or "I order you" (to close the window). The speech act can be described as "asking" or "commanding."

The speech act theory that has informed my perspective, as discussed in this section, has been developed since 1955, when Austin proposed a theory of language as a mode of social action (actually, *doing* things with words; Austin, 1976).

When someone says, "It is cold in here," in a certain situation this may be an act of putting a question or giving a command ("close the window!"). A definite interpretation of speech acts is difficult or impossible, because the meaning of text on the level of illocution belongs partly to the world of subtext, which is a world we cannot observe directly. Furthermore, in saying one thing, people can perform more than one speech act at the same time. *For example, by speaking the sentence "It is cold in here," one could perform the following acts: declaring, complaining, or asking.* And people often are not (very) conscious of the speech acts they are performing.

Related to this, we have to realize that, as Melrose (1994) argues,

> The thesis of an intentional and self-knowing, self-determining *single* subject of language of action, oriented to and moving toward a specific goal, is exploded. Pratt (1986) draws significantly on this critique of the unified subject in her work on speech act theory and ideology, to such an extent that the use of speech act theory in the analysis of writing for the stage (cf. Elam, 1984) is seriously challenged. (p. 169)

Nevertheless, speech act theory is a valuable basis for developing tools to learn to understand and analyze dramatic dialogue, as long as we realize that the interpretations we create on the level of illocution are—or could be—a matter of making choices (subjective connotation). It is, however, possible to make a clear description of the interpretation of illocution itself, related to the effects utterances have on the level of speech acts. In analyzing, for example, the first beat of the dialogue between Tyrone and Mary on the level of the speech acts, we see the following pattern:

T1 statement + congratulation

M2 assertions + challenge

T3 negation / assertion / command / question

M4 negations + statement (supposition or question)

T5 negations + statement

M6 *affirmation* + assertions

T7 supposition (question) / assertion (affirmation)

Here we see that the deictic turn of Tyrone in speech 5—which has been taken over by Mary in speech 6: three times *you*—must have a special meaning on the pragmatic level of the discourse. This concerns their attitude toward what they are saying and hearing in the dialogue and how they act and react on that. The special meaning of the deictic turn in speech 5 is indicated by Mary's *affirmation* in speech 6, after she has challenged and contradicted Tyrone's words in her earlier speeches. She makes a good use of the turn, seemingly affirming the truth of Tyrone's statement in speech 5 but actually changing the subject. This is taken over by Tyrone, probably because he has a high opinion of his condition. Mary knows Tyrone very well, and in acting that way, she shows her intelligence. And possibly Tyrone feels that Mary wants to avoid the subject he wants to speak about. Both characters keep the conversation going. The reader or the spectator of the dialogue begins to understand who the characters are as well as the nature of their relationship.

The most important question with regard to speech acts is whether they result in the desired effects or not. As Weijdema and colleagues (1982, p. 174) have made clear, in practice the illocutionary force of utterances is usually implicit. This means that without interpreting the subtext, the possible nonverbal performance, and the context of characters taking part in a dialogue, we cannot determine the real meaning of words. See, for example, pages 345–346 in the section *The Study of Performance*, the description of the performance of the beat which is composed of the speeches 14 to 22. In analyzing this segment on the level of the speech acts, we can describe the following pattern:

M14 advise / report / assertion / report / hypothesis

T15 affirmation / advise

M16 negation / statement / supposition

T17 affirmation / advise / assertion

M18 negation / assertion / question

T19 negation / assertion

M20 question / negation / assertion / request (command) / statement

T21 negation / assertions / request (command)

M22 *promise* / statement / report

We see, among other things, that Mary's request in speech 20 is met by Tyrone's negation in speech 21 and that his request in this speech is met by Mary's promise in speech 22. This is a surprising fact if we notice Mary's negations in the other lines (16, 18, and 20), which correspond with the conclusion of the analysis of the nonverbal performance that it is not likely that Mary is making a real commitment in speech 22.

This conclusion of Mary possibly not making a real commitment concerns the most important point in analyzing speech acts in dramatic texts. Through creating a speech act by saying something, a speaker aims, consciously or not, at a certain result or outcome of his or her speech act. He or she aims at a certain effect. The analysis of speech acts in a dramatic text, therefore, focuses on the motivation of the speaker and on the effect on the partner of what he or she says in the dialogue. As we have seen, Tyrone's speech acts are not effective and Mary probably is not cooperative.

Cooperation is an essential condition for successful communication and interaction. Because the development of drama is based on contrasts and conflict(s) between and within the characters in dramatic dialogues, it is necessary to analyze when such essential conditions for proper communication and interaction are violated. The main purpose of reading (or making an analysis of) a dialogue on the level of illocution is to determine when and why characters are violating postulates which are conditions and rules of conduct that should be met in order to create a situation of successful communication and interaction. Examples of these postulates are (list is partly based on Van Kesteren, 1981, pp. 490–532):

- *Connection*: creating and maintaining contact with the partner in the discourse
- *Cooperation*: acting together to be able to communicate with each other, above all by talking (and giving the necessary information) about the topic(s) of the discourse
- *Quality*: aiming at producing valuable information
- *Relevance*: connecting what one says with the subject of discourse
- *Sincerity*: what one says must have the quality of being genuine
- *Rationality*: being sensible (reasonableness)
- *Commitment*: being responsible for what one says, to fulfill an obligation, for instance
- *Competence*: being in the position or having the authority or the knowledge (etc.) to say the words one speaks
- *Voluntariness*: speaking what one says without being compelled or compelling the partner in the discourse, not imposing one's will on him or her
- *Liberty*: having the right and the power to decide for oneself what one says and does, also when one is junior in rank or position
- *Friendliness*: feeling and expressing kindness toward the partner in the discourse
- *Aesthetics*: the principle of expressing clearly one's thought and feelings in a way that holds the attention of one's partner in the discourse
- *Quantity*: not using less or more words than necessary

The relation between performing speech acts and, consciously or not, adhering to postulates of successful communication and interaction may be clear. Remaining faithful to such postulates in a process of communication and interaction is an action of doing things in human discourse in a certain way (according to certain rules). The importance of studying acts of violation of the postulates in dramatic dialogue is almost self-evident.

To support the development of teaching students the use of tools of this kind, the main information of part 2 will be summarized in the next part of this chapter.

SUMMARY ACCOUNT DIRECTED TOWARD THE DEVELOPMENT OF A SERIES OF LESSONS

Stage Directions and Information Within Dialogue

Introduction

For readers, one of the functions of dialogue is, in some degree, comparable to that of stage directions: providing the interpreting mind of the reader with minimal information about the characters and their situation and about the arena of the scene in which the dialogue occurs, including the stage setting, the use of space, props, costumes, and other sign systems. Talking with the students and asking them to write about this kind of information is the first step in studying dialogue. The acquired information forms the basis for the students to interpret within a certain context the part of the dramatic story in which the dialogue occurs and which, for a great part, is created by the dialogue at the same time.

It is advisable that students begin the study by singling out dialogues (or a scene) at the beginning of plays, because this choice limits the context of which readers must a have thorough knowledge before they are able to begin to understand what exists and what is happening hidden in and underneath the text they are studying.

First Interpretation

The second step is asking the students to write fully, carefully, and clearly, in their own words, a restatement of the meaning of the dialogue they are studying.

When the restatements of the original text are made, it is important to ask the students to answer for their interpretation of difficult parts of the dialogue. It is predictable that their restatement will be explicit about the interpretation of subtext because, in the process of making the restatement, the students will add information to the dialogue, especially on the level of subtext.

Description of the Characters

The final step in this section is describing the characters who are taking part in the dialogue and their relation to one another and to the dramatic situation. Asking the students to write a short biography, paying special attention to similarities and to contrasts between the characters, will enable them to bring about the intended result: learning to know the characters very well.

The characters can be studied by looking at the following aspects, as far as the information really can be based in the text (the list is partly based on Van Luxemburg, Ball, & Wetsteijn, 1987):

- Age, past, important experiences, social status and cultural background, relation with others
- Things they are saying about themselves
- Things they are saying about each other or about other characters (R3), or about persons (R1)
- Topics they want (or refuse) to talk about
- Things they are saying about certain topics and/or about what is happening in the dramatic situation
- References to time and space
- Their actions and reactions in the dialogue, related to questions with regard to their motivation(s) and objective(s)
- Their manner of speaking related to their past and their status and background, which includes possible information about the use of their voice
- Their manner of doing things (nonverbal behavior related to what they are saying)
- An image related to their sign of the zodiac (independently of the question whether students "believe in it" or not)
- Other aspects students might find important, such as costumes

The information the students describe is based on what the characters say. Therefore, it is important that the students focus their attention on the fact that *the charac-*

ters speak from within themselves and from the situation they live and act in. What the characters say is based on what they feel, and know, and think.

In this way, the students will begin to understand and *feel* who the characters really are (R3) and what their situation and problems are, as well as the growing tension in their dialogue. It is useful to advise the students to *listen* to the dialogue. They could ask two other students to read the dialogue to them.

After the work in this section has been done, it is advisable to talk with the students about the subject of subtext.

Action and Reaction

Introduction

From now on, the students are asked to focus their attention on discussing and interpreting movement within dialogue and describing the structure of the rhythm of this movement as a pattern of actions and reactions in and between the speeches of the characters.

First Draft

Based on their work of the first three steps, the fourth step is for students to make a first draft of the pattern of actions and reactions in the dialogue, related to the course the interaction of the characters takes. Writing this first draft should be based on the (contrast between the) conscious and unconscious motivation(s) and objectives(s) of their acts (Beckerman, 1979).

The results of the interpretation on this level will be that the students are able to determine provisionally certain units of speeches (*beats*) in the dialogue, which can be used to make a first, provisional segmentation of the text.

Synopsis

The discussion about the first draft focuses on the question of how the rhythm in the dialogue is produced, which is related to looking at clear turns in the text—which are changes in the direction of the discourse made by one of the characters and taken over by the other—and questioning how and why these turns occur.

The fifth step, then, is assigning the students the task of writing a synopsis by working up their first draft into a carefully finished synopsis of the interaction (of the actions and reactions) of the characters, related to the topics they speak about. The teacher could ask the students beforehand to decide on which moment, how, and why one of the characters, consciously or not, makes the first perceptible move toward a certain objective of dramatic importance and how and why the other, consciously or not, responds to this. The students should use this moment as the starting point for studying the movement of the interaction of the characters in the dialogue and how the movement builds the structure of, and the growing tension in, the discourse as a whole. This is related to the question of where the movement in the dialogue is going and how this could be observed in a performance of the dialogue on stage.

The task of creating the synopsis requires refinement of the segmentation of the text, making visible and understandable the rhythm of the succession of acts, creating the pragmatic context as a basis for performance. Going to the theater or watching a recording of the play in which the dialogue occurs could be the last stage of the learning process for younger students, although there are many other possibilities to bring the enactment of texts into the classroom (see Wolf et al., 1997, and their references). And it is also possible to transform the work of the next section into tasks on the level of younger students, because teachers working with these students possibly will use the information found in the subsections on pages 342–349 anyway.

The next section of this part of the chapter will give suggestions for further study and for research which trained students can pursue and which will add to their knowledge of using language and dialogue, and of certain aspects of semiotics (again, see the subsections on pages 342–349).

Further Study and Research

Deixis, Speech Acts, and Postulates

The analysis of the dialogue on the level of deixis concerns the further analysis and interpretation of the text related to subtext (deep reading) (part 3, section 5). Pending the making of the analysis, the students should look at clear deictic turns, which mark changes in the direction taken by the discourse. The students will learn to actually *show* the structure of the rhythm of movement in their report as a pattern of actions and reactions of the characters.

Subsequent to this analysis, the teacher could assign the students the task of studying the acts the characters are performing by saying their speeches, related to the question of when and why conditions and rules of successful communication and interaction are violated (see subsection *The Study of Illocution* on pages 346–349).

The next step is that teacher and students talk again about the phenomenon that the interpretation of how characters feel, think, and act is primarily related to—materialized by—the movement in the dialogue. A second point of discussion might be the question of how that movement could be expressed by action in space, in theater. Students will develop further understanding of the fact that text and subtext together form a basis for transforming a dramatic text into performance.

A premise for the discussion will be: in dramatic situations, in which emotions are an important factor and which also occur in situations in our reality (R1), persons or characters will, consciously or not and depending on their culture, try to conceal their emotions, which often can be seen or heard through their nonverbal behavior, among other things related to codes of the use of space.

Performance

As a result of their work in the earlier sections of this chapter, students will have a thorough knowledge of the dialogues they have studied. During the process of learning to read and to study (R2) a dramatic dialogue (R3), the characters in the dialogue take shape in the mind of the students. As one might say, the students have learned to transform the dialogue in their minds into a performance, which becomes part of their inner life. They have written down the results of that learning process and are able to compare them with the work of theater-makers (R1) who have transformed the same text into a performance (R2) on stage, before an audience.

To investigate the (recorded) performance of dialogue in theater, the students have to formulate one or more questions—or put forward a statement supported by the results of their study—about the performance, in order to be able to choose which aspects of the performance they want to investigate. This can be done in the way as has been described in the subsection *The Study of Performance* on pages 344–346.

WRITING DIALOGUE

Introduction

At this point, to complete their learning process, the teacher could give the students the opportunity to write a dialogue and to observe it being performed by other students or by professional or semi-professional players. Although there are, many different possibilities to bring the enactment of texts into the classroom within the context of what has been written in this chapter, the performers should remain as faithful as possible to the texts and to what they feel and think the writers want to tell and show the audience, which then can be discussed after each performance.

This final part of the leaning process will be illustrated by a discussion about the performance of the text *Kevin and Els* (see next subsection). The text is a one-act play written by two students, Marlous Veldt and Jeroen van der Hee, in the afternoon of the first day in a *practicum* (practical work) after a course of lectures on the theory of narrative literature and of drama in film and on television, which in 1997 was organized and given by Peter, Schmitz, a colleague, and me at the University of Leiden (Department of Literature).

At the beginning of the practicum, Rosan Dieho, a Dutch scriptwriter who gave counsel to the students, asked them to write a one-act play for an actress and an actor, about the following subject: "One of the characters in the play has a secret. He or she may conceal it from the other or tell it him or her (in the end, for example). The character with the secret will lose, anyway." Or more generally formulated, as a premise: "When you keep a secret, you may conceal it from somebody or tell it him or her. You will lose, anyway."

To enable the students, who may work in groups of two, to work on a solid basis, it is advisable that they write a half-page outline in narrative form for the play they want to write and then talk about with their teacher before they begin to write the play itself.

Kevin and Els

Int.—Living room/in disorder—twilight/evening

KEVIN (24 years)—long hair, trousers of a track-suit, self-rolled cigarette in his mouth—lolling on a bench—legs on the table—besides his feet an ashtray full of butts—television on—telephone in his hand.

1. KEVIN   Yes … No, Jesus man, you promised to keep it, until this week!
            … No … No, believe me, the money will be there.
We hear the slam of a door and the sound of activities of someone in the
corridor.

    KEVIN   Oh, shit! I have to go. I'll call you again. Yes … No … This week,
            I promise.
KEVIN flings down the telephone.
    KEVIN   Damn!

Quickly KEVIN takes hold of the remote control. Then he sits on the bench
again, in a lazy way. ELS enters room, her arms full of groceries. She puts
them down.

2. ELS   Are you still sitting there?
KEVIN gets his tobacco and begins to roll a cigarette.
    ELS   By the way, did you find the job of your dreams today?

KEVIN lights his cigarette. ELS sighs and takes up the purchases. She goes
to the kitchen, which is connected with the living room by a bar.

3. KEVIN   What's for dinner?
4. ELS   Do you really care? As long as I prepare the meal?
5. KEVIN   Alright, I'll say nothing any more …
6. ELS   Surely you will stay for Christmas, won't you?
7. KEVIN   Of course, the greatest feast of all.
8. ELS   I think I will cook something delicious for a change, rab-
          bit-meat, or something like that, that's what you are so fond of,
          don't you? Then we will set the table, just like we did in the past
          … with the table-cloth … and mother's candlestick, of course.

This gives KEVIN a shock.

9. KEVIN   No, no … I mean …Why?
10. ELS   Damn it all Kevin. I work myself to death, and you … Every
           night you gamble away your money … excuse me, my money.
           Do you think I like that?

KEVIN goes to the kitchen and slowly begins to take the purchases out of
the shopping-basket.

11. KEVIN   Els …
12. ELS   As long as it is not about money …
           KEVIN does not react.
     ELS   Oh yes, just like I thought …
13. KEVIN   It's more than that. You mentioned the candle-stick … Maybe it
             has been a symbol of warmth for you, when mother took it out

with Christmas … And still we only take it out with Christmas. Do you know how much such a thing is worth?

14. ELS   I should not dream! You have already flogged everything you owned, and now this?

15. KEVIN   No, how could you think such a thing? Damn. My own sister. You always know better, don't you?

KEVIN enters the living room again, snatches his coat from the bench and puts it on, ELS goes after him.

16. ELS   Where are you going?

17. KEVIN   Out! Even Christmas with the Salvation Army will be warmer then in this godforsaken house.

KEVIN leaves the room and we hear the slam of the door. Feeling dismayed, ELS lowers herself on the bench. KEVIN has left his tobacco on the table.

18. ELS   I will light a candle for you, Kevin.

Discussing Text and Performance

Introduction

After the performance of a play, the students give their comments on its content and the structure, as well as on the performance, discussing each other's interpretations and valuations and using the metalanguage (toolbox) they have learned.

During the discussion, the students have to talk about the importance of distributing the necessary information carefully over different parts of the text. The main question here is WHO (including the audience) KNOWS WHAT AT DIFFERENT MOMENTS IN THE PLAY? At the beginning of the play, for example, information could be limited to what is necessary to enable the audience to begin to know the characters, to understand their situation, and to become interested to anticipate and to follow what is coming next—related to a secret, a problem, a (possible) conflict, a desire, a longing, a need, an expectation, a wish.

Additional notes about the toolbox that teacher and students can use in talking about text and performance are given here (based, part, on Swain, 1979, pp. 154–168, and on conversations with Rosan Dieho, counselor of the practicum):

- Drama is about conflict(s). Therefore, an opening scene, in which a writer begins to create the characters and the beginning of the dramatic situation, emerges out of (possible) conflict(s). This is why it is necessary to think about on which moment in the story a play should begin (point-of-attack). Conflict in drama can have a subtle character. Drama is not necessarily a matter of fighting and arguing. Unless it has a clear function—like in a farce—writers should avoid conflicts in the nature of "Yes, it is" and "No, it isn't," because this stops dramatic development.
- The premise is a short statement of the underlying idea of the story.
- The speed of dialogue, related to its building tension and suspense, can be valued by measuring and assessing the time taken by the different stages in the development of action in a dialogue, as well as in the development

of a scene or a play as a whole. The latter especially concerns the question of the occurrence of different unexpected, moving, or horrifying turns in the line of begin-middle-end of the plot of the story of a play—in waves advancing toward a crisis (although it is possible for a play to have an open end). At the basis of this process, tension within and between characters is built up through the movement in their interaction. It is through conflict that characters are forced to act and react and to show, in one way or another, signs of the springs of their actions and reactions.

Related to the subject of speed of dialogue is the technique that the speeches of a character, as well as a dialogue as a whole, are not unnecessarily long, because this can have the effect of slowing down the dramatic development (unless this is the writer's purpose).

- No matter how absurd a play may be, its story must be written in a way that, within its context, its content can be believed and understood. Regardless of the question of whether the students identify with (one of) the characters or not, play and performance should enable the students to enter the dramatic situation and the minds of the characters, even if they dislike or are strongly repelled by what they see and hear.
- The function of humor, also in an earnest play.
- The functions of language (Waugh, 1985): A character's speech, for example, besides having a referential function, may also have an expressive function or the function to maintain contact with the partner in a dialogue.
- Subtext exists below the surface of text. Subtext becomes explicit only when necessary and only if it has a clear function—for example, to characterize a character or a relationship between two characters, or to produce an ironical or a comical effect, or a critical situation.
- Where possible, nonverbal action has precedence over verbal action, unless priority of speech has a clear function.
- Information about and function of past history of the characters.
- A character (R3) should not say something that mainly has the function of giving information to the audience (R2), unless this is related to a certain genre of drama—for example, in epic drama or when using asides, such as in plays of the *Commedia dell'Arte*.

What Characters say should arise from within themselves and their (action in) dramatic interaction and not from the writer plotting a story, which would disturb the pace of action. A play must have the sense of living speech, to stimulate the audience to take part in the reality of the characters (R3). In a manner of speaking, the characters tell the story.

- The use of voice and other sounds.
- Much attention should be given to details. Every character, for example, has his or her characteristic way of speaking (words, grammar, slang, hesitation, etc.). Writing dialogue is writing language that will be spoken. The question here is *how* people speak. It is important, therefore, to listen to a character, to judge whether it is credible that he or she really *speaks. But dialogue in drama (R3) is not similar to dialogue in reality (R1), because in drama, every word counts.*
- The effects of silence and pauses.
- The arena and the use of props.

Some examples of the discussion

After the performance of *Kevin* and *Els* on the second day of the practicum, all students said that they understood that Kevin had pawned the candlestick but that they did not know that until the end. The students said that already at the beginning of the play, there was a state of tension because it was clear that Kevin wanted to hold back some information from his sister. Because the members of the audience did not know what the tension was about, they became interested in what would follow. After the first performance, the students discussed several speeches of the characters, for example, speeches 5, 6, and 8:

5.   What Kevin says in speech 5 is not very clever, because it is in the interest to keep the peace.

6.   Although the previous speeches of Els are slightly ironical, because she is irritated, some of the students felt that what she says in speech 6 is the direct opposite of what she means (which was confirmed by the authors), and they thought that this turn in the play was too strong, too heavy.

8.   Els does not know that Kevin took the candlestick to the pawnshop. For this reason, it would be more logical to let Kevin make the first step in speaking about the candlestick. That Els takes that initiative was felt to be "not natural," forced by the development of the plot rather than motivated by what Els may feel and think at that moment. In this way, the structure of the plot filters though the surface of the text (i.e., the text shows the plot).

It became clear that with regard to the candlestick, the text is ambiguous because it is possible to interpret that Els does know what Kevin has done—although the writers said that they did not write speech 8 with the intention of making the meaning ambiguous. She does not know that the candlestick is not in the house anymore.

If, on the other hand, Els knows that the candlestick is not in the house, then it is "natural" for her to mention this at the end of speech 8, and it is quite clear why she would do that. In this respect, it is interesting to consider what she says in speech 4, which also shows ambiguity despite the writers' intention to avoid ambiguity.

Through these sort of experiences and discussions, it becomes clearer to the students why and how writers are able to play with information related to the ways in which readers read and spectators watch and listen. Based on the comments and on the outcomes of the discussion, the students rewrote their play.

In the performance of the second text of *Kevin* and *Els*, the tension at the beginning of the play turned out to be stronger than in the performance of the first text because the writers had changed speech 1, through which it became clear to the audience that the pawnbroker already had sold the candlestick. Nevertheless, the writers had chosen to let Kevin be the first to speak about the candlestick because he had a guilty conscience.

At the beginning of the play, the student-spectators *seemed* to know more than Els (which is a matter of dramatic irony). Later in the play, Els looks at the cupboard, gets up, and walks toward it. Kevin stops her and Els sits down again.

At the end of the play, when Kevin starts to leave the room, Els opens her handbag and takes out the candlestick. Then she says, laughing: "I will light a candle for you, Kevin." Kevin stands in the doorway and looks at her, overwhelmed.

It may be clear that both characters now have a strong motivation for their acts and that this moves the plot of the story toward a crisis and then toward a surprising end. The drama in the second text of the play occurs through a credible confrontation between the characters, and in the end, the real conflict comes to the surface. And then Els solves the crisis in a humorous way.

In this way, the students learn by experience—which is their most important teacher—to create, to observe, and to interpret and value different worlds: their own worlds as well as the worlds of others.

THE WORLD AT LARGE

Miriam, 9 years old now, has learned the ways of the world of drama, not having lost her natural power to play. Through talking with her, on her level, about what she sees and reads, she becomes a more skillful reader and spectator, not only with regard to situations in texts of easy genres but also with regard to situations that are quite difficult to perceive, understand, and explain. This concerns not only situations in drama (R3) but also in the reality in which she lives (R1). What she had learned through playing and drama, that is, to understand the actions and reactions of different people in different roles in different situations, is related to her learning to act in different roles in different realities (R1–3).

They can become independent, critical, and cooperative human beings.

Through the learning process described in this chapter, students will learn how they can understand, explore, and create realities in a process of dialogue with their inner and outer worlds—that is, with realities that evolve outside them and those they develop inside themselves. Students did this when they were very young children. Their nature can become their culture, the basis of their further development in knowledge, abilities, character, and mental powers, in all situations, especially in reality (R1).

The Sun Has No Shadow

This chapter is about the possibility of students studying dramatic situations (R3) through the use of dialogue in theater. In this way, they can learn to make sense of situations in their own reality and in the reality of others (R1). Students and researchers, therefore, might use the *toolbox* (the metalanguage) that has been described in this chapter to develop the way they feel, think, and communicate about observing, listening to, and reading, talking, and writing about other situations (R3 as well as R1 and R2). This will add to their knowledge of how and why people, including themselves, use different kinds of sign systems (languages) to create all kinds of situations. As Horowitz and Freeman (1995) cite, "Stories attract the interest of learners from infancy to old age and are powerful vehicles for developing theories of self and the world (Bruner, 1990, p. 32)".

This concerns many different ways in which we make sense of the world (like children do by playing and using fantasy) not only in processes of interaction with other human beings, but also with the whole universe. I will tell the final story of this below.

One of my other daughters, Esther, when she was almost 3 years old, was playing in the sun, and with her hands she made shadows on the flagstones in the garden. Suddenly she came toward me and asked, "Daddy, does everything have a shadow?" I asked her to find that out in the garden. Which she did. After some time, she came toward me again and said, "Everything has a shadow." And she mentioned the trees, the fences, and the flowers. "I think that also the ants have a shadow," she said, as an afterthought. After a silence, she asked, "Does the sun have a shadow?" I asked her what she thought about it. She did not answer and went away to play.

A long time after that, when we sat down to dinner, she suddenly said, "I think that the sun has no shadow." When I asked her why she thought so, she said, "The sun has no sun."

This story has a little tail. When Esther went to bed, she told me that she felt sad, because of the sun. I asked her why. She looked at me in a state of being puzzled, not understanding why I did not understand. "Because the sun had no sun," she said. In her mind, while she made sense of a situation in reality (R1), in an empirical way, the sun was a living being, with human feelings. Although she felt sad, the way in which she interacted with the sun suited her very well, because it created a relationship between herself and the sun. This made the reality of the sun understandable, because she could compare it, through the *feeling* of a relationship, with her own reality.

In this way, knowledge grows. Ideas, concepts, and theories grow through one's observing, understanding, feeling, and creating realities that other people can hear, see, and understand.

REFERENCES

Aston, E., & Savona, G. (1991). *Theatre as a sign system: A semiotics of text and performance*. London: Routledge.

Austin, J. L. (1976). *How to do things with words: The William James lectures delivered at Harvard University in 1955* (J. O. Urmson & M. Sbisà, Eds.). London: Oxford University Press.

Beckerman, B. (1979). *Dynamics of drama: Theory and method of analysis*. New York: Drama Book Specialists.

Beckett, S. (1990). *Catastrophe*. In S. Beckett, *The complete dramatic works* (pp. 455–461). London: Faber & Faber.

Benedetti, J. (1982). *Stanislavski: An introduction*. London: Methuen.

Benveniste, E. (1970). *Problems of general linguistics*. Miami: University of Miami Press.

Birch, D. (1993). *The language of drama: Critical theory and practice*. London: Macmillan.

Birdwhistell, R. L. (1971). *Kinesics and context: Essays on body-motion communication*. Harmondsworth, England: Penguin.

Bruner, J. (1990). *Arts and meaning*. Cambridge, MA: Harvard University Press.

Burton, D. (1980). *Dialogue and discourse: A sociolinguistic approach to modern drama dialogue and naturally occurring conversation*. London: Routledge & Kegan Paul.

Counsell, C. (1996). *Signs of performance: An introduction to twentieth-century theater*. London: Routledge.

Dascal, M. (Ed.). (1985). *Dialogue: An interdisciplinary approach*. Amsterdam: John Benjamins.

De Marinis, M. (1993). *The semiotics of performance*. Bloomington: Indiana University Press.

De Saussure, F. (1974). *Course in general linguistics* (W. Baskin, Trans.). London: Fontana. (Original work published 1915)

Elam, K. (1980). *The semiotics of theatre and drama*. London: Methuen.

Elam, K. (1984). *Shakespeare's universe of discourse*. Cambridge: Cambridge University Press.

Evans, D. (1985). *Situations and speech: Toward a formal semantics of discourse*. New York: Garland.

Fuchs, A. (1992). *Remarks on deixis*. Köln, Germany: Universität zu Köln, Institut für Sprachwissenchaft.

Green, K. (Ed.). (1995). *New essays in deixis: Discourse, narrative, literature.* Amsterdam: Rodopi.

Greimas, A. J., & Courtés, J. (1982). *Semiotics and language: An analytical dictionary.* Bloomington: Indiana University Press.

Hogendoorn, W. (1976). *Lezen en zien spleen: Een studie in simultaneiteit in het drama* [Reading and observing performance: A study in simultaneity in drama]. Unpublished thesis, University of Leiden, The Netherlands.

Honzl, J. (1943). The hierarchy of dramatic devices. In L. Matejka & I. R. Titunick (Eds.), *Semiotics of art: Prague school contributions.* Cambridge, MA: MIT Press. (Original work published 1943)

Horowitz, R. (1990). Discourse organization in oral and written language: Critical contrasts for literacy and schooling. In J. H. A. L. de Jong & D. K. Stevenson (Eds.), *Individualizing the assessment of language abilities* (pp. 108–126). Clevedon Avon, England: Multilingual Matters.

Horowitz, R., & Freeman, S. H. (1995). Robots versus spaceships: The role of discussion in kindergartners' and second-graders' preferences for science text. *The Reading Teacher, 49*(1), 30–40.

Kennedy, A. K. (1983). *Dramatic dialogue: The dialogue of personal encounter.* Cambridge: Cambridge University Press.

Kowzan, T. (1968). The sign in the theater. *Diagenes, 61,* 52–80.

Kowzan, T. (1976). *Analyse sémiologique du spectacle théâtral* [Semiological analysis of the theatrical performance]. Lyon, France: Université de Lyon II, Centre d'Etudes et de Recherches Théâtrales.

Lamb, W., & Watson, E. (1979). *Body code: The meaning in movement.* London: Routledge & Kegan Paul.

Lewis, R. (1958). *Method—or madness?* New York: Samuel French.

Lyons, J. (1977). *Semantics.* Cambridge: Cambridge University Press.

Martin, J. (1991). *Voice in modern theater.* London: Routledge.

Melrose, S. (1994). *A semiotics of dramatic text.* London: Macmillan.

Nash, W. (1989). Changing the guard at Elsinore. In R. Carter & P. Simpson (Eds.), *Language, discourse, and literature: An introductory reader in discourse stylistics* (pp. 22–42). London: Routledge.

O'Neill, E. (1976). *Long day's journey into night.* London: Jonathan Cape.

Pavis, P. (1987). *Dictionnaire du théâtre* [Dictionary of the theater]. Paris: Missidor Éditions socials.

Peirce, C. S. (1931–1966). *Collected papers of Charles Sanders Peirce.* (C. Hartshorne, P. Weiss, & A. W. Burks, Eds.). Cambridge, MA: Harvard University Press.

Pellegrini, A. D. (1997). Dramatic play, context, and children's communicative behavior. In J. Flood, S. B. Heath, & D. Lapp (Eds.), *Handbook of research on teaching literacy through the communicative and visual arts.* New York: Simon & Schuster.

Pfister, M. (1991). *The theory and analysis of drama.* (J. Halliday, Trans.). Cambridge: Cambridge University Press.

Pratt, M.-L. (1986). Ideology and speech-act theory. *Poetics Today, 7*(1), 59–72.

Rauh, G. (Ed.). (1983). *Essays on deixis.* Tübingen: Gunter Narr Verlag.

Searle, J. R. (1969). *Speech acts: An essay in the philosophy of language.* Cambridge: Cambridge University Press.

Searle, J. R. (1975). Indirect speech acts. In P. Cole & J. L. Morgan (Eds.), *Syntax and sematics: Vol. 3. Speech acts* (pp. 59–82). New York: Academic Press.

Searle, J. R., & Vanderveken, D. (1885). *Foundations of illocutionary logic.* Cambridge: Cambridge University Press.

Serpieri, A., Elam, K., Publiatti, P. G., Kemeny, T., & Rutelli, R. (1981). Toward a segmentation of the dramatic text. *Poetics Today 2*(3), 163–200.

Shakespeare, W. (1913). *Hamlet, Prince of Denmark.* In *Cassel's illustrated Shakespeare* (pp. 824–859). London: Funk and Wagnall. (Original work written 1602–1604)

Stanislavski, C. (1961). *Creating a role.* New York: Theatre Arts Books.

Stanislavski, C. (1989). *An actor prepares.* London: Theatre Arts Books.

Swain, D. V. (1979). *Film scriptwriting: A practical manual.* New York: Hastings.

van Kesteren, A. (1981). *Theaterwetenschap: Methodogie van een jonge wetenschap* [The study of theater. Methodology of a new science]. Unpublished doctoral thesis, University of Leiden, The Netherlands.

van Luxemburg, J., Bal, M., & Wetsteijn, W. G. (1987). *Inleiding inde literaturewetenschap* [Introduction to the study of literature]. Muiderberg, The Netherlands: Coutinho.

van Stapele, P. (1985). Starting the cycle: Possibilities for the analysis of performance. In E. Fischer-Lichte (Ed.), *Das Drama und seine Inscenierung* (pp. 219–232). Tübinge, Germany: Max Nemeyer Verlag.

van Stapele, P. (1986). Handelen, gebeuren, situatie, context: (Para) verbale en nonverbale interactie in de dramatische dialoog. [Acting, occurring, situation, context: (Para-)verbal and non-verbal interaction in the dramatic dialogue]. In J. Creten & K. Jaspaert (Eds.), *Werk-in-uitvoering: Momentopname van de socialinguistiek in België en Nederland* (pp. 317–334). Leuven, Belgium: Acco.

van Stapele, P. (1988). Art is the foundation of education. In T. R. Carson (Ed.), *Toward a renaissance of humanity: Rethinking and reorienting curriculum and instruction* (pp. 99–106). Edmonton: University of Alberta Printing Services.

van Stapele, P. (1989a). Machines come later: Basis of audiovisual mass media education. In P. van Stapele & C. C. Sutton (Eds.), *Audiovisual mass media education* (pp. 190–205). Utrecht, The Netherlands: Tijdschrift voor Theaterwetenschap & World Council for Curriculum and Instruction.

van Stapele, P. (1986b). The segmentation of the dramatic text through the analysis of deixis. In J. Stellman & J. van der Meer (Eds.), *Festschrift für Herta Schmid* [Memorial volume to Herta Schmid]. Amsterdam: University of Amsterdam.

van Stapele, P., Halliday, M. A. K., Gibbons, J., & Nicholas, H. (1990). The analysis of deixis as basis for discourse analysis of dramatic texts. In M. A. K. Halliday, J. Gibbons, & H. Nicholas (Eds.), *Learning and keeping and using language* (Vol. 2, pp. 333–348). Amsterdam: John Benjamins.

van Stapele, P. (1993). *Catastrophe* by Samuel Beckett: Possibilities for the analysis of dramatic text. *Tijdschrift voor Theaterwetenschap, 9*(33), 37–50.

van Stapele, P., Hess-Luttich, E., Muller, J. E., & van Zoest, A. (1998). Space in dialogue: The relation between indices and space in dramatic text. In E. Hess Lüttich, J. E. Müller, & A. J. A. van Zoest (Eds.), *Signs & Space, Zeichen & Raum.* Tübingen, Germany: Gunter Narr Verlag.

van Stapele, P. (2005). *Poetics of the screenplay as drama–text.* (doctoral thesis). Leiden University, The Netherlands.

van Stapele, P. (in press). *Poetics of the screenplay.* The Hague.

Vygotsky, L. S. (1986). *Thought and language.* Cambridge, MA: MIT Press.

Waugh, L. P. (1985). The poetic function and the nature of language. In K. Pomorska & S. Rydy (Eds.), *Roman Jakobson: Verbal art, verbal sign, verbal time* (pp. 143–168). Oxford: Oxford University Press.

Weijdema, W. (1982). *Structuren in verbale interaktie: Strategieën van sprekers en hoorders in het taalgebruik* [Structures in verbal interaction: The strategic use of language by speakers and hearers]. Muiderberg, The Netherlands: Coutinho.

Weis, E. (1982). *The silent scream: Alfred Hitchcock's sound track.* Rutherford, NJ: Fairleigh Dickinson University Press.

Wolf, S., Edmiston, B., & Enciso, P. (1997). Drama worlds: Places of the heart, head, voice, and hand in dramatic interpretation, In J. Flood, S. B. Heath & D. Lapp (Eds.), *Handbook of research on teaching literacy through the communicative and visual arts* (pp. 492–505). New York: Simon & Schuster.

CHAPTER 15

Poetry Reading and Group Discussion in Elementary School

David Ian Hanauer

This chapter is concerned with the central role of talk in the construction of meaning while reading poetry. The issue of relations between classroom talk and meaning construction has been of concern to both literacy teachers and researchers for many years (Cazden, 1988; Dillon, 1988; Horowitz, 1994). This interest has grown with the advent of multiliteracy approaches to language education (Cope & Kalantzis, 2000) and genre research (Freedman & Medway, 1994; Hanauer, 1999; Swales, 1990). As an approach, multiliteracy proposes that all modalities function in the educational setting and need to be explored in conjunction. Genre research has supported the idea that early literacy programs use authentic literary texts as initial reading material and has focused on the social contextualization of these literacy activities. Both of these advances in literacy research have stimulated a renewed interest in the connections between group discussion and the construction of meaning.

In this chapter, I propose that the task of reading poetry inherently involves the explicit discussion and negotiation of meaning by various readers. This proposal is based on an analysis of the genre-specific aspects of poetry reading and the Vygotskyan approach to the importance of peer collaboration. The task of poetry reading, with its special characteristics, offers elementary school educators the opportunity of presenting a reading task that integrates a much wider set of meaning construction processes and personal experiences than other text types. While reading poetry within the context of group discussion, children will be exposed and participate in an explicit meaning construction process based on a close consideration of the text and an extensive use of personal, associative, and emotive experiences.

The chapter begins with the presentation of a model of how poetry is read. This model is based on current theoretical and empirical studies of the nature of poetry reading. The issue of poetry reading and writing in elementary school is then discussed. The model's assumptions in relation to the way information is processed while reading poetry are then applied to the issue of group discussion within the classroom. The chapter ends with an example of the use of poetry reading in a small group discussion.

A MODEL OF POETRY READING

The model of poetry reading discussed in this chapter is situated within the context of genre studies. The genre approach considers *reading* a collective term for various different types of authentic, socially contextualized reading. As presently conceptualized, genre involves the connections among specific prototypical language patterns, a conventionalized way of reading, and particular discursive functions (Freedman & Medway, 1994; Hanauer, 1999; Swales, 1990).

The aim of the present model of poetry reading is to identify those language patterns and reading procedures that are specific to the genre of poetry. In itself, this aim has a long history of investigation, which was mainly conducted in a self-reflective and intuitive manner within the field of literary studies. However, more recently, the issue of poetry reading has been studied within the context of reading research (Hanauer, 2001). This recent development has brought with it both empirical research methods and cognitive models of the reading process.

A synthesis of the theoretical positions and empirical data relating to the reading of poetry reveals two interrelated, genre-specific aspects of poetry reading. The first aspect relates to the importance of formal textual features for the categorization and comprehension of poetry (Hanauer 1995, 1996, 1998, 2001; Hoffstaedter, 1987; Miall & Kuiken, 1996; van Peer, 1986, 1990). While reading a poem, readers direct their attention to the formal features of the poem and use these features as an information source in the comprehension of the poem. The second genre-specific aspect relates to the subjective and polysemantic nature of constructing meaning while reading poetry (de Beaugrande 1987; Fairley, 1979; Harker, 1982; Shimron, 1980; Svensson, 1987; Thorne, 1989). While reading a poem, readers are faced with various possibilities for the way the poem, or sections of the poem, can be understood. These various different understandings result from the structure of poetic language and the reductive nature of information in the poem. The poem presents readers with an information structure with gaps that have to be elaborated and filled in by readers on the basis of their own world knowledge. While reading a poem, readers may activate associative and emotive information, which is then used to construct a meaning for the poem. In the sections that follow, each of these genre-specific aspects of poetry reading is discussed individually.

Directing Attention at Formal Features

Theoretical discussions within the field of literary studies agree that formal textual features are used in the interpretation of poetry. However, different approaches conflict over the reason for directing attention to formal features. The more prevalent theory on this issue is that poetry reading is a convention-driven activity in which many of the specific conventions of poetry reading involve paying attention to the formal features of the poem. In relation to this issue, two specific conventions have been proposed:

1. The convention of unity: As specified by Culler (1975) and Fairley (1989), readers expect all levels of linguistic information to function in unison in establishing the meaning of the poem. In other words, structural patterns, such as rhyme schemes, alliteration, and graphic form, are transformed into semantic information that is included in the meaning construction process. The aim of the reader is to analyze and incorporate as many formal features as possible in the interpretation of the poem. The poem is seen as a whole in which each element of the poem fulfills an important role.

2. The convention of resistance: As specified by Culler (1975), when reading a poem, readers do not expect to immediately comprehend the text. The convention of poetry is that it should resist automatic understanding. In many cases, the formal features of the poem make it difficult to read and comprehend. The reader must employ a series of micro-conventions that transform an opaque text into an intelligible one. These micro-conventions are a set of rules that allow a range of formal features to be interpreted as meaningful for the understanding of the poem. The reader employs literary rules of meaning construction to transform the poem into a meaningful text.

The conflicting view to conventionalist positions in poetry reading comes from formalist theories of how poetry is read. As their name suggests, formalist theories of poetry emphasize the role of formal textual features in the reading process. Whereas conventionalists describe the reading of poetry as a convention-governed process, the formalists describe poetry reading as a language-governed process. In other words, from a formalist viewpoint, it is the way the specific language patterns found in poetry are perceived by the reader that causes the reader to focus attention on the formal features of the poem during reading.

Formalists, such as Roman Jakobson and Jan Mukarovsky, emphasize the importance of specific language patterns, found in poetry, in drawing attention to themselves during reading. For Jakobson (1960), poetry is a genre of texts in which language patterns are perceived in a very conscious and attention-demanding way. This form of language function is termed by Jakobson as the *poetic function* and is defined as "The set towards the MESSAGE as such, focus on the message for its own sake is the poetic function of language" (p. 356). The term *message*, as used by Jakobson, refers to the structure of the utterance itself and not its content. Thus, for Jakobson, a poem is a text in which the reader is made consciously aware of the linguistic patterns of the text by the structure of the language itself. This conscious presence of linguistic features is achieved through the unique way language is constructed in the poetic function. As stated by Jakobson, "The poetic function projects the principle of equivalence from the axis of selection into the axis of combination" (p. 358). According to Jakobson, when reading a poem, the reader will be confronted by a structure of similarities, regularities, and repetitions. These equivalences will force the reader to reconstruct the hierarchical structure of the text. Instead of reading a poem as a linear string, the reader will stop to consider the structure of similarities and contrasts and will, thus, reconstruct the poem according to its specific language patterns. For example, similarities in sound may be taken as semantic similarities and be used in the meaning construction process. So that while reading a poem, the language patterns of the poem direct the reader to a series of new relationships and meanings. For Jakobson, the textual features of the poem are central in that they draw attention to themselves and direct the reading process.

A closely associated theory of poetry was presented by the Prague formalist, Jan Mukarovsky. Like Jakobson, Mukarovsky (1964) defined poetry according to the function of formal linguistic features. The starting point of his theory was a consideration of the relationship between poetic and standard language. For Mukarovsky, poetic language was essentially different from standard language in that it involved systematic violations of the norms of standard language. These violations produced an aesthetic effect by forcing attention on the linguistic sign itself.

As stated by Mukarovsky (1964):

> The function of poetic language consists in the maximum foregrounding of the utterance. Foregrounding is the opposite of automization, that is, the deautomization of an act; the more the act is automatized, the less it is consciously executed; the more it is foregrounded, the more completely conscious does it become. (p. 19)

By deviating from the norm of language, poetic language is foregrounded and consciously perceived by the reader. For Mukarovsky, as for Jakobson, the textual features of the poem draw attention to themselves and direct the reading process of the poem.

The differences between conventionalist and formalist theories of poetry relate to the level of processing. The conventions of poetry reading specified above can be viewed as modulating meta-strategies employed by the reader when reading poetry. As meta-strategies, these conventions direct the reading process in a top-down fashion. The specific patterns of language considered poetic by formalist theories can be described as directing the reading process in a bottom-up manner. These specific types of language pattern slow down the reading process by forcing the reader to pay attention to the unusual or special use of language. A review of empirical research on the role of formal features in poetry reading conducted by Hanauer (2001) supports this description. Hanauer's review shows that the specific linguistic features of poetry are noticed by readers and are thus made available for further manipulation in the meaning construction process.

Current theories of poetry reading and empirical evidence support the position that a poem cannot be understood without an appreciation of the formal features of the poem. The construction of meaning while reading poetry involves directing attention to the formal features of the poem (Hanauer, 2001). While reading the poem, the reader will pay close attention to the formal features of the text for comprehension purposes. The reader will both consciously search for patterns in the formal and semantic aspects of the poem and be affected by the particular features of the text itself. Both the strategic control of the reader and the individual features of the text will direct the meaning construction process.

The Polysemantic Nature of Constructing Meaning While Reading Poetry

As with the issue of the role of formal textual features, theoretical discussions within the field of literary studies agree that reading poetry can involve subjective and multiple interpretations, but they disagree over the reasons for this. Once again, the argument can be described as a conflict between conventionalist and formalist theories. The conventionalist argument proposes that there are specific conventions that make readers search for and be tolerant of multiple understandings of poems. For example, according to the convention of polysemantic reading proposed by Schmidt (1982) and Thorne (1989), readers expect poems to be polysemantic and have multiple meanings. This polysemantic aspect of poetry reading relates both to differences between readers and differences in repeated readings by the same reader. When reading a poem, the reader will pass through several stages of comprehension in which various different aspects of the poem, including its formal features, will be analyzed. At each subsequent analysis, additional options for meaning construction arise and the meaning of the poem may change. According to the convention of polysemantic meaning in poetry reading, readers are tolerant of multiple interpretations in poetry.

A different argument from the conventionalist position has been proposed by Fish (1980). Fish's argument relates to the concept of "interpretive communities." According to this argument, readers of poetry function within the framework of groups of readers and writers who have common ways of constructing meaning in poems (termed by Fish *interpretive strategies*). Because readers belong to various different interpretive communities, they have different ways of constructing meaning and they therefore produce different readings of the same poem. The source of interpretive variation between readers is the use of different interpretive strategies, which highlight different language patterns and use these patterns in various ways. According to Fish (1980), every poem is open to multiple interpretations through the application of different sets of interpretive strategies by the same reader or different readers.

The formalist argument sees the issue of multiple interpretations as a result of the specific use of language found in poems. As argued by Jakobson (1960), equivalence or sameness is used as the major means of constructing the whole poem. On all levels of their linguistic features, poems display an overall structure of similarities and contrasts. For the other functions of language, equivalence plays a significant role only for the axis of selection in that a choice is made of the appropriate linguistic element from a repertoire of equivalent items. However, in the poetic function of language, equivalence is also used as a way of combining linguistic elements. In poems, the formal features of the text display a system of similarities, regularities, and repetitions such as the repetition of syllables, regularities in stress patterns, or similarity in grammatical category. The poem is a hierarchically structured set of patterns of similarity and contrast. When the principle of equivalence is used as a principle of combination, the text is no longer a linear string but is subdivided and reconstructed according to the patterns of similarity and contrast of the formal features of the text.

The emphasis on the formal features of the poem itself and the nonlinear hierarchical structure of those features brings into question the relationship between the linguistic sign and the nonlinguistic sign. The illusion of a direct relationship between the linguistic sign and the nonlinguistic sign is broken by the perceptible presence of the formal features of the poem. By emphasizing the illusory nature of the relationship between the linguistic sign and the nonlinguistic sign and by situating the linguistic sign within a structure of other linguistic signs, a multiplicity of potential meanings is achieved within the poem. For example, in poems, similarity in sound may be taken as a similarity in meaning, or the connotative associations (rather than denotative precision) of a particular linguistic sign are used for meaning construction in poems. As presented by Jakobson, a poem is a structural whole in which all the formal features of language play a role. The whole poem can only be understood in relation to its parts, and its parts can only be understood in relation to the whole poem. The reader perceives multiple meanings in the poem as result of the structure of similarities and contrasts in the language of the poem.

An additional argument relating to the issue of multiple interpretations and formal textual features in poetry has been proposed by Harker (1982). Harker applies schema theory to the issue of how poetry is read and claims that what is special about poetry is that it activates multiple schemata. These multiple schemata are activated as a result of the reduced nature of the information structure in the poem and as a result of the new reality constructed in relation to the poem. Understanding a poem involves using previous knowledge about the world. But this knowledge is not sufficient to comprehend the poem, because, in many cases, a new combination of schemata which construct a new experience is presented in the poem. The reader has to construct this new reality using existing schemata.

As can be seen in the previous section, researchers and theorists agree that reading poems involves multiple interpretations. The various approaches emphasize different variables that affect the construction of multiple and subjective meanings while reading poetry. The conventionalists tend to place their emphasis on the cognitive control systems of the individual that are acquired with educational frameworks. Thus, a reader of poetry who has learned to look for certain patterns in a poem may differ from a reader who has learned to look for different patterns. According to the conventionalist argument, these same readers have been socialized to accept multiple understandings of the same poem as an appropriate result of reading poetry. The formalists place their emphasis on the way specific language patterns affect meaning construction while reading poetry. According to this approach, the reader will perceive certain patterns in the language of the poem and will use these to reconstruct the interrelationships in the poem. This allows new options for meaning construction and creates connections on the semantic level between diverse elements. Different interpretations will result from the various patterns perceived and connections made by the reader. In addition, understanding the poem will involve the activation and integration of multiple schemata. The differences in the components of individual schemata between readers and the way these schemata are integrated will also produce multiple and subjective understandings of the poem.

Summary—A Model of Poetry Reading

Reading a poem involves an interaction between the specific textual features of the poem and the cognitive control system and knowledge base of the reader. The reader will become aware that the text he or she is reading is a poem as a result of the context of reading (e.g., a poetry anthology, a literature class, a teacher's introduction) or as a result of the identification of the specific language patterns as poetic (e.g., graphic form or rhyme scheme). Both of these options will lead to the categorization of the text as a poem. Once the reader has identified the text as a poem, he or she will direct attention to the formal features of the poem and perceive specific formal patterns in the poem. The reader's experience as a reader of poetry, whether in a formal educational or informal context, will affect the types of pattern that the reader is aware of and will look for As a result of directing attention to specific language patterns that are incorporated in the poem, a wide range of meanings will be assigned to individual lexical items, groups of lexical items, and specific formal features. While attention is directed toward the language patterns of the poem, the reading of the poem will proceed in a slow manner and will involve forward, backward, up, and down eye movements. While the reader is reading the poem, multiple schemata will be activated in a direct or associative manner and will be used, by the reader, in the ongoing process of constructing of meaning. The reader will actively and consciously negotiate the meaning that is to be assigned by evaluating the semantic, emotive, and formal structures of the poem. The reader's implicit and explicit knowledge of formal language patterns and conventions of poetry reading as well as general world knowledge are used as central information sources in this process. The reader's awareness of the individual characteristics of the specific poem that is being read will enlarge the possibilities of meaning construction.

POETRY READING IN THE ELEMENTARY SCHOOL CLASSROOM

At present, poetry is not particularly popular and is rarely used in early literacy programs (Denman, 1988; Elster & Hanauer, 2002). The main reason for this is that poetry is seen as difficult to comprehend and beyond the abilities of most primary children. Although not much research has been conducted on reading poetry with primary school children, there is some initial evidence with which to evaluate the claim that poetry reading is a task that is beyond the abilities of most children. In an interesting school-based study, Duthie and Zimet (1992) document how poetry was used in a first-grade literacy program. The educational program that this study relates to involved exposing children to the formal aspects of poetry, the options for constructing meaning in poetry, and the possible functions of poetry. Within the course of the program, the children both read and wrote poetry. Several specific results of this study are important. First, Duthie and Zimet report that working with poetry produced motivation to work with literacy-related tasks in several students who had previously been reluctant to read and write. This result is in opposition to claims that suggest a hierarchical relationship of difficulty between poetry reading and the reading of other text types. In the case of these particular children, reading poetry did not cause or enhance a sense of frustration but rather was a source of motivation.

The second result relates to the content of what was learned by the children. As reported by Duthie and Zimet (1992), within the course of the program, the children seemed to have grasped the central concept of form-content relations in poetry. In other words, the children were aware and could produce written examples of how different forms of language could be used to construct and change meaning. Specifically, the children demonstrated an understanding of sound patterns (alliteration, rhyming, onomatopoeia), graphic patterns (lining, stanza partition, poem shapes), and semantic patterns (simile, invented words). Figure 15.1 presents some examples of these children's work. The children in the Duthie and Zimet study demonstrated the ability to manipulate language patterns to construct specific meanings. This result undercuts the claim that poetry reading is a difficult task beyond the abilities of most children.

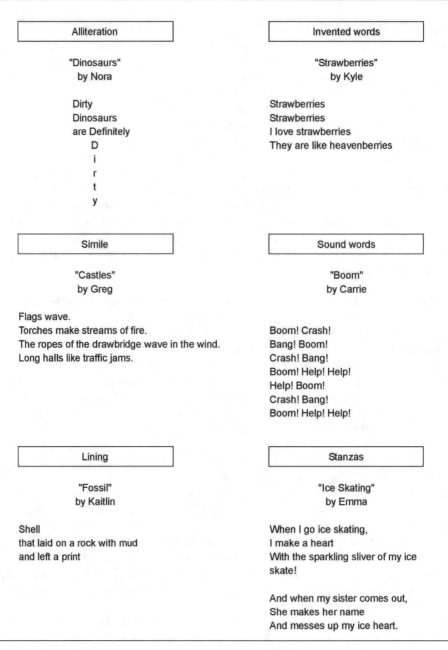

Figure 15.1.   Examples of first-grade children's poetry writing (Duthie & Zimet, 1992).

Additional studies of children's writing and reading of poetry seem to support some of Duthie and Zimet's claims. Hanauer (2004) analyzes the reading and writing of poetry by emergent readers. In his analysis, Hanauer demonstrates the relevance of poetry for young readers (listeners) and writers. Even for very young literacy learners, poetry is shown to be an excellent genre for the expression of truly personally meaningful feelings, thoughts, and experiences. Pontecorvo

(1992) reports on a study she conducted in which 5- and 6-year-olds were requested to write a series of different text types. The text types included a list, a nursery rhyme, and a story. The most important finding of this study is that even preschoolers differentiated in their writing among the various text types. While writing a list or a story, preschoolers tended to relate to the "physical salience" of the object being described and to represent this by writing strings of text with spaces between the text. The spaces were used to differentiate between objects and names. However, the same children, when writing nursery rhymes, almost always produced a continuous string of text in a single flowing writing sequence. As pointed out by Pontecorvo, it seemed that these children were relating to the musical sound patterns of the nursery rhymes. Some of the children related to the graphic aspects of poetry and produced divisions between verses or onomatopoeic forms such as curved lines.

In a different study, Torrance, Lee, and Olson (1994) show how 3- to 7-year-old children produced different mental representations for poems and stories. A text was presented to the children as a story or as a poem and then using the "naughty teddy bear" technique, children were asked to identify verbatim sentences or content knowledge sentences from the texts. Children from all age groups were found to be sensitive to changes in meaning and were capable of differentiating between true and false paraphrases. In addition, at all ages, children found it easier to reject a false verbatim item on the poem condition than in the story. As summarized by the researchers, children of all ages are sensitive to both the specific wording of text and its meaning. The result that increased verbatim recall was achieved for the poem indicates that attention is directed at the specific language used in poems.

Another way of considering the suitability of poetry for elementary school children is to consider their preferences in relation to different types of poetry. Several studies of this kind have been conducted. The classic study in this framework is Terry (1972), who used rating scales and stimuli poetry booklets to evaluate forth, fifth, and sixth-graders' preferences for poetry. A similar study was conducted by Fisher and Natarella (1979) in relation to first-, second-, and third-grade children. Although various findings were presented in these studies, two specific preferences are particularly important. In both studies, in relation to content children preferred poetry that was humorous, that was related to familiar experiences, or that involved animals. In relation to the form of language, children preferred poems that involved sound patterns, such as rhyme and rhythm. These two results were also confirmed by a library circulation study, in which Kupiter and Wilson (1993) investigated the preferences for poetry books of children in three elementary schools. The results show that poetry books with humorous topics in a narrative form that used the sound patterns of rhythm and rhyme were the most popular among the children.

Elster and Hanauer (2002) investigated the way teachers share poetry with children in their elementary school classrooms. The analysis focused on the teacher's reading performance and the responses this elicited from the participating children. Poetry reading was characterized by an expressive reading style, multiple readings in one session, children's active participation in reading along, and extensive discussions focusing on the linguistic features of poems and their potential meanings.

In summary, all of the studies mentioned here suggest that poetry is not beyond the abilities of elementary school children. As seen in several studies, young children, even in first grade, can manipulate formal language patterns to construct and change meaning. Sound patterns and graphic form seem to be particularly salient to young children. Poetry can be a source of motivation and enjoyment for children of all ages. Poems that use sound patterns and have humorous topics or discuss well-known experiences are preferred by children. Taken together these aspects of children's poetry reading form a basis upon which the use of poetry in the elementary classroom can be discussed.

POETRY READING AND GROUP DISCUSSION IN THE ELEMENTARY SCHOOL CLASSROOM

According to the model of poetry reading presented in the previous section, the central aspect of poetry reading is the reader's active and conscious negotiation of the structures of the poem for meaning construction purposes. The reader must carefully consider the individual, formal characteristics of the poem, the presence of multiple schemata, and emotive responses to the poem for the roles they play in the active construction of meaning. The basic principle that informs the following discussion of poetry reading and talk in the elementary school classroom is that by placing the poetry reading task within the context of a group discussion, the individual child is supported and enriched by multiple information sources relating to personal experiences, emotive responses, associative reflections, and perceptions of language patterns while contending with a complex multilevel comprehension task.

Vygotsky (1978) pointed out that problem solving within a group framework can extend a child's ability to comprehend and acquire knowledge. As proposed and demonstrated by Vygotsky (1978), a child who works in collaboration with others can perform on a level that is beyond his or her current level. The group discussion and mutual negotiation of a problem between a child and a more capable peer or adult helps the child to develop both knowledge and abilities to solve complex problems. The assistance provided in the group discussion is internalized by the child and then used autonomously at a later stage (Vygotsky, 1986).

As described by Vygotsky, this internalization process within the context of a group discussion involves the raising of consciousness about specific concepts. This aspect of the internalization process is important in that consciousness is followed by the ability to deliberately control knowledge. According to Vygotsky (1986), the raising of consciousness and the ability to deliberately control knowledge are the two main benefits of schooling. Both of these processes are situated within the context of group discussion, in which assistance is provided to children working on a problem-solving task that the children find engaging.

Vygotsky essentially describes a learning situation in which, by working together and with some limited assistance, children can develop problem-solving abilities and knowledge beyond the level that they could function on alone. The distance between the child's ability to function alone and to function in a group with minimal assistance is termed by Vygotsky as the *zone of proximal development* (Vygotsky, 1978). From a Vygotskyan viewpoint, it is within the zone of proximal development that learning occurs.

It is in relation to the issue of group discussions within the classroom that Vygotsky's theory has had its major impact on educational practices. The concept of a zone of proximal development directs a change in the way teaching is conducted. A child will develop when he or she is involved in an engaging problem-solving task in the context of a supportive group that can provide assistance. The role of the teacher is to construct the environment within which development can take place and to provide assistance when needed. In many ways, responsibility for solving the problem posed by the task is shifted to the child and the group as a whole. Accordingly, the group discussion is a central site within which learning takes place.

Various studies within educational frameworks have specified the importance of group discussion for literacy development. These studies specify three specific advantages of group discussion in the literacy classroom. The first advantage is that group discussion allows the introduction of material and tasks that could not be handled by the child alone. This aspect of group discussion means that young learners can be drawn beyond their current level of functioning and knowledge (Horowitz, 1994; Leal, 1993; Lehman & Scharer, 1996). The second advantage for the literacy classroom is that group discussion raises consciousness about the nature and function of specific linguistic and discursive structures. This explicit discussion of structures may be internalized as an inner dialogue and later utilized by the learner in solving meaning construction or language production problems (Hanauer, 1997; Zyngier, 1994). The third advantage is that within the group discussion, each child has to contend with various viewpoints and interpretations of written text. As opposed to previous educational practices, the classroom discussion is not left at the level of specifying the "facts" of the text (Purves, 1993) or answering directed questions with a single correct answer (Cazden, 1988; Dillon, 1981). By creating collaborative discussion groups between children, multiple perspectives and interpretations are produced and negotiated.

I propose that reading poetry within the context of a group discussion is a particularly good way of extending a child's knowledge of the world, experience of others, and ability to construct meaning from texts. Within the context of group poetry reading, each child will be exposed to the experiences, emotions, perspectives, and meaning construction abilities of other children. The poem within the context of the group discussion is a site for the explicit negotiation of meaning from various perspectives. Children within the group will be exposed and take part in explicit discussions of meaning construction in relation to reduced and ambiguous lines of poetry. Many poems will elicit specific discussion of the meaning of the formal structures of the poem. This group discussion may include the way particular words, phrases, or lines can be understood and may take into account phonological, syntactic, and semantic features of the poem. In addition, the limited information structure found in many poems may elicit personal schema and emotive responses. The children within the group will be exposed to different interpretations of the same lines of poetry.

The reading of poetry within the context of a group discussion is, in many ways, a unique experience in the school framework. The nature of poetry reading involves directly relating to the construction of meaning in texts and can involve a wide set of ways of constructing meaning. The aim of the poetry reading task is to consider the many ways a poem can mean. This aim includes very personal and idiosyncratic understandings of poems and is in opposition to methods of instruction that involve the regurgitation of a predefined expert understanding of the poem. It is the experience of constructing meaning on the basis of textual analysis and personal schema that is important in relation to poetry reading. The group framework should ensure the presence of different interpretations of the same poem.

The following points summarize the advantages for the literacy teacher of reading poetry in the context of a group discussion:

1. While reading poetry in a group discussion, children will participate and be exposed to explicit discussion of the way meaning is constructed.
2. While reading poetry in a group discussion, each child will contend with the construction of meaning on the basis of personal, emotive, and associative memories.
3. While reading poetry in a group discussion, children will be exposed to different understandings of sections of the poem or the poem as a whole.
4. While reading poetry in a group discussion, the meaning construction process will involve various levels of linguistic knowledge.
5. While reading poetry in a group discussion, children will be exposed to a wide range of ways of constructing meaning.

To exemplify these points, in the following section, an example of a group reading of a poem is presented. The group consisted of three children from fourth-grade and a teacher. All participants were native speakers of Hebrew (the translation is by the author). The children were discussing a humorous poem, titled "The Lady With the Baskets" by Chaya Shenhav (see Appendix A). The children were asked to read the poem out loud to one another and then try to see what they understood from the poem.

Tom:	I think it's about a lady who fills the whole bus with baskets … that we don't even know where they came from … Perhaps, she is an alien from outer space … That's what I think.
Teacher:	What do you think Rona?
Rona:	She … eh … is a very fat lady with a lot a lot of baskets that she needs to fill all the seats because she has all these baskets and because she is so fat.
Linor:	Perhaps, the person who wrote this married to a fat woman that … she … he suffers because she is so fat.
Rona:	But Linor … Chaya Shenhav wrote this poem … she's a girl … so … his wife … she's a girl.
Linor:	So perhaps she is very fat and she doesn't want to tell it to anyone so she wrote a poem about it … how fat she is.
Rona:	The lady is fat and she takes up so much room. Perhaps she wants us to know that people should not take up so much room and take all the seats … and then there won't be any room on the bus..and lots of people want to get on buses.
Tom:	I know, perhaps she just wanted to write a funny poem and perhaps she felt that she takes up a lot of room in society.
Teacher:	In society.
Tom:	Yes in society.

Linor: So she is D. P. (a girl from Linor's class) ... She's just the same ...
           Not only is she fat she also takes up all the room because a lot of
           things happen to her ... happen to her a lot of things in class ...
           the class really like D. P. ... there are children who don't partici-
           pate in that snobbery ... it's not good to sit next to her ... it's dif-
           ficult to sit next to her ... me and Maya call this snobbery.

Rona: The lady is not a snob ... It has nothing to do with snobbery.

Teacher: Why do you think the poem keeps repeating the line "On one
           seat there is ..."

Linor: The lady wants ALL the seats.

Rona: So that she can have all the seats.

Linor: She has to have all the seats. No one else must be allowed to get
           anything else ... she's got ... let's say ten seats ... and she's not
           going to let anyone else sit down ... because if she lets someone
           else sit down she won't be able to put her basket on a seat ...

Rona: And if someone else wants to sit.

Linor: She won't let him ... because she's got all the seats ... she could
           put the basket on her knees but she doesn't want to because
           she's selfish.

Tom: I think it's a funny poem about someone who does something
           funny ... and imagines a funny situation.

In the previous transcript of the group reading of the poem, "The Lady With the Baskets," the members of the group presented various ways of understanding this poem. These interpretations were usually introduced by the adverb "perhaps." This indicates the children's recognition of the status of their statements about the meaning of the poem as possible, rather than absolute, ways of understanding the poem. The children do not agree over the meaning of the poem, but they do inter-act to mutually develop their interpretations. In the first section, one such interac-tion occurs between Rona, Tom, and Linor. Rona explains that the point of the poem may be to tell people to leave room on the bus. Tom, who has categorized this poem as a humorous poem, follows up on Rona's statement about "room on the bus" and offers the explanation that it might be about "room in society." This option is immediately picked up by Linor, who then understands the poem as an allegory of a social situation that she knows well from her own classroom experi-ence. Linor informs the group that the lady in the poem is really the girl D.P. from their class. Linor then develops this interpretation into more general statements about class interaction (called "snobbery"). Rona does not accept this interpreta-tion and does not think that the lady in the poem is a snob at all. Tom keeps his interpretation that the poem is a humorous rather than a serious piece.

The children's interpretations relate to different levels of the poem and use dif-ferent personal, emotive, and associative memories. On the level of the form of the poem, Rona and Linor consider the repetition of the phrase "On one seat" as a technique for emphasizing the lady's actions. Linor states emphatically that the lady wants "ALL" all the seats, demonstrating a semantic role for the structural feature of repetition. All three children have a good understanding of the content level of the poem but elaborate on the basic information. For example, the lady is described by the children as being fat. In actual fact, this is not stated explicitly in the poem but does fit in with the overall characterization of the lady as someone who takes up a lot of room. Rona tends to leave her understanding of the poem on the level of description of the scene and analysis of the character's actions and motives. However, she does propose a social-didactic role for this poem—people should leave room for others on buses. Both Linor and Tom relate to the wider context of the poem. Tom makes a genre characterization of the poem and stated its function as "to be funny." This interpretation includes assigning intentions to the poet through an analysis of the poem. Linor interprets this poem in allegorical, personal terms and sees this poem as having a social function. The poem is about a selfish, self-centered person who doesn't leave room for anyone else. Of the three children, Linor reacts in the most emotional way and assigns personal importance to the content of the poem.

As demonstrated in this short example, when reading a poem in a group discussion, children employ personal, emotive, and associative memories to construct meaning on the basis of a textual analysis. The result of meaning construction in this context may be highly individualized, as in the case of Linor's allegorical reading of the poem as a statement about the social interaction in her own class. This type of reading results from the nature of the poetic text—its forms and poetic conventions—and the context of the group discussion. The poetic text invites multiple ways of understanding while not demanding definitive interpretations, and the group discussion elicits interpretive interactions that enrich the construction of individual interpretations. The aim of poetry reading is to develop the reader's knowledge, experience, and ability to construct meaning from texts. Reading poetry in a group discussion allows the child to experience the construction of meaning on a much wider basis than other text types. The group discussion of poetry exposes the child to various viewpoints and the personal experiences of others.

CONCLUSION

In this chapter, I have proposed that reading poetry in the context of a group discussion is a reading task that can widen children's conceptions and experiences of how meaning is constructed in texts. It is a reading and talking task that invites the use of personal emotive schema and close textual analysis. Within the context of a group discussion, each individual child is exposed to the experiences and perspectives of other children. By employing the group poetry reading task, the elementary school literacy teacher can broaden the scope of how meaning is constructed and what personal and textual information sources can be used in meaning construction.

REFERENCES

Cazden, C. B. (1988). *Classroom discourse: The language of teaching and learning.* Portsmouth, NH: Heinemann.

Cope, B., & Kalantzis, M. (Ed.). (2000). *Multiliteracies: Literacy learning and the design of social futures.* London: Routledge

Culler, J. (1975). *Structuralist poetics: structuralism, linguistics, and the study of literature.* London: Routledge & Kegan Paul.

de Beaugrande, R. (1987). Schemas for literary communication. In L. Halasz (Ed.), *Literary discourse: Aspects of social psychological approaches* (pp. 49–99). Berlin/New York: de Gruyter.

Denman, G. (1988). *When you've made it on your own … teaching poetry*. Portsmouth, NH: Heinemann.

Dillon, J. T. (1988). *Questioning and discussion*. Norwood, NJ: Ablex.

Duthie, C., & Zimet, E. K. (1992). Poetry is like directions for your imagination. *The Reading Teacher, 46*(1), 14–24.

Elster, C., & Hanauer, D. (2002). Voicing texts, voices around texts: Reading poems in elementary school classrooms. *Research in the Teaching of English, 37*(1), 89–134.

Fairley, I. R. (1979). Experimental approaches to language in literature: Reader responses to poems. *Style, 13*, 335–364.

Fairley, I. R. (1989). The reader's need for conventions: When is a mushroom not a mushroom? In W. van Peer (Ed.), *The taming of the text* (pp. 292–316). London: Routledge.

Fish, S. (1980). *Is there a text in this class?: The authority of interpretive communities.* Cambridge, MA: Harvard University Press.

Fisher, C. J., & Natarella, M. A. (1979). *Poetry preferences of primary, first, second and third-graders: Studies in language education.* Unpublished doctoral dissertation, University of Georgia, Athens.

Freedman, A., & Medway, P. (1994). *Genre and the new rhetoric.* London: Taylor & Francis.

Hanauer, D. (1995). The effects of educational background on literary and poetic text categorization judgements. In G. Rusch (Ed.), *Empirical approaches to literature* (pp. 338–347). Siegen: LUMIS.

Hanauer, D. (1996). Integration of phonetic and graphic features in poetic text categorization judgements. *Poetics, 23*, 363–380.

Hanauer, D. (1997). Poetry reading in the second language classroom. *Language Awareness, 6*(1), 2–16.

Hanauer, D. (1998). The genre-specific hypothesis of reading: Reading poetry and reading encyclopedic items. *Poetics, 26*(2), 63–80

Hanauer, D. (1999). A genre approach to graffiti at the site of Prime Minister Rabin's assassination. In D. Zissenzwein & D. Schers (Eds.), *Present and future: Jewish culture, identity and language* (pp. 175–184). Tel-Aviv: Tel-Aviv University Press.

Hanauer, D. (2001). What do we know about poetry reading: Theoretical positions and empirical research. In G. Steen & D. Schram (Eds.), *The psychology and sociology of literary text* (pp. 107–128). Amsterdam: John Benjamins.

Hanauer, D. (2004). *Poetry and the meaning of life.* Toronto: Pippin.

Harker, J. W. (1982). Comprehending the discourse of poetry. In A. Flammer & W. Kintsch (Eds.), *Discourse processing* (pp. 570–581). New York: North-Holland.

Hoffstaedter, P. (1987). Poetic text processing and its empirical investigation. *Poetics, 16*, 75–91.

Horowitz, R. (1994). Classroom talk about text: What teenagers and teachers come to know about the world through talk about text. *Journal of Reading, 37*(7), 4–11.

Jakobson, R. (1960). Linguistics and poetics. In T. Sebeok (Ed.), *Style in language.* Cambridge, MA: MIT Press.

Kupiter, K., & Wilson, P. (1993). Updating poetry preferences: A look at the poetry children like. *The Reading Teacher, 47*(1), 28–35.

Leal, D. J. (1993). The power of literary peer-group discussions: How children collaboratively negotiate meaning. *The Reading Teacher, 47*(2), 114–120.

Lehman, B. A., & Scharer, P. L. (1996). Reading alone, talking together: The role of discussion in developing literary awareness. *The Reading Teacher, 50*(1), 26–35.

Miall, D., & Kuiken, D. (1996). *Forms of reading: Recovering the self-as-reader.* Paper presented at the XIV Congress of the International Association of Empirical Aesthetics, Prague.

Mukarovsky, J. (1964). Standard language and poetic language. In P. Garvin (Trans.), *A Prague school reader on esthetics, literary structure, and style.* Washington, DC: Georgetown University Press.

Pontecorvo, C. (1992). Iconicity in children's first written texts. In R. Simone (Ed.), *Iconicity in language* (pp. 278–307). Amsterdam: John Benjamins.

Purves, A. C. (1993). Toward a reevaluation of reader response and school literature. *Language Arts, 70*, 348–361.

Schmidt, S. J. (1982). *Foundations for the empirical study of literature* (R. de Beaugrande, Trans.). Hamburg: Buske.

Shenhav, C. (1991). The lady with the baskets. In H. Geva & V. Karin (Eds.), *Shirim VeLamdin* (p. 9). Ramat-Aviv, Israel: Dror Tasîot Publishing Press.

שנהב, ח.(1991). גברת עם סלים. ח. גבע וו. קרין (עורכות), *שרים ולומדים*. דרור תעשיות בע"מ: רמת אביב

Shimron, J. (1980). Psychological processes behind the comprehension of poetic texts. *Instructional Science, 9*, 43–66.

Svensson, C. (1987). The construction of poetic meaning: A developmental study of symbolic and non-symbolic strategies in the interpretation of contemporary poetry. *Poetics, 16*, 471–503.

Swales, J. (1990). *Genre analysis.* Cambridge: Cambridge University Press.

Terry, C. A. (1972). *A national study of children's poetry preferences in the fourth, fifth and sixth-grades.* Unpublished doctoral dissertation, Ohio State University, Columbus.

Thorne, J. (1989). What is a poem? In W. van Peer (Ed.), *The taming of the text* (pp. 280–291). London: Routledge.

Torrance, N., Lee, E. A., & Olson, D. (1994). *Language form and the say/mean distinction: Verbatim and paraphrase recognition in narrative and nursery rhyme.* Paper presented at the American Educational Research Association conference, San Francisco, CA.

van Peer, W. (1986). *Stylistics and psychology: Investigations of foregrounding.* Wolfboro, NH: Croom Helm.

van Peer, W. (1990). The measurement of metre: Its cognitive and affective functions. *Poetics, 19*, 259–275.

Vygotsky, L. S. (1978). *Mind in society.* Cambridge, MA: Harvard University Press.

Vygotsky, L. S. (1986). *Thought and language.* Cambridge, MA: MIT Press.

Zyngier, S. (1994). Introducing literary awareness. *Language Awareness, 3*(2), 95–108.

APPENDIX A

The Lady With Baskets by Chaya Shenhav

Into the bus got
A lady with baskets,
They saw how she filled
All the seats:

On one seat -
A basket with
Rolls,

On one seat -
A basket with
Tomatoes,

On one seat -
A basket with
Sesame seeds,

On one seat -
A basket with
Cucumbers,
On one seat -
A basket with
Margarine,

On one seat -
A basket with
Humous-techina,

On one seat -
A basket with
All sorts

On one seat -
A basket with
Newspapers.

Son -
Why are you sitting?
Get up at once!
Don't you think that a lady
Needs at least one seat.

CHAPTER 16

Reflective Talk From Poetic Text

Philomena Donnelly
Kieran Egan

"Minds are formed by language, thoughts take their colour from its ideas."

(*J.-J. Rousseau, Emile (1762/1974, p. 73)*)

As a species and as individuals, we began as members of oral cultures. Language emerged in our evolutionary and in our individual development as a natural function of our bodies. However sophisticated our use of language, it never loses the imprint of our bodies. At the simplest level, the basic units of language are products of other bodily functions. The sentence, for example, is shaped by how long it takes us to suck in breath and let it slowly out over our larynx and pharynx (in a process Steven Pinker, 1994, describes as "syntax overriding carbon dioxide," p. 164).

One of the oddities of literacy is that it makes us reflect on this function of our bodies in a detailed way. We can make visible to our eyes the product of our thought as expressed in words. Literacy is a very strange achievement. It involves the externalizing of a natural bodily activity and its preservation in a peculiar coded form that allows us then to reexamine that past activity.

We consider the achievement of this peculiarity to be foundational to all other educational achievements. We teach children to express their thoughts in writing and then reflect on their, and on others', past thoughts. But, of course, this is too simple a way of putting it. We recognize increasingly that the kind of writing system we learn shapes our consciousness of language and that our consciousness of ourselves and of our world is, in some significant degree, a by-product of our ways of creating and interpreting written texts. Writing, as David Olson (1994) has argued so persuasively, plays "a critical role in producing the shift from thinking about things to thinking about representations of those things, that is, thinking about thought" (p. 282).

Consciousness of language use—what is sometimes called, rather ponderously, "metalinguistic awareness"—is clearly important for children's ability to function adequately in a literate environment. Yet we do little explicitly to cultivate such consciousness. The context of the typical classroom, and the pressures on teachers, inclines us to move toward the efficiency of telling children things rather than have them reflect on the language in which the things are expressed. Yet it is this latter form of intellectual activity that would seem to be of special importance at the time that literacy is becoming elaborated in their lives. We do not mean to suggest some simple dichotomy here between "telling" and "reflecting"; obviously, there are times for both. Our concern is that explicit techniques for engaging children in reflecting on language use are not common.

What we want to describe and exemplify in the following pages is a technique that can be used by any teacher to encourage children's reflection on language. We indicate a way in which talk about texts can stimulate the kind of reflection that seems to us of particular importance in learning to become fluently literate.

What follows is built on the work of Matthew Lipman (Lipman, Sharp, & Oscanyon, 1980; see also Lipman, 1993) as this has been interpreted and developed by Joseph Dunne and Philomena Donnelly in Dublin, Ireland. Lipman initiated the Philosophy for Children program in the United States. Thinking, for Lipman, involves learning and exercising particular skills. He lists 30 of these, which he engages children in learning; such things as learning to ask relevant questions, drawing out the consequences of what is said, giving reasons for beliefs, defining terms to avoid ambiguity, and detecting fallacies in reasoning (see Lipman et al., 1980, and his journal *Thinking: The Journal of Philosophy for Children*). Lipman's program comprises a number of stories. Typically, the children with their teacher read a selected passage, and the teacher generates discussion based on the ideas and concepts of the passage. A more informal application of this technique, using questions raised by children in conversation or questions that result from stories he told, is exemplified in Gareth Matthews' (1980, 1984) delightful and fascinating discussions with children.

Dunne is Senior Lecturer in Philosophy of Education at St. Patrick's College of Education, Dublin. During 1989 Dunne, in collaboration with Philomena Donnelly, developed another procedure for doing philosophy with young children.

Exploration of ways to apply Lipman's ideas about the value of philosophy for children led to a procedure we have found both engaging to children and fruitful in achieving the aims of reflection on language. We call the technique "Thinking Time," because this is the name the children themselves invented for the sessions.

THINKING TIME ORGANIZATION

In this section, we describe briefly the process that evolved while working with a class of 33 boys and girls aged 5 to 6 years in Bayside Junior School.

The school lies on the northern coast of Dublin Bay. It has 500 pupils between the ages of 4 and 8 years. There are 18 classroom teachers, one learning support teacher, one resource teacher, and a nonteaching principal. It is a modern, well-equipped, single-story building. The school serves a largely middle-class area, and there is a very low percentage of unemployment among parents. Bayside Senior School is part of the same building. The children transfer from the junior to the senior school where they stay for 4 years. They then transfer to secondary school, usually at the age of 12–13 years.

The procedure we developed works as follows. The classroom tables are pushed to the sides, and the children and teacher sit in a circle with no designated places. The topic for discussion and the opening speaker are chosen by consensus the previous day. This allows time for reflection on the topic. The child opening the discussion makes his or her initial statement and then tips (i.e., touches the arm of) the child next to him or her. If this child wishes to speak, he or she does so, and then tips the next child; otherwise, he or she passes on the tip. This continues around the circle, with the teacher participating when the tip comes to him or her.

When it is the teacher's turn to speak, the teacher can model dialogical forms of language, such as "I agree with ...," "I disagree with ...," "I wonder if this is always true ..." and so on.

The Socratic structure of the dialogue is complemented by the physical structure. Fisher (1990) defines a Socratic structure as "a process approach where the teacher becomes the facilitator of investigations aimed at encouraging children to discuss, listen, clarify and justify their thinking" (p. 164) A Socratic structure offers the children the opportunity to speak in the classroom without the burden of answering a teacher-question. Flanders (1970) showed that two thirds of classroom time is taken up by teachers talking. Thinking Time offers the children the opportunity to speak, to listen, to reflect, to have an opinion, to make a statement, to ask a question, and to be listened to. It gives time to wonder and ponder and, by the sharing of speaking and listening, to try and make sense of the world we share. In speaking, children become conscious of their own minds and learn there can be many answers to a question. They come to recognize that not all questions have one correct answer.

Thinking Time sessions can last from 30 to 40 minutes. To end a session, we do a final "tip" around, during which the children can make a final statement about what has been discussed, offer an answer to the question on which the conversation was based, or offer a definition. There is no one single conclusion accepted above others, nor is there a vote for or against. All thoughts and ideas are accepted and left to further internal reflection. Often, indeed, further thoughts and musings are raised during other class time or during yard time or recess.

TALK AND TEXT

Often it proves best to begin the session with a particular text that lends itself to philosophical reflection. This does not mean that it needs to be abstruse or complicated, just that it raises a profound idea—of the kind that children themselves will raise readily, given the chance (cf. Matthews, 1980, 1984). Poems, stories, pictures, and even pieces of sculpture have proven powerful stimulants to discussion. By using a text children can read, or have read to them, the teacher can assist in language development, awareness of written language, and reflection on the text itself and on the world it refers to. The procedure described in the previous section has worked well in achieving these aims with children and students of all ages. Engaging in a genuine and open conversation about a text helps children, in a way that is cumulative, to further develop their reading and language abilities. In sharing and thinking together, the children learn to reflect and make the text their own in some significant sense. Our experience reflects Vygotsky's (1978) claim that

Any function in the child's culture development appears twice, or in two planes. First it appears on the social plane and then on the psychological plane. First it appears between people as an interpsychological category, and then within the child as an intrapsychological category. This is equally true with regard to voluntary attention, logical memory, the formation of concepts, and the development of volition. (p. 163)

So, let us give an example. It is quite lengthy, but we think you will see if you follow the children's and teacher's words that the talk about our simple 19-word text does indeed exemplify the reflective qualities of thought mentioned in the previous section. It is Emily Dickinson's (1993) short poem about words:

A word is dead

When it is said,

Some say.

I say it just

Begins to live

That day.

Here follows a script from a Thinking Time on this poem with a class of 35 boys and girls, aged 12 to 13, in Bayside Senior School in Dublin. The class teacher and Philomena Donnelly were both present. Donnelly had been involved in Thinking Time sessions with this class over a 6-month period. This session was videotaped and transcribed. Each indentation indicates another child speaking and "T" indicates a teacher is speaking.

We have considered breaking up this rather long section with a meta-commentary, elaborating and drawing attention to features of the text that illustrate our general arguments about this style of talk about text. But we have concluded that it would be better to leave the text as transcribed from the video. The reader can thus, we think, better experience something of the thought processes that the children both generated and followed as they sat in the circle. It is a long piece of transcription and is an unfamiliar form of text, in part because it is, in fact, talk. If readers reflect as they read, we think they will be drawn in to the children's own thinking, and readers will begin to reflect on the important issues the children try to grapple with. Occasionally, their reflections might seem naïve or inadequately articulated. But it is, to us at least, fascinating to see how inarticulate groping for an idea in conversation can be valuable to others in helping them to articulate it, which in turn helps the child who began the struggle to become clearer about what he or she meant (see Sheldon, chap. 3, this vol., for further elaboration of this idea).

Thinking Time: April 6, 1996

- I think words are alive for the amount of time you say them. If I say "Hallelujah ," then it's gone.
- If you keep using the same word …
- A word I think is a sort of alive because when you say it, it's your meaning for that word and it's alive.

- I think words are alive because words have a great meaning in our lives. Some sentences are insignificant when you say them but some great statements are remembered for ever and ever. Things that are said in the Bible and things like that and I think people wouldn't be able to write and speak because if they could not speak they wouldn't have words to write or read.
- I don't think you could think if you couldn't speak because when you think, you think in speech in a way.
- I think words are always alive because you don't know how many times a word is said in a day.
- If humans didn't have a voice to speak then there would be no way of communicating between them and if you think of words you think of what you say in words and if you didn't have a voice you wouldn't know the words to think.
- Words are words and I don't think they're alive and I don't think they're dead. They're just there.
- I think that when you're thinking you automatically think words and you can't control it.
- I don't think words ever die out because we use them every day.
- If you couldn't speak then you couldn't learn anything. Everything you learn if you don't pass it on to someone else then when you die no one else will know.
- I think words come alive when you use them. They live on after you've used them. They live on after you've used them because other people can repeat what you have said.
- Without words I think you must be able to think because otherwise how would languages be invented?
- God gave us voices to speak.
- I think words are alive because when you use them you can have a picture in your mind and whenever you use them the same picture comes.
- Some words are alive. Say, "the," it's just a word. you are not doing anything but if you say "running" it's an action. You're actually doing something.
- I don't think words are ever alive.
- *T—I wonder if it's true to say that if you haven't got a voice you can't think. Some people are born and they can't speak. They're physically dumb but does that mean they can't think? I wonder if that's necessarily true?*
- If you couldn't speak could you think or write? I think you couldn't write because you can think about what you're going to write.
- I think words are alive because in a legend or something it's passed on from generation to generation.
- I don't think words die out because when you use them they are still there when we're finished using them.
- Well if you were dumb and couldn't speak; well you'd still be able to think because you could hear people thinking. You wouldn't be able to say them out but you could say them in your mind.
- If you couldn't speak you'd still be able to think and that. You mightn't be able to say the words but you'd be able to think the words and you'd still be able to communicate. Think about a word, then you could draw it and you could be telepathic.

- Well I think it would be possible to speak, to write and to think and perhaps even to read if you had no words because there are other ways of communicating but I don't think humans wouldn't evolve a way of communication. They might use pictures as Michael said or they might use like perhaps taps on the ground or find some way of communicating; even if it was through speaking.
- Well obviously animals can communicate with each other, food calls, mating calls and they can't speak and they have their own way so they obviously have learned how to communicate. And man has made many great inventions like the telephone; many great achievements but whoever created talk a long time ago must have been a real genius because it's a great achievement to have created all the languages and a form of communication like this.
- I think because we speak it's hard to imagine not speaking even though if we couldn't speak we could still think and use signs to communicate.
- I don't think one person created all these words because some of them use different syllables than we use so it could have been just loads of people from different countries evolved this way of talking.
- People who are dumb and words are alive but have a different meaning.
- People who are dumb; they think in words but they cannot get them out.
- I think words never die out because we always have to use them sometime.
- I think that people can think even though they can't hear because every time they use sign language; mumble out words that resemble the sounds of the words so they must be able to think if they use sign language.
- As far as I'm concerned if words are alive it must have a soul because anything that is alive has a soul as far as we know it and when it dies the soul leaves the thing and I don't think words have souls so they're not alive.
- I think that people just say words automatically but if we didn't know words or if no one invented words we wouldn't miss them. We'd draw pictures or use sign language.
- I think words die when we die because if we lived for another day the words that we were going to say wouldn't be said.
- Words; we use them all the time. If I said "blah blah" you wouldn't know what that meant so I think words do have a meaning and they are alive.
- *T—I wonder if what David said is true? To be alive you must have a soul? I'd say a flower is alive but I wonder if a flower has a soul and I'm also wondering; I have a question. Several people have mentioned words and meaning. Maybe it is the case that words are only alive when they have meaning. Can words be used when they have no meaning? Maybe that's what makes them alive or dead?*
- Reading a book like, you'd want to think about it. If you think about the words it makes you feel like you're there. It makes the book more alive.
- Many people have said that sometimes the book is better than the film but I think they are because it's the words they put in them gives it some meaning and you sort of picture it in your mind in your own way.
- People that are deaf; some people might think they don't know many words because they can't hear them or something like that. They use them in their sign language and they can think inside themselves.

- Without words there wouldn't be books or anything so you'd be losing out on that.
- Maybe words can't be alive because if you just said a word it just goes blank.
- Well the question is who invented words? Did some fella just one day blabber out loads of words and they made meaning for them or what happened?
- I think words could be alive but they die eventually. Like if you know a word but then you forget it, it dies when you forget it.
- I think they are alive once you have a real meaning for them. If you hear a word and you don't really care; if you hear a word and you think over the word and you think about over the sentence that's been said then the word is brought alive in your mind. It's been given meaning to you and I'd say each person may have slightly, only a very slightly, different meaning for each word in the way its used because you have your word and I would say words are definitely alive. As Eimear says in a book it's a lot better than a television program because then you create your own picture in your mind; what the words tell you and you create your own picture.
- Words aren't alive in the same way as humans are alive. Words can't be alive like that. Words are alive in a different way. They are alive in what they mean. If they are used to describe good things in life then they're alive with happiness but then they're a kind of dead if they are about gloom and everything. But words could never be alive the way humans are; words are alive in a life of their own. They have a different meaning of life.
- Words are dead in a sense because they are not solid matter, and they are not gas. They are just very important because without words we'd have no way of communicating and even if we could communicate the way dolphins do by bleeping or whatever, it would still, I'd say, take hundreds of years to evolve such ways of talking as we have now.
- I disagree with teacher because a flower might have its own kind of soul; it might have a flower soul.
- I think when you are talking the words just show everything up.
- I don't think words can ever die because every time you talk you just use the same words again and again and it just goes on and on.
- If you think back to the Stone Age time they didn't have any words. They just communicated by thumping the ground with their sticks.
- Maybe words are alive in a sense and not in another sense because the word *pennyfarthing* was an old bicycle and not many people use that word nowadays. So maybe it's dead and other words.
- I think words are born but they don't really die because even like David just said there, "pennyfarthing" and it isn't used as much now but like people might talk about old bikes and how they used to be.
- I reckon to us words look dead but I reckon they have their own way of living to them. They might have their own way of communicating.
- Humans couldn't advance without words because even if you had a language with pictures you couldn't explain things very well or if someone is not a good artist then no one will know what they're saying.

- *T—I think words are alive and I think words are necessary and we have evidence of this in the fact that language vocabulary keeps increasing all the time.*
- Michael said words die when you speak them but they don't because other people still remember them.
- *T—I agree with Aoife and I was wondering when she was speaking. Maybe we're looking at this the wrong way. Is it the case that we give life to words or when we speak them they are born or maybe it is the other way around. Is it words that give us life? Is it the words that help us to become alive rather than us helping them to live? I was just wondering.*
- Some people might think it is awful without words but if we didn't have words to speak we'd find some other way of communicating.
- I think they're replacing a lot of words and they're changing them to easier words. Like *television,* everyone refers to it as TV now and pennyfarthing is now bicycle or bike. I think they're going to shorten out the English language.
- Words could be alive in their own way. Words could see for all we know because they could think we're dead because we move and stuff.
- Without words you wouldn't be able to say how you feel, if you're happy or sad.
- Humans have lived in big groups and I don't think that would be possible if there wasn't words because humans find comfort in each other because they can explain what they mean and, like loads of people said, pictures and thumping it would be good but I don't think it would be able to explain everything as well as words explain them because with words you can put your feelings into a sentence and then other people can understand what you feel like and I'd say they're alive.
- Well I think when you say a word it's alive and when you forget about it someone else is saying it so it's still alive. So a word isn't dead but you could say all over the world people are saying words because everyone has words. People in Africa when they didn't talk to people in Europe they'd still talk their own language so it's not really that people who don't live together create different ways of communicating. It's that they create different words. So obviously something or someone has given us the ability to create words or something like that.
- I think words will always be with us because from the Stone Age to now we've developed loads and loads, like thousands of words, so I think in the next thousands of years people will make new words.
- I think it's not just words that if you say they are alive they cease because the whole Irish language. Like there's no one in here who would go around speaking Irish and I think it will die in a sense if you could say that as I say as we have advanced already in technology I'd say we could advance some other way of communicating, some easier way.
- I'm just wondering as David said if a language died out like Irish and no one speaks Irish now. The words if they were alive what would they do?
- I don't think words live or die. It's just a way to express something or to tell, to explain what you think and I personally don't think; I think that anyone who thinks a word lives or dies is an idiot.
- When we go to secondary school, we're going to learn a new language like French or German or Spanish and we might emigrate to that country and

start speaking that language and maybe we're going to forget English and take up the Spanish language and then that's one person who's after forgetting the English language.

- Teacher said we might need words and words might need us but I think it's that we both need each other.
- I disagree with Eoin because we've been on this Earth long enough now to find, to have found some way of communicating and expressing our feelings.
- Quite a few people here have said words are alive because they have meaning but pictures can have meanings and they are not alive and words are just sounds and that would mean that if they are alive then every sound is alive.
- I think words are alive because words do have meaning and if words were dead we wouldn't have a clue what they meant.
- I think when you are a child and starting to use words and as you get older you start to use bigger words so maybe that's when words start to come alive.
- Every sound could be alive because animals have a use for them.
- I disagree with what Emma said if we didn't have words we wouldn't be able to express our feelings but if we're sad we might cry and people aren't going to think we're happy if we're crying and we're happy we smile.
- I don't think words are alive or dead because they'll always be there but people mightn't use them.
- *T—I'm wondering is it in the thinking that makes them alive and in the same sense that a picture is only a picture on a wall and it's only when someone looks at it and thinks about it. It's the thinking that makes it come alive in the same way as you said that a book is better than a film. If a book is sitting on your teacher's table and no one ever opens it maybe that's dead but when someone opens it and reads the words maybe it's in the reading of it it comes alive because someone is thinking.*
- Words aren't alive until you put them to work like in a sentence and that's when they come alive and everyone can understand them.
- I think we need words because if a person is rushed into hospital and they're dying the doctor isn't going to have time to draw pictures and to make signs with his hands. We'd find it very difficult.
- I also disagree with Emma because if we didn't have words we'd still be able to express our feelings because we'd still have some type of communication. And I also disagree with David because he said we could emigrate into a different country and start talking their language but that language is never going to die down and we're always going to remember different parts.
- Words are always alive as long as we use them.
- If a person went to secondary school and learned a new language and then emigrated to another country, I don't think they'd forget their own language.
- I don't think words are alive. I just think they're dead. They're just something that's there. They're not alive; it's just something that's there.
- Well words, I'd say words are alive in one sense and not in another sense. They don't breathe like we do but they have a meaning and they mean something to us. They help us live and through us they live and we proba-

bly have a lot better life through them. Eimear said that if someone is rushed into the doctor they wouldn't be able to tell them through pictures what they felt [was] wrong with them. And like a lot of things would just be so much harder without words. We just need them to sort of supply and we need them to come together because people depend on other people to help them and we couldn't get help from other people if we hadn't got words.

- Well people say that words have meaning and they have an explanation. Happy is a mood but mood is another word and what is mood? Mood is your feelings so if you're to give one word a meaning you've got to use another word to give that meaning so after everything you have to use another word to describe that word. Words have different meaning to other people. A deaf person, a deaf person can't hear a word or they might learn to speak a word, but they can't learn to speak unless they hear others speaking. And when a baby is young it only speaks certain words and it calls people different things and words might mean something. I know my sister's words mean different things to her. Things that move are "woof woof" and anything that doesn't move is "yum yum" so things mean different things to different people. Babies don't depend on words but when we grow up we find it hard to think of a world without words.
- I think, well loads of people are saying we couldn't survive without words but if words weren't invented, like back in the Stone Age, we'd probably create another device to communicate because people who are deaf and dumb, they use sign language to communicate so we don't exactly need words and we'd get used to the lifestyle of living without words.
- Words help you and if you were in Antarctica you'd need clothes. They're helping you. Clothes aren't alive so how can words be alive? They're just the same and I totally agree with Brian. A word is just a sound made from your mouth, from your tongue moving of your lips and stuff. It's not alive. You can't create something that isn't alive. You need D.N.A. or something that could create life.
- I think words are not living things. They're just for our use.
- Maybe words die out when we use them badly like in slang. Like instead of saying "the" we say "th-" or something like that. Maybe words will die down.
- In baby books there's like maybe three words for a picture and some books there's just pictures so babies learn how to speak from pictures; sometimes as well by parents explaining.
- I reckon some words are alive and some are dead. Words like "the" are dead but exciting words are alive and also if there was no such thing as words I don't think we'd be sitting here doing Thinking Time.
- Teacher said maybe words come alive when you think about them or when you read them but they can't be alive if they need someone to think for them.
- *T—Some people have been talking about using signs but surely when we're using signs they represent words.*
- I think words never live to die.
- People are saying words are dead but to die you have to live first.
- I think words are just here to help us communicate.

- *T—People were talking about language evolving and all the new words; maybe we've gone too far; maybe we've too many words and we're too careless with the way we use them. What if they were rationed and you were only allowed to use say five hundred words in a day; would we be more careful how we use them and where we use them?*
- Someone said we could create a new device for communication but I don't think that would work because how would you tell people how to work the device if you're not going to use speech?
- I disagree with Aoife because Aoife said words don't breathe but you use breath to say words.
- I think that; I disagree that words have to live to be dead. If something is not there it's not there and I don't think words are alive and don't think they will ever be alive.
- A word I think blooms into life, into meaning, when you say it because you've got some meaning for it but if you lie or if you say something without meaning the word isn't living because you're not putting any meaning into it. You're not giving it life. I think a word needs meaning; it needs people to give it meaning and you need it to help you communicate. Instead there could be other ways like other languages and taps but I don't think it would give as much meaning as a word can. I don't think they could give as much.
- I disagree with the teacher when she said pictures and signs are used to give meaning to words because sign language—when people use sign language they form their hands to represent letters and words and we couldn't use sign language because we'd be using that to represent words. And we wouldn't know what words were so we wouldn't use something like that and we wouldn't say "O.K. We're forming a new language. We stamp three times on the floor and that means Hello or something" because we don't have "hello" to make a word.
- I think words need us to survive and we need words to survive.
- I don't think words are alive because they don't eat, they don't grow, they're not visible but a word you can stretch it but you can't make it grow. You can say "b-l-u-e" but you're only stretching it.
- I' d love to know where words came from and where it began.
- It would be a bit hard if we were all sitting here and writing out pictures and then showing them for words. And if we did do that we'd be thinking it would be very hard to write every single word on one picture. And I totally disagree with Sinead and teacher, because we are born with words and other people who are deaf were born working sign language and if we were born with people stamping their feet we'd grow to learn what that meant.
- According to the poem words are alive if we use them that day but if we use the same words every day it must have more lives than a cat.
- I reckon words only live for a second because when you say a word you're on to a new word like it's over like that. And I agree with Sinead and teacher; if you draw a picture it represents a word.
- I think we couldn't survive without some way of communicating because everything that humans have done they couldn't have done it by themselves. They needed help from someone else. They needed to communicate.

- *T—I agree with Catherine. I think she summed up my feelings about words very well when she said we need them to survive and they need us to survive. Our life would be very difficult if we didn't have a wide range of words to choose from and words would not exist if we choose not to use them.*
- I agree with Brian; words have no brain or anything.
- I disagree with the teacher because people lived and drew pictures before words were invented.
- I think that people are saying that deaf people use sign language. I think that when we're thinking about a word we draw a picture of it in our minds like what we're going to do and then we use the word.
- I also disagree with teacher because there are different signs for words. The caveman might have gone "Oah oah" or something like that and the amount of times you hit your stomach or the amount of "Oah oah"s might describe something.
- Imagine the alphabet if there were no words. There wouldn't be letters. there'd be pictures or something and it would be real complicated. You couldn't just survive on pictures. It would be too complicated for everybody.
- Well you can't live without words. You have to have words. Like if somebody invented a business for food they can't just draw a picture of a factory or food. They wouldn't know how to write the words if they weren't invented.
- Words could be alive. I disagree with Brian because words could be alive. They mightn't be alive in the way we think of what's alive because when we think of alive we think of organs and breathing air but words could be alive in a different way to what we are alive.

REFLECTIONS ON THE DIALOGUE

In reading and rereading the script, we are fascinated with the sense of presence, the sense of now. It is as though one is reading a play. One is caught up with the evolving dialogue/conversation. The thoughts, musings, and questions of the children are all thrown into the communal pot of wonder. It is as though one can hear them listening, almost hear them thinking. There is a sense of a joint search and a certain commitment to the journey. Themes emerge over time. It is the time in Thinking Time that adds the vital ingredient. Most importantly, the language is alive. There are no set scripts, no prepared monologues, and no learned words. Paulo Freire, in *Education: The Practice of Freedom* (1976), defines dialogue as a horizontal relationship between persons engaged in a joint search, and the matrices of such a search are loving, humble, hopeful, trusting, and critical (p. 45). In contrast, he defines anti-dialogue as involving vertical relationships between persons which lack love and therefore is acritical and cannot create a critical attitude: "It is self-sufficient and hopelessly arrogant" (p. 46). He concludes that the anti-dialogue does not communicate but rather issues communiqués.

In *The Human Condition* (1958), Hannah Arendt argues that we can know someone quite different from ourselves only through conversation. Such a conversation builds the community of the classroom between child and child, and child and teacher. The conversation is unpredictable. Children and teacher lose themselves in the dialogue and yet come out of it with a deeper understanding of themselves.

It is through the to-ing and fro-ing of the conversation that interest, understanding, and meaning evolve. There are no set pieces. It is a collective search.

Our claim has been that the reader would be able to see in the talk about text (in the previously presented transcription) evidence of student reflection on language and its leading to sophisticated reflection about their world and experience. We think such phrases as the following, which we have selected almost randomly, support this claim:

- "I think words need us to survive and we need words to survive."
- "I don't think you could think if you couldn't speak because when you think, you think in speech in a way."
- "If you couldn't speak, could you think or write? I think you couldn't write because you can think about what you're going to write."
- "As far as I'm concerned if words are alive it must have a soul because anything that is alive has a soul as far as we know it and when it dies the soul leaves the thing and I don't think words have souls so they're not alive."
- "I think because we speak it's hard to imagine not speaking"

The words with which the students, after some practice with Thinking Time, commonly begin their contributions to the conversation, are also worthy of note:

- "Well, the question is …"
- "I disagree with teacher because …"
- "I reckon …"
- "Some people might think …"
- "I'm just wondering …"
  "Quite a few people here have said …"
  "I also disagree …"
- "I'd love to know …"
- "Imagine …"

We are particularly fond of the last two conversation openers. When a 12-year-old child says to her or his classmates, "I'd love to know …" or "Imagine …," the human desire to learn is evident. Argument, in the philosophical sense of argument, is also present:

- "I think words never live to die."
- "People are saying words are dead but to die you have to live."

Later a child says:

- "I disagree that words have to live to be dead. If something is not there, it's not there."

TEACHING STYLES AND LEARNING STYLES

The more and varied the teaching styles brought to a classroom, the more learning styles are being appealed to. A Socratic approach is just one of them. In such an approach, the teacher becomes the facilitator assisting the children, as Plato puts it, "to give birth to their own ideas" (1964, pp. 15–32). In this process, it is necessary to "festina lente"—make haste slowly. The teacher teaches by modeling forms of speech and thought. Direct instruction has no place during Thinking Time, even though such a style might be very valuable during other parts of the school day.

Listening and reflecting are key elements of any learning style. A listening and reflective teacher will encourage such practices in his or her pupils by modeling them. Listening and reflecting take time and practice. Giving the kind of time and practice evident in the text of talk reproduced in this chapter has beneficial influences that are cumulative and cross-curricular in their effects.

WHAT DO THE CHILDREN GO HOME WITH?

Possibly the most important thing the children go home with is a sense of belonging to a community of reflective people through the process of a text openly shared. A more tangible product of this is evidently improved reasoning and expressive skills. We have not tested for children's conceptual improvements in these areas compared with some control group. But we would expect improvements on reasoning ability, for example, might well reflect the kinds of results Lipman found on the California Test of Mental Maturity, to his surprise, after he initially devised his program (see his account in Lipman, 1993, pp. 372–384). The questions raised by the text are still open at the end. The understanding that emerges is of a complex kind. No conclusion is sought or imposed. The conversation is primarily a philosophy session, but it is worth reflecting how the frequent engagement in such a process would be likely to enhance these children's understanding when they return to read their school texts or any text. Would it be possible to sit and participate in such a dialogue and not be affected by it? Witnessing words and thoughts "bloom into life," as one child put it, is not something one can do passively. To have spoken, to have listened, to have mused, and to have reflected on Emily Dickinson's poem within the community of the classroom brings to life—brings back to living language and thought—the issues the poem has coded in text. From these 19 beautiful words, a class of 12- to 13-year-old girls and boys in a Dublin primary school shared many hundreds of words in conversation and in wonder. From such a text came such talk. It gives us great pleasure to share their words with you.

REFERENCES

Arendt, H. (1958). *The human condition*. Chicago: University of Chicago Press.

Dickinson, E. (1993). *Poems*. New York: Alfred A. Knopf.

Fisher, R. (1990). *Teaching children to think*. Oxford: Blackwell.

Flanders, N. (1970). *Analyzing teacher behaviour*. New York: Addison-Wesley.

Freire, P. (1974). *Education: The practice of freedom*. London: Writers & Readers Publishing Cooperative.

Lipman, M. (Ed.). (1993). *Thinking children and education*. Dubuque, IA: Kendall/Hunt.

Lipman M., Sharp, A. M., & Oscanyon, F. S. (1980). *Philosophy in the classroom*. Philadelphia: Temple University Press.

Matthews, G. (1980). *Philosophy and the young child*. Cambridge, MA: Harvard University Press.

Matthews, G. (1984). *Conversations with children*. Cambridge, MA: Harvard University Press.

Olson, D. (1994). *The world on paper.* Cambridge: Cambridge University Press.
Pinker, S. (1994). *The language instinct: How the mind creates language.* New York: Morrow.
Plato. (1964). *The midwife's apprentice.* London: Routledge & Kegan Paul
Rousseau, J.-J. (1974). *Emile.* London: Everyman Library. (Original work published 1762)
Vygotsky, L. (1978). *Mind in society.* Cambridge, MA: Harvard University Press.

CHAPTER 17

The Talmud Teaches How to Speak About Beliefs and Deeds

Jacob Neusner

A principal way to reasoned learning about the world leads us to reconstruct, in our minds, the arguments that a given proposition provokes. When we contemplate Plato's dialogues, we learn how to recapitulate the arguments for and against a given idea, we work our way through the same analytical procedures, consider the same issues, respond to the same rationality, that Socrates contemplated and Plato portrayed. This "written down talk" gives the text its power, allowing us to construct a drama of our own in response to the moral or philosophical issues under discussion. Now if Plato has given us an ideal model for thought as written talk, a perfect example of a text that makes talk possible and even compelling, Plato also has left room for another model. For Plato's presentation of the moving argument, or the dialectics, of analysis of a problem in the form of conversation focuses on abstract definitions and global propositions. But where are we to find a model of concrete and practical models, relevant to everyday problems, of written talk, texts that provoke us to reconstruct the ideas and arguments that pertain to an immediate dilemma? And how are we to locate the dialectics of discourse when at issue are everyday issues, the actualities of the workaday day?

DIALECTICS AND WRITTEN TALK

Out of antiquity comes a powerful exercise in written thought, an effort to set forth issues in so concrete a way that we may ourselves join in a long-ago conversation and find wisdom and reason, both, in recapitulating, even reconstructing, issues that have been worked through, in this very language that we use, and in these very terms that guide our inquiry, for 2,000 years. It is the Talmud of Babylonia (aka "the Bavli"), the foundation-document of the education of Judaism. The Talmud is made up of a law code, the Mishnah, about 200 CE, and an analytical presentation of that law code and commentary on it, the Gemara or simply "the Talmud," of about 600 CE. Whereas the Mishnah is a carefully crafted piece of writing, the Talmud consists of not spelled out scripts of a fully articulated analytical argument—such as we find in Plato's dialogues—but rather signals that guide us in the reconstruction of that argument. It is a classic case of a text that insists we join in the conversation, a text that is meant to be talked about.

That is why, if you go into a yeshiva devoted to Talmud study, such as flourishes in most of the major cities of the Western world and in the state of Israel, you will find yourself in a very noisy place. Students sit in pairs, the one reading and expounding the text, the other arguing doggedly and conversing vividly about what is read and how explanation unfolds. The Talmud cannot be "read," only declaimed and shaped into the basis for an ongoing argument. It is a document that tolerates the passive reader only with great difficulty but that welcomes the active, engaged student, the one who wishes to join in the argument.

This the Talmud does by forming its most important discussions in the form of dialectical arguments. Here is where "talk about texts" finds a most appropriate case in a text that is meant to stimulate talk, and to do so in a very particular way. The Talmud's distinctive trait is its particular mode of argument, the dialectical one. Rather than define the dialectical argument in abstract terms, I give one concrete case, which shows at each point how people are invited to join in the talk about the text—by the text itself! For the moment it suffices to define a dialectical argument as a give and take in which parties to the argument counter one another's arguments in a progression of exchanges (often, in what seems like an infinite progress to an indeterminate conclusion). That definition will be refined in due course. The passage that we consider occurs at the Babylonian Talmud Baba Mesia 5B–6A, which is to say, Talmud to Mishnah Baba Mesia. 1:1–2. Our interest is in the twists and turns of the argument, on which my comments focus. I give the Mishnah passage in boldfaced type, which shows the text that is being analyzed. The Talmud is in two languages, Hebrew and Aramaic; I give Aramaic in italics. That is where we find ourselves in the heart of the argument, at the dialectical center of things.

The Talmud deals with a case of two claimants to an object each claims to have found. The Mishnah passage is as follows:

MISHNAH BABA MESIA 1:1

A.   Two lay hold of a cloak—

B.   this one says, "I found it!"—

C.   and that one says, "I found it!"—

D.   this one says, "It's all mine!"—

E.   and that one says, "It's all mine!"—

F.   this one takes an oath that he possesses no less a share of it than half,

G.   and that one takes an oath that he possesses no less a share of it than half,

H.   and they divide it up.

The problem then recalls the two women fighting before Solomon about the disposition of the infant child, but the law of the Mishnah and the decision of Solomon scarcely intersect. The issue now is addressed by the Talmud. What we wish to notice is how the Talmud forms a script that permits us to join in the discussion; if we

English commentary and expanded translation of the text, making it readable and comprehensible

Hebrew/Aramaic text of the Talmud, fully vocalized, and punctuated

Literal translation of the Talmud text into English

TRANSLATION AND COMMENTARY

MISHNAH שְׁנַיִם אוֹחֲזִין בְּטַלִּית ¹Two claimants appear before a Bet Din holding on to a garment. ²One of them says: "I found it," and the other says: "I found it." One of them says: "The whole garment is mine," and the other says: "The whole garment is mine." ³The Bet Din resolves such conflicting claims in the following way: One of the two claimants must take an oath that no less than half of the garment is his, and the other claimant must likewise take an oath that no less than half of it is his. ⁴They shall then divide the garment or its value between them.

LITERAL TRANSLATION

MISHNAH ¹Two are holding on to a garment. ²This one says: "I found it," and this one says: "I found it." This one says: "All of it is mine," and this one says: "All of it is mine." ³This one shall swear that he does not have in it less than half of it, and this one shall swear that he does not have in it less than half of it, ⁴and they shall divide [it].

¹אוֹחֲזִין בְּטַלִּית. ²זֶה אוֹמֵר:
"אֲנִי מְצָאתִיהָ," וְזֶה אוֹמֵר:
"אֲנִי מְצָאתִיהָ." זֶה אוֹמֵר:
"כּוּלָּהּ שֶׁלִּי," וְזֶה אוֹמֵר: "כּוּלָּהּ
שֶׁלִּי." ³זֶה יִשָּׁבַע שֶׁאֵין לוֹ בָּהּ פָּחוֹת מֵחֶצְיָהּ, וְזֶה יִשָּׁבַע שֶׁאֵין
לוֹ בָּהּ פָּחוֹת מֵחֶצְיָהּ, ⁴וְיַחֲלוֹקוּ.

RASHI

משנה שנים אוחזין בטלית — דוקא אוחזין, דשניהם מוחזקים בה ואין לזה בה יותר מזה. שאילו היה ביד אחד לבדו, הוי אידך המוציא מחבירו, ועליו להביא ראיה בעדים שהיא שלו. ולי נאמר זה ליטול בשבועה. זה אומר כולה שלי — בגמרא מפרש למה מנה פרטי. זה ושבע — מפרש בגמרא (ג,א) שלקח.

שבועה זו למה. שאין לו בה חצות מחצה — בגמרא (ג,ב), מפרש אמאי תקנו כי הני ליטול בכך שבועה.

NOTES

The order and internal structure of the tractate. Rishonim raise questions with regard to the place of tractate *Bava Metzia* in the general sequence of tractates in the Talmud (see *Tosafot* שנים). They also question the order of the chapters within the tractate itself: The first chapter, שנים אוחזין, would appear to belong to the laws concerning the finding of lost objects. Would it not have been more natural to begin with the fundamental principles underlying these laws (which are found in the second chapter, אלו מציאות) and only then to go on to discuss the various details relating to the subject?

Tosafot explain that the tractates *Bava Kamma*, *Bava Metzia*, and *Bava Batra* are really only divisions of one long tractate called *Nezikin*, comprising thirty chapters. Since the last chapter of *Bava Kamma* deals with the subject of dividing objects between different claimants and the imposition of an oath in such cases, our tractate begins with a discussion of these laws.

Another explanation is given by *Rosh*: In the case presented at the beginning of our tractate we suspect that one of the disputing claimants may have obtained possession of the object illegally. Therefore it was appropriate to present it immediately after similar cases in the last chapter of the previous tractate.

Rashbatz gives a different explanation: The tractate should actually begin with the laws and general principles concerning the finding of lost objects. But the specific case of שנים אוחזין, in which there are two equal claims to the ownership of a found object, contains unusual and interesting principles; hence the Mishnah begins with this

case. This is, indeed, a common practice in the Mishnah, where an individual case of special interest often precedes a discussion of general principles.

שנים אוחזין בטלית **Two men are holding on to a garment.** The Mishnah used the word טלית — "a garment" — and not the more general term חפץ — "an object" — because, as will be explained below, there are various laws which apply specifically to a garment and to the way in which the claimants are holding it which do not apply to other objects (*Torat Hayyim* and other *Aharonim*).

זה ושבע **This one shall swear.** In Jewish law an oath is not considered absolute proof but rather as corroboration of a certain claim. The prohibition against uttering a false oath written in the Ten Commandments (Exodus 20:7), and the words of the Torah and the Prophets regarding the many divine punishments imposed on someone who perjures himself (see Numbers 5; Zechariah 4–5), made people very fearful about taking oaths in general and about taking false oaths in particular. In general the obligation to take an oath is used as a threat against someone whose claim, we suspect, is not well founded, for it is possible that he has brought a case to court even though he is not entirely certain of the justice of his claim. Therefore it is assumed that a person would be very reluctant to take an oath in support of such a claim.

זה ישבע וזה ישבע **This one shall swear... and this one shall swear....** Rishonim (*Rabbenu Hananel* and others) ask why we do not apply here, as we sometimes do in other cases of property whose ownership is in doubt, the principle of כל דאלים גבר — "whoever is the stronger wins" —

BACKGROUND

טלית **Garment.** This is the specific term for the garment worn by men during the Mishnaic and Talmudic periods. This garment was essentially a large, square piece of cloth in which men would wrap themselves, using it as an outer garment. A טלית might be woven in a geometric pattern for decoration, and occasionally decorations made of more expensive materials were added to it. But in general a טלית was a plain piece of cloth, usually with ritual fringes (ציציות) on the four corners. After the Jews were exiled from Eretz Israel and other countries in the Middle East, the טלית remained as a garment used during prayer and various other religious ceremonies. The Mishnah used the טלית as an example for a number of reasons: Since it was generally worn as an outer garment, and since people used to take it off while they worked, it was quite common to find a lost טלית. In addition, the simple form of the טלית easily permitted its division into two or more pieces of cloth without destroying the value of the garment. In cases where the litigants claim objects that cannot be divided physically, they divide the value of the object between them.

Notes highlight points of interest in the text and expand the discussion by quoting other classical commentaries

Hebrew commentary of Rashi, the classic explanation that accompanies all editions of the Talmud

HALAKHAH

שנים אוחזין בטלית **Two claimants are holding on to a garment.** "Where two claimants are holding on to one object (or have possession of one animal), and each claims ownership of the whole object, each of the claimants must take an oath that he has a valid claim to ownership of the

object he is claiming, and that he is entitled to no less than half of it. The claimants then divide the object, or its value, equally between them," in accordance with the Mishnah here and the Gemara's elucidation of it. (*Shulhan Arukh, Hoshen Mishpat* 138:1.)

Figure 17.1. This is a translation and adaptation of the traditional Hebrew edition of *The Talmud*. The overall design and organizational structure of the page is similar to that of the traditional pages. This presentation of tractate *Bava Metzia* was prepared with notes for the purpose of teaching about *The Talmud* by Rabbi Adir Steinsaltz. This figure shows how the key text is at the center of the page and is in Hebrew-Aramaic, completely vocalized and punctuated for the reader. Rabbi Steinsaltz indicates the alongside the center are the main auxiliary commentaries. At the bottom of the page and in the margins are the additions and supplements. He shows that commentary in the left column provides a conceptual understanding of the arguments presented in *The Talmud*, conveying their form, content, context, and significance. Further, the commentary brings out the logic of the questions posed by the Sages and the assumptions that they made. The *Halakhah* section appears below the Notes with references to legal decisions reached over the centuries by the Rabbis based on their dialogues about matters dealt with in *The Talmud*. Source: Steinsaltz, A. (1989). *The Talmud: The Steinsaltz Edition*, Vol. 1, tractate *Bava Matzia*, Part 1, New York: Random House, p. 2A.

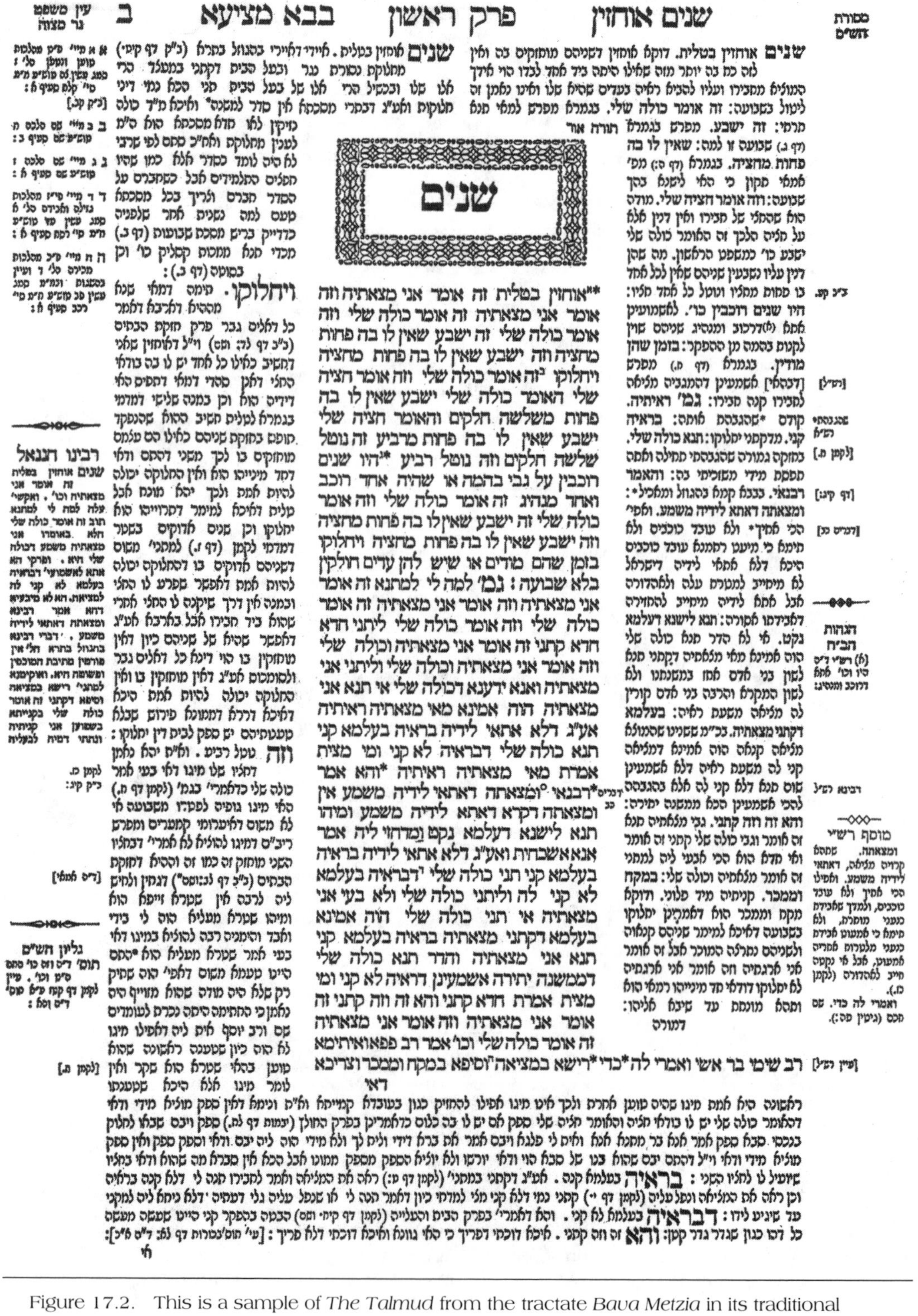
שנים אוחזין פרק ראשון בבא מציעא ב

שנים

*אוחזין בטלית זה אומר אני מצאתיה וזה אומר אני מצאתיה זה אומר כולה שלי וזה אומר כולה שלי זה ישבע שאין לו בה פחות מחציה וזה ישבע שאין לו בה פחות מחציה ויחלוקו זה אומר כולה שלי וזה אומר חציה שלי האומר כולה שלי ישבע שאין לו בה פחות משלשה חלקים והאומר חציה שלי ישבע שאין לו בה פחות מרביע זה נוטל שלשה חלקים וזה נוטל רביע *היו שנים רוכבין על גבי בהמה או שהיה אחד רוכב ואחד מנהיג זה אומר כולה שלי וזה אומר כולה שלי זה ישבע שאין לו בה פחות מחציה וזה ישבע שאין לו בה פחות מחציה ויחלוקו בזמן שהם מודים או שיש להן עדים חולקין בלא שבועה: גמ' למה לי למתנא זה אומר אני מצאתיה וזה אומר אני מצאתיה זה אומר כולה שלי וזה אומר כולה שלי ליתני חדא חדא קתני זה אומר אני מצאתיה וכולה שלי וזה אומר אני מצאתיה וכולה שלי וליתני אני מצאתיה ואנא ידענא דכולה שלי אי תנא אני מצאתיה הוה אמינא מאי מצאתיה ראיתיה אע"ג דלא אתאי לידיה בראיה בעלמא קני תנא כולה שלי דבראיה לא קני ומי מצית אמרת מאי מצאתיה ראיתיה *והא אמר *רבנאי °ומצאתה דאתאי לידיה משמע אין ומצאתה דקרא דאתא לידיה משמע ומיהו תנא לישנא דעלמא נקט ומדחזי ליה אמר אנא אשכחית ואע"ג דלא אתאי לידיה בראיה בעלמא קני תני כולה שלי דבראיה בעלמא לא קני לה וליתני כולה שלי ולא בעי אני מצאתיה אי תני כולה שלי הוה אמינא בעלמא דקתני מצאתיה בראיה בעלמא קני תנא אני מצאתיה והדר תנא כולה שלי דממשנה יתירה אשמעינן דראיה לא קני ומי מצית אמרת חדא קתני והא זה וזה קתני זה אומר אני מצאתיה וזה אומר אני מצאתיה זה אומר כולה שלי וכו' אמר רב פפא ואיתימא רב שימי בר אשי ואמרי לה *כדי *רישא במציאה *וסיפא במקח וממכר וצריכא דאי

Figure 17.2. This is a sample of *The Talmud* from the tractate *Bava Metzia* in its traditional Hebrew-Aramaic language and form. Source: *Bava Metzia*. (5754. *Talmud Bavli*. Jerusalem: Vagshal, p. 2A.

don't read it out loud, we miss the compelling power of the passage, especially its systematic resort to applied reason and practical logic. And, we must not forget, we want to see precisely how a dialectical argument is written down as a text but provokes us to talk, engage in dialogue, with the text:

BABYLONIAN TALMUD BABA MESIA 5B–6A

[5B] IV.1. A.   This one takes an oath that he possesses no less a share of it than half, [and that one takes an oath that he possesses no less a share of it than half, and they divide it up]:

The rule of the Mishnah, which is cited at the head of the sustained discussion, concerns the case of two persons who find a garment. They settle their conflicting claim by requiring each to take an oath that he or she owns title to no less than half of the garment, and then they split the garment between them.

Now how does the Talmud undertake its sustained analysis of this matter? Our first question is one of text criticism: analysis of the Mishnah paragraph's word choice. We say that the oath concerns the portion that the claimant alleges he possesses. But the oath really affects the portion that he does not have in hand at all:

> B.   *Is it concerning the portion that he claims he possesses that he takes the oath, or concerning the portion that he does not claim to possess?* [Daiches: "The implication is that the terms of the oath are ambiguous. By swearing that his share in it is not "less than half," the claimant might mean that it is not even a third or a fourth (which is "less than half"), and the negative way of putting it would justify such an interpretation. He could therefore take this oath even if he knew that he had no share in the garment at all, while he would be swearing falsely if he really had a share in the garment that is less than half, however small that share might be].

> C.   *Said R. Huna, "It is that he says, 'By an oath! I possess in it a portion, and I possess in it a portion that is no more than half a share of it.'"* [The claimant swears that his share is at least half (Daiches, *Baba Mesia, ad loc.*)].

Having asked and answered the question, we now find ourselves in an extension of the argument; the principal trait of the dialectical argument is now before us in three keywords:

[1] but!

[2] maybe the contrary is the case, so—

[3] what about?

The argument then is conducted by the setting aside of a proposition in favor of its opposite. Here we come to the definitive trait of the dialectic argument: its insistence on challenging every proposal with the claim, "Maybe it's the opposite?" This pestering question forces us back on our sense of self-evidence; it makes us consider the contrary of each position we propose to set forth. It makes thought happen. True, the Talmud's voice's "but"—the whole of the dialectic in one word!—presents a formidable nuisance. But so does all criticism, and only the mature mind will welcome criticism. Dialectics is not for children, politicians, propagandists, or egoists. Genuine curiosity about the truth shown by rigorous logic forms the counterpart to musical virtuosity. So the objection proceeds:

C.   *Then let him say, "By an oath! The whole of it is mine!"*

Why claim half when the alleged finder may as well demand the whole cloak?

D.   *But are we going to give him the whole of it?* [Obviously not, there is another claimant, also taking an oath.]

The question contradicts the facts of the case: Two parties claim the cloak, so the outcome can never be that one will get the whole thing.

E.   *Then let him say, "By an oath! Half of it is mine!"*

Then—by the same reasoning—why claim "no less than half," rather than simply, half.

F.   *That would damage his own claim* [which was that he owned the whole of the cloak, not only half of it].

The claimant does claim the whole cloak, so the proposed language does not serve to replicate his actual claim. That accounts for the language that is specified.

G.   *But here too is it not the fact that, in the oath that he is taking, he impairs his own claim?* [After all, he here makes explicit the fact that he owns at least half of it. What happened to the other half?]

The solution merely compounds the problem.

H.   *[Not at all.] For he has said,* "The whole of it is mine!" [And, he further proceeds] "And as to your contrary view, By an oath, I do have a share in it, and that share is no less than half!"

We solve the problem by positing a different solution from the one we suggested at the outset. Why not start where we have concluded? Because if we had done so, we should have ignored a variety of intervening considerations and so should have expounded less than the entire range of possibilities. The power of the dialectical argument now is clear: It forces us to address not the problem and the solution alone, but the problem and the various ways by which a solution may be reached; then, when we do come to a final solution to the question at hand, we have reviewed all of the possibilities. We have seen how everything flows together; nothing is left unattended.

What we have here is not a set piece of two positions, with an analysis of each, such as the formal dialogue exposes with elegance; it is, rather, an unfolding analytical argument, explaining why this, not that, then why not that but rather this; and onward to the other thing and the thing beyond that—a linear argument in constant forward motion. When we speak of a moving argument, this is what we mean: what is not static and merely expository, but what is dynamic and always contentious. It is not an endless argument, an argument for the sake of arguing, or evidence that important to the Talmud and other writings that use the dialectics as a principal mode of dynamic argument is process but not position. To the contrary, the passage is resolved with a decisive conclusion, not permitted to run on.

But the dialectical composition proceeds—continuous and coherent from point to point, even as it zigs and zags. That is because the key to everything is give and take. We proceed to the second cogent proposition in the analysis of the cited Mishnah passage, which asks a fresh question: Why an oath at all?

> 2.A.   [It is envisioned that each party is holding on to a corner of the cloak, so the question is raised:] Now, since this one is possessed of the cloak and standing right there, and that one is possessed of the cloak and is standing right there, why in the world do I require this oath?

Until now we have assumed as fact the premise of the Mishnah's rule, which is that an oath is there to be taken. But why assume so? Surely each party now has what he is going to get. So what defines the point and effect of the oath?

> B.   Said R. Yohanan, "This oath [to which our Mishnah passage refers] happens to be an ordinance imposed only by rabbis,
>
> C.   "so that people should not go around grabbing the cloaks of other people and saying, 'It's mine!'" [But, as a matter of fact, the oath that is imposed in our Mishnah passage is not legitimate by the law of the Torah. It is an act taken by sages to maintain the social order.]

We do not administer oaths to liars; we do not impose an oath in a case in which one of the claimants would take an oath for something he knew to be untrue, since one party really does own the cloak, the other really has grabbed it. The proposition solves the problem—but hardly is going to settle the question. On the contrary, Yohanan raises more problems than he solves. So we ask how we can agree to an oath in this case at all?

> D.   *But why then not advance the following argument: since such a one is suspect as to fraud in a property claim, he also should be suspect as to fraud in oath-taking?*

Yohanan places himself into the position of believing in respect to the oath what we will not believe in respect to the claim on the cloak, for, after all, one of the parties before us must be lying! Why sustain such a contradiction: gullible and suspicious at one and the same time?

> E.   *In point of fact, we do not advance the argument: since such a one is suspect as to fraud in a property claim, he also should be suspect as to fraud in oath-taking, for if you do not concede that fact, then how is it possible that the All-Merciful has ruled, "One who has conceded part of a claim against himself must take an oath as to the remainder of what is subject to claim"?*

If someone claims that another party holds property belonging to him or her, and the one to whom the bailment has been handed over for safekeeping, called the bailee, concedes part of the claim, the bailee must then take an oath in respect to the rest of the claimed property; that is, the part that the bailee maintains does not belong to the claimant at all. So the law itself—the Torah, in fact—has sustained the same contradiction. That fine solution, of course, is going to be challenged:

F.   *Why not simply maintain, since such a one is suspect as to fraud in a property claim, he also should be suspect as to fraud in oath-taking?*

G.   *In that other case, [the reason for the denial of part of the claim and the admission of part is not the intent to commit fraud, but rather,] the defendant is just trying to put off the claim for a spell.*

We could stop at this point without losing a single important point of interest; everything is before us. One of the striking traits of the large-scale dialectical composition is its composite character. Starting at the beginning, without any loss of meaning or sense, we may well stop at the end of any given paragraph of thought. But the dialectics insists on moving forward, exploring, pursuing, and insisting; were we to remove a paragraph in the middle of a dialectical composite, then all that follows would become incomprehensible. That is a mark of the dialectical argument: sustained, continuous, and coherent—yet perpetually in control and capable of resolving matters at any single point. For those of us who consume, but do not produce, arguments of such dynamism and complexity, the task is to discern the continuity, that is to say, not to lose sight of where we stand in the whole movement.

Now, having fully exposed the topic, its problem, and its principles, we take a tangent indicated by the character of the principle before us: when a person will or will not lie or take a false oath. We have a theory on the matter; what we now do is expound the theory, with special reference to the formulation of that theory in explicit terms by a named authority:

H.   This concurs with the position of Rabbah. [For Rabbah has said, "On what account has the Torah imposed the requirement of an oath on one who confesses to only part of a claim against him? It is by reason of the presumption that a person will not insolently deny the truth about the whole of a loan in the very presence of the creditor and so entirely deny the debt. He will admit to part of the debt and deny part of it. Hence we invoke an oath in a case in which one does so, to coax out the truth of the matter."]

I.   For you may know, [in support of the foregoing], that R. Idi bar Abin said R. Hisda [said]: "He who [falsely] denies owing money on a loan nonetheless is suitable to give testimony, but he who denies that he holds a bailment for another party cannot give testimony."

The proposition is now fully exposed. A named authority is introduced, who will concur in the proposed theoretical distinction. He sets forth an extra-logical consideration, which of course the law always will welcome: The rational goal of finding the truth overrides the technicalities of the law governing the oath.

Predictably, we cannot allow matters to stand without challenge, and the challenge comes at a fundamental level, with the predictable give and take to follow:

J.   But what about that which R. Ammi bar. Hama repeated on Tannaite authority: "[If they are to be subjected to an oath,] four sorts of bailees have to have denied part of the bailment and conceded part of the bailment, namely, the unpaid bailee, the borrower, the paid bailee, and the one who rents."

K.   *Why not simply maintain, since such a one is suspect as to fraud in a property claim, he also should be suspect as to fraud in oath-taking?*

L.   *In that case as well, [the reason for the denial of part of the claim and the admission of part is not the intent to commit fraud, but rather,] the defendant is just trying to put off the claim for a spell.*

M.   *He reasons as follows: "I'm going to find the thief and arrest him." Or: "I'll find [the beast] in the field and return it to the owner."*

Once more, "if that is the case" provokes yet another analysis; we introduce a different reading of the basic case before us, another reason that we should not impose an oath:

N.   *If that is the case, then why should one who denies holding a bailment ever be unsuitable to give testimony? Why don't we just maintain that the defendant is just trying to put off the claim for a spell. He reasons as follows: "I'm going to look for the thing and find it."*

O.   *When in point of fact we do rule,* He who denies holding a bailment is unfit to give testimony, *it is in a case in which witnesses come and give testimony against him that at that very moment, the bailment is located in the bailee's domain, and he fully is informed of that fact, or, alternatively, he has the object in his possession at that very moment.*

The solution to the problem at hand also provides the starting point for yet another step in the unfolding exposition. But enough has passed before us to make the main point.

What we have accomplished on our wanderings is a survey of opinion on a theme, to be sure, but opinion that intersects at our particular problem as well. The moving argument serves to carry us hither and yon; its power is to demonstrate that all considerations are raised, all challenges met, all possibilities explored. This is not merely a set-piece argument, where we have proposition, evidence, analysis, conclusion; it is a different sort of thinking altogether, purposive and coherent, but also comprehensive and compelling for its admission of possibilities and attention to alternatives. What we shall see, time and again, is that the dialectical argument is the Talmud's medium of generalization from case to principle and extension from principle to new cases.

THE DIALECTICS OF REPENTANCE

Having seen dialectics in a theoretical problem, let us now turn to a more immediately relevant, practical one: How does the applied reason and practical logic of the Talmud, yielding a text that insists we join in conversation, provoke rational inquiry into issues of ethical interest? For that purpose, we deal with "saying you're sorry," that is to say, how the text embodies thought about repentance. The Mishnah passage concerns the Day of Atonement and sin. In a religious system such as this one, in which there are so many things we are supposed to do or supposed not to do, it is inevitable that we shall do something wrong. We are human. It is not natural to keep all the laws. Some of the ritual ones may be inconvenient. Much more important: Some of the rules about right action to our fellow human beings conflict with our deep needs to be selfish and to hurt other people. So we do sin, and when we do, it is more commonly against other people than it is against God.

In Judaism, the Day of Atonement brings forgiveness and reconciliation between us and God. But what about forgiveness for what we have alone against other people? For that purpose, we have to rely on our own efforts. The Day of Atonement will not do for us what we do not do for ourselves. The Mishnah and the Talmud are able to work out general rules to tell us what to do in ordinary circumstances. This is hardly as easy as it sounds. It is amazing that even though the Mishnah and the Talmud go back for nearly 2,000 years, they are still interesting to us. We live in a completely different age and in a totally different world. How is it possible for us to want to hear what the Mishnah and the Talmud have to tell us about our relationships with other people? The answer is in two parts.

First, because human relationships do remain constant. There are just so many things people can do to and for each other, bad things and good things. Second, because the Mishnah and the Talmud, for their part, are careful to avoid talking about things in a too concrete and specific way. If they are too specific, people will eventually no longer listen to what they have to say.

The Mishnah talks about sin and saying you're sorry ("repentance"), about relying on the Day of Atonement to do what we can and should do for ourselves. The Mishnah speaks of winning the friendship of people whom we have offended. It is surely relevant to ordinary folk in our own day. We have friends whom we have offended. It certainly speaks to our world and about our problems. It is no accident. The conception of the Mishnah and the Talmud is that we can discover rules that will apply everywhere and to all the people. That is why the Mishnah and the Talmud claim in the context of Judaism to be Torah: instruction. Judaism conceives of God as the Teacher, and the holy people, Israel (not to be confused with the contemporary state of Israel) as God's disciples, through the master, Moses. The Torah speaks eternal truths—which God reveals and which Israel the holy people accept as Torah—even though they were written down long after Moses received the Torah at Mount Sinai. The power of Mishnah and Talmud lies in their ability to talk to us. But we are the one who gives the Mishnah and the Talmud their power and influence.

The "we" now permits us to enter the alien text, the language we use inviting us to suspend disbelief for the moment and join a conversation of long ago and far away, in a strange land. When we join that conversation, we discover what it means to live in eternity: to participate in a civilization, in a culture. Clearly, the fundamental principle that governs is, because we form a holy community, the community has to define its norms for proper conduct. That means we do not treat as random, personal, and private matters that, within the Torah, form concerns of a public, communal, and social character. That is because this "we" forms Israel, holy Israel, and all together bear responsibility for the character of our community, each one in his or her conscience expected to respond to the norms of the community as a whole. Judaism is called "a legalistic religion," meaning that it is a religion that teaches norms of behavior and belief. And so it is—and so is every religion that regards the community as critical, the conduct of life together as consequential. Only religions that people invent for themselves, one by one, as modes of entirely private and personal conviction, may be described as not legalistic. But then, the activities of a person that are wholly idiosyncratic and personal may well shade over into the subjective and irrelevant, and if it is anything, the Torah sets itself up as God's will for the whole community of holy Israel. So we should not find surprising the Torah's provision of rules for activities that people may carry out any which way.

We want to examine, in particular, the Talmud's mode of thinking and analyzing practices. Finally, we hope to see what we may learn from the Talmud about things with which we already are familiar. As we recall from the chapter where it originally made its appearance, the Mishnah paragraph—Mishnah tractate Yoma 8:8–9 ‹before us is a set of four sentences, each separate and distinct from the others.

1.   He who says I shall sin and repent, sin and repent they do not give him sufficient power to make repentance

[He who says], I shall sin, and the Day of Atonement will atone ± the Day of Atonement does not atone

2.   Sins that are between man and the Omnipresent the Day of Atonement atones for. Sins that are between man and his fellow the Day of Atonement does not atone for, until one will win the good will of his fellow [once more].

3.   This is what Rabbi Eleazar ben Azariah expounded:

From all our sins shall we be clean before the Lord (Lev. 16:3)

Sins that are between man and the Omnipresent the Day of Atonement atones for.

Sins that are between man and his fellow the Day of Atonement does not atone for until one will win the good will of his fellow.

4.   Said Rabbi Aqiba Happy are you, Oh Israel Before whom are you purified?

Who purifies you?

Your father who is in heaven.

As it is said, And I will sprinkle clean water on us and we will be clean (Ezekiel 36:25).

And it says, "The hope of Israel is the Lord (Jeremiah 17:13)."

Just as the immersion-pool cleans the unclean people,

So the Holy One blessed be he cleans Israel.

The Mishnah-passage repeats its one idea four times, each time in a somewhat different way. The main point is that the Day of Atonement will do us no good if we do not do our share of the work of repentance. We must say that we're sorry for what we have done wrong. The first point is that we cannot sin and take for granted that the Day of Atonement will make up for us. There is nothing magical, nothing that works without regard to what we do and believe in our hearts. The second point is that the Day of Atonement serves only to atone for those sins that we have done against God. But sins that we have done against other people must be atoned for by going to the person whom we have injured and seeking forgiveness. Our Mishnah is going to demand some amplification here. What sort of "mission" to the one whom we have hurt is required? What if the person will not grant us forgiveness? These are questions of belief, but they are going to demand statements of behavior—rules on what we are expected to do.

The third and the fourth points say what the first two points already have said. Eleazar b. Azariah's lesson is precisely what No. 2 already has told us. The Day of Atonement will do us good only if we first seek forgiveness of the one we have injured. Before us proceed to the Talmud, let us see whether we are able to list some of the questions we shall want the Talmud to answer.

First, we shall want to know the source of the Mishnah passage's rule. That source, we need hardly note, is Scripture. So we shall ask, "What is the source of this rule about seeking forgiveness from our friend?" We shall ask the Talmud to tell us whether we must persist, if the friend will not forgive, and if so, to what extent. What if the person whom we have hurt moves away, or dies, before we have a chance to gain forgiveness? What do we do then? These are some of the things we shall not expect the Talmud to tell us, when the Talmud comes before us in its role as an explanation for the Mishnah. What the Talmud will tell us when it proceeds to expand and explain its explanation we can now hardly predict.

Explaining the Mishnah

By this time in our learning of Talmud, we surely can predict that the first thing the about this Mishnah passage is the source of this law. Sometimes the question is asked directly. Other times, the question is answered without being asked. In the first Talmud selection, we find the answer without the question. Naturally, the answer is that we learn the rule in Scripture. This time the relevant book of the Bible is Proverbs, and we shall observe that Proverbs says almost exactly what the Mishnah says. But it says the same thing in a different circumstance and for a different purpose. So the contribution of the Amora, Isaac is to see the relevance of what Scripture says to what Mishnah wants us to do. This we shall see in A–J.

We already know to expect that when we have a statement of an ideal of how we should behave, the Talmud will turn that statement into rules about things we must actually do. We therefore shall not be surprised to find that an important explanation of our Mishnah passage will be a concrete instruction on precisely how to make friends with someone we have offended. The rule will be spun out of a relevant verse of Scripture since, we remember, the Amoraim do not regard Mishnah as an adequate and complete source of truth. They insist on turning, also and especially, to the written Torah, to the Scriptures. Two Amoraim, Hisda (K–O), and Yosé b. R. Hanina (P–Z), supply us with rules based on verses of the Scripture.

A. Said R. Isaac,

B. Whoever offends his fellow,

C. even [merely] through words,

D. has to make peace with him,

E. since it is said,

F. My son, if we have become a surety for our neighbor, if we have struck our hands for a stranger, we are snared by the words of our mouth.

> Do this now, my son, and deliver yourself, since we have come into the hand of our neighbor.   Go, humble yourself, and urge our neighbor (Prov. 6:1–3).

G. If we are wealthy

H. open the palm of your hand to him.

I. And if not

J. send many friends to him.

K. Said R. Hisda,

L. And he needs to make peace with him through three groups of three people,

M. since it is said,

N. He comes before men and says,

O. I have sinned, and I have perverted that which was right, and it did me no profit (Job 33:27).

P. Said R. Yosé b. R. Hanina,

Q. Whoever seeks pardon of his fellow

R. should not seek it from him more than three times,

S. since it is said, Forgive, I pray we now, and now we pray we (Gen. 50:17).

T. But if he dies,

U. one brings ten men,

V. and sets them up at his grave,

W. and says,

Y. "I have sinned against the Lord, the God of Israel,

Z. "and against Mr. So and So, whom I have injured."

Isaac's rule is not quite the same as Mishnah's, as the Mishnah passage speaks of the setting of the Day of Atonement. So why has the Talmudic editor introduced this rule at just this point? For the obvious reason that the Mishnah passage speaks about harm done by a person to another person. It says that the Day of Atonement does not atone in such a case. We must apologize and win the other person's forgiveness. So Isaac's saying (A–J) is quite appropriate for this setting, even though it is not exactly to the point of the Mishnah passage. In fact, what he says is rather straightforward, even self-evident. If we offend our fellow, even by something we have said, we have to make peace.

The proof text then becomes the main element. Proverbs 6:1–3 contains precisely the advice that Isaac wants to give. If someone has a claim of money against us, pay him off. If it is some other sort of complaint, send many friends to him: "Urge our neighbor." Hisda's point is equally clear. The work of making friends should not go on indefinitely. We try our best. But if the other person cannot be pacified, then let it be. Three times, with three people each time, would be ample. We notice that the verse in Job contains three clauses. The person says, "I have sinned," and then, "I have perverted," and finally, "and it did me no profit." So we find three little "confessions," a fair indication of what is required of we as well. Yosé b. R. Hanina then draws out the implications of Hisda's saying. We do it three times—and no more than three times. This is derived not from what Hisda has said but from yet another verse of Scripture, cited at S. Here, too, we see a group of three clauses and each represents a request for pardon and forgiveness.

Finally, we have the rule to cover the special case of someone's dying before we can make up. The Talmud's answer is to go to the grave and to state there the confession of what one has done, together with a prayer for forgiveness. It is the best we can do. We should not misunderstand the point of going to the grave. It is to help the person who seeks forgiveness to locate and focus on the one who has been injured. Going to the grave is for the sake of the one who is alive, not for the sake of the one whose bones are deposited in the ground.

It is time to ask whether—if we were commenting on and explaining this Mishnah passage—we would add to what the Talmud contributes. Can we make up a Talmud to go along with the one given to us by the Amoraim of Babylonia of the third, fourth, and fifth centuries of the Common Era? This is a good opportunity because the teachings of the Amoraim are expressed fairly simply, and they address an issue that we know well. How would we make up—continue—the Talmud? We might add some stories of specific incidents we have witnessed, such as occasions on which someone we know has tried to make friends with a person he or she has made angry or offended. Or we might amplify Yosé's case about someone who dies. We might add that if someone moves away, we write letters or make phone calls.

The concluding unit of our Talmudic passage shows us how the person who put the Talmud together added to these rather straightforward rules and made the Talmudic passage more concrete. This was done by adding a series of three stories about what happened to great rabbis of the Talmudic age.

II.   A. R. Jeremiah had something against R. Abba

B. He went and sat down at the door of R. Abba.

C. As the maid was throwing out water,

D. a few drops of water touched his head.

E. He said, They have made me into a dung-heap.

F. He cited the following verse about himself:

G. He raises up the poor out of the dust (I Samuel 2:8).

H. R. Abba heard.

I. And he came to him.

J. He said to him,

K. Now I must make peace with we.

L. For it is written,

M. Go, humble yourself and urge your neighbor (Prov. 6:3).

The story's purpose is to give the law life. The law takes on new and human meaning when we are told how a particular sage acted. That is why the editor of the Talmud placed this and two other stories alongside the Talmud's explanation and expansion of our Mishnah passage. But the stories also have their own purposes. They make their own points. It is only later on that the person who put the Talmud together as we have it brought them before us and set them out as illustrations of the Talmud's explanation of the Mishnah passage.

Jeremiah's behavior is interesting. Jeremiah had injured Abba. So Jeremiah went straight to the other party and sat down at his door. What was the importance of such a deed? It was to make sure that Abba knew that Jeremiah was aware something had gone wrong. Why? Because Jeremiah understood that the worst thing Abba could do is to bear a grudge. If we are angry and we express it, the ball is in the other person's court. We do not keep things in. We say what we think. If the other party wants to make amends, well and good. But we are not going to hate that other person. The way to avoid hating him or her is to say what we think. Then why be angry any longer? So Jeremiah went and sat down at Abba's door. It was a simple, silent, and eloquent gesture. Let Abba say what was on his mind. What happened? The maid threw out some water, and Jeremiah got slightly wet. Just a few drops touched him. But to him this was too much. So he pitied himself. This is not so impressive. But it had a good result. Jeremiah quoted a verse from Scripture, with the notion that the verse spoke about Jeremiah in particular: "He raises up the poor out of the dust." Now Abba heard that Jeremiah was at his door. He came out and realized what was happening. Then he, too, found an appropriate verse in Scripture—that same verse with which we began our account, cited by Isaac to explain and support the teaching of the Mishnah passage. So we can see that whatever really happened, the story is worked out to remind us of where we are, which is in the Talmudic discussion. This is artful, as in the story itself, the cited verse of Scripture plays an important role as well. Now another story:

A. R. Zeira, when he had something against some one,

B. would go back and forth before him,

C. and make himself available to the other,

D. so that the other would come out

E. and make peace with him.

The storyteller reports something Zeira did under ordinary circumstances, a general rule of behavior, rather than a specific and concrete incident. When someone hurt Zeira, he would go to the other party and say nothing. He simply made himself available. The other person could then see him and do what had to be done. Why has the editor told this story at this point? For the obvious reason that Zeira is said here to have done in general what Jeremiah did in particular. So the story is not told at random or without purpose. It is part of a careful discussion of the notion that if we have a grievance, we should not keep it in. We should go to the other party. We do not have to say a thing. All we have to do is remind the other party by our presence that there is some unfinished business.

The third story then proceeds to illustrate the same thing. But it makes another point as well.

A. Rab [Rab Abba] had something against a certain butcher.

B. He [the butcher] did not come to him [Rab].

C. On the eve of the Day of Atonement, he [Rab] said, I shall go to make peace with him.

D. R. Huna met him.

E. He said to him, Where is the master going?

F. He said to him, "To make peace with so and so."

G. He said, "Abba is going to kill someone."

H. He [Rab] went and stood before him.

I. He [the butcher] was sitting and chopping an [animal's] head.

J. He [the butcher] raised his eyes and saw him.

K. He said to him, "You are Abba! Get out. I have nothing to do with you."

L. While he was chopping the head,

M. a bone flew off,

N. and stuck his throat,

O. and killed him.

The story about Rab goes over the same ground as the stories we already have heard. That is, we have to make ourselves available to the party against whom we have a grievance. We don't sit on our high horse. We go to the other person. That is what Rab did. But our opening Talmudic passage has made a second point. If the editor is not to lose that other point, we have to be reminded of it. What if the other party will not then seek to reconcile with us? This is not quite the point of Isaac and Hisda and Yosé, which is that we make an effort to appease the other party. But the important and new idea is precisely this: What happens if we go to the other party, and that person will not atone for the harm he or she has done to us? What do we do then? So the new and final notion of this carefully constructed set completes the whole. Review the points:

1. If we offend our friend, we have to try to appease him or her (Isaac).
2. We send three groups of people, in succession (Hisda).
3. If the friend will not be appeased, we owe no more (Yosé b. Hanina).
4. If our friend has a grievance against us, we make ourselves available (Jeremiah, thus illustrating the general position of Isaac and Hisda).
5. If we have a grievance against our friend, we make ourselves available (Zeira).
6. If we have a grievance against our friend, we make ourselves available. But if the friend will not then try to make amends, that is not our problem.

In 6, we conclude the line of thought begun by Isaac and Hisda. Now the story about Rab is rather curious. It invokes something we have not seen often in our passages of the Talmud—supernatural power. When Rab is mistreated by the man, the man "accidentally" dies. The storyteller does not have to tell us that it is not an accident, but he does so when he has Huna make his prophetic comment. The storyteller wants us to know that the butcher's accidental death is not accidental. So we are warned in advance, through Huna's baleful comment, that Rab, in all innocence, is protected by Heaven.

Rab behaved correctly. Indeed, the story about Rab is the first point in this sequence that reminds us where we began, the Day of Atonement. Until this story, the subject has never been mentioned! So it is the Day of Atonement. In conformity with the Mishnah's teaching, we should have expected the butcher to come to Rab, as Jeremiah did. But the butcher did not come. So, like Zeira, Rab makes himself available to the butcher. Huna intervenes early to warn us of the story's real meaning. Then, the story resumes (H). If we did not have D–G, the story would flow smoothly. But it also would not make its point. That is why I think the clause is integral and not inserted as a gloss.

Rab goes to the butcher and stands before him—a respectful gesture indeed, considering it is Rab who has the complaint against the butcher. I underline Rab's strange and deliberate behavior. It reminds us that the butcher remains sitting. And, lest we miss the point and think the butcher did stand up, we are told that he merely raised his eyes and saw Rab (J). The butcher remained seated in the presence of one of the great sages of the time. It is a sage, moreover, whom the butcher offended, and it is the eve of the Day of Atonement. All the elements are present for some smashing conclusion. And it is not long in coming. The butcher speaks his own death sentence in K. "You are Abba—get out!" The world is on its head. The person who is injured is injured again. And all of this is done with great brutality—the butcher continues to chop the animal head (L). The rest follows.

The butcher chops the head—the symbol of death—and a bone flies off and sticks in the butcher's throat. He is injured by his own actions, and the bone stabs him in the organ that he has used to injure and offend Rab. The butcher died because he killed himself. The irony of Huna's saying now is clear. Abba (that is, Rab) killed no one. The butcher did not really kill himself. It was an accident. But Huna has already told us the meaning of the accident.

Now why has the one who put the Talmud together told this story here? We notice that there are three halakhic sayings, Isaac's, Hisda's, and Yosé b R Hanina's. Then we have three stories that illustrate halakhah where we started—the Day of Atonement, appeasing our friend. We end at precisely the unanswered question: What happens if we do not appease our friend, whom we have injured, by the eve of the Day of Atonement? True, it is an extreme and unusual case. What happens with Rab happens because, after all, Rab is a holy man and a great sage of Torah. Still, the story in its own context is not making the point that Rab is a holy man and that we should not be mean to rabbis. It makes the point that Rab was the injured party, and he went to the one who had hurt him (as Zeira did) in order to give the other party a chance to deal with his complaint (as Abba did). And this he did on the eve of the Day of Atonement just as the Mishnah says we must do. So the concluding story, which brings us back to the Mishnah passage, also has a powerful effect in answering the question the Mishnah has left open: What happens if we do not do what the Mishnah says? The answer is, God oversees all things. God seals our judgment on the Day of Atonement. If, therefore, on the eve of the Day of Atonement, we do not do what is expected of us, there will be serious results. This artful construction, therefore, has never lost sight of the Mishnah passage it is meant to explain even though, as we ourselves have seen, it is sometimes difficult to keep our eyes on our starting point. In the end, we can rely on the one who put things together. We never are let down. We will recall that once before, we asked ourselves, "Is the Talmud carefully constructed, or is it just one interesting saying or story after another?" We once more observe that the Talmud, as exemplified by this passage, is put together with amazing care. We see there is close attention to form and formality. Three of one thing, then a matching triplet: three teachings, three stories. We see that acute care is paid to the substance as each saying, then each story, carries forward what has been set in the preceding one. And, at the end, we see a remarkable climax—the invocation of God's role in making sense of the whole thing. And at the end, we return to the beginning. We show the relevance to the Mishnah passage of all that the Talmud has said by way of explaining the Mishnah passage.

Expanding the Explanation

The Talmud's next important passage goes on to fresh ideas. It deals with the Confession, the recital of sins that we say on the Day of Atonement. The Day of Atonement atones for our sins, so we must list those sins before God in order to seek forgiveness. The Talmud's discussion carries forward, in a general way, its treatment of our Mishnah passage. The Mishnah passage provides the theme of forgiveness of sins on the Day of Atonement. But the specific treatment of the theme is another matter. The Talmud has two questions about the confession of sins. First, when are we supposed to confess our sins? Second, precisely what prayer do we say to confess our sins? Before we proceed, let us look at the prayer that nowadays we say in the synagogue as the confession of sins on the Day of Atonement. It is known as the *Vidui*, or Confession, and appears in the Mahzor, the Prayer book for the New Year and the Day of Atonement, as follows (in the classic translation of Rabbi Jules Harlow):

> We abuse, we betray, we are cruel. We destroy, we embitter, we falsify. We gossip, we hate, we insult. We jeer, we kill, we lie. We mock, we neglect, we oppress. We pervert, we quarrel, we rebel. We steal, we transgress, we are unkind. We are violent, we are wicked, we are xenophobic. We yield to evil, we are zealots for bad causes.

> We have ignored Your commandments and statutes, and it has not profited us. We are just, we have stumbled. We have acted faithfully, we have been unrighteous.

> We have sinned, we have transgressed. Therefore we have not been saved. Endow us with the will to forsake evil; save us soon. Thus Your prophet Isaiah declared: "Let the wicked forsake his path, and the unrighteous man his plotting. Let him return to the Lord who shall forgive, and to the God of our fathers, forgive and pardon our sins on this transgressions from Your sight. Subdue our impulse to evil; submit us to Your service, that we may return to us. Renew our will to observe Your precepts. Soften our hardened hearts so that we may love and revere We, as it is written in Your Torah: "And the Lord our God will soften our heart and the heart of our children, so that we will love the Lord our God with all our heart and with all our being that we may live."

> We know our sins, whether deliberate or not, whether committed willingly or under compulsion, whether in public or in private. What are we? What is our piety? What is our righteousness, our attainment, our power, our might? What can we say Lord our God and God of our fathers? Compared to us, all the mighty are nothing, the famous are non-existent, the wise lack wisdom, the clever lack reason. For most of their actions are meaninglessness, the days of their lives emptiness. Man's superiority to the beast is an illusion. All life is a fleeting breath.

> What can we say to us, what can we tell ourselves? We know all things, secret and revealed.

> We always forgive transgressions. Hear the cry of our prayers. Pass over the transgressions of a people who turn away from transgression. Blot out our sins from Your sight.

We know the mysteries of the universe, the secrets of everyone alive. We probe our innermost depths. We examine our thoughts and desires. Nothing escapes us, nothing is hidden from You.

May it therefore be Your will, Lord our God and God of our fathers, to forgive us all our sins, to pardon all our iniquities, to grant us atonement for all our transgressions.

We have sinned against You unwillingly and willingly.

And we have sinned against You by misusing our minds. We have sinned against You by immoral sexual acts.

And we have sinned against You knowingly and deceitfully.

And we have sinned against You by supporting immorality. We have sinned against You by deriding parents and teachers.

We have sinned against You by using bad language,

And we have sinned against You by not resisting the impulse to evil.

For all these sins, forgiving God, forgive us, pardon us, grant us atonement.

We have sinned against You by fraud and by falsehood.

And we have sinned against You by scoffing.

We have sinned against You by dishonesty in business.

And we have sinned against You by taking usurious interest.

We have sinned against You by idle chatter.

And we have sinned against You by haughtiness.

We have sinned against You by rejecting responsibility.

And we have sinned against You by plotting against others.

We have sinned against You by irreverence.

And we have sinned against You by rushing to do evil.

We have sinned against You by taking vain oaths.

And we have sinned against You by breach of trust.

For all these sins, forgiving God, forgive us, pardon us, grant us atonement.

Some of the rabbis of the Talmud refer to facts of what now serves as our Confession of sins for the Day of Atonement. Fact of their work is to select among different versions of prayers already available the ones they think should be said in the synagogue. Another task is to make up prayers for people to say. Because the rabbis of the Talmud are both learned and holy, they have special gifts for creating prayers. Still, Jews at all later periods in the history of the Jewish people have joined in this neverending work. The first of the two units of the Talmud deals with the time at which we are supposed to say the confession.

   B. The religious duty [to say] the confession [applies] on the eve of the

      Day of Atonement, at dusk.

   C. But said sages

D. Let one say the confession before he eats and drinks,

E. Lest one be upset during the meal.

F. And even though he said the confession before he ate and drank,

G. he should say the confession after he eats and

H. Lest some mishap took place during the meal.

I. And even though he said the confession in the evening service,

J. Let him say the confession in the morning service;

K. in the morning service, let him say the confession in the additional service;

L. in the additional service, let him say the confession in the afternoon service;

M. in the afternoon service, let him say it in the closing service

N. And where [in the service] does he say it?

O. An individual [praying by himself or herself [says it]

after the [silent] Prayer.

P. And the agent of the congregation says it in the repetition.

The *baraita*, stated in simple, tight clauses, has its own rhythm. Can we see it? Read the passage out loud, and we should be able to hear it. The *baraita* is arranged in matching clauses, which we can pick out (I–J, K–L, etc.). In fact, the *baraita* is divided into three parts. We can tell one from the other in two ways. First, the subjects of the two are different. Second, the two parts are phrased differently. These go together, hand in hand: what is said and the way it is said. The three parts are A–H, I–M, and N–P. The first two parts are so neatly stated that we pass from the one to the other without any real break. Then the third part is set off by a question (N). But the whole is a single, coherent statement: When do we say the Confession? How often do we say the Confession? At what point in the service do we say the Confession?

The main point (A–H) is that one should say the confession prior to eating the final meal before sunset on the eve of the Day of Atonement. That way we may be sure that we have said the Confession correctly. We might have too much to drink at supper. Then, at the *Kol Nidré* service at the commencement of the holy day, we might miss something or make a mistake. That good advice leaves the impression that we say the Confession only once. So I–M hastens to tell us that we say it at each and every service for the Day of Atonement: Evening (which we call *Kol Nidré*), Morning (*Shaharit*), Additional (*Musaf*), Afternoon (*Minhah*), and Closing Service (*Neilah*)—five times in all. The discussion moves forward, but for the point of this essay, we have seen a representative sample.

If we now look back at our Mishnah passage, we see that the Talmud has essentially gone its own way. We have seen this before. Although the Mishnah provides the point of departure, it does not indicate the only road to be followed. As we know, the rabbis of the Talmud do not hesitate to explore issues, ideas, or problems important to them but which are not raised in the Mishnah passage on which they are working. This is another sign of the essential independence and freedom of the rabbis who created the Talmud. They are deeply loyal to the Mishnah. They are eager to clarify it. They want to be sure that every one of its words is defined. They make certain that any questions left open in the Mishnah passage under discussion will be answered thoroughly and that the answers themselves will be fully explained. But they do go their own way. They ask their own questions. Obviously, at this point in their treatment of our Mishnah passage, they have not strayed far from the basic theme, which is the Day of Atonement and the forgiveness of sins. But we see that they also introduce the subjects important in their own day, not only in the time in which the Mishnah was made up.

The Talmud would be received with care and reverence, but it would not prevent those who received it from responding, in their own fresh and interesting ways, to what it said. That is why at the outset we spoke not of asking for answers but of using our own minds to discover the answers. The experience of learning the Talmud teaches the lesson that we must always stand back and make up our own minds. We must always discover for ourselves those things that in the end, we shall affirm and believe. We do not merely ask other people to tell us what is so. We must find out for ourselves. And the only way in which we can find out for ourselves is by using our own minds and not by relying on other people—however learned or holy, however much we admire and wish to follow them—to give us answers.

TALK ABOUT TEXT AND THE EVOLUTION OF CULTURE

While the passages of Baba Mesia and Yoma that we have considered lead readers into a world few find familiar, the power of the discourse, the actualization of applied reason and practical logic to cases that we ourselves can analyze and discuss, has won the Talmud attention far beyond the community of Judaism. The Bavli, once merely the foundation document of Judaism, now finds its place in the high culture of the English-speaking world. Numerous translations and introductions make the work accessible, and considerable response in the marketplace of culture indicates an interest in what the Talmud has to teach. That is as it should be. For the Talmud offers a compelling possibility of culture: the rational reconsideration of the givens of the social order. It shows the way to the systematic translation of high ideals of social and personal conduct into the humble realities of the workaday world. Those high ideals are set forth in Scripture, which the Talmud frames into the rules of the reasoned conduct. Its rigorous and systematic, argumentative, and uncompromisingly rational inquiry sets forth the moral and civil consequences of Scripture's laws and narratives. This the Bavli does in vast detail, the rigorous inquiry of criticism extending into the smallest matters. So the Talmud sets forth an orderly world, resting on reason and tested by rationality, all in accord with consistent principles. To the cultural chaos of our own day, the Talmud shows a way of rationality to a world in quest of reason and order.

The Talmud translates Pentateuchal narratives and laws into a systematic account of its "Israel's" entire social order. In its 37 topical presentations of Mishnah tractates, the Talmud portrays not so much how people are supposed to live—this the Mishnah does—as how they ought to think, the right way of analyzing circumstance and tradition alike. That is what makes encounter with the Bavli urgent for the contemporary situation. To a world such as ours, engaged as it is, at the dawn of a new century by standard reckoning, in a massive enterprise of reconstruction after history's most destructive century, old systems having given way, new ones yet to show their merit and their mettle, the Talmud presents a considerable resource.

The Bavli shows not only a way of reform, but, more valuable still, a way of thinking and talking and rationally arguing about reform. When we follow not only what the sages of the Talmud say, but how they express themselves, their modes of critical thought and—above all—rigorous argument, we encounter a massive, concrete instance of the power of intellect to purify and refine. For the sages of the Talmud, alongside the great masters of Greek philosophy and their Christian and Muslim continuators, exercise the power of rational and systematic inquiry, tenacious criticism, the exchange of not only opinion but reason for opinion, argument, and evidence. They provide a model of how intellectuals take up the tasks of social criticism and pursue the disciplines of the mind in the service of the social order. And that, I think, is what has attracted the widespread interest in the Talmud as shown by repeated translations of, and introductions to, that protean document. Not an antiquarian interest in a long-ago society, nor an ethnic concern with heritage and tradition, but a vivid and contemporary search for plausible examples of the rational world order, animate the unprecedented interest of the world of culture in the character (and also the contents) of the Bavli. The Talmud embodies applied reason and practical logic in quest of the holy society. That model of criticism and reason in the encounter with social reform of which I spoke is unique. The kind of writing that the Talmud represents has serviceable analogues but no known counterpart in the literature of world history and philosophy, theology, religion, and law. That is because the Talmud sets forth not only decisions and other wise and valuable information but also the choices that face reasonable persons and the basis for deciding matters in one way rather than in some other. And the Talmud records the argument, the constant, contentious, uncompromising argument, that endows with vitality the otherwise merely informative corpus of useful insight. "Let logic pierce the mountain"—that is what sages say. Not many have attained the purity of intellect characteristic of this writing. With the back-and-forth argument, the Talmud enlightens and engages. How so? The Talmud sets forth not so much a record of what was said as a set of notes that permit the engaged reader to reconstruct thought and recapitulate reason and criticism. Indeed, the Talmud treats coming generations the way composers treat unborn musicians: They provide the notes for the musicians to reconstruct the music. In the Talmudic framework, then, everything is in the moving, or dialectical argument, the give and take of unsparing rationality, which, through our own capacity to reason, we are expected to reconstitute the issues, the argument, and the prevailing rationality. The Bavli makes enormous demands on its future. It pays a massive compliment to its heirs.

In that aspect, the Talmud recalls the great philosophical dialogues of ancient and medieval times. As we noted at the outset, readers familiar with the dialogues of Socrates as set forth by Plato—those wonderful exchanges concerning abstractions such as truth and beauty, goodness and justice—will find familiar the notion of dialectical argument, with its unfolding, ongoing give and take. But in the concrete statement of the Talmud, they will be puzzled by the chaos of the Talmudic dialectic, its meandering and open-ended character. And they will miss the formal elegance and the perfection of exposition that characterize Plato's writings. So too, the Talmud's presentation of contrary positions and exposition of the strengths and weaknesses of each will hardly surprise jurisprudents. But the inclusion of the model of extensive exposition of debate surprises. Decisions ordinarily record the main points but not the successive steps in argument and counterargument, such as we find here. And, more to the point, we expect decisions, while much of the Talmud's discourse proves open ended.

The very character and the style of the Talmud's presentation certainly demand a kind of reading not ordinarily required of us. But it is one that classroom teachers undertake all the time: reconstructing thought from notes, turning a few words into a whole presentation. What we are given are notes, which we are expected to know how to use in the reconstruction of the issues under discussion, the arguments under exposition. That means we must make ourselves active partners in the thought processes the document sets forth. Not only is the argument open ended, so too the bounds of participation know no limits. Indeed, it is the very reticence of the Talmud to tell us everything we need to know, the remarkable confidence of its compilers that generations over time will join in the argument they precipitate, grasp the principles they embody in concrete cases, find compelling the issues they deem urgent—it is that remarkable faith in the human intellect of age succeeding age that lifts the document above time and circumstance and renders it immortal. In transcending circumstances of time and place and condition, the Talmud attains a place in the philosophical, not merely historical, curriculum of culture. That is why every generation of its heirs and continuators found itself a partner in the ongoing reconstruction of reasoned thought, each adding its commentary to the ever-welcoming text. To a discussion of how we know the world through the discourse of the classroom, the Talmud has a formidable contribution to make. It is a piece of writing that does more than define an entire civilization. Rather, it demonstrates how education, properly carried on, recapitulates the highest rationality of the civilization that sustains the school and is sustained by it.

CHAPTER 18

Children's Collaborative Interpretations of Artworks: The Challenge of Writing Visual Texts Within the Texts of Their Lives

Brent Wilson

INTRODUCTION: THE PURPOSES OF EDUCATION IN THE VISUAL ARTS

For much of the 20th century, teachers believed that art performed its educational function when school children expressed their experiences and their feelings through the creation of paintings and drawings, sculptures, and collages. Art-making in school was for the purpose of enhancing children's "creative and mental growth" (Lowenfeld, 1947). Modernism's strictures even prohibited teachers from showing the works of artists in their classrooms out of a fear that the originality of children's images would be damaged if they were to copy from adults. If teachers discouraged their students from viewing the artwork of artists, then, obviously, they couldn't learn what these artworks might have to teach.

In the 1970s, postmodernism hit art education like a slap in the face. Children's images, heretofore considered original, were found to be utterly filled with appropriations from the popular media and myriad other sources (Wilson & Wilson, 1977). Moreover, educators began to consider the possibility of an education in the visual arts that was "beyond creating" (Getty Center for Education in the Arts, 1985). The content and the methods of art historians, art critics, and philosophers of art—not just artists—were proposed as acceptable models for children to emulate. The classroom study of artworks was no longer forbidden. Moreover, a comprehensive pedagogy, derived from Bruner's (1960) and Barkan's (1962) conceptions of education, began to take hold. Education was seen as a process through which students came to understand the structure of disciplines. The new forms of art education, which collectively came to be called discipline-based art education (DBAE), had as their guiding principle the belief that children could move from naïve to sophisticated modes of functioning within the realm of the visual arts by mastering the content and inquiry processes found in the disciplines of art history, art criticism, aesthetics (the philosophy of art), and the production of art (Clark, Day, & Greer, 1987). Encouraged by the prospects of the new art education promoted by the Getty Education Institute for the Arts, teachers of art began to experiment with comprehensive forms of art instruction that placed the interpretation of artworks at their core.

Beginning in 1988, the Getty established six regional institutes to serve as research and development centers to experiment with and develop new forms of DBAE. These consortia, composed of school districts, colleges and universities, art museums, arts agencies and organizations, and even one state department of education, were established in Florida, Ohio, Minnesota, Nebraska, Texas, and the Southeast Center in Chattanooga, Tennessee (which extended across several southeastern states). The Getty regional institute professional development initiative eventually included over 400 urban, suburban, and rural school districts. I headed a team that evaluated the implementation of DBAE over an 8-year period (Wilson, 1997).

When the change initiative began, elementary classroom teachers and visual arts instructors knew almost nothing about the interpretation of artworks. They soon learned. In the Getty-sponsored professional development institutes, teachers began to collaborate with art historians, museum educators, aestheticians, art critics, and artists to devise strategies for teaching DBAE. Teams of teachers led by their school administrators left their everyday lives to spend a week or more in the galleries of art museums. Indeed, these institutes had something of the character of rites of passage from ordinary worlds into worlds of art (Wilson, 1997, pp. 66–75). In museums that to some seemed strange, even alien and forbidding places, participants were invited to approach artworks as visual texts that would yield meaning—if they were given the opportunity. Led by art historians and other discipline experts, educators sometimes spent 30 minutes or more discussing the meaning of a single painting that, ordinarily, they would view for only a few seconds. Once participants began to experience the joys of interpretive discovery, they demonstrated what they had learned by planning gallery tours and other activities that centered on interpretation. After a week or more of living in galleries, participants no longer viewed art museums as alien; their passage to art worlds was well under way. They learned that their interpretations of artworks could be just as "right," just as valid, as those written by historians and critics. From organizing tours and participating in a variety of other active-learning tasks, it was a short step to planning classroom art activities for their students.

When elementary classroom teachers and art instructors returned to their schools they implemented art instruction that was balanced between the making and studying of artworks. Interpretation of the meaning of artworks[1] was a central feature of the new forms of art education. Although in the study of literature, teachers and children somewhat routinely discussed the meaning of texts and how meaning is conveyed, because of the predominance of art-making activities prior to the introduction of DBAE, the practice of interpretation rarely occurred during art instruction.

Soon after teachers began to present artworks for their students to discuss and interpret, they began to tell me how successful these sessions were. They claimed that classroom discussions of artworks were often more easily initiated, more lively, and more readily sustained than discussions of poems, stories, and text-book material. They explained that during discussions of works of literature and other texts, at least some of their students got lost as they struggled to keep up with language that referred to increasingly abstract concepts. In the sessions where artworks were interpreted, however, teachers reported that, with students contin-ually pointing to the concrete features of artworks, they didn't get lost. Indeed, I was told repeatedly by teachers in different parts of the country that students who almost never said anything in class were eagerly joining in the collaborative discussion of artworks.

BEYOND DISCIPLINE-BASED ART EDUCATION: THE INSPIRED INTERPRETATION OF A VISUAL TEXT

Teachers who attempted to implement DBAE were sometimes taught to discuss artworks from discrete vantage points—from the perspective of the historian, then the critic, and then the aesthetician. Pedagogy, however, is not so easily frag-mented when children just want to get on with their discussion of the interesting things they discover in artworks. During DBAE instruction, forms of interpreta-tion that were neither pure history, nor criticism, nor philosophy, nor artist's talk began to emerge. It was as if practice began to lead theory—or that teacher practice forced the theoreticians of DBAE to reconsider the ways they had fractured the in-terpretive process (Wilson, 1997, pp. 82–109). As the evaluator of the project, I got to sit in hundreds of classrooms observing teachers and students engaged in the practice of DBAE. Indeed, the collaborative interpretation of artworks emerged as one of the most educationally potent features of DBAE. As they clustered around reproductions of paintings, through discussion and deliberation, teachers and stu-dents searched for possible meanings, shared insights, and came to conclusions. In a few DBAE classrooms, children and their teachers even challenged initial as-sumptions, reflected on alternative interpretations, and refined their arguments about the meaning of artworks. In DBAE classrooms, teachers almost always led these communal interpretive sessions.

At Harrison Elementary School in suburban Chattanooga, Tennessee, for exam-ple, Sher Kenaston led her fourth-grade students in a discussion of James Cameron's painting, *Colonel and Mrs. James A. Whiteside, Son Charles and Servants* (1858–1859). The work, painted just before the Civil War, shows the wealthy Whiteside family on their spacious verandah high up on Lookout Mountain with the city of Chattanooga below them (in the painting's background).

Sher Kenaston displayed the Cameron painting in front of the students, who were seated on the floor in a semi-circle. Ms. Kenaston asked, "Why are we doing this?" (They had looked at the print briefly the previous Friday.)[2]

A student responded, "It's in the Hunter Museum."

Ms. Kenaston:	"But there are lots of works in the Hunter. Why study this one?"
Child:	"It's about Tennessee."
Ms. Kenaston:	"Who remembers the artist's name?"

(Ms. Kenaston reminded the students that the artist was James Cameron, that the picture was painted before the Civil War, and that when the artist returned to Chattanooga after the war he was so distressed by the destruction that he ceased painting.)

Ms. Kenaston:	"It's a picture of what?"
Child:	"A family."
Ms. Kenaston:	"Yes, it's a family painted just before the Civil War. Do you think that they are happy or sad, or are they just ..."

"Serious," is the word with which a student filled the blank.

Ms. Kenaston:	"What do you notice between all these figures and Colonel Whiteside?"
Child:	"He's fixin' to open a book; he's got a letter; that's why they are sad."

Ms. Kenaston responded: "I think they are just serious. Why do you think that Cameron painted it?"

(Ms. Kenaston showed the students that the letter contains James Cameron's signature, that this was the artist's way of signing the painting, and that Cameron had probably been asked by Colonel Whiteside to paint his family's portrait.)

She then returned to her line of questioning: "What do you think about the different people? Do you see the little boy? What is he doing?"

Child:	"He is a servant."
Ms. Kenaston:	"Yes, this is just before the Civil War."

"The war was going to free the slaves," responded one of the African American students.

"Yes," Ms. Kenaston replied, "we wouldn't see that today. Who is this?" she asked, pointing to the young woman who is holding the Whiteside infant.

Child:	"She's a slave too."
Ms. Kenaston:	"How do you think she feels toward the baby?"

The same African American student answered: "They wouldn't let them [her] hold the baby."

Ms. Kenaston responded: "Yes, they would. Lots of babies were raised by servants."

A child directed a question to Ms. Kenaston: "You haven't said anything. What do you think? Do you like it?"

Ms. Kenaston didn't tip her hand, she just smiled, shrugged her shoulders, and asked: "What do you think is the most interesting thing about the painting besides the people? If you were on Lookout Mountain, just what would you see? Remember this was in 1859."

There were comparisons between the way Chattanooga looked then and now. One child commented on the "the way he [the artist] mixed it up—the way he puts the mountains—makes it look more real.... It looks like the cliffs are close."

Discussions with fourth-graders seldom move in straight lines. There were comments about the time of day depicted, the clothing worn by the Whiteside family, and then a child declared: "I'll bet they had lots of servants," to which Ms. Kenaston responded: "I'll bet they did. But remember what happened in three years. In eight years what would be missing from the picture? What two people would not be in the picture?"

Child:	"The slaves."
Ms. Kenaston:	"Yes, they would be paid servants."
A child asked:	"Did the slaves fight in the war?"
Ms. Kenaston:	"Some did. Remember, no person had the right to own another."
Child:	"Our parents own us."
Another child:	"No, they don't."
Ms. Kenaston:	"These people were brought over from Africa against their will."
Child:	"Were the slaves paid to be servants?"

(Things were moving so fast that I missed part of the exchange.)

Ms. Kenaston:	"After the war would things look like this?"
Child:	"No."
Ms. Kenaston:	"Why not?"
Child:	"A big battle was fought on Lookout Mountain. The mansion might be destroyed."

There was more discussion of the Civil War destruction and comments about the colors of the painting, the texture, and the contrast between the bumpy texture of the rocks and the smooth floor. A child remarked on the faces of the Whiteside family. Another asserted that the people and the rocks looked "quite natural." A child pointed "over here, the people owned the land," and another pointed out where the train was. Ms. Kenaston told the children, "You will be surprised when we go to the Hunter and you find out how big it is [the painting]." And then she asked, "Does it look like a stage to you? What does Colonel Whiteside have in his hand?"

Child:	"It's a Bible."
Ms. Kenaston:	"What impression did he [Colonel Whiteside] want to give?"
Child:	"He was a Christian."
Child:	"He was a church man."

Joey stood up excitedly. "Wait a minute; if he was a Christian, why did he have slaves right in his house?"

Ms. Kenaston to the class:	"Do you want to answer?"
Child:	"Everybody did it then."
Ms. Kenaston:	"That's the argument you give your parents. 'I want to go down to the mall.' Your parents say, 'Why?' and you say, 'Because everybody will be there.' The Colonel was ignoring his value system, or he ignored it because everyone else was doing it."
Child:	"Maybe they were his kids [the two servants]."
Ms. Kenaston:	"No, they were slaves—you can't get him out of it."
Child:	"It's not true that most people were doing it because in the North they didn't have slaves."

As the discussion drew to a close, Ms. Kenaston asked: "What have we discovered? There is a lot more to this painting than we thought at first."

The discussion touched on the roots of race relationships that continue to trouble our country and that still affect the lives of students. It was obvious that some students connected the issue of slavery to their own beliefs and attitudes. Perhaps even more important, they had begun to assess the contradictions between religious and social values and practices. Indeed, I began to observe that in the most interesting of the interpretive discussions, such as the one conducted by Ms. Kenaston and her students, a new goal for art education was beginning to emerge. The purposes of interpretation went beyond the mere academic exercise of students performing the roles of historian, or critic, or philosopher. The educationally potent part of the practice emerged when students connected their interpretations of artworks to their own lives. In my role as evaluator, I began to search for theories that would account for the practices I was observing.

INTERPRETATION AND THE ACT OF REWRITING TEXTS WITHIN THE TEXTS OF OUR LIVES

The philosopher Arthur Danto reminds us that visual art objects by themselves do not constitute artworks. "My theory of interpretation," he writes, "is ... constitutive, for an object is an artwork *at all* only in relation to an interpretation ... Interpretation in my sense is transfigurative. It transforms objects into works of art" (1986, p. 44). Over the course of its lifetime, an art object may elicit many different interpretations, some based, at least in part, on previous interpretations. Obviously, elementary and secondary school students can benefit from encounters with interpretations previously given—the historically grounded interpretations of the sorts that museum curators and professional critics write. In different eras, objects from the realms of art and visual culture may accumulate many valid interpretations. Moreover, the interests of the interpreters may lead to different acceptable interpretations. Inasmuch as the interests of young people are different from the interests of artists, historians, and critics, it seems reasonable to encourage them to produce their own interpretations of visual works.

Richard Rorty (1992) discusses the motives individuals might have for interpreting artworks. In true pragmatist spirit, Rorty claims that "all anybody ever does with anything is use it" (p. 93). He claims, "Interpreting something, knowing it, penetrating to its essence, and so on are all just various ways of describing some process of putting it [a text] to work" (p. 93). If we were to follow Rorty's lead, artworks could be interpreted in a variety of ways. Nevertheless, interpretation has ethical implications. Rorty wrote:

> Kant ... distinguished between value and dignity. Things, Kant said, have value, but persons have dignity. Texts, are for this purpose [that is to say, for the purpose of reasoning and deliberation], honorary persons. To merely use them—to treat them merely as means and not also as ends in themselves is to act immorally. (p. 106)

Rorty continues,

> For there is, I think a useful distinction ... between knowing what you want to get out of a person or thing or text in advance and hoping that the person or thing or text will help you to want something different—that he or she or it will help you to change your purposes, and thus to change your life. This distinction, I think, helps us highlight the difference between methodical and inspired readings of texts. (p. 106)

In classrooms, what are the practical consequences of Rorty's position? By inviting students and teachers to treat artworks with the same respect accorded humans, Rorty places their educational value in an entirely new light. If accorded dignity, artworks have the potential to reveal things that individuals are unable to imagine before they encounter them. Conversely, if teachers decide beforehand what they wish their students to derive from an artwork and seek no more, they will, in fact, seldom get more. On the other hand, following Rorty's pragmatic lead, the educator could be encouraged to ask of artworks, What are you about that I have not yet recognized? What do you mean that I do not yet know? How might you add to my knowledge of myself, and the common realities of the world in which I live. How do you contribute to my conceptions of how humans should live their lives, to my reconstruction of the past and my visions of the future? In short, how might you as honorary person/visual text contribute to my humanity?

The educational potential of artworks may be calculated according to the extent that they are interpreted and shaped within personal narratives and used to expand students' conceptions of themselves and their worlds. Interpretation, according to Barthes (1985), is a search. Indeed, for Barthes, interpretation is like an ongoing quest that reveals itself as a unique form of writing. He wrote that we never stop adding to the Search. "We never stop writing it [a text]. And no doubt that is what reading is: rewriting the text of the work within the text of our lives" (p. 101).

In DBAE classrooms, I was observing a new form of art education that had evolved into something similar to Danto's artwork-as-interpretation, Rorty's artwork-as-honorary person, and Barthes's writing of a text into an individual life. It wasn't so much that within DBAE a new mode of interpretive discourse had developed; it was that cooperative interpretation had became a general practice in art classrooms that had previously known only art-making. By attempting to emulate the interpretative processes of art critics and historians (coupled with a deemphasis of formal analysis of the elements and principles of design that has pervaded art educational discourse for much of the century), teachers and students had discovered an engaging and rewarding activity that often rivaled the joys students associated with the creation of their own artworks.

HOW DO STUDENTS INTERPRET ARTWORKS WITHOUT THE GUIDANCE OF THEIR TEACHERS?

As I listened to the discussions in DBAE classrooms in different parts of the country, I wondered whether or not students would be able to arrive at insights into artworks and into their own lives without the skillful guidance of teachers. If children participate in interpretive discussions regularly, do they acquire the ability to direct their own conversations and to arrive at interpretive closure without adult leadership? Without teacher prompting and guidance, to what extent do students themselves give well-reasoned interpretations of visual artworks and to what extent do they connect those interpretations to their interests and, as Barthes puts it, rewrite "the text of the work within the text of [their] lives"?

I saw the opportunity to answer these questions by taking advantage of the situation that had already occurred during the DBAE implementation process. In virtually every elementary school I visited, at least some teachers had become excited about the DBAE practice of joining with their students in the collaborative interpretation of artworks. In those same schools, there were other teachers who either knew little about the new art program or who cared little about implementing it.[3] This situation, in which there were classrooms within the same schools where teachers had either implemented or not implemented the program, provided an opportunity to investigate the extent to which DBAE students had, in effect, become different from other students.

I selected students from elementary school classrooms in two Florida districts and a Tennessee district where teachers had fully adopted one of the collaborative interpretive processes developed within DBAE institutes.[4] From the same schools and from the same grades, I also selected students from classrooms where teachers did not teach any form of DBAE. Although I didn't fully monitor the art teaching that occurred in the non-DBAE classrooms, I was able to determine from discussions with school administrators that the teachers and students in these classrooms rarely, if ever, discussed the works of artists. Art instruction in the non-DBAE classrooms was directed toward art-making projects—often associated with holidays such as Thanksgiving and Valentine's Day.

The Experiment

I faced the challenge of devising a situation in which students could interpret artworks without the guidance of a teacher. The solution I arrived at was to divide classrooms of students into smaller groups. From the DBAE and non-DBAE fourth- and fifth-grade classrooms, small groups of students—five seemed just about the right number—were taken to a quiet room where they were seated around a table on which a reproduction of an artwork had been placed. (The artworks used were similar to those the DBAE students had studied, but the specific works were unfamiliar to them.) Once the students were seated at a low table, they were invited to discuss an artwork's meaning. They were also told that the discussion was to proceed without assistance from an adult.

The Interpretive Task

Students were given these instructions:

What is the main idea shown in this work? What does it mean? How do all the things you see in the work and all the things you know about the work help to show the main idea? We would like you to share with one another your thoughts about the work's important ideas. With each main idea you give, tell what it is about the work that helps to show the main idea. In other words, give evidence for your thoughts about the main idea. Talk among yourselves and listen carefully to the ideas presented by each member of the group. And remember, some of the ideas you hear may be better than others. The best "main ideas" are those for which there is the best evidence. If there is no evidence for an idea about the work, perhaps it is not a good main idea.

Among the artworks used to elicit students' interpretations were Frida Kahlo's self-portraits, Dorothea Lange's *Migrant Mother*, Rousseau's jungle scenes, Hokusai's *Great Wave*, and Edward Hicks's *Peaceable Kingdom*.

Students who were accustomed to discussing artworks in class moved easily and eagerly into the interpretive task. Students who had not received DBAE instruction, generally speaking, also engaged in lively discussions without guidance.

After group members had discussed an artwork for 15 or 20 minutes, I asked them to summarize the best ideas they had heard. Most groups were not successful at synthesizing the best ideas. Nevertheless, their summaries reflected views presented by various group members—just as in classroom interpretive discussions.

Finally, each student was asked to write his or her individual thoughts about the work's main idea and all the things that show the main idea. "What do you think the work means, and what evidence do you have to support your view?"

The Analysis of Students' Interpretations

The realm of art criticism is fraught with controversy. Critics and philosophers debate issues such as the characteristics of acceptable interpretations and problems of overinterpretation, underinterpretation, and misinterpretation (Eco, 1992). Assessment of students' interpretations of artworks is, in effect, another act of interpretative judgment. Just as students are asked to provide evidence to support their conclusions regarding an artwork's main idea, I had to provide evidence to support my assessment of students' interpretions. Arts assessment is, in effect, an act of art criticism, or, more accurately, of meta-criticism.

In the arts there are, of course, (a) interpretations for which there is strong evidence (either within the work or the contexts that surround the work's creation and interpretation); (b) interpretations that cannot be discounted even though the evidence to support them is weak; (c) interpretations that cannot be rejected even though there appears to be no available evidence either to support or reject a conclusion; and (d) interpretations that can be discounted because there is evidence that contradicts interpreters' claims. To state that artworks mean things they clearly do not mean and to allow unjustified interpretations to stand is akin to telling lies about artworks. Most certainly, it is treating an artwork dishonorably, as Rorty (1992) might claim.

Students' interpretations of an artwork's main idea provided the principal basis for analyses. If students offered insightful conclusions regarding an artwork's main ideas for which there was substantial evidence, they received high scores.[5] When their conclusions were less insightful and the evidence was less compelling, they received lower scores; and when their conclusions were wrong because there was strong evidence to support a contrary position, their scores reflected their inability to distinguish between reasoned and less reasoned interpretations.

Differences Between DBAE and Non-DBAE Students' Interpretations of Artworks

I found that students from DBAE classrooms where collaborative interpretations of artworks was practiced with their teachers' guidance arrived at more insightful, valid, and well-reasoned interpretations of artworks' "main ideas" than students who did not practice collaborative interpretations with their teachers. It is important to remember that in the experimental situation, both groups were functioning without the assistance of their teachers. The mean score for the DBAE group was 2.339 and for the non-DBAE group it was 1.766. A t test indicated that there was a significant difference between the DBAE and non-DBAE groups' Global Main Idea scores ($t = 3.507$, $df = 101$, $p < .001$). Statistically significant differences notwithstanding, I was more concerned about the educational significance of the differences.

Only 4 of 56 DBAE students managed to provide highly insightful and well-reasoned interpretations of the meaning of a complete artwork. Nevertheless, more than a third (36%) of the DBAE students gave valid and reasoned interpretations of the meaning of an entire artwork and provided evidence to support their interpretations. This finding must be viewed in light of the fact that over one half (57%) of the DBAE students offered both valid and invalid interpretations of artworks simultaneously. In other words, they were unable to weigh evidence with sufficient insight to enable them to retain reasonable interpretations and to reject unreasonable ones. This finding is tremendously important because the students exhibited the same interpretive behaviors that I observed among their teachers. As I observed teachers in many classrooms, I found that they were frequently reluctant to challenge students' wrong-headed interpretations of artworks. It is possible that in some instances, perhaps even in many instances, teachers themselves do not distinguish between well-reasoned and unreasonable interpretations. I concluded that teachers do not challenge wrong-headed interpretations out of the concern that the suggestion "your interpretation is wrong" might discourage discussion and participation. I have also heard many teachers voice a version of the opinion, "in art there are no wrong answers."

Here is a fourth-grade DBAE student's response to Edward Hicks's *Peaceable Kingdom* that illustrates how students can be simultaneously insightful and wrong.

> The evidence that I think about this painting is the animals and people are reuniting together. Also, I think the stream, clouds, and trees, and land have spirits of their own. In this certain picture because the clouds, wind, land, [and] stream also give energy. So it's all the circle of life. The animals and the lion eat the ox but when the lion dies

the lion's body becomes the grass and the ox eats the grass so in this picture it's all the circle of life. I also think the dark colors in this picture show more feelings and tameness and the lighter colors show more wildness and more energy and strength.

In some respects, this is a marvelous response. There is evidence of intertextuality—of relating Hicks's painting to the Disney film *Lion King* and its circle of life—and there is an astonishing characterization, for a fourth-grade student, of the effect of colors on the painting's expressive character. And yet her conclusions about the circle of life are just plain wrong. She missed the main idea of the painting—that there is a connection between William Penn's signing a peace treaty with the Indians, shown in the background, and the reference to the Biblical prophesy of a peaceful coexistence of lambs and lions and children and bears, which fills most of the foreground.

Another fourth-grade DBAE student actually got closer to the painting's meaning than the first. She wrote this brief summary of the work's main idea:

Well, what I think is that Mr. Hicks is trying to expraz [express] is that man and beast can, if they try, live in peace and harmony. Short of [sort of] what Martin Luther King's dream was based on. So that's what I think, and in the end, maybe, just maybe, if we all try, it will be like that.

The young student has used her knowledge of Martin Luther King Jr.'s dream for America to understand another American dream: the Isaiah-inspired millennial vision projected in Hicks's painting. This kind of interpretation, where the understanding of one text is based on an understanding of another text, is an essential component of critical thinking. It exemplifies intertextuality—the relating of ideas from one text to another. Unfortunately, this student's brilliant insight is unelaborated.

The absence of evidence to justify an interpretation raises another significant point. During the group discussion phase of the interpretive task, I consistently observed students who offered an abundance of evidence to justify various interpretations. When it came to writing their individual interpretations, however, students tended to jump directly to their own conclusions. I have to remind myself that, for fourth- and fifth-grade students (and for many of the rest of us), writing is a chore. Often what students are able, or are willing, to write in a short period of time represents only a portion of their thinking. It is important to recognize that students' writing skills at this age often trail behind their oral language skills. I should also note that the students had no notion of what I would be looking for in their writing. If students had been taught explicitly how to frame their interpretations, their written responses might have been much richer.

A third student wrote his interpretation of Hicks's *Peaceable Kingdom* in a form that has some of the character of a poem:

Animals and humans coming together.
Sharing the land.
Showing how the world should be.
The meat eaters and plant eaters (animals) not fighting.
The Pilgrims and Indians not fighting for the land.
Really peaceful.
It shows that the Indians cared for their land and not polluting.

This fourth-grade student did capture aspects of the work's main idea. The only problematic part of his conclusion is the claim that the work shows that the Indians cared for the land. Native Americans may have, but the painting contains no evidence that would support this conclusion. Within DBAE classrooms, I almost never observed teachers pointing to the rhetorical structures and arguments that students offered during collaborative interpretive sessions. From this study and from my observations of classrooms, I have concluded that students' interpretations would be more insightful if greater attention were directed to the justification of claims and the construction of critical arguments.

Offering Evidence: Differences Between DBAE and Non-DBAE Students' Writing About the Features of Artworks and Their Contexts

My primary objective was to determine whether students with different educational experiences, by employing group and individual critical inquiry processes, could make reasoned statements about the global meaning of artworks. At the same time, I was interested in the types of evidence students offered to support their views regarding an artwork's meaning. The instructions given at the beginning of the task asked students to take note of "how ... all the things you see in the work and all the things you know about the work help to show the main idea." Students were also reminded that "the best 'main ideas' are those for which there is the best evidence." I wanted to learn whether DBAE students, whom I assumed might have been instructed either explicitly or implicitly in what to look for in artworks, would respond differently from non-DBAE.

Sensory, Formal, and Expressive Evidence

Through an analysis of each sentence students wrote about the works of art, I found that DBAE students made references to the sensory, formal, and expressive features of artworks with significantly greater frequency than non-DBAE students. The mean score for DBAE students was .312 ($SD = .459$), and for the non-DBAE students it was .155 ($SD = .243$), $t = 2.115$, $df = 101$, $p < .05$. More important than the finding that DBAE students offered these classifications of evidence is the fact that they sometimes used comments about things such as colors and the "feeling" conveyed by artworks as evidence to support their claims about the main idea.

Symbolic and Metaphoric Evidence

Within each sentence, I also classified students' references to symbolic and metaphoric features that they associated with the artworks they had been invited to interpret. Again, I found a significant difference between DBAE and non-DBAE students. The t test indicates that there is a significant difference between DBAE and non-DBAE students' offering of evidence relating to symbol and metaphor. The mean for DBAE students was .201 ($SD = .850$), and for non-DBAE students it was .068 ($SD = .846$), $t = .194$, $df = 101$, $p < .05$. I should note, however, that few students presented this form of evidence. Twenty-two of 56 DBAE students (39%) based their interpretations of artworks' main ideas on this kind of evidence. Only

8 of 47 non-DBAE students (17%) made reference to the symbolic and metaphoric evidence. So how good is the performance of DBAE students?

Insightful art criticism and art historical inquiry involve processes such as (a) interpreting the symbolic meaning of artworks' objects and features; (b) viewing artworks as visual metaphorical statements; and (c) interpreting artworks semiotically—seeing them as signs of things not present (Bal & Bryson, 1991, 1992). Indeed, getting students to interpret artworks in light of their symbolic, metaphoric, and semiotic features would be one of the highest and most important achievements of art education. In addition to providing the means by which students gain original insights into artworks, insightful metaphoric and semiotic interpretations of artworks probably provide the best indication available that students have become critical thinkers. In the ideal art educational world—the one I like to imagine will someday exist—virtually all students' interpretations of artworks would rely on symbolic, metaphoric, and semiotic approaches to interpretation. The DBAE students in this study are still a long distance from the ideal—nevertheless, they performed considerably better than non-DBAE students.

Other Types of Evidence

I compared DBAE and non-DBAE students to determine whether they made reference to subject matter aspects of artworks; the social and intellectual conditions associated with the creation and interpretation of artworks and the artistic, aesthetic, and stylistic factors associated with artworks; and personal factors relating to the life of the works' artists, and whether students connected the artworks to their own lives. It is perhaps not surprising that there were no significant differences in the uses of these classifications between DBAE and non-DBAE students. Students do not need a special type of education in order to comment on the subject matter aspects of artworks. The categories that were constructed to take note of students' awareness of artworks' social, historical, and interpretative contexts rely on knowledge that either the students did not possess or that they did not believe important to reveal during the interpretative process. When it came to the students' commenting on whether they recognized explicit connections between the artworks and their own lives, the absence probably points to a pedagogical omission in DBAE programs. In DBAE programs, teaching students to function as art historians and critics directs their attention to artworks and away from the insights those works might reveal about the self, the self in relationship to society or history, and the future that one might construct for one's self.

Noting Relationships and Making Connections

There is one final aspect of connection-making in which DBAE students outperformed non-DBAE students. I tabulated the number of times students made connections between statements about an artwork's global meaning and evidence that would support their conclusions. I also noted the number of explicit relationships students made between and among different classes of evidence.[6] The *t* test indicates that there is a significant difference between the DBAE and non-DBAE groups with regard to the number of relationships noted. The mean number of relationships noted by DBAE students was 1.259 (SD = .675), and the mean for non-DBAE students was .905 (SD = .810), t = 2.420, df = 101, p < .05.

When students did detect and comment on relationships between and among the different aspects of an artwork and connected them to other texts and ideas, it was a sign of active critical thinking. Indeed, students come to know the nature of things through noting the ways in which they are different from or similar to other things. Education itself might be defined in terms of the number of important and meaningful relationships students are encouraged to make among the different texts (artworks, works of literature, music, dance, theater, history, science, social science, mathematics, etc.) they encounter in school and in their lives outside school.

It is instructive to examine a student's response, in which a variety of relationships are noted. About a Frida Kahlo self-portrait, fifth-grade student Brian wrote:

> The main idea of the work is: I think the picher [picture] is about the troubles in her life and she is either sad or angry at something or someone. She looks like she is traped [trapped] in misery and she really doesn't care about herself, but a friend is helping her out. The thorns in her neck stand for she's in a bad dream. She [is] painted light which means she wasn't very mad compared to Vincent van Gogh who did his work heavily. She is manely [mainly] is [sic] traped [trapped] in her own misery and a friend is trying to get her out. She also is not hiding anything and [is] telling her life with simbols [symbols].

Figure 18.1 provides an analysis of the relationships Brian noted in his written interpretation of the painting.

CONCLUSIONS: INTERPRETING THE INTERPRETATIONS

What does it mean that significant differences were found between DBAE and non-DBAE students in important areas such as the interpretation of a global main idea, providing evidence, and recognizing relationships between an artwork's main ideas and different classifications of evidence? Certainly these findings point to the positive outcomes of art instruction that is directed to the verbal unpacking of visual texts. At the same time, it is disappointing to note that DBAE students were inclined to offer, within the same interpretation, both well-reasoned and wrong-headed interpretations of artworks. Finally, where differences were found to exist between DBAE and non-DBAE students, they are often smaller than desirable. I have concluded that there are relatively simple instructional strategies, which if used, would assure that students would become more insightful readers of visual texts. The most obvious of these strategies would be for teachers to encourage students to weight the veracity of their interpretations and to supply evidence for their conclusions.

The interpretation of artworks relates in important ways to the interpretation of works of literature, theater, music, dance, works from history, the social sciences, visual culture (things such as political cartoons, TV, advertisements, comics, illustrations, product design, architecture and landscape architecture, etc.), and even scientific writing. The pedagogical processes that lead to insightful interpretations of visual artworks have broad applications to virtually all school subjects. And as I observed previously, both DBAE and non-DBAE students eagerly discussed vi-

Brian's Written Interpretation	Comments On Relationships In Brian's Interpretation
1. The main idea of the work is: I think the picture is about the troubles in her life and she is either sad or angry at something or someone.	Brian notes a relationship between the work and its main idea—life's troubles. He then goes on to enumerate relationships between trouble and its types and points to relationships between troubles and their causes.
2. She looks like she is trapped in misery and she really doesn't care about herself, but a friend is helping her out.	The first relationship in this sentence is metaphoric—the woman is trapped in misery. The second is that a friend, one of the animals, is providing assistance—a literal relationship having to do with an action.
3. The thorns in her neck stand for she's in a bad dream.	The relationship in this sentence has to do with the way the thorns, an aspect of subject matter, function symbolically to represent a nightmare. (It should be noted that no evidence exists to support the student's claim; at the same time, there is no evidence that would disconfirm it.)
4. She painted light which means she wasn't very mad compared to Vincent van Gogh who did his work heavily.	The first relationship is drawn between the woman and the technique used to depict her. The second is an intertextual comment on the relationship between the technique used in this painting and van Gogh's impasto technique.
5. She is mainly trapped in her own misery and a friend is trying to get her out.	The student repeats the two relationships drawn in the second paragraph.
6. She also is not hiding anything and [is] telling her life with symbols.	The relationship in this last sentence is between the work's principal idea—conveying information about a life—and the symbolic means used to convey the idea.

Figure 18.1. Relationships Noted in a Fifth-Grade Student's Analysis of Frida Kahlo's Self-Portrait.

sual artworks without hesitation and without adult guidance. Artworks are relatively easy for children to discuss, and it is possible that they might learn to transfer the interpretive process from artworks to less concrete texts.

The DBAE experiment has shown that it possible to construct a critical pedagogy based on students' active reading of relationships among different aspects of visual texts—reading relationships among sensory, formal, expressive, symbolic, and contextual factors of visual texts. The reading of relationships within and among texts is, as Danto (1986) would have it, the way visual objects are transformed into visual artworks. Artworks, when treated honorably have the possibility of, to paraphrase Rorty (1992), helping students to want something different—to interpret texts in order to change their purposes and thus to change their lives. Nevertheless, as I viewed the interpretative processes of young DBAE students, my greatest disappointment was that they did not draw connections between the texts they interpreted and their own lives. Few students made the kinds of connections that I observed Sher Kenaston's students making as they struggled to understand the consequences of slavery and issues of freedom raised by the painting of Colonel Whiteside, his family, and his servants. This is, I think, a failure of DBAE and much of contemporary art education. The interpretation of visual texts is seen as an end in itself, not relating of means and ends that might change students' lives.

Of course, if we were to expect our students to write the texts of artworks within the texts of their lives, then the process of assessing and evaluating the outcomes of art education programs—and other programs based on the interpretation of texts—becomes vastly more complex than it is presently. Assessing the success of educational programs would not simply be a matter of determining how well students interpret texts, but how successfully they act on the moral, ethical, artistic, and aesthetic consequences of the meanings of artworks—in school and beyond. I discovered that acting on the consequences of interpretations is extremely difficult for students. For example, after children had arrived at insightful interpretations of artworks such as Hokusai's *Great Wave*, which shows humans pitted against an awesome force of nature, I asked them to sketch ideas for artworks that would show how the theme applied to their own lives and times. Their visual responses revealed almost no ability to transfer ideas from an artist's work to their own artworks. Yes, this study shows that the best DBAE programs broaden and deepen students' interpretations of visual works. It also shows that students are able to use collaborative interpretative processes without teachers to guide them. But perhaps most importantly, the study reveals that the higher goal of leading students to act on the possible implications of interpretations is vastly more difficult. Perhaps, the next step in the process of deepening the consequences of interpretation is for us as teachers to experiment with pedagogical practices that might lead our students to rewrite the texts of artworks within the texts of their lives.

NOTES

1. The "artworks" were generally presented in the form of poster-sized printed reproductions. Throughout this paper, when I mention artworks in school settings, it is to these reproductions that I refer.
2. This is a slightly abbreviated version of an account published in *The Quiet Evolution* (Wilson, 1997, pp. 152–155).
3. I have dealt extensively with the factors that affected the extent to which DBAE programs were implemented in schools and school districts (see Wilson, 1997, pp. 112–163).
4. The students came from the Sarasota and St. Lucie school districts in Florida and the Hamilton County schools in suburban Chattanooga, Tennessee. The experimental group was composed of 56 DBAE students from fourth and fifth grades and the non-DBAE group was composed of 47 students from the same grades.
5. Students' interpretations were analyzed using content analysis procedures developed by Wilson (1966, 1970, 1971, 1972; see also *Art Technical Report*, 1978). The analysis system

also classified the relationships between students' conclusions about artwork's main ideas and different classifications of evidence. The classifications of evidence included references to an artwork's: (a) artform, media, technical, sensory, expressive, and compositional attributes; (b) its subject matter; (c) symbolic and metaphoric features; (d) social and intellectual conditions relating to the creation or the interpretation of the work; (e) the artistic, aesthetic, and stylistic climates relating to the work; and (f) personal factors relating to the life of the artist. The analysis system also made note of the number of relationships among different classifications of evidence and the connections students made between an artwork and their own lives—their own experiences, values, assumptions, and purposes. A final category classified the extent to which students' critical writing was coherent, well organized, clearly written, expressive, and written with a personal voice.

6. The relationship scores were entered into the data set as averages based on the number of sentences written by each student, thus putting the scores on an equivalent scale. For example, if a student noted a total of five relationships and wrote five sentences, the relationship score was entered as 1.000.

REFERENCES

Art Technical Report. (1978). Denver: Education Commission of the States & National Center for Education Statistics.

Bal, M., & Bryson, N. (1991a). Semiotics and art history. *The Art Bulletin, 73*(2), 174–208.

Bal, M., & Bryson, N. (1991b). Some thoughts on "semiotics and art history": Reply. *The Art Bulletin, 73*(2), 528–531.

Barkan, M. (1962). Transitions in art education. *Art Education, 15*(7), 12–18.

Barthes, R. (1985). Day by day with Roland Barthes. In M. Blonsky (Ed.), *On signs* (pp. 98–117). Baltimore: Johns Hopkins University Press.

Bruner, J. S. (1960). *The process of education.* Cambridge, MA: Harvard University Press.

Clark, G., Day, M., & Greer, D. (1987). Discipline-based art education: Becoming students of art. *The Journal of Aesthetic Education, 21*(2), 129–196.

Danto, A. (1986). *The philosophical disenfranchisement of art.* New York: Columbia University Press.

Eco, U. (with Rorty, R., Culler, J., & Brooke-Rose, C.). (1992). *Interpretation and overinterpretation* (S. Collini, Ed.). Cambridge: Cambridge University Press.

Getty Center for Education in the Arts. (1985). *Beyond creating: The place for art in America's schools.* Los Angeles: Author.

Kauppinen, H., & Wilson, B. (1981). *Kuvaamataidon didaktiikka.* Helsinki: Otava.

Kreitler, H., & Kreitler, S. (1972). *Psychology of the arts.* Durham, NC: Duke University Press.

Lowenfeld, V. (1947). *Creative and mental growth.* New York: Macmillan.

Olsen, L. (1997, April 30). Teachers need nuts, bolts of reforms, experts say. *Education Week, 16*(31), 1, 37.

Rorty, R. (1992). The pragmatist's progress. In U. Eco (S. Collini, Ed.), *Interpretation and overinterpretation* (pp. 89–108). Cambridge: Cambridge University Press.

Wilson, B. (1966). An experimental study designed to alter fifth and sixth grade students' perception of paintings. *Studies in Art Education, 8*(1), 33–42.

Wilson, B. (1970). Relationships among art teachers', art critics' and historians', and non-art-trained individuals' statements about Picasso's Guernica. *Studies in Art Education, 12*(1), 31–39.

Wilson, B. (1971). Evaluation of learning in art education. In B. S. Bloom, J. T. Hastings, & D. F. Madaus (Eds.), *Handbook on formative and summative evaluation of student learning* (pp. 499–558). New York: McGraw-Hill.

Wilson, B. (1972). The relationship between years of art training and the use of aesthetic judgmental criteria among high school students. *Studies in Art Education, 13*(2), 34–43.

Wilson, B. (1997). *The quiet evolution: Changing the face of arts education.* Los Angeles: Getty Education Institute for the Arts.

Wilson, B., & Wilson, M (1977). An iconoclastic view of the imagery sources in the drawings of young people. *Art Education, 30*(1), 4–12.

CHAPTER 19

Changing Musical Perception Through Reflective Conversation

Jeanne Bamberger

Each map is in a way a theory that favors certain approximations. Procedures like selection, simplification, smoothing, displacements to make room, out-of-scale notation for bridges, streams, and roads so narrow that they would become invisible at true scale, enter inescapably.
— *P. Morrison (1991, p. 139)*

We are not so much compositors of sentences from bits as reshapers of prior texts. The modes of reshaping are in large part conventional, but also in some unpredictable part innovative and un-predictable … A text has meaning because it is structuring and remembering and sounding and interacting and referring and not doing something else … all at once. The interactions of these acts is the basic drama of every sentence.
— *A. L. Becker (1984, p. 136)*

PATH-MAKERS AND MAP-MAKERS

Both of the above statements consider how we make sense of texts. If we consider that "text" may be a map, spoken discourse, or a musical score (invented or otherwise), the tensions between these two richly drawn remarks illuminate some of the fundamental issues we encounter in the conversations in this chapter. Each of the two quoted authors construes the notion of text in different ways, illuminating the distinction between path-makers and map-makers. The path-maker's path, like Becker's (1984) compositors of sentences, is a response to ever changing flux, a stream of events, a small drama, flowing through time, making sense not so much through the crystalline logic of stable, consistent reference structures, but rather through a coherent interaction of "acts." In turn, the map-maker, favoring certain approximations, must convert real-time experience in following a path to conventionally biased but useful metaphor. As Morrison suggests, a map is the result of a series of generative, implicitly logical procedures that are "out of time."

The tensions, as we move between the two kinds of meaning-making, subtly capture the tensions in the multiple ways we learn. Do we make sense of the sensory phenomena we encounter by playing out various rule-governed operations? Or does sense-making involve, as Becker (1984) proposes, a set of prior texts that one accumulates throughout one's lifetime, from simple social exchanges to long, semi-memorized recitations. One learns these "texts" in action, by repetitions and corrections, starting with the simplest utterances of a baby. One learns to reshape these texts to new context by imitation and by trial and error (pp. 136–137).

The contrasts between the two approaches to learning also raise questions about the role and meaning of reflection in learning. Although the term *reflection* has accrued many meanings over time, distinguishing between only two can again illustrate the distinctions between path-makers and map-makers. The first, and most common distinction refers to reflection *on* an object, subject, or idea—a stop-and-think. The Oxford dictionary offers the following definition of *reflection:* "the action of turning one's thoughts (back) or fixing the thoughts on or upon a subject; meditation, deep or serious consideration" (p. 177). In this case, reflection is an action, but it is an action that puts an object or subject "out there" at arm's length to look *at* rather than to *use*. Reflection in this sense characterizes map-makers. Stopping the continuous flow of time, map-makers differentiate parts, name, test, and make certain to *say* what they perceive—to hold still in description what might otherwise be unstable, uncertain, or in flux.

Path-makers are characterized by another, more interesting and elusive type of reflection—reflections *of* or *in* actions.[1] Rather than the time-out of stop-and-think reflections, these reflecting actions occur in real time, each move "telling" the path-maker the next move to make. Following a path of familiar landmarks is like balancing a tower of blocks, navigating the bumps on a ski trail, making a crescendo in playing a melody during which we are simultaneously hearing, anticipating, and doing. But these reflections in-the-moment easily go unnoticed; they are so fully embedded in a situation that we tend to see through them, noticing only their consequences. In-the-moment reflections resemble a series of linked moves: a move along an action path that triggers the chain reaction (a newly added block makes the tower of blocks wobble) is reflected in the responding move (a counterbalancing push). But the builder is now in the new situation (the tower is stable), the previous moves no longer exist, transparent to the current result, absorbed into the clear and present present.

John Dewey (1929) makes a similar distinction between these two kinds of reflecting. Dewey positions the distinction in terms of permanence and stability in contrast to evanescence and flux. He speaks, on one hand, of "temporal *qualities*," which characterize immediate, present experience, and on the other, "temporal *order*," which he associates with scientific inquiry.

> Temporal quality is ... not to be confused with temporal order. Quality is quality, direct, immediate and undefinable. Order is a matter of relation, of definition, dating, placing and describing. It is discovered in reflection, not directly had and denoted as is temporal quality. Temporal order is a matter of science; temporal quality is an immediate trait of every occurrence whether in or out of consciousness. Every event as such is passing into other things, in such a way that a later occurrence is an integral part of the *character* or *nature* of present existence.... Moreover, while quality is immediate and absolute, any particular quality is notoriously unstable and transitory. Immediate objects are the last work of evanescence ... flux in which nothing abides. (pp. 110–111, 114)

Although I find Dewey's distinction between temporal qualities and temporal order useful and important, I take issue with Dewey's notion that "nothing abides." I argue that although qualities experienced in moment-to-moment actions in a situation may be elusive, they abide and play a critical role in subsequent actions. The problem arises because we tend to believe in—to attribute "reality" to—only that which we can hold still, take out of time or, in Dewey's sense, put into temporal order by dating, placing, and describing. After all, these become the critical invariances we depend on not only for scientific inquiry but for matters of everyday life.

We tend, along with Dewey, to think of reflecting in-the-moment, including the actions inherent in conversation, along with those involved in aesthetic experience, as something else—nonreflective, noncognitive, and undifferentiated. In so doing, we are left with chalking up the successes of those whose work depends on these reflections situated in the moment's actions, to qualities inaccessible to explanation, to mystery, and magic—the expert cabinet maker, the child building complex Lego structures, the painter, violinist, or composer. But what, then, is guiding these actions in the situation—the craftsman's smart hands, the painter's artistic eyes, or the violinist's musical ears? We must at least posit a knowing mind making sense behind these sense organs (hands, eyes, ears) to which we give autonomous life. We say that "actions speak louder than words," but because the active mind behind the moment's actions doesn't seem to speak at all, we feel uncomfortable attributing the results of these reflecting actions, this sense-making, to "knowledge." We admire and value the results and somehow cherish our failure to account for them.

THE LABORATORY FOR MAKING THINGS

The conversations I retell in the following section are about the tensions between path-making and map-making, between temporal qualities and temporal order, as they play themselves out in the discourse among children and between teacher and students. The setting for these conversations is a project and a place called the Laboratory for Making Things—a large room in a public school in central Cambridge, Massachusetts.

All children from Grades K–8 regularly come to the lab with their teachers to explore and experiment with a wide variety of materials to make things that work and that "make sense"—what we have come to call "working systems." In the lab, children move easily *back and forth* between action and symbolic description, between sensory experience and representations of it, between the virtual world of the computer and the more familiar world of their own powerful know-how in working with materials in real time/space/motion.

As an integral part of this culture, children are accustomed to informal conversations in which they explain how they are making sense of their building materials—blocks, foam core, drums, and Legos (Photo 19.1).

They also typically invent some kind of graphic instructions/notations that could help someone else build what they have built. Such conversations are particularly cherished when they spontaneously arise in response to a child's surprising discovery or when an insight leads to solving a particularly difficult problem. This collaborative reflection leads, in turn, to learning from one another—rethinking

Photo 19.1.   Lucy's House

understandings, descriptions, and subsequently even influencing work on later projects that involve quite different materials.

The lab project was initially motivated by a well-recognized but poorly understood phenomenon: Children who are virtuosos at building and fixing complicated things in the everyday world (bicycles, plumbing, car motors, musical instruments and music, games, and gadgets) are often the same children having trouble learning in school. These are children who have the ability to design and build complex systems, who are experts at devising experiments to analyze and test problems, and who can learn by extracting principles from the successful workings of the objects they make. But they are also children who are frequently described as having trouble with conventional symbolic expressions such as numbers, graphs, and written language. With "knowledge" in schools mostly equated with the ability to manipulate symbols, it is not surprising that attention focuses on what these children cannot do. Instead of being seen as virtuosos, they are seen as "failing to perform."

Thus, my primary research question was this: If we could better understand the nature of the knowledge that children bring to what they do so well, could we help them apply this knowledge to success at school?

A cluster of interrelated questions emerged as we watched the children at work. How do children (or any of us) learn to turn continuously moving, organized actions—such as clapping a rhythm, bouncing a ball, turning wheels, or circling gears—into static, discrete, symbolic descriptions that represent our experience of these objects and our sensory mastery of them? How do we learn to make descriptions that hold still, to be looked at "out there"? And why should anyone want to?

PROVOKING CONVENTION

White Queen: … we had SUCH a thunderstorm last Tuesday—I mean one of the last set of Tuesdays, you know.

Alice (puzzled):   In *our* country there's only one day at a time.

Red Queen: That's a poor thin way of doing things. Now *here,* we mostly have days and nights two or three at a time, and sometimes in the winter we take as many as five nights together—for warmth, you know.

—*L. Carroll (p. 324)*

The six 8- and 9-year-old children who were participants in the lab conversations on the occasions with which I will be primarily concerned, were in their second year as members of the lab culture. Mary Briggs, the special education teacher, had selected them from among those she regularly worked with individually. These children came to the lab once a week after school for about 2 hours. All the sessions were videotaped for further analysis.

The conversations of primary focus all revolve around that most ordinary of tunes, Hot Cross Buns. A first project, which preceded the conversations that eventually ensued, involved building the tune using a set of tuned bells borrowed from the Montessori teaching materials. Because this project (a "prior text") significantly influenced those that followed, I briefly summarize it here.

The Montessori bells are a rather exceptional technological invention. Unlike any other pitch-making materials with which I am familiar, these all look alike except for their bases—bells with brown bases match bells with white bases. Thus, the only way to distinguish one bell from another is to play them with the small mallet and listen. Figure 19.1 shows a picture of the children's typical bell construction.[2]

This finished construction, which is typical of path-makers, is also a kind of "text," and as such, it provokes our accepted conventions while at the same time making them come alive to be scrutinized. For example, map-makers, who depend on their previously constructed fixed reference structures, begin by ordering the

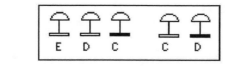

Figure 19.1.   Hot Cross Buns

bells in the conventional manner—as on a keyboard, low-to-high/left-to-right. In contrast, path-makers add bells to their bell path as they need them, one bell at a time, *in order of occurrence in the tune*. In doing so, they necessarily focus their attention on the *position* of each new pitch event (bell) and on its *function* within the tune.

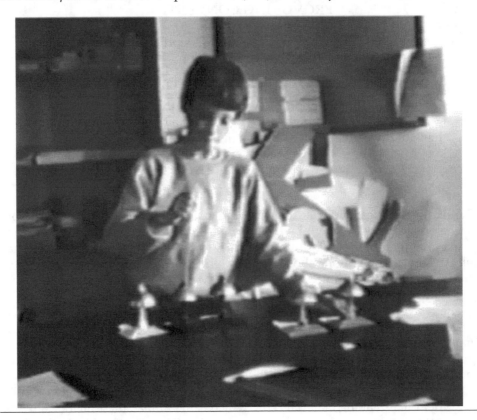

Photo 19.2.   Building Hot Cross Buns

Further, the lab children, who were typical path-makers, consistently need to use two C-bells and two D-bells. For map-makers, in contrast, a single instance of each bell is sufficient—for example, a C-bell can be used wherever it occurs, as it is always heard as "the same." But for path-makers, who take things as they come, the two C-bells are different in every salient respect: The first C-bell is approached from above and has a longer duration, causing it to function as a boundary marker, the ending of the first, small figure. The new C-bell, added immediately after this boundary event, has an entirely different function—it is the beginning of a new figure. It is played faster and follows itself through repetition. Children often leave a space in their bell path to mark this boundary between the two figures.

Most interesting, path-makers do not "hear" across this boundary. Indeed, when crossing the boundary of the two motives in making and playing the tune, the first motive is left behind, the second is just begun, and the two C-bells shift their respective functional meanings: As if facing in different directions, the first is an arrival from before, the second looking toward what is still to come. Leaving a space to mark the boundary between the two C-bells, the cumulating bell-path forms an embodied description of the three-part motivic grouping structure of the tune (Fig. 19.2).

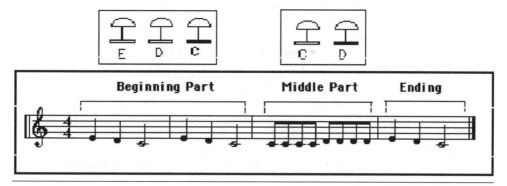

Figure 19.2. Motive Grouping Structure

The first three bells embody the beginning part of the tune which includes immediate repetition of this first little motive or figure. The group of two bells separated by the space in the bell-path embodies the middle part, which includes the second figure. The ending part returns to the initial group of three bells as the first figure returns again. Juxtaposing the meanings implicit in the children's evolving construction with the meanings implicit in our conventional representations alerts us to the alive conceptual background into which the children's new experiences are coming and in terms of which these new experiences will initially be understood and used.

CONVERSATION AS COLLABORATIVE LEARNING

With the tune-building task as background, I focus now on two conversations in which we see collaborative learning in action. The first conversation happened at the beginning of the next session in connection with a new project. I asked the children to *clap only the rhythm* of Hot Cross Buns, at first as a group and then individually. The children were told at the outset that after clapping the rhythm, they were going to "make some instructions that will tell a younger child how to clap the rhythm just as you are going to do." As the children listened to one another's performances, they noticed a puzzle: The middle part, which they called "the fast part," seemed to have become "one thing" instead of two (Fig. 19.3).

Figure 19.3. An Exact Correspondence

As the conversation ensued, Lucy noticed the problem first:

Lucy: When you clap it, the fast part sounds like one big chunk instead of two.
[Lucy claps the "fast part"]:

Ruth (another student):   You wait for a space. But there's really a clap.

[Ruth claps the "fast part" leaving a small pause ("space")]:

Ruth: You know why a space?
Lucy: Because *we* know that it's two, but if you said like to a kindergartner who didn't know the song, Hot Cross Buns, or they knew it but they didn't really know it well, and you just clapped the tune, they wouldn't really get that it's two (Photo 19.3).

Photo 19.3.

Mary: But how do you know it's two?[3]

Ruth: When you hear it ... [*sings* fast part]

[Ruth's comment suggests a question]:

Jeanne: And if you're playing it on the bells, what do you do on the ...
          when you get to "two-a-penny" if you're playing it on the bells?

Lucy: [thoughtfully moves her hand in the air as if she were playing
          the tune on the bells] You pause just a little bit ...

Ruth: Maybe not. Not big, but a clap-worth.

Jeanne: Do you play the whole thing on one bell?

Burt
(another
student): No, you don't.

Lucy: So, if you're playing it on the bells, you have to move to another
          bell in the fast part, and that makes it two; but if you're just
          clapping, it's just one big chunk.

Interrogating their own actions, questioning themselves, the children deliberated over how to "chunk" the tune. This is similar to asking about the parsing of a sentence or finding the edges or the "chunking" of a visual image: When is an ending, when is a beginning; what kinds of features generate boundaries? And ultimately, what is an entity, what is an element; at what level of detail does an entity exist?

Lucy begins the process. Listening to her own and the others' clapping, she notices, "The fast part sounds like one big chunk instead of two." Ruth makes a somewhat ambiguous proposal as a possible causal accounting: "You wait for a space. But there's really a clap." Clapping the middle part, Ruth demonstrates in action that her word, "space," means time; that is, to "wait for a space" means to wait for a little *time*.

Pursuing the questions further, Ruth asks, "You know why a space?" Lucy, focusing on the practical objective of the task, answers, if you didn't leave a space, "they [a kindergartner] wouldn't really get that it's two." Lucy, in the service of "instructing," accounts for the structural function of a space-of-time—it generates a boundary, making the one chunk into two.

Mary, the children's teacher, in her wisdom, probes further, asking the children to reflect on their own assumptions: "But how do *you* know it's two?" Seeing an opportunity to use the children's earlier experience in playing the tune on the bells as a means for carrying their observations further, I intervene: "And if you're playing it on the bells, what do you do ... when you get to "two-a-penny ... ?"

In response, Lucy, playing the tune on imaginary bells, summarizes the collaborative discovery: "If you're playing the bells, you have move to another bell in the fast part, and that makes it two; but if you're just clapping, it's just one big chunk."

In short, through their collaborative conversation, the children develop several new ideas. They discover, for instance, that *change* or contrast helps make structural boundaries. In the process, they also make distinctions between pitch and rhythm: When clapping, you have to interrupt the all-alike claps with a "space" to make two chunks instead of one; when playing the tune on the bells, just moving to a new bell (i.e., changing the pitch) also "makes it two." The children's discussion of structural boundaries and how they are generated continues to play an important role as they work on their invented notations.

LUCY'S TEXT: A SMALL DRAMA

The problem arises from the fact that utterances rarely say what they mean.

—D. R. Olson (1994, p. 68)

As an experiment, we gave the children Cuisenaire rods as materials for making their "instructions." The children were familiar with the rods as materials they used for learning basic arithmetic. All the rods are one centimeter in cross-section, with their lengths analogous to the numerals from 1 to 10—the "1-rod" (as the children call them) is a one-centimeter cube, the "2-rod" is one centimeter wide, two centimeters long, and so on. And each type of rod has a color associated with it. The children were familiar with these materials and their standard usage, so I was curious to see if they would use these implicit symbolic meanings in describing the relative durations of the rhythm. As it turned out, they did so in a wide variety of ways, but I limit the discussion here to a close look at only Lucy's work.

Photo copy 19.4 shows Lucy's instructions. In the following Figure 19.4, the relative lengths of the rods are close to those the children used; the inside designs are intended to indicate differences in color.

Photo 19.4. Lucy's instructions

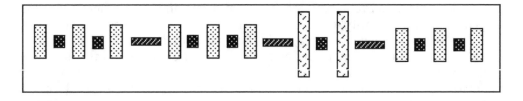

Figure 19.4.   Lucy's Notation

Looking at Lucy's work, it is easy to see that her choice of rods and their arrangement results in the two types of patterns shown in Figure 19.5. One type occurs at the beginning, is repeated immediately, and occurs once again at the end. The second type occurs in the middle—the "fast part" that Lucy and Ruth had puzzled over in the previous conversation.

Figure 19.5.   Beginning and Middle Patterns of Lucy's Notation

Looking in more detail at just the beginning pattern, we see that Lucy has used three different kinds of rods: short upright rods, separated by smaller square rods and followed by a longer, horizontally placed rod (see Fig. 19.6).

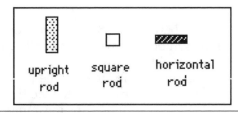

Figure 19.6.   Three Different Kinds of Rods

How are we to understand Lucy's instructions? There are two quite different approaches that one can take. With the first, we see or hear Lucy's "text" in terms of our familiar conventions—in this case, the rules implicit in standard rhythm notation (SRN). Using this approach, we will try to make a mapping between the items in Lucy's "instructions" and the items to which the symbols of SRN refer. However, this approach ignores the fact that Lucy's construction is an active *invention*—a small drama. This suggests a second approach in which we become active participants in the drama, using the evolving text as a means for interrogating what Lucy has found in clapping the rhythm and listening to the others. What has she chosen to give priority to? Are there shifts in focus of attention or level of detail? Has she given new meanings to old, familiar terms?

Considering the first, mapping approach, the variety of rods Lucy uses, together with their arrangement, suggest that she has chosen to guide her readers' actions at a very fine-grained level of detail. For example, one might see the alternation of upright rods and square rods as her effort to make the fine-grained distinction between her clap sound and the "space" or silence between her claps. On this reading, the clap sound is represented by the upright rods, the shorter space/time between claps is represented by the small, square rods, and the longer time between the clap at the end of the figure and the beginning of the repetition is represented by the horizontally placed rod. On this reading, Lucy's selection and arrangement of the rods corresponds closely to a notation of the rhythm in SRN, provided we use the symbols of SRN to show an equally fine-grained level of detail as shown in Figure 19.7.

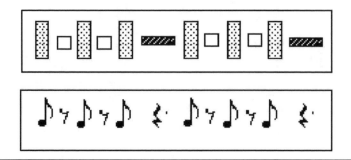

Figure 19.7.   A mapping to SRN

There is clearly a close "fit" between Lucy's construction and a possible notation of the rhythm using the symbolic conventions of SRN. This "fit" is evidence that Lucy is indeed "getting it right."

But what about Lucy's instructions for the middle pattern, the controversial "fast part?" Comparing it with her instructions for the first pattern, the neat fit with SRN seems to break down and with that, the meanings Lucy intends for her rods become puzzling, as well (see Fig. 19.8).

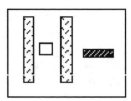

Figure 19.8.   The "Fast Part"

For instance, in mapping the beginning figure to SRN, Lucy's shorter, upright rods represented each clapped event. Why, in this middle part, do we see only *two*, longer upright rods when there are *eight* clapped events? If we invoke correspondence rules such as those applied previously, and if these correspondence rules are our sole criterion, then we would have to say that Lucy is simply getting it wrong.

But what if we take the alternative view? Instead of adopting the approach in which a mapping with the rules of SRN are the privileged criterion, what if we look at Lucy's construction as, indeed, a small drama, a text in action? Joining with her as participants in the drama, we use her construction as a means for interrogating what she has found in the rhythm, while at the same time necessarily interrogating our own deeply internalized assumptions.

With this approach, conventions and their underlying assumptions become a point of departure, and we can go on to ask Are there other aspects of the rhythmic structure that Lucy could be representing in her instructions, and how are these different from those we are able to represent within the constraints given by the symbols of SRN? If we bear in mind that Lucy's choice of rods and their arrangement are an *invention*, we can ask further questions, such as What can we learn about Lucy's focus of attention? Are there implicit "rules" hidden in her evolving actions? What are the features and relations she has chosen to prioritize and at what level of detail? How might these, in turn, relate to Lucy's "hearing" of the tune as reflected in her earlier bell construction?

LEARNING THROUGH COLLABORATIVE CONVERSATION BETWEEN TEACHER AND STUDENT

In the conversation retold, here, (transcribed from the video-tape of the session) Mary and Lucy jointly ponder these puzzlements in Lucy's work. Through their social interchange, they reciprocally and reflectively confront one another's meanings. The conversation is a path of linked actions, each move suggesting the next. Through Mary's responses to Lucy's and the puzzles these create, along with Mary's on-the-spot inquiries, it emerges that each participant is noticing strikingly different kinds of entities. The confusions between the two participants are clear almost from the beginning.

Mary: [pointing to the first long rod in Lucy's middle section]:
        So what does your long rod equal? (Photo 19.5)

Lucy: Fast.

Mary: How many fasts?

Lucy: Three [she pauses]; no, two.

Mary: [tapping out the rhythm on the first long rod—one tap for each syllable]:
         / / /   /
        one a pen-ny.

Lucy: One.

Mary: One what?

Lucy: *One, one-a-penny.*

Photo 19.5.   "What does your long rod equal?"

Mary: One, one-a-penny, which is *four little claps*. But this (picking up the shorter, upright rod in the preceding pattern) is how many claps?

Lucy: One....

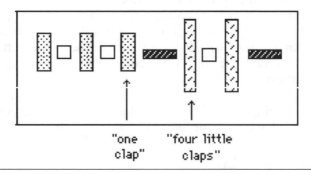

Figure 19.9.

Mary: This is one clap (shorter, upright rod), but all of a sudden, this [picks up longer, upright rod] is how many claps?

Lucy: One.... four.

Ruth: [who was watching]
          Four, it's four

There is a compelling tension in this interchange: two people approaching the same material with each trying to fathom the other. The problems begin with the meaning Lucy gives to Mary's first question, "What does your long rod *equal?*" In the most general sense, according to *Webster's Collegiate Dictionary,* "equal" means "the same as." However, Mary intends her term "equal" to elicit a number—how many claps is the long rod "equal to?" Lucy responds to a different question: "What does your long rod *stand for?*" Sensing that Lucy is giving a different meaning to her "equal," Mary takes up Lucy's term, "fast." Coupling Lucy's term with the meaning, she intends, Mary asks, "How many *fasts?*" Lucy, fumbling as she tries to shift her focus of attention to Mary's meaning, answers, "three," a pause, then "no, two." Mary, pursuing and clarifying her own meaning further, carefully points to the single long rod and taps out for Lucy one tap for each syllable of the verse:

/ / /   /

One a pen-ny.

But Lucy, responds with a puzzling count-up of "one." What could she mean?

Mary, puzzled and in search of the meaning for Lucy's somewhat mysterious answer, "one," asks the critical question, "One *what?*" Lucy's surprising and wonderfully revealing answer implicitly solves the puzzle: "One, one-a-penny." For Lucy the beginning of the "fast part" is just one *chunk,* one "one-a-penny." As if grabbing the motive into one handful, Lucy represents it with a single long rod. The rod stands for, is "equal to," the entire motive.

The tensions in the conversation so far are a striking illustration of two clearly different views bumping into one another but essentially passing each other by. Mary's "how many" questions follow the more conventional, notation-driven rules that focus on consistency whereby each clap is a thing to be represented and each is an equivalent thing to count. Lucy's response points to an aspect of rhythm that differs from Mary's in almost every dimension. As in the previous conversation with Ruth, Lucy's "one-a-penny" motive functions as a single, meaningful structural entity. It is experienced as a whole through the continuous motion of her directed actions in clapping. Rather than the consistency of the map-makers discrete, noncontextual entities, Lucy's one "one-a-penny" exemplifies a pathmaker's sensitivity to context and the "transitory immediacy" of Dewey's temporal quality.

However, Mary, who is unswayed from her initial goal, turns to the logic of explicit comparison. As shown in Figure 19.9, she compares the shorter upright rod in the first part ("… this is one clap") with the problematic longer upright rod in the middle part ("… all of a sudden this is how many claps?"). Lucy, holding her own view despite Mary's explicit comparison, hesitantly responds to Mary's "how many claps," again with "one." Then, shifting her focus and almost reluctantly joining Mary, Lucy says at last, "four."

Mary's responsiveness in the conversation and her effective search for Lucy's meanings are, in their own way, reminiscent of more common interplays between teacher and student but with the roles reversed—teacher now trying to fathom the meanings implicit in the student's actions and texts, rather than, more commonly, the student trying to fathom the meanings of the teacher's actions or text. For instance, Mary is initially focusing on the element most familiar to her and indeed to anyone who has accepted the conventions of SRN—the single event level in which each clap is a thing to count. With her probing and insightful questions, her willingness to put her own assumptions temporarily in abeyance, together with Lucy's responses, Mary comes to see and hear the rhythm in a new way—Lucy's way. In doing so, Mary shifts her attention, perhaps becomes newly aware of an aspect of the structure that differed from hers in both kind and level of detail— namely, the more aggregated *motivic structure* of the rhythm.

It is particularly important to reiterate that it is *through the social interchange, the active interplay* between Mary and Lucy, that their differences in focus emerge and eventually converge. Indeed, it is only through their dialogue that Mary is able to make her assumptions clear to herself as well as to Lucy, and that Lucy is eventually able to *say* what she intended—intentions that were initially hidden in the actions of her evolving instructions. With the configuration holding steady, and with each participant reflecting back the meanings the other sees in it, they both are able to shift their perceptions and to see/hear the rhythm in new ways. In short, we see learning happening in real time.

MORE ENIGMAS

Mary's initial puzzlement, and ours as well, at least in part derives from the shift that occurs within Lucy's text. As the text evolves, Lucy moves from the very fine-grained level of detail we observed in her instructions for the first figure and its repetition to a much more highly aggregated level of structure in the middle part. However, there are other puzzles within the "fast part" even beyond those that Mary found (Fig. 19.10).

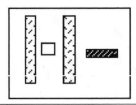

Figure 19.10.   The "Fast Part"

What, for instance, does Lucy intend the small, square rod to stand for, and what is the meaning of the horizontally placed rod at the end? In the earlier reading of the first figure and its repetition, using the conventional approach based on the rules of SRN, we were able to map the small, square rods and the horizontal rods onto symbols of SRN. However, this is certainly not possible with Lucy's instructions for the fast part. As Mary noticed, each upright rod in the first figure was mappable onto a clap, and we could notate them as eighth notes. But in the fast part, upright rods stand for an *aggregate* of claps or a motive, *for which there is no symbol in SRN.* Moreover, within the first figure, the square rods mapped to eighth-note rests, but there is no silence in the middle of the fast part (although Ruth wanted to put one in "to make it two"). The horizontally placed rods we mapped to dotted quarter rests in the first figure, but there is no rest at all separating the end of the fast part from the return of the first motive (see Fig. 19.11).

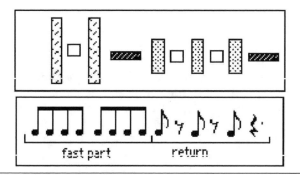

Figure 19.11.   A Mapping to SRN Fails

Once again there are two solutions to this puzzle. On the view that the rules governing SRN determine the single criterion for getting it right, Lucy is inconsistent: She is getting it right in the first part of the tune, but in deviating from conventional rules as she goes along, she gets it wrong in the middle part. On the alternative view, bearing in mind that Lucy's instructions are a small drama, we look instead for the possibility of different foci of attention and for rules that might derive from them, which Lucy has *invented*. In terms of these invented rules, Lucy could be getting it right.

Of course, in taking this latter view, we necessarily confront a danger—we run the risk of having to give up our privileged criterion. In doing so, we may also have to reconsider the "rightness" of the mapping theory in the earlier reading of Lucy's instructions for the beginning figure. There is a certain seductiveness in finding a neat mapping with SRN, but to risk getting that wrong may unearth meanings hidden in our most familiar assumptions, as well as meanings hidden in the initially obscure inventions of another.

A VIRTUAL CONVERSATION WITH LUCY'S TEXT

Intrigued by these puzzles and at least tentatively willing to take the risk, it seemed worthwhile to go back to look once more at the entire construction, focusing now on other possible meanings for the horizontal rods and the small, square rods (see Fig. 19.12).

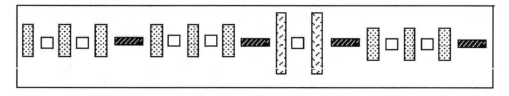

Figure 19.12. Lucy's Text

Using a mapping approach, Lucy's horizontal rods at the ends of each iteration of her beginning pattern were taken to represent a longer time between clapped events. But I noticed that in clapping the rhythm, it is by making these relatively longer "spaces" between clapped sounds that we actually *generate* the structural boundaries that we feel in action and that we hear in listening. That is, there is an intersecting relationship, something like cause and effect, between the longer temporal value of these silences and their *structural function as motive boundary markers*.

But I also noticed that it was impossible to *decouple* which of these meanings Lucy intended—the longer temporal value of the silence, the resultant boundary-making function, or both? Once I recognized this interactive coupling as a problem, I also saw it as a means toward resolving the puzzle of Lucy's horizontal rod at the end of the fast part. For instance, what if in the fast part, Lucy was *decoupling* these two meanings of the horizontal rod, leaving aside its meaning as longer duration and carrying over only its *functional meaning as boundary marker?* Whereas they may have initially served double duty, in going on to the fast part, Lucy could be selectively generalizing such that the meaning of the horizontal rod included only one aspect, not both. On this view, I could understand the horizontal rod as an *invention*—an *iconic* sign Lucy had invented to mark the *grouping* boundaries of the rhythm. If that was right, then the sign is indeed an invention because it conveys an aspect of rhythm that is not included in the meanings conveyed by the symbolic constraints of SRN. That is, the horizontal rods serve as *syntactic markers*, but the symbols of SRN are constrained to refer only to relative time values—they describe *metric* units, not the boundaries of rhythmic groupings such as motives or phrases.

So, by suspending disbelief, letting the text "talk back," looking for sense-making in what initially seemed puzzling and anomalous, I hit on at least a potential "mini theory": If Lucy's horizontal rods were icons for boundary markers, then their meaning in the first figure and its repetitions, as well as in the fast part, was entirely consistent.

Indeed, it is interesting to compare Lucy's icons with those that mark syntactic boundaries in written text as opposed to the actions of spoken language. In the real-time acts of speaking, we mark syntactic boundaries by leaving a "space of time" between syntactic units (clauses, sentences), whereas in writing we use signs such as commas or periods to mark these syntactic boundaries. It is important to note that, like Lucy's, neither these written signs nor any of our other textual symbols tell us anything about *measured time values* in speaking these texts. These are left to interpretation, responsive to the context, the expression, or the feelings we wish to convey.

With these new possibilities in hand, I reconsidered the meaning Lucy might be intending for the small, square rods. I noticed, for instance, that in clapping, it is obviously the silence that occurs between sounds that makes each clap a distinct entity. That is, it is the brief silence-time between claps that *generates boundaries* on this detailed level of structure. As before, the two meanings for Lucy's square rod in the beginning figure—shorter temporal value of a silence and fine-grained functional boundary-marker, are again necessarily coupled—the one generating the other. But if I decoupled the time value of the silence from its structural function, the meaning of the square rod in the fast part became clear: Lucy had again carried over to the fast part only the *functional* meaning of the square rods. The square rod, like the horizontal rod, had become a generalized iconic sign to mark syntactic boundaries. Perhaps in inserting the square rod in the fast part, Lucy was again recalling the children's earlier discussion. The square rod, as an iconic sign, would make sure that the kindergartners "get that it's two."

And looking back at the children's earlier puzzlement over boundaries, I could find further evidence for the importance Lucy and the others had given to boundary conditions. For instance, the fact that they even noticed something puzzling and that that led to their question of whether the "fast part" was one chunk or two revealed in the asking that there was something to be conceived of here. For if a "chunk" was not something conceived of, its boundaries could not become a matter of puzzlement or contention.

Recall Lucy and Ruth's first comments and Ruth's subsequent performance of the "fast part":

Lucy: "When you clap it, the fast part sounds like one big chunk instead of two." [Lucy claps]:

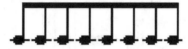

Ruth: You wait for a space. But there's really a clap. [Ruth claps]:

I now saw clearly the influence and the utility of the children's previous experience, their "prior texts in action." Through the questions they put to themselves, their comments, and Ruth's performance, the children had made a discovery—they demonstrated that you could hear the "fast part" as either one chunk or two. But if you wanted to hear two chunks, you had to "wait for a space." And with that in mind, I saw that the position of the "space" in Ruth's performance, along with its small boundary-making function, corresponded exactly to the position of Lucy's square rod in her instructions for the fast part (see Fig. 19.13).

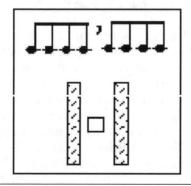

Figure 19.13.   An Exact Correspondence

Recalling my questions about playing the tune on the bells, I recognized more of what the children had learned and what Lucy had made use of. Remembering that Lucy had said, "… if you're playing it on the bells, you have to move to another bell in the fast part, and that makes it two … ," I noticed that Lucy's two long, upright rods in her seemingly anomalous instructions for the middle part, corresponded exactly to the two bells she and the others used for this fast part in their construction and performance of the tune on the bells. Moreover, the children's path-maker strategy with its implicit focus on structural function—the arrangement of the bells in order of occurrence, the inclusion of two bells of the same pitch but differing functions, and the separation of the bells into two groups marked by a space—was quite consistent with Lucy's attention to structural function in her instructions for playing the rhythm, as well. Indeed, the bell construction could have been a model, a previous text, which Lucy shaped to this new context. Perhaps this mapping, as shown in Figure 19.14, was more appropriate than the conventional mapping to the symbols of SRN.

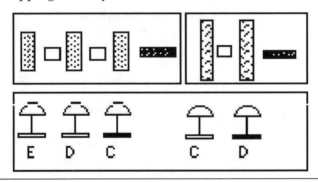

Figure 19.14.   Mapping to a Previous Text

CONVERSATION AND MULTIPLE REPRESENTATIONS

On reflection, Lucy's "text," like her bell construction, seems more a *structural analysis* than an effective set of instructions. However, making this distinction also illuminates the differences in function and utility among multiple possible representations. Every representation is an approximation, a partial description, and it is so in two senses. Each is *incomplete* in that it captures certain features while ignoring others, and each is *partial to* selected features—it "*favors* certain approximations." The rightness of a representation depends on what you want the representation to say and what you want to use it for. For example, the symbols of SRN favor the metric properties of a rhythm, and as a result, SRN is useful for giving instructions to a performer (at least within a certain approximation) with respect to the metric properties we assume to be the important ones. However, as already noted, SRN in its bare form tells us very little about rhythm of another kind—rhythmic grouping structure, phrase boundaries, or how to shape a phrase. This, like the rhythm of spoken text, is left to performers' interpretations, which, in turn, leads to puzzlements over the different possible "hearings" one can make—just the kinds of puzzlements over boundaries that the children posed at the beginning of the session.

In contrast, Lucy's instructions are not very effective in guiding another's performance. Indeed, they are misleading with respect to the number of events performed, and they give the performer only vague cues regarding the relative duration of events. But Lucy's instructions favor different approximations, and once understood as more *about* the rhythm than delivering specific directions, they could be useful to a performer in another way. Her patterns of rods are iconic rather than symbolic—something closer to pictures than to arbitrary notational elements that objectively refer to specific, abstract, formal properties. As such, her patterns are more like the expressive markings that composers or editors add to bare text. Like these markings, Lucy's text could also convey to prospective performers an aspect of musical structure that is usually associated with personal, intimate *feelings*—the expressive, gestural quality of rhythm—aspects that we often consider unexpressible in the rules we learn, or indeed within the neat, symbolic constraints of SRN.

Much as with a musician's performance of his or her own music, Lucy's construction collects together in a unique way varieties of culturally shared, near-and-far prior experiences, which she simultaneously reshapes to new context. Once I understood Lucy's invention by having a conversation back and forth with it, I learned that it expressed qualities of music that are usually expressed on the spot and in action—for example, the subtle fluctuations of tempo that shape a phrase or a whole piece but are not accounted for in SRN. And this produces a paradox: We believe that which we can say to the extent that we give privileged credence and tacit ontological commitment to the conventional notations indigenous to our professional Western culture and to the kinds of objects, features, and relations they display. But what we tacitly value most are those illusive qualities we *recognize* in action (e.g., what we call "a *musical* performance") but find difficult to make explicit within the notational systems and theories we teach. Perhaps what we cherish in our musical culture is what seems most mysterious, and in some sense we want to keep it that way.

> The realm of immediate qualities contains everything of worth and significance. But it is uncertain, unstable and precarious. The first consideration induces us to prize [it] supremely; the second leads us to deny reality to it as compared with alleged underlying things with their fixity and permanence. (Dewey, 1929, p. 114)

CONCLUSIONS: LEARNING TO INVENT MULTIPLE MEANINGS

What are the lessons to be drawn from these stories, especially concerning how and what we teach and learn? To begin with, we quite naturally, perhaps inevitably, bring to our classrooms the particular selections and distillations that have been made from our cultural tales over time—each one, in a way, a theory that favors certain approximations. Giving these distillations names, we teach them through the symbol systems devised to hold them steady on paper. We iron out inconsistencies by mounting rules that we have come to believe in, not only as descriptions but as explanations and accountings: normative behavior and its exceptions that we call "the curriculum." Going backward, we use our analytic stories to reinvent lived experience in the image of our assumptions and notations—those distillations from the past we have come to believe in. Certainly there is a need for a common vocabulary: If we wish to talk to one another, we need to define our terms. However, the analytic stories we tell rarely succeed because it is in the nature of language and of notations to break up and to reify. However, recognizing that what we can say is always partial, a selection, and that these selections may differ from those aspects we select in action (be it performing or listening), we continue to learn through our efforts to match our analyses with what remains unsaid in experience—the seamless meld, the all-at-once, successions of moments create meaning as they disappear in time.

What, then, should teaching be? Rather than trying to blur over, even hide, the tensions between our various ways of understanding and learning, perhaps we should make these tensions productive by putting them into active, constructive confrontation with one another. This would mean, first of all, seeing the conventional curriculum not as a "deliverable" but as a particular selection—a theory that favors certain approximations. As such, we can adopt a stance similar to the anthropologist and use the traditions we teach as an opportunity to inquire into the shared belief systems, the shared sense-making of our professional education culture. In doing so, we also need to recognize that this shared practice has a privileged status and that this increases the importance of inquiring into and learning its privileged ways of making sense—the bases for its selective distillation, simplification, smoothing, and displacement, and the assumptions built into its symbolic modes.

But at the same time, we need to inquire into and help our students inquire into *their* ways of making sense of common texts, examining the relationships between what we teach, what we do in action, and how we variously use and modify these texts in response to new contexts. By giving provisionally equal status to one another's practices-in-action, we can interrogate, distill, and indeed *invent* the implicit rules hidden in and embodied by what has become most familiar. In this way, teaching becomes a collaborative conversation, a creative process rather than merely a process of initiation.

Thus, the conversations retold in this chapter hold a common lesson: By asking in what ways any particular hearing or description might be made commensurate with or transformed into another, we can search for points of convergence and divergence among the multiple meanings made by individuals and among child and adult cultures. After all, the act of choosing a boundary, whether by Lucy's or Mary's criteria, is really a decision to give certain aspects precedence, to put certain elements to use, to notice some things and ignore others. Conversations such as these can serve to "liberate" previously unseen, unsaid, and unused aspects of the phenomena, while at the same time creating the powerful potential for students and teachers to choose selectively and effectively among them, depending on when, where, and what they want to use them for.

* * * * * * * * * * * * * * *

Hence the unsatisfactoriness of all our speculations. On the one hand, so far as they *retain* any multiplicity in their terms, they fail to get us out of the empirical sand-heap world; on the other, so far as they *eliminate* multiplicity the practical man despises their empty barrenness .... When weary of the concrete clash and dust and pettiness, [a person] will refresh himself by a bath in the eternal springs, or fortify himself by a look at the immutable natures. But he will only be a visitor, not a dweller in the region; he will never carry the philosophic yoke upon his shoulders, and when tired of the gray monotony of her problems and insipid spaciousness of her results, will always escape gleefully into the teeming and dramatic richness of the concrete world.

—*W. James (1956, pp. 67–69)*

ACKNOWLEDGMENT

I wish to thank my colleague, Evan Ziporyn, for his contributions to an earlier version of this chapter.

NOTES

1. The term "reflection-in-action" is discussed in other contexts in Schön, 1983.
2. For more on tune-building with the Montessori bells, see Bamberger, 1991.
3. The children's teacher is Mary Briggs who continued to work with these children over a period of 3 years. Her skill in gently inquiring into the sense and reason of the children's comments and their practical work, continued to be truly remarkable. (For more on children's learning in the Laboratory for Making Things and Mary Briggs' work with them, see Bamberger, 2005, 2006.)

REFERENCES

Bamberger, J. (1991). *The mind behind the musical ear: How children develop musical intelligence.* Cambridge: Harvard University Press.

Bamberger, J. (2005). How the conventions of music notation shape musical perception and performance. In D. Hargreaves, D. E. Miell, & R. MacDonald (Eds.), *Musical communications.* Oxford: Oxford University Press.

Bamberger, J. (2006). Restructuring conceptual intuitions through invented notations: From path-making to map-making. In E. Teubal, Dockrell, J., & Tolchinsky, L. (Eds.), *Notational Knowledge.* Rotterdam: Sense Publishers.

Bamberger, J., & Schön, D. A. (1991). Learning as reflective conversation with materials. In F. Steier (Ed.), *Research & reflexivity.* London: Sage.

Becker, A. L. (1984). Biography of a sentence: A Burmese proverb. In E. M. Bruner (Ed.), *Text, play, and story: The construction and reconstruction of self and society, 1983 Proceedings of the American Ethnological Society* (pp. 135–154). Prospect Heights, IL: Waveland Press.

Carroll, L. (1960). *The annotated Alice* (M. Gardner, Ed.). New York: Porter. (Original *Alice in Wonderland* published 1865)

Dewey, J. (1929). *Experience and nature.* New York: Norton.

James, W. (1956). The sentiment of rationality. In *The will to believe* (pp. 63–110). New York: Dover.

Morrison, P. (1991). Necessary white lies. Review of the book *How to lie with maps. Scientific American, 265,* pp. 139–140.

Olson, D. R. (1994). *The world on paper.* Cambridge: Cambridge University Press.

Schön, D. A. (1983). *The reflective practitioner: How professionals think in action.* New York: Basic Books.

The Shorter Oxford English Dictionary, Vol II. (1973). Oxford: Oxford University Press.

CHAPTER 20

Postscript: On the Interaction of Speech and Writing in Classroom Discourse

Carl H. Frederiksen

A central theme of *Talking Texts* is the argument that oral classroom discourse plays a central and pervasive role in shaping students' learning, their cognitive and language development, and their construction of knowledge and meaning in school. An important premise of this argument is that school discourse consists of both oral and written texts, both of which function to scaffold students' learning and development. *Oral texts* are forms of coherent oral conversational discourse that are co-constructed by students as they interact with a teacher and with each other in situations of collaborative classroom activity such as solving problems or engaging in discussions—including discussions of written texts. The introduction of written texts into situations of focused interactive classroom discussion is seen as facilitating the development of coherent oral discourse structures—i.e., the production of oral texts. Thus, it is hypothesized that in such situations classroom dialogue comes to share coherence characteristics with written texts that are used as a focus for classroom discussions ("talk about texts"). In such situations written texts often are used as models or resources to facilitate forms of interactive discourse associated with specific types of collaborative learning activity such as collaborative inquiry, knowledge-building, or problem-solving. Written texts also may be used in activities involving the production of written reports or other discourse products resulting from these activities such as journals, audio-visual presentations to a class, or communications over the web.

The structure and organization of such focused interactive classroom discourse is complex, reflecting an interaction of at least three levels of discourse processing activity: (1) the *cognitive level*, (2) the *social and interactional level*, and (3) the *situational level*. The cognitive level refers to the *cognitive representations and processes of the* participants in a conversational discourse that enable them to produce and interpret dialogue in a particular situation of conversational interaction. These cognitive representations and processes underlie and explain the coherence and organization of the semantic content of the discourse: the topics, inferences, and semantic relations that organize and connect the individual propositional meanings expressed during a conversation into a unified and meaningful structure (such as a narrative, a problem-solving dialogue, an explanation, or a logical argument); and the relationship of cognitive representations of a conversational discourse to the knowledge of its participants (e.g., frames, schemas and conceptual knowledge that are used in its production or comprehension). The social and interactional level refers to the *interactive conversational structure* of the discourse, that is, how the discourse reflects the social context and the patterns and processes of social interaction that are taking place among the participants in the dialogue, including the social roles and relationships among the participants. The situational level refers to the *situational context* of the dialogue, that is, the participation structure of a collabortive classroom activity; the characteristics of the task or activity; and cognitive processes and actions of the participants as they engage in the learning activity—for example their inferences and reasoning in attempting to solve a problem, understand a new concept or topic, or construct a logical argument to support a position on an issue.

These three levels of discourse processing interact in the way that participants in a classroom dialogue engage in distributed cognition through situated conversational interaction and task-oriented activity. Unless it is recorded or transcribed, a classroom discourse is a momentary and episodic event consisting of sequences of conversational turns and actions that are constructed and maintained over time only through the cognitive memory representations, inferences, and processes of conversational interaction of the participants in the dialogue. These processes directly reflect participants' interpretations of the situational context in which the oral discourse occurs. This context includes the social, physical, and activity contexts of the dialogue; and any symbolic (semiotic) objects, images, diagrams, or written language (including written) texts that are available as resources, produced, or used during the classroom dialogue and activity.

In contrast to oral classroom discourse, a *written text* is a permanent product constructed by a writer (or writers) to effectively convey a coherent meaning to a reader, guide a reader's comprehension and construction of meaningful representations, and influence a reader's multidimensional responses to the text. A text is designed for a specific purpose such as to inform, entertain, enlighten, assist, or invoke a poetic response by a reader; and it may be designed to conform to the standards of a particular text genre for use in particular situational contexts or by specific communities of users (e.g., a scientific report, a poem or play, or a history text). The structure and form of a written text reflect many factors including: its linguistic structure, the cohesion and topical organization of the discourse, the particular discourse genre and style, the coherence of its semantic content, the subject-matter domain of the discourse, the structure of knowledge in the domain, and how the text invokes inferences and responses on the part of its intended readers (Frederiksen, 1986; Frederiksen & Donin, 1991).

We are aware of the coherence and structure of written texts because they are "permanent" artifacts that can be subjected to analysis. With the availability of videotaping, it became possible to record and transcribe natural oral discourse and the context in which it occurs, making the coherence and structure of oral texts more visible and subject to analysis. Such analyses will have to include not only analysis of the linguistic and discourse structure of oral texts, their topical and semantic structure, and their conversational structure, but also the manner in which the discourse reflects dynamic processes of conversational interaction, individual and shared cognition, and collaborative action that underlie the dialogue.

Talking Texts focuses particularly on how oral texts that are produced by students through dialogic communication in classroom contexts (often but not always with the participation of a teacher) interact with written texts and come to embody not only coherent meaning structures similar to those found in written texts, but also the influence of written texts on the cognitive reasoning and thinking processes of the participants as they construct the dialogue. When students discuss written texts, or when they collaborate in producing written texts, the content and organization of their oral dialogue reflects and interacts with the content and organization of the written text they are discussing, or that of the text they are writing (or both, if they are using written texts as resources during collaborative writing). *Talking Texts* argues that in discussions involving the use of written texts or the production of written texts, that is, in "talk about texts," this interaction of oral dialogue with written text is a special and significant characteristic of classroom discourse. *Talking Texts* presents papers that are pertinent to the argument that through their participation in focused oral discussions in classrooms, including "talk about texts," children learn to create knowledge structures and develop increasingly advanced cognitive and discursive capabilities within school contexts. These competencies may consist of general communicative, reasoning, thinking and problem solving competencies; or they may consist of competencies associated with particular domains of instruction and learning such as in the natural sciences, history, social science, and the humanities including literature, art, music, and poetry.

This postscript examines the question of how to characterize the interaction of oral and written discourse in interactive situations of collaborative learning and practice such as occur in school or other situations of education and practice. It can be argued that effective collaborative learning situations involve conversational interaction within well-defined contexts of structured participation in situations of shared cognitive activity. Such situations of distributed cognition often involve participants' interaction with artifacts and objects in a task-oriented learning environment—including interaction with written texts, and they often involve the production of artifacts as products of their collaborative activity—including production of written texts. By conceptualizing "talk about texts" as a type of situated classroom activity, we can better understand and analyze how talk and written texts interact in specific learning situations. Moreover, such an analysis of interactive classroom discourse across different subject-matter disciplines can lead to a better understanding of how classroom discourse functions to scaffold students' construction of knowledge and development of competency in these disciplines, and how interaction with written texts facilitates this collaborative learning process.

With this perspective in mind, we will revisit the rich and varied forms and uses of oral and written discourse that have been presented in this unique volume, examining how they provide evidence of interactive uses of oral and written discourse to support students' learning and development of cognitive, social and situational aspects of competency. Finally, we will examine implications of the evidence presented in this volume for future research to better understand the interactions of cognitive and social processes in interactive classroom discourse; the influence of situational constraints in shaping classroom discourse; the particular characteristics of classroom discourse involving "talk about texts"; and the important role of situated classroom discourse, including "talk about texts", in scaffolding students' development of high-level cognitive, discursive, and social competencies within and across subject-matter disciplines.

FORMS AND USES OF ORAL AND WRITTEN DISCOURSE WITHIN EDUCATIONAL CONTEXTS

In organizing this volume, Rosalind Horowitz has asked leading researchers, scholars, and teachers to present examples of research and classroom discourse that show how oral and written discourse function together in school learning in a variety of contexts, and that "illustrate how oral discourse evolves in dialogic communication." In this way she wants to add "a semblance of balance and order to the past century's conflicting theories about oral and written language" in schooling. She aims, through this carefully chosen collection, to contribute to a "rich understanding of how inter-related and essential the oral and written are and how they might work together to create a new discourse that ultimately creates new knowledge." A main thesis of this volume is that oral and written discourse function together in school discourse to develop cognitive and linguistic capacities in students that enable them to move from "novice to expert thinker", and that they are the foundation not only for the development of literacy, but for the development of thinking, reasoning, discussing, and acting in a wide range of fields in the sciences and humanities.

The chapters presented here document relationships that interconnect oral and written language and discourse, both theoretically and practically, in their contexts of use in school settings. The central function of oral and written discourse in developing students' language and cognitive competencies and in enabling them "to move from novice to expert thinker" is supported by many of these examples. Many of the papers employ a constructivist learning perspective or a "neo-Vygotskian" social-developmental perspective to frame their discussion of specific examples of school dialogue, showing how the dialogue functions to scaffold students' learning processes in particular classroom situations. The chapters presented in this volume reflect a great variety of contexts and domains of interactive classroom discourse and include, as well, examples of out-of-school discourse. They also reflect different perspectives on oral and written discourse. It is this diversity that makes the collection of evidence presented here so interesting, as well as the attention the authors pay to the central theme of the volume.

The four parts of this volume address four questions related to the central theme of "talking texts." First, what are the distinctive characteristics of classroom discourse that make it special? Second, what does research on conversational discourse outside the classroom tell us about the oral discourse processing capabilities children bring to the school context? Third, what are the characteristics and forms of effective interactive discourse in classroom contexts? In particular, how do different forms of interactive classroom discourse function to scaffold and support students' construction of meaning and knowledge in specific disciplinary contexts, and their development of general and domain-specific competency in understanding, reasoning, thinking, and communicating effectively through oral and written discourse? Fourth, what are the characteristics of "talk that interacts with text"? More specifically, how does oral discourse that involves discussions about or production of written texts function to scaffold students' learning and development of competency in specific domains (e.g., in science or engineering)? How does classroom discussion of poetry, dialectic texts such as Socratic dialogues in philosophy or written talk from antiquity (the Talmud), or works of art or music function to scaffold students' development of competency in perception, interpretation, reasoning about beliefs and actions, and reflection about language, perception and meaning? And finally, how does talking about texts lead to the production of oral texts by students that increasingly reflect cognitive, linguistic and discourse characteristics of written texts?

Distinctive Characteristics of Oral Classroom Discourse

Given the distinctive yet overlapping nature of oral and written discourse in schooling, Horowitz (chap. 1, this volume) argues that we need to examine carefully the oral discourse styles that occur in school, and their relationship to academic uses of written texts. She identifies six characteristics that distinguish oral classroom discourse: (1) the distinctive and overlapping nature of talk and text, (2) the historical and individual evolution of talk about text, (3) the "co-occurrences, overlays, commingling and commentaries" of talk and text in classroom discussions, (4) institutional expectations and genres of talk in schools, (5) oral discourse styles found in school dialogue, and (6) development of talk in specific domains of academic study in schools. Based on her review of previous research, she finds that oral and written discourse are not so distinct in practice, and that oral discourse styles vary across domains taught in schools.

Horowitz and Olson (chap. 2, this volume) focus specifically on the use of written school texts, and on reading and comprehension in such situations. They ask how it is that children read and understand written school texts, identifying specific challenges school texts present to children. They observe that children confront school texts with prior goals, interests, beliefs, and assumptions about the appropriate uses of texts, and that these influence "how the text is taken." Unlike the "give and take" of oral dialogue, students often regard school texts uncritically as normative and authoritative sources of knowledge and information. These authors show how oral classroom discourse can provide a vehicle to enable students to develop skills in critical reading, and to learn to use text sources effectively and appropriately in specific domains of school learning. Their paper focuses on the crediting of sources, a specific discourse skill that is closely related to critical reading and the development of skill in the use of written texts as sources within the context of academic activities.

These chapters establish that classroom discourse consists of particular and specialized forms of discourse involving both oral discourse and written texts. Written texts used in school pose challenges to students to learn how to read critically and use written sources effectively and appropriately within learning situations and specialized domains of study. Classroom discourse provides an environment for developing skill both in critical reading, and in mastering styles of discourse communication and thought associated with effective learning in classroom situations and academic domains. As students develop competency in participating effectively in classroom discussions and their associated task-oriented academic activities, they develop the language and cognitive competencies they need for subsequent education at the college or university level. Development of these competencies is a central function of schooling. Research on how oral classroom discourse contributes to the development of these competencies can help to establish strategies for using instructional dialogue within classrooms to effectively scaffold students' development of these competencies.

Oral Discourse Competencies Children Bring to School

The papers in Part II document varieties of oral discourse competency that children bring to the school context, and the styles of oral dialogue and conversational structures that students' engage in a variety of settings outside of the classroom. In her paper, Sheldon (chap. 3, this volume) examines conversations of preschool children, emphasizing the richness of preschool children's exposure to and participation in dialogue in their communities in such contexts as families, neighborhoods, nursery schools, and daycare centers. Using recordings of children's conversations made in two daycare centers, she presents examples of children's conversations that demonstrate the extensive conversational skills young children possess when they enter school. Focusing on gender differences, she shows how girls have mastered a repertoire of sophisticated gender-specific conversational strategies such as verbal management of conflict and double-voiced discourse, and the ability to "talk about talk." Sheldon concludes that pre-school children's conversations are dynamic, rule-governed, systematically organized, and co-constructed oral texts. Conversation is a complex skill that is the foundation for learning to read: children produce and interpret oral texts that are far more complex than what they use when they start to read. By recognizing the oral discourse competencies of children entering school, schools can learn how to capitalize on children's well-developed oral conversational skills to facilitate their development of skill in oral classroom discourse communication and reading.

Stentström (chap. 4, this volume) focuses on characteristics of teenage talk, analyzing two examples of the natural dialogue of sixteen year old English schoolgirls: (a) a chat about boys, and (b) a discussion of "smoking, drinking and taking drugs." She focuses particularly on change of topic effects in these conversations. She found that each form of dialogue had its own characteristics: chats functioned as informal social activities and were unbalanced, whereas in discussions the girls considered a subject in detail from different points of view and came to a joint conclusion. Her results on the girls' natural discussions demonstrate many conversational abilities that ought to enable them to participate effectively in small group classroom discussions. Here we see evidence of the sophisticated conversational abilities that teenagers bring to classroom discussions. It would be interesting in future research to obtain data both on students' natural discussions and on their participation in classroom discussions to study directly how students make use of their conversational capabilities when they participate in school discussions.

In her paper, Blum-Kulka (chap. 5, this volume) examines dinner-table conversation in 34 Jewish-American and Israeli middle class families. Her analyses of these conversations shows how the conversation functions to socialize children in the "culturally structured activity of dinner," with parents provided "guided participation" in this conversational activity. She documents many aspects of the skill of participation in these conversations, emphasizing how children at dinner are treated as "ratified participants" in the speech events that are taking place. These conversations are particularly interesting as models of how adults guide children to enable them to learn to participate effectively in this type of discourse. As such, these results can inform research to identify effective mentoring strategies that teachers can use to scaffold students as they learn to participate effectively in classroom discussions.

Bayley and Schecter's paper (chap. 6, this volume) examines how Mexican immigrant families in Texas grapple with issues of language and schooling in dialogues with their children. The results are important for revealing the issues these families are dealing with in trying to support their children's success in English at school while they face complex issues involving tradeoffs between the conflicting goals of success in English language schools vs. language maintenance in Spanish. This paper reveals some of the complex challenges that these children face in developing facility for participating in oral classroom discourse and acquiring literacy skills in English, while continuing to function in Spanish at home and in their community. It documents the many issues facing Spanish-speaking children from the perspective of how their families' attempt to cope with these issues in their discourse interaction with their children.

Geva's paper (chap. 11, this volume) is pertinent both to establishing the oral discourse competencies children bring to schooling, as well as to developing these discourse competencies within school contexts (Part III). Geva reviews research on development of children's use of conjunctions in their oral language, and reports the results of a study of third and fifth grade children's understanding of conjunctions used in written texts. She argues that conjunctions are of particular interest because they signal logical relations in discourse such as cause-effect, contrast, additivity and conditionality. Geva reviews research showing that children display an understanding and use of conjunctions in their oral language. The order of acquisition of different conjunctions follows a "semantic complexity principal" in which older children learn to use conjunctions to encode more complex semantic relationships in text. For example, younger children will use *and* for additive purposes, while older children will use conjunctions in English that more accurately mark additive, causal, temporal and adversative logical relations. In her study of children's understanding and use of conjunctions, she reports results obtained using sentence completion tasks in which a sentence could be completed by choosing one of the conjunctions *because, and*, or *but*. Following the child's completion of the sentence, she presented questions testing the child's ability to choose a correct sentence elaborating the meaning of the conjunction. Sentences were used that were either a familiar content, or an unfamiliar content. Her results showed a developmental progression from grade 3 to grade 5, and a main effect of familiarity. However, in the unfamiliar case the grade difference was smaller, indicating that both the younger and the older children are challenged in using conjunctions correctly with unfamiliar text. In the unfamiliar condition, the relative difficulty of *but* and *and* over *because* was apparent. Thus, developmental changes in using conjunctions correctly in written texts and in correctly interpreting their meaning for unfamiliar texts mirrored results obtained in studies of children's use of conjunctions in oral language.

While his paper is concerned with acquiring competency in understanding the use of dialogue in drama, van Stapele's paper (chap. 14, volume) provides an interesting anecdote and reflection about the extent of children's understanding of story characters, situations, dialogues, and plot structures as reflected in their play (more specifically, "play acting" in which children invent elaborate stories that are enacted through invented dialogue among stuffed animals or other such "characters"). He argues that young children exhibit an understanding of many aspects of story structures in their play acting, creating plots in which characters enact conflicting plans and goals through their dialogue.

Given the particular styles of communication in oral classroom discourse, and the specific characteristics of school texts and oral school discourse (oral discourse in different academic learning situations, and discussions involving "talk about texts"), it is clear that classroom discourse poses particular challenges as well as opportunities to children as they develop competency in these forms of discourse communication and associated cognitive thinking processes. Children entering school must make a transition from the styles of oral conversational dialogue with which they are familiar in home, peer, play, and community settings, to styles of classroom dialogue that occur within school. Moreover, they enter school with varying degrees of familiarity with written texts, stories and other forms of text that they encounter in children's literature including stories read to them or that they may be able to read themselves, and stories that they invent in play. This transition to school discourse will also reflect differences in a child's home culture, community, educational level of the family, and language or dialect (the child's mother tongue and language(s) spoken at home and in the community). A significant issue for educators is to learn how to better capitalize on children's oral discourse competencies to enable them to become skilled both in oral classroom discourse and reading, and to enable children from diverse linguistic, social and cultural backgrounds to become effective participants in oral classroom discourse.

Forms of Interactive Discourse in School Contexts

The papers in Part 3 provide examples of oral classroom discourse consisting of extended, teacher- or tutor-mentored dialogues that are situated in contexts of collaborative learning activities within specific domains. Examples of collaborative learning activities are: developing a reasoned argument to resolve an issue through interactive discussion, constructing a meaningful interpretation for a text, developing differentiated knowledge of a concept and relating it to a story, and acquiring knowledge and skill in complex academic domains (such as algebra and research methods in psychology). These examples illustrate how participation in classroom dialogues can develop domain-specific knowledge and cognitive competencies, as well as more general competencies in oral discourse communication and critical reading.

Nguyen-Jahiel, Anderson, Waggoner and Rowell (chap. 7, this volume) report results of a case study of one experienced teacher's use of a classroom discussion method which they refer to as "collaborative reasoning" to "stimulate critical reading and thinking skills in elementary school students." The classroom discussions reported were based on 20 videotapes of discussions involving a teacher's interaction with a group of eight average reading ability fourth grade students. The immediate goal of the discussions was to facilitate students' development of competency to "use reasoned discourse as a means for choosing among competing ideas." The discussions focused on the big issues in a piece of literature as identified by the teacher, and on helping them learn to reason through these issues as revealed in the text. The teacher was coached to use several types of "instructional moves" that correspond to strategies reported in research on reciprocal teaching (Palincsar & Brown, 1984): prompting, modeling, asking for clarification, challenging students with alternative perspectives, encouraging, summing up, and fostering independence. The teacher introduce strategies of her own: position cards, student argument outlines, and debriefing sessions. The teacher adapted her use of these strategies to the students: which instructional move was used at a given time depended on the students' degree of control over their reasoning, rhetorical strategies, and the students level of independence. The teacher began with modeling reasoning for the students and using many instructional moves, and then gradually faded her support as the students developed independent collaborative reasoning ability. In this study the teacher was able to successfully mentor children's discussions when the cognitive and discourse competencies to be developed by means of the collaborative discussion were clearly defined (learning to produce reasoned arguments to support a position on an issue based on evidence), the tasks were clearly specified (defined by specific literary texts and their issues), and the teacher's mentoring strategies for scaffolding the children's discussions were also well-specified in terms of specific kinds of instructional "moves." Given that the teacher invented strategies of her own, it is likely that teachers who are experienced experts at this form of teaching might use additional strategies beyond those specified by the collaborative reasoning method.

Beck and McKeown (chap. 8, this volume) focus more generally on how teachers can support productive classroom discussions among students by "moving the thinking to the students." They contrast the "traditional initiation-response-evaluation" (IRE) method of conducting a classroom discussion to discussion in which the students are encouraged to freely "express their ideas and views." They argue that to accomplish this objective, they must take an active role in "enabling students to construct meaning" through the use of strategies such as prompting, guiding, challenging, and focusing. Examples of teacher facilitation of classroom dialogue were collected using an instructional approach they developed called "Questioning the Author." In this approach, the teacher poses queries about the author's intended meaning for students to consider as they read a text, and encourages collaborative discussion of how to construct meaning on the basis of ideas encountered in a text. The examples selected, which were based on work with five teachers and 120 fourth and fifth grade students, illustrate the teachers' development of skill in scaffolding "students' cognitive efforts toward making text meaningful." The least-successful teacher used a variant of the IRE method, dominating the classroom discussion and focusing on "getting the facts out" of the story. In contrast, the most successful teacher shared the floor with the students and used a variety of scaffolding strategies for fostering the students' processes in constructing meaning for a story. The third teacher, like the most "expert" teacher, shared the floor with the students but was unable to focus the discussion and scaffold the students' process of meaning construction. Teacher actions in successfully scaffolding students' meaning construction were identified and conceptualized in terms of six "discussion moves": marking, revoicing, turning back, recapping, modeling, and annotating. Like the previous paper, this paper provides evidence of a repertoire of "mentoring strategies" that are closely linked to the specific cognitive-task domain of constructing meaning for narrative stories. This paper highlights the difficulty of shifting from the pervasive IRE format for class discussion, to forms of instructional interaction that foster students' development of cognitive competencies in meaning construction through scaffolding. It highlights differences between "traditional" teacher-directed classroom discourse and more effective forms of teacher-mentored discussion. One implication is that research on oral classroom discourse should focus on forms of teacher-mentored dialogue that are effective in particular domains of learning, and the characteristics of such dialogue.

Saunders and Goldenberg (chap. 9, this volume) report results of a study of effects of use of "instructional conversation" (focused on differentiating a concept from the story: *friendship*, and relating their conceptualization of this concept and its relationship to the events of the story) vs. "recitation instruction" (a type of IRE focused on literal meaning: facts, event sequences) with fourth grade Hispanic students in the first year of transition from Spanish reading to English. In the control lessons, the talk focused on the facts and details of the text, while in the instructional conversation (IC) talk focused on the text in relation to the concept of friendship, the theme of the story. The results show that when literal comprehension was assessed, the two groups did not differ overall, but an assessment based on writing a post-lesson essay "explaining what friendship is" revealed that the IC group produced "more sophisticated and differentiated understandings" of the complex concept of friendship. However, when the students were grouped into high, medium, and low English proficiency groups, literal comprehension was higher under the IC condition than for the control for the high and medium proficiency students, and lower but not significantly different for the low English proficiency students. These results provide preliminary evidence that for Spanish-speaking English language learners, IC focused on high-level concepts in a story can facilitate children's development of higher levels of understanding without having any negative effect on their literal comprehension skills. The study provides an example of how the effects of participation in particular types of oral classroom discourse on students learning and development can be studied.

Hacker and Graesser (chap. 10, this volume) report the results of a study of reciprocal teaching strategies, focusing on dialogue in a tutoring situation which they refer to as "naturalistic tutoring" in which a more advanced student tutors a less advanced student in a particular domain of tutoring. Two tutoring situations were considered: (1) graduate students in psychology tutoring undergraduates on topics in a research methods course; and (2) high school students tutoring seventh grade students in algebra. While the authors recognize that there are many factors that can be considered in explaining the reported superiority of individual tutoring over "classroom instruction," they report that three emerged as having particular importance in their data: (a) collaborative problem solving and question answering, (b) extensive use of problem examples, and (c) deep explanatory reasoning. They focus specifically on collaborative question answering. They describe the dialogue patterns they observe in their tutoring examples in terms of five steps: (1) Tutor asks a question, (2) Student answers, (3) Tutor provides feedback on the student's answer, (4) the Tutor and the Student collaborate through conversational exchanges to improve the answer, (5) the Tutor assesses the Student's understanding of the answer. Step 4, collaboration, is singled out as the most critical component of the dialogue in which their student tutors rely on five specific strategies reported to be used in reciprocal teaching: pumping, prompting, splicing, hinting, and summarizing. While it was not clear from the paper whether or not the student tutors received any instruction in how they should approach the task of tutoring, the results seem to show that when students are asked to tutor less experienced students, they adopt an approach to tutoring that incorporates aspects of the traditional IRE classroom pattern (in steps 1 to 3), but shifts to using reciprocal teaching strategies in what appears to be a period of coaching the student (step 4), followed by dialogue to evaluate their understanding (step 5). In addition, their extensive use of problem examples and deep explanatory reasoning resemble characteristics that are found in studies of tutoring by experienced tutors.

Characteristics of "Talk That Interacts with Text"

These chapters provide examples of how written discourse can be used in conjunction with oral classroom discourse functions as instruments for developing students' general and domain-specific knowledge and cognitive competencies. In two of these papers, written text is used, in conjunction with oral discourse, as an instrument for developing cognitive competencies in specific domains: conducting scientific inquiry, and engineering design.

Polman and Pea (chap. 12, this volume) provide examples in which grade 11 students worked cooperatively in small groups using interactive oral and written communication (face-to-face discussion and communication by means of e-mail messages), to design and conduct an open-ended research project in science requiring: selecting a group topic, writing-up background information, providing a research question, collecting and analyzing data (over the internet), and completing and revising a research report. One group selected the domain of UFO sightings, using a research report on UFO sightings on the internet to verify the truth or falsity of the explanation cited in another report in which UFO sightings were attributed to natural phenomena. The second group examined whether there are preferred paths of hurricane movement in the northern hemisphere of the Americas. In addition to their face-to-face discussions, the students were mentored by a scientist with whom they could communicate by e-mail. Using suggestions from their teacher and (for Group 2, using e-mail suggestions from their scientist mentor), students produced a report of their research. These researchers examine dialogue sequences that they identified as "transformative," sequences which functioned to support students' creation of new conceptual structures that help them gain new insights and re-conceptualize the problem in the conduct of their research projects.

Geisler and Lewis (chap. 13, this volume) present examples of dialogue among engineering students' as they work on a complex design problem (designing a powered mobility device for use by cerebral palsy children). In the dialogue, they make use of source texts, synthesizing information from different sources in order to carry out a "functional analysis" of the problem. They composed "non-linear texts" which facilitated their oral discussion and development of a design, a process the authors describe as "the text-making of world-making." Rather than using the process of text-consulting to construct "free-standing text worlds," text consultation in solving design problems functions to relate text representations of the world to the "world" of the design problem "outside the borders of the text."

Critical reading in such contexts is motivated by the purpose at hand. The teacher appears to have functioned in the role of mentor to help students develop design expertise in a realistic problem-solving context that simulates real-life professional practice.

In three papers, drama scripts and poetic texts were used as the focus of classroom discussions in which classroom discourse and activities were used to develop students' cognitive competencies in understanding, interpreting, analyzing, and reflecting on these texts. Van Stapele's paper (chap. 14, this volume) focuses on the development of skill in reading and analyzing dialogue in drama texts, and the performance of dramas. He outlines an approach to the analysis of drama which focuses on the structure of the dialogue and how dialogue in stage dramas functions as the sole means by which to advance the story. He shows how dramatic dialogues begin with stage directions (which provide minimal information to interpret the story), and subsequently consist entirely of dialogue in which information about the story is found within characters' individual speech acts, movement in the dialogue reflected in patterns of actions and reactions in the dialogue , "beats" (changes in the direction of the dialogue, i.e., who initiates conversational exchanges), changes in deictic references (e.g., "I" and "You") in the dialogue, and characters violations of conversational postulates. He also discusses the importance of observing performances of the play. He then outlines a process for learning to read and study dialogue based on his method of dialogue analysis. Results are presented consisting of a dramatic dialogue written by students with coaching by an experienced scriptwriter, and examples from the students' discussion of the dialogue using a "meta-language" they had learned previously. Besides providing an example of an effective approach to collaborative learning in a complex domain of expertise, the domain of drama interpretation, writing, direction and performance is particularly interesting because dialogue itself is the object of study through carefully scaffolded student dialogue.

Hanauer (chap. 15, this volume) provides us with an interesting cognitive analysis of conventionalist and formalist theories of poetry and of the process of constructing meaning while reading poetry. He presents a model of poetry reading as a process in which specific textual features of a poem interact with the cognitive control system of the reader and the reader's knowledge, a process in which the reader's attention is directed to specific formal features and patterns of the poem. These patterns activate schemata which are used in the process of constructing meaning for the poem. The paper presents an example of poetry reading in the context of small group discussion in the classroom. Hanauer uses this example of children discussing a humorous poem to show how the classroom discourse enables them to participate in discussing how the meaning is constructed, how the meaning evolves as they read the poem, the possibility of multiple understandings of sections of the poem (polysemy), the various levels of language structures (formal text features) that are involved in meaning construction, and multiple subjective ways of constructing meaning. Thus, the classroom discourse makes explicit for the students many aspects he identified in his model of the cognitive processes involved in the expert reading of a poem.

Donnelly and Egan (chap. 16, this volume) present an extended example of a structured classroom discussion obtained with five and six year old boys and girls in a Dublin, Ireland, junior school using a technique they refer to as "thinking time." Children sit in a circle and, mentored by a teacher, engage in a discussion of a topic chosen by consensus on the previous day. A child opens the discussion making an initial statement, touches the arm of the child next to him giving him an opportunity to speak, and this proceeds from child to child around the circle until it is the teachers turn, and this process is repeated. They describe the resulting dialogue as a "Socratic dialogue structure" facilitated by the teacher. In the final "trip" around the discussion circle, the children can make a final statement about the issues which were discussed. They often "begin a session with a particular text that lends itself to philosophical reflection," or they may use a picture or sculpture to invoke discussion. They present a lengthy transcript of an example of this dialogue, and comment on how it provides evidence of "student reflection on language and its leading to sophisticated reflection about their world and experience." They observe that in such dialogues, the teacher acts as a facilitator, assisting the children and modeling forms of speech and thought. What the authors see as most important is that children gain a sense of "belonging to a community of reflective people through the process of text openly shared," leading to improved reasoning and expressive skills.

In his paper, Neusner (chap. 17, this volume) discusses the Talmud as a unique type of written text that incorporates records of "important discussions in the form of dialectical arguments," and he argues that classroom discussion of the Talmud can develop competency in thinking and reasoning about beliefs. He provides us with background and an example from the Talmud and shows how the Talmud is a record of "written thought" consisting of passages of religious law code that are accompanied by accumulated commentaries about the law code stated in the passage. The Talmud is a carefully crafted text that is meant not only to be read, but also "meant to be talked about," welcoming the student as "one who wishes to join in the argument." Neusner observes that the Talmud is itself "talk about texts" recorded as text, to serve as a basis of additional "talk about text." Using examples from the Talmud, he illustrates the characteristic way in which it sets forth not only decisions on matters, but also the choices faced in making a decision, the basis for deciding a matter in one way (or another), and the arguments associated with decisions. He argues that the reading of the Talmud provides a model for classroom dialogue as a means for making students part of a thought process associated with a document. Just as discussion of the Talmud in religious schools fosters processes of skilled dialectic thought, it provides a model of how participation in classroom dialogues can develop competencies in reasoned argumentation and decision making in students.

The final two chapters provide examples of how oral discussions can develop competency in interpreting works of art, and in understanding the structure of musical compositions and their representation. Wilson (chap. 18, this volume) focuses on the interpretation of works of visual art. He reviews how, in response to postmodernism, art educators argued that art education should focus on the study of art as a discipline, with the objective of mastering the content knowledge and inquiry processes found in the disciplines of the visual arts. This led to the establishment of Discipline Based Art Education (DBAE) classrooms that focused on the interpretation of artworks. Discipline-based strategies for teaching art balance the making and the study of artworks. Wilson presents an excerpt from a student discussion in which students were asked to interpret a pre-civil war painting of a family. The student discussion led to a discussion touching on the roots of race relationships and the issue of slavery, and the beginnings of attempts to "assess the contradictions between religious and social values and practices." In parts of the discussion "students connected their interpretations of artworks to their own lives." He uses this example to illustrate that the "educational potential" of a work of art relates to how it is interpreted. The remainder of the paper focuses on students interpretations of artworks, and how participation in such discussions in DBAE classrooms with the mentorship of a teacher helped the children to develop "more insightful, valid and well-reasoned interpretations of artworks' main ideas" (as compared to traditional art instruction which emphasized production of artworks), and to "acquire an ability to direct their own conversations and arrive at interpretative closure without adult leadership." Following presentation of a piece artwork, students were asked to write their "individual thoughts about the work's main idea," identify aspects of the art that show the main ideas (evidence), and explain what the work means, and to cite evidence to support their views. Content analysis procedures were used to evaluate their interpretations, evaluating their conclusions about the work's main ideas and the types of evidence they cited to support their conclusions. The results indicated that the DBAE students were better able to identify main ideas expressed by the work, and cite sensory, formal, and expressive evidence, and symbolic and metaphoric evidence in their interpretations. They also indicated the students were able to relate a work to other types of evidence such as the social conditions associated with its creation, aesthetic and stylistic factors, factors in the history of the artist, and to aspects of their own lives. The study shows how the production of written compositions can be used to assess the effects of instructional approaches the are based on oral classroom discussions that are focused on developing discipline-based expertise.

Bamberger (chap. 19, this volume) takes us into the domain of music, presenting examples of teacher-student discussions in the context of collaborative learning about the structure of musical composition and representation. Working with a special Education Teacher and students in an after school-place called the "Laboratory for Making Things," examples of children's oral conversations with a teacher are presented to collaboratively learn how to build things and make sense of their building objects and activity. The conversations reported take place during a "tune-building task" in which they are given a familiar and simple tune ("Hot Cross Buns"), and they "build the tune" using Montessori bells. They then "clap the rhythm," and "make instructions to tell a younger child how you did it" (using Cuisenaire rods as materials). Bamberger analyzes the children's productions and their discussions to reveal the cognitive processes they are using to build the tune. Her analysis shows that students function either sequentially as "path-makers', moving locally from one note to another, or they function as "map makers," using a more complex structure to group the notes in constructing the tune. The instructional tasks revealed how, through their discussions with the teacher, the children developed and discussed different ways for representing the structure of the tune. Bamberger uses these examples to show how these children were learning to "invent multiple meanings" by engaging in learning through collaborative dialogue with a teacher. This study shows how, in carefully specified task environments, student-teacher discussions can "make visible" as topics for discussion very subtle aspects of the students' cognition and representation in specific task domains.

THE ROLE OF SITUATED CLASSROOM DISCOURSE IN THE DEVELOPMENT OF COGNITIVE, COMMUNICATIVE AND SOCIAL COMPETENCIES: IMPLICATIONS FOR RESEARCH AND PRACTICE

The papers in this collection establish the breadth and diversity of classroom discourse and the many ways in which "talk about text" can influence the nature of classroom discourse. Important challenges for future research will be: to apply consistent discourse analysis methods across domains to analyze interactive classroom discourse as a cognitive, interactive social, and situated process; to establish what forms of classroom discourse are effective in scaffolding students' development of high-level cognitive, communicative and social competencies within and across subject-matter disciplines; and to track students' learning and development of competencies in classroom contexts in which there is consistent use of these forms of classroom discourse.

Based on the large and representative body of evidence presented in this volume, it is clear that if we shift our focus away from traditional teacher-controlled instructional discourse—typically consisting of IRE sequences in which a teacher initiates the dialogue with a question (usually seeking specific information), followed by student responses, and then feedback provided by the teacher—to more complex and effective forms of teacher-mentored student dialogue consisting of discussion focused on a complex and motivating activity such as performing a challenging task, solving an interesting problem, or interpreting a written text or other object (visual art, music), we will be able to see much more varied forms of classroom conversational discourse that function to effectively support students' learning and development of competency within specific subject-matter domains. While the teacher's role and mentoring strategies may vary across these dialogues, the role of the teacher is often one of scaffolding the students' knowledge-building and thinking as well as their dialogue with one-another. For example, a teacher may begin the dialogue with a topic, issue, problem to be solved; or by presenting students with a complex question requiring collaborative discussion and deliberation. If the students need help in getting their discussion started, the teacher may initiate the discussion by proposing a possible contribution to the discussion or step in "solving the problem" to guide the students reasoning or problem-solving. In complex domains, the teacher may model possible arguments pertaining to an issue, or methods for solving a problem. As the students' "take up" the discussion or problem-solving activity themselves, the teacher may then shift to a role as mentor or coach, providing guidance, feedback, and assistance to the students' when it is needed. This scaffolding assistance is gradually faded as the students' ability to independently construct the dialogue and engage in the reasoning and actions needed to solve the problem increases.

This framework of "modeling, scaffolding, and fading" may take a variety of forms depending on the domain of discussion and activity, the composition of the group (including its linguistic and socio-cultural composition), the level of prior knowledge and experience of the students, and the school, classroom and situational context of the dialogue. The teacher's scaffolding will be apparent in both the content and the conversational structure of the dialogue. Yet despite the diversity of such school discourse, this "cognitive apprenticeship" model seems to be consistent with a great variety of non-traditional, small-group, task-oriented classroom dialogue. It is also consistent with a constructivist learning perspective and a "neo-Vygotskian" social-developmental perspective on students' learning and development. Analysis of the socio-cognitive processes involved in partici-pating in such dialogue can uncover the mechanisms and styles of "cognitive ap-prenticeship" (Collins, Brown & Newman, 1989) by which interactive classroom discourse functions to scaffold and shape students' learning, and support their de-velopment of general cognitive, language and discourse competencies and their development of knowledge and cognitive competency in specific academic domains.

To better understand these processes, researchers will need to take the next steps to investigate more directly the socio-cognitive processes by which partici-pation in interactive instructional dialogue in school, or in other educational con-texts, functions to scaffold students' learning, and their development of cognitive competencies and domain-specific knowledge and expertise. Such a research ap-proach will have to show how the interactive social structure of conversational school discourse interacts with the cognitive representation and processing of the discourse in a context of performing a learning task or activity collaboratively. The conversational structure of these instructional dialogues includes conversational moves and mentoring strategies used by the teacher, and the pattern of the stu-dents' contributions to the dialogue with the teacher and with each other. The se-mantic content of the discourse reflects the individual propositional meanings asserted by the participants' and how these meanings reflect their knowledge, in-ferences, reasoning, and problem-solving actions in developing (co-constructing) argument structures, solutions to problems, and representations of knowledge and meaning through their dialogue and collaborative activity.

This research will require the analysis of conversational discourse from multi-ple perspectives that reflect (a) the situational context including the social compo-sition of the group and the specific collaborative learning activity, (b) the patterns and organization of the conversational discourse as reflected in the structure of the dialogue among participants in the learning activity, and (c) the semantic content of the situated discourse as it reflects the inferences and knowledge individual participants bring to the conversation in making their contributions to the dia-logue in the context of participating in the learning activity. Through its conversa-tional structure and its semantic content, the dialogue reflects processes of distributed cognition in the context of performing the collaborative learning activ-ity. By analyzing the contributions each participant makes to the dialogue, we can see how the collaborative activity reflects the contributions of each participant. The students' contributions will reflect their knowledge, cognitive processes, and their level of development of competency in the domain; while the teacher's con-tributions will reflect modeling and coaching strategies in mentoring the students learning, and changes in these strategies as the students' expertise develops.

An example of the analysis of a short excerpt from a dialogue among students and a tutor in a medical problem-based learning (PBL) group is provided by the "My Theory" example of dialogue which was analyzed from multiple perspec-tives in the special issue of *Discourse Processes* edited by Koschmann (Koschmann, 1999; Koshmann & Evensen, 2000). In this example, the medical students were solving a diagnostic problem with coaching support provided by a tutor. Solving the diagnostic problem involved: (a) applying a "differential diagnosis procedure frame" to develop a list of possible diagnoses of the patient's condition based on the clinical evidence, (b) the construction of causal explanations of the patient's clinical symptoms (the evidence), (c) collaborative reasoning to evaluate alternative diagnostic hypotheses as explanations of the case evidence and to select a leading hypothesis, and (d) contributing to a conversational discourse in which participants contributed to the collaborative problem-solving through their participation in the conversation. There was a particular interest in the contributions made by the tutor and how they functioned to guide the students' diagnostic problem solving.

Frederiksen (1999) applied several techniques of content and conversation analysis to this discourse to explore how the interactive discourse reflected these aspects of collaborative problem solving and to study how the tutor's contributions to the discourse functioned to scaffold the students' problem solving. The analysis of the dialogue revealed that: (a) a differential diagnosis frame served to organize the students' conversational discourse, (b) the medical students collaborated in constructing causal models to explain the patient's clinical symptoms through their contributions to the dialogue; (c) the students engaged in collaborative reasoning to select a preferred diagnostic hypothesis; and (d) the conversational interaction structure provided the vehicle for this distributed cognitive activity. In addition, the tutor's interventions, though relatively few in number, occurred at crucial points in the discourse and functioned to guide the students' use of the differential diagnosis frame to organize their diagnosis of the case. This example illustrates how the process of conversational interaction provided a medium for extended collaborative cognitive activity in situations of complex reasoning and problem solving, and how the conversation provided opportunities for the tutor to scaffold the students' problem solving.

Similar techniques have been applied to study expert tutoring in engineering (Frederiksen, Roy, & Bedard, 2006), in statistics (Frederiksen & Donin, 2005), and in the analysis of developing clinical expertise in medicine (Frederiksen, Donin, Koschman, & A. Kelson, 2006). By applying multiple methods to study social interaction and cognitive processes in classroom discourse, we can study how the discourse reflects the underlying cognitive processes of students as they perform a collaborative activity, and how each student contributes to this activity through his or her contributions to the dialogue. The teacher's process of mentoring the students can also be studied by analyzing the extent and location of the teacher's contributions to the dialogue. Students development of competency in such situations will be reflected in a reduction in the tutor's contributions to the dialogue, and in the success of the students problem solving and reasoning process as reflected in the content of their dialogue.

It is essential that stronger and more specific connections be made between the characteristics and processes of interactive classroom discourse, on the one hand, and students' development of cognitive and socio-cognitive competencies, on the other. The importance of this linkage between interactive classroom discourse and its consequences for students' learning and development of competency cannot be underestimated. Many educators and researchers in the fields of cognition and instruction have presented data and theoretical arguments to support the argument that collaborative learning scaffolded by an experienced tutor, coach, or teacher is the most effective means of developing high level cognitive competencies and knowledge, both in school and in higher levels of the education system. Research is needed to show how interactive instructional discourse functions within specific situations to enable students to construct knowledge, arrive at new comprehension and understanding, and learn to think, reason, carry out actions, and solve problems in specific domains of knowledge and activity. Thus, in addition to documenting general effects of collaborative classroom discourse practices, this research will have to show how effective classroom discourse, including discourse involving the production and use of written texts, functions to scaffold students' learning and development of knowledge and competencies in specific disciplinary contexts.

The examples provided in this volume provide evidence suggesting that oral classroom discourse, including interactive discourse combined with written text, can effectively develop cognitive competencies in students. Through studies applying consistent discourse analysis methods to teacher-mentored student dialogue obtained with teachers who are experienced at mentoring groups of students in specific domains of learning, we should be able to better specify processes of expert mentoring that are effective in specific subject-matter domains. Models of expert mentoring, resulting from such studies, can be used to enable more teachers to use effective forms of mentored classroom discourse in their teaching. The great variety of productive classroom dialogues that have been presented in this volume offer the promise of many effective ways in which teaching practices can be enriched by incorporating forms of oral classroom discourse that scaffold students' learning and include talk about written texts. They demonstrate forms of classroom discourse that effectively scaffold students' oral and written discourse, and their development of domain-specific cognitive and discourse competencies. By applying consistent discourse analysis methods across domains, it will be possible to identify general characteristics of classroom discourse that effectively support students learning and development of both general and domain-specific cognitive, communicative and social competencies.

REFERENCES

Collins, A., Brown, J. S., & Newman, S. E. (1989). Cognitive apprenticeship: Teaching the crafts of reading, writing and mathematics. In L. B. Resnick (Ed.), *Knowing, learning and instruction: Essays in honor of Robert Glaser* (pp. 453–494). Hillsdale, NJ: Lawrence Erlbaum Associates.

Frederiksen, C. H. (1999) Learning to reason through discourse in a problem-based learning group. *Discourse Processes, 27*(2), 135–160.

Frederiksen, C. H. (1986). Cognitive models and discourse analysis. In C. R. Cooper & S. Greenbaum (Eds.), *Written communication annual: Vol. I. Studying writing: Linguistic approaches* (pp. 226–227). Beverly Hills, CA: Sage.

Frederiksen, C. H., & Donin, J. (1991). Constructing multiple semantic representations in comprehending and producing discourse. In G. Denhière & J.-P. Rossi (Eds.), *Texts and text processing* (pp. 19–44). Amsterdam, the Netherlands: North-Holland.

Frederiksen, C. H., & Donin, J. (2005). Coaching and the development of expertise: designing computer coaches to emulate human tutoring in complex domains. In S. Pierre (Ed.), *Développement, integration et evaluation des technologies de formation et d'apprentissage* [Development, integration and evaluation of technologies for learning and training]. Montréal, Canada: Presses Internationales Polytechnique.

Frederiksen, C. H., Donin, J., Koschman, T., & Kelson, A. (in press). *Investigating diagnostic problem-solving in medicine through cognitive analysis of clinical discourse.* Paper being revised for publication. May be found at *http://www.mcgill.ca/edu-acsrg/research/competence/*

Frederiksen, C. H., Roy, M., & Bedard, D. (2006). *Expert tutoring in engineering: Tutorial discourse and the development of expertise.* Unpublished manuscript.

Koschmann, T. (1999). Editor's Introduction. The edge of many circles: Making meaning of meaning making. *Discourse Processes, 27*(2), 103–117.

Koschmann, T., & Evensen, D. H. (2000). Five readings of a single text: Transcript of a videoanalysis session. In D. H. Evensen & C. E. Hmelo (Eds.), *Problem-based learning: A research perspective on learning interactions* (pp. 137–166). Mahwah, NJ: Lawrence Erlbaum Associates.

Palinscar, A. S., & Brown, A. L. (1984). Reciprocal teaching of comprehension-fostering and comprehension-monitoring activities. *Cognition and Instruction, 1,* 117–175.

Contributors

Richard C. Anderson
Center for the Study of Reading
University of
    Illinois-Urbana–Champaign
Champaign, Illinois
USA

School of Psychology
Beijing Normal University
Beijing, China

Department of Applied Social Sciences
Faculty of Health and Social Sciences
Hong Kong Polytechnic University
Hung Hom, Hong Kong

Jeanne Bamberger
Music and Urban Education
School of Humanities, Arts, and Social
    Science
Massachusetts Institute of Technology
Cambridge, Massachusetts
USA

Robert J. Bayley
Department of Linguistics
College of Letters and Science
University of California, Davis
Davis, California
USA

Isabel L. Beck
Department of Instruction and Learning
School of Education Learning Research
    and Development Center
University of Pittsburgh
Pittsburgh, Pennsylvania
USA

Shoshana Blum-Kulka
Department of Communication and
    Journalism
Faculty of Social Sciences
Hebrew University of Jerusalem
Mt. Scopus, Jerusalem
Israel

Philomena Donnelly
Early Childhood Education
Faculty of Education
St. Patrick's College
Drumcondra, Dublin
Ireland

Kieran Egan
Faculty of Education
Simon Fraser University
Burnaby, British Columbia
Canada

Carl H. Frederiksen
Department of Education and Counseling
    Psychology
Faculty of Education
McGill University
Montreal, Quebec
Canada

Cheryl Geisler
Rhetoric, Composition, & Information
    Technology
Department of Language, Literature,
    and Communication
Rensselaer Polytechnic Institute
Troy, New York
USA

Esther Geva
Department of Human Development
   and Applied Psychology
Ontario Institute for Studies
   in Education (OISE)
University of Toronto
Toronto, Ontario
Canada

Claude Goldenberg
School of Education
Stanford University
Stanford, California
USA

Arthur C. Graesser
Department of Psychology
College of Arts and Sciences
Center for Applied Psychological
   Research
The University of Memphis
Memphis, Tennessee
USA

Douglas J. Hacker
Department of Educational Psychology
School of Education
The University of Utah
Salt Lake City, Utah
USA

David Ian Hanauer
English Department
The College of Humanities and Social
   Sciences
Indiana University of Pennsylvania
Indiana, Pennsylvania
USA

Rosalind Horowitz
Department of Interdisciplinary
   Learning and Teaching
Department of Educational Psychology
College of Education and Human
   Development
The University of Texas—San Antonio
Downtown Campus
San Antonio, Texas
USA

Barbara Lewis
Center for Communication Practices
Department of Language, Literature,
   and Communication
Rensselaer Polytechnic Institute
Troy, New York
USA

Margaret G. McKeown
Department of Instruction and Learning
School of Education
Learning Research and Development
   Center
The University of Pittsburgh
Pittsburgh, Pennsylvania
USA

Jacob Neusner
History and Theology
The Institute of Advanced Theology
Bard College
Annandale-on-Hudson, New York
USA

Kim T. Nguyen-Jahiel
College of Education
Center for the Study of Reading
The University of Illinois–Urbana–
   Champaign
Champaign, Illinois
USA

David R. Olson
Department of Human Development
   and Applied Psychology
Ontario Institute for Studies in Education
Faculty of Education
University of Toronto
Toronto, Ontario
Canada

Roy D. Pea
Learning Sciences
School of Education
Stanford Center for Innovations
   in Learning (SCiL)
Stanford University
Stanford, California
USA

Joseph L. Polman
Division of Teaching and Learning
    Division of Educational Psychology
College of Education
University of Missouri – St. Louis
St. Louis, Missouri
USA

Betty Rowell
Columbia Center School
Champaign, Illinois
USA

William M. Saunders
Center for Research on Education,
    Diversity, and Excellence
California State University, Long Beach
Long Beach, California
USA

LessonLab Research Institute
Santa Monica, California
USA

Sandra R. Schecter
Theoretical and Applied Linguistics
Faculty of Education
York University
Toronto, Ontario
Canada

Amy Sheldon
Department of Communication Studies
    and Program in Linguistics
College of Liberal Arts
The University of Minnesota–Twin
    Cities
Minneapolis, Minnesota
USA

Anna-Brita Stenström
Department of English
Faculty of Arts
University of Bergen, Norway
Bergen, Norway

Peter van Stapele
Department of Literature
Faculty of Arts
Leiden University
Leiden, The Netherlands

World Education Fellowship
Den Haag, The Netherlands

Martha Waggoner
Danville Public Schools Danville, Illinois
USA

Brent Wilson
School of Visual Arts
College of Art and Architecture
Penn State University
University Park, Pennsylvania
USA

Author Index

Subject Index

A

Activity
co-constructive activity, 335
design engineers, 317
evolving action, 451
repeated activity, 367, 372
task situation-internalization, 40
Arguments; see also Conflict
central issues, 4–6
claims and unsupported claims, 147–150
dialectical arguments, 398, 403, 404, 405;
    Talmudic, 401–403, 405
ethical issues, 405, 406–409
evidence, 189–191, 408–409
facts, 191
for real-life dilemmas, 97, 189–204, 320
    fig. 13.1, 387, 397
line of argument, 199–200, 414
logical positions, 404–405
moving, 397, 402
multiple argument strategies, 5–6, 29, 106
negotiation reasoning, 195; see also collab-
    orative reasoning
fallacies, 382
oral commentary (the Mishnah), 397–398,
    403, 405, 407, 411–412, 413, 414–416
purposes of, 5–6
questions, 193; and self questions, 34–35

B

Background knowledge, 31, 231
Body, talk, and text
imprint of bodies, 381
sense organs, 441

C

Changes; see also Language, over time
conceptual, 64
Children's
bilingual storybooks, 19, 162
friendships, 107, 221
inferences, 93, 371
play, 98, 103–106, 336

reflection on language, 272, 382
siblings, 159, 336
Children's speech
copycat games, 60–61
highly ritualized, 19
language-based, 93–94
meaning-based, 363
parroting, 19, 61
with sibling and peers, 6, 26, 159–161
secrets, 63
structural complexity of, 272
turn-taking, 136, 139–140
Cognition; see also Domains of Knowledge
and causality, 260, 37
Cognitive Apprenticeship Model, 31, 477
consciousness, 31, 372, 373 (see also mind)
constructivism learning, 208, 297
conventionalists vs. formalists, 297, 365
cultural and physical tools, 300
deeper understanding, 57, 273–275
distributed intelligence across persons,
    298–301
"hold still" action, 440
and humor, 371
information processing, 272, 321–322, 325
introspection, 381, 406
multiple interpretations, 367, 368
negotiation of meaning, 72, 209–210,
    256–257
problems and solutions, 291
in real-time, 300
Collaborative Reasoning (CR)
controversial problems, 189
critical reading and thinking, 187, 200–202,
    243
guiding arguments, 187, 195, 307
instructional, 202–204
for language arts, 187–188, 190–198, 204,
    373
medical students' causal mode, 478–479
for scaffolding student problem solving,
    6, 253, 254, 479
strategies of classification, 190, 192–193;
    and answering questions,
    193–194; by prompting, 190,

491

SR

272C17 FM 8254
09/11/07 44400   NC